LINUX

IN A NUTSHELL

Fourth Edition

Ellen Siever, Stephen Figgins,
and Aaron Weber

O'REILLY®

Beijing • Cambridge • Farnham • Köln • Paris • Sebastopol • Taipei • Tokyo

Linux in a Nutshell, Fourth Edition

by Ellen Siever, Stephen Figgins, and Aaron Weber

Copyright © 2003, 2000, 1999, 1997 O'Reilly & Associates, Inc. All rights reserved.
Printed in the United States of America.

Published by O'Reilly & Associates, Inc., 1005 Gravenstein Highway North, Sebastopol, CA 95472.

O'Reilly & Associates books may be purchased for educational, business, or sales promotional use. Online editions are also available for most titles (*safari.oreilly.com*). For more information, contact our corporate/institutional sales department: 800-998-9938 or *corporate@oreilly.com*.

Editor:	Andy Oram
Production Editor:	Emily Quill
Cover Designer:	Edie Freedman
Interior Designer:	David Futato

Printing History:

January 1997:	First Edition.
February 1999:	Second Edition.
August 2000:	Third Edition.
June 2003:	Fourth Edition.

Nutshell Handbook, the Nutshell Handbook logo, and the O'Reilly logo are registered trademarks of O'Reilly & Associates, Inc. Many of the designations used by manufacturers and sellers to distinguish their products are claimed as trademarks. Where those designations appear in this book, and O'Reilly & Associates, Inc. was aware of a trademark claim, the designations have been printed in caps or initial caps. The association between the image of an Arabian horse and the topic of Linux is a trademark of O'Reilly & Associates, Inc.

While every precaution has been taken in the preparation of this book, the publisher and authors assume no responsibility for errors or omissions, or for damages resulting from the use of the information contained herein.

ISBN: 0-596-00482-6
[M]

[10/03]

LINUX

IN A NUTSHELL

Other Linux Resources from O'Reilly

Related titles

Linux Network Administrator's Guide
Running Linux
Linux Device Drivers
Understanding the Linux Kernel
Building Secure Servers with Linux
LPI Linux Certification in a Nutshell

Learning Red Hat Linux
Linux Server Hacks
Linux Security Cookbook
Managing RAID on Linux
Linux Web Server CD Bookshelf
Building Embedded Linux Systems

Linux Books Resource Center

linux.oreilly.com is a complete catalog of O'Reilly's books on Linux and Unix and related technologies, including sample chapters and code examples.

ONLamp.com is the premier site for the open source web platform: Linux, Apache, MySQL and either Perl, Python, or PHP.

Conferences

O'Reilly & Associates bring diverse innovators together to nurture the ideas that spark revolutionary industries. We specialize in documenting the latest tools and systems, translating the innovator's knowledge into useful skills for those in the trenches. Visit *conferences.oreilly.com* for our upcoming events.

Safari Bookshelf (*safari.oreilly.com*) is the premier online reference library for programmers and IT professionals. Conduct searches across more than 1,000 books. Subscribers can zero in on answers to time-critical questions in a matter of seconds. Read the books on your Bookshelf from cover to cover or simply flip to the page you need. Try it today with a free trial.

Table of Contents

Preface

This is a book about Linux, a freely available clone of the Unix operating system whose uses range from embedded systems and personal data assistants (PDAs) to corporate servers, web servers, and massive clusters that perform some of the world's most difficult computations.

Whether you are using Linux for personal software projects, for a small office or home office (the so-called SOHO environment), to provide services to a small group of colleagues, or to administer a site responsible for millions of email and web connections each day, you need quick access to information on a wide range of tools. This book covers all aspects of administering and making effective use of Linux systems. Among its topics are booting, package management, and the configuration of the GNOME and KDE desktops. But foremost in *Linux in a Nutshell* are the immeasurable utilities and commands that make Linux one of the most powerful and flexible systems available.

In addition to the tools and features written specifically for it, Linux has inherited many from the Free Software Foundation's GNU project, the Berkeley Software Distribution (BSD), the X Window System (XFree86), and contributions from major corporations as well as the companies that created the major Linux distributions. More recent projects extend Linux in exciting ways, some through changes to the kernel and some through libraries and applications that radically change the user's experience; the GNOME and KDE desktops are the most prominent examples.

This book is a quick reference for the basic commands and features of the Linux operating system. As with other books in O'Reilly's "In a Nutshell" series, this book is geared toward users who know what they want to do and have some idea how to do it, but can't always remember the correct command or option.

Other Resources

This book doesn't tell you how to install and come up to speed on a Linux system. For that, you will probably want O'Reilly's *Learning Red Hat Linux*, which contains a Linux distribution on CD-ROM and provides help with installation and configuration. Alternatively, *Running Linux* is an in-depth guide suitable for all major distributions. For networking information, check out the *Linux Network Administrator's Guide*. In addition to these and other Linux titles, O'Reilly's wide range of Unix, X, Perl, and Java titles may also be of interest to the Linux user.

Online Documentation

The Internet is full of information about Linux. One of the best resources is the Linux Documentation Project at *http://www.tldp.org* (or one of the dozens of mirror sites around the world), which has numerous short guides called HOWTOs, along with some full manuals. For online information about the GNU utilities covered in this book, consult *http://www.gnu.org* (also widely mirrored). The Free Software Foundation, which is in charge of the GNU project, publishes its documentation in a number of hard-copy and online books about various tools.

Each distribution maintains its own web site, and contains documentation for the software it provides as well as guides to maintaining your system under that distribution.

Web Sites

As befits a hot phenomenon, Linux is the central subject of several web sites and a frequent topic of discussion on others. Some sites offer original content; others just have links to articles posted elsewhere and threaded discussions (which can be a useful service). Among the sites frequented by Linux users are:

http://www.lwn.net
> Linux Weekly News, a site with weekly in-depth articles and frequent news updates

http://www.linuxgazette.com
> Linux Gazette, a site published monthly by *Linux Journal* with articles and tips in many languages

http://linuxsecurity.com
> Linux Security, a collection of security-related news

http://slashdot.org
> Slashdot, a famous discussion list

http://linuxinsider.com
> Linux Insider, a news feed

http://linuxtoday.com
> Linux Today, another news feed

http://newsforge.com
> NewsForge, a more general computing-related news feed

Linux Journal and Linux Magazine

Linux Journal and *Linux Magazine* are monthly magazines for the Linux community, written and published by a number of Linux activists. With both print editions and web sites, they offer articles ranging from novice questions and answers to kernel programming internals. *Linux Journal*, at *http://www.linuxjournal.com*, is the older magazine and is published by S.S.C. Incorporated, *http://www.ssc.com*. *Linux Magazine* is at *http://www.linuxmagazine.com*.

Usenet Newsgroups

Most people can receive Usenet news at work or through their ISPs. While this communications technology has lost ground in the past several years to web-based threaded discussions, it is still a valuable source of help and community connections on many topics. The following Linux-related newsgroups are popular:

comp.os.linux.announce
> A moderated newsgroup containing announcements of new software, distributions, bug reports, and goings-on in the Linux community. All Linux users should read this group. Submissions may be mailed to *linux-announce@news.ornl.gov*.

comp.os.linux.help
> General questions and answers about installing or using Linux.

comp.os.linux.admin
> Discussions relating to systems administration under Linux.

comp.os.linux.development
> Discussions about developing the Linux kernel and the system itself.

comp.os.linux.networking
> Discussions relating to networking with Linux.

comp.os.linux.security
> Help with firewalls, securing servers, and other security issues.

comp.os.linux.x
> Help on getting the X graphical window system to work. This list used to see some of the highest traffic of any Linux group back when distributions had more trouble setting up graphics automatically. This is no longer the case, thanks to the increasing sophistication of autodetection and configuration software.

There are also several newsgroups devoted to Linux in languages other than English, such as *fr.comp.os.linux* in French and *de.comp.os.linux* in German.

Online Linux Support

There are many ways of obtaining help online, where volunteers from around the world offer expertise and services to assist users with questions and problems.

The freenode IRC service is an Internet relay chat network devoted to so-called "peer-directed" projects, particularly those involving free software. Some of its channels are designed to provide online Linux support services.

Internet relay chat is a network service that allows you to talk interactively on the Internet to other users. IRC networks support multiple channels where different groups of people type their thoughts. Whatever you type in a channel is seen by all other users of that channel.

There are a number of active channels on the freenode IRC network where you will find users 24 hours a day, 7 days a week who are willing and able to help you solve any Linux problems you may have, or just chat. You can use this service by installing an IRC client (some distributions install them by default), connecting to server name *irc.freenode.org:6667*, and joining a channel focusing on Linux, such as:

#linpeople	General help and discussion.
#debian	Help for Debian distribution.
#gentoo	Help for Gentoo distribution.
#redhat	Help for Red Hat distribution.
#suse	Help for SuSE distribution.

And so on. Please be sure to read up on the rules of chat etiquette before chatting. In particular, the participants in these groups tend to expect people to read documentation and do some experimentation before asking for help with a problem.

Linux User Groups

Many Linux User Groups around the world offer direct support to users. Typically, Linux User Groups engage in such activities as installation days, talks and seminars, demonstration nights, and purely social events. Linux User Groups are a great way of meeting other Linux users in your area. There are a number of published lists of Linux User Groups. Some of the better-known ones are:

- Groups of Linux Users Everywhere: *http://www.ssc.com/glue/groups*
- LUGregistry: *http://www.linux.org/users*

Conventions

This desktop quick reference follows certain typographic conventions:

Bold
> is used for commands, programs, and options. All terms shown in bold are typed literally.

Italic
> is used to show arguments and variables that should be replaced with user-supplied values. Italic is also used to indicate filenames and directories and to highlight comments in examples.

Constant Width
> is used to show the contents of files or the output from commands.

Constant Width Bold
> is used in examples to show commands or other text that should be typed literally by the user.

Constant Width Italic
> is used in examples to show text that should be replaced with user-supplied values.

%, $
> are used in some examples as the **tcsh** shell prompt (%) and as the Bourne or **bash** shell prompt ($).

[ ] surround optional elements in a description of syntax. (The brackets themselves should never be typed.) Note that many commands show the argument [*files*]. If a filename is omitted, standard input (e.g., the keyboard) is assumed. End with an end-of-file character.

EOF
> indicates the end-of-file character (normally Ctrl-D).

| is used in syntax descriptions to separate items for which only one alternative may be chosen at a time.

> This icon indicates a note, which is an important aside to its nearby text.

> This icon indicates a warning.

A final word about syntax. In many cases, the space between an option and its argument can be omitted. In other cases, the spacing (or lack of spacing) must be followed strictly. For example, **-w***n* (no intervening space) might be interpreted differently from **-w** *n*. It's important to notice the spacing used in option syntax.

We'd Like to Hear from You

We have tested and verified all of the information in this book to the best of our ability, but you may find that features have changed (or even that we have made mistakes!). Please let us know about any errors you find, as well as your suggestions for future editions, by writing:

O'Reilly & Associates, Inc.
1005 Gravenstein Highway North
Sebastopol, CA 95472
(800) 998-9938 (in the United States or Canada)
(707) 829-0515 (international or local)
(707) 829-0104 (fax)

There is a web page for this book, which lists errata, examples, or any additional information. You can access this page at:

http://www.oreilly.com/catalog/linuxnut4/

To comment or ask technical questions about this book, send email to:

bookquestions@oreilly.com

For more information about books, conferences, Resource Centers, and the O'Reilly Network, see the O'Reilly web site at:

http://www.oreilly.com

Acknowledgments

This fourth edition of *Linux in a Nutshell* is the result of the cooperative efforts of many people. Thanks to Andy Oram for his editorial skills, as well as for pitching in to check existing chapters and update and write new material as needed.

For technical review, thanks go to Matt Welsh of *Running Linux* and *Installation and Getting Started Guide* fame, Michael K. Johnson of Red Hat Software, Robert J. Chassell, Phil Hughes of *Linux Journal*, Laurie Lynne Tucker, Arnold Robbins, Julian T. J. Midgley, Matthias Kalle Dalheimer, Terry Dawson, Doug Moreen, Ron Passerini, and Mark Stone.

Introduction

It is hard to chart the rise of Linux over its twelve years of existence without risking the appearance of exaggeration and hyperbole. During the past five years alone, Linux has grown from a student/hacker playground to an upstart challenger in the server market to a well-respected system taking its rightful place in educational and corporate networks. Many serious analysts claim that its trajectory has just begun, and that it will eventually become the world's most widespread operating system.

Linux was first developed by Linus Torvalds at the University of Helsinki in Finland. From his current location in Silicon Valley, Linus continues to centrally coordinate improvements. The Linux kernel continues to develop under the dedicated cultivation of a host of other programmers and hackers all over the world, joined by members of programming teams at major computer companies, all connected through the Internet.

By "kernel," we mean the core of the operating system itself, not the applications (such as the compiler, shells, and so forth) that run on it. Today, the term "Linux" is often used to mean a software environment with a Linux kernel along with a large set of applications and other software components. In this larger meaning, many people prefer the term GNU/Linux, which acknowledges the central role played by tools from the Free Software Foundation's GNU project in the development of the kernel.

Linux systems cannot be technically referred to as a "version of Unix," as they have not undergone the required tests and licensing.* However, Linux offers all the common programming interfaces of standard Unix systems, and as you can see from this book, all the common Unix utilities have been reimplemented on Linux. It is a powerful, robust, fully usable system for those who like Unix.

---

* Before an operating system can be called "Unix," it must be branded by The Open Group.

The historical impact of Linux goes beyond its role as a challenge to all versions of Unix as well as Microsoft Windows, particularly on servers. Linux's success has also inspired countless other free software or open source (defined at *http://opensource.org*) projects, including Samba, GNOME, and a mind-boggling collection of innovative projects that you can browse at numerous sites like SourceForge (*http://sourceforge.net*). As both a platform for other developers and a development model, Linux gave a tremendous boost to the GNU project, and has also become a popular platform for Java development. In short, Linux is a central participant in the most exciting and productive free software movement ever seen.

If you haven't obtained Linux yet, or have it but don't know exactly how to get started using it, see "Other Resources" in the preface.

The Excitement of Linux

Linux is, first of all, free software: anyone can download the source from the Internet or buy it on a low-cost CD-ROM. But Linux is becoming well known because it's more than free software—it's unusually good software. You can get more from your hardware with Linux and be assured of fewer crashes; even its security is better than many commercial alternatives.

Linux first appeared in organizations as ad hoc installations by hackers running modest web servers or development systems at universities and research institutions, but now extends deeply into corporations around the world. People deploying Linux for mission-critical systems tend to talk about its ample practical advantages, such as the ability to deliver a lot of bang for the buck and the ease of deploying other powerful tools on Linux such as Apache, Samba, and Java environments. They also cite Linux's ability to grow and sprout new features of interest to large numbers of users. But these advantages can be traced back to the concept of software freedom, which is the root of the broad wave of innovation driving Linux.

As free software, Linux revives the grand creativity and the community of sharing that Unix was long known for. The unprecedented flexibility and openness of Unix—which newcomers usually found confusing and frustrating, but eventually found they couldn't live without—continually inspired extensions, new tools like Perl, and experiments in computer science that sometimes ended up in mainstream commercial computer systems.

Many programmers fondly remember the days when AT&T provided universities with Unix source code at no charge, and the University of Berkeley started distributing its version in any manner that allowed people to get it. For these older hackers, Linux brings back the spirit of working together—all the more so because the Internet is now so widespread. And for the many who are too young to remember the first round of open systems or whose prior experience has been constricted by trying to explore and adapt proprietary operating systems, now is the time to discover the wonders of freely distributable source code and infinitely adaptable interfaces.

The economic power behind Linux's popularity is its support for an enormous range of hardware. People who are accustomed to MS-DOS and Microsoft

Windows are often amazed at how much faster their hardware appears to work with Linux—it makes efficient use of its resources.

For the first several years, users were attracted to Linux for a variety of financial and political reasons, but soon they discovered an unexpected benefit: Linux works better than many commercial systems. With the Samba file and print server, for instance, Linux serves a large number of end-user PCs without crashing. With the Apache web server, it provides more of the useful features web administrators want than competing products do. Embedded versions of the Linux kernel are in growing use because, although they are larger than the most stripped-down operating systems, they deliver a range of powerful features within a remarkably small footprint.

Opinions still differ on how suitable Linux is as a general-purpose desktop system. But the tremendous advances in usability and stability of the desktop software and its applications are undisputed. Soon (if not today), one will find Linux in many offices and other end-user environments. Meanwhile, the strides made by Linux in everyday computing tasks are reflected in the new audio and CD-related commands found in this edition.

Distribution and Support

While it is convenient to download one or two new programs over the Internet and fairly feasible to download something as large as the Linux kernel, getting an entire working system over the Internet is difficult without a high-speed Internet connection. Over the years, therefore, commercial and noncommercial packages called *distributions* have emerged. The first distribution consisted of approximately 50 diskettes, at least one of which would usually turn out to be bad and have to be replaced. When CD-ROM drives became widespread, Linux really took off.

After getting Linux, the average user is concerned next with support. While Usenet newsgroups offer very quick responses and meet the needs of many intrepid users, you can also buy support from the vendors of the major distributions and a number of independent experts. Linux is supported at least as well as commercial software. When you buy a distribution from a vendor, you typically are entitled to a period of free support as well.

Intel's x86 family and other compatible chips are still by far the most common hardware running Linux, but Linux is also now commercially available on a number of other hardware systems, notably the PowerPC, the 64-bit Intel Itanium processor, Sun Microsystems' SPARC, and the Alpha (created by Digital Equipment Corporation).

Commands on Linux

Linux commands are not the same as standard Unix ones. They're better! This is because most of them are provided by the GNU project run by the Free Software Foundation (FSF). GNU means "GNU's Not Unix"—the first word of the phrase is expanded with infinite recursion.

Benefiting from years of experience with standard Unix utilities and advances in computer science, programmers on the GNU project have managed to create versions of standard tools that have more features, run faster and more efficiently, and lack the bugs and inconsistencies that persist in the original standard versions.

While GNU provided the programming utilities and standard commands like **grep**, many of the system and network administration tools on Linux came from the Berkeley Software Distribution (BSD). In addition, some people wrote tools that specifically allow Linux to deal with special issues such as filesystems. This book documents all the standard Unix commands that are commonly available on most Linux distributions.

The third type of software most commonly run on Linux is the X Window System, ported by the XFree86 project to standard Intel chips. While this book cannot cover the wide range of utilities that run on X, we briefly cover some of the useful customizations you can make to your KDE, GNOME, or **fvwm2** desktop.

What This Book Offers

Originally based on the classic O'Reilly & Associates quick reference, *Unix in a Nutshell*, this book has been expanded to include much information that is specific to Linux. These enhancements include chapters on:

- Package managers (which make it easy to install, update, and remove related software files)
- The KDE and GNOME desktops and the **fvwm2** window manager
- Boot parameters
- The CVS version control system

The book also contains dozens of Linux-specific commands, along with tried-and-true Unix commands that have been supporting users for decades (though they continue to sprout new options).

This book does not cover the graphical tools contained in most distributions of Linux. Many of these, to be sure, are quite useful and can form the basis of everyday work. Examples of these tools include OpenOffice (the open source version of the StarOffice suite distributed by Sun Microsystems), Evolution (a mail, calendar, and office productivity tool from Ximian), Mozilla (the open source cousin of the Netscape web browser), and the GIMP (a graphic image manipulation program and the inspiration for the GNOME project). But they are not Linux-specific, and their graphical models do not fit well into the format of this book.

While you can do a lot of valuable work with the graphical applications, the core of Linux use is the text manipulation and administration done from the command line, within scripts, or using text editors such as **vi** and Emacs. Linux is still mostly a command-driven system, and this book continues to focus on this level of usage. In your day-to-day work, you'll likely find yourself moving back and forth between graphical programs and the commands listed in this book.

Every distribution of Linux is slightly different, but you'll find that the commands we document are the ones you use most of the time, and that they work the same on all distributions. Basic commands, programming utilities, system administration, and network administration are all covered. However, some areas were so big that we had to leave them out. The many applications that depend on the X Window System didn't make the cut. Nor did the many useful programming languages like Java, Perl, and Python with which users can vastly expand the capabilities of their systems. XML isn't covered here either. These subjects would stretch the book out of its binding.

Linux in a Nutshell doesn't teach you Linux—it is, after all, a quick reference—but novices as well as highly experienced users will find it of great value. When you have some idea of what command you want but aren't sure just how it works or what combinations of options give you the exact output required, this book is the place to turn. It can also be an eye-opener, making you aware of options that you never knew about before.

Once you're over the hurdle of installing Linux, the first thing you need to do is get to know the common utilities run from the shell prompt. If you know absolutely nothing about Unix, we recommend you read a basic guide (introductory chapters in the O'Reilly books *Learning Red Hat Linux* and *Running Linux* can get you started.) This chapter and Chapter 2 offer a context for understanding different kinds of commands (including commands for programming, system administration, and network administration). Chapter 3 is the central focus of the book, containing about one half its bulk.

The small chapters immediately following Chapter 3 help you get your system set up. Since most users do not want to completely abandon other operating systems (whether a Microsoft Windows system, OS/2, or some Unix flavor), Linux often resides on the same computer as other systems. Users can then boot the system they need for a particular job. Chapter 4 describes the commonly used booting options on Intel systems, including LILO (Linux Loader), GRUB (the GRand Unified Bootloader), and Loadlin. Chapter 5 covers the Red Hat package manager (**rpm**)—which is supported by many distributions, including Red Hat, SuSE, Mandrake, and Caldera—and the Debian package manager. Package managers are useful for installing and updating software; they make sure you have all the files you need in the proper versions.

All commands are interpreted by the *shell*. The shell is simply a program that accepts commands from the user and executes them. Different shells sometimes use slightly different syntax to mean the same thing. Under Linux, two popular shells are **bash** and **tcsh** (which on Linux has supplanted the older **csh**), and they differ in subtle ways. (One of the nice things about Linux and other Unix systems is that you have a variety of shells to choose from, each with strengths and weaknesses.) We offer an introduction to shells in Chapter 6, thorough coverage of **bash** in Chapter 7, and a guide to **tcsh** in Chapter 8. You may decide to read these after you've used Linux for a while, because they mostly cover powerful, advanced features that you'll want when you're a steady user.

To get any real work done, you'll have to learn some big, comprehensive utilities, notably an editor and some scripting tools. Two major editors are used on Linux:

vi and Emacs. Emacs is covered in Chapter 10 and **vi** in Chapter 11. Chapters 12 and 13 cover two classic Unix tools for manipulating text files on a line-by-line basis: **sed** and **gawk** (the GNU version of the traditional **awk**). O'Reilly offers separate books about these topics that you may find valuable, as they are not completely intuitive upon first use. (Emacs does have an excellent built-in tutorial, though; to invoke it, press **Ctrl-H** followed by **t** for "tutorial.")

CVS (Concurrent Versions System) and RCS (Revision Control System) manage files so you can retrieve old versions and maintain different versions simultaneously. Originally used by programmers who have complicated requirements for building and maintaining applications, these tools have turned out to be valuable for anyone who maintains files of any type, particularly when coordinating a team of people. CVS has become a distribution channel for thousands of free software projects. Chapter 14 presents RCS commands, and Chapter 15 presents CVS commands.

Graphical desktops are covered in four chapters. Chapter 16 is a brief overview to the major options on Linux systems. It is followed by Chapter 17 on the GNOME desktop, Chapter 18 on the KDE desktop, and Chapter 19 on the **fvwm2** window manager.

Our goal in producing this book is to provide convenience, and that means keeping the book (relatively) small. It certainly doesn't have everything the manual pages have; but you'll find that it has what you need 95% of the time.

Sources and Licenses

Some distributions contain the source code for Linux; it is also easily available for download at *http://www.kernel.org* and elsewhere. Source code is similarly available for all the utilities on Linux (unless your vendor offers a commercial application or library as a special enhancement). You may never bother looking at the source code, but it's key to Linux's strength. Under the Linux license, the source code has to be provided by the vendor, and it permits those who are competent at such things to fix bugs, provide advice about the system's functioning, and submit improvements that benefit everyone. The license is the GNU project's well-known General Public License, also known as the GPL or "copyleft," invented and popularized by the Free Software Foundation.

The FSF, founded by Richard Stallman, is a phenomenon that many people might believe to be impossible if it did not exist. (The same goes for Linux, in fact—15 years ago, who would have imagined a robust operating system developed by collaborators over the Internet and made freely redistributable?) One of the most popular editors on Unix, GNU Emacs, comes from the FSF. So do **gcc** and **g++** (C and C++ compilers), which for a while set the standard in the industry for optimization and fast code. One of the largest projects within GNU is the GNOME desktop, which encompasses several useful general-purpose libraries and applications that use these libraries to provide consistent behavior and interoperability.

Dedicated to the sharing of software, the FSF provides all its code and documentation on the Internet and allows anyone with a whim for enhancements to alter the source code. One of its projects is the Debian distribution of Linux.

To prevent hoarding, the FSF requires that the source code for all enhancements be distributed under the same GPL that it uses. This encourages individuals or companies to make improvements and share them with others. The only thing someone cannot do is add enhancements and then try to sell the product as commercial software—that is, to withhold the source code. That would be taking advantage of the FSF and the users. You can find the GPL in any software covered by that license, or online at *http://www.gnu.org/copyleft/gpl.html*.

As we said earlier, many Linux tools come from BSD instead of GNU. BSD is also free software. The license is significantly different, but that probably don't concern you as a user. The effect of the difference is that companies are permitted to incorporate the software into their proprietary products, a practice that is severely limited by the GNU license.

Beginner's Guide

If you're just beginning to work on a Linux system, the abundance of commands might prove daunting. To help orient you, the following lists present a sampling of commands on various topics.

Communication

ftp	File Transfer Protocol.
login	Sign on.
rlogin	Sign on to remote system.
rsh	Run shell or single command on remote system (not particularly secure).
ssh	Run shell or single command on remote system (secure).
talk	Exchange messages interactively with other terminals.
telnet	Connect to another system.
tftp	Trivial File Transfer Protocol.
uudecode	Decode file prepared for mailing by **uuencode**.
uuencode	Encode file containing binary characters for mailing.
vacation	Respond to mail automatically.

Comparisons

cmp	Compare two files, byte by byte.
comm	Compare items in two sorted files.
diff	Compare two files, line by line.
diff3	Compare three files.

File Management

cat	Concatenate files or display them.
chfn	Change user information for finger, email, etc.
cksum	Compute checksum.
chmod	Change access modes on files.
chsh	Change login shell.

cp	Copy files.
csplit	Split a file into pieces with a specific size or at specific locations.
dd	Copy files in raw disk form.
file	Determine a file's type.
head	Show the first few lines of a file.
less	Display files by screenful.
ln	Create filename aliases.
ls	List files or directories.
merge	Merge changes from different files.
mkdir	Create a directory.
more	Display files by screenful.
mv	Move or rename files or directories.
newgrp	Change current group.
pwd	Print working directory.
rcp	Copy files to remote system.
rm	Remove files.
rmdir	Remove directories.
split	Split files evenly.
tail	Show the last few lines of a file.
wc	Count lines, words, and characters.

Media

cdda2wav	Rip a CD to create a computer-friendly WAV format.
cdparanoia	Rip a CD while providing extra features.
cdrdao	Copy a CD.
cdrecord	Record to a CD.
eject	Eject a removable disk or tape.
mpg321	Play an MP3 file.
volname	Provide the volume name of a CD-ROM.

Printing

lpq	Show status of print jobs.
lpr	Send to the printer.
lprm	Remove print job.
lpstat	Get printer status.
pr	Format and paginate for printing.

Programming

ar	Create and update library files.
as	Generate object file.
bison	Generate parsing tables.
cpp	Preprocess C code.
flex	Lexical analyzer.
g++	GNU C++ compiler.
gcc	GNU C compiler.

ld	Link editor.
m4	Macro processor.
make	Create programs.
ranlib	Regenerate archive symbol table.
rpcgen	Translate RPC to C code.
yacc	Generate parsing tables.

Program Maintenance

cvs	Manage different versions (revisions) of source files.
etags	Generate symbol list for use with the Emacs editor.
gdb	GNU debugger.
gprof	Display object file's profile data.
imake	Generate makefiles for use with **make**.
make	Maintain, update, and regenerate related programs and files.
nm	Display object file's symbol table.
patch	Apply patches to source code.
rcs	Manage different versions (revisions) of source files.
size	Print the size of an object file in bytes.
strace	Trace system calls and signals.
strip	Strip symbols from an object file.

Searching

apropos	Search manpages for topic.
egrep	Extended version of **grep**.
fgrep	Search files for literal words.
find	Search the system for files by name and take a range of possible actions.
grep	Search files for text patterns.
locate	Search a preexisting database to show where files are on the system.
strings	Search binary files for text patterns.
whereis	Find command.

Shell Programming

echo	Repeat command-line arguments on the output.
expr	Perform arithmetic and comparisons.
printf	Format and print command-line arguments.
sleep	Pause during processing.
test	Test a condition.

Storage

bzip2	Compress files to free up space.
cpio	Create and unpack file archives.
gunzip	Expand compressed (*.gz* and *.Z*) files.
gzip	Compress files to free up space.

shar	Create shell archive.
tar	Copy files to or restore files from an archive medium.
zcat	Display contents of compressed files.

System Status

at	Execute commands later.
atq	Show jobs queued by **at**.
atrm	Remove job queued by **at**.
chgrp	Change file group.
chown	Change file owner.
crontab	Automate commands.
date	Display or set date.
df	Show free disk space.
du	Show disk usage.
env	Show environment variables.
finger	Display information about users.
kill	Terminate a running command.
printenv	Show environment variables.
ps	Show processes.
stty	Set or display terminal settings.
who	Show who is logged in.

Text Processing

col	Process control characters.
cut	Select columns for display.
emacs	Work environment with powerful text editing capabilities.
ex	Line editor underlying **vi**.
expand	Convert tabs to spaces.
fmt	Produce roughly uniform line lengths.
fold	Break lines.
gawk	Process lines or records one by one.
ghostscript	Display PostScript or PDF file.
groff	Format **troff** input.
ispell	Interactively check spelling.
join	Merge different columns into a database.
paste	Merge columns or switch order.
rev	Print lines in reverse.
sed	Noninteractive text editor.
sort	Sort or merge files.
tac	Print lines in reverse.
tr	Translate (redefine) characters.
uniq	Find repeated or unique lines in a file.
vi	Visual text editor.
xargs	Process many arguments in manageable portions.

Miscellaneous

banner	Make posters from words.
bc	Arbitrary precision calculator.
cal	Display calendar.
clear	Clear the screen.
man	Get information on a command.
nice	Reduce a job's priority.
nohup	Preserve a running job after logging out.
passwd	Set your login password.
script	Produce a transcript of your login session.
su	Become a superuser.
tee	Simultaneously store output in file and send to screen.
which	Print pathname of a command.

2

System and Network Administration Overview

Common Commands

Following are lists of commonly used system administration commands.

Clocks

hwclock	Manage hardware clock.
rdate	Get time from network time server.
zdump	Print list of time zones.
zic	Create time conversion information files.

Daemons

apmd	Advanced Power Management daemon.
atd	Queue commands for later execution.
bootpd	Internet Boot Protocol daemon.
fingerd	Finger daemon.
ftpd	File Transfer Protocol daemon.
identd	Identify user running TCP/IP process.
imapd	IMAP mailbox server daemon.
inetd	Internet services daemon.
klogd	Manage **syslogd**.
lpd	Printer daemon.
mountd	NFS mount request server.
named	Internet domain name server.
nfsd	NFS daemon.
pppd	Maintain Point-to-Point Protocol (PPP) network connections.
rdistd	Remote file distribution server.
rexecd	Remote execution server.
rlogind	**rlogin** server.

routed	Routing daemon.
rpc.rusersd	Remote users server.
rpc.statd	NFS status daemon.
rshd	Remote shell server.
rwhod	Remote who server.
sshd	Secure shell daemon.
syslogd	System logging daemon.
talkd	Talk daemon.
tcpd	TCP network daemon.
tftpd	Trivial File Transfer Protocol daemon.
update	Buffer flush daemon.
ypbind	NIS binder process.
yppasswdd	NIS password modification server.
ypserv	NIS server process.

Hardware

agetty	Start user session at terminal.
arp	Manage the ARP cache.
cardctl	Control PCMCIA cards.
cardmgr	PCMCIA card manager daemon.
cfdisk	Maintain disk partitions (graphical interface).
fdisk	Maintain disk partitions.
hdparm	Get and set hard drive parameters.
kbdrate	Manage the keyboard's repeat rate.
ramsize	Print information about RAM disk.
setkeycodes	Change keyboard scancode-to-keycode mappings.
setserial	Set serial port information.
slattach	Attach serial lines as network interfaces.

Host Information

arch	Print machine architecture.
dig	Query Internet domain name servers. Replaces **nslookup**.
dnsdomainname	Print DNS domain name.
domainname	Print NIS domain name.
free	Print memory usage.
host	Print host and zone information.
hostname	Print or set hostname.
nslookup	Query Internet domain name servers. (Deprecated)
uname	Print host information.

Installation

cpio	Copy file archives.
install	Copy files into locations providing user access and set permissions.
rdist	Distribute files to remote systems.
tar	Copy files to or restore files from an archive medium.

Mail

fetchmail	Retrieve mail from remote servers.
formail	Convert input to mail format.
mailq	Print a summary of the mail queue.
makemap	Update **sendmail**'s database maps.
rmail	Handle **uucp** mail.
sendmail	Send and receive mail.

Managing Filesystems

To Unix systems, a *filesystem* is a device (such as a partition) that is formatted to store files. Filesystems can be found on hard drives, floppies, CD-ROMs, or other storage media that permit random access.

The exact format and means by which the files are stored are not important; the system provides a common interface for all *filesystem types* that it recognizes. Under Linux, filesystem types include the Second Extended (ext2) Filesystem, which you probably use to store Linux files. This filesystem was developed primarily for Linux and supports 256-character filenames and 4-terabyte maximum filesystem size. (It is "second" because it is the successor to the extended filesystem type.) Other common filesystem types include the MS-DOS filesystem, which allows files on MS-DOS partitions and floppies to be accessed under Linux, and the ISO 9660 filesystem used by CD-ROMs.

The 2.4 kernel adds optional support for an enhanced version of the ext2 filesystem, the Third Extended (ext3) Filesystem. Many Linux distributions ship kernels with this support preconfigured. The ext3 filesystem is essentially an ext2 filesystem with an added journal. Since it is in all other ways identical to the ext2 system, it is both forward and backward compatible with ext2—all ext2 utilities work with ext3 filesystems. When the kernel interacts with an ext3 filesystem, writes to disk are first written to a log or journal before they are written to disk. This slows down writes to the filesystem, but reduces the risk of data corruption in the event of a power outage. It also speeds up reboots after a system unexpectedly loses power. When rebooting with an ext2 filesystem, the **fsck** utility scans the entire disk to ensure that all data blocks are listed as either used or free, that each data block is claimed by only one file or directory, and that all files are available in the directory tree. When rebooting an ext3 filesystem using a supported kernel, it need only check the journal and complete any tasks that were left uncompleted.

To change an ext2 filesystem into an ext3 filesystem, simply add a journal using the **tune2fs** utility with the **-j** option on the unmounted device. If the filesystem is listed in */etc/fstab*, change its specified filesystem from ext2 to ext3, or **auto** (**mountd** will automatically detect the right system).

You can specify the level of journaling the kernel should use in the mount options field (or using **mount -o**). There are three data options:

data=journal

Log all filesystem data and metadata changes. All changes to the filesystem are written twice, once to the journal and once to the filesystem itself. This is the slowest but safest mode.

data=ordered

Log filesystem metadata. Flush data updates to disk before changing metadata. This is the default mode. This slows writes a small amount, but ensures the filesystem is always in sync with changes to its metadata.

data=writeback

Log filesystem metadata. Use the ext2 write process to write data changes. This is the fastest journaling mode. While it maintains filestructure integrity, the contents of files may contain old, stale data when the filesystem is restarted from an unexpected shutdown.

The last field in the */etc/fstab* entry specifies at what point in the boot process the filesystem should be verified with **fsck**. It should never need to be checked because journaling ensures filesystem integrity. You can set this field to **0**. You can also turn off the automatic check of the filesystem that normally occurs every 20th time the system is mounted using **tune2fs -i 0 -c 0**.

Although not covered in this edition of Linux in a Nutshell, Linux supports three other open source journaling filesystems: IBM's Journaled Filesystem (JFS), SGI's Extensible Filesystem (XFS), and the Naming System Venture's Reiser Filesystem (ReiserFS). In some situations these can be faster than ext3. Some Linux distributions use these alternative filesystems by default.

debugfs	Debug ext2 filesystem.
dosfsck	Check and repair a DOS or VFAT filesystem.
dumpe2fs	Print information about superblock and blocks group.
e2fsck	Check and repair an ext2 filesystem.
e2image	Store disaster recovery data for an ext2 filesystem.
fdformat	Format floppy disk.
fsck	Another name for **e2fsck**.
fsck.ext2	Check and repair an ext2 filesystem.
fsck.minix	Check and repair a MINIX filesystem.
fuser	List processes using a filesystem.
mke2fs	Make a new ext2 filesystem.
mkfs	Make new filesystem.
mkfs.ext2	Another name for **mke2fs**.
mkfs.ext3	Yet another name for **mke2fs**.
mkfs.minix	Make new MINIX filesystem.
mklost+found	Make *lost+found* directory.
mkraid	Set up a RAID device.
mkswap	Designate swap space.
mount	Mount a filesystem.
raidstart	Activate a RAID device.
raidstop	Turn off a RAID device.
rdev	Describe or change values for root filesystem.
resize2fs	Enlarge or shrink an ext2 filesystem.

rootflags	List or set flags to use in mounting root filesystem.
showmount	List exported directories.
swapoff	Cease using device for swapping.
swapon	Begin using device for swapping.
sync	Write filesystem buffers to disk.
tune2fs	Manage an ext2 filesystem.
umount	Unmount a filesystem.

Managing the Kernel

depmod	Create module dependency listing.
insmod	Install new kernel module.
lsmod	List kernel modules.
modinfo	Print kernel module information.
modprobe	Load new module and its dependent modules.
rmmod	Remove module.
sysctl	Examine or modify kernel parameters at runtime.

Networking

chat	Establish dial-up IP connections.
dip	Establish dial-up IP connections.
gdc	Administer **gated** routing daemon.
ifconfig	Manage network interfaces.
ipchains	Administer firewall facilities (2.2 kernel).
iptables	Administer firewall facilities (2.4 kernel).
named	Translate between domain names and IP addresses.
nameif	Assign names to network devices.
netstat	Print network status.
nfsstat	Print statistics for NFS and RPC.
nsupdate	Submit dynamic DNS update requests.
portmap	Map daemons to ports.
rarp	Manage RARP table.
route	Manage routing tables.
routed	Dynamically keep routing tables up to date.
rpcinfo	Report RPC information.
ruptime	Check how long remote system has been up.
rwho	Show who is logged into remote system.
traceroute	Trace network route to remote host.

Printing

checkpc	Examine and repair printer settings.
lpc	Control line printer.
tunelp	Tune the printer parameters.

Security and System Integrity

badblocks	Search for bad blocks.
chroot	Change root directory.

Starting and Stopping the System

bootpd	Internet Boot Protocol daemon.
bootpgw	Internet Boot Protocol gateway.
bootptest	Test **bootpd**.
halt	Stop or shut down system.
init	Change runlevel.
reboot	Shut down, then reboot system.
runlevel	Print system runlevel.
shutdown	Shut down system.
telinit	Change the current runlevel.
uptime	Display uptimes of local machines.

System Activity and Process Management

A number of additional commands in Chapter 3 are particularly useful in controlling processes, including **kill**, **killall**, **killall5**, **pidof**, **ps**, and **who**.

fuser	Identify processes using file or filesystem.
ipcrm	Remove interprocess communication message queue, semaphore array, or shared memory segment.
ipcs	Print interprocess communication information.
renice	Change the priority of running processes.
top	Show most CPU-intensive processes.
vmstat	Print virtual memory statistics and process statistics.

Users

chpasswd	Change multiple passwords.
groupadd	Add a new group.
groupdel	Delete a group.
groupmod	Modify groups.
grpck	Check the integrity of group system files.
grpconv	Convert group file to shadow group file.
lastlog	Generate report of last user login times.
newusers	Add new users in a batch.
pwck	Check the integrity of password system files.
pwconv	Convert password file to shadow passwords.
rusers	Print **who**-style information on remote machines.
rwall	Print a message to remote users.
useradd	Add a new user.
userdel	Delete a user and that user's home directory.
usermod	Modify a user's information.

w	List logged-in users.
wall	Write to all users.
whoami	Show how you are currently logged in.

Miscellaneous

anacron	Schedule commands for periodic execution.
atrun	Schedule commands for later execution.
cron	Schedule commands for specific times.
dmesg	Print bootup messages after the system is up.
ldconfig	Update library links and do caching.
logger	Send messages to the system logger.
logrotate	Compress and rotate system logs.
run-parts	Run all scripts in a directory.

Overview of Networking

Networks connect computers so that the different systems can share information. For users and system administrators, Unix systems have traditionally provided a set of simple but valuable network services that let you check whether systems are running, refer to files residing on remote systems, communicate via electronic mail, and so on.

For most commands to work over a network, each system must be continuously running a server process in the background, silently waiting to handle the user's request. This kind of process is called a *daemon*. Common examples, on which you rely for the most basic functions of your Linux system, are **named** (which translates between numeric IP addresses and more human-readable alphanumeric names), **lpd** (which sends documents to a printer, possibly over a network), and **ftpd** (which allows you to connect to another machine via **ftp**).

Most Unix networking commands are based on Internet protocols. These are standardized ways of communicating across a network on hierarchical layers. The protocols range from addressing and packet routing at a relatively low layer to finding users and executing user commands at a higher layer.

The basic user commands that most systems support over Internet protocols are generally called TCP/IP commands, named after the two most common protocols. You can use all of these commands to communicate with other Unix systems besides Linux systems. Many can also be used to communicate with non-Unix systems, as a wide variety of systems support TCP/IP.

This section also covers NFS and NIS—which allow for transparent file and information sharing across networks—and **sendmail**.

TCP/IP Administration

ftpd	Server for file transfers.
gated	Manage routing tables between networks.
host	Print host and zone information.

ifconfig	Configure network interface parameters.
named	Translate between domain names and IP addresses.
netstat	Print network status.
nslookup	Query domain name servers.
ping	Check that a remote host is online and responding.
pppd	Create PPP serial connection.
rdate	Notify time server that date has changed.
route	Manage routing tables.
routed	Dynamically keep routing tables up to date.
slattach	Attach serial lines as network interfaces.
sshd	Server for secure shell connections.
telnetd	Server for Telnet sessions from remote hosts.
tftpd	Server for restricted set of file transfers.

NFS and NIS Administration

domainname	Set or display name of current NIS domain.
makedbm	Rebuild NIS databases.
portmap	DARPA port to RPC program number mapper.
rpcinfo	Report RPC information.
ypbind	Connect to NIS server.
ypcat	Print values in NIS database.
ypinit	Build new NIS databases.
ypmatch	Print value of one or more NIS keys.
yppasswd	Change user password in NIS database.
yppasswdd	Update NIS database in response to **yppasswd**.
yppoll	Determine version of NIS map at NIS server.
yppush	Propagate NIS map.
ypserv	NIS server daemon.
ypset	Point **ypbind** at a specific server.
yptest	Check NIS configuration.
ypwhich	Display name of NIS server or map master.
ypxfr	Transfer NIS database from server to local host.

Overview of TCP/IP

TCP/IP is a set of communications protocols that define how different types of computers talk to one another. It's named for its two most common protocols, the Transmission Control Protocol and the Internet Protocol. The Internet Protocol moves data between hosts: it splits data into packets, which are then forwarded to machines via the network. The Transmission Control Protocol ensures that the packets in a message are reassembled in the correct order at their final destination and that any missing datagrams are re-sent until they are correctly received. Other protocols provided as part of TCP/IP include:

Address Resolution Protocol (ARP)
    Translates between Internet and local hardware addresses (Ethernet, etc.)

Internet Control Message Protocol (ICMP)
    Error-message and control protocol

Point-to-Point Protocol (PPP)
> Enables TCP/IP (and other protocols) to be carried across both synchronous and asynchronous point-to-point serial links

Reverse Address Resolution Protocol (RARP)
> Translates between local hardware and Internet addresses (opposite of ARP)

Simple Mail Transport Protocol (SMTP)
> Used by **sendmail** to send mail via TCP/IP

Simple Network Management Protocol (SNMP)
> Performs distributed network management functions via TCP/IP

User Datagram Protocol (UDP)
> Provides data transfer, but without the reliable delivery capabilities of TCP

TCP/IP is covered in-depth in the three-volume set *Internetworking with TCP/IP* (Prentice Hall). The commands in this chapter and the next are described in more detail in *TCP/IP Network Administration* and *Linux Network Administrator's Guide* both published by O'Reilly.

In the architecture of TCP/IP protocols, data is passed down the stack (toward the Network Access Layer) when it is sent to the network, and up the stack when it is received from the network (see Figure 2-1).

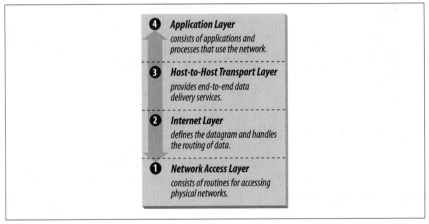

Figure 2-1. Layers in the TCP/IP protocol architecture

IP Addresses

The IP (Internet protocol) address is a 32-bit binary number that differentiates your machine from all others on the network. Each machine must have a unique IP address. An IP address contains two parts: a network part and a host part. The number of address bits used to identify the network and host differ according to the class of the address. There are three main address classes: A, B, and C (see Figure 2-2). The leftmost bits indicate what class each address is.

A standard called Classless Inter-Domain Routing (CIDR) extends the class system's idea of using initial bits to identify where packets should be routed.

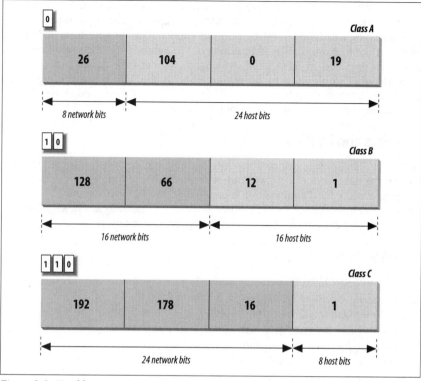

Figure 2-2. IP address structure

Under CIDR, a new domain can be created with any number of fixed leftmost bits (not just a multiple of 8).

Another new standard called IPv6 changes the method of addressing and increases the number of fields. An IPv6 address is 128 bits. When written, it is usually divided into eight 16-bit hexadecimal blocks separated by colons. For example:

```
FE80:0000:0000:0000:0202:B3FF:FE1E:8329
```

To shorten this, leading zeros may be skipped, and any one set of consecutive zeros can be replaced with double colons. For example, the above address can be reduced to:

```
FE80::202:B3FF:FE1E:8329
```

When IPv4 and IPv6 networks are mixed, the IPv4 address can be packed into the lower four bytes, yielding an address like 0:0:0:0:0:0:192.168.1.2, or ::192.168.1.2, or even ::C0A8:102.

Because improvements in IPv4, including CIDR, have relieved much of the pressure to migrate to IPv6, organizations have been slow to adopt IPv6. Some use it experimentally, but communication between organizations using IPv6 internally are still usually encapsulated inside IPv4 datagrams, and it will be a while before IPv6 becomes common.

If you wish to connect to the Internet, contact an Internet Service Provider (ISP) and have them assign you a network address or range of addresses. If you are not connecting to an outside network, you can choose your own network address as long as it conforms to the IP address syntax. You should use the special reserved addresses provided in RFC 1597, which lists IP network numbers for private networks that don't have to be registered with the IANA (Internet Assigned Numbers Authority). An IP address is different from an Ethernet address, which is assigned by the manufacturer of the physical Ethernet card.

Gateways and Routing

Gateways are hosts responsible for exchanging routing information and forwarding data from one network to another. Each portion of a network that is under a separate local administration is called an *autonomous system* (AS). Autonomous systems connect to each other via exterior gateways. An AS also may contain its own system of networks, linked via interior gateways.

Gateway protocols

Gateway protocols include:

EGP (Exterior Gateway Protocol)
BGP (Border Gateway Protocol)
> Protocols for exterior gateways to exchange information

RIP (Routing Information Protocol)
> Interior gateway protocol; most popular for LANs

Hello Protocol
OSPF (Open Shortest Path First)
> Interior gateway protocols

Routing daemons

While most networks will use a dedicated router as a gateway, GNU Zebra and **routed**, the routing daemons, can be run on a host to make it function as a gateway. Only one of them can run on a host at any given time. Zebra is the gateway routing daemon that replaces the older **gated** routing daemon. It allows a host to function as both an exterior and interior gateway, and simplifies the routing configuration by combining the protocols RIP, Hello, BGP, EGP, and OSPF into a single package. We do not cover GNU Zebra in this book.

routed, a network routing daemon that uses RIP, allows a host to function as an interior gateway only, and manages the Internet routing tables. For more details on **routed**, see Chapter 3.

Routing tables

Routing tables provide information needed to route packets to their destinations. This information includes destination network, gateway to use, route status, and number of packets transmitted. Routing tables can be displayed with the **netstat** command.

Name Service

Each host on a network has a name that points to information about that host. Hostnames can be assigned to any device that has an IP address. Name service translates the hostnames (which are easy for people to remember) to IP addresses (the numbers the computer deals with).

DNS and BIND

The Domain Name System (DNS) is a distributed database of information about hosts on a network. Its structure is similar to that of the Unix filesystem—an inverted tree, with the root at the top. The branches of the tree are called *domains* (or *subdomains*) and correspond to IP addresses. The most popular implementation of DNS is the BIND (Berkeley Internet Name Domain) software.

DNS works as a client/server application. The *resolver* is the client, the software that asks questions about host information. The *name server* is the process that answers the questions. The server side of BIND is the **named** daemon. You can interactively query name servers for host information with the **dig** and **host** commands. See Chapter 3 for more details on **named**, **dig**, and **host**.

The name server of a domain is responsible for keeping (and providing on request) the names of the machines in its domain. Other name servers on the network forward requests for these machines to the nameserver.

Domain names

The full domain name is the sequence of names from the current domain back to the root, with a period separating the names. For instance, *oreilly.com* indicates the domain *oreilly* (for O'Reilly & Associates), which is under the domain *com* (for commercial). One machine under this domain is *www.oreilly.com*. Top-level domains include:

aero
> Air-transport industry

biz
> Commercial organizations

com
> Commercial organizations

coop
> Cooperatives

edu
> United States educational organizations

gov
> United States government organizations

info
> Informative sites

int
> International organizations

mil

United States military departments

museum

Museums

name

Names of individuals

net

Commercial Internet organizations, usually Internet service providers

org

Miscellaneous organizations

pro

Professionals, including accountants, lawyers, and physicians

Some domains (e.g., *edu, gov,* and *mil*) are sponsored by organizations that restrict their use; others (e.g., *com, info, net,* and *org*) are unrestricted. Countries also have their own two-letter top-level domains based on two-letter country codes. One special domain, *arpa,* is used for technical infrastructure purposes. The Internet Corporation for Assigned Names and Numbers (ICANN) oversees top-level domains and provides contact information for sponsored domains.

Configuring TCP/IP

Certain commands are normally run in the system's startup files to enable a system to connect to a network. These commands can also be run interactively.

ifconfig

The network interface represents the way that the networking software uses the hardware—the driver, the IP address, and so forth. To configure a network inter-face, use the **ifconfig** command. With **ifconfig**, you can assign an address to a network interface, setting the netmask, broadcast address, and IP address at boot time. You can also set network interface parameters, including the use of ARP, the use of driver-dependent debugging code, the use of one-packet mode, and the address of the correspondent on the other end of a point-to-point link. For more information on **ifconfig**, see Chapter 3.

Serial-line communication

There are two protocols for serial-line communication: Serial Line IP (SLIP) and Point-to-Point Protocol (PPP). These protocols let computers transfer information using the serial port instead of a network card and a serial cable instead of an Ethernet cable. SLIP is rarely used anymore, having been replaced by PPP.

PPP was intended to remedy some of SLIP's failings—it can hold packets from non-Internet protocols, it implements client authorization and error detection/correction, and it dynamically configures each network protocol that passes through it. Under Linux, PPP exists as a driver in the kernel and as the daemon **pppd**. For more information on **pppd**, see Chapter 3.

Troubleshooting TCP/IP

The following commands can be used to troubleshoot TCP/IP. For more details on these commands, see Chapter 3.

ifconfig
> Provide information about the basic configuration of the network interface.

netstat
> Display network status.

ping
> Indicate whether a remote host can be reached.

nslookup
> Query the DNS name service.

traceroute
> Trace route taken by packets to reach network host.

Overview of Firewalls and Masquerading

A firewall computer is a secure system that sits between an internal network and an external network (i.e., the Internet). It is configured with a set of rules that it uses to determine what traffic is allowed to pass and what traffic is barred. While a firewall is generally intended to protect the network from malicious or even accidentally harmful traffic from the outside, it can also be configured to monitor traffic leaving the network. As the sole entry point into the system, the firewall makes it easier to construct defenses and monitor activity.

The firewall can also be set up to present a single IP address to the outside world, even though multiple IP addresses may be used internally. This is known as *masquerading*. Masquerading can act as additional protection, hiding the very existence of a network. It also saves the trouble and expense of obtaining multiple IP addresses.

IP firewalling and masquerading are implemented in Linux Version 2.4 with *netfilter*, also known as **iptables**. In Linux Version 2.2, they are implemented with the **ipchains** facility. The 2.0 kernels used a command called **ipfwadm**, which will not be covered here. The two newer commands are very similar, but differ in some of the organization of their rules. The firewalling facilities built into the 2.4 kernel are also designed to be extensible—if there is some function missing from the implementation, you can add it.

Most distributions come with firewall support already built into the kernel. If this is not the case in your distribution, you need to compile firewall support into the kernel by running **make config** with the 2.4 kernel and selecting the following network options:

- Network packet filtering (replaces **ipchains**)
- TCP/IP networking

Then select the following options from the IP: Netfilter Configuration menu:

- IP tables support (required for filtering/masq/NAT)
- Packet filtering

There are several extended target and matching rule modules you may wish to compile as well. The behavior of those extension modules is described under the **iptables** command. If you have an existing firewall designed for the 2.2 kernel or the 2.0 kernel, you can compile support for these older-style commands and use them with your new kernel instead of the newer **iptables** style of netfiltering.

For **ipchains** support in the 2.2 kernel, select these options:

- Network firewalls
- TCP/IP networking
- IP: firewalling

If you want to support a transparent proxy service on your firewall, select the following option:

- IP: transparent proxy support

If you want your firewall to support masquerading, select the following options as well:

- IP: masquerading
- IP: ICMP masquerading

The packet filtering facilities provide built-in rule sets. Each network packet is checked against each rule in the rule set until the packet either matches a rule or is not matched by any rule. These sets of rules are called *chains*. In the 2.4 kernel, these chains are organized into tables that separate filtering functions from masquerading and packet mangling functions. In either the 2.4 or 2.2 kernel, if a match is found, the counters on that rule are incremented and any target for that rule is applied. A target might accept, reject, or masquerade a packet, or even pass it along to another chain for processing. Details on the chains provided in both **iptables** and **ipchains** can be found under the description of the appropriate command.

In addition to these chains, you can create your own user-defined chains. You might want a special chain for your PPP interfaces or for packets from a particular site. To call a user-defined chain, you just make it the target for a match.

It is possible to make it through a chain without matching any rules that have a target. If no rule matches the packet in a user-defined chain, control returns to the chain from which it was called, and the next rule in that chain is checked. If no rule matches the packet in a built-in chain, a default policy for that chain is used. The default policy can be any of the special targets that determine what is done with a packet. The valid targets for each command are detailed in Chapter 3.

In the 2.4 kernel, you use the **iptables** command to define the rules. Once you have the rules defined you can use **iptables-save** to create a file with all the rule definitions, and **iptables-restore** to restore those definitions when you reboot. The equivalent 2.2 kernel commands are **ipchains**, **ipchains-save**, and **ipchains-restore**.

For more information on the kinds of decisions you need to make and the considerations that go into defining the rules, see a general book on firewalls such as *Building Internet Firewalls* (O'Reilly). For more details on **ipchains** or **iptables**, consult the *Linux Network Administrator's Guide* (O'Reilly), or one of the relevant HOWTOs, such as the "Linux 2.4 Packet Filtering HOWTO." These HOWTOs and a number of tutorials are available on the Netfilter web site at *http://www.netfilter.org/*.

Overview of NFS

The Network File System (NFS) is a distributed filesystem that allows users to mount remote filesystems as if they were local. NFS uses a client/server model in which a server exports directories to be shared, and clients mount the directories to access the files in them. NFS eliminates the need to keep copies of files on several machines by letting the clients all share a single copy of a file on the server. NFS is an RPC-based application-level protocol. For more information on the architecture of network protocols, see "Overview of TCP/IP" earlier in this chapter.

Administering NFS

To set up NFS clients and servers you must start the NFS daemons on the servers, export filesystems from the NFS servers, and mount the filesystems on the clients. The */etc/exports* file is the NFS server configuration file; it controls which files and directories are exported and what kinds of access are allowed. Names and addresses for clients that should be allowed or denied access to NFS are kept in the */etc/hosts.allow* and */etc/hosts.deny* files.

Daemons

NFS server daemons, called *nfsd daemons*, run on the server and accept RPC calls from clients. NFS servers also run the **mountd** daemon to handle mount requests. On the client, caching and buffering are handled by **biod**, the block I/O daemon. The **portmap** daemon maps RPC program numbers to the appropriate TCP/IP port numbers.

Exporting Filesystems

To set up an NFS server, first check that all the hosts that will mount your filesystem can reach your host. Next, edit the */etc/exports* file on the server. Each entry in this file indicates the name of a directory to be exported, domain names of machines that will have access to that particular mount point, and any options specific to that machine. A typical entry looks like:

```
/projects hostname1(rw) hostname2(ro)
```

If you are running **mountd**, the files will be exported as the permissions in */etc/exports* allow. See the **exports** manpage for all available export options.

Mounting Filesystems

To enable an NFS client, mount a remote filesystem after NFS is started, either by using the **mount** command or by specifying default remote filesystems in */etc/ fstab*. For example:

```
# mount servername:/projects /mnt/nfs/projects
```

A **mount** request calls the server's **mountd** daemon, which checks the access permissions of the client and returns a pointer to a filesystem. Once a directory is mounted, it remains attached to the local filesystem until it is unmounted with the **umount** command or until the local system is rebooted.

Usually, only a privileged user can mount filesystems with NFS. However, you can enable users to mount and unmount selected filesystems using the **mount** and **umount** commands if the **user** option is set in */etc/fstab*. This can reduce traffic by having filesystems mounted only when needed. To enable user mounting, create an entry in */etc/fstab* for each filesystem to be mounted.

Overview of NIS

The Network Information System (NIS) refers to the service formerly known as Sun Yellow Pages (YP). It is used to make configuration information consistent on all machines in a network. It does this by designating a single host as the master of all the system administration files and databases and distributing this information to all other hosts on the network. The information is compiled into databases called maps. NIS is built on the RPC protocol. There are currently two NIS servers freely available for Linux, **yps** and **ypserv**. We describe **ypserv** in this book.

Servers

In NIS, there are two types of servers—master servers and slave servers. Master servers are responsible for maintaining the maps and distributing them to the slave servers. The files are then available locally to requesting processes.

Domains

An NIS domain is a group of hosts that use the same set of maps. The maps are contained in a subdirectory of */var/yp* having the same name as the domain. The machines in a domain share password, host, and group file information. NIS domain names are set with the **domainname** command.

NIS Maps

NIS stores information in database files called *maps*. Each map consists of a pair of **dbm** database files, one containing a directory of keys (a bitmap of indices) and the other containing data values. The non-ASCII structure of **dbm** files necessitates using NIS tools such as **yppush** to move maps between machines.

The file */var/yp/YP_MAP_X_LATE* contains a complete listing of active NIS maps as well as NIS aliases for NIS maps. All maps must be listed in this file in order for NIS to serve them.

Map Manipulation Utilities

The following utilities are used to administer NIS maps:

makedbm
> Make **dbm** files. Modify only **ypserv**'s map and any nondefault maps.

ypinit
> Build and install NIS databases. Manipulate maps when NIS is being initialized. Should not be used when NIS is already running.

yppush
> Transfer updated maps from the master server.

Administering NIS

NIS is enabled by setting up NIS servers and NIS clients. The descriptions given here describe NIS setup using **ypserv**, which does not support a master/slave server configuration. All NIS commands depend on the RPC **portmap** program, so make sure it is installed and running before setting up NIS.

Setting Up an NIS Server

Setting up an NIS server involves the following steps:

1. Set a domain name for NIS using **domainname**
2. Edit the *ypMakefile*, which identifies which databases to build and what sources to use in building them
3. Copy the *ypMakefile* to */var/yp/Makefile*
4. Run **make** from the */var/yp* directory, which builds the databases and initializes the server
5. Start **ypserv**, the NIS server daemon

Setting Up an NIS Client

Setting up an NIS client involves only the following steps:

1. Set the domain name for NIS using **domainname**, which should be the same name used by the NIS server
2. Run **ypbind**

NIS User Accounts

NIS networks have two kinds of user accounts: distributed and local. Distributed accounts must be administered from the master machine; they provide information that is uniform on each machine in an NIS domain. Changes made to distributed accounts are distributed via NIS maps. Local accounts are administered from the local computer; they provide account information unique to a specific machine. They are not affected by NIS maps, and changes made to local accounts do not affect NIS. When NIS is installed, preexisting accounts default to local accounts.

RPC and XDR

RPC (Remote Procedure Call) is the session protocol used by both NFS and NIS. It allows a host to make a procedure call that appears to be local but is really executed remotely on another machine on the network. RPC is implemented as a library of procedures, plus a network standard for ordering bytes and data structures called XDR (eXternal Data Representation).

3

Linux Commands

This chapter presents the Linux user, programmer, and system administration commands. These are entered into a shell at the console or on a virtual terminal on a graphical desktop.

Each entry is labeled with the command name on the outer edge of the page. The syntax line is followed by a brief description and a list of available options. Many commands come with examples at the end of the entry. If you need only a quick reminder or suggestion about a command, you can skip directly to the examples.

Typographic conventions for describing command syntax are listed in the Preface. For help in locating commands, see the index at the back of this book.

We've tried to be as thorough as possible in listing options. The basic command information and most options should be correct; however, there are many Linux distributions and many versions of commands. New options are added and sometimes old options are dropped. You may, therefore, find some differences between the options you find described here and the ones on your system. When there seems to be a discrepancy, check the manpage. For most commands you can also use the option **--help** to get a brief usage message. (Even when it isn't a valid option, it will usually result in an "invalid option" error along with the usage message.)

Traditionally, commands take single-letter options preceded by a single hyphen, like **-d**. A more recent convention allows long options preceded by two hyphens, like **--debug**. Often, a feature can be invoked through either the old style or the new style of options.

Alphabetical Summary of Commands

aclocal

aclocal [*options*]

GNU **autoconf** tool. Place **m4** macro definitions needed by **auto-conf** into a single file. The **aclocal** command first scans for macro definitions in **m4** files in its default directory (*/usr/share/aclocal* on some systems) and in the file *acinclude.m4*. It next scans for macros used in the *configure.in* file. It generates an *aclocal.m4* file that contains definitions of all **m4** macros required by autoconf.

Options

--**acdir**=*dir*
> Look for macro files in directory *dir* instead of the default directory.

--**help**
> Print help message, then exit.

--**output**=*file*
> Save output to *file* instead of *aclocal.m4*.

--**print-ac-dir**
> Print the name of the directory to be searched for **m4** files, then exit.

--**verbose**
> Print names of files being processed.

--**version**
> Print version number, then exit.

-**I** *dir*
> Additionally, search directory *dir* for **m4** macro definitions.

addr2line

addr2line [*options*] [*addresses*]

Translate hexadecimal program addresses into filenames and line numbers for the executable given with the **-e** option, or *a.out* if **-e** is not specified. If *addresses* are given on the command line, display the filename and line number for each address. Otherwise, read the addresses from standard input and display the results on standard output (useful for use in a pipe). **addr2line** prints two question marks (??) if it cannot determine a filename, and 0 if it cannot determine the line number. **addr2line** is used for debugging.

Options

-**b** *bfdname*, --**target**=*bfdname*
> Set the binary file format using its binary file descriptor name, *bfdname*. Use the **-h** option for a list of supported formats for your system.

-**C**, --**demangle**[=*style*]
> Decode (demangle) low-level symbol names into user names. See the **-h** help output for a list of styles supported by your compiler.

-e *file*, **--exe**=*file*

Specify the filename of the executable to use. The default is *a.out*.

-f, **--functions**

Display function names in addition to filenames and line numbers.

-h, **--help**

Display help information and exit.

-s, **--basenames**

Strip directories off filenames and show only the basenames.

---

agetty

agetty [*options*] *port baudrate* [*term*]

System administration command. The Linux version of **getty**. Set terminal type, modes, speed, and line discipline. **agetty** is invoked by **init**. It is the second process in the series **init-getty-login-shell**, which ultimately connects a user with the Linux system. **agetty** reads the user's login name and invokes the **login** command with the user's name as an argument. While reading the name, **agetty** attempts to adapt the system to the speed and type of device being used.

You must specify a *port*, which **agetty** will search for in the */dev* directory. You may use -, in which case **agetty** reads from standard input. You must also specify *baudrate*, which may be a comma-separated list of rates through which **agetty** will step. Optionally, you may specify the *term*, which is used to override the TERM environment variable.

Options

-f *file*

Specify the use of *file* instead of */etc/issue* upon connection to terminal. It is overridden by **-i**.

-h   Specify hardware, not software, flow control.

-H *hostname*

Write login *hostname* into the *utmp* file. By default, no login host is specified.

-I *string*

Specify *string* to be sent to tty or modem.

-i   Suppress printing of */etc/issue* before printing the login prompt.

-l *program*

Specify the use of *program* instead of */bin/login*.

-m   Attempt to guess the appropriate baud rate.

-n   Don't prompt for a login name.

-t *timeout*

Specify that **agetty** should exit if the **open** on the line succeeds and there is no response to the login prompt in *timeout* seconds.

-L Do not require carrier detect; operate locally only. Use this when connecting terminals.

-w Wait for carriage return or linefeed before sending login prompt. Use when sending an initialization string.

---

anacron

anacron [*options*] [*job*]

System administration command. Normally started in a system startup file. Execute commands periodically. By default, the **anacron** command reads a list of jobs from a configuration file, /etc/anacrontab. The file consists of shell variables to use when running commands, followed by a list of tasks to run. Each task specifies how often in days it should be run, a delay in minutes to wait before running the task, a unique job identifier used to store a timestamp, and the shell command to execute. Timestamps for the last run of each task are stored in the /var/spool/anacron file. For each task, **anacron** compares the stored timestamp against the current time. If the command has not been executed within the specified frequency, the command is run. Upon completion **anacron** records the new date in the timestamp file. Limit **anacron** to a specified task by giving its unique *job* identifier on the command line.

The **anacron** command is often used to support the **cron** daemon on systems that are not run continuously.

Options

-d Run in foreground rather than as a background process. Send messages to standard error.

-f Run tasks ignoring timestamps.

-h Print help message, then exit.

-n Run tasks now, ignoring delay specifications.

-q Suppress messages to standard error when using the **-d** option.

-s Execute tasks serially. Do not start new task until previous task is completed.

-t *file*
Read tasks from *file* instead of from /etc/anacrontab.

-u Update timestamps for tasks, but don't run them.

-V Print version number, then exit.

---

apmd

apmd [*options*]

System administration command. **apmd** handles events reported by the Advanced Power Management BIOS driver. The driver reports on battery level and requests to enter sleep or suspend mode. **apmd** will log any reports it gets via **syslogd** and take steps to make sure that basic sleep and suspend requests are handled gracefully. You can fine-tune the behavior of **apmd** by specifying an **apmd_proxy** command to run when it receives an event.

Options

-c *n*, --check *n*

> Set the number of seconds to wait for an event before rechecking the power level. Default is to wait indefinitely. Setting this causes the battery levels to be checked more frequently.

-P *command*, --apmd_proxy *command*

> Specify the **apmd_proxy** command to run when APM driver events are reported. This is generally a shell script. The *command* will be invoked with parameters indicating what kind of event was received. The parameters are listed in the next section.

-p *n*, --percentage *n*

> Log information whenever the power changes by *n* percent. The default is 5. Values greater than 100 will disable logging of power changes.

-V, --version

> Print version and exit.

-v, --verbose

> Verbose mode; all events are logged.

-W, --wall

> Use **wall** to alert all users of a low battery status.

-w *n*, --warn *n*

> Log a warning at ALERT level when the battery charge drops below *n* percent. The default is 10. Negative values disable low battery level warnings.

-q, --quiet

> Disable low battery level warnings.

-?, --help

> Print help summary and exit.

Parameters

The **apmd** proxy script will be invoked with the following parameters:

start

> Invoked when the daemon starts.

stop

> Invoked when the daemon stops.

suspend [system | user]

> Invoked when a suspend request has been made. The second parameter indicates whether the request was made by the system or by the user.

standby [system | user]

> Invoked when a standby request has been made. The second parameter indicates whether the request was made by the system or by the user.

resume [suspend | standby | critical]

Invoked when the system resumes normal operation. The second parameter indicates the mode the system was in before resuming. **critical** suspends indicate an emergency shutdown. After a **critical** suspend the system may be unstable, and you can use the **resume** command to help you recover from the suspension.

change power

Invoked when system power is changed from AC to battery or from battery to AC.

change battery

Invoked when the APM BIOS driver reports that the battery is low.

change capability

Invoked when the APM BIOS driver reports that some hardware that affects its capability has been added or removed.

---

apropos

apropos *string* ...

Search the short manual page descriptions in the **whatis** database for occurrences of each *string* and display the result on the standard output. Like **whatis**, except that it searches for strings instead of words. Equivalent to **man -k**.

---

apt

apt

The Advanced Package Tool, the Debian package management system. A freely available packaging system for software distribution and installation. For detailed information on **apt** and its commands, see Chapter 5.

---

ar

ar *key* [*args*] [*posname*] [*count*] *archive* [*files*]

Maintain a group of *files* that are combined into a file *archive*. Used most commonly to create and update static library files as used by the link editor (**ld**). Compiler frontends often call **ar** automatically. Only one key letter may be used, but each can be combined with additional *args* (with no separations between). *posname* is the name of a file in *archive*. When moving or replacing *files*, you can specify that they be placed before or after *posname*.

Keys

d   Delete *files* from *archive*.

m   Move *files* to end of *archive*.

p   Print *files* in *archive*.

q   Append *files* to *archive*.

r   Replace *files* in *archive*.

t   List the contents of *archive* or list the named *files*.

x   Extract contents from *archive* or only the named *files*.

Arguments

a   Use with **r** or **m** key to place *files* in the archive after *posname*.

b   Same as **a,** but before *posname*.

c   Create *archive* silently.

f   Truncate long filenames.

i   Same as **b.**

l   For backward compatibility; meaningless in Linux.

N   Use *count* parameter. Where multiple entries with the same name are found, use the *count* instance.

o   Preserve original timestamps.

P   Use full pathname. Useful for non-POSIX-compliant archives.

s   Force regeneration of *archive* symbol table (useful after running **strip**).

S   Do not regenerate symbol table.

u   Use with **r** to replace only *files* that have changed since being put in *archive*.

v   Verbose; print a description of actions taken.

V   Print version number.

Example

Replace **mylib.a** with object files from the current directory:

```
ar r mylib.a `ls *.o`
```

---

arch

arch

Print machine architecture type to standard output. Equivalent to **uname -m**.

---

arp

arp [*options*]

TCP/IP command. Clear, add to, or dump the kernel's Address Resolution Protocol (ARP) cache (*/proc/net/arp*). ARP is used to translate protocol addresses to hardware interface addresses. Modifying your ARP cache can change which interfaces handle specific requests. ARP cache entries may be marked with the following flags: C (complete), M (permanent), and P (publish). In kernels before 2.2, a published entry was used for creating an ARP proxy, a technique by which one system can act as a gateway to another system on the same subnet. While **arp** can create a proxy for a single system, subnet proxies are now handled by the **arp** kernel module. See the Linux 2.4 Advanced Routing HOWTO for details. We have retained the subnet proxy information here for older kernels.

Options

host option arguments may be given as either a hostname or an IP address. When using the **-D** option, they may also be given as a hardware interface address (e.g., eth0, eth1).

-a [*hosts*], **--display** [*hosts*]
> Display entries for *hosts* or, if none are specified, all entries.

-d *host,* **--delete** *host*
> Remove the specified *host*'s entry.

-D, --use-device
> Use the hardware address associated with the specified interface. This may be used with **-s** when creating a proxy entry.

-d *host* [**pub**]*,* **--delete** *host* [**pub**]
> Remove *host*'s entry. To delete a proxy entry, use the **pub** argument and specify the interface associated with the proxy using **-i**.

-f *file,* **--file** *file*
> Read entries from *file* and add them.

-H *type,* **--hw-type** *type,* **-t** *type*
> Search for *type* entries when examining the ARP cache. *type* is usually **ether** (Ethernet), which is the default, but may be **ax25** (AX.25 packet radio), **arcnet** (ARCnet), **pronet** (PROnet), or **netrom** (NET/ROM).

-i *interface,* **--device** *interface*
> Select an interface. If you are dumping the ARP cache, this option will cause the command to display only the entries using that interface. When setting entries, this will cause the interface to be associated with that entry. If you do not use this option when setting an entry, the kernel will guess.

-n, --numeric
> Display host IP addresses instead of their domain names.

-s *host hardware-address* [**netmask** *mask*] [**pub**], **--set** *host hardware-address* [**netmask** *mask*] [**pub**]
> Add a permanent entry for *host* at *hardware-address*. A *hardware-address* for type **ether** hardware is 6 hexadecimal bytes, colon-separated. The **pub** argument can be used to set the publish flag, creating a proxy entry. On kernels before 2.2x, you can specify a netmask on behalf of which the current system should handle requests.

-v, --verbose
> Verbose mode.

Examples

Display entry for host **eris**:

```
arp -a eris
```

Set a permanent cache entry for host **illuminati**, whose hardware address you know:

```
arp -s illuminati 00:05:23:73:e6:cf
```

Set an ARP proxy for host **fnord** using the **eth0** interface's hardware address:

> `arp -Ds fnord eth0 pub`

Remove the **fnord** ARP proxy:

> `arp -i eth0 -d fnord pub`

---

as

as [*options*] *files*

Generate an object file from each specified assembly language source *file*. Object files have the same root name as source files but replace the *.s* suffix with *.o*. There may be some additional system-specific options.

Options

-- [| *files*]

Read input files from standard input, or from *files* if the pipe is used.

-a[**cdhlmns**][=*file*]

With only the **-a** option, list source code, assembler listing, and symbol table. The other options specify additional things to list or omit:

-ac

Omit false conditionals.

-ad

Omit debugging directives.

-ah

Include the high-level source code, if available.

-al

Include an assembly listing.

-am

Include macro expansions.

-an

Suppress forms processing.

-as

Include a symbol listing.

=*file*

Set the listing filename to *file*.

--defsym *symbol=value*

Define the *symbol* to have the value *value*, which must be an integer.

-f   Skip whitespace and comment preprocessing.

--fatal-warnings

Treat warnings as errors.

--gstabs

Generate stabs debugging information.

--gdwarf2

Generate DWARF2 debugging information.

-o *objfile*

Place output in object file *objfile* (default is *file*.o).

--statistics

Print information time and space assembler uses.

-v   Display the version number of the assembler.

-I *path*

Include *path* when searching for **.include** directives.

-J   Don't warn about signed overflow.

-R   Combine both data and text in text section.

-W   Don't show warnings.

-Z   Generate object file even if there are errors.

---

at

at [*options*] *time*

Execute commands at a specified *time* and optional *date*. The commands are read from standard input or from a file. (See also **batch**.) End input with EOF. *time* can be formed either as a numeric hour (with optional minutes and modifiers) or as a keyword. It can contain an optional *date*, formed as a month and date, a day of the week, or a special keyword (**today** or **tomorrow**). An increment can also be specified.

The **at** command can always be issued by a privileged user. Other users must be listed in the file */etc/at.allow* if it exists; otherwise, they must not be listed in */etc/at.deny*. If neither file exists, only a privileged user can issue the command.

Options

-c *job* [*job...*]

Display the specified jobs on the standard output. This option does not take a time specification.

-d *job* [*job...*]

Delete the specified jobs. Same as **atrm**.

-f *file*

Read job from *file*, not from standard input.

-l   Report all jobs that are scheduled for the invoking user. Same as **atq**.

-m   Mail user when job has completed, regardless of whether output was created.

-q *letter*

Place job in queue denoted by *letter*, where *letter* is any single letter from a–z or A–Z. Default queue is **a**. (The batch queue defaults to **b**.) Higher-lettered queues run at a lower priority.

-V   Display the version number.

Time

hh:mm [*modifiers*]

Hours can have one digit or two (a 24-hour clock is assumed by default); optional minutes can be given as one or two digits; the colon can be omitted if the format is *h*, *hh*, or *hhmm* (e.g., valid times are 5, 5:30, 0530, 19:45). If modifier **am** or **pm** is added, *time* is based on a 12-hour clock. If the keyword **zulu** is added, times correspond to Greenwich Mean Time.

midnight | noon | teatime | now

Use any one of these keywords in place of a numeric time. **teatime** translates to 4:00 p.m.; **now** must be followed by an *increment* (described in a moment).

Date

month num[, *year*]

month is one of the 12 months, spelled out or abbreviated to its first three letters; *num* is the calendar date of the month; *year* is the four-digit year. If the given *month* occurs before the current month, **at** schedules that month next year.

day

One of the seven days of the week, spelled out or abbreviated to its first three letters.

today | tomorrow

Indicate the current day or the next day. If *date* is omitted, **at** schedules **today** when the specified *time* occurs later than the current time; otherwise, **at** schedules **tomorrow**.

Increment

Supply a numeric increment if you want to specify an execution time or day *relative* to the current time. The number should precede any of the keywords **minute**, **hour**, **day**, **week**, **month**, or **year** (or their plural forms). The keyword **next** can be used as a synonym of **+ 1**.

Examples

In typical usage, you run **at** and input commands that you want executed at a particular time, followed by EOF.

```
$ at 1:00 am tomorrow
at> ./total_up > output
at> mail joe < output
at> <EOT>              Entered by pressing Ctrl-D
job 1 at 2003-03-19 01:00
```

The two commands could also be placed in a file and submitted as follows:

```
$ at 1:00 am tomorrow < scriptfile
```

More examples of syntax follow. Note that the first two commands are equivalent.

```
$ at 1945 December 9
$ at 7:45pm Dec 9
$ at 3 am Saturday
$ at now + 5 hours
$ at noon next day
```

atd

atd *options*

System administration command. Normally started in a system startup file. Execute jobs queued by the **at** command.

Options

-b *n*

Wait at least *n* seconds after beginning one job before beginning the next job. Default is 60.

-d Print error messages to standard error instead of using **syslog**.

-l *average*

When system load average is higher than *average*, wait to begin a new job. Default is 0.8.

-s Process queue once, then exit.

atq

atq [*options*]

List the user's pending jobs, unless the user is a privileged user; in that case, list everybody's jobs. Same as **at -l**, and related to **batch** and **atrm**.

Options

-q *queue*

Query only the specified queue and ignore all other queues.

-v Show jobs that have completed but have not yet been deleted.

-V Print the version number.

atrm

atrm [*options*] *job* [*job...*]

Delete jobs that have been queued for future execution. Same as **at -d**.

Options

-q *queue*

Remove job from the specified queue.

-V Print the version number and then exit.

audiosend

audiosend [*email@address*]

Send an audio recording as an email from a properly equipped workstation (Sun and Sony, with microphones). After prompting for address, subject, and Cc: fields, the program asks the user to record a message, then allows him to re-record, send, or cancel.

autoconf

autoconf [*options*] [*template_file*]

Generate a configuration script from **m4** macros defined in *template_file*, if given, or in a *configue.ac* or *configure.in* file in the current working directory. The generated script is almost invariably called *configure*.

Options

-d, --debug
> Don't remove temporary files.

-f, --force
> Replace files generated previously by **autoconf**.

-h, --help
> Print help message, then exit.

-i, --initialization
> When tracing calls with the **-t** option, report calls made during initialization.

-o *file*, **--output=***file*
> Save output to *file*.

-t *macro*, **--trace=***macro*
> Report the list of calls to *macro*.

-v, --verbose
> Verbosely print information about the progress of **autoconf**.

-I *dir*, **--include=***dir*
> Search in directory *dir* for input files.

-V, --version
> Print version number, then exit.

-W *category*, **--warnings=***category*
> Print any warnings related to *category*. Accepted categories are:

> **cross**
>> Cross compilation.

> **obsolete**
>> Obsolete constructs.

> **syntax**
>> Questionable syntax.

> **all**
>> All warnings.

> **no-***category*
>> Turn off warnings for *category*.

> **none**
>> Turn off all warnings.

> **error**
>> Treat warnings as errors.

---

autoheader

autoheader [*options*] [*template_file*]

GNU **autoconf** tool. Generate a template file of C **#define** statements from **m4** macros defined in *template_file*, if given, or in a *configue.ac* or *configure.in* file in the current working directory. The generated template file is almost invariably called *config.h.in*.

Options

-d, --debug
    Don't remove temporary files.

-f, --force
    Replace files generated previously by **autoheader**.

-h, --help
    Print help message, then exit.

-o *file*, **--output=***file*
    Save output to *file*.

-v, --verbose
    Verbosely print information about the progress of **autoheader**.

-I *dir*, **--include=***dir*
    Search in directory *dir* for input files.

-V, --version
    Print version number, then exit.

-W *category*, **--warnings=***category*
    Print any warnings related to *category*. Accepted categories are:

obsolete
    Obsolete constructs.

all
    All warnings.

no-*category*
    Turn off warnings for *category*.

none
    Turn off all warnings.

error
    Treat warnings as errors.

---

automake

automake [*options*] [*template_file*]

GNU **automake** tool. Creates GNU standards-compliant *Makefile.in* files from *Makefile.am* template files and can be used to ensure that projects contain all files and install options required to be standards-compliant. Note that Versions 1.4 and 1.6 differ enough that many distributions include an *automake14* package for backward compatibility.

Options

-a, --add-missing
    Add any missing files **automake** requires to the directory by creating symbolic links to **automake**'s default versions.

-c, --copy
    Used with the **-a** option. Copy missing files instead of creating symbolic links.

--cygnus
    Specifies project has a Cygnus-style source tree.

-f, --force-missing
> Used with the **-a** option. Replace required files even if a local copy already exists.

--foreign
> Treat project as a non-GNU project. Check only for elements required for proper operation.

--gnu
> Treat project as a GNU project with the GNU project structure.

--gnits
> A stricter version of **--gnu**, performing more checks to comply with GNU project structure rules.

--help
> Print help message, then exit.

-i, --ignore-deps
> Disable automatic dependency tracking.

--libdir=_dir_
> Used with the **-a** option. Search in directory _dir_ for default files.

--no-force
> Update only _Makefile.in_ files that have updated dependents.

-v, --verbose
> List files being read or created by **automake**.

--version
> Print version number, then exit.

-Werror
> Treat warnings as errors.

---

autoreconf

autoreconf [_options_]

GNU **autoconf** tool. Update configure scripts by running **autoconf**, **autoheader**, **aclocal**, **automake**, and **libtoolize** in specified directories and subdirectories. This command is seldom invoked manually. It is usually called automatically from other **autoconf** tools.

Options

-d, --debug
> Don't remove temporary files.

-f, --force
> Remake all configure scripts, even when newer than their template files.

-h, --help
> Print help message, then exit.

-i, --install
> Add any default files missing from package by copying versions included with **autoconf** and **automake**.

-s, --symlink
Used with the **-i** option. Create symbolic links to default files instead of copying them.

-v, --verbose
Verbosely print information about the progress of **autoreconf**.

-I *dir*, **--include**=*dir*
Search in directory *dir* for input files.

-V, --version
Print version number, then exit.

-W *category*, **--warnings**=*category*
Print any warnings related to *category*. Accepted categories are:

cross
Cross compilation.

obsolete
Obsolete constructs.

syntax
Questionable syntax.

all
All warnings.

no-*category*
Turn off warnings for *category*.

none
Turn off all warnings.

error
Treat warnings as errors.

---

autoscan

autoscan [*options*] [*directory*]

GNU **autoconf** tool. Create or maintain a preliminary *configure.ac* file named *configure.scan* based on source files in specified *directory*, or current directory if none given. If a *configure.ac* file already exists, **autoconf** will check it for completeness and print suggestions for correcting any problems it finds.

Options

-d, --debug
Don't remove temporary files.

-h, --help
Print help message, then exit.

-v, --verbose
Verbosely print information about the progress of **autoscan**.

-I *dir*, **--include**=*dir*
Search in directory *dir* for input files. Use multiple times to add multiple directories.

-B *dir,* **--prepend-include=***dir*
> Search *dir* for input files before searching in other directories.
> Use multiple times to add multiple directories.

-V, **--version**
> Print version number, then exit.

---

autoupdate

autoupdate [*options*] [*file*]

GNU **autoconf** tool. Update the configure template file *file,* or *configure.ac* if no file is specified. This command is seldom invoked manually. It is usually called automatically from other **autoconf** tools.

Options
-d, **--debug**
> Don't remove temporary files.

-f, **--force**
> Remake all configure scripts, even when newer than their template files.

-h, **--help**
> Print help message, then exit.

-v, **--verbose**
> Verbosely print information about the progress of **autoupdate**.

-I *dir,* **--include=***dir*
> Search in directory *dir* for input files.

-V, **--version**
> Print version number, then exit.

---

badblocks

badblocks [*options*] *device block-count*

System administration command. Search *device* for bad blocks. You must specify the number of blocks on the device (*block-count*).

Options
-b *blocksize*
> Expect *blocksize*-byte blocks.

-c *blocksize*
> Test *blocksize*-byte blocks at a time. Default is 16.

-f   Force a read/write or nondestructive write test on a mounted device. Use only when */etc/mtab* incorrectly reports a device as mounted.

-i *file*
> Skip test of known bad blocks listed in *file*.

-n   Perform a nondestructive test by writing to each block and then reading back from it while preserving data.

-o *file*
> Direct output to *file*.

-p *number*

    Repeat search of device until no new bad blocks have been found in *number* passes. Default is 0.

-v   Verbose mode.

-w   Test by writing to each block and then reading back from it.

---

banner

banner [*option*] [*characters*]

Print *characters* as a poster. If no *characters* are supplied, **banner** prompts for them and reads an input line from standard input. By default, the results go to standard output, but they are intended to be sent to a printer.

Option

-w *width*

    Set width to *width* characters. Note that if your banner is in all lowercase, it will be narrower than *width* characters. If **-w** is not specified, the default width is 132. If **-w** is specified but *width* is not provided, the default is 80.

Example

`/usr/games/banner -w50 Happy Birthday! |lpr`

---

basename

basename *name* [*suffix*]
basename *option*

Remove leading directory components from a path. If *suffix* is given, remove that also. The result is printed to standard output.

Options

--help

    Print help message and then exit.

--version

    Print the version number and then exit.

Examples

```
% basename /usr/lib/libm.a
libm.a
```

```
% basename /usr/lib/libm.a .a
libm
```

---

bash

bash [*options*] [*file* [*arguments*]]
sh [*options*] [*file* [*arguments*]]

Standard Linux shell, a command interpreter into which all other commands are entered. For more information, see Chapter 7.

batch

batch [*options*] [*time*]

Execute commands entered on standard input. If *time* is omitted, execute commands when the system load permits (when the load average falls below 0.8). Very similar to **at**, but does not insist that the execution time be entered on the command line. See **at** for details.

Options

-f *file*
> Read job from *file*, not standard input.

-m Mail user when job has completed, regardless of whether output was created.

-q *letter*
> Place job in queue denoted by *letter*, where *letter* is one letter from a–z or A–Z. The default queue is **b**. (The **at** queue defaults to **a**.) Higher-lettered queues run at a lower priority.

-V Print the version number and then exit.

-v Display the time a job will be executed.

bc

bc [*options*] [*files*]

bc is a language (and compiler) whose syntax resembles that of C, but with unlimited-precision arithmetic. **bc** consists of identifiers, keywords, and symbols, which are briefly described in the following entries. Examples are given at the end.

Interactively perform arbitrary-precision arithmetic or convert numbers from one base to another. Input can be taken from *files* or read from the standard input. To exit, type **quit** or EOF.

Options

-h, --help
> Print help message and exit.

-i, --interactive
> Interactive mode.

-l, --mathlib
> Make functions from the math library available.

-s, --standard
> Ignore all extensions, and process exactly as in POSIX.

-w, --warn
> When extensions to POSIX **bc** are used, print a warning.

-q, --quiet
> Do not display welcome message.

-v, --version
> Print version number.

Identifiers

An identifier is a series of one or more characters. It must begin with a lowercase letter but may also contain digits and underscores. No uppercase letters are allowed. Identifiers are used as names for variables, arrays, and functions. Variables normally store arbitrary-precision numbers. Within the same program you may name a variable, an array, and a function using the same letter. The following identifiers would not conflict:

x Variable *x*.

x[*i*]

> Element *i* of array *x*. *i* can range from 0 to 2047 and can also be an expression.

x(y,z)

> Call function *x* with parameters *y* and *z*.

Input-output keywords

ibase, **obase**, **scale**, and **last** store a value. Typing them on a line by themselves displays their current value. You can also change their values through assignment. The letters A–F are treated as digits whose values are 10–15.

ibase = *n*

> Numbers that are input (e.g., typed) are read as base *n* (default is 10).

obase = *n*

> Numbers that are displayed are in base *n* (default is 10). Note: once **ibase** has been changed from 10, use A to restore **ibase** or **obase** to decimal.

scale = *n*

> Display computations using *n* decimal places (default is 0, meaning that results are truncated to integers). **scale** is normally used only for base-10 computations.

last

> Value of last printed number.

Statement keywords

A semicolon or a newline separates one statement from another. Curly braces are needed when grouping multiple statements.

if (*rel-expr*) {*statements*} [**else** {*statements*}]

> Do one or more *statements* if relational expression *rel-expr* is true. Otherwise, do nothing, or if **else** (an extension) is specified, do alternative *statements*. For example:

```
if (x==y) {i = i + 1} else {i = i - 1}
```

while (*rel-expr*) {*statements*}

> Repeat one or more *statements* while *rel-expr* is true; for example:

```
while (i>0) {p = p*n; q = a/b; i = i-1}
```

for (*expr1; rel-expr; expr2*) {*statements*}

Similar to **while**; for example, to print the first 10 multiples of 5, you could type:

```
for (i=1; i<=10; i++) i*5
```

GNU **bc** does not require three arguments to **for**. A missing argument 1 or 3 means that those expressions will never be evaluated. A missing argument 2 evaluates to the value 1.

break

Terminate a **while** or **for** statement.

print *list*

GNU extension. It provides an alternate means of output. *list* consists of a series of comma-separated strings and expressions; **print** displays these entities in the order of the list. It does not print a newline when it terminates. Expressions are evaluated, printed, and assigned to the special variable **last**. Strings (which may contain special characters, i.e., characters beginning with \\) are simply printed. Special characters can be:

a   Alert or bell

b   Backspace

f   Form feed

n   Newline

r   Carriage return

q   Double quote

t   Tab

\\   Backslash

continue

GNU extension. When within a **for** statement, jump to the next iteration.

halt

GNU extension. Cause the **bc** processor to quit when executed.

quit

GNU extension. Cause the **bc** processor to quit whether line is executed or not.

limits

GNU extension. Print the limits enforced by the local version of **bc**.

Function keywords

define *f(args)* {

Begin the definition of function *f* having the arguments *args*. The arguments are separated by commas. Statements follow on successive lines. End with }.

auto *x, y*

> Set up *x* and *y* as variables local to a function definition, initialized to 0 and meaningless outside the function. Must appear first.

return(*expr*)

> Pass the value of expression *expr* back to the program. Return 0 if (*expr*) is left off. Used in function definitions.

sqrt(*expr*)

> Compute the square root of expression *expr*.

length(*expr*)

> Compute how many significant digits are in *expr*.

scale(*expr*)

> Same as **length**, but count only digits to the right of the decimal point.

read( )

> GNU extension. Read a number from standard input. Return value is the number read, converted via the value of **ibase**.

Math library functions

These are available when **bc** is invoked with -l. Library functions set **scale** to 20.

s(*angle*)

> Compute the sine of *angle*, a constant or expression in radians.

c(*angle*)

> Compute the cosine of *angle*, a constant or expression in radians.

a(*n*)

> Compute the arctangent of *n*, returning an angle in radians.

e(*expr*)

> Compute **e** to the power of *expr*.

l(*expr*)

> Compute the natural log of *expr*.

j(*n, x*)

> Compute the Bessel function of integer order *n*.

Operators

These consist of operators and other symbols. Operators can be arithmetic, unary, assignment, or relational:

arithmetic

> + - * / % ^

unary

> - ++ --

assignment

> =+ =- =* =/ =% =^ =

relational

> < <= > >= == !=

Other symbols

/* */ Enclose comments.

( ) Control the evaluation of expressions (change precedence). Can also be used around assignment statements to force the result to print.

{ } Use to group statements.

[ ] Indicate array index.

"text"

Use as a statement to print *text*.

Examples

Note in these examples that when you type some quantity (a number or expression), it is evaluated and printed, but assignment statements produce no display.

ibase = 8	*Octal input*
20	*Evaluate this octal number*
16	*Terminal displays decimal value*
obase = 2	*Display output in base 2 instead of base 10*
20	*Octal input*
10000	*Terminal now displays binary value*
ibase = A	*Restore base-10 input*
scale = 3	*Truncate results to 3 decimal places*
8/7	*Evaluate a division*
1.001001000	*Oops! Forgot to reset output base to 10*
obase=10	*Input is decimal now, so A isn't needed*
8/7	
1.142	*Terminal displays result (truncated)*

The following lines show the use of functions:

define p(r,n){	*Function p uses two arguments*
auto v	*v is a local variable*
v = r^n	*r raised to the n power*
return(v)}	*Value returned*
scale=5	
x=p(2.5,2)	$x = 2.5 \wedge 2$
x	*Print value of x*
6.25	
length(x)	*Number of digits*
3	
scale(x)	*Number of places right of decimal point*
2	

---

biff

biff [*arguments*]

Notify user of mail arrival and sender's name. **biff** operates asynchronously. Mail notification works only if your system is running the **comsat(8)** server. The command **biff y** enables notification, and the command **biff n** disables notification. With no arguments, **biff** reports **biff**'s current status.

bison

bison [*options*] *file*

Given a *file* containing context-free grammar, convert into tables for subsequent parsing while sending output to *file.c*. This utility is to a large extent compatible with **yacc,** and in fact is named for it. All input files should use the suffix *.y*; output files will use the original prefix. All long options (those preceded by --) may instead be preceded by +.

Options

-b *prefix,* **--file-prefix**=*prefix*
> Use *prefix* for all output files.

-d, **--defines**
> Generate *file.h,* producing **#define** statements that relate **bison**'s token codes to the token names declared by the user.

-r, **--raw**
> Use **bison** token numbers, not **yacc**-compatible translations, in *file.h.*

-k, **--token-table**
> Include token names and values of YYNTOKENS, YYNNTS, YYNRULES, and YYNSTATES in *file.c.*

-l, **--no-lines**
> Exclude **#line** constructs from code produced in *file.c.* (Use after debugging is complete.)

-n, **--no-parser**
> Suppress parser code in output, allowing only declarations. Assemble all translations into a switch statement body and print it to *file.act.*

-o *file,* **--output-file**=*file*
> Output to *file.*

-p *prefix,* **--name-prefix**=*prefix*
> Substitute *prefix* for **yy** in all external symbols.

-t, **--debug**
> Compile runtime debugging code.

-v, **--verbose**
> Verbose mode. Print diagnostics and notes about parsing tables to *file.output.*

-V, **--version**
> Display version number.

-y, **--yacc, --fixed-output-files**
> Duplicate **yacc**'s conventions for naming output files.

bootpd

bootpd [*options*] [*configfile* [*dumpfile*]]

TCP/IP command. Internet Boot Protocol server. **bootpd** normally is run by */etc/inetd* by including the following line in the file */etc/inetd.conf:*

> **bootps dgram udp wait root /etc/bootpd bootpd**

This causes **bootpd** to be started only when a boot request arrives. It may also be started in standalone mode, from the command line. Upon startup, **bootpd** first reads its configuration file, */etc/bootptab* (or the *configfile* listed on the command line), then begins listening for BOOTREQUEST packets.

bootpd looks in */etc/services* to find the port numbers it should use. Two entries are extracted: **bootps** (the **bootp** server listening port) and **bootpc** (the destination port used to reply to clients).

If **bootpd** is compiled with the **-DDEBUG** option, receipt of a SIGUSR1 signal causes it to dump its memory-resident database to the file */etc/bootpd.dump* or the *dumpfile* specified on the command line.

Options

-c *directory*

    Force **bootpd** to work in *directory*.

-d *level*

    Specify the debugging level. Omitting *level* will increment the level by 1.

-t *timeout*

    Specify a timeout value in minutes. A timeout value of 0 means wait forever.

Configuration file

The **bootpd** configuration file has a format in which two-character, case-sensitive tag symbols are used to represent host parameters. These parameter declarations are separated by colons. The general format is:

    hostname:*tg*=*value*:*tg*=*value*:*tg*=*value*

where *hostname* is the name of a **bootp** client and *tg* is a tag symbol. The currently recognized tags are listed in the following section.

Tags

Tag	Meaning
bf	Bootfile
bs	Bootfile size in 512-octet blocks
cs	Cookie server address list
ds	Domain name server address list
gw	Gateway address list
ha	Host hardware address
hd	Bootfile home directory
hn	Send hostname
ht	Host hardware type (see Assigned Numbers RFC)
im	Impress server address list
ip	Host IP address

Tag	Meaning
lg	Log server address list
lp	lpr server address list
ns	IEN-116 name server address list
rl	Resource location protocol server address list
sm	Host subnet mask
tc	Table continuation
to	Time offset in seconds from UTC
ts	Time server address list
vm	Vendor magic cookie selector

There is also a generic tag, **T***n*, where *n* is an RFC 1048 vendor field tag number. Generic data may be represented as either a stream of hexadecimal numbers or as a quoted string of ASCII characters.

bootpgw

bootpgw [*options*] *server*

TCP/IP command. Internet Boot Protocol Gateway. Maintain a gateway that forwards **bootpd** requests to *server*. In addition to dealing with BOOTREPLY packets, also deal with BOOT-REQUEST packets. **bootpgw** is normally run by */etc/inetd* by including the following line in the file */etc/inetd.conf*:

```
bootps dgram udp wait root /etc/bootpgw bootpgw
```

This causes **bootpgw** to be started only when a boot request arrives. **bootpgw** takes all the same options as **bootpd**, except **-c**.

bootptest

bootptest [*options*] *server* [*template*]

TCP/IP command. Test *server*'s **bootpd** daemon by sending requests every second for 10 seconds or until the server responds. Read options from the *template* file, if provided.

Options

-f *file*
Read the boot filename from *file*.

-h Identify client by hardware address, not IP address.

-m *magic-number*
Provide *magic-number* as the first word of the vendor options field.

bzcmp

bzcmp [*options*] *file1 file2*

Apply **cmp** to the data from files in the **bzip2** format without requiring on-disk decompression. See **bzip2** and **cmp** for usage.

bzdiff

bzdiff [*options*] *file1 file2*

Apply **diff** to data from files in the **bzip2** format without requiring on-disk decompression. See **bzip2** and **cmp** for usage.

bzgrep

bzgrep [options] pattern [file...]

Apply **grep** to data from files in the **bzip2** format without requiring on-disk decompression. See **bzip2** and **grep** for usage.

bzip2

bzip2 [options] filenames
bunzip2 [options] filenames
bzcat [option] filenames
bzip2recover filenames

File compression and decompression utility similar to **gzip**, but uses a different algorithm and encoding method to get better compression. **bzip2** replaces each file in *filenames* with a compressed version of the file and with a *.bz2* extension appended. **bunzip2** decompresses each file compressed by **bzip2** (ignoring other files, except to print a warning). **bzcat** decompresses all specified files to standard output, and **bzip2recover** is used to try to recover data from damaged files.

Additional related commands include **bzcmp**, which compares the contents of bzipped files; **bzdiff**, which creates diff (difference) files from a pair of **bzip** files; **bzgrep**, to search them; and the **bzless** and **bzmore** commands, which apply the more and less commands to **bzip** output as **bzcat** does with the **cat** command. See **cat**, **cmp**, **diff**, and **grep** for information on how to use those commands.

Options

--   End of options; treat all subsequent arguments as filenames.

-dig

Set block size to *dig* × 100KB when compressing, where *dig* is a single digit from 1 to 9.

-c, --stdout

Compress or decompress to standard output.

-d, --decompress

Force decompression.

-f, --force

Force overwrite of output files. Default is not to overwrite. Also forces breaking of hard links to files.

-k, --keep

Keep input files; don't delete them.

-L, --license, -V, --version

Print license and version information and exit.

-q, --quiet

Print only critical messages.

-s, --small

Use less memory, at the expense of speed.

-t, --test

Check the integrity of the files, but don't actually compress them.

-v, --verbose
>Verbose mode. Show the compression ratio for each file processed. Add more -v's to increase the verbosity.

-z, --compress
>Force compression, even if invoked as **bunzip2** or **bzcat**.

--repetitive-fast, --repetitive-best
>Sometimes useful in versions earlier than 0.9.5 (which has an improved sorting algorithm) for providing some control over the algorithm.

---

bzless

bzless [*options*] *file*

Applies **less** to data files in the **bzip2** format without requiring on-disk decompression. See **bzip2** and **less** for usage.

---

bzmore

bzmore [*options*] *file*

Applies **more** to data files in the **bzip2** format without requiring on-disk decompression. See **bzip2** and **more** for usage.

---

c++

c++ [*options*] *files*

See **g++**.

---

c++filt

c++filt [*options*] [*symbol*]

Decode the specified C++ or Java function name *symbol*, or read and decode symbols from standard input if no symbol is given. This command reverses the name mangling used by C++ and Java compilers to support function overloading, multiple functions that share the same name.

Options

-_, --strip-underscores
>Remove initial underscores from symbol names.

--help
>Print usage information, then exit.

-j, --java
>Print names using Java syntax.

-n, --no-strip-underscores
>Preserve initial underscores on symbol names.

-s *format*, --format=*format*
>Expect symbols to have been coded in the specified format. Format may be one of the following:

>**arm**
>>C++ Annotated Reference Manual.

>**edg**
>>EDG (Intel) compiler.

gnu
> Gnu compiler (the default).

gnu-new-abi
> Gnu compiler with the new application binary interface (for **gcc** 3.x.)

hp
> HP compiler.

lucid
> Lucid compiler.

--version
> Print version number, then exit.

---

cal

cal [*options*] [[*month*] *year*]

Print a 12-month calendar (beginning with January) for the given *year,* or a one-month calendar of the given *month* and *year. month* ranges from 1 to 12. *year* ranges from 1 to 9999. With no arguments, print a calendar for the current month.

Options

-j Display Julian dates (days numbered 1 to 365, starting from January 1).

-m Display Monday as the first day of the week.

-y Display entire year.

Examples

```
cal 12 1995
cal 1994 > year_file
```

---

cardctl

cardctl [*options*] *command*

System administration command. Control PCMCIA sockets or select the current scheme. The current scheme is sent along with the address of any inserted cards to configuration scripts (by default located in */etc/pcmcia*). The **scheme** command displays or changes the scheme. The other commands operate on a named card socket number, or all sockets if no number is given.

Commands

config [*socket*]
> Display current socket configuration.

eject [*socket*]
> Prepare the system for the card(s) to be ejected.

ident [*socket*]
> Display card identification information.

insert [*socket*]
> Notify system that a card has been inserted.

reset [*socket*]
> Send reset signal to card.

resume [*socket*]
> Restore power to socket and reconfigure for use.

scheme [*name*]
> Display current scheme or change to specified scheme *name*.

status [*socket*]
> Display current socket status.

suspend [*socket*]
> Shut down device and cut power to socket.

Options

-c *directory*
> Look for card configuration information in *directory* instead of /etc/pcmcia.

-f *file*
> Use *file* to keep track of the current scheme instead of /var/ run/pcmcia-scheme.

-s *file*
> Look for current socket information in *file* instead of /var/run/ stab.

---

cardmgr

cardmgr [*options*]

System administration command. The PCMCIA card daemon. **cardmgr** monitors PCMCIA sockets for devices that have been added or removed. When a card is detected, it attempts to get the card's ID and configure it according to the card configuration database (usually stored in /etc/pcmcia/config). By default, **cardmgr** does two things when it detects a card: it creates a system log entry and it beeps. Two high beeps mean it successfully identified and configured a device. One high beep followed by one low beep means it identified the device, but was unable to configure it successfully. One low beep means it could not identify the inserted card. Information on the currently configured cards can be found in /var/run/stab.

Options

-c *directory*
> Look for the card configuration database in *directory* instead of /etc/pcmcia.

-d   Use **modprobe** instead of **insmod** to load the PCMCIA device driver.

-f   Run in the foreground to process the current cards, then run as a daemon.

-m *directory*
> Look in *directory* for card device modules. Default is /lib/ modules/RELEASE, where RELEASE is the current kernel release.

-o   Configure the cards present in one pass, then exit.

-p_file_
> Write **cardmgr**'s process ID to _file_ instead of _/var/run/cardmgr._
> _pid._

-q   Run in quiet mode. No beeps.

-s _file_
> Write current socket information to _file_ instead of _/var/run/_
> _stab._

-v   Verbose mode.

-V   Print version number and exit.

---

cat

cat [_options_] [_files_]

Read (concatenate) one or more _files_ and print them on standard output. Read standard input if no _files_ are specified or if - is specified as one of the files; input ends with EOF. You can use the > operator to combine several files into a new file or >> to append files to an existing file.

Options

-A, --show-all
> Same as -vET.

-b, --number-nonblank
> Number all nonblank output lines, starting with 1.

-e   Same as -vE.

-E, --show-ends
> Print $ at the end of each line.

-n, --number
> Number all output lines, starting with 1.

-s, --squeeze-blank
> Squeeze down multiple blank lines to one blank line.

-t   Same as -vT.

-T, --show-tabs
> Print TAB characters as ^I.

-u   Ignored; retained for Unix compatibility.

-v, --show-nonprinting
> Display control and nonprinting characters, with the exception of LINEFEED and TAB.

Examples

cat ch1	_Display a file_
cat ch1 ch2 ch3 > all	_Combine files_
cat note5 >> notes	_Append to a file_
cat > temp1	_Create file at terminal; end with EOF_
cat > temp2 << STOP	_Create file at terminal; end with **STOP**_

---

cc

cc [_options_] _files_

See **gcc**.

cdda2wav

cdda2wav [*options*] [*output.wav*]

Convert Compact Disc Digital Audio (CDDA) to the WAV format. This process is often called "ripping" a CD-ROM, and is generally performed before using an encoder to convert the file to a compressed music format such as OGG or MP3. By default, **cdda2wav** reads data from the */dev/cdrom* device and outputs one WAV file per track.

Options

Some of the following options use sectors as a unit of measurement. Each sector of data on a CD represents approximately 1/75 second of play time.

-D, --device *devicename*
> Specify the device. The device must work with the **-i** (**--interface**) settings.

-A , --auxdevice *drivename*
> Specify a different drive for ioctl purposes.

-I, --interface *ifname*
> Specify the type of interface. For Linux systems, the most appropriate value is usually *cooked_ioctl*.

-s, --stereo
> Record in stereo. Use **-m** (**--mono**) to record in mono.

-x, --max
> Set recording quality (and amount of hard disk usage) to maximum.

-b, --bits-per-sample *n*
> Set the quality of samples to *n* bits per sample per channel. Possible values are 8, 12, and 16.

-r, --rate *n*
> Set the sample rate in samples per second. To get a list of possible values, use the **-R** option.

-R, --dump-rates
> Output a list of possible sample rates and dividers. This option is typically used alone.

-P, --set-overlap *n*
> Use *n* sectors of overlap for jitter correction.

-n, --sectors-per-request *n*
> Read *n* sectors in each request.

-t, --track *tracknumber*
> Set start track and, optionally, end track. Separate the tracks with the + character.

-i, --index *n*
> Set the start index to *n* when recording.

-o, --offset *n*
> Start recording *n* sectors before the beginning of the first track.

-O, --output-format

Choose the output file format. Normal file options are *wav*, *aiff*, *aifc*, *au*, and *sun*. You can also use *cdr* and *raw* for header-less files dumped into recording devices.

-d, --duration

Set to a number followed by **f** for frames (sectors) or **s** for seconds. Set time to zero to record an entire track. For example, to copy two minutes, enter **120s**.

-B, --bulk

Copy each track into its own file.

-w, --wait

Wait for a signal before recording anything.

-e, --echo

Copy audio data to a sound device rather than to a file.

-p, --set-pitch *n*

Adjust the pitch by *n* percent when copying data to an audio device.

-S, --speed-select *n*

Specify the speed at which your system will read the CD-ROM. Set the value to the multiple of normal playback speed given as your CD-ROM drive speed (4, 16, 32, and so forth). Setting the speed lower than the maximum can prevent errors in some cases.

-q, --quiet

Quiet mode; the program will not send any data to the screen.

-J, --version

Display version and quit.

Examples

For most systems, you should be able to copy a complete CD to a single WAV file with the following command:

```
cdda2wav
```

To copy a complete CD to a set of WAV files, one per track:

```
cdda2wav -B
```

---

cdparanoia

cdparanoia [*options*] *span* [*outfile*]

Like **cdda2wav**, **cdparanoia** records Compact Disc audio files as WAV, AIFF, AIFF-C, or raw format files. It uses additional data-verification and sound-improvement algorithms to make the process more reliable, and is used by a number of graphical recording programs as a backend.

Options

-v, --verbose

Verbose mode.

-q, --quiet

Quiet mode.

-e, --stderr-progress
Send all progress messages to stderr instead of stdout; used by wrapper scripts.

-V, --version
Print version information and quit.

-Q, --query
Display CD-ROM table of contents and quit.

-s, --search-for-drive
Search for a drive, even if */dev/cdrom* exists.

-h, --help
Display options and syntax.

-p, --output-raw
Output headerless raw data.

-r, --output-raw-little-endian
Output raw data in little-endian byte order.

-R, --output-raw-big-endian
Output raw data in big-endian byte order.

-w, --output-wav
Output in WAV format. This is the default.

-f, --output-aiff
Output in AIFF format.

-a, --output-aifc
Output in AIFF-C format.

-c, --force-cdrom-little-endian
Force **cdparanoia** to treat the drive as a little-endian device.

-C, --force-cdrom-big-endian
Force **cdparanoia** to treat the drive as a big-endian device.

-d, --force-cdrom-device *devicename*
Specify a device name to use instead of the first readable CD-ROM available.

-S, --force-read-speed *n*
Set the read speed to *n* on drives that support it. This is useful if you have a slow drive or are low on memory.

-Z, --disable-paranoia
Disable data verification and correction. Causes **cdparanoia** to behave exactly as **cdda2wav** would.

-z, --never-skip[*=retries*]
If a read fails (for example, due to a scratch in the disc), try again and again. If you specify a number, **cdparanoia** will try that number of times. If you do not, **cdparanoia** will retry until it succeeds.

-Y, --disable-extra-paranoia
Use data verification and correction only at read boundaries. Not recommended.

-X, --abort-on-skip
If a read fails and must be skipped, skip the entire track and delete any partially completed output file.

Progress symbols

The output during operation **cdparanoia** includes both smiley faces and more standard progress symbols. They are:

:-)   Operation proceeding normally.

:-| Operation proceeding normally, but with jitter during reads.

:-/   Read drift.

8-| Repeated read problems in the same place.

:-O   SCSI/ATAPI transport error (hardware problem not related to the disc itself).

:-(Scratch detected.

;-(Unable to correct problem.

8-X   Unknown and uncorrectable error.

:^D   Finished.

     Blank space in the progress indicator means that no corrections were necessary.

-    Jitter correction was required.

+   Read errors.

!   Errors even after correction; repeated read errors.

e   Corrected transport errors.

V   An uncorrected error or a skipped read.

The span argument

The **cdparanoia** command takes exactly one argument, which describes how much of the CD to record. It uses numbers followed by bracketed times to designate track numbers and time within them. For example, the string **1[2:23]-2[5]** indicates a recording from the two-minute and twenty-three-second mark of the first track up to the fifth second of the second track. The time format is demarcated by colons, *hours:minutes:seconds:.sectors*, with the last item, *sectors*, preceded by a decimal point (a sector is 1/75 of a second). It's best to put this argument within quotes.

If you use the **-B** option, the span argument is not required.

cdrdao

cdrdao *command* [*options*] *toc-file*

Write all content specified in description file *toc-file* to a CD-R disk drive in one step. This is called disk-at-once (DAO) mode, as opposed to the more commonly used track-at-once (TAO) mode. DAO mode allows you to change the length of gaps between tracks and define data to be written in these gaps (like hidden bonus tracks or track intros). The toc file can be created by hand or generated from an existing CD using **cdrdao**'s **read-toc** command. A cue file, as generated by other audio programs, can be used instead of a toc file. The file format for toc files is discussed at length in the **cdrdao** manpage.

Commands

The first argument must be a command. Note that not all options are available for all commands.

show-toc

Print a summary of the CD to be created.

read-toc

Read from a CD and create a disk image and toc file that will allow creation of duplicates.

read-cddb

Check a CDDB server for data about the CD represented by a given toc file, then write that data to the toc file as CD-TEXT data.

show-data

Print out the data that will be written to the CD-R. Useful for checking byte order.

read-test

Check the validity of the audio files described in the toc file.

disk-info

Display information about the CD-R currently in the drive.

msinfo

Display multisession information. Useful mostly for wrapper scripts.

scanbus

Scan the system bus for devices.

simulate

A dry run: do everything except write the CD.

unlock

Unlock the recorder after a failure. Run this command if you cannot eject the CD after using **cdrdao**.

write

Write the CD.

copy

Copy the CD. If you use a single drive, you will be prompted to insert the CD-R after reading. An image file will be created unless you use the **--on-the-fly** flag and two CD drives.

Options

--device *bus,id,logicalunit*

Set the SCSI address of the CD-R using the bus number, ID number, and logical unit number.

--source-device *bus,id,logicalunit*

Used only with the **copy** command. Set the SCSI address of the source device.

--driver *driver-id:option-flags*

Force **cdrdao** to use the driver you choose with the driver options named, instead of the driver it autodetects.

--source-driver *driver-id:option-flags*

Used only with the copy command. Set the source device driver and flags.

speed *value*

Set the write speed to *value*. The default is the highest available; use a lower value if higher values give poor results.

--datafile *filename*

When used with the **read-toc** command, specifies the data file placed in the toc file. When used with **read-cd** and **copy**, specifies the name of the image file created.

read-raw

Used only with the **read-cd** command. Write raw data to the image file.

--buffers *n*

Set the number of seconds of data to be buffered. Default is 32; set to a higher number if your read source is unreliable or is slower than the CD-R.

--multi

Record as a multisession disc.

--overburn

If you are using a disc with more storage space than **cdrdao** detects, use this option to keep writing even when **cdrdao** thinks you're out of space.

--eject

Eject the disc when done.

--swap

Swap byte order for all samples.

--session *n*

Used only with the **read-toc** and **read-cd** commands when working with multisession CDs. Specifies the number of the session to be processed.

--reload

Allow the drive to be opened before writing without interrupting the process. Used with simulation runs.

--force

Override warnings and perform the action anyway.

--paranoia-mode *n*

Specifies *n*, from 0 to 3, for the amount of error correction in the CD read. 0 is none, 3 is full (see **cdparanoia** for information about error correction). Set error correction to a lower number to increase read speed. The default is 3.

--keepimage

Used only with the **copy** command. Keeps the image file created during the copy process.

--on-the-fly
> Do not create an image file: pipe data directly from source to CD-R.

--with-cddb
> Use CDDB to fetch information about the disc and save it as CD-TEXT data. Used with the **copy**, **read-toc**, and **read-cd** commands.

cddb-servers *server,server*
> Enter hosts for servers. Servers may include ports, paths, and proxies; you can list multiple servers separated by spaces or commas.

--cddb-timeout *s*
> Set the timeout for CDDB server connections to *s* seconds.

--cddb-directory *localpath*
> CDDB data that is fetched will be saved in the directory *localpath*.

--save
> Save current options to the settings file *$HOME/.cdrdao*.

-n Do not wait 10 seconds before writing the disc.

-v *verbose-level*
> Set the amount of information printed to the screen. 0, 1, and 2 are fine for most users; greater numbers are useful for debugging.

---

cdrecord

cdrecord [*general-options*] **dev**=*device* [*track-options*]
track1,track2...

Record data or audio compact discs. This program normally requires root access, and has a large number of options and settings. A number of useful examples can be found in the manpage, which is quite extensive.

General options

General option flags go directly after the **cdrecord** command. Options affecting the track arguments are placed after the device argument and before the track arguments themselves. The general options are:

--version
> Print version information and exit.

-v Verbose mode. Use one **v** for each level of verbosity: **-vv** would be very verbose, and **-vvv** would be even more so.

-V As with the **-v**, a verbose mode counter. However, this applies only to SCSI transport messages. This will slow down the application.

--debug=*n*, **-d**
> Set the debug level to an integer (greater numbers are more verbose), or use multiple **-d** flags as with the **-v** and **-V** flags.

--kdebug=_n_, **--kd=**_n_

Set the kernel's debug notification value to _n_ during SCSI command execution. Works through the scg-driver.

-s, --silent

Silent mode. Do not print any SCSI error commands.

--force

Override errors if possible. May allow you to blank an otherwise broken CD-RW.

--dummy

Perform a dry run, doing all the steps of recording with the laser turned off. This will let you know whether the process is going to work.

--dao

Disk-at-once mode. Works only with MMC drives that support non-raw session-at-once modes.

--multi

Set to record in multisession mode. Must be present on all sessions but the last one for a multisession disc.

--msinfo

Get multisession information from the CD. Used only with multisession discs onto which you can still record more sessions.

--toc

Display the table of contents for the CD currently in the drive. Works for CD-ROM as well as CD-R and CD-RW drives.

--atip

Display the ATIP (Absolute Time In Pregroove) information for a disc. Only some drives allow you to read this information.

--fix

Close ("fixate") the session, preventing future multisession recordings and allowing the disc to be played in standard audio CD players (some can also play a disc that has not been closed).

--nofix

Do not close the disc after writing.

--load

Load media and exit. Works with tray-loading mechanisms only.

--eject

Eject disc after recording. Some hardware may need to eject a disc after a dummy recording and before the actual recording.

--speed=_n_

Set the speed to _n_, a multiple of the audio speed. Normally, **cdrecord** will get this from the CDR_SPEED environment variable. If your drive has trouble with higher numbers, try 0 as a value.

blank=*type*
> Erase data from a CD-RW in one of the following ways:
>
> **help**
>> Display a possible list of blanking methods.
>
> **all**
>> Erase all information on the disc. May take a long time.
>
> **fast**
>> Perform a quick erase of the disc, erasing only the PMA, TOC, and pregap.
>
> **track**
>> Blank a track.
>
> **unreserve**
>> Unreserve a track previously marked as reserved.
>
> **trtail**
>> Blank the tail of a track only.
>
> **unclose**
>> Unclose the last session.
>
> **session**
>> Blank the last session.

fs=*n*
> Set the fifo buffer size to *n*, in bytes. You may use **k**, **m**, **s**, or **f** to specify kilobytes, megabytes, or units of 2048 and 2352 bytes, respectively. The default is 4MB.

timeout=*n*
> Set the timeout to *n* seconds. Defaults to 40.

driver=*name*
> Lets you specify a driver for your system. Suggested for experts only. The special drivers cdr_simul and dvd_simul are used for simulation and profiling tests.

driveropts=*optlist*
> Specify a comma-separated list of driver options. To get a list of valid options, use **driveropts=help** and **--checkdrive**.

--checkdrive
> Check to see if there are valid drivers for the current drive. Returns 0 if the drive is valid.

--scanbus
> Scan SCSI devices.

--reset
> Attempt to reset the SCSI bus. Does not work on all systems.

--useinfo
> Use *.inf* files to override audio options set elsewhere.

mcn=*n*
> Set the Media Catalog Number to *n*.

The device argument

The device argument should be specified not as a file but as three integers representing the bus, target, and logical unit, as in the **cdrdao** command. To check the available options, use the **--scanbus** option.

Track options and arguments

Track options may be mixed with track arguments, and normally apply to the track immediately after them or to all tracks after them. The track arguments themselves should be the files that you will be writing to the CD. Options are:

isrc=*n*

> Set the International Standard Recording Number for the track following this argument.

index=*a,b,c*

> Set the index list for the next track. The values should be increasing comma-separated integers, starting with index 1 and counting in sectors (75ths of a second). For example, you could set three indices in a track with **index=0,750,7500** and they would occur at the beginning of the track, after 10 seconds, and after 100 seconds.

--audio

> Write all tracks after this track in digital audio format (playable by standard CD players). If you do not use this flag or the **--data** flag, **cdrecord** will assume that *.au* and *.wav* files are to be recorded as raw audio and that all other files are data.

--swab

> Declare that your data is in byte-swapped (little-endian) byte order. This is not normally necessary.

--data

> Record subsequent tracks as CD-ROM data. If you do not use this flag or the **--audio** flag, all files except for those ending in *.wav* or *.au* are assumed to be data.

--mode2

> Write all subsequent tracks in CD-ROM mode 2 format.

--xa1, --xa2

> Write subsequent tracks in CD-ROM XA mode 1 or CD-ROM XA mode 2 format.

--cdi

> Write subsequent tracks in CDI format.

--isosize

> The size of the next track should match the size of the ISO-9660 filesystem. This is used when duplicating CDs or copying from raw-data filesystems.

--pad

    Insert 15 sectors of blank data padding between data tracks. Applies to all subsequent tracks or until you use the **--nopad** argument, and is overridden by the **padsize**=*n* argument.

padsize=*n*

    Insert *n* sectors of blank data padding after the next track. Applies only to the track immediately after it.

--nopad

    Do not insert blank data between data tracks following this flag. This is the default behavior.

tsize=*n*

    Set the size of the next track. Useful only if you are recording from a raw disk for which **cdrecord** cannot determine the file size. If you are recording from an ISO 9660 filesystem, use the **--isosize** flag instead.

---

cfdisk

cfdisk [*options*] [*device*]

System administration command. Partition a hard disk. Normally, *device* will be */dev/hda*, */dev/hdb*, */dev/sda*, */dev/sdb*, */dev/hdc*, */dev/hdd*, and so on. See also **fdisk**.

Options

-a   Highlight the current partition with a cursor, not reverse video.

-c *cylinders*

    Specify the number of cylinders.

-g   Ignore driver-provided geometry; guess one instead.

-h *heads*

    Specify the number of heads.

-s *sectors*

    Specify the number of sectors per track.

-v   Print version number and exit.

-z   Do not read the partition table; partition from scratch.

-P *format*

    Display the partition table in *format*, which must be **r** (raw data), **s** (sector order), or **t** (raw format).

Commands

up arrow, down arrow

    Move among partitions.

b   Toggle partition's bootable flag.

d   Delete partition (allow other partitions to use its space).

g   Alter the disk's geometry. Prompt for what to change: cylinders, heads, or sectors (**c**, **h**, or **s**, respectively).

h   Help.

m   Attempt to ensure maximum usage of disk space in the partition.

n   Create a new partition. Prompt for more information.

p   Display the partition table.

q   Quit without saving information.

t   Prompt for a new filesystem type, and change to that type.

u   Change the partition size units, rotating from megabytes to sectors to cylinders and back.

W   Save information.

---

chage

chage [*options*] *user*

Change information about user password expirations. If run without any option flags, **chage** will prompt for values to be entered; you may also use option flags to change or view information.

Options

-l   This flag is used without any others, and causes **chage** to display the current password expiration attributes for the user.

-m *mindays*
   Minimum number of days between password changes. Default is zero, meaning that the user may change the password at any time.

-M *maxdays*
   Maximum number of days between password changes.

-d *lastday*
   Date of last password change. This may be expressed as a date in YYYY-MM-DD format, or as the number of days between January 1, 1970 and the last password change.

-I *inactive-days*
   If a password expires and the user does not log in for this number of days, the account will be locked, and the user must contact a system administrator before logging in. Set to 0 to disable the feature.

-E *expiredate*
   Set the date when the account will be locked. This is not a date for password expiration, but for account expiration. It may be expressed as a YYYY-MM-DD date or as a number of days since January 1, 1970.

-W *warning*
   The number of days before password expiration that a user will be warned to change passwords.

---

chat

chat [*options*] [*script*]

System administration command. Set up or initiate dial-up Internet connections; often used in conjunction with **pppd**, the PPP daemon. On some systems, **chat** takes the place of the **dip** program. A chat *script* is composed of a simple but expressive syntax of paired expect and send strings and sometimes substrings. A script string may contain either text expected from the modem or text to be sent, a chat directive, a substitution character, or a mixture of all three. When reading from a file, lines beginning with # are treated as comments.

Options

-e   Start script with the **ECHO** directive turned on.

-E   Allow script to read environment variables by using shell $*VARIABLE* syntax.

-f *file*

   Read chat script from *file* instead of standard input.

-r *file*

   Send the output of the **REPORT** directive to *file*. By default, they are sent to standard error.

-s   Send all error and log information to standard error, even when using the **-v** option.

-S   Silent mode; send neither error nor log messages to **syslogd**.

-t *n*

   Set the default timeout value to *n* seconds. When not specified, the default timeout value is 45 seconds.

-T *string*

   Set the string to be used instead of the \T substitution character. This is usually a phone number.

-U *string*

   Set the string to be used instead of the \U substitution character. This is usually a second phone number.

-v   Verbose mode; log the chat script state and text sent to and received from the modem to **syslogd**.

-V   Standard error verbose mode; identical to **-v,** but send information to standard error instead of **syslogd**.

Chat directives

Scripts are built from paired strings, an expect string and a send string. A null string formed with two single quotes, ' ', tells **chat** to expect nothing and just send the send string. A hyphen, -, may be used in an expect string to specify an alternate expect and send in the event the first expect fails. **chat** will wait, expecting the first part of the string, and if it fails to receive it, it will perform the second part of the string, often a directive. For example:

```
ogin:-BREAK-ogin:
```

is interpreted by **chat** to mean expect the string "ogin:"; if it is not received before the timeout period, send a break signal to the modem, then expect "ogin:" again.

BREAK is an example of a chat directive, which is a special keyword that directs **chat** to take some action. Most directives are meant for use as expect strings. Some are meant to be special reply strings. **BREAK** can be used as a reply, or, as the above example shows, can be inserted into an expect substring. The following chat directives are recognized by **chat**:

ABORT *string*

If the modem returns the specified *string*, abort the script. This is often used to capture a modem status sent as a string, such as **BUSY** or **NO CARRIER**.

BREAK *string*

Reply string. Send a break signal to the modem. If the modem returns the specified *string*, abort the script. This is often used to capture a modem status sent as a string, such as **BUSY** or **NO CARRIER**.

CLR_ABORT *string*

Clear an **ABORT** string from memory.

CLR_ABORT *string*

Clear a **REPORT** string from memory.

ECHO *status*

Set **ECHO** to *status* **ON** or **OFF**. When on, **chat** will echo output from the modem to standard error.

EOT

Reply string. **EOT** is used as a send string. It instructs **chat** to send an end-of-file character. This can also be embedded in a string using the character sequence **^D**.

REPORT *string*

When the script receives *string*, write it and any characters following it to standard error.

HANGUP *status*

Set HANGUP to *status* **ON** or **OFF**. When on, **chat** will treat a modem hanging up as an error. When off, it will continue to process the script. You usually want to set this to on after the modem has connected.

SAY *string*

Print the string to the standard error. This can be used to communicate with the script's user.

TIMEOUT *n*

Set the timeout value for subsequent expect strings to *n* seconds.

Substitution characters

"   The null string. When used in place of a send string, **chat** sends a return character. When used in an expect string, **chat** expects nothing and just sends the send string.

\b   Backspace character.

\c Used at the end of a string. Suppresses the newline character automatically added to send strings. Not valid in expect strings.

\d Pause one second. Not valid in expect strings.

\n The newline character.

\N, \0
> The null character.

\p Pause one tenth of a second. Not valid in expect strings.

\xd5
> Mask this string. Write the string ?????? instead when writing to the system log. Not valid in expect strings.

\r The carriage return character.

\t The tab character.

\T The string specified with the **-T** option, usually a phone number. Not valid in expect strings.

\U The string specified with the **-U** option, usually a second phone number. Not valid in expect strings.

**** The backslash character.

\\ddd
> An ASCII character expressed in octal. Not valid in expect strings.

^char
> Substitute a control character for *char*.

@file
> Substitute the contents of *file*. Not valid in expect strings.

$NAME
> When using the **-E** option, substitute the value of the specified environment variable *NAME*, or substitute nothing if the variable is not set.

Exit codes

0 Script terminated normally.

1 Invalid parameter or expect string. Script failed.

2 Error during execution. Script failed.

3 Expect string timeout with no further instructions. Script halted.

4 and up
> Script exited on an **ABORT** condition. The exit code indicates the abort string—4 is the first, 5 the second, and so on.

---

chattr

chattr [*options*] `mode files`

Modify file attributes. Specific to Linux Second and Third Extended Filesystem (ext2 and ext3). Behaves similarly to symbolic **chmod**, using +, -, and =. *mode* is in the form *opcode attribute*. See also **lsattr**.

Options

-R   Modify directories and their contents recursively.

-V   Print modes of attributes after changing them.

-v *version*
> Set the file's version.

Opcodes

+   Add attribute.

-   Remove attribute.

=   Assign attributes (removing unspecified attributes).

Attributes

A   Don't update access time on modify.

a   Append only for writing. Can be set or cleared only by a privileged user.

c   Compressed.

d   No dump.

i   Immutable. Can be set or cleared only by a privileged user.

j   Journalled file. This is useful only in cases where you are using an ext3 filesystem mounted with the **data="ordered"** or **data="writeback"** attributes. The **data="journalled"** option for the filesystem causes this operation to be performed for all files in the system and makes this option irrelevant.

S   Synchronous updates.

s   Secure deletion. The contents are zeroed on deletion, and the file cannot be undeleted or recovered in any way.

u   Undeletable. This causes a file to be saved even after it has been deleted, so that a user can undelete it later.

Example

> `chattr +a myfile`   *As superuser*

---

checkpc

checkpc [*options*]

System administration command. Examine and optionally repair the LPRng printer capability database and related files. Entries in this database control the printing and spooling of print jobs. The **checkpc** command reports incorrect entries in */etc/printcap* and ensures that files and directories used by LPRng exist and have the correct permissions.

Options

-a   Don't create missing accounting files specified in **:af** entries.

-c   Print verbose configuration details.

-D   Run with debugging flags on.

-f   Fix database by creating missing files and changing incorrect file permissions.

-h Print help message and exit.

-l Don't create missing logging files specified in **:lf** entries.

-p Print information about printcap database.

-r Remove old job files. Use **-A** to set the maximum age for job files.

-s Don't create missing filter status files specified in **:ps** entries.

-t *size[unit]*
> Truncate log files to specified *size*. You may specify the unit of that size in **k** or **M** for kilobytes or megabytes. The default is megabytes.

-A *age[unit]*
> Report junk or job files older than *age*. A unit of **D**, **H**, **M**, or **S** may be used to specify that *age* represents days, hours, minutes, or seconds. The default is days.

-P *printer*
> Check or fix entries only for the specified *printer*.

-V Verbose mode. Report on progress of **checkpc** including all entries checked and repairs made.

---

chfn

chfn [*options*] [*username*]

Change the information that is stored in */etc/passwd* and displayed to the **finger** query. Without *options*, **chfn** enters interactive mode and prompts for changes. To make a field blank, enter the keyword **none**. Only a privileged user can change information for another user. For regular users, **chfn** prompts for the user's password before making the change.

Options

-f, --full-name
> Specify new full name.

-h, --home-phone
> Specify new home phone number.

-o, --office
> Specify new office number.

-p, --office-phone
> Specify new office phone number.

-u, --usage, --help
> Print help message and then exit.

-v, --version
> Print version information and then exit.

Example

```
chfn -f "Ellen Siever" ellen
```

chgrp

chgrp [*options*] *newgroup files*
chgrp [*options*]

Change the group of one or more *files* to *newgroup*. *newgroup* is either a group ID number or a group name located in */etc/group*. Only the owner of a file or a privileged user may change the group.

Options

-c, --changes
Print information about files that are changed.

-f, --silent, --quiet
Do not print error messages about files that cannot be changed.

--help
Print help message and then exit.

-R, --recursive
Traverse subdirectories recursively, applying changes.

--reference=*filename*
Change the group to that associated with *filename*. In this case, *newgroup* is not specified.

-v, --verbose
Verbosely describe ownership changes.

--version
Print version information and then exit.

chmod

chmod [*options*] *mode files*
chmod [*options*] **--reference=***filename files*

Change the access *mode* (permissions) of one or more *files*. Only the owner of a file or a privileged user may change the mode. *mode* can be numeric or an expression in the form of *who opcode permission*. *who* is optional (if omitted, default is **a**); choose only one *opcode*. Multiple modes are separated by commas.

Options

-c, --changes
Print information about files that are changed.

-f, --silent, --quiet
Do not notify user of files that **chmod** cannot change.

--help
Print help message and then exit.

-R, --recursive
Traverse subdirectories recursively, applying changes.

--reference=*filename*
Change permissions to match those associated with *filename*.

-v, --verbose
> Print information about each file, whether changed or not.

--version
> Print version information and then exit.

Who

u User.

g Group.

o Other.

a All (default).

Opcode

+ Add permission.

- Remove permission.

= Assign permission (and remove permission of the unspecified fields).

Permissions

r Read.

w Write.

x Execute.

s Set user (or group) ID.

t Sticky bit; used on directories to prevent removal of files by non-owners.

u User's present permission.

g Group's present permission.

o Other's present permission.

Alternatively, specify permissions by a three-digit octal number. The first digit designates owner permission; the second, group permission; and the third, other's permission. Permissions are calculated by adding the following octal values:

4 Read.

2 Write.

1 Execute.

Note that a fourth digit may precede this sequence. This digit assigns the following modes:

4 Set user ID on execution to grant permissions to process based on the file's owner, not on permissions of the user who created the process.

2 Set group ID on execution to grant permissions to process based on the file's group, not on permissions of the user who created the process.

1 Set sticky bit.

Examples

Add execute-by-user permission to *file*:

    chmod u+x *file*

Either of the following will assign read/write/execute permission by owner (7), read/execute permission by group (5), and execute-only permission by others (1) to *file*:

    chmod 751 *file*
    chmod u=rwx,g=rx,o=x *file*

Any one of the following will assign read-only permission to *file* for everyone:

    chmod =r *file*
    chmod 444 *file*
    chmod a-wx,a+r *file*

The following makes the executable setuid, assigns read/write/execute permission by owner, and assigns read/execute permission by group and others:

    chmod 4755 *file*

---

chown

    chown [*options*] *newowner files*
    chown [*options*] --reference=*filename files*

Change the ownership of one or more *files* to *newowner*. *newowner* is either a user ID number or a login name located in */etc/passwd*. **chown** also accepts users in the form *newowner:newgroup* or *newowner.newgroup*. The last two forms change the group ownership as well. If no owner is specified, the owner is unchanged. With a period or colon but no group, the group is changed to that of the new owner. Only the current owner of a file or a privileged user may change the owner.

Options

-c, --changes
> Print information about files that are changed.

--dereference
> Follow symbolic links.

-f, --silent, --quiet
> Do not print error messages about files that cannot be changed.

-h, --no-dereference
> Change the ownership of each symbolic link (on systems that allow it) rather than the referenced file.

-v, --verbose
> Print information about all files that **chown** attempts to change, whether or not they are actually changed.

-R, --recursive
> Traverse subdirectories recursively, applying changes.

--reference=_filename_
> Change owner to the owner of _filename_ instead of specifying a new owner explicitly.

--help
> Print help message and then exit.

--version
> Print version information and then exit.

---

chpasswd **chpasswd** [_option_]

System administration command. Change user passwords in a batch. **chpasswd** accepts input in the form of one _username:password_ pair per line. If the **-e** option is not specified, _password_ is encrypted before being stored.

Option

-e Passwords given are already encrypted.

---

chroot **chroot** _newroot_ [_command_]

System administration command. Change root directory for _command_ or, if none is specified, for a new copy of the user's shell. This command or shell is executed relative to the new root. The meaning of any initial / in pathnames is changed to _newroot_ for a command and any of its children. In addition, the initial working directory is _newroot_. This command is restricted to privileged users.

---

chsh **chsh** [_options_] [_username_]

Change your login shell, either interactively or on the command line. Warn if _shell_ does not exist in _/etc/shells_. Specify the full path to the shell. **chsh** prompts for your password. Only a privileged user can change another user's shell.

Options

-l, --list-shells
> Print valid shells, as listed in _/etc/shells_, and then exit.

-s _shell_, **--shell** _shell_
> Specify new login shell.

-u, --help
> Print help message and then exit.

-v, --version
> Print version information and then exit.

Example
> **chsh -s /bin/tcsh**

chvt

chvt *N*

Switch to virtual terminal *N* (that is, switch to */dev/ttyN*). If you have not created */dev/ttyN*, it will be created when you use this command. There are keyboard shortcuts for this functionality as well. From a graphical desktop, you can press Ctrl-Alt-F1 through F12 to switch to different virtual terminals. In text mode, you can skip the Ctrl key and just use Alt-F1 through F12. To switch back to graphical mode, use Alt-F7.

cksum

cksum [*files*]

Compute a cyclic redundancy check (CRC) checksum for all *files*; this is used to ensure that a file was not corrupted during transfer. Read from standard input if the character - or no files are given. Display the resulting checksum, the number of bytes in the file, and (unless reading from standard input) the filename.

clear

clear

Clear the terminal display.

cmp

cmp [*options*] *file1 file2* [*skip1* [*skip2*]]

Compare *file1* with *file2*. Use standard input if *file1* is - or missing. This command is normally used for comparing binary files, although files can be of any type. (See also **comm** and **diff**.) *skip1* and *skip2* are optional offsets in the files at which the comparison is to start.

Options

-c, --print-chars
    Print differing bytes as characters.

-i *num*, --ignore-initial=*num*
    Ignore the first *num* bytes of input.

-l, --verbose
    Print offsets and codes of all differing bytes.

-s, --quiet, --silent
    Work silently; print nothing, but return exit codes:

    0   Files are identical.

    1   Files are different.

    2   Files are inaccessible.

Example

Print a message if two files are the same (exit code is 0):

    cmp -s old new && echo 'no changes'

col

col [*options*]

A postprocessing filter that handles reverse linefeeds and escape characters, allowing output from **tbl** or **nroff** to appear in reasonable form on a terminal.

Options

-b   Ignore backspace characters; helpful when printing manpages.

-f   Process half-line vertical motions, but not reverse line motion. (Normally, half-line input motion is displayed on the next full line.)

-l *n*
Buffer at least *n* lines in memory. The default buffer size is 128 lines.

-x   Normally, **col** saves printing time by converting sequences of spaces to tabs. Use **-x** to suppress this conversion.

Examples

Run *myfile* through **tbl** and **nroff**, then capture output on screen by filtering through **col** and **more**:

```
tbl myfile | nroff | col | more
```

Save manpage output for the **ls** command in *out.print*, stripping out backspaces (which would otherwise appear as ^H):

```
man ls | col -b > out.print
```

colcrt

colcrt [*options*] [*files*]

A postprocessing filter that handles reverse linefeeds and escape characters, allowing output from **tbl** or **nroff** to appear in reasonable form on a terminal. Put half-line characters (e.g., subscripts or superscripts) and underlining (changed to dashes) on a new line between output lines.

Options

-   Do not underline.

-2   Double space by printing all half-lines.

colrm

colrm [*start* [*stop*]]

Remove specified columns from a file, where a column is a single character in a line. Read from standard input and write to standard output. Columns are numbered starting with 1; begin deleting columns at (including) the *start* column, and stop at (including) the *stop* column. Entering a tab increments the column count to the next multiple of either the *start* or *stop* column; entering a backspace decrements it by 1.

Example

```
colrm 3 5 < test1 > test2
```

column

column [*options*] [*files*]

Format input from one or more *files* into columns, filling rows first. Read from standard input if no files are specified.

Options

-c *num*
  Format output into *num* columns.

-s *char*
  Delimit table columns with *char*. Meaningful only with -t.

-t Format input into a table. Delimit with whitespace, unless an alternate delimiter has been provided with -s.

-x Fill columns before filling rows.

comm

comm [*options*] *file1* *file2*

Compare lines common to the sorted files *file1* and *file2*. Three-column output is produced: lines unique to *file1*, lines unique to *file2*, and lines common to both files. **comm** is similar to **diff** in that both commands compare two files. But **comm** can also be used like **uniq**; **comm** selects duplicate or unique lines between *two* sorted files, whereas **uniq** selects duplicate or unique lines within the *same* sorted file.

Options

- Read the standard input.

-*num*
  Suppress printing of column *num*. Multiple columns may be specified and should not be space-separated.

--help
  Print help message and exit.

--version
  Print version information and exit.

Example

Compare two lists of top-10 movies, and display items that appear in both lists:

```
comm -12 siskel_top10 ebert_top10
```

compress

compress [*options*] *files*

Compress one or more *files*, replacing each with the compressed file of the same name with .Z appended. If no file is specified, compress standard input. Each file specified is compressed separately. **compress** ignores files that are symbolic links. See also **gzip** and **bzip2**, which are more commonly used now.

Options

-b *maxbits*
    Limit the maximum number of bits.

-c   Write output to standard output, not to a .Z file.

-d   Decompress instead of compressing. Same as **uncompress**.

-f   Force generation of an output file even if one already exists.

-r   If any of the specified files is a directory, compress recursively.

-v   Print compression statistics.

-V   Print version and compilation information and then exit.

---

cp

cp [*options*] *file1* *file2*
cp [*options*] *files* *directory*

Copy *file1* to *file2*, or copy one or more *files* to the same names under *directory*. If the destination is an existing file, the file is overwritten; if the destination is an existing directory, the file is copied into the directory (the directory is *not* overwritten).

Options

-a, --archive
    Preserve attributes of original files where possible. The same as **-dpR**.

-b, --backup
    Back up files that would otherwise be overwritten.

-d, --no-dereference
    Do not dereference symbolic links; preserve hard link relationships between source and copy.

-f, --force
    Remove existing files in the destination.

-i, --interactive
    Prompt before overwriting destination files.

-l, --link
    Make hard links, not copies, of nondirectories.

-p, --preserve
    Preserve all information, including owner, group, permissions, and timestamps.

-P, --parents
    Preserve intermediate directories in source. The last argument must be the name of an existing directory. For example, the command:

    cp --parents jphekman/book/ch1 newdir

    copies the file *jphekman/book/ch1* to the file *newdir/jphekman/book/ch1*, creating intermediate directories as necessary.

-r, -R, --recursive
    Copy directories recursively.

-S *backup-suffix*, **--suffix=***backup-suffix*

Set suffix to be appended to backup files. This may also be set with the **SIMPLE_BACKUP_SUFFIX** environment variable. The default is ~. You need to explicitly include a period if you want one before the suffix (for example, specify *.bak*, not *bak*).

-s, **--symbolic-link**

Make symbolic links instead of copying. Source filenames must be absolute.

-u, **--update**

Do not copy a file to an existing destination with the same or newer modification time.

-v, **--verbose**

Before copying, print the name of each file.

-V *type*, **--version-control=***type*

Set the type of backups made. You may also use the **VERSION_CONTROL** environment variable. The default is **existing**. Valid arguments are:

t, numbered

Always make numbered backups.

nil, existing

Make numbered backups of files that already have them; otherwise, make simple backups.

never, simple

Always make simple backups.

-x, **--one-file-system**

Ignore subdirectories on other filesystems.

Example

Copy the contents of the *guest* directory recursively into the *archives/guest/* directory, and display a message for each file copied:

```
cd /archives && cp -av /home/guest guest
```

---

cpio

cpio *flags* [*options*]

Copy file archives from or to tape or disk, or to another location on the local machine. Each of the three flags **-i**, **-o**, or **-p** accepts different options.

Flags

-i, **--extract** [*options*] [*patterns*]

Copy in (extract) from an archive files whose names match selected *patterns*. Each pattern can include Bourne shell filename metacharacters. (Patterns should be quoted or escaped so that they are interpreted by **cpio**, not by the shell.) If *pattern* is omitted, all files are copied in. Existing files are not overwritten by older versions from the archive unless **-u** is specified.

-o, --create [*options*]

    Copy out to an archive a list of files whose names are given on the standard input.

-p, --pass-through [*options*] *directory*

    Copy (pass) files to another directory on the same system. Destination pathnames are interpreted relative to the named *directory*.

Comparison of valid options

Options available to the **-i**, **-o**, and **-p** flags are shown here (the **-** is omitted for clarity):

```
i:   bcdf mnrtsuv B SVCEHMR IF
o:   0a c          vABL VC HM O F
p:   0a d lm       uv L V     R
```

Options

-0, --null

    Expect list of filenames to be terminated with null, not newline. This allows files with a newline in their names to be included.

-a, --reset-access-time

    Reset access times of input files after reading them.

-A, --append

    Append files to an existing archive, which must be a disk file. Specify this archive with **-O** or **-F**.

-b, --swap

    Swap bytes and half-words to convert between big-endian and little-endian 32-bit integers.

-B   Block input or output using 5120 bytes per record (default is 512 bytes per record).

--blocksize=*size*

    Set input or output blocksize to $size \times 512$ bytes.

-c   Read or write header information as ASCII characters; useful when source and destination machines are different types.

-C *n*, **--io-size=***n*

    Like **-B**, but blocksize can be any positive integer *n*.

-d, --make-directories

    Create directories as needed.

-E *file*, **--pattern-file=***file*

    Extract from the archives filenames that match patterns in *file*.

-f, --nonmatching

    Reverse the sense of copying; copy all files *except* those that match *patterns*.

-F *file*, **--file=***file*

    Use file as the archive, not stdin or stdout. *file* can reside on another machine, if given in the form *user@hostname:file* (where *user@* is optional).

--force-local

Assume that *file* (provided by **-F**, **-I**, or **-O**) is a local file, even if it contains a colon (:) indicating a remote file.

-H *type*, **--format=***type*

Use *type* format. Default for copy-out is **bin**; default for copy-in is autodetection of the format. Valid formats (all caps also accepted) are:

bin
> Binary.

odc
> Old (POSIX.1) portable format.

newc
> New (SVR4) portable format.

crc
> New (SVR4) portable format with checksum added.

tar
> Tar.

ustar
> POSIX.1 tar (also recognizes GNU tar archives).

hpbin
> HP-UX's binary (obsolete).

hpodc
> HP-UX's portable format.

-I *file*

Read *file* as an input archive. May be on a remote machine (see **-F**).

-k   Ignored. For backward compatibility.

-l, **--link**

Link files instead of copying.

-L, **--dereference**

Follow symbolic links.

-m, **--preserve-modification-time**

Retain previous file modification time.

-M *msg*, **--message=***msg*

Print *msg* when switching media, as a prompt before switching to new media. Use variable **%d** in the message as a numeric ID for the next medium. **-M** is valid only with **-I** or **-O**.

-n, **--numeric-uid-gid**

When verbosely listing contents, show user ID and group ID numerically.

--no-absolute-filenames

Create all copied-in files relative to the current directory.

--no-preserve-owner

Make all copied files owned by yourself, instead of the owner of the original. Can be used only if you are a privileged user.

-O *file*
>   Archive the output to *file*, which may be a file on another
>   machine (see **-F**).

--only-verify-crc
>   For a CRC-format archive, verify the CRC of each file; don't
>   actually copy the files in.

--quiet
>   Don't print the number of blocks copied.

-r   Rename files interactively.

-R [*user*][*:group*], **--owner** [*user*][*:group*]
>   Reassign file ownership and group information to the user's
>   login ID (privileged users only).

-s, --swap-bytes
>   Swap bytes of each two-byte half-word.

-S, --swap-half-words
>   Swap half-words of each four-byte word.

--sparse
>   For copy-out and copy-pass, write files that have large blocks
>   of zeros as sparse files.

-t, --list
>   Print a table of contents of the input (create no files). When
>   used with the **-v** option, resembles output of **ls -l**.

-u, --unconditional
>   Unconditional copy; old files can overwrite new ones.

-v, --verbose
>   Print a list of filenames processed.

-V, --dot
>   Print a dot for each file read or written (this shows **cpio** at
>   work without cluttering the screen).

--version
>   Print version number and then exit.

Examples

Generate a list of files whose names end in *.old* using **find**; use the
list as input to **cpio**:

```
find . -name "*.old" -print | cpio -ocBv > /dev/rst8
```

Restore from a tape drive all files whose names contain **save** (subdirectories are created if needed):

```
cpio -icdv "*save*" < /dev/rst8
```

Move a directory tree:

```
find . -depth -print | cpio -padm /mydir
```

---

cpp

cpp [*options*] [*ifile* [*ofile*]]

GNU C language preprocessor. **cpp** is normally invoked as the first
pass of any C compilation by the **gcc** command. The output of **cpp**

is a form acceptable as input to the next pass of the C compiler. The *ifile* and *ofile* options are, respectively, the input and output for the preprocessor; they default to standard input and standard output.

Options

-$** Do not allow **$ in identifiers.

-ansi

Use 1990 ISO C standard. This is equivalent to **-std=c89.**

-dD

Similar to **-dM,** but exclude predefined macros and include results of preprocessing.

-dM

Suppress normal output. Print series of **#define**s that create the macros used in the source file.

-dN

Similar to **-dD,** but don't print macro expansions.

-dI

Print **#include** directives in addition to other output.

-fpreprocessed

Treat file as already preprocessed. Skip most processing directives, remove all comments, and tokenize file.

-ftabstop=*width*

Set distance between tabstops so columns will be reported correctly in warnings and errors. Default is 8.

-fno-show-column

Omit column numbers in warnings and errors.

-gcc

Define **__GNUC__, __GNUC_MINOR__,** and **__GNUC_PATCHLEVEL__** macros.

--help

Print usage message and exit.

-idirafter *dir*

Search *dir* for header files when a header file is not found in any of the included directories.

-imacros *file*

Process macros in *file* before processing main files.

-include *file*

Process *file* before main file.

-iprefix *prefix*

When adding directories with **-iwithprefix**, prepend *prefix* to the directory's name.

-isystem *dir*

Search *dir* for header files after searching directories specified with **-I** but before searching standard system directories.

-iwithprefix *dir*

Append *dir* to the list of directories to be searched when a header file cannot be found in the main include path. If **-iprefix** has been set, prepend that prefix to the directory's name.

-iwithprefixbefore *dir*

Insert *dir* at the beginning of the list of directories to be searched when a header file cannot be found in the main include path. If **-iprefix** has been set, prepend that prefix to the directory's name.

-lang-c, **-lang-c++**, **-lang-objc**, **-lang-objc++**

Expect the source to be in C, C++, Objective C, or Objective C++, respectively.

-lint

Display all lint commands in comments as **#pragma lint** *command*.

-nostdinc

Search only specified, not standard, directories for header files.

-nostdinc++

Suppress searching of directories believed to contain C++-specific header files.

-o *file*

Write output to *file*. (Same as specifying a second filename in the command line.)

-pedantic

Warn verbosely.

-pedantic-errors

Produce a fatal error in every case in which **-pedantic** would have produced a warning.

-std=*standard*

Specify C *standard* of input file. Accepted values are:

iso9899:1990, c89

1990 ISO C standard.

iso9899:199409

1994 amendment to the 1990 ISO C standard.

iso9899:1999, c99, iso9899:199x, c9x

1999 revised ISO C standard.

gnu89

1990 C Standard with gnu extensions. The default value.

gnu99, gnu9x

1999 revised ISO C standard with gnu extensions.

-traditional

Behave like traditional C, not ANSI.

-trigraphs

Convert special three-letter sequences, meant to represent missing characters on some terminals, into the single character they represent.

-undef
> Suppress definition of all nonstandard macros.

-v   Verbose mode.

-version
> Print version number, then process file.

--version
> Print version number then exit.

-w   Don't print warnings.

-x *language*
> Specify the language of the input file. *language* may be **c**, **c++**, **objective-c**, or **assembler-with-cpp**. By default, language is deduced from the filename extension. If the extension is unrecognized, the default is **c**.

-A *name*[*=def*]
> Assert *name* with value *def* as if defined by **#assert**. To turn off standard assertions, use **-A-**.

-A *-name*[*=def*]
> Cancel assertion *name* with value *def*.

-C   Retain all comments except those found on **cpp** directive lines. By default, **cpp** strips C-style comments.

-D*name*[*=def*]
> Define *name* with value *def* as if by a **#define**. If no *=def* is given, *name* is defined with value 1. **-D** has lower precedence than **-U**.

-E   Preprocess the source files, but do not compile. Print result to standard output. This option is usually passed from **gcc**.

-H   Print pathnames of included files, one per line, on standard error.

-I*dir*
> Search in directory *dir* for **#include** files whose names do not begin with / before looking in directories on standard list. **#include** files whose names are enclosed in double quotes and do not begin with / will be searched for first in the current directory, then in directories named on **-I** options, and last in directories on the standard list.

-I-   Split includes. Search directories specified by **-I** options preceding this one for header files included with quotes (**#include** "file.h") but not for header files included with angle brackets (**#include** <file.h>). Search directories specified by **-I** options following this one for all header files.

-M [**-MG**]
> Suppress normal output. Print a rule for **make** that describes the main source file's dependencies. If **-MG** is specified, assume that missing header files are actually generated files, and look for them in the source file's directory.

-MF *file*
> Print rules generated by **-M** or **-MM** to *file*.

-MD *file*
> Similar to **-M**, but output to *file*; also compile the source.

-MM
> Similar to **-M**, but describe only those files included as a result of **#include** "*file*".

-MMD *file*
> Similar to **-MD**, but describe only the user's header files.

-MQ *target*
> Similar to **-MT**, but quote any characters that are special to **make**.

-MT *target*
> Specify the *target* to use when generating a rule for **make**. By default the target is based on the name of the main input file.

-P Preprocess input without producing line-control information used by next pass of the C compiler.

-U*name*
> Remove any initial definition of *name*, where *name* is a reserved symbol predefined by the preprocessor or a name defined on a **-D** option. Names predefined by **cpp** are **unix** and **i386** (for Intel systems).

-Wall
> Warn both on nested comments and trigraphs.

-Wcomment, -Wcomments
> Warn when encountering the beginning of a nested comment.

-Wtraditional
> Warn when encountering constructs that are interpreted differently in ANSI than in traditional C.

-Wtrigraph, -Wcomments
> Warn when encountering trigraphs, three-letter sequences meant to represent missing characters on some terminals.

Special names

cpp understands various special names, some of which are:

__DATE__
> Current date (e.g., Jan 10 2003).

__FILE__
> Current filename (as a C string).

__LINE__
> Current source line number (as a decimal integer).

__TIME__
> Current time (e.g., 12:00:00).

These special names can be used anywhere, including in macros, just like any other defined names. **cpp**'s understanding of the line number and filename may be changed using a **#line** directive.

Directives

All **cpp** directive lines start with # in column 1. Any number of blanks and tabs is allowed between the # and the directive. The directives are:

#assert *name (string)*

Define a question called *name*, with an answer of *string*. Assertions can be tested with **#if** directives. The predefined assertions for **#system**, **#cpu**, and **#machine** can be used for architecture-dependent changes.

#unassert *name*

Remove assertion for question *name*.

#define *name token-string*

Define a macro called *name*, with a value of *token-string*. Subsequent instances of *name* are replaced with *token-string*.

#define *name(arg, ... , arg) token-string*

This allows substitution of a macro with arguments. *token-string* will be substituted for *name* in the input file. Each call to *name* in the source file includes arguments that are plugged into the corresponding *args* in *token-string*.

#undef *name*

Remove definition of the macro *name*. No additional tokens are permitted on the directive line after *name*.

#ident *string*

Put *string* into the comment section of an object file.

#include *"filename"*, **#include**<*filename*>

Include contents of *filename* at this point in the program. No additional tokens are permitted on the directive line after the final " or >.

#line *integer-constant "filename"*

Cause **cpp** to generate line-control information for the next pass of the C compiler. The compiler behaves as if *integer-constant* is the line number of the next line of source code and *filename* (if present) is the name of the input file. No additional tokens are permitted on the directive line after the optional *filename*.

#endif

End a section of lines begun by a test directive (**#if**, **#ifdef**, or **#ifndef**). No additional tokens are permitted on the directive line.

#ifdef *name*

Lines following this directive and up to matching **#endif** or next **#else** or **#elif** will appear in the output if *name* is currently defined. No additional tokens are permitted on the directive line after *name*.

#ifndef *name*

Lines following this directive and up to matching **#endif** or next **#else** or **#elif** will appear in the output if *name* is not currently defined. No additional tokens are permitted on the directive line after *name*.

#if *constant-expression*

Lines following this directive and up to matching **#endif** or next **#else** or **#elif** will appear in the output if *constant-expression* evaluates to nonzero.

#elif *constant-expression*

An arbitrary number of **#elif** directives are allowed between an **#if**, **#ifdef**, or **#ifndef** directive and an **#else** or **#endif** directive. The lines following the **#elif** and up to the next **#else**, **#elif**, or **#endif** directive will appear in the output if the preceding test directive and all intervening **#elif** directives evaluate to zero, and the *constant-expression* evaluates to nonzero. If *constant-expression* evaluates to nonzero, all succeeding **#elif** and **#else** directives will be ignored.

#else

Lines following this directive and up to the matching **#endif** will appear in the output if the preceding test directive evaluates to zero, and all intervening **#elif** directives evaluate to zero. No additional tokens are permitted on the directive line.

#error

Report fatal errors.

#warning

Report warnings, but then continue processing.

---

cron

cron

System administration command. Normally started in a system startup file. Execute commands at scheduled times, as specified in users' files in */var/spool/cron*. Each file shares its name with the user who owns it. The files are controlled via the command **crontab**. The **cron** command will also read commands from the */etc/crontab* file and from the */etc/cron.d/* directory.

---

crontab

crontab [`options`] [`file`]

View, install, or uninstall your current *crontab* file. A privileged user can run **crontab** for another user by supplying **-u** *user*. A *crontab* file is a list of commands, one per line, that will execute automatically at a given time. Numbers are supplied before each command to specify the execution time. The numbers appear in five fields, as follows:

Minute	0-59
Hour	0-23
Day of month	1-31
Month	1-12
	Jan, Feb, Mar, ...
Day of week	0-6, with 0 = Sunday
	Sun, Mon, Tue, ...

Use a comma between multiple values, a hyphen to indicate a range, and an asterisk to indicate all possible values. For example, assuming these *crontab* entries:

```
59 3 * * 5    find / -print | backup_program
0 0 1,15 * *  echo "Timesheets due" | mail user
```

the first command backs up the system files every Friday at 3:59 a.m., and the second command mails a reminder on the 1st and 15th of each month.

The superuser can always issue the **crontab** command. Other users must be listed in the file */etc/cron.allow* if it exists; otherwise, they must not be listed in */etc/cron.deny*. If neither file exists, only the superuser can issue the command.

Options

The **-e**, **-l**, and **-r** options are not valid if any *files* are specified.

-e   Edit the user's current *crontab* file (or create one).

-l   Display the user's *crontab* file on standard output.

-r   Delete the user's *crontab* file.

-u *user*
Indicate which *user*'s *crontab* file will be acted upon.

---

csh   **csh** [*options*] [*file* [*arguments*]]

C shell, a command interpreter into which all other commands are entered. On Linux, **csh** has been replaced with an enhanced version of the shell called **tcsh**. For more information, see Chapter 8.

---

csplit   **csplit** [*options*] *file arguments*

Separate *file* into context-based sections and place sections in files named xx00 through xx*n* (*n* < 100), breaking *file* at each pattern specified in *arguments*. See also **split**.

Options

-   Read from standard input.

-b *suffix,* **--suffix-format**=*suffix*
Append *suffix* to output filename. This option causes **-n** to be ignored. *suffix* must specify how to convert the binary integer to readable form by including one of the following: **%d**, **%i**, **%u**, **%o**, **%x**, or **%X**. The value of *suffix* determines the format for numbers as follows:

%d   Signed decimal.

%i   Same as **%d**.

%u   Unsigned decimal.

%o   Octal.

%x   Hexadecimal.

%X   Same as **%x**.

-f *prefix*, **--prefix=***prefix*

Name new files *prefix*00 through *prefixn* (default is xx00 through xx*n*).

-k, --keep-files

Keep newly created files even when an error occurs (which would normally remove these files). This is useful when you need to specify an arbitrarily large repeat argument, {*n*}, and you don't want an out-of-range error to cause removal of the new files.

-n *num*, **--digits=***num*

Use output filenames with numbers *num* digits long. The default is 2.

-s, -q, --silent, --quiet

Suppress all character counts.

-z, --elide-empty-files

Do not create empty output files. However, number as if those files had been created.

Arguments

Any one or a combination of the following expressions may be specified as arguments. Arguments containing blanks or other special characters should be surrounded by single quotes.

/expr/[*offset*]

Create file from the current line up to the line containing the regular expression *expr*. *offset* should be of the form +*n* or -*n*, where *n* is the number of lines below or above *expr*.

%expr%[*offset*]

Same as */expr/*, except no file is created for lines previous to line containing *expr*.

num

Create file from current line up to (but not including) line number *num*. When followed by a repeat count (number inside { }), put the next *num* lines of input into another output file.

{*n*} Repeat argument *n* times. May follow any of the preceding arguments. Files will split at instances of *expr* or in blocks of *num* lines. If * is given instead of *n*, repeat argument until input is exhausted.

Examples

Create up to 20 chapter files from the file **novel**:

```
csplit -k -f chap. novel '/CHAPTER/' '{20}'
```

Create up to 100 address files (xx00 through xx99), each four lines long, from a database named **address_list**:

```
csplit -k address_list 4 {99}
```

ctags [*options*] *files*

Create a list of function and macro names defined in a programming source *file*. More than one file may be specified. **ctags** understands many programming languages, including C, C++, FORTRAN, Java, Perl, Python, flex, yacc, and bison. The output list (named *tags* by default) contains lines of the form:

> *name*   *file*   *context*

where *name* is the function or macro name, *file* is the source file in which *name* is defined, and *context* is a search pattern that shows the line of code containing *name*. After the list of tags is created, you can invoke **vi** on any file and type:

> **:set tags=***tagsfile*
> **:tag** *name*

This switches the **vi** editor to the source file associated with the *name* listed in *tagsfile* (which you specify with -t).

etags produces an equivalent file for tags to be used with Emacs.

Options

-a   Append tag output to existing list of tags.

-e   Create tag files for use with **emacs**.

-h *extensionlist*
Interpret files with filename extensions specified in *extensionlist* as header files. The default list is ".h.H.hh.hpp.hxx.h++. inc.def". To indicate that files without extensions should be treated as header files, insert an additional period in the list before another period or at the end of the list, or use just a period by itself. To use this option multiple times and have the specified lists ANDed together, use a plus sign as the first character in the list. To restore the default, use the word "default".

-n   Use numeric **ex** commands to locate tags. Same as **--excmd= number**.

-o *file*, -f *file*, **--output=***file*
Write to *file*.

--packages-only
Include tag entries for members of structure-like constructs.

-R   Recursively read files in subdirectories of the directory given on the command line.

-u   Don't sort tag entries.

-x   Produce a tabular listing of each function, and its line number, source file, and context.

-B   Search for tags backward through files.

-I *tokenlist*
Specify a list of tokens to be specially handled. If given as a file, use **ex** pattern commands to locate tags. Same as **--excmd= pattern**.

-N   Use **ex** pattern commands to locate tags. Same as **--excmd=pattern**.

-S, --ignore-indentation
Normally **ctags** uses indentation to parse the tag file; this option tells **ctags** to rely on indentation less.

-T, --typedefs-and-c++
Include tag entries for typedefs, structs, enums, unions, and C++ member functions.

-V, --version
Print the version number and exit.

---

cut

cut *options* [*files*]

Cut out selected columns or fields from one or more *files*. In the following options, *list* is a sequence of integers. Use a comma between separate values, and a hyphen to specify a range (e.g., **1-10,15,20** or **50-**). See also **paste** and **join**.

Options

-b *list*, **--bytes** *list*
Specify *list* of positions; only bytes in these positions will be printed.

-c *list*, **--characters** *list*
Cut the column positions identified in *list*.

-d *c*, **--delimiter** *c*
Use with **-f** to specify field delimiter as character *c* (default is tab); special characters (e.g., a space) must be quoted.

-f *list*, **--fields** *list*
Cut the fields identified in *list*.

-n   Don't split multibyte characters.

-s, --only-delimited
Use with **-f** to suppress lines without delimiters.

--output-delimiter=*string*
Use *string* as the output delimiter. By default, the output delimiter is the same as the input delimiter.

--help
Print help message and exit.

--version
Print version information and exit.

Examples

Extract usernames and real names from */etc/passwd*:

```
cut -d: -f1,5 /etc/passwd
```

Find out who is logged on, but list only login names:

```
who | cut -d" " -f1
```

Cut characters in the fourth column of *file*, and paste them back as the first column in the same file:

```
cut -c4 file | paste - file
```

CVS

cvs [*options*] *cvs-command* [*command-options*] [*command-args*]

CVS (Concurrent Versions System) is a version control system. Like earlier version control systems such as RCS, CVS tracks versions, permits the storage and retrieval of earlier versions, and allows tracking of the history of a file or an entire project. In addition, it permits multiple users on different systems across a network to work in a file simultaneously and merge their changes. All CVS commands start with **cvs**, followed by any global options, the command to execute, and any command options or arguments. For more information on CVS and its commands, see Chapter 15.

Linux Commands

---

date

date [*options*] [*+format*] [*date*]

Print the current date and time. You may specify a display *format*. *format* can consist of literal text strings (blanks must be quoted) as well as field descriptors, whose values will appear as described in the following entries (the listing shows some logical groupings). A privileged user can change the system's date and time.

Options

+format

Display current date in a nonstandard format. For example:

```
$ date +"%A %j %n%k %p"
Tuesday 248
15 PM
```

The default is **%a %b %e %T %Z %Y** (e.g., Tue Sep 5 14:59:37 EDT 2000).

-d *date,* --date *date*

Display *date*, which should be in quotes and may be in the format *d* **days** or *m* **months** *d* **days** to print a date in the future. Specify **ago** to print a date in the past. You may include formatting (see the following section).

-f *datefile,* --file=*datefile*

Like -d, but printed once for each line of *datefile*.

-I [*timespec*], --iso-8601[*=timespec*]

Display in ISO-8601 format. If specified, *timespec* can have one of the values **date** (for date only), **hours**, **minutes**, or **seconds** to get the indicated precision.

-r *file,* --reference=*file*

Display the time *file* was last modified.

-R, --rfc-822

Display the date in RFC 822 format.

--help
> Print help message and exit.

--version
> Print version information and exit.

-s *date*, **--set** *date*
> Set the date.

-u, **--universal**
> Set the date to Greenwich Mean Time, not local time.

Format

The exact result of many of these codes is locale-specific and depend upon your language setting, particularly the **LANG** environment variable. See **locale**.

% Literal %.

- (hyphen)
> Do not pad fields (default: pad fields with zeros).

_ (underscore)
> Pad fields with space (default: zeros).

%a Abbreviated weekday.

%b Abbreviated month name.

%c Country-specific date and time format.

%d Day of month (01–31).

%h Same as **%b**.

%j Julian day of year (001–366).

%k Hour in 24-hour format, without leading zeros (0–23).

%l Hour in 12-hour format, without leading zeros (1–12).

%m Month of year (01–12).

%n Insert a new line.

%p String to indicate AM or PM.

%r Time in **%I:%M:%S %p** (12-hour) format.

%s Seconds since "the epoch," which is 1970-01-01 00:00:00 UTC (a nonstandard extension).

%t Insert a tab.

%w Day of week (Sunday = 0).

%x Country-specific date format based on locale.

%y Last two digits of year (00–99).

%z RFC 822-style numeric time zone.

%A Full weekday.

%B Full month name.

%D Date in **%m/%d/%y** format.

%H Hour in 24-hour format (00–23).

%I Hour in 12-hour format (01–12).

%M Minutes (00–59).

%S Seconds (00–59).

%T Time in **%H:%M:%S** format.

%U Week number in year (00–53); start week on Sunday.

%V Week number in year (01–52); start week on Monday.

%W Week number in year (00–53); start week on Monday.

%X Country-specific time format based on locale.

%Y Four-digit year (e.g., 1996).

%Z Time zone name.

Strings for setting date

Strings for setting the date may be numeric or nonnumeric. Numeric strings consist of time, day, and year in the format *MMDDhhmm[[CC]YY][.ss]*. Nonnumeric strings may include month strings, time zones, a.m., and p.m.

time
> A two-digit hour and two-digit minute (*hhmm*); *hh* uses 24-hour format.

day
> A two-digit month and two-digit day of month (*MMDD*); default is current day and month.

year
> The year specified as either the full four-digit century and year or just the two-digit year; the default is the current year.

Examples

Set the date to July 1 (**0701**), 4 a.m. (**0400**), 1995 (**95**):

    date 0701040095

The command:

    date +"Hello%t Date is %D %n%t Time is %T"

produces a formatted date as follows:

    Hello   Date is 05/09/93
          Time is 17:53:39

---

dd
    dd *options*

Make a copy of an input file (**if**) using the specified conditions, and send the results to the output file (or standard output if **of** is not specified). Any number of options can be supplied, although **if** and **of** are the most common and are usually specified first. Because **dd** can handle arbitrary blocksizes, it is useful when converting between raw physical devices.

Options

bs=*n*
> Set input and output blocksize to *n* bytes; this option overrides **ibs** and **obs**.

cbs=_n_

Set the size of the conversion buffer (logical record length) to _n_ bytes. Use only if the conversion _flag_ is **ascii, ebcdic, ibm, block,** or **unblock.**

conv=_flags_

Convert the input according to one or more (comma-separated) _flags_ listed next. The first five _flags_ are mutually exclusive.

ascii

EBCDIC to ASCII.

ebcdic

ASCII to EBCDIC.

ibm

ASCII to EBCDIC with IBM conventions.

block

Variable-length records (i.e., those terminated by a newline) to fixed-length records.

unblock

Fixed-length records to variable-length records.

lcase

Uppercase to lowercase.

ucase

Lowercase to uppercase.

noerror

Continue processing after read errors.

notrunc

Don't truncate output file.

swab

Swap each pair of input bytes.

sync

Pad input blocks to **ibs** with trailing zeros.

count=_n_

Copy only _n_ input blocks.

ibs=_n_

Set input blocksize to _n_ bytes (default is 512).

if=_file_

Read input from _file_ (default is standard input).

obs=_n_

Set output blocksize to _n_ bytes (default is 512).

of=_file_

Write output to _file_ (default is standard output).

seek=_n_

Skip _n_ output-sized blocks from start of output file.

skip=_n_

Skip _n_ input-sized blocks from start of input file.

--help
> Print help message and then exit.

--version
> Print the version number and then exit.

You can multiply size values (*n*) by a factor of 1024, 512, or 2 by appending the letter **k**, **b**, or **w**, respectively. You can use the letter **x** as a multiplication operator between two numbers.

Examples

Convert an input file to all lowercase:

> **dd if=caps_file of=small_file conv=lcase**

Retrieve variable-length data and write it as fixed-length to **out**:

> *data_retrieval_cmd* | **dd of=out conv=sync,block**

---

deallocvt

deallocvt *N*

Deallocate and destroy the unused virtual console */dev/ttyN*. Multiple consoles may be named with additional spaces and integers: **deallocvt 1 4** will deallocate the */dev/tty1* and */dev/tty4*. Consoles are considered unused if they are not in the foreground, have no open processes, and have no selected text. The command will not destroy consoles that are still active.

---

debugfs

debugfs [[*option*] *device*]

System administration command. Provide direct access to data structure of an ext2 filesystem in order to debug problems with the device. *device* is the special file corresponding to the device containing the ext2 filesystem (e.g., */dev/hda3*). **debugfs** may be used on a mounted filesystem device.

Option

-b *blocksize*
> Use the specified *blocksize* for the filesystem.

-c   Catastrophic mode. Open the filesystem in read-only mode, do not read the inode and group bitmaps initially.

-f *file*
> Read commands from *file*. Exit when done executing commands.

-i   Specify file system *device* is an ext2 image file created by **e2image**.

-s *block*
> Read the superblock from the specified *block*.

-w   Open the filesystem in read-write mode.

-R *command*
> Execute the given *command* (see list below) then exit.

-V   Print version number, then exit.

Commands

cat *file*
> Dump the contents of an inode to standard output.

cd *directory*
> Change the current working directory to *directory*.

chroot *directory*
> Change the root directory to be the specified inode.

close
> Close the currently open filesystem.

clri *file*
> Clear the contents of the inode corresponding to *file*.

dump *file out_file*
> Dump the contents of an inode to *out_file*.

expand_dir *directory*
> Expand *directory*.

feature [[-]*feature*]
> Set filesystem *feature* listed on the command line, then print current feature settings. Use - to clear a *feature*.

find_free_block [*goal*]
> Find first free block starting from *goal* (if specified) and allocate it.

find_free_inode [*dir* [*mode*]]
> Find a free inode and allocate it.

freeb *block*
> Mark *block* as not allocated.

freei *file*
> Free the inode corresponding to *file*.

help
> Print a list of commands understood by **debugfs**.

icheck *block*
> Do block-to-inode translation.

initialize *device blocksize*
> Create an ext2 filesystem on *device*.

kill_file *file*
> Remove *file* and deallocate its blocks.

lcd *directory*
> Change current working *directory* on native filesystem.

ln *source_file dest_file*
> Create a link.

logdump [-**ac**] [-**b***block*] [-**i***inode*] [-**f***journal_file*] [*out_file*]
> Print the ext3 journal for the filesytem. Use options to specify the location of the journal by block, inode, or filename, or to specify a file to which the journal should be printed.

ls [-l] [-d] [*pathname*]

> Emulate the **ls** command. Use -l for verbose format and -d to list deleted entries.

modify_inode *file*

> Modify the contents of the inode corresponding to *file*.

mkdir *directory*

> Make *directory*.

mknod *file* [p|[[c|b] *major minor*]]

> Create a special device file.

ncheck *inode*

> Do inode-to-name translation.

open [-b *blocksize*] [-c] [-f] [-i] [-w] [-s *block*] *device*

> Open a filesystem.

pwd

> Print the current working directory.

quit

> Quit **debugfs**.

rdump *directory dest_directory*

> Recursively dump *directory* and its contents to *dest_directory* on the native filesystem.

rm *file*

> Remove *file*.

rmdir *directory*

> Remove *directory*.

setb *block*

> Mark *block* as allocated.

seti *file*

> Mark in use the inode corresponding to *file*.

set_super_value [-l] *field value*

> Set superblock *field* to *value*. Use -l to print a list of valid fields.

show_super_stats [-h]

> List the contents of the superblock and block group descriptors. Use -**h** to list only the superblock contents.

stat *file*

> Dump the contents of the inode corresponding to *file*.

testb *block*

> Test whether *block* is marked as allocated.

testi *file*

> Test whether the inode corresponding to *file* is marked as allocated.

unlink *file*

> Remove a link.

write *source_file file*

> Create a file in the filesystem named *file*, and copy the contents of *source_file* into the destination file.

depmod   **depmod** [*options*] *modules*

System administration command. Create a dependency file for the modules given on the command line. This dependency file can be used by **modprobe** to automatically load the relevant *modules*. The normal use of **depmod** is to include the line **/sbin/depmod -a** in one of the files in */etc/rc.d* so that the correct module dependencies will be available after booting the system.

Options
-a, --all
> Create dependencies for all modules listed in */etc/modules.conf*.

-b *dir*, **--basedir** *dir*
> Specify a base directory to use instead of */lib/modules*.

-e, --errsyms
> Print a list of all unresolved symbols.

-d   Debug mode. Show all commands being issued.

-h, --help
> Print help message, then exit.

-n, --show
> Write dependency file to standard output.

-q, --quiet
> Don't display error messages about missing symbols.

-r, --root
> Allow root to load modules not owned by root.

-s, --syslog
> Write error messages to the syslog daemon instead of to standard error.

-v   Print a list of all processed modules.

-A, --quick
> Check timestamps and update the dependency file if anything has changed.

-C *file*, **--config** *file*
> Use the specified configuration file instead of */etc/modules.conf*. May also be set using the MODULECONF environment variable.

-F *file*, **--kernelsyms** *file*
> Use the specified kernel symbol file to build dependencies. Usually this is either a copy of a system's *System.map* file or the output of */proc/ksyms*.

-V, --version
> Print version number.

Files

/etc/modules.conf
> Information about modules: which ones depend on others, and which directories correspond to particular types of modules.

/sbin/insmod, /sbin/rmmod
> Programs that **depmod** relies on.

---

devdump

devdump `isoimage`

Interactively display the contents of the device or filesystem image *isoimage*. **devdump** displays the first 256 bytes of the first 2048-byte sector and waits for commands. The prompt shows the extent number (zone) and offset within the extent, and the contents display at the top of the screen.

Commands

+   Search forward for the next instance of the search string.

a   Search backward within the image.

b   Search forward within the image.

f   Prompt for a new search string.

g   Prompt for a new starting block and go there.

q   Exit.

---

df

df [`options`] [`name`]

Report the amount of free disk space available on all mounted filesystems or on the given *name*. (**df** cannot report on unmounted filesystems.) Disk space is shown in 1KB blocks (default) or 512-byte blocks (if the environment variable POSIXLY_CORRECT is set). *name* can be a device name (e.g., */dev/hd**), the directory name of a mounting point (e.g., */usr*), or a directory name (in which case **df** reports on the entire filesystem in which that directory is mounted).

Options

-a, --all
> Include empty filesystems (those with 0 blocks).

--block-size=*n*
> Show space as *n*-byte blocks.

-h, --human-readable
> Print sizes in a format friendly to human readers (e.g., 1.9G instead of 1967156).

-H, --si
> Like **-h**, but show as power of 1000 rather than 1024.

-i, --inodes
> Report free, used, and percent-used inodes.

-k, --kilobytes
> Print sizes in kilobytes.

-l, --local
> Show local filesystems only.

-m, --megabytes
> Print sizes in megabytes.

--no-sync
> Show results without invoking **sync** first (i.e., without flushing the buffers). This is the default.

-P, --portability
> Use POSIX output format (i.e., print information about each filesystem on exactly one line).

--sync
> Invoke **sync** (flush buffers) before getting and showing sizes.

-t *type*, **--type=***type*
> Show only *type* filesystems.

-T, --print-type
> Print the type of each filesystem in addition to the sizes.

-x *type*, **--exclude-type=***type*
> Show only filesystems that are not of type *type*.

--help
> Print help message and then exit.

--version
> Print the version and then exit.

---

diff

diff [*options*] [*diroptions*] *file1 file2*

Compare two text files. **diff** reports lines that differ between *file1* and *file2*. Output consists of lines of context from each file, with *file1* text flagged by a < symbol and *file2* text by a > symbol. Context lines are preceded by the **ed** command (**a**, **c**, or **d**) that would be used to convert *file1* to *file2*. If one of the files is -, standard input is read. If one of the files is a directory, **diff** locates the filename in that directory corresponding to the other argument (e.g., **diff my_dir junk** is the same as **diff my_dir/junk junk**). If both arguments are directories, **diff** reports lines that differ between all pairs of files having equivalent names (e.g., *olddir/program* and *newdir/program*); in addition, **diff** lists filenames unique to one directory, as well as subdirectories common to both. See also **cmp**.

Options

-a, --text
> Treat all files as text files. Useful for checking to see if binary files are identical.

-b, --ignore-space-change
> Ignore repeating blanks and end-of-line blanks; treat successive blanks as one.

-B, --ignore-blank-lines

Ignore blank lines in files.

-c   Context **diff**: print 3 lines surrounding each changed line.

-C *n*, **--context**[=*n*]

Context **diff**: print *n* lines surrounding each changed line. The default context is 3 lines.

-d, --minimal

To speed up comparison, ignore segments of numerous changes and output a smaller set of changes.

-D *symbol*, **--ifdef**=*symbol*

When handling C files, create an output file that contains all the contents of both input files, including **#ifdef** and **#ifndef** directives that reflect the directives in both files.

-e, --ed

Produce a script of commands (**a, c, d**) to re-create *file2* from *file1* using the **ed** editor.

-F *regexp*, **--show-function-line**[=*regexp*]

For context and unified **diff**, show the most recent line containing *regexp* before each block of changed lines.

-H   Speed output of large files by scanning for scattered small changes; long stretches with many changes may not show up.

--help

Print brief usage message.

--horizon-lines=*n*

In an attempt to find a more compact listing, keep *n* lines on both sides of the changed lines when performing the comparison.

-i, --ignore-case

Ignore case in text comparison. Uppercase and lowercase are considered the same.

-I *regexp*, **--ignore-matching-lines**=*regexp*

Ignore lines in files that match the regular expression *regexp*.

-l, --paginate

Paginate output by passing it to **pr**.

-L *label*, **--label** *label*, **--label**=*label*

For context and unified **diff**, print *label* in place of the filename being compared. The first such option applies to the first filename and the second option to the second filename.

--left-column

For two-column output (**-y**), show only left column of common lines.

-n, --rcs

Produce output in RCS **diff** format.

-N, --new-file

Treat nonexistent files as empty.

-p, --show-c-function

When handling files in C or C-like languages such as Java, show the function containing each block of changed lines. Assumes **-c,** but can also be used with a unified **diff**.

-P, --unidirectional-new-file

If two directories are being compared and the first lacks a file that is in the second, pretend that an empty file of that name exists in the first directory.

-q, --brief

Output only whether files differ.

-r, --recursive

Compare subdirectories recursively.

-s, --report-identical-files

Indicate when files do not differ.

-S *filename,* **--starting-file=***filename*

For directory comparisons, begin with the file *filename,* skipping files that come earlier in the standard list order.

--suppress-common-lines

For two-column output (**-y**), do not show common lines.

-t, --expand-tabs

Produce output with tabs expanded to spaces.

-T, --initial-tab

Insert initial tabs into output to line up tabs properly.

-u   Unified **diff**: print old and new versions of lines in a single block, with 3 lines surrounding each block of changed lines.

-U *n,* **--unified**[**=***n*]

Unified **diff**: print old and new versions of lines in a single block, with *n* lines surrounding each block of changed lines. The default context is 3 lines.

-v, --version

Print version number of this version of **diff**.

-w, --ignore-all-space

Ignore all whitespace in files for comparisons.

-W *n,* **--width=***n*

For two-column output (**-y**), produce columns with a maximum width of *n* characters. Default is 130.

-x *regexp,* **--exclude=***regexp*

Do not compare files in a directory whose names match *regexp*.

-X *filename,* **--exclude-from=***filename*

Do not compare files in a directory whose names match patterns described in the file *filename*.

-y, --side-by-side

Produce two-column output.

-*n*   For context and unified **diff**, print *n* lines of context. Same as specifying a number with **-C** or **-U**.

---

diff3

diff3 [*options*] *file1 file2 file3*

Compare three files and report the differences. No more than one of the files may be given as - (indicating that it is to be read from standard input). The output is displayed with the following codes:

====

All three files differ.

====1

file1 is different.

====2

file2 is different.

====3

file3 is different.

diff3 is also designed to merge changes in two differing files based on a common ancestor file (i.e., when two people have made their own set of changes to the same file). diff3 can find changes between the ancestor and one of the newer files and generate output that adds those differences to the other new file. Unmerged changes occur where both of the newer files differ from each other and at least one of them differs from the ancestor. Changes from the ancestor that are the same in both of the newer files are called *merged changes*. If all three files differ in the same place, it is called an *overlapping change*.

This scheme is used on the command line with the ancestor being *file2*, the second filename. Comparison is made between *file2* and *file3*, with those differences then applied to *file1*.

Options

-3, --easy-only
Create an **ed** script to incorporate into *file1* unmerged, nonoverlapping differences between *file1* and *file3*.

-a, --text
Treat files as text.

-A, --show-all
Create an **ed** script to incorporate all changes, showing conflicts in bracketed format.

-e, --ed
Create an **ed** script to incorporate into *file1* all unmerged differences between *file2* and *file3*.

-E, --show-overlap
Create an **ed** script to incorporate unmerged changes, showing conflicts in bracketed format.

-x, --overlap-only
Create an **ed** script to incorporate into *file1* all differences where all three files differ (overlapping changes).

-X Same as **-x**, but show only overlapping changes, in bracketed format.

-m, --merge
> Create file with changes merged (not an **ed** script).

-L *label,* **--label=***label*
> Use *label* to replace filename in output.

-i
> Append the **w** (save) and **q** (quit) commands to **ed** script output.

-T, --initial-tab
> To line tabs up properly in output, begin lines with a tab instead of two spaces.

-v, --version
> Print version information and then exit.

---

dig

dig [*@server*] [*options*] [*name*] [*type*] [*class*] [*query-options*]
dig *@server name type*
dig *-h*

The **dig** command is used to query DNS servers; it is more flexible than the deprecated **nslookup** command. If you use it without any options or arguments, it will search for the root server. The standard arguments are:

server
> The server to query. If no server is supplied, **dig** will check the name servers listed in */etc/resolv.conf*. The address may be an IPv4 dotted address or an IPv6 colon-delimited address. It may also be a hostname, which **dig** will resolve (through the name servers in */etc/resolv.conf*).

name
> The domain name to look up.

type
> The type of query to perform, such as **A, ANY, MX, SIG**, and so forth. The default is **A**, but you may use any valid BIND9 query type.

Options

You may use the following option flags with **dig**:

-b *address*
> Set the source IP address for the query.

-c *class*
> Set the class of query. The default value is **IN** (internet), but you can choose **HS** for Hesiod or **CH** for CHAOSNET.

-f *filename*
> Operate in batch mode, performing the queries in the file you specify.

-p *portnumber*
> Choose the port number for the query. The default value is the standard DNS port, 53.

-t *type*

Set the type of query, as with the query argument. The default value is **A**, but you may use any valid BIND9 query.

-x *addr*

Use the **-x** flag for reverse lookups, specifying an IPv4 or IPv6 address. You do not need the name, class, or type arguments if you use the **-x** flag.

-k *filename*

Specify a TSIG key file; used for signed transactions. You can also use the **-y** key, although this is less secure.

-y *keyname:keyvalue*

Enter the actual key name and value when conducting a signed transaction. Because the key and value can be seen in the output of **ps**, this is not recommended for use on multiuser systems; use **-k** instead.

Query options

There are a large number of query options for **dig**. Each query option is preceded by +, and many have an opposite version beginning with **no**. For example, the **tcp** flag is passed as **+tcp**, and negated with **+notcp**. Because there are so many options, only a few are discussed here. For greater detail, see the **dig** manpage.

+tcp, **+notcp**

Use (or do not use) the TCP protocol instead of the default UDP.

+domain=*searchdomain*

Perform a search in the domain specified; this is equivalent to using the **+search** option and having "searchdomain" as the sole entry in the search list or domain directive of */etc/resolv.conf*.

+search, **+nosearch**

Use (or do not use) the search list provided in */etc/resolv.conf*. The default is not to use the search list.

+time=*T*

Timeout for queries, in seconds. The default is 5, and the minimum is 1.

+tries=*N*

The number of times to retry UDP queries. The default is 3, and the minimum is 1.

---

dip

dip [*options*] [*chat scriptfile*]

System administration command. Set up or initiate dial-up Internet connections. **dip** can be used to establish connections for users dialing out or dialing in. Commands can be used in interactive mode or placed in a script file for use in dial-out connections. To establish dial-in connections, **dip** is often used as a shell, and may be executed using the commands **diplogin** or **diplogini**.

Options

-a   In dial-in mode, prompt for username and password. Same as the **diplogini** command.

-i   Initiate a login shell for a dial-in connection. Same as the **diplogin** command.

-k   Kill the most recent **dip** process or the process running on the device specified by the **-l** option.

-l *device*
> Used with the **-k** option. Specifies a tty *device*.

-m *mtu*
> Maximum Transfer Unit. The default is 296.

-p *protocol*
> The *protocol* to use: SLIP, CSLIP, PPP, or TERM.

-t   Command mode. This is usually done for testing.

-v   Verbose mode.

Commands

Most of these commands can be used either in interactive mode or in a script file.

beep *times*
> Beep the terminal the specified number of *times*.

bootp
> Retrieve local and remote IP addresses using the BOOTP protocol.

break
> Send a BREAK.

chatkey *keyword code*
> Map a modem response keyword to a numeric code.

config [**interface**|**routing**] [**pre**|**up**|**down**|**post**] *arguments*
> Modify **interface** characteristics or the **routing** table before the link comes up, when it is up, when it goes down, or after it is down. The syntax for *arguments* is the same as for arguments for the **ifconfig** or **route** commands.

databits 7|8
> Set the number of data bits.

dec $*variable* [*value*]
> Decrement $*variable* by *value*. The default is 1.

default
> Set default route to the IP address of the host connected to.

dial *phonenumber* [*timeout*]
> Dial *phonenumber*. Abort if remote modem doesn't answer within *timeout* seconds. Set **$errlvl** according to the modem response.

echo on|off
> Enable or disable the display of modem commands.

exit [*n*]

Exit the script. Optionally return the number *n* as the exit status.

flush

Clear the input buffer.

get *$variable* [**ask**|**remote** [*timeout*]] *value*

Set *$variable* to *value*. If **ask** is specified, prompt the user for a value. If **remote** is specified, retrieve the value from the remote system. Abort after *timeout* seconds.

goto *label*

Jump to the section identified by *label*.

help

List available commands.

if *expr* **goto** *label*

Jump to the section identified by *label* if the expression evaluates to true. An expression compares a variable to a constant using one of these operators: =, !=, <, >, <=, or >=.

inc *$variable* [*value*]

Increment *$variable* by *value*. The default is 1.

init *string*

Set the *string* used to initialize the modem. The default is ATE0 Q0 V1 X1.

mode *protocol*

Set the connection *protocol*. Valid values are **SLIP**, **CSLIP**, **PPP**, and **TERM**. The default is **SLIP**.

netmask *mask*

Set the subnet mask.

parity E|O|N

Set the line parity to even, odd, or none.

password

Prompt user for password.

proxyarp

Install a proxy ARP entry in the local ARP table.

print *$variable*

Display the content of *$variable*.

psend *command*

Execute *command* in a shell, and send output to the serial device. Commands are executed using the user's real UID.

port *device*

Specify the serial device the modem is attached to.

quit

Exit with a nonzero exit status. Abort the connection.

reset

Reset the modem.

securid

Prompt user for the variable part of an ACE System SecureID password, and send it together with the stored prefix to the remote system.

securidf *prefix*

Store the fixed part of an ACE System SecureID password.

send *string*

Send *string* to the serial device.

shell *command*

Execute command in a shell using the user's real UID.

skey [*timeout*]

Wait for an S/Key challenge, then prompt user for the secret key. Generate and send the response. Abort if challenge is not received within *timeout* seconds. S/Key support must be compiled into **dip**.

sleep *time*

Wait *time* seconds.

speed *bits-per-second*

Set the port speed. Default is 38400.

stopbits 1|2

Set the number of stop bits.

term

Enable terminal mode. Pass keyboard input directly to the serial device.

timeout *time*

Set the number of seconds the line can be inactive before the link is closed.

wait *text* [*timeout*]

Wait *timeout* seconds for *text* to arrive from the remote system. If *timeout* is not specified, wait forever.

---

dir

dir [*options*] [*file*]

List directory contents. **dir** is equivalent to the command **ls -C -b** (list files in columns, sorted vertically, special characters escaped) and it takes the same arguments as **ls**. This is an alternate invocation of the **ls** command and is provided for the convenience of those converting from Microsoft Windows and the DOS shell.

---

dircolors

dircolors [*options*] [*file*]

Set the color options for **ls** by changing the LS_COLORS environment variable. If you specify a file, **dircolors** will read it to determine which colors to use. Otherwise, it will use a default set of colors.

Options

The program takes three options in addition to the standard **--help** and **--version** flags:

-p, --print-database
> Display the default colors. You can copy this information into a file and change it to suit your preferences, and then run the program with the file as its argument to set the colors to your new values.

-c, --csh, --c-shell
> Use csh (C shell) syntax when setting the LS_COLORS variable.

-b, --sh, --bourne-shell
> Use the Bourne shell syntax when setting the LS_COLORS variable.

dirname

> **dirname** *pathname*
>
> Print *pathname*, excluding the last level. Useful for stripping the actual filename from a pathname. If there are no slashes (no directory levels) in *pathname*, **dirname** prints . to indicate the current directory. See also **basename**.

dmesg

> **dmesg** [*options*]
>
> System administration command. Display the system control messages from the kernel ring buffer. This buffer stores all messages since the last system boot, or the most recent ones if the buffer has been filled.
>
> ### Options
>
> **-c** Clear buffer after printing messages.
>
> **-n***level*
> > Set the level of system message that will display on console.
>
> **-s***buffersize*
> > Specify *buffersize* of kernel ring buffer. This is useful if you have changed the kernel default.

dnsdomain-name

> **dnsdomainname**
>
> TCP/IP command. Print the system's DNS domain name. See also **hostname**.

dnssec-keygen

> **dnssec-keygen** [*options*] *domain-name*
>
> System administration command. Generate encrypted Secure DNS (DNSSEC) or Transaction Signatures (TSIG) keys for *domain-name*. When the key is completed, **dnssec-keygen** prints the key identifier to standard output and creates public and private key files whose names are based on the key identifier and the filename

extensions *.key* and *.private*. It creates both files even when using an asymmetric algorithm like HMAC-MD5. For more information on Secure DNS, see *DNS and BIND* (O'Reilly), or read RFC 2535.

Options

-a *algorithm*

> Specify the cryptographic *algorithm* to use. Accepted values are **RSAMD5, RSA, DSA, DH,** or **HMAC-MD5.**

-b *bitsize*

> Specify the key *bitsize*. Accepted values depend on the encryption algorithm used.

-c *class*

> The domain record for which the key is being generated should contain *class*. When this option is not given, a *class* of **IN** is assumed.

-e Use a large exponent when generating an RSA key.

-g *generator*

> Specified the number to use as a generator when creating a DH (Diffie Hellman) key. Accepted values are **2** and **5.**

-h Print a help message, then exit.

-n *type*

> The owner of the key must be of the specified *type*. Accepted values are **ZONE, HOST, ENTITY,** or **USER.**

-p *protocol*

> Specify the protocol value for the generated key. Accepted values are given in RFC 2535 and other DNS Security RFCs. By default the value is either **2** (email) or **3** (DNSSEC).

-r *device*

> Specify the *device* to use as a source of randomness when creating keys. This can be a device file, a file containing random data, or the string **keyboard** to specify keyboard input. By default, */dev/random* will be used when available, and keyboard input will be used when it is not.

-s *type*

> Specify whether the key can be used for authentication, confirmation, both, or neither. Accepted values for *type* are **AUTHCONF, NOAUTHCONF, NOAUTH,** or **NOCONF.**

---

dnssec-makekeyset

dnssec-makekeyset [*options*] *key-identifiers*

System administration command. Generate a domain keyset from one or more DNS Security keys generated by **dnssec-keygen.** Keysets can be sent to parent zone administrators to be signed with the zone key. The keyset is written to a file with the name *keyset-domainname*. For more information on Secure DNS, see *DNS and BIND* (O'Reilly), or read RFC 2535.

Options

-a Verify all generated signatures.

-e *end-time*
> Specify the date and time the records will expire. The *end-time* may be specified in *yyyymmddhhmmss* notation, or as *+N* seconds from the *start-time*. The default is 30 days from *start-time*.

-h Print help message, then exit.

-p Use pseudo-random data to sign the zone key.

-r *device*
> Specify the *device* to use as a source of randomness when creating keys. This can be a device file, a file containing random data, or the string **keyboard** to specify keyboard input. By default, */dev/random* will be used when available, and keyboard input will be used when it is not.

-s *start-time*
> Specify the date and time the records become valid. The *end-time* may be specified in *yyyymmddhhmmss* notation, or as *+N* seconds from the current time. The default is the current time.

-t *ttl*
> Specify the TTL (time to live) in seconds for the KEY and SIG records. Default is 3600 seconds.

---

dnssec-signkey

dnssec-signkey [*options*] *keyset key-identifiers*

System administration command. Sign a secure DNS *keyset* with the key signatures specified in the list of *key-identifiers*. A zone administrator would use this command to sign a child zone's keyset with the parent zone's keys. For more information on Secure DNS, see *DNS and BIND* (O'Reilly), or read RFC 2535.

Options

-a Verify generated signatures.

-c *class*
> Specify the DNS *class* of the keyset.

-e *end-time*
> Specify the date and time the records will expire. The *end-time* may be specified in *yyyymmddhhmmss* notation, or as *+N* seconds from the *start-time*. The default is 30 days from *start-time*.

-h Print help message, then exit.

-p Use pseudo-random data to sign the zone key.

-r *device*
> Specify the *device* to use as a source of randomness when creating keys. This can be a device file, a file containing random data, or the string **keyboard** to specify keyboard input. By default, */dev/random* will be used when available, and keyboard input will be used when it is not.

-s *start-time*

Specify the date and time the records become valid. The *end-time* may be specified in *yyyymmddhhmmss* notation, or given as *+N* seconds from the current time. The default is the current time.

---

dnssec-signzone   `dnssec-signzone` [*options*] *zonefile* [*key-identifiers*]

System administration command. Sign a secure DNS *zonefile* with the signatures in the specified list of *key-identifiers*. If signed keysets associated with the zone are found in the current directory, include their signatures in the signed zone file. The **dnssec-signzone** command writes the signed zone information to a file named **db-***domainname*.**signed**. This file should be referenced in a zone statement in a *named.conf* file. For more information on Secure DNS, see *DNS and BIND* (O'Reilly), or read RFC 2535.

Options

-a   Verify generated signatures.

-c *class*

Specify the DNS *class* of the keyset.

-d *directory*

Search *directory* for signed key files.

-e *end-time*

Specify the date and time the records will expire. The *end-time* may be specified in *yyyymmddhhmmss* notation, or given as *+N* seconds from the *start-time*. The default is 30 days from *start-time*.

-h   Print help message, then exit.

-i *days*

When signing a previously signed zone, replace any records due to expire within the specified number of *days*. The default is one quarter of the number of days between the signature's *start-time* and *end-time*.

-n *threads*

Specify the number of *threads* to use when signing the zone file. The default is one for each detected CPU.

-o *origin*

Specify the zone *origin*. The name of the zone file is the default origin.

-p   Use pseudo-random data to sign the zone key.

-r *device*

Specify the *device* to use as a source of randomness when creating keys. This can be a device file, a file containing random data, or the string **keyboard** to specify keyboard input. By default, */dev/random* will be used when available, and keyboard input will be used when it is not.

-s *start-time*

Specify the date and time the records become valid. The *end-time* may be specified in *yyyymmddhhmmss* notation, or given as +*N* seconds from the current time. The default is the current time.

-t   Print statistics when complete.

domainname

domainname [*name*]

NFS/NIS command. Set or display name of current NIS domain. With no argument, **domainname** displays the name of the current NIS domain. Only a privileged user can set the domain name by giving an argument; this is usually done in a startup script.

dosfsck

dosfsck [*options*] *device*
fsck.msdos [*options*] *device*

System administration command. Similar to **fsck**, but specifically intended for MS-DOS filesystems. When checking an MS-DOS filesystem, **fsck** calls this command. Normally **dosfsck** stores all changes in memory, then writes them when checks are complete.

Options

-a   Automatically repair the system; do not prompt the user.

-d *file*

Drop the named file from the file allocation table. Force checking, even if kernel has already marked the filesystem as valid. **dosfsck** will normally exit without checking if the system appears to be clean.

-f   Save unused cluster chains to files.

-l   List pathnames of files being processed.

-r   Repair the system, prompting user for advice.

-t   Mark unreadable clusters as bad.

-u *file*

Attempt to undelete the named file.

-v   Verbose mode.

-w   Write changes to disk immediately.

-y   When queried, answer "yes."

-A   Filesystem is an Atari version of MS-DOS.

-F   Flush buffer caches before checking.

-V   Repeat test to verify all errors have been corrected.

du

du [*options*] [*directories*]

Print disk usage (as the number of 1KB blocks used by each named directory and its subdirectories; default is the current directory).

Options

-a, --all

Print disk usage for all files, not just subdirectories.

-b, --bytes

Print sizes in bytes.

-c, --total

In addition to normal output, print grand total of all arguments.

-D, --dereference-args

Follow symbolic links, but only if they are command-line arguments.

-h, --human-readable

Print sizes in human-readable format.

-H, --si

Like **-h**, but show as power of 1000 rather than 1024.

-k, --kilobytes

Print sizes in kilobytes (this is the default).

-l, --count-links

Count the size of all files, whether or not they have already appeared (i.e., via a hard link).

-L, --dereference

Follow symbolic links.

--exclude=*pattern*

Exclude files that match *pattern*.

--max-depth=*num*

Report sizes for directories only down to *num* levels below the starting point (which is level 0).

-m, --megabytes

Print sizes in megabytes.

-s, --summarize

Print only the grand total for each named directory.

-S, --separate-dirs

Do not include the sizes of subdirectories when totaling the size of parent directories.

-x, --one-file-system

Display usage of files in current filesystem only.

-X, --exclude-from=*file*

Exclude files that match any pattern in *file*.

--help

Print help message and then exit.

--version

Print the version and then exit.

dumpe2fs   dumpe2fs *device*

System administration command. Print information about *device*'s superblock and blocks group.

Options

-b   List blocks marked as bad.

-f   Force display of filesystems with unknown feature flags.

-h   Display superblock information only.

-i   Specify device is an image file created by **e2image**.

-ob *superblock*
      Specify location of the superblock.

-oB *blocksize*
      Specify *blocksize* to use when examining filesystem.

-x   Print block numbers in hexadecimal.

-V   Print version number and exit.

dumpkeys   dumpkeys [*options*]

Print information about the keyboard driver's translation tables to standard output. Further information is available in the manual pages under *keytables*.

Options

-1, --separate-lines
      Print one line for each modifier/keycode pair and prefix **plain** to each unmodified keycode.

-c*charset*, **--charset=***charset*
      Specify character set with which to interpret character code values. The default character set is **iso-8859-1**. The full list of valid character sets is available with the **--help** option.

--compose-only
      Print compose key combinations only. Requires compose key support in the kernel.

-f, --full-table
      Output in canonical, not short, form: for each key, print a row with modifier combinations divided into columns.

--funcs-only
      Print function key string definitions only; do not print key bindings or string definitions.

-h, --help
      Print help message and the version.

-i, --short-info
      Print in short-info format, including information about acceptable keycode keywords in the keytable files; the number of actions that can be bound to a key; a list of the ranges of action codes (the values to the right of a key definition); and the number of function keys that the kernel supports.

--keys-only

> Print key bindings only; do not print string definitions.

-l, --long-info

> Print the same information as in **--short-info**, plus a list of the supported action symbols and their numeric values.

-n, --numeric

> Print action code values in hexadecimal notation; do not attempt to convert them to symbolic notation.

-S *num*, **--shape**=*num*

> Print using *num* to determine table shape. Values of *num* are:
>
> 0   Default.
>
> 1   Same as **--full-table**.
>
> 2   Same as **--separate-lines**.
>
> 3   One line for each keycode up to the first hole, then one line per modifier/keycode pair.

---

e2fsck

e2fsck [*options*] *device*
fsck.ext2 [*options*] *device*

System administration command. Similar to **fsck**, but specifically intended for Linux Second Extended Filesystems. When checking a second extended filesystem, **fsck** calls this command. This command is also used for the third extended filesystem (ext3), which is a journaling version of the second extended filesystem.

Options

-b *superblock*

> Use *superblock* instead of the default superblock.

-d   Debugging mode.

-f   Force checking, even if kernel has already marked the filesystem as valid. **e2fsck** will normally exit without checking if the system appears to be clean.

-l *file*

> Consult *file* for a list of bad blocks, in addition to checking for others.

-n   Ensure that no changes are made to the filesystem. When queried, answer "no."

-p   "Preen." Repair all bad blocks noninteractively.

-t   Display timing statistics.

-v   Verbose.

-y   When queried, answer "yes."

-B *size*

> Expect to find the superblock at *size*; if it's not there, exit.

-F   Flush buffer caches before checking.

-L *file*

> Consult *file* for list of bad blocks instead of checking filesystem for them.

---

e2image

e2image [*option*] *device file*

System administration command. Store disaster recovery data for ext2 filesystem on *device* to image file *file*. Weekly filesystem images can be an important part of a disaster recovery plan.

Option

-r Create a raw image file that can be checked and debugged using filesystem utilities such as **e2fsck** or **debugfs**. Raw images are created as sparse files. Either compress the image file before moving it, or use the **-sparse=always** option when copying it with **cp**.

e2label

e2label *device* [*label*]

System administration command. Display the filesystem label on an ext2 filesystem *device*. Change filesystem label to *label* if specified.

echo

echo [**options**] [*string*]

Send (echo) the input *string* to standard output. This is the **/bin/echo** command. **echo** also exists as a command built into the C shell and **bash**. The following character sequences have special meanings:

\a Alert (bell).

\b Backspace.

\c Suppress trailing newline.

\f Form feed.

\n Newline.

\r Carriage return.

\t Horizontal tab.

\v Vertical tab.

\\ Literal backslash.

nnn The octal character whose ASCII code is *nnn*.

Options

-e Enable character sequences with special meaning. (In some versions, this option is not required in order to make the sequences work.)

-E Disable character sequences with special meaning.

-n Suppress printing of newline after text.

--help
    Print help message and then exit.

--version
    Print version information and then exit.

Examples

```
/bin/echo "testing printer" | lp
/bin/echo "TITLE\nTITLE" > file ; cat doc1 doc2 >> file
/bin/echo "Warning: ringing bell \a"
```

---

egrep

egrep [*options*] [*regexp*] [*files*]

Search one or more *files* for lines that match an extended regular expression *regexp*. **egrep** doesn't support the regular expressions \(, \), \n, \<, \>, \{, or \}, but does support the other expressions, as well as the extended set +, ?, |, and ( ). Remember to enclose these characters in quotes. Regular expressions are described in Chapter 9. Exit status is 0 if any lines match, 1 if none match, and 2 for errors.

See **grep** for the list of available options. Also see **fgrep**.

Examples

Search for occurrences of **Victor** or **Victoria** in *file*:

```
egrep 'Victor(ia)*' file
egrep '(Victor|Victoria)' file
```

Find and print strings such as **old.doc1** or **new.doc2** in *files*, and include their line numbers:

```
egrep -n '(old|new)\.doc?' files
```

---

eject

eject [*options*] [*device*]

Eject removable media such as a CD-ROM, floppy, tape, or JAZ or ZIP disk. You may name the device by */dev* or */mnt* filename. The */dev* and */mnt* prefixes are optional for any items in the */dev* and */mnt* directories. If no device is named, it is assumed that "cdrom" should be ejected.

Options

The eject command takes the following option flags:

-h   Display help information.

-v, --verbose
    Verbose mode: display additional information about actions.

-d, --default
    List the default device name rather than doing anything.

-a, --auto on|1|off|0
    Set the auto-eject mode to on or off (equivalent to 1 or 0). If auto-eject mode is on, the device is ejected when closed or unmounted.

-c, --changerslot *slotnumber*
    If using a CD-ROM changer, select a CD from one of the slots. Slots are enumerated starting with 0, and the CD-ROM drive must not be playing music or mounted to read data.

-t, --trayclose

Close the CD-ROM drive. Not all drives will respond to this command.

-x, --cdspeed *speed*

Set the speed multiplier for the CD-ROM to an integer, usually a power of 2. Not all devices support this command. Setting the speed to 0 indicates that the drive should operate at its maximum speed.

-n, --noop

Do not perform any actions; merely display the actions that would be performed.

-r, --cdrom

Use CD-ROM commands to eject the drive. Normally, the system will try all methods (CD-ROM, SCSI, floppy, tape) to eject.

-s, --scsi

Use SCSI commands to eject the drive. Normally, the system will try all methods (CD-ROM, SCSI, floppy, tape) to eject.

-f, --floppy

Use floppy commands to eject the drive. Normally, the system will try all methods (CD-ROM, SCSI, floppy, tape) to eject.

-q, --tape

Use tape commands to eject the drive. Normally, the system will try all methods (CD-ROM, SCSI, floppy, tape) to eject.

-p, --proc

Use the mounted files listed in */proc/mounts* rather than in */etc/mtab*.

-V, --version

Display version information, then quit.

---

elvtune

elvtune [*options*] *devices*

System administration command. Set the latency in the elevator algorithm used to schedule I/O activities for the specified block *devices*. If no options are given, print the current settings for *devices*.

Options

-b *N*

Set the maximum coalescing factor allowed on writes when reads are pending to *N*.

-h Print help message, then exit.

-r *N*

Set the maximum read latency (basically, the number of sectors to read before writes are allowed) to *N*. The default is 8192.

-v Print version number, then exit.

-w *N*

Set the maximum write latency (sectors to write before allowing a read) to *N*. The default is 16384.

---

emacs

emacs [*options*] [*files*]

A text editor and all-purpose work environment. For more information, see Chapter 10.

---

env

env [*option*] [*variable=value* ...] [*command*]

Display the current environment or, if an environment *variable* is specified, set it to a new *value* and display the modified environment. If *command* is specified, execute it under the modified environment.

Options

-, -i, --ignore-environment
Ignore current environment entirely.

-u *name*, **--unset** *name*
Unset the specified variable.

--help
Print help message and then exit.

--version
Print version information and then exit.

---

etags

etags [*options*] *files*

Create a list of function and macro names defined in a programming source *file*. **etags** generates tags for use by **emacs**. (**ctags** produces an equivalent tags file for use with vi.) More than one file may be specified. **etags** understands many programming languages, including C, C++, FORTRAN, Java, Perl, Python, flex, yacc, and bison. The output list (named *TAGS* by default) contains lines of the form:

   name   *file*   *context*

where *name* is the function or macro name, *file* is the source file in which *name* is defined, and *context* is a search pattern that shows the line of code containing *name*. After the list of tags is created, you can invoke Emacs on any file and type:

   M-x visit-tags-table

You will be prompted for the name of the tag table; the default is *TAGS*. To switch to the source file associated with the *name* listed in *tagsfile*, type:

   M-x find-tag

You will be prompted for the tag you would like Emacs to search for.

Options

-a, --append
> Append tag output to existing list of tags.

-d, --defines
> Include tag entries for C preprocessor definitions.

-i *file*, **--include**=*file*
> Add a note to the tags file that *file* should be consulted in addition to the normal input file.

-l *language*, **--language**=*language*
> Consider the files that follow this option to be written in *language*. Use the **-h** option for a list of languages and their default filename extensions.

-o *file*, **--output**=*file*
> Write to *file*.

-r *regexp*, **--regex**=*regexp*
> Include a tag for each line that matches *regexp* in the files following this option.

-C, --c++
> Expect *.c* and *.h* files to contain C++, not C, code.

-D, --no-defines
> Do not include tag entries for C preprocessor definitions.

-H, -h, --help
> Print usage information.

-R, --noregex
> Don't include tags based on regular-expression matching for the files that follow this option.

-S, --ignore-indentation
> Normally **etags** uses indentation to parse the tag file; this option tells it to rely on it less.

-V, --version
> Print the version number.

---

ex

ex [*options*] *file*

An interactive command-based editor. For more information, see Chapter 11.

. expand

expand [*options*] [*files*]

Convert tabs in given files (or standard input, if the file is named -) to appropriate number of spaces; write results to standard output.

Options

-*tabs*, -t *tabs*, **--tabs** *tabs*
> *tabs* is a comma-separated list of integers that specify the placement of tab stops. If exactly one integer is provided, the tab stops are set to every *integer* spaces. By default, tab stops

are 8 spaces apart. With **-t** and **--tabs**, the list may be separated by whitespace instead of commas.

-i, --initial

Convert tabs only at the beginning of lines.

--help

Print help message and then exit.

--version

Print version information and then exit.

---

expr

expr *arg1 operator arg2* [*operator arg3* ...]

Evaluate arguments as expressions and print the results. Arguments and operators must be separated by spaces. In most cases, an argument is an integer, typed literally or represented by a shell variable. There are three types of operators: arithmetic, relational, and logical, as well as keyword expressions. Exit status for **expr** is 0 (expression is nonzero and nonnull), 1 (expression is 0 or null), or 2 (expression is invalid).

Arithmetic operators

Use these to produce mathematical expressions whose results are printed:

+   Add *arg2* to *arg1*.

-    Subtract *arg2* from *arg1*.

*   Multiply the arguments.

/   Divide *arg1* by *arg2*.

%   Take the remainder when *arg1* is divided by *arg2*.

Addition and subtraction are evaluated last, unless they are grouped inside parentheses. The symbols *, (, and) have meaning to the shell, so they must be escaped (preceded by a backslash or enclosed in single quotes).

Relational operators

Use these to compare two arguments. Arguments can also be words, in which case comparisons are defined by the locale. If the comparison statement is true, the result is 1; if false, the result is 0. Symbols > and < must be escaped.

=, ==

Are the arguments equal?

!=   Are the arguments different?

>   Is *arg1* greater than *arg2*?

>=   Is *arg1* greater than or equal to *arg2*?

<   Is *arg1* less than *arg2*?

<=   Is *arg1* less than or equal to *arg2*?

Logical operators

Use these to compare two arguments. Depending on the values, the result can be *arg1* (or some portion of it), *arg2*, or 0. Symbols | and & must be escaped.

| Logical OR; if *arg1* has a nonzero (and nonnull) value, the result is *arg1*; otherwise, the result is *arg2*.

&   Logical AND; if both *arg1* and *arg2* have a nonzero (and nonnull) value, the result is *arg1*; otherwise, the result is 0.

:   Like **grep**; *arg2* is a pattern to search for in *arg1*. *arg2* must be a regular expression. If part of the *arg2* pattern is enclosed in \ (\) (escaped parentheses), the result is the portion of *arg1* that matches; otherwise, the result is simply the number of characters that match. By default, a pattern match always applies to the beginning of the first argument (the search string implicitly begins with a ^). Start the search string with .* to match other parts of the string.

Keywords

index *string character-list*
> Return the first position in *string* that matches the first possible character in *character-list*. Continue through *character-list* until a match is found, or return 0.

length *string*
> Return the length of *string*.

match *string regex*
> Same as *string : regex*.

quote *token*
> Treat *token* as a string, even if it would normally be a keyword or an operator.

substr *string start length*
> Return a section of *string*, beginning with *start*, with a maximum length of *length* characters. Return null when given a negative or nonnumeric *start* or *length*.

Examples

Division happens first; result is 10:

```
expr 5 + 10 / 2
```

Addition happens first; result is 7 (truncated from 7.5):

```
expr \( 5 + 10 \) / 2
```

Add 1 to variable *i*. This is how variables are incremented in shell scripts:

```
i=`expr $i + 1`
```

Print 1 (true) if variable **a** is the string "hello":

```
expr $a = hello
```

Print 1 (true) if **b** plus 5 equals 10 or more:

```
expr $b + 5 \>= 10
```

Find the 5th, 6th, and 7th letters of the word *character*:

    `expr substr character 5 3`

In the examples that follow, variable **p** is the string "version.100". This command prints the number of characters in **p**:

    `expr $p : '.*'`   *Result is 11*

Match all characters and print them:

    `expr $p : '\(.*\)'`   *Result is "version.100"*

Print the number of lowercase letters at the beginning of **p**:

    `expr $p : '[a-z]*'`   *Result is 7*

Match the lowercase letters at the beginning of **p**:

    `expr $p : '\([a-z]*\)'`   *Result is "version"*

Truncate **$x** if it contains five or more characters; if not, just print **$x**. (Logical OR uses the second argument when the first one is 0 or null, i.e., when the match fails.)

    `expr $x : '\(.....\)' \| $x`

In a shell script, rename files to their first five letters:

    `mv $x `expr $x : '\(.....\)' \| $x``

(To avoid overwriting files with similar names, use **mv -i**.)

---

false   `false`

A null command that returns an unsuccessful (nonzero) exit status. Normally used in **bash** scripts. See also **true**.

---

fdformat   `fdformat` [*option*] *device*

Low-level format of a floppy disk. The device for a standard format is usually */dev/fd0* or */dev/fd1*.

Option

-n   Do not verify format after completion.

---

fdisk   `fdisk` [*options*] [*device*]

System administration command. Maintain disk partitions via a menu. **fdisk** displays information about disk partitions, creates and deletes disk partitions, and changes the active partition. It is possible to assign a different operating system to each of the four possible primary partitions, though only one partition is active at any given time. You can also divide a physical partition into several logical partitions. The minimum recommended size for a Linux system partition is 40MB. Normally, *device* will be */dev/hda*, */dev/hdb*, */dev/sda*, */dev/sdb*, */dev/hdc*, */dev/hdd*, and so on. See also **cfdisk**.

Options

-b *sectorsize*

Set the size of individual disk sectors. May be 512, 1024, or 2048. Most systems now recognize sector sizes, so this is not necessary.

-l   List partition tables and exit.

-u   Report partition sizes in sectors instead of cylinders.

-s *partition*

Display the size of *partition*, unless it is a DOS partition.

-v   Print version number, then exit.

Commands

a   Toggle a bootable flag on current partition.

b   Edit disklabel of a BSD partition.

c   Toggle DOS compatibility flag.

d   Delete current partition.

l   List all partition types.

m   Main menu.

n   Create a new partition; prompt for more information.

o   Create an empty DOS partition table.

p   Print a list of all partitions and information about each.

q   Quit; do not save.

t   Replace the type of the current partition.

u   Modify the display/entry units, which must be cylinders or sectors.

v   Verify: check for errors, and display a summary of the number of unallocated sectors.

w   Save changes and exit.

x   Switch to expert commands.

---

fetchmail

`fetchmail [options] [servers...]`

System administration command. Retrieve mail from mail servers and forward it to the local mail delivery system. **fetchmail** retrieves mail from servers that support the common mail protocols POP2, POP3, IMAP2bis, and IMAP4. Messages are delivered via SMTP through port 25 on the local host and through your system's mail delivery agent (such as *sendmail*), where they can be read through the user's mail client. **fetchmail** settings are stored in the *~/.fetchmailrc* file. Parameters and servers can also be set on the command line, which will override settings in the *.fetchmailrc* file. **fetchmail** is compatible with the **popclient** program, and users can use both without having to adjust file settings.

Options

-a, --all

Retrieve all messages from server, even ones that have already been seen but are left on the server. The default is to retrieve only new messages.

-auth *type*

Specify an authentication type. *type* can be: **password**, **kerberos_v5**, **kerberos**, **gssapi**, **cram-md5**, **otp**, **ntlm**, **ssh**, or **any**. When using the default value, **any**, **fetchmail** will use the highest authentication available. In decreasing order of security: **gssapi**, **kerberos**, **cram**, **x-otp**, **ntlm**, then **login**. Using **ssh** suppresses authentication. Use **ssh** when using an end-to-end secure connection.

-B *n*, **--fetchlimit** *n*

Set the maximum number of messages (*n*) accepted from a server per query.

-b *n*, **--batchlimit** *n*

Set the maximum number of messages sent to an SMTP listener per connection. When this limit is reached, the connection will be broken and reestablished. The default of 0 means no limit.

-bsmtp *file*

Append fetched mail to the specified batched sendmail (BSMTP) *file*. If *file* is -, send to standard output.

-c, --check

Check for mail on a single server without retrieving or deleting messages. Works with IMAP, but not well (if at all) with other protocols.

-D [*domain*], **--smtpaddress** [*domain*]

Specify the *domain* name placed in RCPT TO lines sent to SMTP. The default is the local host.

-d *n*, **--daemon** *n*

Detach from current process and run as a daemon, fetching mail every *n* seconds. A user may run only one **fetchmail** daemon process. See option **--quit**.

-E *header*, **--envelope** *header*

Change the header assumed to contain the mail's envelope address (usually "X-Envelope-to:") to *header*.

-e *n*, **--expunge** *n*

Tell an IMAP server to EXPUNGE (i.e., purge messages marked for deletion) after *n* deletes. A setting of 0 indicates expunging only at the end of the session. Normally, an **expunge** occurs after each delete.

-F, --flush

For POP3 and IMAP servers, remove previously retrieved messages from the server before retrieving new ones.

-f *file,* **--fetchmailrc** *file*
Specify a nondefault name for the **fetchmail** configuration file.

--fetchdomains *hosts*
Specify the domains to which mail should be sent when operating in ETRN or ODMR mode.

-I *specification,* **--interface** *specification*
Require that the mail server machine is up and running at a specified IP address (or range) before polling. The *specification* is given as *interface/ipaddress/mask.* The first part indicates the type of TCP connection expected (*sl0, ppp0,* etc.), the second is the IP address, and the third is the bit mask for the IP, assumed to be 255.255.255.255.

-i *file,* **--idfile** *file*
Store POP3 UIDs in *file* instead of the default *.fetchids* file.

--invisible
Supress Received header and and spoof the MTA so it looks like mail comes directly from the mailserver host.

-K, **--nokeep**
Delete all retrieved messages from the mail server.

-k, **--keep**
Keep copies of all retrieved messages on the mail server.

-L *file,* **--logfile** *file*
Redirect status messages to the specified *file.* This option is primarily for use in debugging. See the **--syslog** option.

-l *size,* **--limit** *size*
Set the maximum message size that will be retrieved from a server. Messages larger than this size will be left on the server and marked unread.

-lmtp
Deliver fetched mail via LMTP instead of SMTP. The server, specified with the **-S** option, must explicitly include the port to be used.

-M *interface,* **--monitor** *interface*
In daemon mode, monitor the specified TCP/IP *interface* for any activity besides itself, and skip the poll if there is no other activity. Useful for PPP connections that automatically time out with no activity.

-m *command,* **--mda** *command*
Pass mail directly to mail delivery agent instead of sending to port 25. The *command* is the path and options for the mailer, such as **/usr/lib/sendmail -oem**. A **%T** in the command will be replaced with the local delivery address, and an **%F** will be replaced with the message's **From** address.

-N, **--nodetach**
Run command in the foreground. Useful for debugging a configuration file that normally would run **fetchmail** as a daemon. Also causes **fetchmail** to ignore **-L** or **--syslog** options.

-n, --norewrite

Do not expand local mail IDs to full addresses. This option will disable expected addressing and should be used only to find problems.

--nobounce

Do not bounce error messages back to the sender; send them to the postmaster instead.

--nosyslog

Turn off logging to **syslogd**. This option overrides resource file settings and the **-L** option.

-P *n*, **--port** *n*

Specify a port to connect to on the mail server. The default port numbers for supported protocols are usually sufficient.

-p *proto*, **--protocol** *proto*

Specify the protocol to use when polling a mail server. *proto* can be:

AUTO

Attempt IMAP, POP3, then POP2.

POP2

Post Office Protocol 2.

POP3

Post Office Protocol 3.

APOP

POP3 with MD5 authentication.

KPOP

POP3 with Kerberos v4 authentication on port 1109.

RPOP

POP3 with RPOP authentication.

SDPS

Demon Internet's Standard Dial-up POP3 Service.

IMAP

IMAP2bis, IMAP4, or IMAP4rev1. **fetchmail** autodetects their capabilities.

ETRN

Extended SMTP with Extended TURN command.

ODMR

On Demand Mail Relaying.

--plugin *command*

Use external program to establish the TCP connection. The *command* is the path and options for the external program. Use escape codes **%h** and **%p** in *command* to pass the hostname and port as arguments to the external program. When using this command, **fetchmail** will write to the program's standard input and read from its standard output.

--plugout *command*

Same as the **--plugin** option, but used to establish SMTP connections.

--plugout *principal*

Authenticate using the specified service *principal*. Used with POP3 or IMAP with Kerberos authentication.

--postmaster *name*

If unable to deliver mail, deliver it to *name*. Set *name* to "" to have undeliverable mail discarded.

-Q *string,* **--qvirtual** *string*

Remove the prefix *string*, which is the local user's hostid, from the address in the envelope header (such as "Delivered-To:").

-q, **--quit**

Kill a running daemon process before performing any other commands.

-r *folder,* **--folder** *folder*

Retrieve the specified mail *folder* from the mail server.

-S *hostlist,* **-smtphost** *hostlist*

Attempt to forward mail to one of the SMTP hosts listed in the comma-separated *hostlist*. The hosts are tried in the order they are given. The host may be a domain name, IP address, or the directory path to an LMTP socket. Port numbers can be appended to domain names and IP addresses using */port* notation.

-s, **--silent**

Suppress status messages during a **fetch**.

--showdots

Always print progress dots. By default **fetchmail** prints progress dots only when the current tty is standard output.

--smtpname *user*

Specify the user and domain name to use in RCPT TO lines sent to SMTP. *user* should be in the form *user@domain*. By default, **fetchmail** uses the local user and domain.

-syslog

Redirect status and error messages to the **syslog** daemon.

--ssl

Encrypt connection to mail server using Secure Socket Layer.

--sslcert *file*

Specify the *file* containing the client-side public SSL certificate.

--sslkey *file*

Specify the *file* containing the client-side private SSL key.

--sslproto *proto*

Specify a specific SSL protocol to use. *proto* may be **ssl2**, **ssl3**, or **tls1**.

--sslcertck

Fail unless the server's certificate has been signed by a local list of trusted certificates. *proto* may be **ssl2**, **ssl3**, or **tls1**.

--sslcertpath *directory*

Specify the directory containing trusted certificates to be used with **--sslcertck**.

--sslfingerprint *hash*

Fail unless the server's key fingerprint matches the specified fingerprint *hash*. *hash* is an MD5 hash of the server's key given in hexadecimal notation, using colons to separate groups of two digits. Letter hex digits must be in uppercase.

-t *n*, **--timeout** *n*

Set the non-response timeout to *n* seconds.

--tracepolls

Add information about the account and server being polled to the Received header of each message received.

-U, --uidl

For POP3, track the age of kept messages via unique ID listing.

-u *name*, **--username** *name*

Specify the user *name* to use when logging into the mail server.

-V, --version

Print the version information for **fetchmail** and display the options set for each mail server. Perform no **fetch**.

-v, --verbose

Display all status messages during a **fetch**.

-w *n*, **--warnings** *n*

When issuing warnings about oversized messages, wait *n* seconds after each warning before sending another warning.

-Z *nnn*, **--antispam** *nnn*

Specify the SMTP error *nnn* to signal a spam block from the client. If *nnn* is −1, this option is disabled. Multiple SMTP codes may be given as a comma-separated list. By default **fetchmail** discards messages with error codes 571, 550, 501, and 554.

---

fgconsole

fgconsole

Print the number of the current virtual console. For example, if you are using */dev/tty1*, the command would return 1.

---

fgrep

fgrep [*options*] *pattern* [*files*]

Search one or more *files* for lines that match a literal text string *pattern*. Exit status is 0 if any lines match, 1 if not, and 2 for errors.

See **grep** for the list of available options. Also see **egrep**.

Examples

Print lines in *file* that don't contain any spaces:

```
fgrep -v ' ' file
```

Print lines in *file* that contain the words in the file **spell_list**:

```
fgrep -f spell_list file
```

file

file [*options*] *files*

Classify the named *files* according to the type of data they contain. **file** checks the magic file (usually */usr/share/magic*) to identify some file types.

Options

-b   Brief mode; do not prepend filenames to output lines.

-c   Check the format of the magic file (*files* argument is invalid with -c). Usually used with -m.

-f *file*
    Read the names of files to be checked from *file*.

-L   Follow symbolic links. By default, symbolic links are not followed.

-m *file*
    Search for file types in *file* instead of */usr/share/magic*.

-n   Flush standard output after checking a file.

-s   Check files that are block or character special files in addition to checking ordinary files.

-v   Print the version.

-z   Attempt checking of compressed files.

Many file types are understood. Output lists each filename, followed by a brief classification such as:

```
ascii text
c program text
c-shell commands
data
empty
iAPX 386 executable
directory
[nt]roff, tbl, or eqn input text
shell commands
symbolic link to ../usr/etc/arp
```

Example

List all files that are deemed to be **troff/nroff** input:

```
file * | grep roff
```

---

find

find [*pathnames*] [*conditions*]

An extremely useful command for finding particular groups of files (numerous examples follow this description). **find** descends the directory tree beginning at each *pathname* and locates files that meet the specified *conditions*. The default pathname is the current directory. The most useful conditions include -**print** (which is the default if no other expression is given), -**name** and -**type** (for general use), -**exec** and -**size** (for advanced use), and -**mtime** and -**user** (for administrators).

Conditions may be grouped by enclosing them in \(\) (escaped parentheses), negated with ! (use \! in **tcsh**), given as alternatives by separating them with **-o**, or repeated (adding restrictions to the match; usually only for **-name**, **-type**, or **-perm**). Note that "modification" refers to editing of a file's contents, whereas "change" means a modification, or permission or ownership changes. In other words, **-ctime** is more inclusive than **-atime** or **-mtime**.

Conditions and actions

-atime +n | -n | n

> Find files that were last accessed more than n (+n), less than n (-n), or exactly n days ago. Note that **find** changes the access time of directories supplied as *pathnames*.

-ctime +n | -n | n

> Find files that were changed more than n (+n), less than n (-n), or exactly n days ago. A change is anything that changes the directory entry for the file, such as a **chmod**.

-depth

> Descend the directory tree, skipping directories and working on actual files first, and then the parent directories. Useful when files reside in unwritable directories (e.g., when using **find** with **cpio**).

-exec *command* { } \;

> Run the Linux *command*, from the starting directory on each file matched by **find** (provided *command* executes successfully on that file, i.e., returns a 0 exit status). When *command* runs, the argument { } substitutes the current file. Follow the entire sequence with an escaped semicolon (\;). In some shells, the braces may need to be escaped as well.

-follow

> Follow symbolic links and track the directories visited (don't use with **-type l**).

-group *gname*

> Find files belonging to group *gname*. *gname* can be a group name or a group ID number.

-inum *n*

> Find files whose inode number is *n*.

-links *n*

> Find files having *n* links.

-mount, -xdev

> Search only for files that reside on the same filesystem as *pathname*.

-mtime +n | -n | n

> Find files that were last modified more than n (+n), less than n (-n), or exactly n days ago. A modification is a change to a file's data.

-name *pattern*

> Find files whose names match *pattern*. Filename metacharacters may be used but should be escaped or quoted.

-newer *file*

> Find files that were modified more recently than *file*; similar to **-mtime**. Affected by **-follow** only if it occurs after **-follow** on the command line.

-ok *command* { }\;

> Same as **-exec**, but prompts user to respond with **y** before *command* is executed.

-perm *nnn*

> Find files whose permission flags (e.g., **rwx**) match octal number *nnn* exactly (e.g., 664 matches **-rw-rw-r--**). Use a minus sign before *nnn* to make a "wildcard" match of any unspecified octal digit (e.g., **-perm -600** matches **-rw-******), where * can be any mode).

-print

> Print the matching files and directories, using their full pathnames. Return true.

-regex *pattern*

> Like **-path**, but uses **grep**-style regular expressions instead of the shell-like globbing used in **-name** and **-path**.

-size *n*[c]

> Find files containing *n* blocks, or if **c** is specified, *n* characters long.

-type *c*

> Find files whose type is *c*. *c* can be **b** (block special file), **c** (character special file), **d** (directory), **p** (fifo or named pipe), **l** (symbolic link), **s** (socket), or **f** (plain file).

-user *user*

> Find files belonging to *user* (name or ID).

-daystart

> Calculate times from the start of the day today, not 24 hours ago.

-maxdepth *num*

> Do not descend more than *num* levels of directories.

-mindepth *num*

> Begin applying tests and actions only at levels deeper than *num* levels.

-noleaf

> Normally, **find** assumes that each directory has at least two hard links that should be ignored (a hard link for its name and one for "."; i.e., two fewer "real" directories than its hard link count indicates). **-noleaf** turns off this assumption, a useful practice when **find** runs on non-Unix-style filesystems. This forces **find** to examine all entries, assuming that some might prove to be directories into which it must descend (a time-waster on Unix).

-amin +*n* | -*n* | *n*
> Find files last accessed more than *n* (+*n*), less than *n* (-*n*), or exactly *n* minutes ago.

-anewer *file*
> Find files that were accessed after *file* was last modified. Affected by **-follow** when after **-follow** on the command line.

-cmin +*n* | -*n* | *n*
> Find files last changed more than *n* (+*n*), less than *n* (-*n*), or exactly *n* minutes ago.

-cnewer *file*
> Find files that were changed after they were last modified. Affected by **-follow** when after **-follow** on the command line.

-empty
> Continue if file is empty. Applies to regular files and directories.

-false
> Return false value for each file encountered.

-fstype *type*
> Match files only on *type* filesystems. Acceptable types include **minix, ext, ext2, xia, msdos, umsdos, vfat, proc, nfs, iso9660, hpfs, sysv, smb,** and **ncpfs**.

-gid *num*
> Find files with numeric group ID of *num*.

-ilname *pattern*
> A case-insensitive version of **-lname**.

-iname *pattern*
> A case-insensitive version of **-name**.

-ipath *pattern*
> A case-insensitive version of **-path**.

-iregex *pattern*
> A case-insensitive version of **-regex**.

-lname *pattern*
> Search for files that are symbolic links, pointing to files named *pattern*. *pattern* can include shell metacharacters and does not treat **/** or **.** specially. The match is case-insensitive.

-mmin +*n* | -*n* | *n*
> Find files last modified more than *n* (+*n*), less than *n* (-*n*), or exactly *n* minutes ago.

-nouser
> The file's user ID does not correspond to any user.

-nogroup
> The file's group ID does not correspond to any group.

-path *pattern*
> Find files whose names match *pattern*. Expect full pathnames relative to the starting pathname (i.e., do not treat **/** or **.** specially).

Examples

List all files (and subdirectories) in your home directory:

```
find $HOME -print
```

List all files named *chapter1* in the */work* directory:

```
find /work -name chapter1
```

List all files beginning with *memo* owned by *ann*:

```
find /work -name 'memo*' -user ann -print
```

Search the filesystem (begin at root) for manpage directories:

```
find / -type d -name 'man*' -print
```

Search the current directory, look for filenames that don't begin with a capital letter, and send them to the printer:

```
find . \! -name '[A-Z]*' -exec lpr { }\;
```

Find and compress files whose names don't end with *.gz*:

```
gzip `find . \! -name '*.gz' -print`
```

Remove all empty files on the system (prompting first):

```
find / -size 0 -ok rm { } \;
```

Search the system for files that were modified within the last two days (good candidates for backing up):

```
find / -mtime -2 -print
```

Recursively **grep** for a pattern down a directory tree:

```
find /book -print | xargs grep '[Nn]utshell'
```

If the files *kt1* and *kt2* exist in the current directory, their names can be printed with the command:

```
$ find . -name 'kt[0-9]'
./kt1
./kt2
```

Since the command prints these names with an initial *./* path, you need to specify the *./* when using the **-path** option:

```
$ find . -path './kt[0-9]'
./kt1
./kt2
```

The **-regex** option uses a complete pathname, like **-path**, but treats the following argument as a regular expression rather than a glob pattern (although in this case the result is the same):

```
$ find . -regex './kt[0-9]'
./kt1
./kt2
```

---

finger

finger [*options*] *users*

Display data about one or more *users*, including information listed in the files *.plan* and *.project* in each user's home directory. You can specify each user either as a login name (exact match) or as a first or last name (display information on all matching names).

Networked environments recognize arguments of the form *user@host* and *@host*.

Options

-l   Force long format (default): everything included by the **-s** option and home directory, home phone, login shell, mail status, *.plan*, *.project*, and *.forward*.

-m   Suppress matching of users' "real" names.

-p   Omit *.plan* and *.project* files from display.

-s   Show short format: login name, real name, terminal name, write status, idle time, office location, and office phone number.

---

fingerd

`in.fingerd` [*options*]

TCP/IP command. Remote user information server. **fingerd** provides a network interface to the **finger** program. It listens for TCP connections on the **finger** port and, for each connection, reads a single input line, passes the line to **finger**, and copies the output of **finger** to the user on the client machine. **fingerd** is started by **inetd** and must have an entry in **inetd**'s configuration file, */etc/inetd.conf*.

Options

-f   Allow **finger** forwarding in the form of *user@host1@host2*.

-p *command,* -L *path*
    Use alternate **finger** program specified by *command*.

-l   Log **finger** requests.

-t *n*
    Set timeout period to *n* seconds.

-u   Reject requests in the form of *@host*.

-w   Include additional information, such as uptime and the name of the operating system.

---

flex

`flex` [*options*] [*file*]

flex (Fast Lexical Analyzer Generator) is a faster variant of **lex**. It generates a lexical analysis program (named *lex.yy.c*) based on the regular expressions and C statements contained in one or more input *files*. See also bison, yacc, and the O'Reilly book *lex & yacc*.

Options

-b   Generate backup information to *lex.backup*.

-d   Debug mode.

-f   Use faster compilation (limited to small programs).

-h   Help summary.

-i   Scan case-insensitively.

-l   Maximum **lex** compatibility.

-o *file*
> Write output to *file* instead of *lex.yy.c.*

-p   Print performance report.

-s   Exit if the scanner encounters input that does not match any of its rules.

-t   Print to standard output. (By default, **flex** prints to *lex.yy.c.*)

-v   Print a summary of statistics.

-w   Suppress warning messages.

-B   Generate batch (noninteractive) scanner.

-F   Use the fast scanner table representation.

-I   Generate an interactive scanner (default).

-L   Suppress **#line** directives in *lex.yy.c.*

-P *prefix*
> Change default **yy** prefix to *prefix* for all globally visible variable and function names.

-V   Print version number.

-7   Generate a 7-bit scanner.

-8   Generate an 8-bit scanner (default).

-+   Generate a C++ scanner class.

-C   Compress scanner tables but do not use equivalence classes.

-Ca Align tables for memory access and computation. This creates larger tables but gives faster performance.

-Ce Construct equivalence classes. This creates smaller tables and sacrifices little performance (default).

-Cf Generate full scanner tables, not compressed.

-CF Generate faster scanner tables, like **-F**.

-Cm Construct metaequivalence classes (default).

-Cr Bypass use of the standard I/O library; use **read( )** system calls instead.

---

fmt

fmt [*options*] [*files*]

Convert text to specified width by filling lines and removing newlines. Concatenate files on the command line, or read text from standard input if - (or no file) is specified. By default, preserve blank lines, spacing, and indentation. **fmt** attempts to break lines at the end of sentences and avoid breaking lines after a sentence's first word or before its last.

Options

-c, --crown-margin
> Crown margin mode. Do not change indentation of each paragraph's first two lines. Use the second line's indentation as the default for subsequent lines.

-p *prefix*, **--prefix**=*prefix*
> Format only lines beginning with *prefix*.

-s, **--split-only**
> Suppress line-joining.

-t, **--tagged-paragraph**
> Tagged paragraph mode. Same as crown mode when the indentations of the first and second lines differ. If the indentation is the same, treat the first line as its own separate paragraph.

-u, **--uniform-spacing**
> Reduce spacing to a maximum of one space between words and two between sentences.

-w *width*, **--width**=*width*
> Set output width to *width*. The default is 75.

--help
> Print help message and then exit.

--version
> Print version information and then exit.

---

fold

`fold` [*option*] [*files*]

Break the lines of the named *files* so that they are no wider than the specified width (default is 80). **fold** breaks lines exactly at the specified width, even in the middle of a word. Reads from standard input when given - as a file.

Options

-b, **--bytes**
> Count bytes, not columns (i.e., consider tabs, backspaces, and carriage returns to be one column).

-s, **--spaces**
> Break at spaces only, if possible.

-w, **--width** *width*, -*width*
> Set the maximum line width to *width*. The flags **-w 6**, **--width 6**, and **-6** will all set the maximum width to six columns.

---

formail

`formail` [*options*]

Filter standard input into mailbox format. Useful for splitting mail digests or passing the contents of a mail file to another program such as a spam filter for additional processing. If no sender is apparent, provide the sender *foo@bar*. By default, escape bogus **From** lines with >.

Options

+*skip*
> Do not split first *skip* messages.

-*total*
> Stop after splitting *total* messages.

-a *headerfield*
> Append *headerfield* to header, unless it already exists. If *headerfield* is **Message-ID** or **Resent-Message-ID** with no contents, generate a unique message ID.

-b Do not escape bogus **From** lines.

-c When header fields are more than one line long, concatenate the lines.

-d Do not assume that input must be in strict mailbox format. This option disables recognition of the **Content-Length** field so you can split digests or use nonstandard mailbox formats

-e Allow messages to begin one immediately after the other; do not require empty space between them.

-f Do not edit non-mailbox-format lines. By default, *formail* prepends **From** to such lines.

-i *headerfield*
> Append *headerfield* whether or not it already exists. Rename each existing *headerfield* to **Old-***headerfield*, unless it is empty.

-k For use only with **-r**. Keep the body as well as the fields specified by **-r**.

-m *minfields*
> Require at least *minfields* before recognizing the beginning of a new message. Default is 2.

-n Allow simultaneous **formail** processes to run.

-p *prefix*
> Escape lines with *prefix* instead of >.

-q Do not display write errors, duplicate messages, and mismatched **Content-Length** fields. This is the default; use **-q-** to turn it off.

-r Throw away all existing fields, retaining only **X-Loop**, and generate autoreply header instead. You can preserve particular fields with the **-i** option.

-s Must be the last option; everything following it will be assumed to be its arguments. Divide input to separate mail messages, and pipe them to the program specified or concatenate them to standard output (by default).

-t Assume sender's return address to be valid. (By default, **formail** favors machine-generated addresses.)

-u *headerfield*
> Delete all but the first occurrence of *headerfield*.

-x *headerfield*
> Display the contents of *headerfield* on a single line.

-z When necessary, add a space between field names and contents. Remove ("zap") empty fields.

-A *headerfield*
> Append *headerfield* whether or not it already exists.

-B Assume that input is in BABYL **rmail** format.

-D *maxlen idcache*
> Remember old message IDs (in *idcache*, which will grow no larger than approximately *maxlen*). When splitting, refuse to output duplicate messages. Otherwise, return true on discovering a duplicate. With **-r**, look at the sender's mail address instead of the message ID.

-I *headerfield*
> Append *headerfield* whether or not it already exists. Remove existing fields.

-R *oldfield newfield*
> Change all fields named *oldfield* to *newfield*.

-U *headerfield*
> Delete all but the last occurrence of *headerfield*.

-Y Format in traditional Berkeley style (i.e., ignore **Content-Length** fields).

-X *headerfield*
> Display the field name and contents of *headerfield* on a single line.

---

free

free [*options*]

Display statistics about memory usage: total free, used, physical, swap, shared, and buffers used by the kernel.

Options

-b Calculate memory in bytes.

-k Default. Calculate memory in kilobytes.

-m Calculate memory in megabytes.

-o Do not display "buffer adjusted" line. The **-o** switch disables the display "-/+ buffers" line that shows buffer memory subtracted from the amount of memory used and added to the amount of free memory.

-s *time*
> Check memory usage every *time* seconds.

-t Display all totals on one line at the bottom of output.

-V Display version information.

---

fsck

fsck [*options*] [*filesystem*] ...

System administration command. Call the filesystem checker for the appropriate system type to check and repair unmounted filesystems. If a filesystem is consistent, the number of files, number of blocks used, and number of blocks free are reported. If a filesystem is inconsistent, **fsck** prompts before each correction is attempted. **fsck**'s exit code can be interpreted as the sum of all conditions that apply:

1	Errors were found and corrected.
2	Reboot suggested.
4	Errors were found but not corrected.
8	**fsck** encountered an operational error.
16	**fsck** was called incorrectly.
128	A shared library error was detected.

Options

--   Pass all subsequent options to filesystem-specific checker. All options that **fsck** doesn't recognize will also be passed.

-s   Serial mode. Check one filesystem at a time.

-t *fstype*
      Specify the filesystem type. Do not check filesystems of any other type.

-A   Check all filesystems listed in */etc/fstab*. The root filesystem is checked first.

-C   Display completion (progress) bar.

-N   Suppress normal execution; just display what would be done.

-P   Meaningful only with **-A**: check root filesystem in parallel with other systems. This option is potentially dangerous.

-R   Meaningful only with **-A**: check all filesystems listed in */etc/fstab* except the root filesystem.

-T   Suppress printing of title.

-V   Verbose mode.

---

fsck.minix

`fsck.minix [`*options*`]` `device`

System administration command. Similar to **fsck**, but specifically intended for Linux MINIX filesystems.

Options

-a   Automatic mode; repair without prompting.

-f   Force checking, even if kernel has already marked the filesystem. **fsck.minix** will normally exit without checking if the system appears to be clean.

-l   List filesystems.

-m   Enable MINIX-like "mode not cleared" warnings.

-r   Interactive mode; prompt before making any repairs.

-s   Display information about superblocks.

-v   Verbose mode.

---

ftp

`ftp [`*options*`]` `[`*hostname*`]`

Transfer files to and from remote network site *hostname*. **ftp** prompts the user for a command. The commands are listed after the options. Some of the commands are toggles, meaning they turn on a feature when it is off and vice versa. Note that versions may have different options.

Options

-d   Enable debugging.

-g   Disable filename globbing.

-i   Turn off interactive prompting.

-n   No autologin upon initial connection.

-v   Verbose. Show all responses from remote server.

Commands

![command [args]]
> Invoke an interactive shell on the local machine. If arguments are given, the first is taken as a command to execute directly, with the rest of the arguments as that command's arguments.

$macro-name [args]
> Execute the macro *macro-name* that was defined with the **macdef** command. Arguments are passed to the macro unglobbed.

account *[passwd]*
> Supply a supplemental password that will be required by a remote system for access to resources once a login has been successfully completed. If no argument is given, the user will be prompted for an account password in a non-echoing mode.

append *local-file [remote-file]*
> Append a local file to a file on the remote machine. If *remote-file* is not given, the local filename is used after being altered by any **ntrans** or **nmap** setting. File transfer uses the current settings for *type*, *format*, *mode*, and *structure*.

ascii
> Set the file transfer type to network ASCII (default).

bell
> Sound a bell after each file transfer command is completed.

binary
> Set file transfer type to support binary image transfer.

bye
> Terminate FTP session and then exit **ftp**.

case
> Toggle remote computer filename case mapping during **mget**. The default is off. When **case** is on, files on the remote machine with all-uppercase names will be copied to the local machine with all-lowercase names.

cd *remote-directory*
> Change working directory on remote machine to *remote-directory*.

cdup

Change working directory of remote machine to its parent directory.

chmod [*mode*] [*remote-file*]

Change file permissions of *remote-file*. If options are omitted, the command prompts for them.

close

Terminate FTP session and return to command interpreter.

cr

Toggle carriage return stripping during ASCII-type file retrieval.

delete *remote-file*

Delete file *remote-file* on remote machine.

debug [*debug-value*]

Toggle debugging mode. If *debug-value* is specified, it is used to set the debugging level.

dir [*remote-directory*] [*local-file*]

Print a listing of the contents in the directory *remote-directory* and, optionally, place the output in *local-file*. If no directory is specified, the current working directory on the remote machine is used. If no local file is specified or - is given instead of the filename, output comes to the terminal.

disconnect

Synonym for **close**.

form *format*

Set the file transfer form to *format*. Default format is *file*.

get *remote-file* [*local-file*]

Retrieve the *remote-file* and store it on the local machine. If the local filename is not specified, it is given the same name it has on the remote machine, subject to alteration by the current **case**, **ntrans**, and **nmap** settings. If local file is -, output comes to the terminal.

glob

Toggle filename expansion for **mdelete**, **mget**, and **mput**. If globbing is turned off, the filename arguments are taken literally and not expanded.

hash

Toggle hash sign (#) printing for each data block transferred.

help [*command*]

Print help information for *command*. With no argument, **ftp** prints a list of commands.

idle [*seconds*]

Get/set idle timer on remote machine. *seconds* specifies the length of the idle timer; if omitted, the current idle timer is displayed.

image

Same as **binary**.

lcd [*directory*]

Change working directory on local machine. If *directory* is not specified, the user's home directory is used.

ls [*remote-directory*] [*local-file*]

Print listing of contents of directory on remote machine, in a format chosen by the remote machine. If *remote-directory* is not specified, current working directory is used.

macdef *macro-name*

Define a macro. Subsequent lines are stored as the macro *macro-name*; a null line terminates macro input mode. When **$i** is included in the macro, loop through arguments, substituting the current argument for **$i** on each pass. Escape **$** with \.

mdelete *remote-files*

Delete the *remote-files* on the remote machine.

mdir *remote-files local-file*

Like **dir**, except multiple remote files may be specified.

mget *remote-files*

Expand the wildcard expression *remote-files* on the remote machine and do a **get** for each filename thus produced.

mkdir *directory-name*

Make a directory on the remote machine.

mls *remote-files local-file*

Like **nlist**, except multiple remote files may be specified, and the local file must be specified.

mode [*mode-name*]

Set file transfer mode to *mode-name*. Default mode is stream mode.

modtime [*file-name*]

Show last modification time of the file on the remote machine.

mput [*local-files*]

Expand wildcards in *local-files* given as arguments and do a **put** for each file in the resulting list.

newer *remote-file* [*local-file*]

Get file if remote file is newer than local file.

nlist [*remote-directory*] [*local-file*]

Print list of files in a directory on the remote machine to *local-file* (or to the screen if *local-file* is not specified). If *remote-directory* is unspecified, the current working directory is used.

nmap [*inpattern outpattern*]

Set or unset the filename mapping mechanism. The mapping follows the pattern set by *inpattern*, a template for incoming filenames, and *outpattern*, which determines the resulting mapped filename. The sequences **$1** through **$9** are treated as variables; for example, the *inpattern* **$1.$2**, along with the input file *readme.txt*, would set **$1** to **readme** and **$2** to **txt**. An *outpattern* of **$1.data** would result in an output file of *readme.data.* **$0** corresponds to the complete filename. [*string1*, *string2*] is replaced by *string1* unless that string is null, in which case it's replaced by *string2*.

ntrans [*inchars* [*outchars*]]

Set or unset the filename character translation mechanism. Characters in a filename matching a character in *inchars* are replaced with the corresponding character in *outchars*. If no arguments are specified, the filename mapping mechanism is unset. If arguments are specified:

- Characters in remote filenames are translated during **mput** and **put** commands issued without a specified remote target filename.

- Characters in local filenames are translated during **mget** and **get** commands issued without a specified local target filename.

open *host* [*port*]

Establish a connection to the specified *host* FTP server. An optional *port* number may be supplied, in which case **ftp** will attempt to contact an FTP server at that port.

prompt

Toggle interactive prompting.

proxy *ftp-command*

Execute an FTP command on a secondary control connection (i.e., send commands to two separate remote hosts simultaneously).

put *local-file* [*remote-file*]

Store a local file on the remote machine. If *remote-file* is left unspecified, the local filename is used after processing according to any **ntrans** or **nmap** settings in naming the remote file. File transfer uses the current settings for *type*, *file*, *structure*, and *transfer mode*.

pwd

Print name of the current working directory on the remote machine.

quit

Synonym for **bye**.

quote *arg1 arg2*...

Send the arguments specified, verbatim, to the remote FTP server.

recv *remote-file* [*local-file*]

Synonym for **get**.

reget *remote-file* [*local-file*]

Retrieve a file (like **get**), but restart at the end of *local-file*. Useful for restarting a dropped transfer.

remotehelp [*command-name*]

Request help from the remote FTP server. If *command-name* is specified, remote help for that command is returned.

remotestatus [*filename*]
> Show status of the remote machine or, if *filename* is specified, of *filename* on remote machine.

rename [*from*] [*to*]
> Rename file *from* on remote machine to *to*.

reset
> Clear reply queue.

restart *marker*
> Restart the transfer of a file from a particular byte count.

rmdir [*directory-name*]
> Delete a directory on the remote machine.

runique
> Toggle storing of files on the local system with unique filenames. When this option is on, rename files as **.1** or **.2**, and so on, as appropriate, to preserve unique filenames, and report each such action. Default value is off.

send *local-file* [*remote-file*]
> Synonym for **put**.

sendport
> Toggle the use of PORT commands.

site [*command*]
> Get/set site-specific information from/on remote machine.

size *filename*
> Return size of *filename* on remote machine.

status
> Show current status of **ftp**.

struct [*struct-name*]
> Set the file transfer structure to *struct-name*. By default, stream structure is used.

sunique
> Toggle storing of files on remote machine under unique filenames.

system
> Show type of operating system running on remote machine.

tenex
> Set file transfer type to that needed to talk to TENEX machines.

trace
> Toggle packet tracing.

type [*type-name*]
> Set file transfer **type** to *type-name*. If no type is specified, the current type is printed. The default type is network ASCII.

umask [*mask*]
> Set user file-creation mode mask on the remote site. If *mask* is omitted, the current value of the mask is printed.

user *username* [*password*] [*account*]

    Identify yourself to the remote FTP server. **ftp** will prompt the user for the password (if not specified and the server requires it) and the account field.

verbose

    Toggle verbose mode.

? [*command*]

    Same as **help**.

---

ftpd

in.ftpd [*options*]

TCP/IP command. Internet File Transfer Protocol server. The server uses the TCP protocol and listens at the port specified in the **ftp** service specification. **ftpd** is started by **inetd** and must have an entry in **inetd**'s configuration file, */etc/inetd.conf*. There are several FTP daemons available. On many Linux distributions the default is **wu-ftpd**, which we document here.

Options

-a   Read access information from configuration file */etc/ftpaccess*.

-d, -v

    Write debugging information to **syslogd**.

-i   Log all files received in the transfer log */var/log/xferlog*.

-l   Log each FTP session in **syslogd**.

-o   Log all files sent in the transfer log */var/log/xferlog*.

-p*port*

    Use *port* as the FTP control port instead of reading the appropriate port from */etc/services*. Works only in standalone mode.

-q   Use PID files to record the process IDs of running daemons. This is the default. These files are needed to determine the current number of users.

-r*dir*

    Change system root (**chroot**) to specified directory when loaded.

-s   Run **ftpd** standalone in the foreground.

-t*timeout*

    Set default timeout period to *timeout* seconds.

-u*umask*

    Set default umask to *umask*.

-w   Record user logins in the **wtmp** file. This is the default.

-x   Used with options -i and -o. Log file transfers to **syslogd** as well as the tranfer log.

-z *option*

    Set Transport Security Layer (TSL) option for Secure Socket Layers. See **wu-ftpd** documentation for more details.

-A Do not read access information from configuration file */etc/ ftpaccess*. This is the default.

-I Do not use **ident** to determine client's remote username.

-L Log all commands sent to **ftpd** in **syslogd**. This option is over-riden by option -a.

-P*port*
Use *port* as the FTP data port instead of reading the appropriate port from */etc/services*.

-Q Do not use PID files to record the process IDs of running daemons. Without PID files, there is no imposed limit to the number of concurrent users.

-S Run **ftpd** standalone in the background.

-T*maxtimeout*
Set maximum timeout period in seconds. Default limit is 15 minutes.

-U Record user logins in the **utmp** file. By default, logins are not recorded.

-V Print version, then exit.

-W Do not record user logins in the **wtmp** file.

-X Used with options -i and -o. Log file transfers to **syslogd** instead of the tranfer log.

---

fuser

fuser [*options*] [*files* | *filesystems*]

Identifies and outputs the process IDs of processes that are using the *files* or local *filesystems*. Each process ID is followed by a letter code: **c** if process is using *file* as the current directory; **e** if executable; **f** if an open file; **m** if a shared library; and **r** if the root directory. Any user with permission to read */dev/kmem* and */dev/ mem* can use **fuser**, but only a privileged user can terminate another user's process. **fuser** does not work on remote (NFS) files.

If more than one group of files is specified, the options may be respecified for each additional group of files. A lone dash (-) cancels the options currently in force, and the new set of options applies to the next group of files. Like a number of other administrator commands, **fuser** is usually installed to the */sbin* directory. You may need to add that directory to your path or execute the command as */sbin/fuser*.

Options

- Return all options to defaults.

-*signal*
Send *signal* instead of SIGKILL.

-a Display information on all specified files, even if they are not being accessed by any processes.

-i Request user confirmation to kill a process. Ignored if -**k** is not also specified.

-k   Send SIGKILL signal to each process.

-l   List signal names.

-m   Expect *files* to exist on a mounted filesystem; include all files accessing that filesystem.

-n *space*

Set the namespace checked for usage. Acceptable values are **file** for files, **udp** for local UPD ports, and **tcp** for local TCP ports.

-s   Silent.

-u   User login name, in parentheses, also follows process ID.

-v   Verbose.

-V   Display version information.

---

g++

g++ [*options*] *files*

Invoke **gcc** with the options necessary to make it recognize C++. **g++** recognizes all the file extensions **gcc** does, in addition to C++ source files (*.C, .cc,* or *.cxx* files) and C++ preprocessed files (*.ii* files). See also **gcc**.

---

gawk

gawk [*options*] '*script*' [*var=value...*] [*files*]
gawk [*options*] **-f** *scriptfile* [*var=value...*] [*files*]

The GNU version of **awk**, a program that does pattern matching, record processing, and other forms of text manipulation. For more information, see Chapter 13.

---

gcc

gcc [*options*] *files*

GNU Compiler Collection. **gcc**, formerly known as the GNU C Compiler, compiles multiple languages (C, C++, Objective-C, Ada, FORTRAN, and Java) to machine code. Here we document its use to compile C, C++, or Objective-C code. **gcc** compiles one or more programming source files; for example, C source files (*file.c*), assembler source files (*file.s*), or preprocessed C source files (*file.i*). If the file suffix is not recognizable, assume that the file is an object file or library. **gcc** normally invokes the C preprocessor, compiles the process code to assemble language code, assembles it, and then links it with the link editor. This process can be stopped at one of these stages using the **-c, -S,** or **-E** option. The steps may also differ depending on the language being compiled. By default, output is placed in *a.out*. In some cases, **gcc** generates an object file having a *.o* suffix and a corresponding root name.

Preprocessor and linker options given on the **gcc** command line are passed on to these tools when they are run. These options are briefly described here, but some are more fully described under entries for **cpp, as,** and **ld**. The options that follow are divided into general, preprocessor, linker, and warning options. **gcc** accepts many system-specific options not covered here.

Note: **gcc** is the GNU form of **cc**; on most Linux systems, the command **cc** will invoke **gcc**. The command **g++** will invoke **gcc** with the appropriate options for interpreting C++.

General options

-a   Provide profile information for basic blocks.

-aux-info *file*
Print prototyped declarations and information on their origins to *file*.

-ansi
Enforce full ANSI conformance.

-b *machine*
Compile for use on *machine* type.

-c   Create linkable object file for each source file, but do not call linker.

-dumpmachine
Print compiler's default target machine, then exit.

-dumpspecs
Print built-in specification strings, then exit.

-dumpversion
Print version number, then exit.

-f*option*
Set the specified compiler *option*. Many of these control debugging, optimization of code, and special language options. Use the **--help -v** options for a full listing.

-g   Include debugging information for use with **gdb**.

-g*level*
Provide *level* amount of debugging information. *level* must be 1, 2, or 3, with 1 providing the least amount of information. The default is 2.

--help
Print most common basic options, then exit. When used with option **-v**, print options for all of **gcc**'s subprocesses. For options specific to a target, use **--target-help**.

-m*option*
Set the specified machine specific *option*. Use the **--target-help** option for a full listing.

-o *file*
Specify output file as *file*. Default is *a.out*.

-p   Provide profile information for use with **prof**.

-pass-exit-codes
On error, return highest error code as the exit code instead of 1.

-pedantic
Warn verbosely.

-pedantic-errors

Generate an error in every case in which **-pedantic** would have produced a warning.

-pg Provide profile information for use with **gprof**.

-print-file-name=_file_

Print the full path to the library specified by filename _file_, then exit. This is the library **gcc** would use for linking.

-print-search-dirs

Print installation directory and the default list of directories **gcc** will search to find programs and libraries, then exit.

-pipe

Transfer information between stages of compiler by pipes instead of temporary files.

-save-temps

Save temporary files in the current directory when compiling.

-std=_standard_

Specify C _standard_ of input file. Accepted values are:

iso9899:1990, c89

1990 ISO C standard.

iso9899:199409

1994 amendment to the 1990 ISO C standard.

iso9899:1999, c99, iso9899:199x, c9x

1999 revised ISO C standard.

gnu89

1990 C Standard with GNU extensions (the default value).

gnu99, gnu9x

1999 revised ISO C standard with GNU extensions.

-time

Print statistics on the execution of each subprocess.

-v Verbose mode. Print subprocess commands to standard error as they are executed. Include **gcc** version number and preprocessor version number. To generate the same output without executing commands, use the option -###.

-w Suppress warnings.

-x _language_

Expect input file to be written in _language_, which may be **c, objective-c, c-header, c++, ada, f77, ratfor, assembler, java, cpp-output, c++-cpp-output, objc-cpp-output, f77-cpp-output, assembler-with-cpp,** or **ada.** If **none** is specified as _language_, guess the language by filename extension.

-B_path_

Specify the _path_ directory in which the compiler files are located.

-E Preprocess the source files, but do not compile. Print result to standard output. This option is useful to meaningfully pass some **cpp** options that would otherwise break **gcc**, such as **-C**, **-M**, or **-P**.

-I*dir*

Include *dir* in list of directories to search for include files. If *dir* is -, search those directories specified by **-I** before the **-I-** only when **#include** "*file*" is specified, not **#include** <*file*>.

-L*dir*

Search *dir* in addition to standard directories.

-O[*level*]

Optimize. *level* should be 1, 2, 3, or 0 (the default is 1). 0 turns off optimization; 3 optimizes the most.

-S Compile source files into assembler code, but do not assemble.

-V *version*

Attempt to run **gcc** version *version*.

-Wa,*options*

Pass *options* to the assembler. Multiple options are separated by commas.

-Wl,*options*

Pass *options* to the linker. Multiple options are separated by commas.

-Wp,*options*

Pass *options* to the preprocessor. Multiple options are separated by commas.

-Xlinker *options*

Pass *options* to the linker. A linker option with an argument requires two **-Xlinker**s, the first specifying the option and the second specifying the argument. Similar to **-Wl**.

Preprocessor options

gcc will pass the following options to the preprocessor:

-$** Do not allow **$ in identifiers.

-dD, -dI, -dM, -dN

Suppress normal output; print preprocessor instructions instead. See **cpp** for details.

-idirafter *dir*

Search *dir* for header files when a header file is not found in any of the included directories.

-imacros *file*

Process macros in *file* before processing main files.

-include *file*

Process *file* before main file.

-iprefix *prefix*

When adding directories with **-iwithprefix**, prepend *prefix* to the directory's name.

-isystem *dir*

Search *dir* for header files after searching directories specified with **-I** but before searching standard system directories.

-iwithprefix *dir*

Append *dir* to the list of directories to be searched when a header file cannot be found in the main include path. If **-iprefix** has been set, prepend that prefix to the directory's name.

-iwithprefixbefore *dir*

Insert *dir* at the beginning of the list of directories to be searched when a header file cannot be found in the main include path. If **-iprefix** has been set, prepend that prefix to the directory's name.

-nostdinc

Search only specified, not standard, directories for header files.

-nostdinc++

Suppress searching of directories believed to contain C++-specific header files.

-trigraphs

Convert special three-letter sequences, meant to represent missing characters on some terminals, into the single character they represent.

-undef

Suppress definition of all nonstandard macros.

-A *name[=def]*

Assert *name* with value *def* as if defined by **#assert**. To turn off standard assertions, use **-A-**.

-A *-name[=def]*

Cancel assertion *name* with value *def*.

-C   Retain all comments except those found on **cpp** directive lines. By default, the preprocessor strips C-style comments.

-D*name[=def]*

Define *name* with value *def* as if by **#define**. If no *=def* is given, *name* is defined with value 1. **-D** has lower precedence than **-U**.

-H   Print pathnames of included files, one per line, on standard error.

-M, -MG, -MF, -MD, -MMD, -MQ, -MT

Suppress normal output and print Makefile rules describing file dependencies. Print a rule for **make** that describes the main source file's dependencies. If **-MG** is specified, assume that missing header files are actually generated files, and look for them in the source file's directory. Most of these options imply **-E**. See **cpp** for further details.

-U*name*

Remove definition of symbol *name*.

Linker options

gcc will pass the following options to the linker:

-l*lib*
> Link to *lib*.

-nostartfiles
> Force linker to ignore standard system startup files.

-nostdlib
> Suppress linking to standard library files.

-s　Remove all symbol table and relocation information from the executable.

-shared
> Create a shareable object.

-shared-libgcc
> Link to a shared version of **libgcc** if available.

-static
> Suppress linking to shared libraries.

-static-libgcc
> Link to a static version of **libgcc** if available.

-u *symbol*
> Force the linker to search libraries for a definition of *symbol*, and to link to the libraries found.

Warning options

-pedantic
> Warn verbosely.

-pedantic-errors
> Produce a fatal error in every case in which **-pedantic** would have produced a warning.

-w　Don't print warnings.

-W　Warn more verbosely than normal.

-Waggregate-return
> Warn if any functions that return structures or unions are defined or called.

-Wall
> Enable **-W**, **-Wchar-subscripts**, **-Wcomment**, **-Wformat**, **-Wimplicit**, **-Wmain**, **-Wmissing-braces**, **-Wparentheses**, **-Wreturn-type**, **-Wsequence-point**, **-Wswitch**, **-Wtemplate-debugging**, **-Wtrigraphs**, **-Wuninitialized**, **-Wunknown-pragmas**, and **-Wunused**.

-Wcast-align
> Warn when encountering instances in which pointers are cast to types that increase the required alignment of the target from its original definition.

-Wcast-qual

Warn when encountering instances in which pointers are cast to types that lack the type qualifier with which the pointer was originally defined.

-Wchar-subscripts

Warn when encountering arrays with subscripts of type **char**.

-Wcomment

Warn when encountering the beginning of a nested comment.

-Wconversion

Warn in particular cases of type conversions.

-Werror

Exit at the first error.

-Wformat

Warn about inappropriately formatted **printf**s and **scanf**s.

-Wimplicit

Warn when encountering implicit function or parameter declarations.

-Winline

Warn about illegal inline functions.

-Wmain

Warn about malformed main functions.

-Wmissing-braces

Enable more verbose warnings about omitted braces.

-Wmissing-declarations

Warn if a global function is defined without a previous declaration.

-Wmissing-prototypes

Warn when encountering global function definitions without previous prototype declarations.

-Wnested-externs

Warn if an **extern** declaration is encountered within a function.

-Wno-import

Don't warn about use of **#import**.

-Wparentheses

Enable more verbose warnings about omitted parentheses.

-Wpointer-arith

Warn when encountering code that attempts to determine the size of a function or void.

-Wredundant-decls

Warn if anything is declared more than once in the same scope.

-Wreturn-type

Warn about violations of sequence point rules defined in the C standard.

-Wreturn-type
> Warn about functions defined without return types or with improper return types.

-Wshadow
> Warn when a local variable shadows another local variable.

-Wstrict-prototypes
> Insist that argument types be specified in function declarations and definitions.

-Wswitch
> Warn about switches that skip the index for one of their enumerated types.

-Wtraditional
> Warn when encountering code that produces different results in ANSI C and traditional C.

-Wtrigraphs
> Warn when encountering trigraphs.

-Wuninitialized
> Warn when encountering uninitialized automatic variables.

-Wundef
> Warn when encountering a non-macro identifier in an **#if** directive.

-Wunknown-pragmas
> Warn when encountering a **#pragma** directive not understood by **gcc**.

-Wunused
> Warn about unused variables, functions, labels, and paramaters.

Pragma directives

#pragma interface [*header-file*]
> Used in header files to force object files to provide definition information via references instead of including it locally in each file. C++-specific.

#pragma implementation [*header-file*]
> Used in main input files to force generation of full output from *header-file* (or, if it is not specified, from the header file with the same base name as the file containing the pragma directive). This information will be globally visible. Normally the specified header file contains a **#pragma interface** directive.

---

gdb
    gdb [*options*] [*program* [*core*|*pid*]]

> GDB (GNU DeBugger) allows you to step through the execution of a program in order to find the point at which it breaks. It fully supports C and C++, and provides partial support for FORTRAN, Java, Chill, assembly, and Modula-2. The program to be debugged is normally specified on the command line; you can also specify a core or, if you want to investigate a running program, a process ID.

Options

-b *bps*

Set line speed of serial device used by GDB to *bps*.

-batch

Exit after executing all the commands specified in *.gdbinit* and **-x** files. Print no startup messages.

-c *file*, **-core**=*file*

Consult *file* for information provided by a core dump.

-cd=*directory*

Use *directory* as **gdb**'s working directory.

-d *directory*, **-directory**=*directory*

Include *directory* in path that is searched for source files.

-e *file*, **-exec**=*file*

Use *file* as an executable to be read in conjunction with source code. May be used in conjunction with **-s** to read the symbol table from the executable.

-f, -fullname

Show full filename and line number for each stack frame.

-h, -help

Print help message, then exit.

-n, -nx

Ignore *.gdbinit* file.

-q, -quiet

Suppress introductory and copyright messages.

-s *file*, **-symbols**=*file*

Consult *file* for symbol table. With **-e**, also uses *file* as the executable.

-tty=*device*

Set standard in and standard out to *device*.

-write

Allow **gdb** to write into executables and core files.

-x *file*, **-command**=*file*

Read **gdb** commands from *file*.

Common commands

These are just some of the more common **gdb** commands; there are too many to list them all.

bt　Print the current location within the program and a stack trace showing how the current location was reached. (**where** does the same thing.)

break

Set a breakpoint in the program.

cd　Change the current working directory.

clear

Delete the breakpoint where you just stopped.

commands

    List commands to be executed when a breakpoint is hit.

c   Continue execution from a breakpoint.

delete

    Delete a breakpoint or a watchpoint; also used in conjunction with other commands.

display

    Cause variables or expressions to be displayed when program stops.

down

    Move down one stack frame to make another function the current one.

frame

    Select a frame for the next **continue** command.

info

    Show a variety of information about the program. For instance, **info breakpoints** shows all outstanding breakpoints and watchpoints.

jump

    Start execution at another point in the source file.

kill

    Abort the process running under **gdb**'s control.

list

    List the contents of the source file corresponding to the program being executed.

next

    Execute the next source line, executing a function in its entirety.

print

    Print the value of a variable or expression.

ptype

    Show the contents of a datatype, such as a structure or C++ class.

pwd

    Show the current working directory.

quit

    Exit **gdb**.

reverse-search

    Search backward for a regular expression in the source file.

run

    Execute the program.

search

    Search for a regular expression in the source file.

set variable

    Assign a value to a variable.

signal
> Send a signal to the running process.

step
> Execute the next source line, stepping into a function if necessary.

undisplay
> Reverse the effect of the **display** command; keep expressions from being displayed.

until
> Finish the current loop.

up
> Move up one stack frame to make another function the current one.

watch
> Set a watchpoint (i.e., a data breakpoint) in the program.

whatis
> Print the type of a variable or function.

---

getkeycodes

getkeycodes

Print the kernel's scancode-to-keycode mapping table.

---

gpm

gpm [*options*]

System administration command. Provide a mouse server and cut-and-paste utility for use on the Linux console. **gpm** acts like a daemon, responding to both mouse events and client input. If no clients are connected to the active console, **gpm** provides cut-and-paste services.

Options

-2 Force two buttons. If there is a middle button, it is treated as the right button.

-3 Force three buttons. With a three-button mouse, the left button makes a selection, the right button extends the selection, and the middle button pastes it. Using this option with a two-button mouse results in being unable to paste.

-a *accel*
> Set the acceleration for a single motion longer than the delta specified with the **-d** option.

-A [*limit*]
> Start up with pasting disabled for security. If specified, *limit* gives the time in seconds during which a selection can be pasted. If too much time has passed, the paste is not allowed.

-b *baud*
> Specify the baud rate.

-B *seq*

Set a three-digit button sequence, mapping the left, middle, and right buttons to buttons 1, 2, and 3. The default is 123. The sequence 321 is useful if you are left-handed, or 132 for a two-button mouse.

-d *delta*

Set the delta value for use with **-a**. When a mouse motion event is longer than the specified delta, use *accel* as a multiplier. *delta* must be 2 or greater.

-D   Debugging mode. When set, **gpm** does not put itself into the background, and it logs messages to standard error instead of syslog.

-g *num*

For a glidepoint device, specify the button to be emulated by a tap. *num* must be 1, 2, or 3 and refers to the button number before any remapping is done by the **-B** option. Applies to **mman** and **ps2** protocol decoding.

-h   Print a help message and exit.

-i *interval*

Specify the upper time limit, in milliseconds, between mouse clicks for the clicks to be considered a double or triple click.

-k   Kill a running **gpm**. For use with a bus mouse to kill **gpm** before running X. See also **-R**.

-l *charset*

Specify the **inword( )** lookup table, which determines what characters can appear in a word. *charset* is a list of characters. The list can include only printable characters. Specify a range with -, and use \ to escape the following character or to specify an octal character.

-m *filename*

Specify the mouse file to open. The default is */dev/mouse*.

-M   Enable the use of more than one mouse. Options appearing before **-M** apply to the first mouse; those appearing after it apply to the second mouse. Forces the use of **-R**.

-o *extra-options*

Specify a comma-separated list of additional mouse-specific options. See the **gpm** info page for a description of the mouse types and the possible options.

-p   Keep the pointer visible while text is being selected. The default is not to show the pointer.

-r *num*

Specify the responsiveness. A higher number causes the cursor to move faster.

-R *name*

Act as a repeater and pass any mouse data received while in graphical mode to the fifo */dev/gpmdata* in the protocol specified by *name* (default is **msc**). In addition to certain of the protocol types available with **-t**, you can specify **raw** to repeat the data with no protocol translation.

-s *num*
Specify the sample rate for the mouse device.

-S [*commands*]
Enable special-command processing (see the next section). Custom *commands* can be specified as a colon-separated list to associate commands with the left button, middle button, and right button. If a command is omitted, it defaults to sending a signal to **init**.

-t *type*
Specify the mouse protocol type. Use **-t help** for a list of types; those marked with an asterisk (*) can be used with **-R**.

-v   Print version information and exit.

-V [*increment*]
Make **gpm** more or less verbose by the specified *increment*. The default verbosity level is 5 and the default increment is 1. A larger value of *increment* causes more messages to be logged. The increment can be negative, but must be specified with no space (e.g., **-V-3**).

Special commands

Special commands, activated with the **-S** option, are associated with each mouse button. You can also use **-S** to customize the commands. To execute a special command, triple-click the left and right buttons (hold down one of the buttons and triple-click the other). A message appears on the console and the speaker beeps twice. At that point, release the buttons and press the desired button within three seconds to activate the associated special command. The default special commands are:

Left button
Reboot by signalling **init**.

Middle button
Shut down the system with **/sbin/shutdown -h now**.

Right button
Reboot with **/sbin/shutdown -r now**.

---

gprof

gprof [*options*] [*object_file*]

Display the profile data for an object file. The file's symbol table is compared with the call graph profile file *gmon.out* (previously created by compiling with **gcc -pg**). Many of **gprof**'s options take a symbol specification argument, or symspec, to limit the option to specified files or functions. The symspec may be a filename, a function, or a line number. It can also be given as *filename:function* or *filename:linenumber* to specify a function or line number in a specific file. **gprof** expects filenames to contain a period and functions to not contain a period.

Options

-a, --no-static

Do not display statically declared functions. Since their information might still be relevant, append it to the information about the functions loaded immediately before.

-b, --brief

Do not display information about each field in the profile.

-c, --static-call-graph

Consult the object file's text area to attempt to determine the program's static call graph. Display static-only parents and children with call counts of 0.

--demangle[*=style*], **--no-demangle**

Specify whether C++ symbols should be demangled or not. They are demangled by default. If profiling a program built by a different compiler, you may need to specify the mangling style.

--function-ordering

Print suggested function order based on profiling data.

--file-ordering *file*

Print suggested link line order for *.o* files based on profiling data. Read function name to object file mappings from *file*. This file can be created using the **nm** command.

-i, --file-info

Print summary information on data files, then exit.

-k *from to*

Remove arcs between the routines *from* and *to*.

-m *n*, **--min-count**[*=n*]

Don't print count statistics for symbols executed less than *n* times.

-n[*symspec*], **--time**[*=symspec*]

Propogate time statistics in call graph analysis.

-p[*symspec*], **--flat-profile**[*=symspec*]

Print profile statistics.

-q[*symspec*], **--graph**[*=symspec*]

Print call graph analysis.

-s, --sum

Summarize profile information in the file *gmon.sum*.

-v, --version

Print version and exit.

-w *n*, **--width**=*n*

Print function index formatted to width *n*.

-x, --all-lines

When printing annotated source, annotate every line in a basic block, not just the beginning.

-y, --separate-files
> Print annotated-source output to separate files instead of standard output. The annotated source for each source file is printed to *filename-ann*.

-z, --display-unused-functions
> Include zero-usage calls.

-A[*symspec*], **--annotated-source**[=*symspec*]
> Print annotated source code.

-C[*symspec*], **--exec-counts**[=*symspec*]
> Print statistics on the number of times each function is called. When used with option **-l**, count basic-block execution.

-F *routine*
> Print only information about *routine*. Do not include time spent in other routines.

-I *dirs,* **--directory-path**=*dirs*
> Set directory path to search for source files. The *dirs* argument may be given as a colon-separated list of directories.

-J[*symspec*], **--no-annotated-source**[=*symspec*]
> Don't print annotated source code.

-L, --print-path
> Print the path information when printing filenames.

-N[*symspec*], **--no-time**[=*symspec*]
> Don't propogate time statistics in call graph analysis.

-P[*symspec*], **--no-flat-profile**[=*symspec*]
> Don't print profile statistics

-Q[*symspec*], **--no-graph**[=*symspec*]
> Don't print call graph analysis.

-T, --traditional
> Print output in BSD style.

-Z[*symspec*], **--no-exec-counts**[=*symspec*]
> Don't print statistics on the number of times each function is called.

---

grep

grep [*options*] *pattern* [*files*]

Search one or more *files* for lines that match a regular expression *pattern*. Regular expressions are described in Chapter 9. Exit status is 0 if any lines match, 1 if none match, and 2 for errors. See also **egrep** and **fgrep**.

Options

-a, --text
> Don't suppress output lines with binary data; treat as text.

-b, --byte-offset
> Print the byte offset within the input file before each line of output.

-c, --count
> Print only a count of matched lines. With **-v** or **--revert-match** option, count nonmatching lines.

-d *action*, **--directories**=*action*
> Define an *action* for processing directories. Possible actions are:

> **read**
> > Read directories like ordinary files (default).

> **skip**
> > Skip directories.

> **recurse**
> > Recursively read all files under each directory. Same as **-r**.

-e *pattern*, **--regexp**=*pattern*
> Search for *pattern*. Same as specifying a pattern as an argument, but useful in protecting patterns beginning with -.

-f *file*, **--file**=*file*
> Take a list of patterns from *file*, one per line.

-h, --no-filename
> Print matched lines but not filenames (inverse of -l).

-i, --ignore-case
> Ignore uppercase and lowercase distinctions.

-l, --files-with-matches
> List the names of files with matches but not individual matched lines; scanning per file stops on the first match.

--mmap
> Try to use memory mapping (**mmap**) to read input in order to save time.

-n, --line-number
> Print lines and their line numbers.

-q, --quiet, --silent
> Suppress normal output in favor of quiet mode; scanning stops on the first match.

-r, --recursive
> Recursively read all files under each directory. Same as **-d recurse**.

-s, --no-messages
> Suppress error messages about nonexistent or unreadable files.

-v, --invert-match
> Print all lines that don't match *pattern*.

-w, --word-regexp
> Match on whole words only. Words are divided by characters that are not letters, digits, or underscores.

-x, --line-regexp
> Print lines only if *pattern* matches the entire line.

-A *num*, **--after-context**=*num*
> Print *num* lines of text that occur after the matching line.

-B *num*, **--before-context**=*num*
> Print *num* lines of text that occur before the matching line.

-C[*num*], **--context**[=*num*], **-***num*
> Print *num* lines of leading and trailing context. Default context is 2 lines.

-E, **-extended-regexp**
> Act like **egrep**, recognizing extended regular expressions such as **(UN|POS)IX** to find **UNIX** and **POSIX**.

-F, **--fixed-strings**
> Act like **fgrep**, recognizing only fixed strings instead of regular expressions. Useful when searching for characters that **grep** normally recognizes as metacharacters.

-G, **--basic-regexp**
> Expect the regular expressions traditionally recognized by **grep** (the default).

-H, **--with-filename**
> Display, before each line found, the name of the file containing the line. This is done by default if multiple files are submitted to a single **grep** command.

-V, **--version**
> Print the version number and then exit.

-Z, **--null**
> When displaying filenames, follow each with a zero byte instead of a colon.

Examples

List the number of users who use **tcsh**:

```
grep -c /bin/tcsh /etc/passwd
```

List header files that have at least one **#include** directive:

```
grep -l '^#include' /usr/include/*
```

List files that don't contain *pattern*:

```
grep -c pattern files | grep :0
```

---

groff

groff [*options*] [*files*]
troff [*options*] [*files*]

Frontend to the **groff** document-formatting system, which normally runs **troff** along with a postprocessor appropriate for the selected output device. Options without arguments can be grouped after a single dash (-). A filename of - denotes standard input.

Options

-a Generate an ASCII approximation of the typeset output.

-b Print a backtrace.

-C Enable compatibility mode.

-d*cs*, **-d***name*=*s*
> Define the character *c* or string *name* to be the string *s*.

-e Preprocess with **eqn**, the equation formatter.

-E Don't print any error messages.

-f*fam*

Use *fam* as the default font family.

-F*dir*

Search *dir* for subdirectories with *DESC* and font files before the default */usr/lib/groff/font*.

-h Print a help message.

-i Read standard input after all *files* have been processed.

-l Send the output to a print spooler (as specified by the print command in the device description file).

-L*arg*

Pass *arg* to the spooler. Each argument should be passed with a separate **-L** option.

-m*name*

Read the macro file *tmac.name*.

-M*dir*

Search directory *dir* for macro files before the default directory */usr/lib/groff/tmac*.

-n*num*

Set the first page number to *num*.

-N Don't allow newlines with **eqn** delimiters; equivalent to **eqn**'s **-N** option.

-o*list*

Output only pages specified in *list*, a comma-separated list of page ranges.

-p Preprocess with **pic**.

-P*arg*

Pass *arg* to the postprocessor. Each argument should be passed with a separate **-P** option.

-r*cn, -name=n*

Set the number register *c* or *name* to *n*. *c* is a single character and *n* is any **troff** numeric expression.

-R Preprocess with **refer**.

-s Preprocess with **soelim**.

-S Use safer mode (i.e., pass the **-S** option to **pic** and use the **-msafer** macros with **troff**).

-t Preprocess with **tbl**.

-T*dev*

Prepare output for device *dev*; the default is **ps**.

-v Make programs run by **groff** print out their version number.

-V Print the pipeline on stdout instead of executing it.

-w*name*

Enable warning *name*. You can specify multiple **-w** options. See the **troff** manpage for a list of warnings.

-W*name*
> Disable warning *name*. You can specify multiple **-W** options. See the **troff** manpage for a list of warnings.

-z Suppress **troff** output (except error messages).

-Z Do not postprocess **troff** output. Normally **groff** automatically runs the appropriate postprocessor.

Devices

ascii
> Typewriter-like device.

dvi
> T$_E$X dvi format.

latin1
> Typewriter-like devices using the ISO Latin-1 character set.

ps PostScript.

X75
> 75-dpi X11 previewer.

X100
> 100-dpi X11 previewer.

lj4
> HP LaserJet4-compatible (or other PCL5-compatible) printer.

Environment variables

GROFF_COMMAND_PREFIX
> If set to be X, **groff** will run **Xtroff** instead of **troff**.

GROFF_FONT_PATH
> Colon-separated list of directories in which to search for the *devname* directory.

GROFF_TMAC_PATH
> Colon-separated list of directories in which to search for the macro files.

GROFF_TMPDIR
> If set, temporary files will be created in this directory; otherwise, they will be created in TMPDIR (if set) or */tmp* (if TMPDIR is not set).

GROFF_TYPESETTER
> Default device.

PATH
> Search path for commands that **groff** executes.

groffer

groffer [*viewing_options*] [*man_options*] [*groff_options*] [*file-spec...*]
groffer *filespec*

Groffer displays manpages and **groff** documents. It accepts the option flags from both *man* and *groff*. The filespec argument can be a filename or a manpage or section specified in the format *man:page* or *man:section*. For more information, see **groff** and **man**.

groupadd

groupadd [*options*] *group*

System administration command. Create new group account *group*. Options -**f** and -**r** are added by RedHat and may not be available on all distributions.

Options

-**f**   Exit with error if group being added already exists. If a *gid* requested with -**g** already exists and the -**o** option has not been specified, assign a different *gid* as if -**g** had not been specified.

-**g***gid*
> Assign numerical group ID. (By default, the first available number above 500 is used.) The value must be unique unless the -**o** option is used.

-**o**   Accept a nonunique *gid* with the -**g** option.

-**r**   Add a system account. Assign the first available number lower than 499.

---

groupdel

groupdel *group*

System administration command. Remove *group* from system account files. You may still need to find and change permissions on files that belong to the removed group.

---

groupmod

groupmod [*options*] *group*

System administration command. Modify group information for *group*.

Options

-**g** *gid*
> Change the numerical value of the group ID. Any files that have the old *gid* must be changed manually. The new *gid* must be unique unless the -**o** option is used.

-**n** *name*
> Change the group name to *name*.

-**o**   Override. Accept a nonunique *gid*.

---

groups

groups [*options*] [*users*]

Show the groups that each *user* belongs to (default user is the owner of the current group). Groups are listed in */etc/passwd* and */etc/group*.

Options

--**help**
> Print help message.

--**version**
> Print version information.

---

grpck

grpck [*option*] [*files*]

System administration command. Remove corrupt or duplicate entries in the */etc/group* and */etc/gshadow* files. Generate warnings for other errors found. **grpck** will prompt for a "yes" or "no" before deleting entries. If the user replies "no," the program will exit. If run in a read-only mode, the reply to all prompts is "no." Alternate group and gshadow *files* can be checked. If other errors are found, the user will be encouraged to run the **groupmod** command.

Option

-r   Read-only mode.

Exit codes

0   Success.

1   Syntax error.

2   One or more bad group entries found.

3   Could not open group files.

4   Could not lock group files.

5   Could not write group files.

---

grpconv

grpconv
grpunconv

System administration command. Like **pwconv**, the **grpconv** command creates a shadowed group file to keep your encrypted group passwords safe from password-cracking programs. **grpconv** creates the */etc/gshadow* file based on your existing */etc/groups* file and replaces your encrypted password entries with **x**. If you add new entries to the */etc/groups* file, you can run **grpconv** again to transfer the new information to */etc/gshadow*. It will ignore entries that already have a password of **x** and convert those that do not. **grpunconv** restores the encrypted passwords to your */etc/groups* file and removes the */etc/gshadow* file.

---

gs

gs [*options*] [*files*]

GhostScript, an interpreter for Adobe Systems' PostScript and PDF (Portable Document Format) languages. Used for document processing. With - in place of *files*, standard input is used.

Options

-- *filename arg1* ...
  Take the next argument as a filename, but use all remaining arguments to define **ARGUMENTS** in *userdict* (not *system-dict*) as an array of those strings before running the file.

-g*number1*x*number2*
  Specify width and height of device; intended for systems like the X Window System.

-q Quiet startup.

-r*number,* **-r***number1***x***number2*
Specify X and Y resolutions (for the benefit of devices, such as printers, that support multiple X and Y resolutions). If only one number is given, it is used for both X and Y resolutions.

-D*name=token,* **-d***name=token*
Define a name in *systemdict* with the given definition. The token must be exactly one token (as defined by the token operator) and must not contain any whitespace.

-D*name,* **-d***name*
Define a name in *systemdict* with a null value.

-I*directories*
Add the designated list of directories at the head of the search path for library files.

-S*name=string,* **-s***name=string*
Define a name in *systemdict* with a given *string* as value.

Special names
-dDISKFONTS
Causes individual character outlines to be loaded from the disk the first time they are encountered.

-dNOBIND
Disables the **bind** operator. Useful only for debugging.

-dNOCACHE
Disables character caching. Useful only for debugging.

-dNODISPLAY
Suppresses the normal initialization of the output device. May be useful when debugging.

-dNOPAUSE
Disables the prompt and pause at the end of each page.

-dNOPLATFONTS
Disables the use of fonts supplied by the underlying platform (e.g., the X Window System).

-dSAFER
Disables the **deletefile** and **renamefile** operators and the ability to open files in any mode other than read-only.

-dWRITESYSTEMDICT
Leaves *systemdict* writable.

-sDEVICE=*device*
Selects an alternate initial output device.

-sOUTPUTFILE=*filename*
Selects an alternate output file (or pipe) for the initial output device.

---

gunzip

gunzip [*options*] [*files*]

Uncompress *files* compressed by **gzip**. See **gzip** for a list of options.

---

gzexe

gzexe [*option*] [*files*]

Compress executables. When run, these files automatically uncompress, thus trading time for space. **gzexe** creates backup files (*filename~*), which should be removed after testing the original.

Option
-d   Decompress files.

gzip

gzip [*options*] [*files*]
gunzip [*options*] [*files*]
zcat [*options*] [*files*]

Compress specified files (or read from standard input) with Lempel-Ziv coding (LZ77). Rename compressed file to *filename.gz*; keep ownership modes and access/modification times. Ignore symbolic links. Uncompress with **gunzip**, which takes all of **gzip**'s options except those specified. **zcat** is identical to **gunzip -c** and takes the options -**fhLV**, described here. Files compressed with the **compress** command can be decompressed using these commands.

Options
-*n*, --**fast**, --**best**
Regulate the speed of compression using the specified digit *n*, where -**1** or --**fast** indicates the fastest compression method (less compression) and -**9** or --**best** indicates the slowest compression method (most compression). The default compression level is -**6**.

-**a**, --**ascii**
ASCII text mode: convert end-of-lines using local conventions. This option is supported only on some non-Unix systems.

-**c**, --**stdout**, --**to-stdout**
Print output to standard output, and do not change input files.

-**d**, --**decompress**, --**uncompress**
Same as **gunzip**.

-**f**, --**force**
Force compression. **gzip** would normally prompt for permission to continue when the file has multiple links, its *.gz* version already exists, or it is reading compressed data to or from a terminal.

-**h**, --**help**
Display a help screen and then exit.

-**l**, --**list**
Expects to be given compressed files as arguments. Files may be compressed by any of the following methods: **gzip**, **deflate**, **compress**, **lzh**, or **pack**. For each file, list uncompressed and compressed sizes (the latter being always -**1** for files compressed by programs other than **gzip**), compression ratio, and uncompressed name. With -**v**, also print compression

method, the 32-bit CRC of the uncompressed data, and the timestamp. With **-N**, look inside the file for the uncompressed name and timestamp.

-L, --license
Display the **gzip** license and quit.

-n, --no-name
When compressing, do not save the original filename and timestamp by default. When decompressing, do not restore the original filename if present, and do not restore the original timestamp if present. This option is the default when decompressing.

-N, --name
Default. Save original name and timestamp. When decompressing, restore original name and timestamp.

-q, --quiet
Print no warnings.

-r, --recursive
When given a directory as an argument, recursively compress or decompress files within it.

-S *suffix*, **--suffix** *suffix*
Append *.suffix*. Default is **gz**. A null suffix while decompressing causes **gunzip** to attempt to decompress all specified files, regardless of suffix.

-t, --test
Test compressed file integrity.

-v, --verbose
Print name and percent size reduction for each file.

-V, --version
Display the version number and compilation options.

---

halt

halt [*options*]

System administration command. Insert a note in the file */var/log/wtmp*; if the system is in runlevel 0 or 6, stop all processes; otherwise, call **shutdown -h**.

Options

-d Suppress writing to */var/log/wtmp*.

-f Call **halt** even when **shutdown -nf** would normally be called (i.e., force a call to **halt**, even when not in runlevel 0 or 6).

-h Place hard drives in standby mode before halt or power off.

-i Shut down network interfaces before halt.

-n No sync before reboot or halt.

-p Perform power off when halting system.

-n Suppress normal call to **sync**.

-w Suppress normal execution; simply write to */var/log/wtmp*.

hdparm [*options*] [*device*]

Read or set the hard drive parameters. This command can be used to tune hard drive performance; it is mostly used with IDE drives, but can also be used with SCSI drives.

Options

The **hdparm** command accepts many option flags, including some that can result in filesystem corruption if misused. Flags can be used to set or get a parameter. To get a parameter, just pass the flag without a value. To set a parameter, follow the flag with a space and the appropriate value.

-a [*n*]

Get or set the number of sectors to read ahead in the disk. The default is 8 sectors (4KB); a larger value is more efficient for large, sequential reads, and a smaller value is better for small, random reads. Many IDE drives include this functionality in the drive itself, so this feature is not always necessary.

-A   Enable or disable the IDE read-ahead feature. Usually on by default.

-b [*n*]

Get or set the bus state for the drive.

-B   Get the Advanced Power Management (APM) data if the drive supports it.

-c [*n*]

Get or set 32-bit I/O values for IDE drives. Acceptable values are 0 (32-bit support off), 1 (32-bit support on), and 3 (on, but only with a sync sequence).

-C   Check the power status of the drive. This will tell you unknown, active/idle, standby, or sleeping. Use **-S**, **-y**, **-Y**, and -Z to set the power status.

-d [*n*]

Get or set the **using_dma** flag for the drive, which may be 0 or 1.

-D   Enable or disable defect handling features that are controlled by the hard drive itself.

-E *n*

Set CD-ROM read speed to *n* times normal audio playback speed. Not normally necessary.

-f   Flush and sync the buffer cache on exit.

-g   Query and display drive size and geometry information, such as number of cylinders, heads, and sectors.

-h   Display a short help message.

-i   Display the drive identification information obtained at boot time. If the drive has changed since boot, this information may not be current.

-I   Display more detailed identification information for the drive.

-k [*n*]

Get or set the **keep_settings_over_reset** variable. Valid settings are 0 and 1, and a value of 1 will keep the **-dmu** options when rebooting (soft reset only).

-K [*n*]

Get or set the **keep_features_over_reset** variable. Valid settings are 0 and 1, and a value of 1 will keep settings for the flags **-APSWXZ** over a soft reset.

-L *n*

Set the door lock flag for the drive. Used for Syquest, ZIP, and JAZ drives.

-m [*n*]

Get or set the number of sectors used for multiple sector count reading. A value of 0 disables the feature, and values of 2, 4, 8, 16, and 32 are common. Drives that try to support this feature and fail may suffer corruption and data loss.

-n [*n*]

Set to 0 or 1 to disable or enable the "ignore write errors" flag. This can cause massive data loss if used incorrectly, and is for development purposes only.

-p *n*

Tune the IDE interface to use PIO mode *n*, usually an integer between 0 and 5. Incorrect values can result in massive data loss. Support for the PIO mode setting feature varies between IDE chips, so tuning it is not for the faint of heart.

-P *n*

Set the internal prefetch sector count. Not all drives support the feature.

-q   Suppress output for the flag after this one, unless it is the **-i**, **-v**, **-t**, or **-T** flag.

-r [*n*]

Get or set the flag for read-only on the device. A value of 1 marks the device as read-only.

-R   This option should be used by experts only. It registers an IDE interface. See the **-U** option for further details.

-S *n*

Set the amount of time a disk is inactive before it spins down and goes into standby mode. Settings from 1 to 240 represent chunks of five seconds (for timeout values between 5 seconds and 20 minutes); values from 241 to 251 are increments of 30 minutes (for 30 minutes to 5.5 hours). A value of 252 sets the timeout to 21 minutes, 253 to the vendor default, and 255 to 20 minutes and 15 seconds.

-T   Time cache reads to determine performance.

-t   Time device reads to determine performance.

-u [*n*]

Get or set the interrupt-unmask value for the drive. A value of 1 lets the drive unmask other interrupts and can improve performance; used with older kernels and hardware it can cause data loss.

-U   Unregister an IDE interface. Use this feature and the **-R** feature only with hot-swappable hardware, such as very high-end servers and some laptops. It can damage or hang other systems and should be used with caution.

-v   Display all appropriate settings for device except **-i**.

-W   Enable or disable the write-cache feature for the drive. The default varies between drive manufacturers.

-X *n*

Set the IDE transfer mode. Possible values include 34 (multi-word DMA mode2 transfers) and 66 (UltraDMA mode2 transfers), or any PIO mode number plus 8. This option is suggested for experts only, and is useful only with newer EIDE/IDE/ATA2 drives. Often used in combination with **-d**.

-y   Put the IDE drive into standby (spin-down) mode, saving power.

-Y   Put the IDE drive into sleep mode.

-z   Force kernel to reread the partition table.

-Z   Disable automatic powersaving on some drives, which can prevent them from idling or spinning down at inconvenient moments. This will increase the electrical power consumption of your system.

---

head

head [*options*] [*files*]

Print the first few lines (default is 10) of one or more *files*. If *files* is missing or -, read from standard input. With more than one file, print a header for each file.

Options

-c *num*[**b**|**k**|**m**], **--bytes** *num* [**b**|**k**|**m**]

Print first *num* bytes or, if *num* is followed by **b**, **k**, or **m**, first *num* 512-byte blocks, 1-kilobyte blocks, or 1-megabyte blocks.

--help

Display help and then exit.

-n *num*, **--lines** *num*, *-num*

Print first *num* lines. Default is 10.

-q, --quiet, --silent

Quiet mode; never print headers giving filenames.

-v, --verbose

Print filename headers, even for only one file.

--version

Output version information and then exit.

Examples

Display the first 20 lines of **phone_list**:

> `head -20 phone_list`

Display the first 10 phone numbers having a 202 area code:

> `grep '(202)' phone_list | head`

---

hexdump

`hexdump [`*`options`*`] `*`file`*

Display specified file or input in hexadecimal, octal, decimal, or ASCII format. Option flags are used to specify the display format.

Options

-b   Use a one-byte octal display, meaning the input offset is in hexadecimal and followed by sixteen three-column octal data bytes, filled in with zeroes and separated by spaces.

-c   Use a one-byte character display, meaning the input offset is in hexadecimal and followed by sixteen three-column entries, filled in with zeroes and separated with spaces.

-C   Canonical mode. Display hexadecimal offset, two sets of eight columns of hexadecimal bytes, then a | followed by the ASCII representation of those same bytes.

-d   Use a two-byte decimal display. The input offset is again in hexadecimal, but the display has only eight entries per line, of five columns each, containing two bytes of unsigned decimal format.

-e *format_string*

> Choose a format string to be used to transform the output data. Format strings consist of:

> *Iteration count*
>> The iteration count is optional. It determines the number of times to use the transformation string. The number should be followed by a slash character (/) to distinguish it from the byte count.

> *Byte count*
>> The number of bytes to be interpreted by the conversion string. It should be preceded by a slash character to distinguish it from the iteration count.

> *Format characters*
>> The actual format characters should be surrounded by quotation marks and are interpreted as **fprintf** (see **printf**) formatting strings, although the *, **h**, **l**, **n**, **p**, and **q** options will not work as expected. Format string usage is discussed at greater length in the **hexdump** manpage.

-f *filename*

> Choose a file that contains several format strings. The strings should be separated by newlines; the # character marks a line as a comment.

-n *length*
> Limit the number of bytes of input to be interpreted.

-o
> Two-byte octal display, meaning a hexadecimal offset followed by eight five-column data entries of two bytes each, in octal format.

-s *offset*
> Skip to specified *offset*. The offset number is assumed to be decimal unless it starts with **0x** or **0X** (hexadecimal), or **O** (octal). Numbers may also be designated in megabytes, kilobytes, or half-kilobytes with the addition of **m**, **k**, or **b** at the end of the number.

-v
> Display all input data, even if it is the same as the previous line. Normally, a duplicate line is replaced by an asterisk (*).

-x
> Display data in a two-byte hexadecimal format. The offset is, as usual, in hexadecimal, and is followed by eight space-separated entries, each of which contains four-column, two-byte chunks of data in hexadecimal format.

---

host

host [*options*] *name* [*server*]

System administration command. Print information about hosts or zones in DNS. Hosts may be IP addresses or hostnames; **host** converts IP addresses to hostnames by default and appends the local domain to hosts without a trailing dot. Default servers are determined in */etc/resolv.conf*. For more information about hosts and zones, read Chapters 1 and 2 of *DNS and BIND* (O'Reilly).

Options

-a Same as **-t ANY**.

-c *class*
> Search for specified resource record class (**IN**, **CH**, **CHAOS**, **HS**, **HESIOD**, or **ANY**). Default is IN.

-d Verbose output. Same as **-v**.

-l
> Perform reverse lookups for IPv6 addresses using IP6.INT domain and "nibble" labels instead of IP6.ARPA and binary labels.

-n Perform zone transfer. Same as **-t AXFR**.

-r
> Do not ask contacted server to query other servers, but require only the information that it has cached.

-t *type*
> Look for *type* entries in the resource record. *type* may be any recognized query type, such as A, AXFR, CNAME, NS, SOA, SIG, or ANY. If *name* is a hostname, **host** will look for A records by default. If *name* is an IPv4 or IPv6 address, it will look for PTR records.

-v
> Verbose. Include all fields from resource record, even time-to-live and class, as well as "additional information" and "authoritative nameservers" (provided by the remote nameserver).

-w   Never give up on queried server.

-C   Display SOA records from all authoritative name servers for the specified zone.

-N *n*

Consider names with fewer than *n* dots in them to be relative. Search for them in the domains listed in the **search** and **domain** directives of */etc/resolv.conf*. The default is usually 1.

-R *n*

Retry query a maximum of *n* times. The defalt is 1.

-T   Use TCP instead of UDP to query name server. This is implied in queries that require TCP, such as AXFR requests.

-W *n*

Wait a maximum of *n* seconds for reply.

---

hostid

      `hostid`

      Print the ID number in hexadecimal of the current host.

---

hostname

      `hostname` [*option*] [*nameofhost*]

      Set or print name of current host system. A privileged user can set the hostname with the *nameofhost* argument.

Options

-a, --alias

Display the alias name of the host (if used).

-d, --domain

Print DNS domain name.

-f, --fqdn, --long

Print fully qualified domain name.

-F *file*, **--file** *file*

Consult *file* for hostname.

-h, --help

Print a help message and then exit.

-i, --ip-address

Display the IP address(es) of the host.

-n, --node

Display or set the DECnet node name.

-s, --short

Trim domain information from the printed name.

-v, --verbose

Verbose mode.

-V, --version

Print version information and then exit.

-y, --yp, --nis

Display the NIS domain name. A privileged user can set a new NIS domain name with *nameofhost*.

---

htdigest

htdigest [-c] *filename realm username*

Create or update user authentication files used by the Apache web server. The -c option is used if you wish to create the file, and will overwrite any existing files rather than update them. The three arguments are the file you wish to use as the authentication file, the realm name to which the user belongs, and the username you will update in the password file. You will be prompted for a password when you run the command.

The Apache manual contains information about authentication mechanisms, including more detail about using **htdigest** and the ways in which you can control access to the resources served by Apache.

hwclock

hwclock [*option*]

System administration command. Read or set the hardware clock. This command maintains change information in */etc/adjtime*, which can be used to adjust the clock based on how much it drifts over time. **hwclock** replaces the **clock** command. The single-letter options are included for compatibility with the older command.

Options

You may specify only one of the following options:

-a, --adjust
Adjust the hardware clock based on information in */etc/adjtime* and set the system clock to the new time.

--getepoch
Print the kernel's hardware clock epoch value, then exit.

-r, --show
Print the current time stored in the hardware clock.

-s, --hctosys
Set the system time in accordance with the hardware clock.

--setepoch, --epoch=*year*
Set the hardware clock's epoch to *year*.

--set --date=*date*
Set the hardware clock to the specified *date*, a string appropriate for use with the **date** command.

-v, --version
Print version and exit.

-w, --systohc
Set the hardware clock in accordance with the system time.

The following may be used with the above options.

--debug
Print information about what **hwclock** is doing.

--localtime
The hardware clock is stored in local time.

--noadjfile

> Disable */etc/adjtime* facilities.

--test

> Do not actually change anything. This is good for checking syntax.

-u, --utc

> The hardware clock is stored in Universal Coordinated Time.

---

iconv

iconv [*options*] *files*

Convert the contents of one or more *files* from one character encoding to another and write the results to standard output.

Options

-c Omit invalid output characters.

-f *code1*, **--from-code**=*code1*

> Convert input characters from the *code1* encoding.

-?, --help

> Print help message and exit.

-l, --list

> Print a list of valid encodings to standard output.

-o *file*, **--output**=*file*

> Write the converted output to *file* instead of standard output.

-s, --silent

> Operate silently; don't print warning messages.

-t *code2*, **--to-code**=*code2*

> Convert input characters to the *code2* encoding.

--usage

> Print a brief usage message showing only the command syntax and then exit.

-V, --version

> Print version information and exit.

--verbose

> Operate verbosely; print progress messages.

---

id

id [*options*] [*username*]

Display information about yourself or another user: user ID, group ID, effective user ID and group ID if relevant, and additional group IDs.

Options

-g, --group

> Print group ID only.

-G, --groups

> Print supplementary groups only.

-n, --name

> With **-u**, **-g**, or **-G**, print user or group name, not number.

-r, --real
> With **-u**, **-g**, or **-G**, print real, not effective, user ID or group ID.

-u, --user
> Print user ID only.

--help
> Print help message and then exit.

--version
> Print version information.

---

identd

in.identd [*options*] [*kernelfile* [*kmemfile*]]

TCP/IP command. Provide the name of the user whose process is running a specified TCP/IP connection. You may specify the kernel and its memory space.

Options

-b   Run standalone; not for use with **inetd**.

-d   Allow debugging requests.

-g*gid*
> Attempt to run in the group *gid*. Useful only with **-b**.

-h   Print help message, then exit.

-i   Run as a daemon, one process per request.

-l   Run using **init**.

-m   Allow multiple requests per session.

-n   Return user IDs instead of usernames.

-o   When queried for the type of operating system, always return OTHER.

-p*port*
> Listen at *port* instead of the default, port 113.

-t*seconds*
> Exit if no new requests have been received before *seconds* seconds have passed. Note that, with **-i** or **-w**, the next new request will result in **identd** being restarted. Default is infinity (never exit).

-u*uid*
> Attempt to run as *uid*. Useful only with **-b**.

-w   Run as a daemon, one process for all requests.

-C*file*
> Read configuration information from *file* instead of */etc/identd. conf*.

-E   Enable DES encryption using the last key from key file */etc/ identd.key*.

-K*n*
> Use a maximum of *n* threads to perform kernel lookups. Default is 8.

-L*facility*
> Use the specified **syslog** *facility* instead of *daemon.key*.

-N Do not provide a username or user ID if the file *.noident* exists in the user's home directory.

-P*file*
> Store the process number for the **identd** daemon in *file*. By default it's */etc/identd.pid*.

-V Print version and exit.

ifconfig

ifconfig [*interface*]
ifconfig [*interface address_family parameters addresses*]

TCP/IP command. Assign an address to a network interface and/or configure network interface parameters. **ifconfig** is typically used at boot time to define the network address of each interface on a machine. It may be used at a later time to redefine an interface's address or other parameters. Without arguments, **ifconfig** displays the current configuration for a network interface. Used with a single *interface* argument, **ifconfig** displays that particular interface's current configuration.

Arguments

interface
> String of the form *name unit*, for example, en0.

address_family
> Since an interface may receive transmissions in differing protocols, each of which may require separate naming schemes, you can specify the *address_family* to change the interpretation of the remaining parameters. You may specify **inet** (for TCP/IP, the default), **ax25** (AX.25 Packet Radio), **ddp** (Appletalk Phase 2), or **ipx** (Novell).

parameters
> The following *parameters* may be set with **ifconfig**:
>
> **add** *address/prefixlength*
> > Add an IPv6 address and prefix length.
>
> **allmulti/-allmulti**
> > Enable/disable sending of incoming frames to the kernel's network layer.
>
> **arp/-arp**
> > Enable/disable use of the Address Resolution Protocol in mapping between network-level addresses and link-level addresses.
>
> **broadcast** [*address*]
> > (**inet** only) Specify address to use to represent broadcasts to the network. Default is the address with a host part of all 1s (i.e., **x.y.z.255** for a class C network).
>
> **debug/-debug**
> > Enable/disable driver-dependent debugging code.

del *address/prefixlength*
Delete an IPv6 address and prefix length.

down
Mark an interface "down" (unresponsive).

hw *class address*
Set the interface's hardware class and address. *class* may be **ether** (Ethernet), **ax25** (AX.25 Packet Radio), or **ARCnet**.

io_addr *addr*
I/O memory start address for device.

irq *addr*
Set the device's interrupt line.

metric *n*
Set routing metric of the interface to *n*. Default is 0.

mem_start *addr*
Shared memory start address for device.

media *type*
Set media type. Common values are **10base2**, **10baseT**, and **AUI**. If **auto** is specified, **ifconfig** will attempt to autosense the media type.

mtu *n*
Set the interface's Maximum Transfer Unit (MTU).

multicast
Set the multicast flag.

netmask *mask*
(**inet** only) Specify how much of the address to reserve for subdividing networks into subnetworks. *mask* can be specified as a single hexadecimal number with a leading **0x**, with a dot notation Internet address, or with a pseudo-network name listed in the network table */etc/networks*.

pointopoint/-pointopoint [*address*]
Enable/disable point-to-point interfacing, so that the connection between the two machines is dedicated.

promisc/-promisc
Enable/disable promiscuous mode. Promiscuous mode allows the device to receive all packets on the network.

txqueuelen *n*
Specify the transmit queue length.

tunnel *addr*
Create an IPv6-in-IPv4 (SIT) device, tunneling to IPv4 address *addr*.

up
Mark an interface "up" (ready to send and receive).

addresses
Each address is either a hostname present in the hostname database (*/etc/hosts*), or an Internet address expressed in the Internet standard dot notation.

imake

imake *options*

C preprocessor (**cpp**) interface to the **make** utility. **imake** ("include make") solves the portability problem of **make** by allowing machine dependencies to be kept in a central set of configuration files, separate from the descriptions of the various items to be built. The targets are contained in the *Imakefile*, a machine-independent description of the targets to be built, written as **cpp** macros. **imake** uses **cpp** to process the configuration files and the *Imakefile*, and to generate machine-specific *Makefiles*, which can then be used by **make**.

One of the configuration files is a template file, a master file for **imake**. This template file (default is *Imake.tmpl*) #**include**s the other configuration files that contain machine dependencies such as variable assignments, site definitions, and **cpp** macros, and directs the order in which the files are processed. Each file affects the interpretation of later files and sections of *Imake.tmpl*. Comments may be included in **imake** configuration files, but the initial # needs to be preceded with an empty C comment:

    /**/#

For more information, see **cpp** and **make**. Also check out the Nutshell Handbook *Software Portability with imake* (O'Reilly).

Options

-e Execute the generated *Makefile*. Default is to leave this to the user.

-f *filename*
　　Name of per-directory input file. Default is *Imakefile*.

-s *filename*
　　Name of **make** description file to be generated. If *filename* is a -, the output is written to stdout. The default is to generate, but not execute, a *Makefile*.

-v Print the **cpp** command line used to generate the *Makefile*.

-C *filename*
　　Use the specified name for the temporary input file for **cpp** instead of the default *Imakefile.c*.

-D*define*
　　Set directory-specific variables. This option is passed directly to **cpp**.

-I*directory*
　　Directory in which **imake** template and configuration files may be found. This option is passed directly to **cpp**.

-T*template*
　　Name of master template file used by **cpp**. This file is usually located in the directory specified with the -**I** option. The default file is *Imake.tmpl*.

-U*define*
　　Unset directory-specific variables. This option is passed directly to **cpp**.

Tools

Following is a list of tools used with **imake**:

makedepend [*options*] *files*

Create header file dependencies in *Makefile*s. **make depend** reads the named input source *files* in sequence and parses them to process **#include**, **#define**, **#undef**, **#ifdef**, **#ifndef**, **#endif**, **#if**, and **#else** directives so that it can tell which **#include** directives would be used in a compilation. **makedepend** determines the dependencies and writes them to the *Makefile*. **make** then knows which object files must be recompiled when a dependency has changed. **makedepend** has the following options:

-- options --

Ignore any unrecognized options following a double hyphen. A second double hyphen terminates this action. Recognized options between the hyphens are processed normally.

-a Append dependencies to any existing ones instead of replacing existing ones.

-f*filename*

Write dependencies to *filename* instead of to *Makefile*.

-m Print a warning when encountering a multiple inclusion.

-o *suffix*

Specify an object file suffix to use instead of the default *.o*.

-p *prefix*

Specify a prefix to prepend to object names. The prefix may be a directory.

-s*string*

Use *string* as delimiter in file, instead of **# DO NOT DELETE THIS LINE — make depend depends on it**.

-v Verbose. List all files included by main source file.

-w *n*

Format output no wider than *n* characters. Default is 78.

-D*name*

Define *name* with the given value (first form) or with value 1 (second form).

-I*dir*

Add directory *dir* to the list of directories searched.

-Y*dir*

Search only *dir* for include files. Ignore standard include directories.

mkdirhier *dir...*

Create directory *dir* and all missing parent directories during file installation operations.

xmkmf [*option*] [*topdir*] [*curdir*]

Bootstrap a *Makefile* from an *Imakefile*. *topdir* specifies the location of the project root directory. *curdir* (usually omitted) is specified as a relative pathname from the top of the build tree to the current directory. The **-a** option is equivalent to the following command sequence:

```
% xmkmf
% make Makefiles
% make includes
% make depend
```

Configuration files

Following is a list of the **imake** configuration files:

Imake.tmpl
> Master template for **imake**. *Imake.tmpl* includes all the other configuration files, plus the *Imakefile* in the current directory.

Imake.params
> Contains definitions that apply across sites and vendors.

Imake.rules
> Contains **cpp** macro definitions that are configured for the current platform. The macro definitions are fed into **imake**, which runs **cpp** to process the macros. Newlines (line continuations) are indicated by the string @@\ (double at sign, backslash).

site.def
> Contains site-specific (as opposed to vendor-specific) information, such as installation directories, what set of programs to build, and any special versions of programs to use during the build. The *site.def* file changes from machine to machine.

Project.tmpl
> File containing X-specific variables.

Library.tmpl
> File containing library rules.

Server.tmpl
> File containing server-specific rules.

.cf The *.cf* files are the vendor-specific *VendorFiles* that live in *Imake.vb*. A *.cf* file contains platform-specific definitions, such as version numbers of the operating system and the compiler and workarounds for missing commands. The definitions in *.cf* files override the defaults, defined in *Imake.params*.

The Imakefile

The *Imakefile* is a per-directory file that indicates targets to be built and installed and rules to be applied. **imake** reads the *Imakefile* and expands the rules into *Makefile* target entries. An *Imakefile* may also include definitions of **make** variables and list the dependencies of the targets. The dependencies are expressed as **cpp** macros, defined in *Imake.rules*. Whenever you change an *Imakefile*, you need to rebuild the *Makefile* and regenerate header file dependencies. For more information on **imake**, see *Software Portability with imake* (O'Reilly).

imapd

imapd

TCP/IP command. The Interactive Mail Access Protocol (IMAP) server daemon. **imapd** is invoked by **inetd** and listens on port 143 for requests from IMAP clients. IMAP allows mail programs to access remote mailboxes as if they were local. IMAP is a richer protocol than POP because it allows a client to retrieve message-level information from a server mailbox instead of the entire mailbox. IMAP can be used for online and offline reading. The popular Pine mail client contains support for IMAP.

inetd

inetd [*options*] [*configuration_file*]

TCP/IP command. The internet services daemon. (On some systems this command is replaced by **xinetd**.) Initialized at bootup, **inetd** creates sockets on behalf of other services and listens to them simultaneously. When it receives an incoming connection request, it spawns the appropriate server and passes it the connection.

The following servers are commonly started by **inetd**: **bootpd, bootpgw, fingerd, ftpd, imapd, rexecd, rlogind, rshd, talkd, telnetd**, and **tftpd**. In addition to launching other services, **inetd** runs a few basic services of its own, including **daytime**, which returns the system's time of day, and **chargen**, which generates a string of characters.

Configuration file

inetd reads information on the services it should support from the specified *configuration_file*, or from the default configuration file */etc/inetd.conf*. **inetd** rereads its configuration file when it receives a hangup signal, SIGHUP. Services may be added, deleted, or modified when the configuration file is reread. Lines beginning with # are treated as comments. Each entry in the configuration file is a single line composed of the following fields:

service
The service name as found in */etc/services*.

type
Socket type, either **stream** for TCP-based services or **dgram** for UDP-based services.

protocol
The transport protocol used by the service. This must be a protocol found in */etc/protocols*. It's usually either **tcp** or **udp**.

wait
For **dgram** sockets, this field specifies whether **inetd** should wait until the service is done to listen on the socket again, or should resume listening right away. The value can be either **wait** or **nowait**. Single-threaded servers like most RPC servers should use **wait**. Multithreaded servers should use **nowait**.

user

> The user ID the process should run under. May be given a name or number. To specify a group name as well, append a dot (.) to the user ID, followed by the group ID.

server

> The full path to the server program to be executed. For **inetd**'s own services, the value of this field is **internal**. Many entries specify the TCP logging tool **tcpd** in this field to wrap the server whose command is given in the next field.

cmdline

> The command-line arguments to be passed to the server, beginning with the name of the server program itself (**argv[0]**). **inetd**'s internal services have no command lines.

Options

-d   Turn on socket-level debugging and print debugging information to stdout.

-q *length*

> Specify the maximum number of pending connections to allow in a socket queue. The default is 128. The minimum value is 8.

Files

/etc/inetd.conf

> Default configuration file.

/var/run/inetd.pid

> **inetd**'s process ID.

---

info

'**info** [*options*] [*topics*]

GNU hypertext reader. Display online documentation previously built from Texinfo input. Info files are arranged in a hierarchy and can contain menus for subtopics. When entered without options, the command displays the top-level info file (usually */usr/local/ info/dir*). When *topics* are specified, find a subtopic by choosing the first *topic* from the menu in the top-level info file, the next *topic* from the new menu specified by the first *topic*, and so on. The initial display can also be controlled by the -**f** and -**n** options. If a specified *topic* has no info file but does have a manpage, **info** displays the manpage; if there is neither, the top-level info file is displayed.

Options

-d *directories,* --**directory** *directories*

> Search *directories*, a colon-separated list, for info files. If this option is not specified, use the **INFOPATH** environment variable or the default directory (usually */usr/local/info*).

--**dribble** *file*

> Store each keystroke in *file*, which can be used in a future session with the --**restore** option to return to this place in **info**.

-f *file,* **--file** *file*
> Display specified info file.

-n *node,* **--node** *node*
> Display specified node in the info file.

-o *file,* **--output** *file*
> Copy output to *file* instead of displaying it at the screen.

--help
> Display brief help.

--restore *file*
> When starting, execute keystrokes in *file.*

--subnodes
> Display subtopics.

--version
> Display version.

--vi-keys
> Use **vi**-like key bindings.

---

init

init [*bootflags*] [*runlevel*]

System administration command. Initialize system.

Boot flags

-a Set the **AUTOBOOT** environment variable to *yes.* The boot loader will do this automatically when booting with the default command line.

-b Boot directly into a single user shell for emergency recovery.

-z *characters*
> The specified *characters* are ignored, but will make the command line take up a bit more room on the stack. *init* uses the extra space to show the curent runlevel when running the **ps** command.

Files

init is the first process run by any Unix machine at boot time. It verifies the integrity of all filesystems and then creates other processes, using **fork** and **exec**, as specified by */etc/inittab.* Which processes may be run are controlled by *runlevel.* All process terminations are recorded in */var/run/utmp* and */var/log/wtmp.* When the runlevel changes, **init** sends SIGTERM and then, after 20 seconds, SIGKILL to all processes that cannot be run in the new runlevel.

Runlevels

The current runlevel may be changed by **telinit**, which is often just a link to **init**. The default runlevels vary from distribution to distribution, but these are standard:

0 Halt the system.

1, s, S
> Single-user mode.

---

6   Reboot the system.

q, Q
> Reread */etc/inittab*.

Check the */etc/inittab* file for runlevels on your system.

---

insmod

insmod [*options*] *file* [*symbol=value* ...]

System administration command. Load the module *file* into the kernel, changing any symbols that are defined on the command line. If the module file is named *file.o* or *file.mod*, the module will be named *file*.

Options

-e *file*, **--persist**=*file*
> Read persistent data from *file*. If module has no persistent data, this option is ignored. If the *file* parameter is the null string "", use default file location.

-f, --force
> Force loading of module, even if problems are encountered.

-h, --help
> Print help message, then exit.

-k, --autoclean
> Mark module to be removed when inactive.

-m, --map
> Print a load map to standard output.

-n, --noload
> Do everything needed to load file, but do not load it. Used to debug command line.

-o *name*, **--name**=*name*
> Name module *name* instead of using the object file's name.

-p, --probe
> Check to see that the module can be successfully loaded.

-q, --quiet
> Don't print warnings or error messages.

-r, --root
> Load modules not owned by the root account. By default these are rejected. This is a security risk.

-s, --syslog
> Send messages to syslog instead of standard output.

-v, --verbose
> Print additional information about progress of **insmod**.

-x, --noexport
> If module does not explicitly export its own symbol table, do not export modules' external symbols.

-y, --noksymoops
> Do not add symbols used for debugging Oops to **ksyms**. These are required if the module has persistent data.

-L, --lock
Set a file lock on the module.

-N, --numeric-only
When checking the module version against the kernel version, only check the numeric part. This is the default for kernel version 2.5 or later.

-O *file*, **--blob**=*file*
Save binary blob of what is loaded into the kernel to *file*.

-P *prefix*, **--prefix**=*prefix*
Specify symbol versions to prefix to module names.

-S, --Kallsyms
Always load modules with **kallsyms** data, even when the kernel does not support it.

-X, --export
If module does not explicitly export its own symbol table, export all modules' external symbols. This is the default behavior.

-V, --version
Print version, then exit.

-Y, --ksymoops
Add symbols used for debugging Oops to **ksyms**. These are required if the module has persistent data.

---

install

install [*options*] [*source*] *destination*

System administration command. Used primarily in Makefiles to update files. **install** copies files into user-specified directories. Similar to **cp**, but attempts to set permission modes, owner, and group. The *source* may be a file or directory, or a list of files and directories. The *destination* should be a single file or directory.

Options

-b, --backup[=*control*]
Back up any existing files. When using the long version of the command, the optional *control* parameter controls the kind of backup. When no control is specified, **install** will attempt to read the control value from the **VERSION_CONTROL** environment variable. Accepted values are:

none, off
Never make backups.

numbered, t
Make numbered backups.

existing, nil
Match existing backups, numbered or simple.

simple, never
Always make simple backups.

-d, --directory
Create any missing directories.

-g *group,* **--group** *group*
> Set group ID of new file to *group* (privileged users only).

--help
> Print help message, then exit.

-m *mode,* **--mode** *mode*
> Set permissions of new file to *mode* (octal or symbolic). By default, the mode is 0755.

-o [*owner*], **--owner**[=*owner*]
> Set ownership to *owner* or, if unspecified, to root (privileged users only).

-p, **--preserve-timestamps**
> Preserve access and modification times on source files and directories.

-s, **--strip**
> Strip symbol tables.

-v, **--verbose**
> Print name of each directory as it is created.

--version
> Print version, then exit.

-C Do not overwrite file when the target exists and is identical to the new file. Preserve original timestamp.

-D Create leading components of destination except the last, then copy source to destination.

-S *suffix,* **--suffix**=*suffix*
> Use *suffix* instead of the default backup suffix, usually **~**.

---

ipchains

ipchains `command` [`options`]

System administration command. Edit IP firewall rules in the 2.2 Linux kernel. A 2.2 Linux kernel compiled with firewall support will examine the headers of all network packets and compare them to matching rules to see what it should do with the packet. A firewall rule consists of some matching criteria and a target, which is a result to be applied if the packet matches the criteria. The rules are organized into chains. You can use these rules to build a firewall or just reject certain kinds of network connections.

Firewall rules are organized into *chains*, ordered checklists that the kernel works through looking for matches. There are three built-in chains: **input, output,** and **forward**. Packets entering the system are tested against the **input** chain; those exiting the system are checked against the **output** chain. If an incoming packet is destined for some other system, it is checked against the **forward** chain. Each of these chains has a default target (a *policy*) in case no match is found. User-defined chains can be created and used as targets for packets, but they have no default policies. If no match can be found in a user-defined chain, the packet is returned to the chain from which it was called and tested against the next rule in that chain.

---

ipchains changes only the rules in the running kernel. When the system is powered off, all those changes are lost. You can use the **ipchains-save** command to make a script you can later run with **ipchains-restore** to restore your firewall settings. Such a script is often called at bootup, and many distributions have an **ipchains** initialization script that uses the output from **ipchains-save**.

Commands

ipchains is always invoked with one of the following commands:

-A *chain rules,* **--append** *chain rules*
 Append new *rules* to *chain*.

-I *chain number rules,* **--insert** *chain number rules*
 Insert *rules* into *chain* at the ordinal position given by *number*.

-D *chain rules,* **--delete** *chain rules*
 Delete *rules* from *chain*. Rules can be specified by their ordinal number in the chain as well as by a general rule description.

-R *chain number rule,* **--replace** *chain number rule*
 Replace a rule in *chain*. The rule to be replaced is specified by its ordinal *number*.

-C *chain rule,* **--check** *chain rules*
 Construct a network packet that matches the given *rule* and check how *chain* will handle it. The rule must describe the source, destination, protocol, and interface of the packet to be constructed.

-L [*chain*], **--list** *$PARAMETER*
 List the rules in *chain*. If no chain is specified, list the rules in all chains.

-ML, **--masquerading --list**
 List masquerading connections.

-MS *tcp tcpfin udp,* **--masquerading --set** *tcp tcpfin udp*
 Set timeout value in seconds for masquerading connections. **-MS** always takes three parameters, specifying the timeout values for TCP sessions, for TCP sessions that have received a FIN packet, and for UDP packets.

-F *chain,* **--flush** *chain*
 Remove all rules from *chain*.

-Z [*chain*], **--zero** [*chain*]
 Reset the packet and byte counters in *chain*. If no chain is specified, all chains will be reset. When used without specifying a chain and combined with the **-L** command, lists the current counter values before they are reset.

-N *chain,* **--new-chain** *chain*
 Create a new *chain*. The chain's name must be unique.

-X [*chain*], **--delete-chain** *chain*
 Delete *chain*. Only user-defined chains can be deleted, and there can be no references to the chain to be deleted. If no argument is given, all user-defined chains will be deleted.

-P *chain target,* **--policy** *chain target*
> Set the policy for a built-in *chain;* the target itself cannot be a chain.

-S *tcp tcpfin udp,* **--set** *tcp tcpfin udp*
> Set masquerade timeout values for TCP sessions, TCP sessions after receiving a FIN packet, and UDP sessions. Timeout values of 0 preserve the previous setting. This option valid only when used with **-M**.

-h [icmp]
> Print a brief help message. If the option **icmp** is given, print a list of valid ICMP types.

-V, --version
> Print version number, then exit.

Targets

A target can be the name of a chain or one of the following special values:

ACCEPT
> Let the packet through.

DENY
> Drop the packet.

MASQ
> Masquerade the packet so it appears that it originated from the current system. Reverse packets from masqueraded connections are unmasqueraded automatically. This is a legal target only for the **forward** chain, or user-defined chains used in forwarding packets. To use this target, the kernel must be compiled with support for IP masquerading.

REDIRECT [*port*]
> Redirect incoming packets to a local *port* on which you are running a transparent proxy program. If the specified port is 0 or is not given, the destination port of the packet is used as the redirection port. **REDIRECT** is a legal target only for the **input** chain or for user-defined chains used in handling incoming packets. The kernel must be compiled with support for transparent proxies.

REJECT
> Drop the packet and send an ICMP message back to the sender indicating that the packet was dropped.

RETURN
> Return to the chain from which this chain was called and check the next rule. If **RETURN** is the target of a rule in a built-in chain, then the built-in chain's default policy is applied.

Rule specification parameters

These options are used to create rules for use with the preceding commands. Rules consist of some matching criteria and usually a target to jump to (**-j**) if the match is made. Many of the parameters for these matching rules can be expressed as a negative with an exclamation point (!) meaning "not." Those rules will match everything except the given parameter.

-p [!] *name,* **--protocol [!]***$PARAMETER*
> Match packets of protocol *name.* The value of *name* can be given as a name or number as found in the file */etc/protocols.* The most common values are **tcp, udp, icmp,** or the special value **all.** The number 0 is equivalent to **all,** and this is the default value when this option is not used.

-s [!] *address[/mask]* **[!]** *[port],* **--source [!]** *address[/mask]* **[!]** *[port]*
> Specifies the source *address* and *port* of the packet that will match this rule. The address may be supplied as a hostname, a network name, or an IP address. The optional *mask* is the netmask to use and may be supplied either in the traditional form (e.g., /255.255.255.0) or in the modern form (e.g., /24). The optional *port* specifies the TCP, UDP, or ICMP type that will match. You may supply a port specification only if you've supplied the **-p** parameter with one of the **tcp, udp** or **icmp** protocols. A colon can be used to indicate an inclusive range of ports or ICMP values to be used (e.g., 20:25 for ports 20 through 25). If the first *port* parameter is missing, the default value is 0. If the second is omitted, the default value is 65535.

-d [!] *address[/mask]* **[!]** *[port],* **--destination [!]** *address[/mask]* *[port]*
> Match packets with the destination *address.* The syntax for this command's parameters is the same as for the **-s** option.

-j *target,* **--jump** *target*
> Jump to a special target or a user-defined chain. If this option is not specified for a rule, matching the rule only increases the rule's counters and the packet is tested against the next rule.

-i [!] *name,* **--interface** *name*
> Match packets from interface *name[+]. name* is the network interface used by your system (e.g., **eth0** or **ppp0**). A + can be used as a wildcard, so **ppp+** would match any interface name beginning with **ppp.**

[!] -f, [!]--fragment *$PARAMETER*
> The rule applies to everything but the first fragment of a fragmented packet.

--source-port *[!] port*
> Match packets from the source *port.* The syntax for specifying ports can be found in the preceding description of the **-s** option.

--destination-port *[!] port*
> Match packets with the destination *port.* The syntax for specifying ports can be found in the preceding description of the **-s** option.

--icmp-type *[!] type*
> Match packets with ICMP type name or number of *type.*

Options

-b, --bidirectional
Put rule in both the input and output chain so that packets will be matched in both directions.

-v, --verbose
Verbose mode.

-n, --numeric
Print all IP address and port numbers in numeric form. By default, names are displayed when possible.

-l, --log
Log information for the matching packet to the system log.

-t *andmask xormask*, **--TOS** *andmask xormask*
Change the Type Of Service field in the packet's header. The TOS field is first ANDed with the 8-bit hexadecimal mask *andmask*, then XORed with the 8-bit hexadecimal mask *xormask*. Rules that would affect the least significant bit (LSB) portion of the TOS field are rejected.

-x, --exact
Expand all numbers in a listing (-L). Display the exact values of the packet and byte counters instead of rounded figures.

[!] -y, --syn
Match only incoming TCP connection requests, those with the SYN bit set and the ACK and FIN bits cleared. This blocks incoming TCP connections but leaves outgoing connections unaffected.

--line-numbers
Used with the **-L** command. Add the line number to the beginning of each rule in a listing indicating its position in the chain.

--no-warnings
Disable all warnings.

---

ipchains-restore   `ipchains-restore` [*options*]

System administration command. Restore firewall rules. **ipchains-restore** takes commands generated by **ipchains-save** and uses them to restore the firewall rules for each chain. Often used by initialization scripts to restore firewall settings on boot.

Options

-f   Force updates of existing chains without asking.

-v   Print rules as they are being restored.

-p   If a nonexisting chain is targeted by a rule, create it.

---

ipchains-save   `ipchains-save` [*chain*] [*option*]

System administration command. Print the IP firewall rules currently stored in the kernel to stdout. If no *chain* is given, all

---

chains will be printed. Output is usually redirected to a file, which can later be used by **ipchains-restore** to restore the firewall.

Option

-v Print out rules to stderr as well as stdout, making them easier to see when redirecting output.

---

ipcrm

ipcrm [*options*]

System administration command. Remove interprocess communication (IPC) message queues, shared memory segments, or semaphore arrays. These may be specified either by numeric identifier or by key, using the following options.

Options

-m *identifier, -M key*
> Remove specified shared memory segment and its associated data structures after the last detach is performed.

-q *identifier, -Q key*
> Remove specified message queue and its associated data structures.

-s *identifier, -S key*
> Remove specified semaphore array and its associated data structures.

---

ipcs

ipcs [*options*]

System administration command. Print report on interprocess communication (IPC) message queues, shared memory segments, and semaphore arrays for which the current process has read access. Options can be used to specify the type of resources to report on and the output format of the report.

Options

Resource specification options:

-a Report on all IPC facilities: shared memory segments, message queues, and semaphore arrays. This is the default.

-m Report on shared memory segments.

-q Report on message queues.

-s Report on semaphore arrays.

Output format options:

-c Print creator and owner user IDs for IPC facilities.

-l Print resource maximum and minimum limits.

-p Print creator and last operation process identifiers.

-t Print attach, detach, and change times for shared memory segments, last operation and change times for semaphore arrays, and send, receive, and change times for message queues.

-u Print summary of current resource usage.

Other options:

-h   Print help message, then exit.

-i *identifier*
> Used in combination with the **-m**, **-q**, or **-s** options. Report only on the resource specified by numeric *identifier*.

---

iptables

iptables *command* [*options*]

System administration command. Configure *netfilter* filtering rules. In the 2.4 kernel, the **ipchains** firewall capabilities are replaced with the *netfilter* kernel module. *netfilter* can be configured to work just like **ipchains**, but it also comes with the module **iptables**, which is similar to **ipchains** but extensible. **iptables** rules consist of some matching criteria and a target, a result to be applied if the packet matches the criteria. The rules are organized into chains. You can use these rules to build a firewall, masquerade your local area network, or just reject certain kinds of network connections.

There are three built-in tables for **iptables**: one for network filtering (**filter**), one for Network Address Translation (**nat**), and the last for specialized packet alterations (**mangle**). Firewall rules are organized into chains, ordered checklists of rules that the kernel works through looking for matches. The **filter** table has three built-in chains: **INPUT**, **OUTPUT**, and **FORWARD**. The **INPUT** and **OUTPUT** chains handle packets originating from or destined for the host system. The **FORWARD** chain handles packets just passing through the host system. The **nat** table also has three built-in chains: **PREROUTING**, **POSTROUTING**, and **OUTPUT**. **mangle** has only two chains: **PREROUTING** and **OUTPUT**.

netfilter checks packets entering the system. After applying any **PREROUTING** rules, it passes them to the **INPUT** chain, or to the **FORWARD** chain if the packet is just passing through. Upon leaving, the system packets are passed to the **OUTPUT** chain and then on to any **POSTROUTING** rules. Each of these chains has a default target (a policy) in case no match is found. User-defined chains can also be created and used as targets for packets but do not have default policies. If no match can be found in a user-defined chain, the packet is returned to the chain from which it was called and tested against the next rule in that chain.

iptables changes only the rules in the running kernel. When the system is powered off, all changes are lost. You can use the **iptables-save** command to make a script you can run with **iptables-restore** to restore your firewall settings. Such a script is often called at bootup. Many distributions have an **iptables** initialization script that uses the output from **iptables-save**.

Commands

iptables is always invoked with one of the following commands:

-A *chain rules*, --**append** *chain rules*
> Append new *rules* to *chain*.

-I *chain number rules,* **--insert** *chain number rules*
> Insert *rules* into *chain* at the ordinal position given by *number*.

-D *chain rules,* **--delete** *chain rules*
> Delete *rules* from *chain*. Rules can be specified by their ordinal number in the chain as well as by a general rule description.

-R *chain number rule,* **--replace** *chain number rule*
> Replace a rule in *chain*. The rule to be replaced is specified by its ordinal *number*.

-C *chain rule,* **--check** *chain rules*
> Check how *chain* will handle a network packet that matches the given *rule*. The rule must describe the source, destination, protocol, and interface of the packet to be constructed.

-L [*chain*], **--list** *$PARAMETER*
> List the rules in *chain*, or all chains if *chain* is not specified.

-F [*chain*], **--flush** *chain*
> Remove all rules from *chain*, or from all chains if *chain* is not specified.

-Z [*chain*], **--zero** [*chain*]
> Zero the packet and byte counters in *chain*. If no chain is specified, all chains will be reset. When used without specifying a chain and combined with the **-L** command, list the current counter values before they are reset.

-N *chain,* **--new-chain** *chain*
> Create a new *chain*. The chain's name must be unique. This is how user-defined chains are created.

-X [*chain*], **--delete-chain** [*chain*]
> Delete the specified user-defined *chain*, or all user-defined chains if *chain* is not specified.

-P *chain target,* **--policy** *chain target*
> Set the default policy for a built-in *chain*; the target itself cannot be a chain.

-E *old-chain new-chain,* **--rename-chain** *old-chain new-chain*
> Rename *old-chain* to *new-chain*.

-h [**icmp**]
> Print a brief help message. If the option **icmp** is given, print a list of valid ICMP types.

Targets

A target may be the name of a chain or one of the following special values:

ACCEPT
> Let the packet through.

DROP
> Drop the packet.

QUEUE
> Send packets to the user space for processing.

RETURN

Stop traversing the current chain and return to the point in the previous chain from which this one was called. If **RETURN** is the target of a rule in a built-in chain, the built-in chain's default policy is applied.

Rule specification parameters

These options are used to create rules for use with the preceding commands. Rules consist of some matching criteria and usually a target to jump to (**-j**) if the match is made. Many of the parameters for these matching rules can be expressed as a negative with an exclamation point (!) meaning "not." Those rules will match everything except the given parameter.

-p [!] *name,* **--protocol** [!]*$PARAMETER*

Match packets of protocol *name.* The value of *name* can be given as a name or number as found in the file */etc/protocols.* The most common values are **tcp, udp, icmp,** or the special value **all.** The number 0 is equivalent to **all,** and this is the default value when this option is not used. If there are extended matching rules associated with the specified protocol, they will be loaded automatically. You need not use the **-m** option to load them.

-s [!] *address[/mask]* **[!]** *[port],* **--source** [!] *address[/mask]* [!] *[port]*

Match packets with the source *address.* The address may be supplied as a hostname, a network name, or an IP address. The optional mask is the netmask to use and may be supplied either in the traditional form (e.g., /255.255.255.0) or in the modern form (e.g., /24).

-d [!] *address[/mask]* **[!]** *[port],* **--destination** [!] *address[/mask]* *[port]*

Match packets from the destination *address.* See the description of **-s** for the syntax of this option.

-j *target,* **--jump** *target*

Jump to a special target or a user-defined chain. If this option is not specified for a rule, matching the rule only increases the rule's counters, and the packet is tested against the next rule.

-i [!] *name[+],* **--in-interface** *name[+]*

Match packets being received from interface *name. name* is the network interface used by your system (e.g., **eth0** or **ppp0**). A + can be used as a wildcard, so **ppp+** would match any interface name beginning with **ppp.**

-o [!] *name[+],* **--out-interface** *name[+]*

Match packets being sent from interface *name.* See the description of **-i** for the syntax for *name.*

[!] -f, [!]--fragment *$PARAMETER*

The rule applies only to the second or further fragments of a fragmented packet.

-c *packets bytes,* **--set-counters** *packets bytes*

Initialize packet and byte counters to the specified values.

Options

-v, --verbose

Verbose mode.

-n, --numeric

Print all IP address and port numbers in numeric form. By default, text names are displayed when possible.

-x, --exact

Expand all numbers in a listing (**-L**). Display the exact value of the packet and byte counters instead of rounded figures.

-m *module*, **--match** *module*

Explicitly load matching rule extensions associated with *module*. See the next section.

-h [**icmp**], **--help** [**icmp**]

Print help message. If **icmp** is specified, a list of valid ICMP type names will be printed. **-h** can also be used with the **-m** option to get help on an extension module.

--line-numbers

Used with the **-L** command. Add the line number to the beginning of each rule in a listing, indicating its position in the chain.

--modprobe=*command*

Use specified *command* to load any necessary kernel modules while adding or inserting rules into a chain.

Match extensions

Several kernel modules come with netfilter to extend matching capabilities of rules. Those associated with particular protocols are loaded automatically when the **-p** option is used to specify the protocol. Others need to be loaded explicitly with the **-m** option.

tcp

Loaded when **-p tcp** is the only protocol specified.

--source-port [**!**] [*port*][*:port*], **--sport** [**!**] [*port*][*:port*]

Match the specified source ports. Using the colon specifies an inclusive range of services to match. If the first port is omitted, 0 is the default. If the second port is omitted, 65535 is the default. You can also use a dash instead of a colon to specify the range.

--destination-port [**!**] [*port*][*:port*], **--dport** [**!**] [*port*][*:port*]

Match the specified destination ports. The syntax is the same as for **--source-port**.

--tcp-flags [**!**] *mask comp*

Match the packets with the TCP flags specified by *mask* and *comp*. *mask* is a comma-separated list of flags that should be examined. *comp* is a comma-separated list of flags that must be set for the rule to match. Valid flags are **SYN, ACK, FIN, RST, URG, PSH, ALL**, and **NONE**.

--tcp-option [**!**] *n*

Match if TCP option is set.

--mss *n*[*:n*]

> Match if TCP SYN or SYN/ACK packets have the speci-
> fied MSS value or fall within the specified range. Use this
> to control the maximum packet size for a connection.

[!] --syn

> Match packets with the SYN bit set and the ACK and FIN
> bits cleared. These are packets that request TCP connec-
> tions; blocking them prevents incoming connections.
> Shorthand for **--tcp-flags SYN,RST,ACK SYN**.

udp

> Loaded when **-p udp** is the only protocol specified.

--source-port [!] [*port*][*:port*], **--sport** [!] [*port*][*:port*]

> Match the specified source ports. The syntax is the same
> as for the **--source-port** option of the TCP extension.

--destination-port [!] [*port*][*:port*], **--dport** [!] [*port*][*:port*]

> Match the specified destination ports. The syntax is
> the same as for the **--source-port** option of the TCP
> extension.

icmp

> Loaded when **-p icmp** is the only protocol specified.

--icmp-type [!] *type*

> Match the specified ICMP *type*. *type* may be a numeric
> ICMP type or one of the ICMP type names shown by the
> command **iptables -p icmp -h**.

mac

> Loaded explicitly with the **-m** option.

--mac-source [!] *address*

> Match the source *address* that transmitted the packet.
> *address* must be given in colon-separated hexbyte nota-
> tion (for example, **--mac-source 00:60:08:91:CC:B7**).

limit

> Loaded explicitly with the **-m** option. The **limit** extensions are
> used to limit the number of packets matched. This is useful
> when combined with the **LOG** target. Rules using this exten-
> sion match until the specified limit is reached.

--limit *rate*

> Match addresses at the given *rate*. *rate* is specified as a
> number with an optional **/second**, **/minute**, **hour**, or **/day**
> suffix. When this option is not set, the default is **3/hour**.

--limit-burst [*number*]

> Set the maximum *number* of packets to match in a burst.
> Once the number has been reached, no more packets are
> matched for this rule until the number has recharged. It
> recharges at the rate set by the **--limit** option. When not
> specified, the default is **5**.

multiport

> Loaded explicitly with the **-m** option. The **multiport** exten-
> sions match sets of source or destination ports. These rules

can be used only in conjunction with **-p tcp** and **-p udp**. Up to 15 ports can be specified in a comma-separated list.

--source-port [*ports*]
> Match the given source *ports*.

--destination-port [*ports*]
> Match the given destination *ports*.

--port [*ports*]
> Match if the packet has the same source and destination port and that port is one of the given *ports*.

mark
> Loaded explicitly with the **-m** option. This module works with the **MARK** extension target.

--mark *value*[*/mask*]
> Match the given unsigned mark value. If a mask is specified, it is logically ANDed with the mark before comparison.

owner
> Loaded explicitly with the **-m** option. The **owner** extensions match the user, group, process, and session IDs of a local packet's creator. This makes sense only as a part of the **OUTPUT** chain.

--uid-owner *userid*
> Match packets created by a process owned by *userid*.

--gid-owner *groupid*
> Match packets created by a process owned by *groupid*.

--pid-owner *processid*
> Match packets created by process ID *processid*.

--sid-owner *sessionid*
> Match packets created by a process in the session *sessionid*.

--cmd-owner *command*
> Match if packet was created by a process with the name *command*.

state
> Loaded explicitly with the **-m** option. This module matches the connection state of a packet.

--state *states*
> Match the packet if it has one of the states in the comma-separated list *states*. Valid states are **INVALID, ESTABLISHED, NEW**, and **RELATED**.

tos
> Loaded explicitly with the **-m** option. This module matches the Type of Service field in a packet's header.

--tos *value*
> Match the packet if it has a TOS of *value*. *value* can be a numeric value or a Type of Service name. **iptables -m tos -h** will give you a list of valid TOS values.

tostate

> Loaded explicitly with the **-m** option. This module matches the connection state of a packet.
>
> **--state** *states*
>
>> Match the packet if it has one of the states in the comma-separated list *states*. Valid states are **INVALID, ESTABLISHED, NEW,** and **RELATED**.

ah

> Loaded explicitly with the **-m** option. This module matches the SPIs in the AH header of IPSec packets.
>
> **--ahspi** [!] *n*[:*n*]
>
>> Match the SPIs in the AH header against the specified value or range of values.

esp

> Loaded explicitly with the **-m** option. This module matches the SPIs in the ESP header of IPSec packets.
>
> **--ahspi** [!] *n*[:*n*]
>
>> Match the SPIs in the ESP header against the specified value or range of values.

length

> Loaded explicitly with the **-m** option. This module matches the length of a packet.
>
> **--length** *n*[:*n*]
>
>> Match if the length of the packet is the same as the specified value or is within the range of values.

ttl

> Loaded explicitly with the **-m** option. This module matches the time-to-live (TTL) field in the IP header.
>
> **--ttl** *n*
>
>> Match if the TTL is the same as the specified value.

Target extensions

Extension targets are optional additional targets supported by separate kernel modules. They have their own associated options.

LOG

> Log the packet's information in the system log.
>
> **--log-level** *level*
>
>> Set the syslog level by name or number (as defined by *syslog.conf*).
>
> **--log-prefix** *prefix*
>
>> Begin each log entry with the string *prefix*. The prefix string may be up to 30 characters long.
>
> **--log-tcp-sequence**
>
>> Log the TCP sequence numbers. This is a security risk if your log is readable by users.

--log-tcp-options
> Log options from the TCP packet header.

--log-ip-options
> Log options from the IP packet header.

MARK
Used to mark packets with an unsigned integer value you can use later with the **mark** matching extension. Valid only with the **mangle** table.

--set-mark *value*
> Mark the packet with *value*.

REJECT
Drop the packet and, if appropriate, send an ICMP message back to the sender indicating the packet was dropped. If the packet was an ICMP error message, an unknown ICMP type, or a nonhead fragment, or if too many ICMP messages have already been sent to this address, no message is sent.

--reject-with *type*
> Send specified ICMP message type. Valid values are **icmp-net-unreachable**, **icmp-host-unreachable**, **icmp-port-unreachable**, or **icmp-proto-unreachable**. If the packet was an ICMP ping packet, *type* may also be **echo-reply**.

TOS
Set the Type of Service field in the IP header. **TOS** is a valid target only for rules in the **mangle** table.

--set-tos *value*
> Set the TOS field to *value*. You can specify this as an 8-bit value or as a TOS name. You can get a list of valid names using **iptables -j TOS -h**.

SNAT
Modify the source address of the packet and all future packets in the current connection. **SNAT** is valid only as a part of the **POSTROUTING** chain in the **nat** table.

--to-source *address*[*-address*][*port-port*]
> Specify the new source address or range of addresses. If a **tcp** or **udp** protocol has been specified with the **-p** option, source ports may also be specified. If none is specified, map the new source to the same port if possible. If not, map ports below 512 to other ports below 512, those between 512 and 1024 to other ports below 1024, and ports above 1024 to other ports above 1024.

DNAT
Modify the destination address of the packet and all future packets in the current connection. **DNAT** is valid only as a part of the **POSTROUTING** chain in the **nat** table.

--to-destination *address*[*-address*][*port-port*]
> Specify the new destination address or range of addresses. The arguments for this option are the same as the **--to-source** argument for the **SNAT** extension target.

MASQUERADE

Masquerade the packet so it appears that it originated from the current system. Reverse packets from masqueraded connections are unmasqueraded automatically. This is a legal target only for chains in the **nat** table that handle incoming packets and should be used only with dynamic IP addresses (like dial-up.) For static addresses use **DNAT**.

--to-ports *port[-port]*

Specify the port or range of ports to use when masquerading. This option is valid only if a **tcp** or **udp** protocol has been specified with the **-p** option. If this option is not used, the masqueraded packet's port will not be changed.

REDIRECT

Redirect the packet to a local *port*. This is useful for creating transparent proxies.

--to-ports *port[-port]*

Specify the port or range of ports on the local system to which the packet should be redirected. This option is valid only if a **tcp** or **udp** protocol has been specified with the **-p** option. If this option is not used, the redirected packet's port will not be changed.

ULOG

Userspace logging. Multicast matching packets though a netlink socket, which is a socket linking kernel space and userspace. One or more userspace processes can subscribe to the multicast groups and receive the packets.

--ulog-nlgroup *n*

Send packet to the specified netlink group (1–32). The default group is 1.

--ulog-prefix *prefix*

Prefix packet messages with the specified prefix of 32 characters or less.

--ulog-cprange *n*

Copy up to *n* bytes of the packet to the netlink socket. The default value, 0, copies an entire packet, regardless of size.

--ulog-qthreshold *n*

Transmit packets when *n* packets have been queued. Default value is 1.

TCPMSS

Alter the MSS value of TCP SYN packets.

--set-mss *n*

Set the MSS value to *n*.

--clamp-mss-to-pmtu

Set the MSS value to the outgoing interface's MTU (maximum transmission unit) minus 40.

iptables-restore   **iptables-restore** [*options*]

System administration command. Restore firewall rules from information provided on standard input. **iptables-restore** takes commands generated by **iptables-save** and uses them to restore the firewall rules for each chain. This is often used by initialization scripts to restore firewall settings on boot.

Options

-c, --counters
> Restore packet and byte counter values.

-n, --noflush
> Don't delete previous table contents.

iptables-save   **iptables-save** [*options*]

System administration command. Print the IP firewall rules currently stored in the kernel to stdout. Output may be redirected to a file that can later be used by **iptables-restore** to restore the firewall.

Options

-c, --counters
> Save packet and byte counter values.

-t *name*, **--table** *name*
> Print data from the specified table only.

isodump   **isodump** *isoimage*

Interactively display the contents of the ISO9660 image *isoimage*. Used to verify the integrity of the directory inside the image. **isodump** displays the first portion of the root directory and waits for commands. The prompt show the extent number (zone) and offset within the extent, and the contents display at the top of the screen.

Commands

+   Search forward for the next instance of the search string.

a   Search backward within the image.

b   Search forward within the image.

f   Prompt for a new search string.

g   Prompt for a new starting block and go there.

q   Exit.

isoinfo   **isoinfo** [*options*]

Display information about ISO9660 images. You can use **isoinfo** to list the contents of an image, extract a file, or generate a **find**-like file list. The **-i** option is required to specify the image to examine.

Options

-d   Print information from the primary volume descriptor (PVD) of the ISO9660 image, including information about Rock Ridge and Joliet extensions if they are present.

-f   Generate output similar to the output of a **find . -print** command. Do not use with **-l**.

-h   Print help information and exit.

-i *isoimage*
> Specify the path for the ISO9660 image to examine.

-j *charset*
> Convert any Joliet filenames to the specified character set.

-J   Extract filename information from any Joliet extensions.

-l   Generate output similar to the output of an **ls -lR** command. Do not use with **-f**.

-N *sector*
> To help examine single-session CD files that are to be written to a multisession CD. Specify the sector number at which the ISO9660 image is to be written when sent to the CD writer.

-p   Display path table information.

-R   Extract permission, filename, and ownership information from any Rock Ridge extensions.

-T *sector*
> To help examine multisession images that have already been burned to a multisession CD. Use the specified sector number as the start of the session to display.

-x *path*
> Extract the file at the specified path to standard output.

---

isosize

isosize [*option*] *iso9660-img-file*

Display the length of an ISO9660 filesystem contained in the specified file. The image file can be a normal file or a block device such as */dev/sr0*. With no options, the length is displayed in bytes. Only one of the two options can be specified.

Options

-d *num*
> Display the size in bytes divided by *num*.

-x   Display the number of blocks and the blocksize (although the output refers to blocks as sectors).

---

isovfy

isovfy *isoimage*

Verify the integrity of the specified ISO9660 image and write the results to standard output.

ispell

`ispell` [*options*] [*files*]

Compare the words of one or more named *files* with the system dictionary. Display unrecognized words at the top of the screen, accompanied by possible correct spellings, and allow editing via a series of commands.

Options

-b   Back up original file in *filename.bak*.

-d *file*
    Search *file* instead of standard dictionary file.

-m   Suggest different root/affix combinations.

-n   Expect **nroff** or **troff** input file.

-p *file*
    Search *file* instead of personal dictionary file.

-t   Expect T_EX or L^AT_EX input file.

-w *chars*
    Consider *chars* to be legal, in addition to a–z and A–Z.

-x   Do not back up original file.

-B   Search for missing blanks (resulting in concatenated words) in addition to ordinary misspellings.

-C   Do not produce error messages in response to concatenated words.

-L *number*
    Show *number* lines of context.

-M   List interactive commands at bottom of screen.

-N   Suppress printing of interactive commands.

-P   Do not attempt to suggest more root/affix combinations.

-S   Sort suggested replacements by likelihood that they are correct.

-T *type*
    Expect all files to be formatted by *type*.

-W *n*
    Never consider words that are *n* characters or fewer to be misspelled.

-V   Use hat notation (^L) to display control characters, and **M-** to display characters with the high bit set.

Interactive commands

?   Display help screen.

space
    Accept the word in this instance.

number
    Replace with suggested word that corresponds to *number*.

!*command*
> Invoke shell and execute *command* in it. Prompt before exiting.

a
> Accept word as correctly spelled, but do not add it to personal dictionary.

i
> Accept word and add it (with any current capitalization) to personal dictionary.

l
> Search system dictionary for words.

q
> Exit without saving.

r
> Replace word.

u
> Accept word and add lowercase version of it to personal dictionary.

x
> Skip to the next file, saving changes.

^L
> Redraw screen.

^Z
> Suspend **ispell**.

join

join [*options*] *file1 file2*

Join lines of two sorted files by matching on a common field. If either *file1* or *file2* is -, read from standard input.

Options

-a *filenum*
> Print a line for each unpairable line in file *filenum*, in addition to the normal output.

-e *string*
> Replace missing input fields with *string*.

-i, --ignore-case
> Ignore case differences when comparing keys.

-1 *fieldnum1*
> The join field in *file1* is *fieldnum1*. Default is the first field.

-2 *fieldnum2*
> The join field in *file2* is *fieldnum2*. Default is the first field.

-o *fieldlist*
> Order the output fields according to *fieldlist*, where each entry in the list is in the form *filenum.fieldnum*. Entries are separated by commas or blanks.

-t *char*
> Specifies the field-separator character (default is whitespace).

-v *filenum*
> Print only unpairable lines from file *filenum*.

--help
> Print help message and then exit.

--version
> Print the version number and then exit.

kbd_mode

kbd_mode [*option*]

Print or set the current keyboard mode, which may be **RAW**, **MEDIUMRAW, XLATE,** or **UNICODE**.

Options

-a Set mode to **XLATE** (ASCII mode).

-k Set mode to **MEDIUMRAW** (keycode mode).

-s Set mode to **RAW** (scancode mode).

-u Set mode to **UNICODE** (UTF-8 mode).

kbdrate

kbdrate [*options*]

System administration command. Control the rate at which the keyboard repeats characters, as well as its delay time. Using this command without options sets a repeat rate of 10.9 characters per second; the default delay is 250 milliseconds. When Linux boots, however, it sets the keyboard rate to 30 characters per second.

Options

-s Suppress printing of messages.

-r *rate*

Specify the repeat rate, which must be one of the following numbers (all in characters per second): 2.0, 2.1, 2.3, 2.5, 2.7, 3.0, 3.3, 3.7, 4.0, 4.3, 4.6, 5.0, 5.5, 6.0, 6.7, 7.5, 8.0, 8.6, 9.2, 10.0, 10.9, 12.0, 13.3, 15.0, 16.0, 17.1, 18.5, 20.0, 21.8, 24.0, 26.7, or 30.0.

-d *delay*

Specify the delay, which must be one of the following (in milliseconds): 250, 500, 750, or 1000.

kernelversion

kernelversion

This command tells you what version of the Linux kernel you are using. It is also used by *modultils* and the */etc/modules.conf* file to determine where to put kernel modules. It accepts no arguments or options.

kill

kill [*options*] [*pids* | *commands*]

Send a signal to terminate one or more process IDs. You must own the process or be a privileged user. If no signal is specified, TERM is sent.

This entry describes the **/bin/kill** command, which offers several powerful features. There are also built-in shell commands of the same name; the **bash** version is described in Chapter 7 and the **tcsh** version in Chapter 8.

In particular, **/bin/kill** allows you to specify a command name, such as **gcc** or **xpdf**, instead of a process ID (PID). All processes running that command with the same UID as the process issuing **/bin/kill** will be sent the signal.

If **/bin/kill** is issued with a *pid* of 0, it sends the signal to all processes of its own process group. If **/bin/kill** is issued with a *pid* of −1, it sends the signal to all processes except process 1 (the system's *init* process).

Options

-a   Kill all processes of the given name (if privileges allow), not just processes with the same UID. To use this option, specify the full path (e.g., **/bin/kill -a gcc**).

-l   List all signals.

-p   Print the process ID of the named process, but don't send it a signal. To use this option, specify the full path (e.g., **/bin/kill -p**).

-signal

The signal number (from */usr/include/sys/signal.h*) or name (from **kill -l**). With a signal number of 9 (HUP), the kill cannot be caught by the process; use this to kill a process that a plain **kill** doesn't terminate. The default is TERM.

---

killall

`killall` [*options*] *names*

Kill processes by command name. If more than one process is running the specified command, kill all of them. Treat command names that contain a **/** as files; kill all processes that are executing that file.

Options

-signal

Send *signal* to process (default is TERM). *signal* may be a name or a number.

-e   Require an exact match to kill very long names (i.e., longer than 15 characters). Normally, **killall** kills everything that matches within the first 15 characters. With **-e**, such entries are skipped. (Use **-v** to print a message for each skipped entry.)

-g   Kill the process group to which the process belongs.

-i   Prompt for confirmation before killing processes.

-l   List known signal names.

-q   Quiet; do not complain of processes not killed.

-v   Verbose; after killing process, report success and process ID.

-V   Print version information.

-w   Wait for all killed processes to die. Note that **killall** may wait forever if the signal was ignored or had no effect, or if the process stays in zombie state.

killall5

killall5

The System V equivalent of **killall**, this command kills all processes except those on which it depends.

klogd

klogd [*options*]

System administration command. Control which kernel messages are displayed on the console, prioritize all messages, and log them through **syslogd**. On many operating systems, **syslogd** performs all the work of **klogd**, but on Linux the features are separated. Kernel messages are gleaned from the */proc* filesystem and from system calls to **syslogd**. By default, no messages appear on the console. Messages are sorted into eight levels, 0–7, and the level number is prepended to each message.

Priority levels

0   Emergency situation (**KERN_EMERG**).

1   A crucial error has occurred (**KERN_ALERT**).

2   A serious error has occurred (**KERN_CRIT**).

3   An error has occurred (**KERN_ERR**).

4   A warning message (**KERN_WARNING**).

5   The situation is normal but should be checked (**KERN_NOTICE**).

6   Information only (**KERN_INFO**).

7   Debugging messages (**KERN_DEBUG**).

Options

-c *level*
   Print all messages of a higher priority (lower number) than *level* to the console.

-d   Debugging mode.

-f *file*
   Print all messages to *file*; suppress normal logging.

-i   Signal executing daemon to reload kernel module symbols.

-k *file*
   Use *file* as source of kernel symbols.

-n   Avoid auto-backgrounding. This is needed when **klogd** is started from **init**.

-o   One-shot mode. Prioritize and log all current messages, then immediately exit.

-p   Reload kernel module symbol information whenever an Oops string is detected.

-s   Suppress reading of messages from the */proc* filesystem. Read from kernel message buffers instead.

-v   Print version, then exit.

-x   Don't translate instruction pointers (EIP). **klogd** will not read
the *System.map* file.

-I   Signal executing daemon to reload both static kernel symbols
and kernel module symbols.

-2   Print two lines for each symbol, one showing the symbol and
the other showing its numerical value (address).

Files
/usr/include/linux/kernel.h, */usr/include/sys/syslog.h*
Sources for definitions of each logging level.

/proc/kmsg
A file examined by **klogd** for messages.

/var/run/klogd.pid
klogd's process ID.

---

ksyms   **ksyms** [*options*]

System administration command. Print a list of all exported kernel
symbols (name, address, and defining module, if applicable).

Options
-a, --all
Include symbols from unloaded modules.

-h, --noheader
Suppress header message.

-m, --info
Include starting address and size. Useful only for symbols in
loaded modules.

-H, --help
Print help message, then exit.

-V, --version
Print version, then exit.

File
/proc/ksyms
Another source of the same information.

---

last   **last** [*options*] [*username*] [*ttynumber*]

Display a list of the most recent logins, taken from the file */var/log/
wtmp* by default. If you specify a tty number or username, the
output will display only the logins for that user or terminal.

Options
-n *number, -number*
Choose how many lines of logins to display. Thus, **last -7** or
last -n 7 displays seven lines.

-R   Do not show the hostname from which logins originated.

-a   Display the hostname from which logins originated.

-d Display both IP address and hostname.

-f *filename*
> Get the list of logins from a file you choose. The default source is */var/log/wtmp*.

-i Display IP address and hostname. Display the IP address in the numbers-and-dots notation.

-o Read an old-style (libc5 application) *wtmp* file. Not likely to be useful on newer systems.

-x Display shutdown messages and runlevel messages.

---

lastb

lastb [*options*] [*username*] [*ttynumber*]

Display a list of recent bad login attempts (from the */var/log/btmp* file). Accepts the same option flags and arguments as *last*.

---

lastlog

lastlog [*options*]

System administration command. Print the last login times for system accounts. Login information is read from the file */var/log/lastlog*.

Options

-t*n*
> Print only logins more recent than *n* days ago.

-u*name*
> Print only login information for user *name*.

---

ld

ld [*options*] *objfiles*

Combine several *objfiles*, in the specified order, into a single executable object module (*a.out* by default). **ld** is the link editor and is often invoked automatically by compiler commands. **ld** accepts many options, the most common of which are listed here.

Options

-b *format*, **--format**=*format*
> If **ld** is configured to accept more than one kind of object file, this command can be used to specify the input format. *format* should be a GNU Binary File Descriptor (BFD) as described in the BFD library. Use **objdump -i** to list available formats.

-call_shared
> Link with dynamic libraries.

-d, -dc, -dp
> Force the assignment of space to common symbols.

-defsym *symbol*=*expression*
> Create the global *symbol* with the value *expression*.

-demangle[=*style*]
> Force demangling of symbol names. Optionally set the demangling style. Turn off demangling with **-nodemangle**.

-e *symbol*
> Set *symbol* as the address of the output file's entry point.

-f *name*
> Set the **DT_AUXILIARY** field of ELF shared object to *name*.

-fini *name*
> Set the **DT_FINI** field of ELF shared object to the address of function *name*. The default function is **_fini**.

-h *name*
> Set the **DT_SONAME** field of ELF shared object to *name*.

--help
> Print help message, then exit.

-i   Produce a linkable output file; attempt to set its magic number to OMAGIC.

-init *name*
> Set the **DT_INIT** field of ELF shared object to the address of function *name*. The default function is **_init**.

-l*arch*, **--library**=*archive*
> Include the archive file *arch* in the list of files to link.

-m *linker*
> Emulate *linker*. List supported emulations with the -V option.

-n   Make text read-only; attempt to set NMAGIC.

-o *output*
> Place output in *output*, instead of *a.out*.

-oformat *format*
> Specify output format.

-q   Retain relocation sections and contents in linked executables.

-r   Produce a linkable output file; attempt to set its magic number to OMAGIC.

-rpath *dir*
> Add directory *dir* to the runtime library search path. Ignore additional paths normally read from the **LD_RUN_PATH** environment variable.

-rpath-link *dirs*
> Specify path to search for shared libraries required by another shared library. The *dirs* argument can be a single directory, or multiple directories separated by colons. This overrides search paths specified in shared libraries themselves.

-s   Do not include any symbol information in output.

-shared
> Create a shared library.

-static
> Do not link with shared libraries.

-sort-common
> Do not sort global common symbols by size.

-t   Print each input file's name as it is processed.

--target-help
> Print target-specific options, then exit.

-u *symbol*
> Force *symbol* to be undefined.

-v, --version
> Show version number.

--verbose
> Print information about **ld**; print the names of input files while attempting to open them.

-warn-common
> Warn when encountering common symbols combined with other constructs.

-warn-once
> Provide only one warning per undefined symbol.

-x With **-s** or **-S**, delete all local symbols. These generally begin with **L**.

-z *keyword*
> Mark the object for special behavior specified by *keyword*. **ld** recognizes the following keywords:

> **combreloc**
>> Object combines and sorts multiple relocation sections for dynamic symbol lookup caching.

> **defs**
>> Disallow undefined symbols.

> **initfirst**
>> Initialize object first at runtime.

> **interpose**
>> Interpose object's symbol table before all but the primary executable's symbol table.

> **loadfltr**
>> Process object's filter immediately at runtime.

> **multidefs**
>> Allow multiple definitions of a single symbol. Use the first definition.

> **nocombreloc**
>> Disable combining multiple relocation sections.

> **nocopyreloc**
>> Disable copy relocation.

> **nodefaultlib**
>> Ignore default library search path when seeking dependencies for object.

> **nodelete**
>> Do not unload object at runtime.

> **nodlopen**
>> Object is not available to **dlopen**.

nodump
> Object cannot be dumped by **dldump**.

now
> Non-lazy runtime binding.

origin
> Object may contain $ORIGIN.

-E, --export-dynamic
> Add all symbols to dynamic symbol table, not just those refer-
> enced by linked objects.

-EB
> Link big-endian objects.

-EL
> Link little-endian objects.

-F *name*
> Set **DT_FILTER** field of ELF shared object to *name*.

-L*dir*, **--library-path**=*dir*
> Search directory *dir* before standard search directories (this
> option must precede the **-l** option that searches that directory).

-M   Display a link map on standard output.

-Map *file*
> Print a link map to *file*.

-N   Allow reading of and writing to both data and text. Mark
> ouput if it supports Unix magic numbers. Do not page-align
> data.

-O *level*
> Optimize. *level* should be 1, 2, 3, or 0. The default is 1. 0 turns
> off optimization; 3 optimizes the most.

-R *file*
> Obtain symbol names and addresses from *file*, but suppress
> relocation of *file* and its inclusion in output.

-S   Do not include debugger symbol information in output.

-T *file*
> Execute script *file* instead of the default linker script.

-Tbss *address*
> Begin bss segment of output at *address*.

-Tdata *address*
> Begin data segment of output at *address*.

-Ttext *address*
> Begin text segment of output at *address*.

-Ur
> Synonymous with **-r** except when linking C++ programs,
> where it resolves constructor references.

-X   With **-s** or **-S**, delete local symbols beginning with **L**.

-V   Show version number and emulation linkers for **-m** option.

ldconfig

`ldconfig [options] directories`

System administration command. Examine the libraries in the given *directories*, */etc/ld.so.conf*, */usr/lib*, and */lib*; update links and cache where necessary. Usually run in startup files or after the installation of new shared libraries.

Options

-D   Debug mode. Suppress all normal operations.

-l   Library mode. Expect libraries as arguments, not directories. Manually link specified libraries.

-n   Suppress examination of */usr/lib* and */lib* and reading of */etc/ld. so.conf*; do not cache.

-N   Do not cache; only link.

-p   Print all directories and candidate libraries in the cache. Used without arguments.

-v   Verbose mode. Include version number, and announce each directory as it is scanned and links as they are created.

-X   Do not link; only rebuild cache.

Files

/lib/ld.so
> Linker and loader.

/etc/ld.so.conf
> List of directories that contain libraries.

/etc/ld.so.cache
> List of the libraries found in those libraries mentioned in */etc/ ld.so.conf*.

ldd

`ldd [options] programs`

Display a list of the shared libraries each *program* requires.

Options

-d, --data-relocs
> Process data relocations. Report missing objects.

-r, --function-relocs
> Process relocations for both data objects and functions. Report any that are missing.

-v, --verbose
> Display **ldd**'s version.

--help
> Print help message, then exit.

--version
> Display the linker's version, then exit.

less   less [*options*] [*filename*]

less is a program for paging through files or other output. It was written in reaction to the perceived primitiveness of **more** (hence its name). Some commands may be preceded by a number.

Options

-[z]*num*, **--window=***num*
> Set number of lines to scroll to *num*. Default is one screenful. A negative *num* sets the number to *num* lines less than the current number.

+[+]*command*
> Run *command* on startup. If *command* is a number, jump to that line. The option ++ applies this command to each file in the command-line list.

-?, --help
> Print help screen. Ignore all other options; do not page through file.

-a, --search-screen
> When searching, begin after last line displayed. (Default is to search from second line displayed.)

-b*buffers*, **-buffers=***buffers*
> Use *buffers* buffers for each file (default is 10). Buffers are 1 KB in size.

-c, --clear-screen
> Redraw screen from top, not bottom.

-d, --dumb
> Suppress dumb-terminal error messages.

-e, --quit-at-eof
> Automatically exit after reaching EOF twice.

-f, --force
> Force opening of directories and devices; do not print warning when opening binaries.

-g, --hilite-search
> Highlight only string found by past search command, not all matching strings.

-h*num*, **--max-back-scroll=***num*
> Never scroll backward more than *num* lines at once.

-i, --ignore-case
> Make searches case-insensitive, unless the search string contains uppercase letters.

-j*num*, **--jump-target=***num*
> Position target line on line *num* of screen. Target line can be the result of a search or a jump. Count lines beginning from 1 (top line). A negative *num* is counted back from bottom of screen.

-k*file*, **--lesskey-file=***file*
Read *file* to define special key bindings.

-m, **--long-prompt**
Display **more**-like prompt, including percent of file read.

-n, **--line-numbers**
Do not calculate line numbers. Affects **-m** and **-M** options and = and **v** commands (disables passing of line number to editor).

-o*file*, **--log-file=***file*
When input is from a pipe, copy output to *file* as well as to screen. (Prompt for overwrite authority if *file* exists.)

-p*pattern*, **--pattern=***pattern*
At startup, search for first occurrence of *pattern*.

-q, **--quiet**, **--silent**
Disable ringing of bell on attempts to scroll past EOF or before beginning of file. Attempt to use visual bell instead.

-r, **--raw-control-chars**
Display "raw" control characters instead of using ^{x} notation. This sometimes leads to display problems, which might be fixed by using **-R** instead.

-s, **--squeeze-blank-lines**
Print successive blank lines as one line.

-t*tag*, **--tag=***tag*
Edit file containing *tag*. Consult *./tags* (constructed by **ctags**).

-u, **--underline-special**
Treat backspaces and carriage returns as printable input.

-w, **--hilite-unread**
Show the line to which a movement command has skipped, phrases displayed by a search command, or the first unread line during a normal scroll by highlighting text in reverse video.

-x*n*, **--tabs=***n*
Set tab stops to every *n* characters. Default is 8.

-y*n*, **--max-forw-scroll=***n*
Never scroll forward more than *n* lines at once.

-B, **--auto-buffers**
Do not automatically allocate buffers for data read from a pipe. If **-b** specifies a number of buffers, allocate that many. If necessary, allow information from previous screens to be lost.

-C, **-CLEAR-SCREEN**
Redraw screen by clearing it and then redrawing from top.

-E, **--QUIT-AT-EOF**
Automatically exit after reaching EOF once.

-F, **--quit-if-one-screen**
Exit without displaying anything if first file can fit on a single screen.

-G, --HILITE-SEARCH
Never highlight matching search strings.

-I, --IGNORE-CASE
Make searches case-insensitive, even when the search string contains uppercase letters.

-J, --status-column
Used with **-w** or **-W**, highlight a single column on the left edge of the screen instead of the whole text of an unread line.

-K*charset*
Use the specified *charset*.

-M Prompt more verbosely than with **-m**, including percentage, line number, and total lines.

-N, --LINE-NUMBERS
Print line number before each line.

-O*file*, **--LOG-FILE=***file*
Similar to **-o**, but do not prompt when overwriting file.

-P[mM=]*prompt*
Set the prompt displayed by **less** at the bottom of each screen to *prompt*. The **m** sets the prompt invoked by the **-m** option, the **M** sets the prompt invoked by the **-M** option, and the **=** sets the prompt invoked by the **=** command. Special characters (described in the manpage for **less**), can be used to print statistics and other information in these prompts.

-Q, --QUIET, --SILENT
Never ring terminal bell.

-R, --RAW-CONTROL-CHARS
Like **r**, but adjust screen to account for presence of control characters.

-S, --chop-long-lines
Cut, do not fold, long lines.

-T*file*, **--tag-file=***file*
With the **-t** option or **:t** command, read *file* instead of *./tags*.

-U, --UNDERLINE-SPECIAL
Treat backspaces and carriage returns as control characters.

-V, --version
Display version and exit.

-W, --HILITE-UNREAD
Show phrases displayed by a search command, or the first unread line of any forward movement that is more than one line, by highlighting text in reverse video.

-X, --no-init
Do not send initialization and deinitialization strings from termcap to terminal.

Commands

Many commands can be preceded by a numeric argument, referred to as *number* in the command descriptions.

SPACE, ^V, f, ^F
> Scroll forward the default number of lines (usually one windowful).

z   Similar to **SPACE**, but allows the number of lines to be specified, in which case it resets the default to that number.

RETURN, ^N, e, ^E, j, ^J
> Scroll forward. Default is one line. Display all lines, even if the default is more lines than the screen size.

d, ^D
> Scroll forward. Default is one-half the screen size. The number of lines may be specified, in which case the default is reset.

b, ^B, ESC-v
> Scroll backward. Default is one windowful.

w   Like **b**, but allows the number of lines to be specified, in which case it resets the default to that number.

y, ^Y, ^P, k, ^K
> Scroll backward. Default is one line. Display all lines, even if the default is more lines than the screen size.

u, ^U
> Scroll backward. Default is one-half the screen size. The number of lines may be specified, in which case the default is reset.

r, ^R, ^L
> Redraw screen.

R   Like **r**, but discard buffered input.

F   Scroll forward. When an EOF is reached, continue trying to find more output, behaving similarly to **tail -f**.

g, <, ESC-<
> Skip to a line. Default is 1.

G, >, ESC->
> Skip to a line. Default is the last one.

p, %
> Skip to a position *number* percent of the way into the file.

{   If the top line on the screen includes a {, find its matching }. If the top line contains multiple {s, use *number* to determine which one to use in finding a match.

}   If the bottom line on the screen includes a }, find its matching {. If the bottom line contains multiple }s, use *number* to determine which one to use in finding a match.

(If the top line on the screen includes a (, find its matching). If the top line contains multiple (s, use *number* to determine which one to use in finding a match.

)   If the bottom line on the screen includes a), find its matching
    (. If the bottom line contains multiple)s, use *number* to deter-
    mine which one to use in finding a match.

[If the top line on the screen includes a [, find its matching]. If
    the top line contains multiple [s, use *number* to determine
    which one to use in finding a match.

]   If the bottom line on the screen includes a], find its matching
    [. If the bottom line contains multiple]s, use *number* to deter-
    mine which one to use in finding a match.

ESC-^F
    Behave like { but prompt for two characters, which it substi-
    tutes for { and } in its search.

ESC-^B
    Behave like } but prompt for two characters, which it substi-
    tutes for { and } in its search.

m   Prompt for a lowercase letter and then use that letter to mark
    the current position.

'   Prompt for a lowercase letter and then go to the position
    marked by that letter. There are some special characters:

    ^   Beginning of file.

    $ End of file.

^X^X
    Same as '.

/pattern
    Find next occurrence of *pattern*, starting at second line
    displayed. Some special characters can be entered before
    pattern:

    !   Find lines that do not contain *pattern*.

    *   If current file does not contain *pattern*, continue through
        the rest of the files in the command-line list.

    @   Search from the first line in the first file specified on the
        command line, no matter what the screen currently
        displays.

?pattern
    Search backward, beginning at the line before the top line.
    Treats !, *, and @ as special characters when they begin
    pattern, as / does.

ESC-/*pattern*
    Same as /*.

ESC-?*pattern*
    Same as ?*.

n   Repeat last *pattern* search.

N   Repeat last *pattern* search in the reverse direction.

ESC-n

Repeat previous search command but as though it were prefaced by *.

ESC-N

Repeat previous search command but as though it were prefaced by * and in the reverse direction.

ESC-u

Toggle search highlighting.

:e [*filename*]

Read in *filename* and insert it into the command-line list of filenames. Without *filename*, reread the current file. *filename* may contain special characters:

%   Name of current file

Name of previous file

^X^V, E

Same as **:e**.

:n   Read in next file in command-line list.

:p   Read in previous file in command-line list.

:x   Read in first file in command-line list.

:f, =, ^G

Print filename, position in command-line list, line number on top of window, total lines, byte number, and total bytes.

-   Expects to be followed by a command-line option letter. Toggle the value of that option or, if appropriate, prompt for its new value.

-+   Expects to be followed by a command-line option letter. Reset that option to its default.

--   Expects to be followed by a command-line option letter. Reset that option to the opposite of its default, where the opposite can be determined.

_   Expects to be followed by a command-line option letter. Display that option's current setting.

+*command*

Execute *command* each time a new file is read in.

q, :q, :Q, ZZ

Exit.

v   Not valid for all versions. Invoke editor specified by **$VISUAL** or **$EDITOR,** or **vi** if neither is set.

! [*command*]

Not valid for all versions. Invoke **$SHELL** or **sh**. If *command* is given, run it and then exit. Special characters:

%   Name of current file.

Name of previous file.

!!   Last shell command.

| *mark-letter* **command**

> Not valid for all versions. Pipe fragment of file (from first line on screen to *mark-letter*) to *command*. *mark-letter* may also be:

> ^   Beginning of file.

> $ End of file.

> **., newline**
>> Current screen is piped.

Prompts

The prompt interprets certain sequences specially. Those beginning with **%** are always evaluated. Those beginning with **?** are evaluated if certain conditions are true. Some prompts determine the position of particular lines on the screen. These sequences require that a method of determining that line be specified. See the **-P** option and the manpage for more information.

---

lesskey

lesskey [**-o** *output-file* | **--output**=*output-file*] [*input-file*]

Configure keybindings for the **less** command using a configuration file. The input file defaults to *~/.lesskey* and the output file to *~/.less* unless you specify otherwise.

Configuration file format

The configuration file for **lesskey** has one to three sections. These are marked by a line containing a # symbol and the name of the section: **#command**, **#line-edit**, and **#env**.

The #command section

> The command section determines the keys used for actions within **less**. Each line should contain the key or key combination you wish to define, a space or tab, and the name of the action to perform. You may also add an extra string at the end, which will be performed at the end of the first action.

> Keys you define should be entered as you plan to type them, with the exception of the caret (^), space, tab, and backslash (\) characters, which should be preceded by a backslash. In addition, the following special keys are represented by escape sequences that begin with a backslash:

>> Backspace: \b
>> Escape: \e
>> Newline: \n
>> Return: \r
>> Tab: \t
>> Up arrow: \ku
>> Down arrow: \kd
>> Right arrow: \kr
>> Left arrow: \kl
>> Page up: \kU
>> Page down: \kD
>> Home: \kh

End: \ke

Delete: \kx

The actions that can be defined are:

invalid (creates error)
noaction
forw-line
back-line
forw-line-force
forw-scroll
back-scroll
forw-screen
back-screen
forw-window
back-window
forw-screen-force
forw-forever
repaint-flush
repaint
undo-hilite
goto-line
percent
left-scroll
right-scroll
forw-bracket
back-bracket
goto-end
status
forw-search
back-search
repeat-search
repeat-search-all
set-mark
goto-mark
examine
next-file
index-file
prev-file
toggle-option
display-option
pipe
visual
shell
firstcmd
help
version (display version)
digit (display number)
quit

The #line-edit section

The line editing section lets you choose keys for the line-editing capabilities of **less** in a similar manner to the

#**command** section, although without the "extra" string after the command. The line editing actions that can be defined are:

forw-complete
back-complete
expand
literal
right
left
word-left
word-right
insert
delete
word-delete
word-backspace
home
end
up
down

The #env section

The third section, like the second, is optional, and you can use it to override environment variables that affect **less**. Each line consists of a variable, the equals sign (=), and the value to which you wish to set the variable. The most important ones are **LESS**, which allows you to select additional flags to pass to **less** when you run it, and **LESSCHARSET**, which lets you choose a character set. Check the **less** manpage for a complete list of environment variables that affect the program.

---

lftp

lftp [*options*] [*url*]

File transfer program with more features than **ftp**. The **lftp** command allows FTP and HTTP protocol transfers, plus other protocols including FISH (SSH based), FTPS, and HTTPS. It uses a shell-like command interface and offers job control in a manner similar to **bash**. **lftp** has two important reliability features: it resumes failed or interrupted transactions, and it goes into the background automatically if it is quit in the middle of a file transfer.

Options

-d   Run in debug mode.

-e *commands*
    Start, execute the specified commands, and then wait for further instructions.

-p *portnumber*
    Connect to the specified port number.

-u *user*[,*pass*]
    Login to the server with the username (and, optionally, password) you specify.

-f *scriptfile*

Run the specified script file of **lftp** commands, then exit.

-c *commands*

Run the commands specified, then exit.

Commands

The **lftp** commands are similar to those for **ftp**. However, **lftp** lacks or uses different mechanisms for a number of commands, including **$**, **ascii**, **binary**, **case**, and **macdef**. It also adds the following:

alias [*name* [*value*]]

Create an alias for a command. For example, you could set *dir* to be an alias for **ls -lf**.

anon

Set the username to anonymous. This is the default username.

at

Execute a command at a given time, as with the **at** command in an actual shell.

bookmark [*arguments*]

The **lftp** bookmark command used with the following arguments will add, delete, edit, import, or list bookmarks, respectively:

- **add** *name url*
- **del** *name*
- **edit**
- **import** *type*
- **list**

cache

Work with the local memory cache. This command should be followed by the arguments:

stat

Display the status for the cache.

on|off

Turn caching on or off.

flush

Empty the cache.

size *n*

Set the maximum size for the cache. Setting it to -1 means unlimited.

expire *nu*

Set the cache to expire after *n* units of time. You can set the unit to seconds (**s**), minutes (**m**), hours (**h**), or days (**d**). For example, for a cache that expires after an hour, use the syntax **cache expire 1h**.

close

> Where the **ftp** version of this command just stops all sessions, this version closes idle connections with the current server. If you have connections to multiple servers and wish to close all idle connections, add the -**a** flag.

command *cmd args*

> Execute the specified **lftp** command, with the specified arguments, ignoring any aliases created with the **alias** command.

mirror [*options*] [*remotedir* [*localdir*]]

> Copy a directory exactly. The **mirror** command accepts the following arguments:

> **-c, --continue**
>> If mirroring was interrupted, resume it.

> **-e, --delete**
>> Delete local files that are not present at the remote site.

> **-s, --allow-suid**
>> Keep the suid/sgid bits as set on the remote site.

> **-n, --only-newer**
>> Get only those files from the remote site that have more recent dates than the files on the local system. Cannot be used with the -**c** argument.

> **-r, --no-recursion**
>> Do not get any subdirectories.

> **--no-umask**
>> Do not use umask when getting file modes. See **umask** for more information about file modes.

> **-R, --reverse**
>> Mirror files from the local system to the remote system. With this argument, make sure that you specify the local directory first and the remote directory second. If you do not specify both directories, the second is assumed to be the same as the first. If you choose neither, the operation occurs in the current working directories.

> **-L, --dereference**
>> When mirroring a link, download the file the link points to rather than just the link.

> **-N, --newer-than** *filename*
>> Get all files newer than the file *filename*.

> **-P, --parallel**[=*n*]
>> Download *n* files in parallel.

> **-i, --include** *regex*
>> Get only the files whose names match the regular expression *regex*. See **grep** for more information about regular expressions.

-x, --exclude *regex*

Do not get the files whose names match *regex*. See **grep** for more information about regular expressions.

-t, time-prec *n*

Set the precision of time measurement for file comparison; if file dates differ by amounts less than **n**, they are assumed to be the same. You can specify *n* in seconds (**s**), minutes (**m**), hours (**h**), or days (**d**).

-T, --loose-time-prec *n*

Set the precision for loose time comparisons. You can specify *n* in seconds (**s**), minutes (**m**), hours (**h**), or days (**d**).

-v, --verbose=*n*

Set the verbose level. You can set *n* from 0 (no output) to 3 (full output) using a number or by repeating the *v*. For example, **-vvv** is level 3 verbose mode.

--use-cache

Use the cache to get directory listings.

--remove-source-files

Move, rather than copy, files when mirroring.

set [setting | value]

Set one of the preference variables for **lftp**. If run without arguments, list the variables that have been changed; without arguments and with the **-a** or **-d** flags, list all values or default values, respectively.

See the **lftp** manpage for a complete list of preference variables that can be set.

wait [n | all]

Wait for the job or jobs you specify by number, or all jobs, to terminate.

---

lftpget

lftpget [*options*] *url*

Uses the **lftp** program to fetch the specified URL, which may be HTTP, FTP, or any of the protocols supported by **lftp**.

Options

lftpget takes only three options:

-c Continue or restart a paused transaction.

-d Display debugging output.

-v Verbose mode; display more information about transactions.

---

link

link *file1 file2*

Create a link between two files. This is the same as the **ln** command, but it has no error checking because it uses the **link( )** system call directly.

ln

ln [*options*] *sourcename* [*destname*]
ln [*options*] *sourcenames destdirectory*

Create pseudonyms (links) for files, allowing them to be accessed by different names. The first form links *sourcename* to *destname*, where *destname* is usually either a new filename or (by default) a file in the current directory with the same name as *sourcename*. If *destname* is an existing file, it is overwritten; if *destname* is an existing directory, a link named *sourcename* is created in that directory. The second form creates links in *destdirectory*, each link having the same name as the file specified.

Options

-b, --backup=[*control*]

Back up any existing files. When using the long version of the command, the optional *control* parameter controls the kind of backup. When no control is specified, **ln** will attempt to read the control value from the **VERSION_CONTROL** environment variable. Accepted values are:

none, off

Never make backups.

numbered, t

Make numbered backups.

existing, nil

Match existing backups, numbered or simple.

simple, never

Always make simple backups.

-d, -F, --directory

Allow hard links to directories. Available to privileged users.

-f, --force

Force the link (don't prompt for overwrite permission).

--help

Print a help message and then exit.

-i, --interactive

Prompt for permission before removing files.

-n, --no-dereference

Replace symbolic links to directories instead of dereferencing them. **--force** is useful with this option.

-s, --symbolic

Create a symbolic link. This lets you link across filesystems, and also see the name of the link when you run **ls -l** (otherwise, there's no way to know the name that a file is linked to).

-S *suffix*, **--suffix**=*suffix*

Append *suffix* to files when making backups, instead of the default ~.

--target-directory= *diectory*

Create links in the specified *diectory*.

-v, --verbose
> Verbose mode.

--version
> Print version information and then exit.

loadkeys

loadkeys [*options*] [*filename*]

Load a keymap from a specified file, usually one of the keymaps stored in */lib/kbd/keymaps*. If you create your own keymap file, the related commands **showkey**, **keymaps**, and **dumpkeys** will be useful as well.

Options

-c, --clearcompose
> Clear the compose, or accent, table in the kernel.

-d, --default
> Load the default keymap. The same as running **loadkeys defkeymap**.

-h, --help
> Display help and usage information.

-m, --mktable
> Instead of loading the table, output maps as C language declarations.

-q, --quiet
> Operate in quiet mode.

-s, --clearstrings
> Clear the string table in the kernel.

-v, --verbose
> Operate verbosely. For extra effect, repeat.

locale

locale [*options*] [*name*]

Print report on current locale settings. Locales determine the country-specific settings for a system, including character encodings, the formatting of dates, honorifics, diagnostic messages, currency, printer paper sizes, and default measurements. Locale settings are essentially a dictionary of settings specified by keyword. The keywords are grouped together into related categories whose names begin with **LC_**. Each category has a related environment variable of the same name from which it will read its locale setting. Supply keyword or category names as *name* to examine their values. Multiple names may be given. You can also use the special keyword **charmap** to see the current character mapping. When executed with no arguments, **locale** prints the value of all locale-related environment variables.

Options

-a Print all available locale settings installed on the system.

-c Print the category related to each *name* argument.

-k   Print keywords along with their settings for each *name* argument.

-m   Print all available character maps.

Environment variables

LANG
> The default value for unset internationalization variables. If not set, the system's default value is used.

LC_ADDRESS
> Postal settings, country, and language names and abbreviation.

LC_COLLATE
> String and character sorting and comparison settings.

LC_CTYPE
> Character attributes, including case conversion mappings, and categories of characters (whitespace, digit, lower, upper, punctuation, etc.).

LC_IDENTIFICATION
> Information related to the current locale definition, including its title, source, revision, and contact information for its author.

LC_MEASUREMENT
> Measurement units, metric or other.

LC_MESSAGES
> Settings for yes/no prompts and other informative and diagnostic messages.

LC_MONETARY
> Currency formats and symbols.

LC_NAME
> Formats for names and honorifics.

LC_NUMERIC
> Non-monetary number formats.

LC_PAPER
> Default paper sizes for printing and pagination.

LC_TELEPHONE
> Telephone number formats.

LC_TIME
> Date and time formats.

LC_ALL
> When set, overrides the values of all other internationalization variables.

NLSPATH
> The path for finding message catalogues used in processing messages.

Examples

Print the category name and all keywords for date and time settings:

```
locale -ck LC_TIME
```

Print the strings used for days of the week and months of the year:

```
locale day mon
```

---

locate

locate [*options*] *pattern*

Search database(s) of filenames and print matches. *, ?, [, and] are treated specially; / and . are not. Matches include all files that contain *pattern* unless *pattern* includes metacharacters, in which case **locate** requires an exact match.

Options

-d *path*, **--database**=*path*
> Search databases in *path*. *path* must be a colon-separated list.

-h, **--help**
> Print a help message and then exit.

--version
> Print version information and then exit.

---

lockfile

lockfile [*options*] *filenames*

Create semaphore file(s), used to limit access to a file. When **lockfile** fails to create some of the specified files, it pauses for 8 seconds and retries the last one on which it failed. The command processes flags as they are encountered (i.e., a flag that is specified after a file will not affect that file).

Options

-*sleeptime*
> Number of seconds **lockfile** waits before retrying after a failed creation attempt. Default is 8.

-!   Invert return value. Useful in shell scripts.

-l *lockout_time*
> Time (in seconds) after a lockfile was last modified at which it will be removed by force. See also **-s**.

-ml, **-mu**
> If the permissions on the system mail spool directory allow it or if **lockfile** is suitably setgid, **lockfile** can lock and unlock your system mailbox with the options **-ml** and **-mu**, respectively.

-r *retries*
> Stop trying to create *files* after *retries* retries. The default is –1 (never stop trying). When giving up, remove all created files.

-s *suspend_time*
After a lockfile has been removed by force (see **-l**), a suspension of 16 seconds takes place by default. (This is intended to prevent the inadvertent immediate removal of any lockfile newly created by another program.) Use **-s** to change the default 16 seconds.

---

logger

logger [*options*] [*message...*]

TCP/IP command. Add entries to the system log (via **syslogd**). If no message is given on the command line, standard input is logged.

Options

-d   When writing to a socket with **-s**, use a datagram instead of a stream.

-f *file*
Read *message* from *file*.

-i   Include the process ID of the **logger** process.

-p *pri*
Enter message with the specified priority *pri*. Default is **user. notice**.

-s   Log message to standard error as well as to the system log.

-t *tag*
Mark every line in the log with the specified *tag*.

-u *socket*
Write log to *socket* instead of to the syslog.

-   Accept no futher options. Consider whatever is to the right of the hyphen as the message to be logged.

---

login

login [*name* | *option*]

Log into the system. **login** asks for a username (*name* can be supplied on the command line) and password (if appropriate).

If successful, **login** updates accounting files, sets various environment variables, notifies users if they have mail, and executes startup shell files.

Only the root user can log in when */etc/nologin* exists. That file is displayed before the connection is terminated. Furthermore, root may connect only on a tty that is listed in */etc/securetty*. If *~/.hush-login* exists, execute a quiet login. If */var/adm/lastlog* exists, print the time of the last login.

Options

-f   Suppress second login authentication.

-h *host*
Specify name of remote host. Normally used by servers, not humans; may be used only by root.

-p   Preserve previous environment.

logname

logname [*option*]

Consult */var/run/utmp* for user's login name. If found, print it; otherwise, exit with an error message.

Options

--help
Print a help message and then exit.

--version
Print version information and then exit.

---

logrotate

logrotate [*options*] *config_files*

System administration command. Manipulate log files according to commands given in *config_files*.

Options

-d, --debug
Debug mode. No changes will be made to log files.

-f, --force
Force rotation of log files.

-h, --help
Describe options.

-m *command,* **--mail** *command*
Use the specified *command* to mail log files. The default is **/bin/ mail -s**.

-s *file,* **--state** *file*
Save state information in *file*. The default is */var/lib/logrotate. status*.

--usage
Show syntax and options.

-v, --verbose
Describe what is being done and what log files are affected.

Commands

compress
Compress old versions of log files with **gzip**.

compresscmd *command*
Use *command* to compress log files. Default is **gzip**.

compressext *extension*
Append filename **extension** to compressed files instead of the **compress** command's default.

compressoptions *options*
Specify *options* to pass to the **compress** command. Default for **gzip** is **-9** for maximum compression.

copy
Copy log file, but do not change the original.

copytruncate

Copy log file, then truncate it in place. For use with programs whose logging cannot be temporarily halted.

create [*permissions*] [*owner*] [*group*]

After rotation, re-create log file with the specified *permissions*, *owner*, and *group*. *permissions* must be in octal. If any of these parameters is missing, the log file's original attributes will be used.

daily

Rotate log files every day.

delaycompress

Don't compress log file until the next rotation.

endscript

End a **postrotate** or **prerotate** script.

extension *extension*

Give rotated log files the specified *extension*. Any compression extension will be appended to this.

ifempty

Rotate log file even if it is empty. Overrides the default **notifempty** option.

include *file*

Read the *file* into current file. If *file* is a directory, read all files in that directory into the current file.

mail *address*

Mail any deleted logs to *address*.

mailfirst

When using the **mail** command, mail the newly rotated log instead of the one being deleted.

maillast

When using the **mail** command, mail the log that is about to expire. This is the default behavior.

missingok

Skip missing log files. Do not generate an error.

monthly

Rotate log files only the first time **logrotate** is run in a month.

nocompress

Override **compress**.

nocopy

Override **copy**.

nocopytruncate

Override **copytruncate**.

nocreate

Override **create**.

nodelaycompress

Override **delaycompress**.

nomail
> Override **mail**.

nomissingok
> Override **missingok**.

noolddir
> Override **olddir**.

nosharedscipts
> Override **sharedscripts**. Run **prerotate** and **postrotate** scripts for each log rotated. This is the default.

notifempty
> Override **ifempty**.

olddir *directory*
> Move logs into *directory* for rotation. *directory* must be on the same physical device as the original log files.

postrotate
> Begin a script of directives to apply after the log file is rotated. The script ends when the **endscript** directive is read.

prerotate
> Begin a script of directives to apply before a log file is rotated. The script ends when the **endscript** directive is read.

rotate *number*
> The *number* of times to rotate a log file before removing it.

size *n*[**k**|**M**]
> Rotate log file when it is greater than *n* bytes. *n* can optionally be followed by **k** for kilobytes or **M** for megabytes.

sharedscripts
> Run **prescript** and **postscript** only once for the session.

start *n*
> Use *n* as the starting number for rotated logs. Default is 0.

tabooext [+] *extlist*
> Replace taboo extension list with the given *extlist*. If + is specified, add to existing list. The default list is **.rpmorig .rpmsave ,v .swp .rpmnew ~**.

weekly
> Rotate log files if more than a week has passed since their last rotation.

uncompresscmd *command*
> Use *command* to uncompress log files. Default is **gunzip**.

---

look

look [*options*] *string* [*file*]

Search for lines in *file* (*/usr/dict/words* by default) that begin with *string*.

Options

-a Use alternate dictionary */usr/dict/web2*.

-d Compare only alphanumeric characters.

-f   Search is not case-sensitive.

-t *character*
    Stop checking after the first occurrence of *character*.

---

losetup

losetup [*options*] *loopdevice* [*file*]

System administration command. Set up and control loop devices. Attach a loop device to a regular file or block device, detach a loop device, or query a loop device. A loop device can be used to mount an image file as if it were a normal device.

Options

-d   Detach specified *loopdevice*.

-e *encryption*
    Use specified *encryption* when performing writes and reads. Accepted values are **NONE**, **DES**, and **XOR**. When using DES encryption, you will be prompted for initialization values.

-o *offset*
    Start reading data at *offset* bytes from the beginning of *file*.

---

lpc

lpc [*options*] [*command*]

System administration command. LPRng line printer control program. If executed without a command, **lpc** accepts commands from standard input. Some of the commands accept a *jobid* parameter. A *jobid* can be one or more job numbers, user names, **lpd** key characters, or key character and glob patterns of the form *X=pattern*. It can also be the keyword **all**, which matches all jobs.

Options

-a   Alias for the **-Pall** command. Operate on all printer spool queues listed in the *printcap* **all** field.

-A   Use authentication as specified in the **AUTH** environment variable.

-P*printer*
    Specify the print spool queue to operate on. A *printer* may also specify a host (e.g., *printer@host*). The default queue is the queue for whatever printer is listed in the **PRINTER** environment variable, or the first entry in the */etc/printcap* file. If the keyword **all** is given instead of a printer name, **lpc** will operate on printers specified in the **all** field of the */etc/printcap* file on the appropriate host. If no **all** field is specified, then **lpc** will use **lpd** on the appropriate host to find all available printers.

-S*server*
    Send commands to the specified *server* instead of whatever server is listed in */etc/printcap* or set using the **-P** option.

-U*user*
    Execute commands as if they were made by *user*.

-V   Print version number, then exit.

Commands

?, help [*commands*]

Get a list of commands or help on specific commands.

active [*printer@host*]

Report whether **lpd** server is active.

abort all|*printer*

Terminate current printer daemon and disable printing for the specified *printer*.

class all|*printer restriction*

Restrict class of jobs being printed. **restriction** may be a class, a glob match on a particular control file entry of the form *X=globmatch*, or the word **off** to remove any existing restrictions.

clean all|*printer*

Remove files that cannot be printed from the specified printer queues.

client all|*printer*

Show LPRng client configuration and printcap information.

defaultq

List the default **lpc** queue.

defaults

List **lpc**'s default configuration information.

disable all|*printer*

Disable specified printer queues.

down all|*printer message*

Disable specified printer queues and put *message* in the printer status file.

enable all|*printer*

Enable the specified printer queues.

exit, quit

Exit **lpc**.

help

Print help message.

hold *printer* [*jobid*]

Hold jobs in the queue. Release with the **release** command.

holdall all|*printer*

Automatically hold all new jobs until they are released with the **release** command.

kill all|*printer*

The same as performing **abort** followed by **start**. Although it is a convenient shorthand, sometimes the **start** command will not work due to race conditions.

lpd [*printer@host*]

Determine if **lpd** process is running. Report PID if it is.

lpq *printer* [*options*]

Run **lpq** command from inside **lpc**.

lprm *printer jobid*
> Run **lprm** command from inside **lpc** to remove one or more print jobs.

move *source jobid destination*
> Move specified jobs from *source* printer to *destination* printer.

msg *printer message*
> Change printer status message to *message*. An empty *message* removes the current status message.

noholdall all|*printer*
> Cancel **holdall** command.

quit, exit
> Exit **lpc** program.

redirect *source destination*
> Redirect all jobs sent to *source* printer to *destination* printer. If *destination* is **off**, turn off redirection.

redo *printer jobid*
> Reprint *jobs*.

release *printer* [*jobid*]
> Release held jobs for printing.

reread [*printer@host*]
> Request **lpd** server to reread configuration and printcap information.

server all|*printer*
> Show printcap entries as used by **lpd**.

start all|*printer*
> Enable the printer queues and start printing daemons for the specified printers.

status all|*printer*
> Return the status of the specified printers.

stop all|*printer*
> Disable the specified printer daemons after any current jobs are completed.

topq *printer* [*jobid*] [*users*]
> Put the specifed jobs at the top of the printer's queue in the order the jobs are listed.

up all|*printer*
> Enable print queues and restart daemons for the specified printers.

---

lpd   **lpd** [*options*]

TCP/IP command. LPRng line printer daemon. **lpd** is usually invoked at boot time from the *rc2* file. It makes a single pass through the printer configuration file (traditionally */etc/printcap*) to find out about the existing printers, and prints any files left after a crash. It then accepts requests to print files in a queue, transfer files to a spooling area, display a queue's status, or remove jobs from a

---

queue. In each case, it forks a child process for each request, then continues to listen for subsequent requests.

A file lock in each spool directory prevents multiple daemons from becoming active simultaneously. After the daemon has set the lock, it scans the directory for files beginning wth *cf*. Lines in each *cf* file specify files to be printed or nonprinting actions to be performed. Each line begins with a key character, which specifies information about the print job or what to do with the remainder of the line. Key characters are:

c   **cifplot** file.

d   **DVI** file.

f   Formatted file—name of a file to print that is already formatted.

g   Graph file.

l   Formatted file, but suppress pagebreaks and printing of control characters.

n   **ditroff** file.

p   File filtered using **pr**.

t   **troff** file.

v   File containing raster image.

C   Classification—string to be used for the classification line on the burst page.

H   Hostname—name of machine where **lpd** was invoked.

I   Indentation—number of characters to indent output.

J   Job name—string to be used for the jobname on the burst page.

L   Literal—contains identification information from the password file and causes the banner page to be printed.

M   Mail—send mail to the specified user when the current print job completes.

N   Filename—original name of data file to be printed.

P   Person—login name of person who invoked **lpd**.

T   Title—string to be used as the title for **pr**.

U   Unlink—name of file to remove upon completion of printing.

W   Width—page width in number of characters.

Options

-p *port*

Bind **lpd** to *port* instead of the default determined by **getservbyname**, usually port 515.

-F   Run **lpd** in foreground instead of as a daemon.

-L *file*

Log error and debugging messages to *file* instead of **syslogd**.

-V   Print version, then exit.

Files

/etc/lpd.conf
   LPRng configuration file.

/etc/printcap
   Printer description file.

/etc/lpd.perms
   Printer permissions.

/var/spool/*
   Spool directories.

/var/spool/*/printcap
   Printer-specific description file.

/var/spool/*/printer
   Queue lock file.

/var/spool/*/control.printer
   Queue control.

/var/spool/*/active.printer
   Active job.

/dev/lp*
   Printer devices.

---

lpq

lpq [*options*] [*jobid*]

Check the print spool queue for status of print jobs. For each job, display username, rank in the queue, filenames, job number, and total file size (in bytes). If *user* is specified, display information only for that user. *jobid* can be one or more job numbers, usernames, **lpd** key characters, or key character and glob patterns of the form *X=pattern*.

Options

-a   Report on all printers listed in the server's printcap database.

-l   Verbose mode. Print information about each file comprising a job. Use -l multiple times to increase the information provided.

-s   Print one-line status summary for each queue and subqueue.

-A   Use authentication.

-L   Maximum verbosity. Print all available information about each file comprising a job in a long display format.

-P*printer*
     Specify which printer to query. Without this option, **lpq** uses the printer set in the **PRINTER** or other printer-related environment variables or the default system printer.

-V   Print version, then exit.

-t*n*   Display spool queues every *n* seconds.

---

lpr

lpr [*options*] [*files*]

The LPRng print spooler. Send *files* to the printer spool queue. If no *files* are given, accept standard input. On most Linux distributions, the LPRng print spooler replaces the BSD print spooler. Some systems use the alternative CUPS printing system. Both printing systems have **lpr** commands with options that are mostly compatible with BSD's **lpr**. We document LPRng's **lpr** command here.

Options

-b, -l

Expect a binary or literal file on which minimial processing should be done. The file is assigned filter **f**, which passes it through the default input filter (**:if** or **:filter** in the printcap file).

-f Use a filter that interprets the first character of each line as a standard carriage control character.

-h Do not print the burst page.

-i [*cols*]

Indent the output. Default is 8 columns. Specify number of columns to indent with the *cols* argument.

-k Send data directly to the remote printer instead of creating a temporary file. This may cause problems if the job is killed when transferring the file, but can speed up large jobs.

-l Use a filter that allows control characters to be printed and suppresses pagebreaks.

-m *address*

Send mail to *address* if print job is unsuccessful.

-w *n*

Set page width to *n* characters.

-A Use authentication.

-B Filter all job files as specified in the printcap database, then combine them into a single job file to be sent to the spooler.

-C *class*

Set the job classification used on the burst page and to assign priorities. *class* should be a letter from **A** to **Z**, **A** being the lowest priority and **Z** the highest.

-F *filter*

Set the print *filter* to use when printing *files*. *filter* should be a lowercase letter. The default is **f**. The command used for each filter is defined in the printer's printcap file.

-G Filter individual jobs before sending them to the spooler.

-J *name*

Replace the job name on the burst page with *name*. If omitted, use the first file's name or **STDIN**.

-K *n, #n*

> Print *n* copies of each listed file.

-P*printer*

> Output to *printer* instead of the printer specified in the **PRINTER** environment variable or the system default.

-R *name*

> Place additional accounting information in the **R** field of the control file.

-T *title*

> Use *title* as the title when using **pr**.

-U *user*

> Specify a username for the job. Available only for privileged users.

-V Verbose mode. Print additional information about progress of the print job. Additional **-V** options may be given to increase the level of information printed.

-X *command*

> Use the specified external *command* to filter files.

-Y *host%port*

> Bypass the print spooler. Connect directly to the specified host and port and send the filtered file.

-Z *options*

> Pass additional *options* through to the print spooler.

Obsolete options

The following options are all obsolete, though still functional. They may be removed in later versions of **lpr**. We include them here for those working with older systems or updating legacy shell scripts.

-c Expect data produced by **cifplot**. Use filter **c**.

-d Expect data produced by T_EX in the DVI (device-independent) format. Use filter **d**.

-g Expect standard plot data produced by the **plot** routines. Use filter **g**.

-n Expect data from **ditroff** (device-independent **troff**). Use filter **n**.

-p Expect data preprocessed by the **pr** command. Use default filter **f**. This function may not be supported on some systems.

-r Remove *files* upon completion of spooling. Mostly for compatibility with Berkeley **lpr**.

-t Expect data from **troff** (phototypesetter commands). Use filter **t**.

-v Expect a raster image for devices like the Benson Varian. Use filter **v**.

lprm

lprm [*options*] [*jobid*]

Remove a print job from the print spool queue. You must specify a job number or numbers, which can be obtained from **lpq**. A *jobid* can be one or more job numbers, usernames, **lpd** key characters, or key character and glob patterns of the form *X=pattern*. It can also be the keyword **all**, which matches all jobs. Only a privileged user may remove files belonging to another user.

Options

-a Remove all jobs available to the user. Same as using the *jobid* **ALL**.

-A Use authentication.

-P *printer*
　　Specify printer queue. Normally, the default printer or printer specified in the **PRINTER** environment variable is used.

-U *user*
　　Remove files as if command were executed by *user*. Only a privileged user can use this option.

-V Print version, then exit.

---

lpstat

lpstat [*options*] [*queues*]

Show the status of the print queue or queues. With options that take a *list* argument, omitting the list produces all information for that option. *list* can be separated by commas or, if enclosed in double quotes, by spaces. For the LPRng print service, **lpstat** is a frontend to the **lpq** program.

Options

-a [*list*]
　　Show whether the *list* of printer or class names is accepting requests.

-c [*list*]
　　Show information about printer classes named in *list*.

-d Show the default printer destination.

-f [*list*]
　　Verify that the *list* of forms is known to **lp**.

-l Use after -f to describe available forms, after -p to show printer configurations, or after -s to describe printers appropriate for the specified character set or print wheel.

-o [*list*]
　　Show the status of output requests. *list* contains printer names, class names, or request IDs.

-p [*list*]
　　Show the status of printers named in *list*.

-r Show whether the print scheduler is on or off.

-s   Summarize the print status (show almost everything).

-t   Show all status information (report everything).

-u [*list*]
> Show request status for users on *list*. Use **all** to show information on all users.

-A   Use authentication.

---

ls

ls [*options*] [*names*]

List contents of directories. If no *names* are given, list the files in the current directory. With one or more *names*, list files contained in a directory *name* or that match a file *name*. *names* can include filename metacharacters. The options let you display a variety of information in different formats. The most useful options include **-F**, **-R**, **-l**, and **-s**. Some options don't make sense together (e.g., **-u** and **-c**).

Options

-1, --format=single-column
> Print one entry per line of output.

-a, --all
> List all files, including the normally hidden files whose names begin with a period.

-b, --escape
> Display nonprinting characters in octal and alphabetic format.

-c, --time-ctime, --time=status
> List files by status change time (not creation/modification time).

--color =*when*
> Colorize the names of files depending on the type of file. Accepted values for *when* are **never**, **always**, or **auto**.

-d, --directory
> Report only on the directory, not its contents.

-f   Print directory contents in exactly the order in which they are stored, without attempting to sort them.

--full-time
> List times in full, rather than use the standard abbreviations.

-g   Long listing like **-l**, but don't show file owners.

-h   Print sizes in kilobytes and megabytes.

--help
> Print a help message and then exit.

-i, --inode
> List the inode for each file.

--indicator-style=none
> Display filenames without the flags assigned by **-p** or **-f** (default).

-k, --kilobytes
If file sizes are being listed, print them in kilobytes. This option overrides the environment variable **POSIXLY_ CORRECT**.

-l, --format=long, --format=verbose
Long format listing (includes permissions, owner, size, modification time, etc.).

-m, --format=commas
Merge the list into a comma-separated series of names.

-n, --numeric-uid-gid
Like -l, but use group ID and user ID numbers instead of owner and group names.

-o   Long listing like -l, but don't show group information.

-p, --filetype, --indicator-style=_file-type_
Mark directories by appending / to them.

-q, --hide-control-chars
Show nonprinting characters as ? (default for display to a terminal).

-r, --reverse
List files in reverse order (by name or by time).

-s, --size
Print file size in blocks.

--show-control-chars
Show nonprinting characters verbatim (default for printing to a file).

--si   Similar to -h, but uses powers of 1000 instead of 1024.

-t, --sort=time
Sort files according to modification time (newest first).

-u, --time=atime, --time=access, --time=use
Sort files according to file access time.

--version
Print version information on standard output, then exit.

-x, --format=across, --format=horizontal
List files in rows going across the screen.

-v, --sort=version
Interpret the digits in names such as _file.6_ and _file.6.1_ as versions, and order filenames by version.

-w, --width=_n_
Format output to fit _n_ columns.

-A, --almost-all
List all files, including the normally hidden files whose names begin with a period. Does not include the . and .. directories.

-B, --ignore-backups
Do not list files ending in ~ unless given as arguments.

-C, --format=vertical
List files in columns (the default format).

-D, --dired
List in a format suitable for Emacs **dired** mode.

-F, --classify, --indicator-style=classify
Flag filenames by appending / to directories, * to executable files, @ to symbolic links, | to FIFOs, and = to sockets.

-G, --no-group
In long format, do not display group name.

-H, --dereference-command-line
When symbolic links are given on the command line, follow the link and list information from the actual file.

-I, --ignore *pattern*
Do not list files whose names match the shell pattern *pattern* unless they are given on the command line.

-L, --dereference
List the file or directory referenced by a symbolic link rather than the link itself.

-N, --literal
Display special graphic characters that appear in filenames.

-Q, --quote-name
Quote filenames with "; quote nongraphic characters.

-R, --recursive
List directories and their contents recursively.

-S, --sort=size
Sort by file size, largest to smallest.

-R*file***, --reload-state** *file*
Load state from *file* before starting execution.

-U, sort=none
Do not sort files.

-X, sort=extension
Sort by file extension, then by filename.

---

lsattr

lsattr [*options*] [*files*]

Print attributes of *files* on a Linux Second Extended File System. See also **chattr**.

Options

-a   List all files in specified directories.

-d   List attributes of directories, not of contents.

-v   List version of files.

-R   List directories and their contents recursively.

-V   List version of **lsmod**, then exit.

lsmod	**lsmod**

System administration command. List all loaded modules: name, size (in 4KB units), and, if appropriate, a list of referring modules. The same information is available in */proc/modules* if the */proc* directory is enabled on the system.

Options

-h, --help
> Show usage.

-V, --version
> Show version of this command.

m4	**m4** [*options*] [*macros*] [*files*]

Macro processor for C and other files.

Options

-e, --interactive
> Operate interactively, ignoring interrupts.

-d*flags*, --debug=*flags*
> Specify *flag*-level debugging.

--help
> Print help message, then exit.

-l*n*, --arglength=*n*
> Specify the length of debugging output.

-o *file*, --error-output=*file*
> Place output in *file*. Despite the name, print error messages on standard error.

-p, --prefix-built-ins
> Prepend **m4_** to all built-in macro names.

-s, --synclines
> Insert **#line** directives for the C preprocessor.

-t*name*, --trace*name*
> Insert *name* into symbol table as undefined. Trace macro from the point it is defined.

--version
> Print version, then exit.

-B*n*
> Set the size of the pushback and argument collection buffers to *n* (default is 4096).

-D*name*[=*value*], --define=*name*[=*value*]
> Define *name* as *value* or, if *value* is not specified, define *name* as null.

-E, --fatal-warnings
> Consider all warnings to be fatal, and exit after the first of them.

-F*file,* **--freeze-state** *file*
> Record **m4**'s frozen state in *file* for later reloading.

-G, --traditional
> Behave like traditional **m4**, ignoring GNU extensions.

-H*n,* **--hashsize=***n*
> Set symbol-table hash array to *n* (default is 509).

-I*directory,* **--include=***directory*
> Search *directory* for include files.

-Q, --quiet, --silent
> Suppress warning messages.

-R*file,* **--reload-state** *file*
> Load state from *file* before starting execution.

-U*name,* **--undefine=***name*
> Undefine *name.*

---

mail

mail [*options*] [*users*]

Read mail or send mail to other *users*. The **mail** utility allows you to compose, send, receive, forward, and reply to mail. **mail** has two main modes: compose mode, in which you create a message, and command mode, in which you manage your mail.

While **mail** is a powerful utility, it can be tricky for a novice user. It is most commonly seen nowadays in scripts. Most Linux distributions include several utilities that are richer in features and much easier to use: mailers built in to browsers such as Netscape and Mozilla, graphical mail programs distributed with GNOME (Evolution) and KDE (Kmail), and the terminal-based, full-screen utilities **pine** and **elm**. The GNU Emacs editor can also send and receive mail.

This section presents **mail** commands, options, and files. To get you started, here are two of the most basic commands.

To enter interactive mail-reading mode, type:

    mail

To begin writing a message to *user*, type:

    mail user

Enter the text of the message, one line at a time, pressing Enter at the end of each line. To end the message, enter a single period (.) in the first column of a new line and press Enter.

Command-line options
-b *list*
> Set blind carbon copy field to comma-separated *list.*

-c *list*
> Set carbon copy field to comma-separated *list.*

-d   Print debugging information.

-f [*file*]
> Process contents of *file* instead of */var/spool/mail/$user*. If *file* is omitted, process *mbox* in the user's home directory.

-i Do not respond to tty interrupt signals.

-n Do not consult */etc/mail.rc* when starting up.

-p Read mail in POP mode.

-s *subject*
> Set subject to *subject*.

-u Process contents of */var/spool/mail/$user* (the default).

-v Verbose; print information about mail delivery to standard output.

-N When printing a mail message or entering a mail folder, do not display message headers.

-P Disable POP mode.

Compose-mode commands

~! Execute a shell escape from compose mode.

~? List compose-mode escapes.

~b *names*
> Add names to or edit the **Bcc:** header.

~c *names*
> Add names to or edit the **Cc:** header.

~d Read in the *dead.letter* file.

~e Invoke text editor.

~f *messages*
> Insert *messages* into message being composed.

~F *messages*
> Similar to **~f**, but include message headers.

~h Add to or change all headers interactively.

~m *messages*
> Similar to **~f**, but indent with a tab.

~M *messages*
> Similar to **~m**, but include message headers.

~p Print message header fields and message being sent.

~q Abort current message composition.

~r *filename*
> Append file to current message.

~s *string*
> Change **Subject:** header to *string*.

~t *names*
> Add names to or edit the **To:** list.

~v Invoke editor specified with the **VISUAL** environment variable.

~| command
> Pipe message through *command*.

~: mail-command
> Execute *mail-command*.

~~string
> Insert *string* in text of message, prefaced by a single tilde (~). If string contains a ~, it must be escaped with a \.

Command-mode commands

?   List summary of commands (help screen).

!   Execute a shell command.

- num
> Print *num*th previous message; defaults to immediately previous.

alias (a)
> Print or create alias lists.

alternates (alt)
> Specify remote accounts on remote machines that are yours. Tell mail not to reply to them.

chdir (c)
> **cd** to home or specified directory.

copy (co)
> Similar to **save**, but do not mark message for deletion.

delete (d)
> Delete message.

dp   Delete current message and display next one.

edit (e)
> Edit message.

exit (ex, x)
> Exit **mail** without updating folder.

file (fi)
> Switch folders.

folder (fold)
> Read messages saved in a file. Files can be:
>
> \#   Previous
>
> %   System mailbox
>
> *%user*
>> *user*'s system mailbox
>
> &   mbox
>
> *+folder*
>> File in *folder* directory.

folders
> List folders.

headers (h)
> List message headers at current prompt.

---

headers+ (h+)
> Move forward one window of headers.

headers- (h-)
> Move back one window of headers.

help
> Same as ?.

hold (ho)
> Hold messages in system mailbox.

ignore
> Append list of fields to ignored fields.

mail *user* **(m)**
> Compose message to *user*.

mbox
> Move specified messages to *mbox* on exiting (the default).

next (n)
> Type next message or next message that matches argument.

preserve (pr)
> Synonym for **hold**.

print [*list*] **(p)**
> Display each message in *list*.

Print [*list*] **(P)**
> Similar to **print**, but include header fields.

quit (q)
> Exit **mail** and update folder.

reply (r)
> Send mail to all on distribution list.

Reply (R)
> Send mail to author only.

respond
> Same as **reply**.

retain
> Always include this list of header fields when printing messages. With no arguments, list retained fields.

save (s)
> Save message to folder.

saveignore
> Remove ignored fields when saving.

saveretain
> Override **saveignore** to retain specified fields.

set (se)
> Set or print **mail** options.

shell (sh)
> Enter a new shell.

size
> Print size of each specified message.

source

> Read commands from specified file.

top

> Print first few lines of each specified message.

type (t)

> Same as **print**.

Type (T)

> Same as **Print**.

unalias

> Discard previously defined aliases.

undelete (u)

> Restore deleted message.

unread (U)

> Mark specified messages as unread.

unset (uns)

> Unset **mail** options.

visual (v)

> Edit message with editor specified by the **VISUAL** environment variable.

write (w)

> Write message, without header, to file.

xit (x)

> Same as **exit**.

z   Move **mail**'s attention to next windowful of text. Use **z-** to move it back.

Options

These options are used inside the *.mailrc* file. The syntax is **set** *option* or **unset** *option*.

append

> Append (do not prepend) messages to *mbox*.

ask

> Prompt for subject.

askbcc

> Prompt for blind carbon copy recipients.

askcc

> Prompt for carbon copy recipients.

asksub

> Prompt for **Subject** line.

autoprint

> Print next message after a delete.

chron

> Display messages in chronological order, most recent last.

debug

> Same as **-d** on command line.

dot

Interpret a solitary . as an EOF.

folder

Define directory to hold mail folders.

hold

Keep message in system mailbox upon quitting.

ignore

Ignore interrupt signals from terminal. Print them as @.

ignoreeof

Do not treat ^D as an EOF.

metoo

Do not remove sender from groups when mailing to them.

noheader

Same as -N on command line.

nokerberos

Retrieve POP mail via POP3, not KPOP, protocol.

nosave

Do not save aborted letters to *dead.letter*.

pop-mail

Retrieve mail with POP3 protocol, and save it in *mbox.pop*.

prompt

Set prompt to a different string.

Replyall

Switch roles of **Reply** and **reply**.

quiet

Do not print version at startup.

searchheaders

When given the specifier */x:y*, expand all messages that contain the string *y* in the *x* header field.

verbose

Same as -v on command line.

verbose-pop

Display status while retrieving POP mail.

Special files

calendar

Contains reminders that the operating system mails to you.

.maildelivery

Mail delivery configuration file.

.mailrc

Mail configuration file.

triplog

Keeps track of your automatic response recipients.

tripnote

Contains automatic message.

mailq

mailq [*options*]

System administration command. List all messages in the **sendmail** mail queue. Equivalent to **sendmail -bp**.

Options

-Ac Show queue specified in */etc/mail/submit.cf* instead of queue specified in */etc/mail/sendmail.cf*.

-v Verbose mode.

mailstats

mailstats [*options*]

System administration command. Display a formatted report of the current **sendmail** mail statistics.

Options

-c Use configuration in */etc/mail/submit.cf* instead of */etc/mail/sendmail.cf*.

-f *file*
    Use **sendmail** statistics file *file* instead of the file specified in the **sendmail** configuration file.

-o Don't show the name of the mailer in the report.

-p Print stats without headers or separators. Output suitable for use by other programs. Reset statistics.

-C *file*
    Use **sendmail** configuration file *file* instead of the default *sendmail.cf* file.

-P Print stats without headers or separators. Output suitable for use by other programs. Do not reset statistics.

mailto

mailto [*options*] *recipients*

Send mail with MIME types and text formatting. This program has a very similar interface to that of the *mail* program, with two differences: it only sends mail, and it adds a number of text formatting and MIME handling features, described here. For features not covered here, check the **mail** command. **mailto** uses the **metamail** backend and relies on the **mailcap** configuration files.

Text formatting

Mail formatting is handled with escape sequences that begin with the tilde (~) character. Those for text formatting are:

~b Turn bold text on or off.

~i Turn italic text on or off.

~jc, ~jl, ~jr
    Set justification to center, left, or right.

~k Toggle whether to send a blind copy to yourself.

~n Hard line break (newline).

~>, ~<
> Increase or decrease left margin.

~<R, ~>R
> Increase or decrease right margin.

~Q Quotation mode (indent and mark selection as excerpt).

~z Append ~/.*signature* as the signature for this message.

Including objects in mail

You can include a variety of objects in your messages, again using tilde escape sequences. To do so, enter ~*, and the program will prompt you for the type of data you wish to add. The available content types will vary from installation to installation.

make

make [*options*] [*targets*] [*macro definitions*]

Update one or more *targets* according to dependency instructions in a description file in the current directory. By default, this file is called *makefile* or *Makefile*. Options, targets, and macro definitions can be in any order. Macro definitions are typed as:

> *name=string*

For more information on **make**, see *Managing Projects with make* (O'Reilly).

Options

-d, --debug
> Print detailed debugging information.

-e, --environment-overrides
> Override **makefile** macro definitions with environment variables.

-f *makefile*, **--file**=*makefile*, **--makefile**=*makefile*
> Use *makefile* as the description file; a filename of - denotes standard input.

-h, --help
> Print options to **make** command.

-i, --ignore-errors
> Ignore command error codes (same as **.IGNORE**).

-j [*jobs*], **--jobs** [=*jobs*]
> Attempt to execute *jobs* jobs simultaneously or, if no number is specified, as many jobs as possible.

-k, --keep-going
> Abandon the current target when it fails, but keep working with unrelated targets.

-l [*load*], **--load-average** [=*load*], **--max-load** [=*load*]
> Attempt to keep load below *load*, which should be a floating-point number. Used with **-j**.

-n, --just-print, --dry-run, --recon
> Print commands but don't execute (used for testing).

-o *file,* **--old-file=***file,* **--assume-old=***file*
> Never remake *file* or cause other files to be remade on account of it.

-p, --print-data-base
> Print rules and variables in addition to normal execution.

-q, --question
> Query; return 0 if file is up to date; nonzero otherwise.

-r, --no-built-in-rules
> Do not use default rules.

-s, --silent, --quiet
> Do not display command lines (same as **.SILENT**).

-t, --touch
> Touch the target files without remaking them.

-v, --version
> Show version of **make**.

-w, --print-directory
> Display the current working directory before and after execution.

--warn-undefined-variables
> Print warning if a macro is used without being defined.

-C *directory,* **--directory** *directory*
> **cd** to *directory* before beginning **make** operations. A subsequent **-C** directive will cause **make** to attempt to **cd** into a directory relative to the current working directory.

-I *directory,* **--include-dir** *directory*
> Include *directory* in list of directories containing included files.

-S, --no-keep-going, --stop
> Cancel previous **-k** options. Useful in recursive **make**s.

-W *file,* **--what-if** *file,* **--new-file** *file,* **--assume-new** *file*
> Behave as though *file* has been recently updated.

Description file lines

Instructions in the description file are interpreted as single lines. If an instruction must span more than one input line, use a backslash (\) at the end of the line so that the next line is considered a continuation. The description file may contain any of the following types of lines:

Blank lines
> Blank lines are ignored.

Comment lines
> A pound sign (#) can be used at the beginning of a line or anywhere in the middle. **make** ignores everything after the #.

Dependency lines
> Depending on one or more targets, certain commands that follow will be executed. Possible formats include:

```
targets : dependencies
targets : dependencies ; command
```

Subsequent commands are executed if dependency files (the names of which may contain wildcards) do not exist or are newer than a target. If no prerequisites are supplied, then subsequent commands are always executed (whenever any of the targets are specified). No tab should precede any targets.

Conditionals

Conditionals are evaluated when the makefile is first read and determine what **make** sees, i.e., which parts of the makefile are obeyed and which parts are ignored. The general syntax for a conditional is:

```
conditional
Text if true
else
Text if false
endif
```

ifeq (*arg1, arg2*), **ifeq** "*arg1*" "*arg2*"

True if the two arguments are identical. The arguments should either be placed in parentheses and separated by a comma— (arg1, arg2)—or individually quoted with either single or double quotes.

ifneq (*arg1, arg2*), **ifneq** "*arg1*" "*arg2*"

True if the two arguments are not identical. The arguments should either be placed in parentheses and separated by a comma or individually quoted with either single or double quotes.

ifdef *variable*

True if *variable* has a nonempty value.

ifndef *variable*

True if *variable* has an empty value.

Suffix rules

These specify that files ending with the first suffix can be prerequisites for files ending with the second suffix (assuming the root filenames are the same). Either of these formats can be used:

```
.suffix.suffix:
.suffix:
```

The second form means that the root filename depends on the filename with the corresponding suffix.

Commands

Commands are grouped below the dependency line and are typed on lines that begin with a tab. If a command is preceded by a hyphen (-), **make** ignores any error returned. If a command is preceded by an at sign (@), the command line won't echo on the display (unless **make** is called with -**n**).

Macro definitions

These have the following form:

```
name = string
```

or:

```
define name
string
endef
```

Blank space is optional around the =.

Include statements
> Similar to the C include directive, these have the form:
>
> ```
> include files
> ```

Internal macros

$? The list of prerequisites that have been changed more recently than the current target. Can be used only in normal description file entries, not in suffix rules.

$@ The name of the current target, except in description file entries for making libraries, where it becomes the library name. Can be used both in normal description file entries and in suffix rules.

$< The name of the current prerequisite that has been modified more recently than the current target.

$* The name (without the suffix) of the current prerequisite that has been modified more recently than the current target. Can be used only in suffix rules.

$% The name of the corresponding *.o* file when the current target is a library module. Can be used both in normal description file entries and in suffix rules.

$^ A space-separated list of all dependencies with no duplications.

$+ A space-separated list of all dependencies, including duplications.

Pattern rules

These are a more general application of the idea behind suffix rules. If a target and a dependency both contain %, GNU **make** will substitute any part of an existing filename. For instance, the standard suffix rule:

```
$(cc) -o $@ $<
```

can be written as the following pattern rule:

```
%.o : %.c
$(cc) -o $@ $<
```

Macro modifiers

D The directory portion of any internal macro name except $?. Valid uses are:

```
$(*D)    $$(@D)    $(?D)    $(<D)
$(%D)    $(@D)     $(^D)
```

F The file portion of any internal macro name except **$?**. Valid uses are:

```
$(*F)    $$(@F)   $(?F)    $(<F)
$(%F)    $(@F)    $(^F)
```

Functions

$(subst *from,to,string*)
Replace all occurrences of *from* with *to* in *string*.

$(patsubst *pattern,to,string*)
Similar to **subst**, but treat **%** as a wildcard within *pattern*. Substitute *to* for any word in *string* that matches *pattern*.

$(strip *string*)
Remove all extraneous whitespace.

$(findstring *substring,mainstring*)
Return *substring* if it exists within *mainstring*; otherwise, return null.

$(filter *pattern,string*)
Return those words in *string* that match at least one word in *pattern*. *pattern* may include the wildcard **%**.

$(filter-out *pattern,string*)
Remove those words in *string* that match at least one word in *pattern*. *pattern* may include the wildcard **%**.

$(sort *list*)
Return *list*, sorted in lexical order.

$(dir *list*)
Return the directory part (everything up to the last slash) of each filename in *list*.

$(notdir *list*)
Return the nondirectory part (everything after the last slash) of each filename in *list*.

$(suffix *list*)
Return the suffix part (everything after the last period) of each filename in *list*.

$(basename *list*)
Return everything but the suffix part (everything up to the last period) of each filename in *list*.

$(addsuffix *suffix,list*)
Return each filename given in *list* with *suffix* appended.

$(addprefix *prefix,list*)
Return each filename given in *list* with *prefix* prepended.

$(join *list1,list2*)
Return a list formed by concatenating the two arguments word by word (e.g., **$(join a b,.c .o)** becomes **a.c b.o**).

$(word *n,string*)
Return the *n*th word of *string*.

$(wordlist *start,end,string*)

Return words in *string* between word *start* and word *end*, inclusive.

$(words *string*)

Return the number of words in *string*.

$(firstword *list*)

Return the first word in the list *list*.

$(wildcard *pattern*)

Return a list of existing files in the current directory that match *pattern*.

$(foreach *variable,list,string*)

For each whitespace-separated word in *list*, expand its value and assign it to *variable*; then expand *string*, which usually contains a function referencing *variable*. Return the list of results.

$(if *condition,then-string*[*,else-string*])

Expand string *condition* if it expands to a nonempty string, then expand the *then-string*. If *condition* expands to an empty string, return the empty string, or if specified, expand and return the *else-string*.

$(call *variable,parameters*)

Expand each item in comma-separated list *parameters* and assign it to a temporary variable, **$(** *n*), where *n* is an incremented number beginning with 0. Then expand *variable*, a string referencing these temporary variables, and return the result.

$(origin *variable*)

Return one of the following strings that describes how *variable* was defined: **undefined, default, environment, environment override, file, command line, override,** or **automatic.**

$(shell *command*)

Return the results of *command*. Any newlines in the result are converted to spaces. This function works similarly to backquotes in most shells.

$(error *string*)

When evaluated, generate a fatal error with the message *string*.

$(warning *string*)

When evaluated, generate a warning with the message *string*.

Macro string substitution

$(*macro:s1=s2*)

Evaluates to the current definition of **$(** *macro*), after substituting the string *s2* for every occurrence of *s1* that occurs either immediately before a blank or tab or at the end of the macro definition.

Special target names

.DEFAULT:
Commands associated with this target are executed if **make** can't find any description file entries or suffix rules with which to build a requested target.

.DELETE_ON_ERROR:
If this target exists in a makefile, delete the target of any rule whose commands return a nonzero exit status.

.EXPORT_ALL_VARIABLES:
If this target exists, export all macros to all child processes.

.IGNORE:
Ignore error codes. Same as the -i option.

.INTERMEDIATE:
This target's dependencies should be treated as intermediate files.

.NOTPARALLEL:
If this target exists in a makefile, run **make** serially, ignoring option -j.

.PHONY:
Always execute commands under a target, even if it is an existing, up-to-date file.

.PRECIOUS:
Files you specify for this target are not removed when you send a signal (such as an interrupt) that aborts **make** or when a command line in your description file returns an error.

.SECONDARY:
Like .INTERMEDIATE, this target's dependencies should be treated as intermediate files, but never automatically deleted.

.SILENT:
Execute commands, but do not echo them. Same as the -s option.

.SUFFIXES:
Suffixes associated with this target are meaningful in suffix rules. If no suffixes are listed, the existing list of suffix rules is effectively "turned off."

Linux
Commands

---

makedbm

makedbm [*options*] *infile outfile*
makedbm [*option*]

NFS/NIS command. Create or dump an NIS **dbm** file. **makedbm** will take a text *infile* and convert it to a **gdbm** database file named *outfile*. This file is suitable for use with **ypserv**. Each line of the input file is converted to a single record. All characters up to the first TAB or SPACE form the key, and the rest of the line is the data. If a line ends with \&, the data for that record is continued on to the next line. The # character is given no special treatment. *infile* can be -, in which case the standard input is read.

---

makedbm generates two special keys: the **YP_MASTER_NAME** key, which is the value of the current host (unless another name is specified with **-m**), and the **YP_LAST_MODIFIED** key, which is the date of *infile* (or the current time if *infile* is -).

Options

-a   Add support for mail aliases.

-b   Insert **YP_INTERDOMAIN** key into map. This indicates that **ypserv** should fall back to DNS lookups when a host's address is not found in NIS.

-c   Send a **YPPROC_CLEAR** signal to **ypserv**, causing it to clear all cached entries.

-i *file_name*
      Create a **YP_INPUT_NAME** key with the value *file_name*.

-l   Convert keys of the given map to lowercase.

-m *master_name*
      Specify the value of the **YP_MASTER_NAME** key. The default value is the current hostname.

--no-limit-check
      Don't enforce NIS size limits for keys or data.

-o *file_name*
      Create a **YP_OUTPUT_NAME** key with the value *file_name*.

-r   Treat lines beginning with # as comments. Do not include them in the data file.

-s   Add the key **YP_SECURE**, indicating that **ypserv** should accept connections to the database only from secure NIS networks.

-u *filename*
      Undo a **gdbm** file—print out a **dbm** file, one entry per line, with a single space separating keys from values.

Example

It is easy to write shell scripts to convert standard files such as */etc/passwd* to the key value form used by **makedbm**. For example, the **awk** program:

```
BEGIN { FS =":";OFS = "\t";}
{ print $1, $0}
```

takes the */etc/passwd* file and converts it to a form that can be read by **makedbm** to make the NIS file *passwd.byname*. That is, the key is a username and the value is the remaining line in the */etc/passwd* file.

---

makemap   makemap [*options*] *type name*

System administration command. Create database maps for use by **sendmail** in keyed map lookups. **makemap** will read from standard input and create a database file of type *type* with filename

---

name.**db**. If the **TrustedUser** option is set in */etc/sendmail.cf* and **makemap** is invoked as root, the ouput file will be owned by **TrustedUser**.

Input should be formatted as:

> key value

Comment lines with **#**. Indicate parameter substitution with **%n**. Specify a literal **%** character by entering it twice: **%%**. The *type* may be **btree** or **hash**.

Options

-c *size*
> Specify hash or B-Tree cache size.

-d Allow duplicate entries. Valid only with **btree** type maps.

-e Allow empty value data fields.

-f Suppress conversion of uppercase to lowercase.

-l List supported map types.

-o Append to existing file instead of replacing it.

-r If some keys already exist, replace them. (By default, **makemap** will exit when encountering a duplicated key.)

-s Ignore safety checks.

-t *delimiter*
> Use *delimiter* instead of whitespace.

-u Undo a map—print out the specified database file, one entry per line.

-v Verbose mode.

-C *file*
> Look up **TrustedUser** in the specified **sendmail** configuration *file*.

-N Append the zero-byte string terminator specified in **sendmail**'s configuration file to mapped entries.

---

man

man [*options*] [*section*] [*title*]

Display information from the online reference manuals. **man** locates and prints the named *title* from the designated reference *section*.

Traditionally, manpages are divided into nine sections, where section 1 consists of user commands, section 2 contains system calls, and so forth. By default, all sections are consulted, so the *section* option serves to bypass the most common entry and find an entry of the same name in a different section (e.g., **man 2 nice**).

Numerous other utilities, such as **info**, **xman**, and the Konqueror browser, can also display manpages.

Options

-7, --ascii

Expect a pure ASCII file, and format it for a 7-bit terminal or terminal emulator.

-a, --all

Show all pages matching *title*.

-b Leave blank lines in output.

-d, --debug

Display debugging information. Suppress actual printing of manual pages.

-f, --whatis

Same as **whatis** command.

-k, --apropos

Same as **apropos** command.

-l, --local-file

Search local files, not system files, for manual pages. If **i** is given as *filename*, search standard input.

-m *systems,* **--systems=***systems*

Search *systems'* manual pages. *systems* should be a comma-separated list.

-p *preprocessors,* **--preprocessor=***preprocessors*

Preprocess manual pages with *preprocessors* before turning them over to **nroff**, **troff**, or **groff**. Always runs **soelim** first to read in files to be included in this one. *preprocessors* can be any combination of **e** for equations, **p** for pictures, **t** for tables, and **r** for bibliographical references.

-r *prompt,* **--prompt=***prompt*

Set prompt if **less** is used as pager.

-t, --troff

Format the manual page with **/usr/bin/groff -Tgv -mandoc**. Implied by **-T** and **-Z**.

-u, --update

Perform a consistency check between manual page cache and filesystem.

-w, -W, --path, --where

Print pathnames of entries on standard output.

-D Display debugging information about how the page was retrieved.

-K *directory*

A kind of super-**k** option. Search for a term in all manpages and display the name of each page, along with a prompt asking whether you want to view the page.

-L *locale,* **--locale=***locale*

Assume current locale to be *locale*; do not consult the **setlocale( )** function.

-M *path,* **--manpath**=*path*
> Search for manual pages in *path*. Ignore **-m** option.

-Ppager, **--pager**=*pager*
> Select paging program *pager* to display the entry.

-S *sections*
> Sections to look in for an entry. Like specifying *section* on the command line, except that multiple section numbers can be specified, separated by colons.

-T *device,* **--troff-device**[=*device*]
> Format **groff** or **troff** output for *device*, such as **dvi**, **latin1**, **X75**, and **X100**.

-Z, **--ditroff**
> Do not allow postprocessing of manual page after **groff** has finished formatting it.

Section names

Manual pages are divided into sections for various audiences:

1   Executable programs or shell commands.

2   System calls (functions provided by the kernel).

3   Library calls (functions within system libraries).

4   Special files (usually found in */dev*).

5   File formats and conventions (e.g., */etc/passwd*).

6   Games.

7   Macro packages and conventions.

8   System administration commands (usually only for a privileged user).

9   Kernel routines (nonstandard).

---

manpath

manpath [*options*]

Attempt to determine path to manual pages. Check **$MANPATH** first; if that is not set, consult */etc/man.conf*, user environment variables, and the current working directory. The **manpath** command is a symbolic link to **man**, but most of the options are ignored for **manpath**.

Options

-d, **--debug**
> Print debugging information.

-h   Print help message and then exit.

---

mattrib

mattrib [*options*] *filenames*

Change attributes of MS-DOS files. See **mtools** for more information.

Attributes

To set an attribute, use one of the following letters preceded by a +
(to turn the attribute on) or - (to turn it off):

a   Archive; mark the file as a new file that should be archived by
    backup programs.

r   Read-only.

s   System; files with this attribute are marked as operating
    system files.

h   Hide this file when displaying directory contents with DIR.

Options

-/ When listing attributes, descend into all subdirectories
    recursively.

-X Concise output.

-P Display commands for **mformat** that can reproduce the
    current attributes and settings for a given disk.

---

mbadblocks   `mbadblocks drive`

Check MS-DOS filesystems for bad blocks. See **badblocks** and
mtools. As with other **mtools** items, the drive is named with a
letter rather than as a Unix device.

---

mcat   `mcat [option] drive`

Dump raw data, especially for a disk image on a remote floppy
accessed through the **floppyd** tool. See **cat** and **mtools** for more
information. The only option accepted, **-w**, accepts data from stdin
and writes it to the given device.

---

mcd   `mcd drive`

Change directory on an MS-DOS disk. See **cd** and **mtools** for more
information.

---

mcopy   `mcopy [options] sourcefile target`

Copy files between Unix and MS-DOS format partitions. See **cp**
and **mtools** for more information.

Options

The **mcopy** option flags differ from the flags passed to the Unix **cp**
command. The flags are:

-t Convert Unix line breaks to MS-DOS line breaks and vice
    versa when copying text files.

-b Operate in batch mode; use for large copies of data.

-s Copy recursively.

-P Preserve attributes of copied files.

-Q If one copy fails, stop copying the rest. Useful if you think you may run out of disk space.

-a Assume that all incoming files are ASCII and convert carriage return/line feed to plain line feed.

-T Convert line breaks as with **-a**, but also convert PC-8 characters to ISO-8859-1 characters. Replace untranslatable characters with # or . for Unix and DOS respectively.

-n Do not ask for confirmation when overwriting Unix files. Use **-o** to turn off confirmation for overwriting DOS files.

-m Preserve file modification time.

-v Display the names of files as they are copied.

-D *clash-option*
Specify the action to take if the specified directory name already exists. See **mmd** for the possible clash options.

---

mdel, mdeltree

`mdel [option] file`
`mdeltree [option] tree`

Delete an MS-DOS file or file tree. See **rm** and **mtools** for more information.

Option

-v Run in verbose mode, printing the names of the MS-DOS files to be deleted.

---

mdir

`mdir [options] dir`

List directory contents on an MS-DOS filesystem. See **ls**, **dir**, and **mtools** for more information.

Options

-/ Display output recursively, listing the contents of subdirectories.

-a Include hidden files in the output.

-b Produce a concise listing, showing each directory or file on a separate line, with no heading or summary information.

-f Operate in fast mode, without determining the amount of free space. Not required on FAT32 filesystems, which store the free space information explicitly.

-w Produce wide output, printing filenames across the page with no file size or creation date information.

-V Print version information and exit.

---

mdu

`mdu [option] dir`

Display disk usage, in clusters, for a directory and its subdirectories and files on an MS-DOS filesystem. See **du** and **mtools** for more information, and see **minfo** for the cluster size. Only one of **-a** or **-s** can be specified.

Options

-a Show the space used by individual files in a directory as well as the total space.

-s Show only the total space used.

---

merge

merge [*options*] *file1 file2 file3*

Perform a three-way file merge. The effect is easiest to understand if *file2* is considered the original version of a file, *file3* an altered version of *file2*, and *file1* a later altered version of *file2*.

After the merge, *file1* contains both the changes from *file2* to *file1* and the changes from *file2* to *file3*. In other words, *file1* keeps its changes and incorporates the changes in *file3* as well. **merge** does not change *file2* or *file3*.

If a line from *file2* was changed in different ways in both *file1* and *file3*, **merge** recognizes a conflict. By default, the command outputs a warning and puts brackets around the conflict, with lines preceded by <<<<<<< and >>>>>>>. A typical conflict looks like this:

```
<<<<<<< file1
relevant lines from file1
=======
relevant lines from file3
>>>>>>> file3
```

If there are conflicts, the user should edit the result and delete one of the alternatives.

Options

-e Don't warn about conflicts.

-p Send results to standard output instead of overwriting *file1*.

-q Quiet; do not warn about conflicts.

-A Output conflicts using the **-A** style of **diff3**. This merges all changes leading from *file2* to *file3* into *file1* and generates the most verbose output.

-E Output conflict information in a less verbose style than **-A**; this is the default.

-L *label*
   Specify up to three labels to be used in place of the corresponding filenames in conflict reports. That is:

```
merge -L x -L y -L z file_a file_b file_c
```

   generates output that looks as if it came from *x*, *y*, and *z* instead of from *file_a*, *file_b*, and *file_c*.

-V Print version number.

mesg

mesg [`option`]

Change the ability of other users to send **write** messages to your terminal. With no options, display the permission status.

Options

n Forbid **write** messages.

y Allow **write** messages (the default).

metamail

metamail [`options`] [`filename`]

Normally invisible to users, **metamail** is used to send and display rich text or multimedia email using MIME typing metadata. Mail-reading programs normally call **metamail** to determine how to handle the data, but **metamail** can be called directly by developers who want to use it for their own mail software, or by system administrators and power users adding lines to their *printcap* files. Any argument passed to **metamail** that is not preceded by a hyphen (-) is assumed to be the name of a file to read. If no filename is specified, standard input is assumed.

Options

-b The message is not in RFC 822 format; treat as the body of the message. Requires **-c**.

-B Display the message in the background, if noninteractive. Cannot be used with **-p** or **-P**.

-c *type*
   Use the specified content type instead of the one in the headers.

-d Don't ask before running an interpreter to view the message. The default is to ask.

-e Remove ("eat") leading newlines in the message body. Useful for MH-format mail.

-f *addr*
   Specify the name of the message sender. The default is to try to determine the name from the header.

-h Specify that a message is to be printed. Automatically sets **-d**.

-m *mailer*
   Specify the mail program to be called by **metamail**.

-p If necessary, display the output one page at a time. The default is to pipe the output through **more**, but the environment variable **METAMAIL_PAGER** can be set to specify an alternative command. Use **-p** rather than piping the message to a pager.

-P Like **-p**, but also print "Press RETURN to go on" at the end of each page. Cannot be used with **-B**.

-q Run quietly.

-r Specify that **metamail** can be run as root.

-R Run */usr/ucb/reset* to reset the terminal before performing any other I/O.

-s *subject*
Specify the **Subject** field. By default, the subject is determined from the headers.

-T Turn off the effect of the environment variable **MM_TRANS-PARENT**. Intended to be used recursively by **metamail**, and should be used only when the program restarts itself in a terminal emulator window.

-w Don't consult a *mailcap* file to determine how to display the data, but simply decode each part and write to a file in its raw format (which might be binary). Depending on how **metamail** is called, the filename is determined from the message headers, by asking the user, or by generating a unique temporary filename.

-x Tell **metamail** that it is not running on a terminal. The environment variable **MM_NOTTY** can be set instead of specifying **-x**.

-y Try to "yank" a MIME-format message from the body of the message.

-z Delete the input file when done.

---

metasend

metasend [*options*] [*filename*]

A largely developer-oriented interface for sending non-text email using MIME typing metadata. If no arguments are specified, **metasend** prompts the user for the information it needs. See **mailto** for a possible alternative with a friendlier interface.

Options

-/ *subtype*
Specify the MIME multipart subtype other than mixed.

-b Batch mode. All information must be provided on the command line.

-c *cc*
Specify any CC addresses.

-D *string*
Specify a string to be used as the **Content-description** value.

-e *encoding*
Specify the encoding to use. Possible values are **base64**, **quoted-printable**, **7bit** (no encoding is done), or **x-uue**.

-E The file to be included is already MIME-encoded and doesn't need any **Content-** or other header fields added.

-f *file*
The file to be included. If more than one file is specified with separate **-f** options (see **-n**), they are combined into a single multipart MIME object.

-F *from*
> The **From** address.

-i *content-id*
> The content ID value for the MIME entity. Must be a valid content ID enclosed in angle brackets (<>).

-I *content-id*
> The content ID value for a multipart entity being created by **metasend**. Must be a valid content ID enclosed in angle brackets (<>).

-m *type*
> The MIME content type.

-n
> Specify that an additional file is to be included. Must appear after one occurrence of at least -m, -c, and -f and must be specified for each included file.

-ooutfile
> Send the output to the specified file instead of delivering as mail.

-P *preamblefile*
> Specify a file containing alternative text for the preamble portion of a multipart MIME message.

-s *subject*
> The **Subject** field.

-S *splitsize*
> Specify the maximum size before the file is split into parts to be sent separately.

-t *to*
> The **To** field.

-z
> Delete temporary files even if the send fails.

---

mformat

mformat [*options*] drive

Format a blank disk in MS-DOS format. See **mtools** for more information about how to handle MS-DOS filesystems. After using **mformat** to format a disk, you should use **mbadblocks** to check for bad blocks.

Options

The **mformat** command accepts many of the same options as the MS-DOS **FORMAT** command:

-v [*label*]
> Choose a label for this volume. Maximum length is 11 characters.

-f *N*
> If you are using a floppy disk, use this flag and note the size of the disk in kilobytes as 160, 180, 320, 360, 720, 1200, 1440, or 2280. For most relatively recent systems, only the last two are relevant. If you are not using a floppy, you must use the **-h**, **-t**, or **-n** flags.

-t *N*

The number of tracks on the disk.

-h *N*

The number of heads, or sides, on the disk (either 1 or 2).

-n The number of sectors per track.

You can also use a number of option flags that are not included in the MS-DOS version of **FORMAT**, including:

-F Format as a FAT32 partition.

-S *N*

Size code. You are defining a sector that is the N+7th power of two.

-X Format as an XDF (OS/2) disk.

-2 Use a 2m format.

-3 Don't use a 2m format, even if the disk looks like a 2m disk.

-C Create a disk image file. Useful only for virtual disks.

-M *N*

Set the software sector size to be different from the physical sector size.

-N *serialno*

Choose a serial number. Use **-a** for an Atari-style serial number, stored in the OEM label.

-c *N*

Set the cluster size to N sectors.

-r *N*

Set the root directory size to *N* sectors for 12- and 16-bit FAT formats.

-L *N*

Set the length of the File Allocation Table (FAT).

---

mimencode   .   **mimencode** [*options*] [*filename*] [**-o** *output_file*]

Translate to and from MIME encoding formats, the proposed standard for Internet multimedia mail formats. By default, **mimencode** reads standard input and sends a base64-encoded version of the input to standard output.

Options

-b Use the (default) base64 encoding.

-o *output_file*

Send output to the named file rather than to standard output.

-p Translate decoded CRLF sequences into the local newline convention during decoding, and do the reverse during encoding. This is meaningful only when the default base64 encoding is in effect.

-q Use the quoted-printable encoding instead of base64.

-u Decode the standard input rather than encode it.

minfo

minfo [*options*] *drive*

Display information about an MS-DOS filesystem. See **mtools** for more information.

mkdir

mkdir [*options*] *directories*

Create one or more *directories*. You must have write permission in the parent directory in order to create a directory. See also **rmdir**. The default mode of the new directory is 0777, modified by the system or user's **umask**.

Options

-m, --mode *mode*
> Set the access *mode* for new directories. See **chmod** for an explanation of acceptable formats for *mode*.

-p, --parents
> Create intervening parent directories if they don't exist.

--verbose
> Print a message for each directory created.

--help
> Print help message and then exit.

--version
> Print version number and then exit.

Examples

Create a read-only directory named **personal**:

    mkdir -m 444 personal

The following sequence:

    mkdir work; cd work
    mkdir junk; cd junk
    mkdir questions; cd ../..

can be accomplished by typing this:

    mkdir -p work/junk/questions

mkdosfs

mkdosfs [*options*] *device* [*blocks*]
mkfs.msdos [*options*] *device* [*blocks*]

System administration command. Format *device* as an MS-DOS filesystem. You may specify the number of blocks on the device or allow **mkdosfs** to guess.

Options

-b *backup-sector*
> Specify sector for backup boot sector. The default value depends on the number of reserved sectors, but is usually sector 6.

-c Scan *device* for bad blocks before execution.

-f *n*

Specify number of File Allocation Tables (FATs) to create (either **1** or **2**).

-i *volume-id*

Use the specified 32-bit hexadecimal *volume-id* instead of calculating a number based on the time of creation.

-l *file*

Read list of bad blocks from *file*.

-m *message-file*

Set the message to be used when the filesystem is booted without an installed operating system to the contents of the file *message-file*. The message may be up to 418 bytes in size. If filename is a hyphen, read text from standard input.

-n *label*

Set volume name for filesystem to *label*. The volume name may be up to 11 characters long.

-r *maximum-entries*

Set the *maximum-entries* allowed in the root directory. The default is 112 or 224 for floppies and 512 for hard disks.

-s *sectors*

Set the number of disk *sectors* per cluster. The number must be a power of 2.

-v Print verbose information about progress.

-A Create an Atari MS-DOS filesystem.

-C Create and format a file suitable for use on a floppy disk. The *device* given on the command line should be a filename, and the number of *blocks* must also be specified.

-F *fat-size*

Create File Allocation Tables (FATs) of size *fat-size*. By default this will be between 12 and 16 bits. Set to 32 to create a FAT32 filesystem.

-I Force installation to a device without partitions. This is useful when formating magneto-optical disks.

-R *reserved-sectors*

Create the specified number of *reserved-sectors*. The default depends on the size of the File Allocation Table (FAT). For 32-bit FAT, the default is 32; for all other sizes, the default is 1.

-S *sector-size*

Create logical sectors of *sector-size* bytes. Size must be a power of 2 and at least 512 bytes.

---

mke2fs

mke2fs [*options*] *device* [*blocks*]
mkfs.ext2 [*options*] *device* [*blocks*]

System administration command. Format *device* as a Linux Second Extended Filesystem. You may specify the number of blocks on the device or allow **mke2fs** to guess.

Options

-b *block-size*
Specify block size in bytes.

-c Scan *device* for bad blocks before execution.

-f *fragment-size*
Specify fragment size in bytes.

-i *bytes-per-inode*
Create an inode for each *bytes-per-inode* of space. *bytes-per-inode* must be 1024 or greater; it is 4096 by default.

-j Create an ext3 journal. This is the same as invoking **mkfs.ext3**.

-l *filename*
Consult *filename* for a list of bad blocks.

-m *percentage*
Reserve *percentage* percent of the blocks for use by privileged users.

-n Don't create the filesystem, just show what would happen if it were run. This option is overridden by **-F**.

-o *os*
Set filesystem operating system type to *os*. The default value is usually **Linux**.

-q Quiet mode.

-r *revision*
Set filesystem revision number to *revision*.

-v Verbose mode.

-F Force **mke2fs** to run even if filesystem is mounted or device is not a block special device. This option is probably best avoided.

-J *parameterlist*
Use specified *parameterlist* to create an ext3 journal. The following two parameters may be given in a comma-separated list:

size=*journal-size*
Create a journal of *journal-size* megabytes. The size may be between 1024 filesystem blocks and 102,400 filesystem blocks in size (e.g., 1-100 megabytes if using 1K blocks, 4–400 megabytes if using 4K blocks).

device=*journal-device*
Use an external *journal-device* to hold the filesystem journal. The *journal-device* can be specified by name, by volume label, or by UUID.

-L *label*
Set volume *label* for filesystem.

-M *directory*
Set the last mounted directory for filesystem to *directory*.

-N *inodes*

Specify number of *inodes* to reserve for filesystem. By default, this number is calculated from number of blocks and inode size.

-O *featurelist*

Use specified *featurelist* to create filesystem. The **sparse_super** and **filetype** features are used by default on kernels 2.2 and later. The following parameters may be given in a comma-separated list:

filetype

Store file type information in directory entries.

has_journal

Create an ext3 journal. Same as using the **-j** option.

journal_dev

Prepare an external journaling device by creating an ext3 journal on *device* instead of formatting it.

sparse_super

Save space on large filesystem by creating fewer super-block backup copies.

-R stride=*size*

Configure filesystem for a RAID array. Set stride size to *size* blocks per stripe.

-S Write only superblock and group descriptors; suppress writing of inode table and block and inode bitmaps. Useful only when attempting to salvage damaged systems.

-T *use*

Set bytes-per-inode based on the intended *use* of the filesystem. Supported filesystem types are:

news

Four kilobytes per inode.

largefile

One megabyte per inode.

largefile4

Four megabytes per inode.

-V Print version number, then exit.

---

mkfifo

`mkfifo` [*option*] *names*

Make one or more named pipes (FIFOs) with the specified names.

Options

-m *mode*, **--mode=***mode*

Set permission mode. Default is 666 with the bits in the umask subtracted.

--help

Print help information and exit.

--version

Print version information and exit.

---

mkfs

mkfs [*options*] [*fs-options*] *filesys* [*blocks*]

System administration command. Construct a filesystem on a device (such as a hard disk partition). *filesys* is either the name of the device or the mountpoint. **mkfs** is actually a frontend that invokes the appropriate version of **mkfs** according to a filesystem type specified by the -t option. For example, a Linux Second Extended Filesystem uses **mkfs.ext2** (which is the same as **mke2fs**); MS-DOS filesystems use **mkfs.msdos**. *fs-options* are options specific to the filesystem type. *blocks* is the size of the file-system in 1024-byte blocks.

Options

-V   Produce verbose output, including all commands executed to create the specific filesystem.

-t *fs-type*
   Tells **mkfs** what type of filesystem to construct.

Filesystem-specific options

These options must follow generic options and cannot be combined with them. Most filesystem builders support these three options:

-c   Check for bad blocks on the device before building the filesystem.

-l *file*
   Read the file *file* for the list of bad blocks on the device.

-v   Produce verbose ouput.

---

mkfs.ext3

mkfs.ext3 [*options*] *device size*

Create a journaling ext3 filesystem. Options are identical to **mke2fs**. See **mkfs**.

---

mkfs.minix

mkfs.minix [*options*] *device size*

System administration command. Create a MINIX filesystem. See **mkfs**.

---

mkisofs

mkisofs [*options*] **-o** *file pathspecs*

Generate an ISO9660/Joliet/HFS filesystem for writing to a CD with a utility such as **cdrecord**. (HFS is the native Macintosh Hierarchical File System.) **mkisofs** takes a snapshot of a directory tree and generates a binary image that corresponds to an ISO9660 or HFS filesystem when it is written to a block device. Each specified *pathspec* describes the path of a directory tree to be copied into the ISO9660 filesystem; if multiple paths are specified, the files in all the paths are merged to form the image.

Options

-A *id,* **-appid** *id*

Specify a text string *id* that describes the application to be written into the volume header.

-abstract *file*

Specify the abstract filename. Overrides an **ABST**=*file* entry in *.mkisofsrc.*

-allow-lowercase

Allow ISO9660 filenames to be lowercase. Violates the ISO9660 standard.

-allow-multidot

Allow more than one dot in ISO9660 filenames. Violates the ISO9660 standard.

-b *image*

Specify the path and filename of the boot image to be used for making a bootable CD based on the El Torito specification.

-B *sun-images*

Specify a comma-separated list of boot images needed to make a bootable CD for a Sun Sparc system.

-biblio *file*

Specify bibliographic filename. Overrides a **BIBLIO**=*file* entry in *.mkisofsrc.*

-boot-info-table

Specify that a 56-byte table with information on the CD layout is to be patched in at offset 8 of the boot file. If specified, the table is patched into the source boot file, so make a copy if the file isn't recreatable.

-boot-load-seg *addr*

Specify the load segment address of the boot image for a no-emulation El Torito CD.

-boot-load-size *size*

Specify the number of virtual 512-byte sectors to load in no-emulation mode. The default is to load the entire boot file. The number may need to be a multiple of 4 to prevent problems with some BIOSes.

-c *catalog*

Specify the path, relative to the source *pathspec*, and the filename of the boot catalog for an El Torito bootable CD. Required for making a bootable CD.

-C *last-start,next-start*

Required for creating a CDExtra or a second or higher-level session for a multisession CD. *last-start* is the first sector number in the last session on the disk, and *next-start* is the first sector number for the new session. Use the command:

```
cdrecord -msinfo
```

to get the values. Use **-C** with **-M** to create an image that is a continuation of the previous session; without **-M**, create an

---

image for a second session on a CDExtra (a multisession CD with audio data in the first session and an ISO9660 filesystem image in the second).

-[no-]cache-inodes

Cache [do not cache] inode and device numbers to find hard links to files. The default on Linux is to cache. Use **-no-cache-inodes** for filesystems that do not have unique inode numbers.

-check-oldnames

Check all filenames imported from old sessions for **mkisofs** compliance with ISO9660 file-naming rules. If not specified, check only those files with names longer than 31 characters.

-check-session *file*

Check all old sessions for **mkisofs** compliance with ISO9660 file-naming rules. This option is the equivalent of:

```
-M file -C 0,0 -check-oldnames
```

where *file* is the pathname or SCSI device specifier that would be specified with **-M**.

-copyright *file*

Specify the name of the file that contains the copyright information. Overrides a **COPY**=*file* entry in *.mkisofsrc*.

-d Omit trailing period from files that do not have one. Violates the ISO9660 standard, but works on many systems.

-D Do not use deep directory relocation. Violates the ISO9660 standard, but works on many systems.

-dir-mode *mode*

Specify the mode for directories used to create the image. Automatically enables the Rock Ridge extensions.

-eltorito-alt-boot

Start with a new set of El Torito boot parameters. Allows putting more than one El Torito boot image on a CD (maximum is 63).

-exclude-list *file*

Check filenames against the globs contained in the specified file and exclude any that match.

-f Follow symbolic links when generating the filesystem.

-file-mode *mode*

Specify the mode for files used to create the image. Automatically enables the Rock Ridge extensions.

-force-rr

Do not use automatic Rock Ridge detection for the previous session.

-G *image*

Specify the path and filename of the generic boot image for making a generic bootable CD.

-gid *gid*

Set the group ID to *gid* for the source files. Automatically enables the Rock Ridge extensions.

-graft-points

Allow the use of graft points for filenames, which permits paths to be grafted at locations other than the root directory. **-graft-points** checks all filenames for graft points and divides the filename at the first unescaped equals sign (=).

-gui

Switch the behavior for a GUI. Currently, the only effect is to make the output more verbose.

-hard-disk-boot

Specify that the boot image to be used to create an El Torito bootable CD is a hard disk image and must begin with a master boot record containing a single partition.

-hidden *glob*

Set the hidden (existence) ISO9660 directory attribute for paths or filenames matching the shell-style pattern *glob*. To match a directory, the path must not end with a trailing /.

-hidden-list *file*

Specify a file containing a list of *globs* that are to be hidden with **-hidden**.

-hide *glob*

Find paths or files that match the shell-style pattern *glob* and hide them from being seen on the ISO9660 or Rock Ridge directory. The files are still included in the image file. If the pattern matches a directory, the contents of the directory are hidden. To match a directory, the path must not end with a trailing /. Use with the **-hide-joliet** option.

-hide-joliet *glob*

Hide paths or files that match the shell-style pattern *glob* so they will not be seen in the Joliet directory. If the pattern matches a directory, the contents of the directory are hidden. To match a directory, the path must not end with a trailing /. Should be used with **-hide**.

-hide-joliet-list *file*

Specify a file containing a list of *globs* to be hidden with **-hide-joliet**.

-hide-joliet-trans-tbl

Hide the *TRANS.TBL* files from the Joliet tree.

-hide-list *file*

Specify a file containing a list of *globs* to be hidden with **-hide**.

-hide-rr-moved

Rename the directory *RR_MOVED* to *.rr_moved* to hide it as much as possible from the Rock Ridge directory tree. Use the **-D** option to omit the file entirely.

-input-charset *charset*

Specify the character set for characters used in local filenames. Specify **help** in place of a *charset* for a list of valid character sets.

-iso-level *level*

Set the ISO9660 conformance level. Possible values are:

1 Filenames are restricted to 8.3 characters and files may have only one section.

2 Files may have only one section.

3 No restrictions.

-J Generate Joliet directory records in addition to regular ISO9660 filenames.

-jcharset *charset*

The equivalent of **-input-charset -J**.

-l Allow full 31-character filenames instead of restricting them to the MS-DOS-compatible 8.3 format.

-L Allow ISO9660 filenames to begin with a period.

-log-file *file*

Send all messages to the specified log file.

-m *glob*

Exclude files matching the shell-style pattern *glob*.

-M *path*

Specify the path to an existing ISO9660 image to be merged. *path* can also be a SCSI device specified in the same syntax as **cdrecord**'s **dev=** parameter. May be used only with **-C**.

-max-iso9660-filenames

Allow up to 37 characters in ISO9660 filenames. Forces **-N**. Violates the ISO9660 standard.

-N Omit version numbers from ISO9660 filenames. Violates the ISO9660 standard. Use with caution.

-new-dir-mode *mode*

Specify the mode to use for new directories in the image. The default is 0555.

-nobak, -no-bak

Do not include backup files on the ISO9660 filesystem.

-no-boot

Mark the El Torito CD to be created as not bootable.

-no-emul-boot

Specify that the boot image for creating an El Torito bootable CD is a no-emulation image.

-no-iso-translate

Do not translate the # and ~ characters. Violates the ISO9660 standard.

-no-rr

Do not use Rock Ridge attributes from previous sessions.

-no-split-symlink-components

Do not split symlink components.

-no-split-symlink-fields

Do not split symlink fields.

-o *file*
> Specify the filename of the output ISO9660 filesystem image.

-output-charset *charset*
> Specify the output character set for Rock Ridge filenames. The default is the input character set.

-p *prepid*
> Specify a text string of up to 128 characters describing the preparer of the CD. Overrides a **PREP=** parameter set in the file *.mkisofsrc*.

-P *pubid*
> Specify a text string of up to 128 characters describing the publisher of the CD to be written to the volume header. Overrides a **PUBL=** parameter set in *.mkisofsrc*.

-[no -]pad
> Pad [do not pad] the ISO9660 filesystem by 16 sectors (32KB). If the resulting size is not a multiple of 16 sectors, add sectors until it is. The default is **-pad**.

-path-list *file*
> Specify a file that contains a list of *pathspec* directories and filenames to add to the ISO9660 filesystem. Note that at least one *pathspec* must be given on the command line.

-print-size
> Print estimated filesystem size and exit.

-quiet
> Run in quiet mode; do not display progress output.

-r Like **-R**, but set UID and GID to zero, set all file read bits to write, and turn off all file write bits. If any execute bit is set for a file, set all execute bits; if any search bit is set for a directory, set all search bits; if any special mode bits are set, clear them.

-R Generate SUSP (System Use Sharing Protocol) and Rock Ridge records using the Rock Ridge protocol.

-relaxed-filenames
> Allow ISO9660 filenames to include seven-digit ASCII characters except lowercase characters. Violates the ISO9660 standard.

-sort *file*
> Sort file locations according to the rules in the specified file, which contains pairs of filenames and weights, with one space or tab between them. A higher weight puts the file closer to the beginning of the media.

-sysid *id*
> Specify the system ID. Overrides a **SYSI=** parameter set in the file *.mkisofsrc*.

-T Generate the file *TRANS.TBL* in each directory for establishing the correct filenames on non–Rock Ridge–capable systems.

-table-name *table*

Use *table* as the translation table name instead of *TRANS.TBL*. Implies **-T**. For a multisession image, the table name must be the same as the previous session.

-U Allow untranslated filenames. Violates the ISO9660 standard. Forces the options **-d**, **-l**, **-L**, **-n**, **-relaxed-filenames**, **-allow-lowercase**, **-allow-multidot**, **-no-iso-translate**. Use with extreme caution.

-ucs-level *num*

Set the Unicode conformance level to the specified number, which can be between 1 and 3 (default is 3).

-use-fileversion

Use file version numbers from the filesystem. The version number is a string from 1 to 32767. The default is to set a version of 1.

-v Run in verbose mode. Specify twice to run even more verbosely.

-V *volid*

Specify the volume ID (volume name or label) to be written to the master block. Overrides a **VOLI=** parameter specified in the file *.mkisofsrc*.

-volset *id*

Specify the volume set ID. Overrides a **VOLS=** parameter specified in *.mkisofsrc*.

-volset-seqno *num*

Set the volume set sequence number to *num*. Must be specified after **-volset-size**.

-volset-size *num*

Set the volume set size (the number of CDs in a set) to *num*. Must be specified before **-volset-seqno**.

-x *path*

Exclude *path* from being written to the CD, where *path* is the complete pathname derived from the concatenation of the pathname from the command line and the path relative to this directory. May be specified more than once to exclude multiple paths.

HFS options

-apple

Create an ISO9660 CD with Apple's extensions.

-auto *file*

Set *file* as the Autostart file to make the HFS CD use the QuickTime 2.0 Autostart feature. *file* must be the name of an application or document at the top level of the CD and must be less than 12 characters long.

-boot-hfs-file *file*

Install *file* as the driver file that may make the CD bootable on a Macintosh.

-cluster-size *size*

Specify the size in bytes of a cluster or allocation units of PC Exchange files. Implies the use of **--exchange**.

-hfs

Create a hybrid ISO9660/HFS CD. Use with **-map**, **-magic**, and/or the various **--HFS** options.

-hfs-bless *folder*

"Bless" the specified directory (folder), specified as the full pathname as **mkisofs**. This is usually the System Folder and is used in creating HFS bootable CDs. The pathname must be in quotes if it contains spaces.

-hfs-creator *creator*

Set the four-character default creator for all files.

-hfs-type *type*

Set the four-character default type for all files.

-hfs-unlock

Leave the HFS volume unlocked so other applications can modify it. The default is to lock the volume.

-hfs-volid *id*

Specify the volume name for the HFS partition. This name is assigned to the CD on a Macintosh and replaces the ID set with the **-V** option.

-hide-hfs *glob*

Hide files or directories matching the shell-style pattern *glob* from the HFS volume, although they still exist in the ISO9660 and/or Joliet directory. May be specified multiple times.

-hide-hfs-list *file*

The specified file contains a list of globs to be hidden.

-input-hfs-charset *charset*

Specify the input character set used for HFS filenames when used with the **-mac-name** option. The default is cp10000 (Mac Roman).

-mac-name

Use the HFS filename as the starting point for the ISO9660, Joliet, and Rock Ridge filenames.

-magic *file*

Use the specified magic file to set a file's creator and type information based on the file's *magic number*, which is usually the first few bytes of the file. The magic file contains entries consisting of four tab-separated columns specifying the byte offset, type, test, and a message.

-map *file*

Use the specified mapping file to set a file's creator and type information based on the filename extension. Only files that are not known Apple or Unix file types need to be mapped. The mapping file consists of five-column entries specifying the extension, file translation, creator, type, and a comment. Creator and type are both four-letter strings.

-no-desktop
> Do not create empty Desktop files. The default is to create such files.

-output-hfs-charset *charset*
> Specify the output character set used for HFS filenames. Defaults to the input character set.

-part
> Generate an HFS partition table. The default is not to generate the table.

-probe
> Search the contents of files for known Apple or Unix file types.

--format
> Look for Macintosh files of the specified file format type. The valid formats are **cap** (Apple/Unix File System (AUFS) CAP files), **netatalk**, **double**, **ethershare**, **ushare**, **exchange**, **sgi**, **xinet**, **macbin**, **single**, **dave**, and **sfm**.

mklost+found

`mklost+found`

System administration command. Create a *lost+found* directory in the current working directory. Intended for Linux Second Extended Filesystems.

mknod

mknod [*options*] *name type* [*major minor*]

Create a special file (a file that can send or receive data). Special files can be character files (read one character at a time), block files (read several characters at a time), or FIFO pipes (see **mkfifo**).

To choose which type of device to create, use one of the arguments:

p
> Create a FIFO file (named pipe). You do not need to specify the major and minor device numbers.

b
> Create a block file. You must specify the major and minor device numbers the file represents.

c *or* **u**
> Create a character file. You must specify the major and minor device numbers the file represents.

Linux's */dev/MAKEDEV* utility is useful for creating one or more devices of a given type in a single command.

Options

--help
> Print usage information and exit.

-m *mode,* **--mode=***mode*
> Set the file mode of the device, as with **chmod**. The default mode is **a=rw** unless you have chosen other settings via **umask**.

--version
> Print version information and exit.

mkpasswd

`mkpasswd [options] [user]`

Generate a new password for the specified user. The passwords produced are hard to guess and therefore more secure than passwords made up by actual people. Some operating systems distribute a different **mkpasswd** command, which regenerates the user password database; if your system has this version, check the manpage for instructions on how to use it.

If you do not specify a user, **mkpasswd** will display a new password. If you do specify a user, make sure that you have permission to set their password; this will usually mean being root.

Options

-l *n*

   Generate a password that is *n* characters long. The default is 9.

-d *n*

   Generate a password with at least *n* digits in it. The default is 2.

-c *n*

   Generate a password with at least *n* lowercase letters in it. The default is 2.

-C *n*

   Set the minimum number of uppercase letters in the password. The default is 2.

-s *n*

   Generate a password with at least *n* special characters in it. The default is 1.

-p *programname*

   Set the program used to actually set the password. If you do not choose one, the system will try to use **yppasswd**, or, if that is not installed, **passwd**.

-2

   Choose characters in the password so that, on a QWERTY-style keyboard, they alternate between left and right hand keys. This makes it harder for someone to guess what the password is if they watch you type it, but can make automated attacks easier.

-v

   Verbose mode; display the interaction between **mkpasswd** and the system as it sets the password.

mkraid

`mkraid [options] devices`

System administration command. Set up RAID array *devices* as defined in the */etc/raidtab* configuration file. **mkraid** can be used to initialize a new array or upgrade older RAID device arrays for the new kernel. Initialization will destroy any data on the disk devices used to create the array.

Options

-c *file*, **--configfile** *file*
> Use *file* instead of */etc/raidtab*.

-f, **--force**
> Initialize the devices used to create the RAID array even if they currently have data.

-h, **--help**
> Print a usage message and then exit.

-o, **--upgrade**
> Upgrade an older array to the current kernel's RAID version. Preserve data on the old array.

-V, **--version**
> Print version information and then exit.

---

mkswap

`mkswap [option] device [size]`

System administration command. Create swap space on *device*. You may specify its *size* in blocks; each block is a page of about 4KB.

Option

-c   Check for bad blocks before creating the swap space.

---

mktemp

`mktemp [options] template`

Generate a unique temporary filename for use in a script. The filename is based on the specified template, which may be any filename with at least six Xs appended (e.g., */tmp/mytemp. XXXXXX*). **mktemp** replaces the Xs with the current process number and/or a unique letter combination. The file is created with mode 0600 (unless **-u** is specified) and the filename is written to standard output.

Options

-d   Make a directory, not a file.

-q   Fail silently in case of error. Useful to prevent error output from being sent to standard error.

-u   Operate in "unsafe" mode and unlink the temporary file before **mktemp** exits. Use of this option is not recommended.

---

mlabel

`mlabel [options] drive[label]`

Label an MS-DOS filesystem (maximum of 11 characters). See **mtools** for more information.

Options

-c   Overwrite any existing labels.

-s   Show the existing label.

-n   Create a random serial number for the disk.

-N *serialno*
     Choose a new serial number for the disk. It should be an 8-digit hexadecimal number with no spaces in it.

---

mmd

mmd [*option*] *dirname*

Create a directory on an MS-DOS filesystem. See **mkdir** and **mtools** for more information.

Option

-D *clash-option*
     Specify the action to take if the specified directory name already exists. The possible clash options are as follows. (The primary name is the long name if it exists and the short name otherwise; the secondary name is the short name if a long name exists.)

a   Auto-rename the primary name.

A   Auto-rename the secondary name.

m   Ask the user what to do with the primary name.

M   Ask the user what to do with the secondary name.

o   Overwrite the primary name.

O   Overwrite the secondary name.

r   Rename the primary name, prompting the user for the name.

R   Rename the secondary name, prompting the user for the name.

s   Skip the primary name.

S   Skip the secondary name.

---

mmount

mmount *drive* [*mount-arguments*]

Mount an MS-DOS filesystem, passing the *mount-arguments* to **mount**. If no *mount-arguments* are specified, the device name is used. See **mount** and **mtools** for more information.

---

mmove

mmove [*options*] *sourcefile targetfile*
mmove [*options*] *sourcefiles targetdir*

Move or rename an MS-DOS file or directory within a single file-system. If no drive letter is specified for the target file or directory, the source drive is assumed. If no drive letter is specified for either the source or the target, drive **a:** is assumed. See **mv** and **mtools** for more information.

Options

-D *clash-option*
> Specify the action to take if the specified target file or directory already exists. See **mmd** for the possible clash options.

-v   Verbose; display names of the files or directories being moved.

---

modinfo

modinfo [*options*] *object-file*

System administration command. Print information about kernel module *object-file*. Information is read from tag names in the modinfo section of the module file. By default it will print the module's filename, description, author, license, and parameters.

Options

-a, --author
> Print author information.

-d, --description
> Print module description.

-f *format-string*, **--format** *format-string*
> Format output to match *string*. The format string is essentially a **printf** style string. Fields to be replaced are specified by a percent sign followed by a tag name in curly braces, e.g., **%{author}** and **%{filename}**. A line containing the field **%{parm}** will be repeated for each known module parameter. **author, description, filename, licenses,** and **parm** can also be represented by the shorter versions, **%a, %d, %n, %l,** and **%p.**

-h, --help
> Print usage message, then exit.

-l, --license
> Print module license information.

-n, --filename
> Print the module's filename.

-p, --parameters
> Print the module's typed parameters.

-V, --version
> Print version number of the module.

---

modprobe

modprobe [*options*] [*modules*]

System administration command. With no options, attempt to load the specified module, as well as all modules on which it depends. If more than one module is specified, attempt to load further modules only if the previous module failed to load. When specifying a module, use only its name without its path or trailing *.o.*

Options

-a, --all

 Load all listed modules, not just the first one.

-c, --showconfig

 Print **modprobe**'s current configuration.

-d, --debug

 Print debugging information about module.

-h, --help

 Print help message, then exit.

-k, --autoclean

 Mark module to be removed when inactive by setting its auto-clean flag. This option is passed on to **insmod**.

-l, --list

 List modules. This option may be combined with **-t** to specify a type of module.

-n, --show

 Don't load or remove modules; only show what would happen if modules were loaded or removed.

-q, --quiet

 Suppress warnings from **insmod** when it fails to load a module. Continue processing other modules. This option is passed on to **insmod**.

-r, --remove

 Remove the specified modules, as well as the modules on which they depend.

-s, --syslog

 Send error messages to **syslogd** instead of to standard error. This option is passed on to **insmod**.

-t *type,* **--type** *type*

 Load only a specific type of module. Consult */etc/modules.conf* for the directories in which all modules of that type reside.

-v, --verbose

 Print commands as they are executed.

-C *file,* **--config** *file*

 Read additional configuration from *file* instead of */etc/modules. conf.*

-V, --version

 Print version, then exit.

Files

/etc/modules.conf

 Information about modules: which ones depend on others, and which directories correspond to particular types of modules.

/sbin/insmod, /sbin/rmmod, /sbin/depmod

 Programs that **modprobe** relies on.

more

more [*options*] [*files*]

Display the named *files* on a terminal, one screenful at a time. See **less** for an alternative to **more**.

Options

+*num*
> Begin displaying at line number *num*.

-**num** *number*
> Set screen size to *number* lines.

+/*pattern*
> Begin displaying two lines before *pattern*.

-c Repaint screen from top instead of scrolling.

-d Display the prompt "Hit space to continue, Del to abort" in response to illegal commands; disable bell.

-f Count logical rather than screen lines. Useful when long lines wrap past the width of the screen.

-l Ignore form-feed (Ctrl-L) characters.

-p Page through the file by clearing each window instead of scrolling. This is sometimes faster.

-s Squeeze; display multiple blank lines as one.

-u Suppress underline characters.

Commands

All commands in **more** are based on **vi** commands. You can specify a number before many commands to have them executed multiple times. For instance, **3:p** causes **more** to skip back three files, the same as issuing **:p** three times. The optional number is indicated by *num* in the following list.

SPACE
> Display next screen of text.

z Display next *num* lines of text, and redefine a screenful to *num* lines. Default is one screenful.

RETURN
> Display next *num* lines of text, and redefine a screenful to *num* lines. Default is one line.

d, ^D
> Scroll *num* lines of text, and redefine scroll size to *num* lines. Default is one line.

q, Q, INTERRUPT
> Quit.

s Display next screen of text.

f Skip forward two screens of text.

b, ^B
> Skip backward one screen of text.

'   Return to point where previous search began.

=   Print number of current line.

/pattern
        Search for *pattern*, skipping to *num*th occurrence if an argu-
        ment is specified.

n   Repeat last search, skipping to *num*th occurrence if an argu-
        ment is specified.

!*cmd*, :!*cmd*
        Invoke shell and execute *cmd* in it.

v   Invoke **vi** editor on the file at the current line.

^L   Redraw screen.

:n   Skip to next file.

:p   Skip to previous file.

:f   Print current filename and line number.

.   Reexecute previous command.

Examples

Page through *file* in "clear" mode, and display prompts:

        more -cd *file*

Format *doc* to the screen, removing underlines:

        nroff *doc* | **more -u**

View the manpage for the **more** command; begin at the first
appearance of the word "scroll":

        man more|more +/scroll

---

mount   mount [*options*] [[*device*] *directory*]

                   System administration command. Mount a file structure. The file
                   structure on *device* is mounted on *directory*. If no *device* is speci-
                   fied, **mount** looks for an entry in */etc/fstab* to find what device is
                   associated with the given directory. The directory, which must
                   already exist and should be empty, becomes the name of the root
                   of the newly mounted file structure. If **mount** is invoked with no
                   arguments, it displays the name of each mounted device, the direc-
                   tory on which it is mounted, its filesystem type, and any mount
                   options associated with the device.

                   ### Options

                   -a   Mount all filesystems listed in */etc/fstab*. Use **-t** to limit this to
                        all filesystems of a particular type.

                   -f   Fake mount. Go through the motions of checking the device
                        and directory, but do not actually mount the filesystem.

                   -h   Print help message, then exit.

                   -l   When reporting on mounted filesystems, show filesystem
                        labels for filesystems that have them.

                   -n   Do not record the mount in */etc/mtab*.

-o *option*

Qualify the mount with a mount option. Many filesystem types have their own options. The following are common to most filesystems:

async

Read input and output to the device asynchronously.

atime

Update inode access time for each access. This is the default behavior.

auto

Allow mounting with the **-a** option.

defaults

Use all options' default values (**async, auto, dev, exec, nouser, rw, suid**).

dev

Interpret any special devices that exist on the filesystem.

exec

Allow binaries to be executed.

_netdev

Filesystem is a network device requiring network access.

noatime

Do not update inode access time for each access.

noauto

Do not allow mounting via the **-a** option.

nodev

Do not interpret any special devices that exist on the filesystem.

noexec

Do not allow the execution of binaries on the filesystem.

nosuid

Do not acknowledge any **suid** or **sgid** bits.

nouser

Only privileged users will have access to the filesystem.

remount

Expect the filesystem to have already been mounted, and remount it.

ro

Allow read-only access to the filesystem.

rw

Allow read/write access to the filesystem.

suid

Acknowledge **suid** and **sgid** bits.

sync

Read input and output to the device synchronously.

user

Allow unprivileged users to mount or unmount the filesystem. The defaults on such a system will be **nodev**, **noexec**, and **nosuid**, unless otherwise specified.

users

Allow any user to mount or unmount the filesystem. The defaults on such a system will be **nodev**, **noexec**, and **nosuid**, unless otherwise specified.

-r   Mount filesystem read-only.

-s   Where possible, ignore mount options specified by -o that are not supported by the filesystem.

-t *type*

Specify the filesystem type. Possible values include **adfs**, **affs**, **autofs**, **coda**, **cramfs**, **devpts**, **efs**, **ext2**, **ext3**, **hfs**, **hpfs**, **iso9660**, **jfs**, **msdos**, **ncpfs**, **nfs**, **ntfs**, **proc**, **qnx4**, **reiserfs**, **romfs**, **smbfs**, **sysv**, **tmpfs**, **udf**, **ufs**, **umsdos**, **vfat**, **xfs**, and **xiafs**. The default type is **iso9660**. The type **auto** may also be used to set **mount** to autodetect the filesystem. When used with **-a**, this option can limit the types mounted. Use a comma-separated list to specify more than one type to mount, and prefix a type with **no** to exclude that type.

-v   Display mount information verbosely.

-w   Mount filesystem read/write. This is the default.

-F   When used with **-a**, fork a new process to mount each system.

-L *label*

Mount filesystem with the specified label.

-O *option*

Limit systems mounted with **-a** by its filesystem options. (As used with **-o**.) Use a comma-separated list to specify more than one option, and prefix an option with **no** to exclude filesystems with that option. Options **-t** and **-O** are cumulative.

-U *uuid*

Mount filesystem with the specified *uuid*.

-V   Print version, then exit.

Files

/etc/fstab

List of filesystems to be mounted and options to use when mounting them.

/etc/mtab

List of filesystems currently mounted and the options with which they were mounted.

/proc/partitions

Used to find filesystems by label and uuid.

mountd

`rpc.mountd` [*options*]

NFS/NIS command. NFS mount request server. **mountd** reads the file */etc/exports* to determine which filesystems are available for mounting by which machines. It also provides information about which filesystems are mounted by which clients. See also **nfsd**.

Options

-d *kind*, --debug *kind*
> Specify debugging facility. Accepted values for *kind* are **general**, **call**, **auth**, **parse**, and **all**.

-f *file*, --exports-file *file*
> Read the export permissions from *file* instead of */etc/exports*.

-h, --help
> Print help message, then exit.

-n, --no-tcp
> Use UDP for mounts.

-o *n*, --descriptors *n*
> Allow no more than *n* open file descriptors. The default is 256.

-p *n*, --port *n*
> Bind to specified port instead of accepting a port from **portmapper**.

-v, --version
> Print the version number, then exit.

-F, --foreground
> Run **mountd** in the foreground.

-N *n*, --no-nfs-version *n*
> Do not offer NFS version *n*.

-V *n*, --nfs-version *n*
> Explicity offer NFS version *n*.

Files

/etc/exports
> Information about mount permissions.

/var/lib/nfs/rmtab
> List of filesystems currently mounted by clients.

---

mpartition

`mpartition` [*options*] *drive*

Create the MS-DOS partition specified by *drive*; used mostly on proprietary Unix systems where **fdisk** is unavailable. See **mtools** for more information. When a partition is being created, the default is for the number of sectors and heads and the length to be automatically determined, but they can also be specified as options.

Options

-a   Activate the partition, making it the bootable partition.

-b *offset*
> The starting offset of the partition to be created, in sectors. The default is the start of the disk (partition 1) or immediately after the end of the previous partition.

-B *bootsector*
> Read the template master boot record from the file specified by *bootsector*. Can be specified with **-I**.

-c   Create the partition.

-d   Deactivate the partition, making it nonbootable.

-f   Allow overriding of safeguards that perform consistency checking before any change is made to a partition. Can be specified with any operation that modifies the partition table.

-h *heads*
> The number of heads for a partition being created.

-I   Initialize the partition table and remove all partitions.

-l *length*
> The size of the partition to be created, in sectors.

-p   Print a command line to re-create the partition. With -v, print the current partition table.

-r   Remove the partition.

-s *sectors*
> The number of sectors per track of the partition to be created.

-t *cylinders*
> The number of cylinders of the partition to be created.

-v   With -p, print the current partition table; otherwise, for commands that modify the partition table, print it after it has been modified.

-vv   Print a hexadecimal dump of the partition table when reading and writing it.

---

mpg123

     mpg123 [*options*] *file*

     Command-line MP3 player. See **mpg321**.

---

mpg321

     mpg321 [*options*] *file*
     mpg123 [*options*] *file*

     Command-line MP3 players, often used as backends for GUI music players. The files played may be local files or URLs. **mpg321** and **mpg123** behave the same way, except that **mpg123** lacks the option **--skip-printing-frames**.

Options

-o *devicetype*

> Name the type of audio device you are using. Valid types are **oss** (Open Sound System), **sun** (Sun audio system), **alsa** (Advanced Linux Sound Architecture), **alsa09** (ALSA, version 0.9), **esd** (Enlightened Sound Daemon), and **arts** (Analog Real-Time Synthesizer).

-a, --audiodevice *device*

> Name the actual device (e.g., */dev/sound/dsp1*) you are using. This option is ignored if you have chosen **-o arts**. For **esd** running on remote systems, you must specify the host, and for **alsa**, you must specify the card and device (default is **0:0**).

-g, --gain *n*

> Set the volume (gain) to an integer between 1 and 100.

-k, --skip *n*

> Do not play the first *n* frames of the file or stream.

-n, --frames *n*

> Play only the first *n* frames of the file or stream.

-@, --list *filename*

> Specify a playlist file. The format of *filename* is just a list of filenames, one file per line, to be played.

-z, --shuffle

> Shuffle the files in the playlist and any files supplied on the command line, and play the list once. Each file will be played once.

-Z, --random

> Each time one file is finished playing, choose a new file at random. Files may be played more than once, and **mpg321** will continue playing songs at random until it is stopped.

-v, --verbose

> Verbose mode. Display additional information about the file, including ID3 tags and time played/time remaining.

-s, --stdout

> Mostly useful for developers, this option uses stdout instead of an audio device for its output. The output is 16-bit PCM, little-endian data.

-w, --wav *filename*

> Instead of playing the song, write the output to the *.wav* file you specify. Choosing - as the filename sends the WAV data to stdout. This option is usually used with the **--cdr** option.

--cdr *filename*

> Write to a CDR file. Choosing - as the filename sends the data to stdout.

--au *filename*

> Instead of playing the file, write the output to the *.au* file you specify. Choosing - as the filename sends the data to stdout.

-t, --test
> Test mode. Do not play or write any data.

-q, --quiet
> Quiet mode. This still plays the file, but does not display any data about the file or about **mpg321**.

-R   Operate in "remote control" mode, allowing seek and pause. This option is useful almost exclusively for developers of graphical frontends for **mpg321**.

--stereo
> Play in stereo. If audio is mono, send two identical streams as stereo output.

--aggressive
> Aggressive mode takes a higher priority in the system if possible. It requires root access because it can preempt processes owned by other users.

--skip-printing-frames *n*
> Save CPU cycles by displaying a status update only once every *n* frames. This option is not available in **mpg123**.

--help, --longhelp
> Display usage information.

-V, --version
> Display the version of **mpg321** and then quit.

---

mrd   **mrd** [*option*] *directory*

Delete an MS-DOS directory. The directory should be empty. To delete a full directory and its contents, use **mdeltree**. See **rmdir** and **mtools** for more information.

Option

-v   Operate in verbose mode, displaying each directory as it is deleted.

---

mren   **mren** [*options*] *file name*

Rename an MS-DOS file. See **rename** and **mtools** for more information.

Options

-D *clash-option*
> Specify the action to take if the specified new name already exists. See **mmd** for the possible clash options.

-v   Operate verbosely, showing the names of files and directories as they are renamed.

-V   Print version information and exit.

---

mshowfat

mshowfat `file`

Display the FAT clusters associated with a file on an MS-DOS system. See **mtools** for more information.

---

mt

mt [`option`] `operation` [`count`]

Control a magnetic tape drive used to back up or restore system data. The *operation* argument determines what action will be taken, and unless the -**f** or --**file** option is used, the action is applied to the default tape drive named in the **TAPE** environment variable. The *count* argument determines how many times the operation is to be repeated. If not specified, it defaults to 1.

Options

-f, --file=*device*

Name the tape device to use. This may be a local device, character special file (see **mknod**), or a remote device, named as *host:/path/to/drive* or *user@host:path/to/drive*.

--rsh-command=*command*

Choose a different command to use when connecting to a remote drive. The default is set in **MT_RSH**, and is normally either **ssh** or **rsh**.

-V, --version

Print version number and exit.

Operations

mt can perform the following operations on tape drives. Operations applicable only to SCSI tape drives are marked as such.

eof, weof *n*

Write *n* end-of-file (EOF) notations at the current location on the tape.

fsf *n*

Move forward *n* files, positioning the tape at the first block of the next file.

bsf *n*

Move backward *n* files, positioning the tape at the first block of the previous file.

fsr *n*

Move forward *n* records.

bsr *n*

Move backward *n* records.

bsfm *n*

Move backward *n* file marks, to a position on side of the file mark closer to the beginning of the tape.

fsfm *n*

Move forward *n* file marks, to a position on side of the file mark closer to the beginning of the tape.

asf *n*

> Move to file number *n* on the tape. This is the same as rewinding the tape and moving forward *n* spaces with **fsf**.

eom

> Move to the end of recording on the tape. Usually used when preparing to record new data onto the tape.

rewind

> Return to the beginning of the tape.

offline, rewoffl

> Rewind and unload the tape (if drive supports unload).

status

> Display the status of the tape drive.

retension

> Used when the tape has become loosely wound, usually because it has been dropped, shaken, or transported. Rewinds the tape, moves forward to the end of the tape, then rewinds again.

erase

> Erase the tape.

fss *n*

> SCSI drives only. Move forward *n* set marks.

bss *n*

> SCSI drives only. Move backward *n* set marks.

wset *n*

> SCSI drives only. Write *n* set marks at current position.

eod, seod

> Move to the end of valid data on the tape. Similar to **eom**, but used with streamer tapes.

setblk *n*

> SCSI drives only. Set the block size to *n* bytes per record.

setdensity *n*

> SCSI drives only. Set the data density for your tape drive to *n*. The appropriate value should be in the tape or tape drive documentation. For more information, see the **densities** operation.

drvbuffer *n*

> SCSI drives only. Set the buffer value. For no buffer, choose 0, and for normal buffering, choose 1. Other values may have different effects depending on the drive.

stoptions *n*

> SCSI drives only. Set the driver bits for the device; items are added as with **chmod**. 1 is for write buffering, 2 for asynchronous writing, 4 for read-ahead, and 8 for debugging output.

stwrthreshold *n*

> SCSI drives only. Set the write threshold for the tape drive to *n* kilobytes. This value may not be higher than the driver buffer value.

seek *n*

SCSI drives only. Seek to block *n* on the tape.

tell

SCSI drives only. Tell the number of the current block on the tape.

densities

SCSI tapes only. Display information about data densities on stdout.

datacompression [*n*]

Works on some SCSI-2 DAT tapes only. If *n* is 0, turn data compression off. If *n* is 1, display the compression status. Other values turn compression on.

mtools   *command* [*options*] [*arguments*]

A collection of tools for working with MS-DOS files and filesystems, especially for accessing files on floppy disks without mounting them as Unix filesystems. The various commands are **mattrib, mbadblocks, mcat, mcd, mcopy, mdel, mdeltree, mdir, mdu, mformat, minfo, mlabel, mmd, mmount, mmove, mpartition, mrd, mren, mshowfat, mtoolstest, mtype,** and **mzip.**

For the purposes of **mtools**, all MS-DOS file names begin with a drive letter and colon, followed by the path. **mtools** accepts both / and \ for directory separators. For example, an MS-DOS file might be referred to as *a:/directory/subdirectory/file.txt.* If you use the backslash or any standard Unix wildcards or special characters, put the filename in quotation marks.

FAT filesystem filenames are normally a maximum of eight characters long with a three-letter extension, and are not case-sensitive. Even in the more recent VFAT system, which does preserve case sensitivity, two files with the same letters in their names, regardless of case, cannot coexist. Unix filenames that are too long, that use reserved characters (; + = [ ] ' , \ " * \ \ < > / ? : or |), or that conflict with MS-DOS devices (PRN, for example) are converted to VFAT names. This means replacing reserved characters with an underscore (_) and shortening files as needed, replacing several characters with a single tilde (~).

mtoolstest   mtoolstest

Display the configuration for **mtools**. See **mtools** for more information.

mtype   mtype [*options*] *files*

Display the contents of an MS-DOS file, as with the MS-DOS command **type**. See **mtools** for more information.

Options

-s   Strip the high bit from the data.

-t   View as a text file, changing carriage return/line feeds to line feeds.

---

mv

mv [*option*] *sources target*

Move or rename files and directories. The source (first column) and target (second column) determine the result (third column):

Source	Target	Result
File	*name* (nonexistent)	Rename file to *name*.
File	Existing file	Overwrite existing file with source file.
Directory	*name* (nonexistent)	Rename directory to *name*.
Directory	Existing directory	Move directory to be a subdirectory of existing directory.
One or more files	Existing directory	Move files to directory.

Options

-b, --backup
Back up files before removing.

-f, --force
Force the move, even if *target* file exists; suppress messages about restricted access modes.

--help
Print a help message and then exit.

-i, --interactive
Query user before removing files.

-u, --update
Do not remove a file or link if its modification date is the same as or newer than that of its replacement.

-v, --verbose
Print the name of each file before moving it.

--version
Print version information and then exit.

-S *suffix,* **--suffix=***suffix*
Override the **SIMPLE_BACKUP_SUFFIX** environment variable, which determines the suffix used for making simple backup files. If the suffix is not set either way, the default is a tilde (~).

-V *value,* **--version-control=***value*
Override the **VERSION_CONTROL** environment variable, which determines the type of backups made. The acceptable values for version control are:

t, numbered
Always make numbered backups.

nil, existing
> Make numbered backups of files that already have them, simple backups of the others. This is the default.

never, simple
> Always make simple backups.

---

mzip

mzip [*options*] [*drive:*]

Set modes or eject an MS-DOS-formatted ZIP or JAZ disk. See **mtools** for information about handling MS-DOS filesystems. Unix-formatted ZIP and JAZ drives can be handled as you would a floppy or other removable media, using the **mount** and **umount** commands.

Note that a ZIP drive is usually referred to as drive Z:, and a JAZ drive as drive J:.

Options

- **-e**   Eject the disk.
- **-f**   Force eject (even if the disk is mounted). Must be used in combination with **-e**.
- **-r**   Put disk into read-only mode.
- **-w**   Put disk into read/write mode.
- **-P**   Prevent writing to the disk without a password.
- **-x**   Prevent read or write access to the disk without a password.
- **-u**   Make the disk writable, but restore write protection on eject.
- **-q**   Query and display the disk status.

---

named

named [*options*]

TCP/IP command. Internet domain name server. **named** is used by resolver libraries to provide access to the Internet distributed naming database. With no arguments, **named** reads */etc/named.conf* for any initial data and listens for queries on a privileged port. See RFC 1034 and RFC 1035 for more details.

There are several **named** binaries available at different Linux archives, displaying various behaviors. Here we describe **named** as provided by Internet Software Consortium's Berkeley Internet Name Domain (BIND) version 9.2.x.

Options

-c *file*
> Read configuration information from *file* instead of */etc/named.conf*.

-d *debuglevel*
> Print debugging information. *debuglevel* is a number indicating the level of messages printed.

-f   Run **named** in the foreground.

-g   Run **named** in the foreground and send all log messages to standard error.

-n *n*
> Specify the number of processors in a multiprocessor system. Normally **named** can autodetect the number of CPUs.

-p *port*
> Use *port* as the port number. Default is 53.

-t *dir*
> Change root to specified directory after reading command arguments but before reading the configuration file. Useful only when running with option **-u**.

-u *user*
> Set the user ID to *user* after completing any privileged operations.

-v   Print version, then exit.

File

/etc/named.conf
> Read when **named** starts up.

---

namei

namei [*options*] *pathname* [*pathname* . . .]

Follow a pathname until a terminal point is found (e.g., a file, directory, char device, etc.). If **namei** finds a symbolic link, it shows the link and starts following it, indenting the output to show the context. **namei** prints an informative message when the maximum number of symbolic links this system can have has been exceeded.

Options

-m   Show mode bits of each file type in the style of **ls** (e.g., "rwxr-xr-x").

-x   Show mountpoint directories with a **D** rather than a **d**.

File type characters

For each line of output, **namei** prints the following characters to identify the file types found:

-    A regular file.

?   An error of some kind.

b   A block device.

c   A character device.

d   A directory.

f: The pathname **namei** is currently trying to resolve.

l   A symbolic link (both the link and its contents are output).

s   A socket.

| **nameif** | **nameif** [*options*] [*name macaddress*] |

System administration command. Assign an interface *name* to a network device specified by *macaddress*, the unique serial number that identifies a network card. If no *name* and *macaddress* are given, **nameif** will attempt to read addresses from the configuration file */etc/mactab*. Each line of the configuration file should contain either a comment beginning with # or an interface name and MAC address.

Options

-c *filename*
> Read interface names and MAC addresses from *filename* instead of */etc/mactab*.

-s Send any error messages to **syslog**.

File

/proc/ksyms
> List of interface names and MAC addresses used to rename interfaces.

| **netstat** | **netstat** [*options*] |

TCP/IP command. Show network status. Print information on active sockets, routing tables, interfaces, masquerade connections, or multicast memberships. By default, **netstat** lists open sockets.

Options

The first five options(**-g**, **-i**, **-r**, **-s**, and **-M**) determine what kind of information **netstat** should display.

-g, --groups
> Show multicast group memberships.

-i, --interface[=*name*]
> Show all network interfaces, or just the interface specified by *name*.

-r, --route
> Show kernel routing tables.

-s, --statistics
> Show statistics for each protocol.

-M, --masquerade
> Show masqueraded connections.

-a, --all
> Show all entries.

-c, --continuous
> Display information continuously, refreshing once every second.

-e, --extend
> Increase level of detail in reports. Use twice for maximum detail.

-l, --listening
> Show only listening sockets.

-n, --numeric
> Show network addresses, ports, and users as numbers.

--numeric-hosts
> Show host addresses as numbers, but resolve others.

--numeric-ports
> Show ports as numbers, but resolve others.

--numeric-users
> Show user ID numbers for users, but resolve others.

-o, --timers
> Include information on network timers.

-p, --program
> Show the process ID and name of the program owning the socket.

--protocol=*family*
> Show connections only for the specified address *family*. Accepted values are **inet, unix, ipx, ax25, netrom**, and **ddp**.

-t, --tcp
> Limit report to information on TCP sockets.

-u, --udp
> Limit report to information on UDP sockets.

-v, --verbose
> Verbose mode.

-w, --raw
> Limit report to information on raw sockets.

-C   Print routing information from the route cache.

-F   Print routing information from the forward information database (FIB). This is the default.

-N, --symbolic
> Where possible, print symbolic host, port, or user names instead of numerical representatitons. This is the default behavior.

---

newaliases

newaliases

Rebuild the mail aliases database, */etc/aliases*, after a change. Return 0 on success, or a number greater than 0 if there was an error. **newaliases** must be run whenever */etc/aliases* has been changed for the change to take effect. Identical to **sendmail -bi**.

---

newgrp

newgrp [*group*]

Change user's group ID to the specified group. If no group is specified, change to the user's login group. The new group is then used for checking permissions.

newusers   newusers *file*

System administration command. Create or update system users from entries in *file*. Each line in *file* has the same format as an entry in */etc/passwd* except that passwords are unencrypted, and group IDs can be given as a name or number. During an update, the password age field is ignored if the user already exists in the */etc/shadow* password file. If a group name or ID does not already exist, it will be created. If a home directory does not exist, it will be created.

nfsd   rpc.nfsd [*option*] *n*

System administration command. Launch *n* kernel threads for the Network File System (NFS) kernel module. The threads will handle client filesystem requests. By default only one thread is launched. Most systems require eight or more, depending on the number of NFS clients using the system. Use **nfsstat** to check NFS performance.

Option

-p *port*
> Listen for NFS requests on *port* instead of the default port 2049.

nfsstat   nfsstat [*options*]

System administration command. Print statistics on NFS and remote procedure call (RPC) activity for both clients and server.

Options

-c   Display only client-side statistics.

-n   Display only NFS statistics.

-r   Display only RPC statistics.

-s   Display only server-side statistics.

-o *facility*
> Only display statistics for the specified *facility*. The following are valid values for *facility*:

> **fh**   Server file handle cache.

> **net** Network layer statistics.

> **nfs** Same as **-n**.

> **rc**   Server request reply cache.

> **rpc** Same as **-r**.

nice   nice [*option*] [*command* [*arguments*]]

Execute a *command* (with its *arguments*) with lower priority (i.e., be "nice" to other users). With no arguments, **nice** prints the default scheduling priority (niceness). If **nice** is a child process, it prints the parent process's scheduling priority. Niceness has a range of –20 (highest priority) to 19 (lowest priority).

Options

--help
> Print a help message and then exit.

-n *adjustment,* *-adjustment,* **--adjustment**=*adjustment*
> Run *command* with niceness incremented by *adjustment* (1–19); default is 10. A privileged user can raise priority by specifying a negative *adjustment* (e.g., –5).

--version
> Print version information and then exit.

---

nm

nm [*options*] [*objfiles*]

Print the symbol table (name list) in alphabetical order for one or more object files. If no object files are specified, perform operations on *a.out*. Output includes each symbol's value, type, size, name, and so on. A key letter categorizing the symbol can also be displayed.

Options

-a, --debug-syms
> Print debugger symbols.

--defined-only
> Display only defined symbols.

-f *format,* **--format**=*format*
> Specify output format (**bsd**, **sysv**, or **posix**). Default is **bsd**.

-g, --extern-only
> Print external symbols only.

--help
> Print help message, then exit.

-l, --line-numbers
> Print source filenames and line numbers for each symbol from available debugging information.

-n, -v, --numeric-sort
> Sort the external symbols by address.

-p, --no-sort
> Don't sort the symbols at all.

-r, --reverse-sort
> Sort in reverse, alphabetically or numerically.

-s, --print-armap
> Include mappings stored by **ar** and **ranlib** when printing archive symbols.

--size-sort
> Sort by size.

-t *radix,* **--radix**=*radix*
> Use the specified *radix* for printing symbol values. Accepted values are **d** for decimal, **o** for octal, and **x** for hexadecimal.

--target=*format*
> Specify an object code *format* other than the system default.

-u, --undefined-only
Report only the undefined symbols.

-A, -o, -print-file-name
Print input filenames before each symbol.

-C, --demangle[=*style*]
Translate low-level symbol names into readable versions. You may specify a style to use when demangling symbol names from a foreign compiler.

-D, --dynamic
Print dynamic, not normal, symbols. Useful only when working with dynamic objects (some kinds of shared libraries, for example).

-P, --portability
Same as **-f posix**.

-S, --print-size
Print the size of defined symbols.

-V, --version
Print **nm**'s version number on standard error.

---

nohup

nohup *command* [*arguments*]
nohup *option*

Run the named *command* with its optional command *arguments*, continuing to run it even after you log out (make *command* immune to hangups; i.e., **no hangup**). Terminal output is appended to the file *nohup.out* by default. Modern shells preserve background commands by default; this command is necessary only in the original Bourne shell.

Options
--help
Print usage information and exit.

--version
Print version information and exit.

---

nslookup

nslookup [**-option...**] [*host_to_find* | -[*server*]]

TCP/IP command. Query Internet domain name servers. **nslookup** is deprecated; its functionality is replaced by the **dig** and **host** commands. **nslookup** may not be included in some distributions.

nslookup has two modes: interactive and noninteractive. Interactive mode allows the user to query name servers for information about various hosts and domains or to print a list of hosts in a domain. It is entered either when no arguments are given (default name server will be used) or when the first argument is a hyphen and the second argument is the hostname or Internet address of a name server. Noninteractive mode is used to print just the name and requested information for a host or domain. It is used when the name of the host to be looked up is given as the first argument. Any of the *keyword=value* pairs listed under the interactive **set**

command can be used as an option on the command line by prefacing the keyword with a -. The optional second argument specifies a name server.

Options

All of the options under the **set** interactive command can be entered on the command line, with the syntax -*keyword*[=*value*].

Interactive commands

exit

> Exit **nslookup**.

finger [*name*] [>|>>*filename*]

> Connect with finger server on current host, optionally creating or appending to *filename*.

help, ?

> Print a brief summary of commands.

host [*server*]

> Look up information for *host* using the current default server, or *server* if specified.

ls -[ahd] *domain* [>|>>*filename*]

> List information available for *domain*, optionally creating or appending to *filename*. The **-a** option lists aliases of hosts in the domain. **-h** lists CPU and operating system information for the domain. **-d** lists all contents of a zone transfer.

lserver *domain*

> Change the default server to *domain*. Use the initial server to look up information about *domain*.

root

> Change default server to the server for the root of the domain namespace.

server *domain*

> Change the default server to *domain*. Use the current default server to look up information about *domain*.

set *keyword*[=*value*]

> Change state information affecting the lookups. Valid keywords are:

> **all**

> > Print the current values of the frequently used options to **set**.

> **class=***name*

> > Set query class to **IN** (Internet), **CHAOS**, **HESIOD**, or **ANY**. Default is **IN**.

> **domain=***name*

> > Change default domain name to *name*.

> **[no]debug**

> > Turn debugging mode on or off.

> **[no]d2**

> > Turn exhaustive debugging mode on or off.

[no]defname
Append default domain name to every lookup.

[no]ignoretc
Ignore truncate error.

[no]recurse
Tell name server to query or not query other servers if it does not have the information.

[no]search
With *defname*, search for each name in parent domains of current domain.

[no]vc
Always use a virtual circuit when sending requests to the server.

port=*port*
Connect to name server using *port*.

querytype=*value*
See **type=***value*.

retry=*number*
Set number of retries to *number*.

root=*host*
Change name of root server to *host*.

srchlist=*domain*
Set search list to *domain*.

timeout=*number*
Change timeout interval for waiting for a reply to *number* seconds.

type=*value*
Change type of information returned from a query to one of:

A	Host's Internet address
ANY	Any available information
CNAME	Canonical name for an alias
HINFO	Host CPU and operating system type
MD	Mail destination
MG	Mail group member
MINFO	Mailbox or mail list information
MR	Mail rename domain name
MX	Mail exchanger
NS	Name server for the named zone
PTR	Hostname or pointer to other information
SOA	Domain start-of-authority
TXT	Text information
UINFO	User information
WKS	Supported well-known services

view *filename*
Sort and list output of previous **ls** command(s) with **more**.

nsupdate

nsupdate [*options*] [*filename*]

System administration command. Interactively submit dynamic DNS update requests to a name server. Use **nsupdate** to add or remove records from a zone without manually editing the zone file. Commands may be entered interactively or read from *filename*. An update message is built from multiple commands, some establishing prerequisites, some adding or deleting resource records. Messages are executed as a single transaction. A blank line or the **send** command will send the current message. Lines beginning with a semicolon are treated as comments. For additional information on dynamic DNS updates, see RFC 2136.

Options

-d   Print additional tracing information usable for debugging.

-k *keyfile*
    Read encrypted transaction signature key from *keyfile*. The key should be encrypted using the HMAC-MD5 algorithm. Keyfiles are generated by the **dnssec-keygen** command.

-v   Use TCP instead of UDP to send update requests.

-y *keyname:secret*
    Generate transaction signature from specified *keyname* and *secret*.

Interactive commands

key *keyname secret*
    Generate transaction signature from specified *keyname* and *secret*. This command overrides command-line options **-k** or **-y**.

local *address* [*port*]
    Use local *address* and, if specified, *port* to send updates.

prereq nxdomain *domain-name*
    Perform updates only if there are no preexisting records with the name *domain-name*.

prereq nxrset *domain-name* [*class*] *type*
    Perform updates only if there are no preexisting records of the specified *type* and *class* for *domain-name*. When no *class* is given, **IN** is assumed.

prereq yxdomain *domain-name*
    Perform updates only if there is a preexisting record with the name *domain-name*.

prereq nxrset *domain-name* [*class*] *type* [*data*.
    Perform updates only if there is a preexisting record of the specified *type* and *class* for *domain-name*. If *data* is given, the RDATA of the specified resource must match it exactly. When no *class* is given, **IN** is assumed.

send
    Send the current message. Same as entering a blank line.

server *servername* [*port*]
> Update records on DS server *servername* instead of the master server listed in the **MNAME** field of the appropriate zone's SOA record.

show
> Print all commands in current message.

update add *domain-name* [*ttl*] [*class*] *type data*
> Add a resource record with the specified values.

update delete *domain-name* [*ttl*] [*class*] [*type* [*data*]]
> Delete resource records for *domain-name*. The *ttl* field is always ignored, but if other fields are given, only delete records that match all criteria.

zone *zonename*
> Apply updates to the specified *zonename*. If no **zone** command is given, **nsupdate** attempts to determine the correct zone based on other input.

---

objcopy

objcopy [*options*] *infile* [*outfile*]

Copy the contents of the input object file to another file, optionally changing the file format in the process (but not the endianness). If *outfile* is not specified, **objcopy** creates a temporary file and renames it to *infile* when the copy is complete, destroying the original input file. The GNU Binary File Descriptor (BFD) library is used to read and write the object files.

Options

--add-section *section=file*
> Add a new section to the output object file with the specified section name and the contents taken from the specified file. Available only for formats that allow arbitrarily named sections.

--alt-machine-code=*n*
> If the output architecture has alternate machine codes, use the *n*th code instead of the default.

-b *n,* **--byte**=*n*
> Copy only every *n*th byte. Header data is not affected. The value of *n* can be from 0 to *interleave*–1, where *interleave* is specified by **-i** (default is 4). This option is useful for creating files to program ROM and is typically used with **srec** as the output format.

-B *bfdarch,* **--binary-architecture**=*bfdarch*
> Set the output architecture to *bfdarch* (e.g., i386) for transforming a raw binary file into an object file. Otherwise, this option is ignored. After the conversion, your program can access data inside the created object file by referencing the special symbols **_binary_objfile_start**, **_binary_objfile_end**, and **_binary_objfile_size**.

--change-addresses=*incr*, --adjust-vma=*incr*

Change the VMA and LMA addresses of all sections, plus the start address, by adding *incr*. Changing section addresses is not supported by all object formats. Sections are not relocated.

--change-leading-char

For object formats that use a special character (such as an underscore) to begin symbols, change the leading character when converting between formats. If the character is the same in both formats, the option has no effect. Otherwise, it adds, removes, or changes the leading character as appropriate for the output format.

--change-section-address *section*{=|+|-}*val*, **--adjust-section-vma** *section*{=|+|-}*val*

Set or change the VMA and LMA addresses of the specified section. With =, set the section address to the specified value; otherwise, add or subtract the value to get the new address.

--change-section-lma *section*{=|+|-}*val*

Set or change the LMA address of the specified section. With =, set the section address to the specified value; otherwise, add or subtract the value to get the new address.

--change-section-vma *section*{=|+|-}*val*

Set or change the VMA address of the specified section. With =, set the section address to the specified value; otherwise, add or subtract the value to get the new address.

--change-start *incr*, **--adjust-start** *incr*

Add *incr* to the start address to get a new start address. Not supported by all object formats.

--change-warnings, --adjust-warnings

Issue a warning if the section specified in one of the options **--change-section-address**, **--change-section-lma**, or **--change-section-vma** does not exist.

--debugging

Convert debugging information if possible.

-F *bfdname*, **--target=***bfdname*

Set the binary format for both input and output files to the binary file descriptor name *bfdname*. No format translation is done. Use the **-h** option for a list of supported formats for your system.

-g, --strip-debug

Do not copy debugging information.

-G *symbol*, **--keep-global-symbol=***symbol*

Copy only the specified global symbol, making all other symbols local to the file. May be specified multiple times.

--gap-fill=*val*

Fill gaps between sections with the specified value; applies to the load address (LMA) of the sections.

-h, --help

Print help information, including a list of supported target object formats, then exit.

-i *interleave,* **--interleave**=*interleave*

Copy one out of every *interleave* bytes. Use **-b** to set the byte to copy (default is 4). This option is ignored if **-b** is not specified.

-I *bfdname,* **--input-target**=*bfdname*

Set the binary file format of the input file using its binary file descriptor name, *bfdname*.

-j *section,* **--only-section**=*section*

Copy only the specified section. May be specified multiple times.

-K *symbol,* **--keep-symbol**=*symbol*

Copy only the specified symbol from the source file. May be specified multiple times.

--keep-global-symbols=*filename*

Apply the option **--keep-global-symbol** to each symbol listed in the specified file. The file should have one symbol per line, with comments beginning with a hash mark (#). May be specified multiple times.

--keep-symbols=*file*

Apply the option **--keep-symbol** to each symbol listed in the specified file. The file should have one symbol per line, with comments beginning with a hash mark (#). May be specified multiple times.

-L *symbol,* **--localize-symbol**=*symbol*

Make the specified symbol local. May be specified multiple times.

--localize-symbols=*filename*

Apply the option **--localize-symbol** to each symbol listed in the specified file. The file should have one symbol per line, with comments beginning with a hash mark (#). May be specified multiple times.

-N *symbol,* **--strip-symbol**=*symbol*

Do not copy the specified symbol. May be specified multiple times.

--no-change-warnings, --no-adjust-warnings

Do not issue a warning even if the section specified in one of the options **--change-section-address**, **--change-section-lma**, or **--change-section-vma** does not exist.

-O *bfdname,* **--output-target**=*bfdname*

Set the binary file format of the output file using its binary file descriptor name, *bfdname*. The format **srec** generates S-records (printable ASCII versions of object files), and **binary** generates a raw binary file. Use **-h** for other available formats.

-p, --preserve-dates
> Preserve the input file's access and modification dates in the output file.

--pad-to=*addr*
> Pad the output file up to the load address. Use the fill value specified by **--gap-fill** (default is 0).

-R *section*, --remove-section=*section*
> Do not copy any section with the specified name. May be specified multiple times.

--redefine-sym *old=new*
> Change the name of the symbol *old* to *new*.

--remove-leading-char
> If the first character of a global symbol is a special character (such as an underscore) used by the input object file format, remove it. Unlike **--change-leading-char**, this option always changes the symbol name when appropriate, regardless of the output object format.

--rename-section *oldname=newname*[,*flags*]
> Rename a section from *oldname* to *newname*, optionally also changing the flags to *flags*.

-S, --strip-all
> Do not copy relocation and symbol information.

--set-section-flags *section=flags*
> Set flags for the specified section as a comma-separated string of flag names. Not all flags are meaningful for all object formats. The possible flags are **alloc**, **code**, **contents**, **data**, **debug**, **load**, **noload**, **readonly**, **rom**, and **share**.

--set-start=*val*
> Set the start address of the new file to the specified value. Not supported by all object formats.

--srec-forceS3
> Force all **srec** output records to be type S3 records.

--srec-len=*ival*
> Set the maximum length of **srec** output records to the specified value. The length includes the **address**, **data**, and **crc** fields.

--strip-symbols=*filename*
> Apply the option **--strip-symbol** to each symbol listed in the specified file. The file should have one symbol per line, with comments beginning with a hash mark (#). May be specified multiple times.

--strip-unneeded
> Strip all symbols not needed for relocation processing.

-v, --verbose
> Run in verbose mode, listing all object files modified; for archives, list all archive members.

-V, --version
Print version information and exit.

-W *symbol,* **--weaken-symbol=***symbol*
Make the specified symbol weak. May be specified multiple times.

--weaken
Make all global symbols weak.

--weaken-symbols=*filename*
Apply the option **--weaken-symbol** to each symbol listed in the specified file. The file should have one symbol per line, with comments beginning with a hash mark (#). May be specified multiple times.

-x, --discard-all
Do not copy nonglobal symbols.

-X, --discard-locals
Do not copy compiler-generated local symbols (usually those starting with L or ..).

---

objdump

objdump [*options*] *objfiles*

Display information about one or more object files. If an archive is specified, **objdump** displays information on each object file in the archive. At least one of the options **-a, -d, -D, -f, -g, -G, -h, -H, -p, -r, -S, -t, -T, -V,** or **-x** must be given to tell **objdump** what information to show.

Options

-a, --archive-header
If any input files are archives, display the archive header information. The output includes the object file format of each archive member.

--adjust-vma=*offset*
Add *offset* to all section headers before dumping information. Useful if the section addresses do not correspond to the symbol table.

-b *bfdname,* **--target=***bfdname*
Set the binary file format using its binary file descriptor name, *bfdname*. Use the **-h** option for a list of supported formats for your system.

-C [*style*], **--demangle**[=*style*]
Decode (demangle) low-level symbol names into user-level names, optionally specifying a mangling style. Removes any initial underscores and makes C++ function names readable.

-d, --disassemble
Display assembler mnemonic names for the machine instructions. Disassemble only sections that are expected to contain instructions.

-D, --disassemble-all
> Disassemble all sections, not just those expected to contain instructions.

-EB, --endian=big
-EL, --endian=little
> Specify whether the object files are big- or little-endian, for disassembling. Useful for disassembling formats such as S-records (printable ASCII versions of object files) that do not include that information.

-f, --file-header
> Display overall header summary information.

--file-start-context
> When using **-S** and displaying source code from a file that hasn't been displayed yet, include context from the start of the file.

-g, --debugging
> Display debugging information.

-G, --stabs
> Display any stabs (debugging symbol table entries) information, in addition to the contents of any sections requested.

-h, --section-header, --header
> Display section header summary information.

-H, --help
> Display help information and exit.

-i, --info
> Display the architectures and object formats available on your system for use with **-b** or **-m**.

-j *name,* **--section=***name*
> Display information for section *name*.

-l, --line-numbers
> Label the display with filename and source code line numbers corresponding to the object code or relocation entries shown. Use with **-d, -D,** or **-r**.

-m *arch,* **--architecture=***arch*
> Specify the architecture for disassembling object files. Useful when disassembling files such as S-records that do not include this information.

-M *options,* **--disassembler-options=***options*
> Pass target-specific information to the disassembler. Supported only on some targets.

--no-show-raw-insn
> Do not show instructions in hexadecimal when disassembling. This is the default with **--prefix-addresses**.

-p, --private-headers
> Display information specific to the object format. For some formats, no additional information is displayed.

--prefix-addresses

When disassembling, print the complete address on each line.

-r, --reloc

Display relocation entries. With **-b** or **-D**, the entries are intermixed with the disassembly.

-R, --dynamic-reloc

Print dynamic relocation entries. Meaningful only for dynamic objects such as certain types of shared libraries.

-s, --full-contents

Display the full contents of any requested sections.

-S, --source

Display source code intermixed with disassembly, if possible. Implies **-d**.

--show-raw-insn

When disassembling, show instructions in hexadecimal as well as symbolic form. This is the default except with **--prefix-addresses**.

--start-address=_addr_

Start displaying data at the specified address. Applies to **-d**, **-r**, and **-s**.

--stop-address=_addr_

Stop displaying data at the specified address. Applies to **-d**, **-r**, and **-s**.

-t, --syms

Print symbol table entries.

-T, --dynamic-syms

Print dynamic symbol table entries. Meaningful only for dynamic objects such as certain types of shared libraries.

-V, --version

Print version information and exit.

-w, --wide

Format lines for output devices wider than 80 characters, and do not truncate symbol table names.

-x, --all-header

Display all available header information. Equivalent to specifying **-a -f -h -r -t**.

-z, --disassemble-zeroes

Disassemble blocks of zeroes. The default is to skip such blocks.

---

od

od [_options_] [_files_]
od --traditional [_file_] [[**+**]_offset_ [[**+**]_label_]]

Dump the specified files to standard output. The default is to dump in octal format, but other formats can be specified. With multiple files, concatenate them in the specified order. If no files are specified or *file* is -, read from standard input. With the second form, using the **--traditional** option, only one file can be specified.

Options

For the following options, see the later "Arguments" section for an explanation of the arguments *bytes*, *size*, and *type*. If no options are specified, the default is **-A o -t d2 -w 16**.

-a   Print as named characters. Same as **-ta**.

-A*radix*, **--address-radix**=*radix*
> Specify the radix (base) for the file offsets printed at the beginning of each output line. The possible values are:
>
> **d**   Decimal.
>
> **n**   None; do not print an offset.
>
> **o**   Octal; the default.
>
> **x**   Hexadecimal.

-b   Print as octal bytes. Same as **-toC**.

-c   Print as ASCII characters or backslash escapes. Same as **-tc**.

-d   Print as unsigned decimal shorts. Same as **-tu2**.

-f   Print as floating point. Same as **-tfF**.

-h   Print as hexadecimal shorts. Same as **-tx2**.

--help
> Display a usage message and exit.

-i   Print as decimal shorts. Same as **-td2**.

-j*bytes*, **--skip-bytes**=*bytes*
> Skip the specified number of input bytes before starting.

-l   Print as decimal longs. Same as **-td4**.

-N*bytes*, **--read-bytes**=*bytes*
> Format and print only the specified number of input bytes.

-o   Print as octal shorts. Same as **-to2**.

-s*bytes*, **--strings**[=*bytes*]
> Output strings that are at least *bytes* ASCII graphic characters long (default 3 if *bytes* is not specified for **--strings**).

-t*type*, **--format**=*type*
> Format the output according to *type*, where *type* is a string of one or more of the characters listed in the "Arguments" section. If more than one type is specified, each output line is written once in each specified format. If a trailing z is appended to *type*, **od** appends any printable characters to the end of each output line.

--traditional
> Accept arguments in the traditional form, which takes a single file specification with an optional offset and label as shown in the second form of the command. *offset* is an octal number indicating how many input bytes to skip over. *label* specifies an initial pseudo-address, which is printed in parentheses after

any normal address. Both the offset and the label can begin with an optional plus sign (+), and can have a trailing decimal point (.) to force the offset to be interpreted as a decimal number and/or a trailing b to multiply the number of bytes skipped by *offset* by 512.

-v, --output-duplicates

Print all lines, including duplicates. By default, only the first of a series of identical lines is printed, and an asterisk is printed at the beginning of the following line to indicate that there were duplicates.

--version

Display version information and exit.

-w*bytes,* **--width**[*=bytes*]

Dump *bytes* input bytes to each output line. Defaults to 16 if this option is omitted. If **--width** is specified but *bytes* is omitted, the default is 32.

-x Print as hexadecimal shorts. Same as **-tx2**.

Arguments

bytes

Specify a number of bytes. Treated as hexadecimal if it begins with 0x or 0X, as octal if it begins with 0, or as decimal otherwise. Append b to multiply by 512, k to multiply by 1024, or m to multiply by 10248576.

size

Specified as part of *type* to indicate how many bytes to use in interpreting each number. Types **a** and **c** do not take a size. For other types, *size* is a number. For type **f**, *size* can also be one of the following:

D Double.

F Float.

L Long double.

For the remaining types (**d**, **o**, **u**, **x**), *size* can be one of the following in addition to a number:

C Character.

I Integer.

L Long.

S Short.

type

Specify the format type. The possible types are:

a Named character.

c ASCII character or backslash escape.

d*size*

Signed decimal, with *size* bytes per integer.

f_size_
> Floating point, with _size_ bytes per integer.

o   Octal, with _size_ bytes per integer.

u   Unsigned decimal, with _size_ bytes per integer.

x   Hexadecimal, with _size_ bytes per integer.

---

openvt

openvt [_options_] [--] [_command_] [_arguments_]

Locate the first available virtual terminal (VT) and run _command_ with any _arguments_ given. If no command is specified, the shell **$SHELL** is started.

Options

--   Required before the command name to pass options to the command.

-c _vt_
> Use the specified VT number instead of the first available. You must have write access to _vt_.

-l   Run the command as a login shell, prepending a dash (-) to the command name.

-s   Switch to the new VT when the command is started.

-u   Determine the owner of the current VT and log in as that user. You must be root to use this option, which is also suitable for calling by init. Don't use with **-l**.

-v   Verbose mode.

-w   Wait for the command to complete. If used with **-s**, switch back to the controlling terminal when the command is done.

---

passwd

passwd [_user_]

Create or change a password associated with a _user_ name. Only the owner or a privileged user may change a password. Owners need not specify their _user_ name.

---

paste

paste [_options_] _files_

Merge corresponding lines of one or more _files_ into tab-separated vertical columns. See also **cut**, **join**, and **pr**.

Options

-   Replace a filename with the standard input.

-d_char_, **--delimiters**=_char_
> Separate columns with _char_ instead of a tab. You can separate columns with different characters by supplying more than one _char_.

--help
> Print a help message and then exit.

-s, --serial
> Merge lines from one file at a time.

--version
> Print version information and then exit.

Examples

Create a three-column *file* from files *x*, *y*, and *z*:

```
paste x y z > file
```

List users in two columns:

```
who | paste - -
```

Merge each pair of lines into one line:

```
paste -s -d"\t\n" list
```

---

patch

`patch [options] [original [patchfile]]`

Apply the patches specified in *patchfile* to *original*. Replace the original with the new, patched version; move the original to *original.orig* or *original~*. The patch file is a difference listing produced by the **diff** command.

Options

-b, --backup
> Back up the original file.

--backup-if-mismatch, --no-backup-if-mismatch
> When not backing up all original files, these options control whether a backup should be made when a patch does not match the original file. The default is to make backups unless **--posix** is specified.

-c, --context
> Interpret *patchfile* as a context diff.

-d *dir*, --directory=*dir*
> **cd** to *directory* before beginning **patch** operations.

--dry-run
> Print results of applying a patch, but don't change any files.

-e, --ed
> Treat the contents of *patchfile* as **ed** commands.

-f, --force
> Force all changes, even those that look incorrect. Skip patches if the original file does not exist; force patches for files with the wrong version specified; assume patches are never reversed.

-g *num*, --get *num*
> Specify whether to check the original file out of source control if it is missing or read-only. If *num* is a positive number, get the file. If it is negative, prompt the user. If it is 0, do not check files out of source control. The default is negative or the

value of the **PATCH_GET** environment variable when set, unless the **--posix** option is given. Then the default is 0.

--help
> Print help message, then exit.

-i *file*, **--input=***file*
> Read patch from *file* instead of stdin.

-l, **--ignore-whitespace**
> Ignore whitespace while pattern matching.

-n, **--normal**
> Interpret patch file as a normal diff.

-o *file*, **--output=***file*
> Print output to *file*.

-p[*num*], **--strip**[**=***num*]
> Specify how much of preceding pathname to strip. A *num* of 0 strips everything, leaving just the filename. 1 strips the leading **/**. Each higher number after that strips another directory from the left.

--quoting-style=*style*
> Set the quoting style used when printing names. The default style is **shell** unless set by the environment variable **QUOTING_STYLE**. *style* may be one of the following:
>
> **c**   Quote as a C language string.
>
> **escape**
>> Like **c**, but without surrounding double-quote characters.
>
> **literal**
>> Print without quoting.
>
> **shell**
>> Quote for use in shell when needed.
>
> **shell-always**
>> Quote for use in shell even if not needed.

--posix
> Conform more strictly to the POSIX standard.

-r *file*, **--reject-file=***file*
> Place rejects (hunks of the patch file that **patch** fails to place within the original file) in *file*. Default is *original.rej*.

-s, **--silent**, **--quiet**
> Suppress commentary.

-t, **--batch**
> Skip patches if the original file does not exist.

-u, **--unified**
> Interpret patch file as a unified context diff.

--verbose
> Verbose mode.

-v, **--version**
> Print version number and exit.

-z *suffix,* **--suffix=***suffix*
> Back up the original file in *original.suffix.*

-B *prefix,* **--prefix=***prefix*
> Prepend *prefix* to the backup filename.

-D *string,* **--ifdef=***string*
> Mark all changes with:
> ```
> #ifdef
>     string
> #endif
> ```

-E, --remove-empty-files
> If **patch** creates any empty files, delete them.

-F *num,* **--fuzz=***num*
> Specify the maximum number of lines that may be ignored (fuzzed over) when deciding where to install a hunk of code. The default is 2. Meaningful only with context diffs.

-N, --forward
> Ignore patches that appear to be reversed or to have already been applied.

-R, --reverse
> Do a reverse patch: attempt to undo the damage done by patching with the old and new files reversed.

-T, --set-time
> When original file timestamps match the times given in the patch header, set timestamps for patched files according to the context diff headers. Use option **-f** to force date changes. Assume timestamps are in local time.

-V *method,* **--version-control=***method*
> Specify method for creating backup files (overridden by **-B**):

> **t, numbered**
> > Make numbered backups.

> **nil, existing**
> > Back up files according to preexisting backup schemes, with simple backups as the default. This is **patch**'s default behavior.

> **never, simple**
> > Make simple backups.

-Y *prefix,* **--basename-prefix=***prefix*
> Use the specified *prefix* with a file's basename to create backup filenames. Useful for specifying a directory.

-Z, --set-utc
> When original file timestamps match the times given in the patch header, set timestamps for patched files according to the context diff headers. Use option **-f** to force date changes. Assume timestamps are in Coordinated Universal Time (UTC).

Environment variables

TMPDIR, TMP, TEMP
> Specify the directory for temporary files; */tmp* by default.

SIMPLE_BACKUP_SUFFIX
> Suffix to append to backup files instead of *.orig* or ~.

QUOTING_STYLE
> Specify how output should be quoted (see **--quoting-style**).

PATCH_GET
> Specify whether **patch** should retrieve missing or read-only files from source control (see **-g**).

POSIXLY_CORRECT
> When set, **patch** conforms more strictly to the POSIX standard (see **--posix**).

VERSION_CONTROL, PATCH_VERSION_CONTROL
> Specify what method to use in naming backups (see **-V**).

---

pathchk

        `pathchk` [*option*] *filenames*

Determine validity and portability of *filenames*. Specifically, determine if all directories within the path are searchable and if the length of the *filenames* is acceptable.

Options

-p, --portability
> Check portability for all POSIX systems.

--help
> Print a help message and then exit.

--version
> Print version information and then exit.

---

perl

        `perl`

A powerful text-processing language that combines many of the most useful features of shell programs, C, **awk**, and **sed**, as well as adding extended features of its own. For more information, see *Learning Perl* and *Programming Perl* (both from O'Reilly).

---

pidof

        `pidof` [*options*] *programs*

Display the process IDs of the listed program or programs. **pidof** is actually a symbolic link to **killall5**.

Options

-o *pids*
> Omit all processes with the specified process IDs.

-s   Return a single process ID.

-x   Also return process IDs of shells running the named scripts.

ping   ping [*options*] *host*

System administration command. Confirm that a remote host is online and responding. **ping** is intended for use in network testing, measurement, and management. Because of the load it can impose on the network, it is unwise to use **ping** during normal operations or from automated scripts.

Options

-a   Make **ping** audible. Beep each time response is received.

-b   Ping a broadcast address.

-c *count*
> Stop after sending (and receiving) *count* **ECHO_RESPONSE** packets.

-d   Set **SO_DEBUG** option on socket being used.

-f   Flood **ping**-output packets as fast as they come back or 100 times per second, whichever is more. This can be very hard on a network and should be used with caution. Only a privileged user may use this option.

-i *wait*
> Wait *wait* seconds between sending each packet. Default is to wait 1 second between each packet. This option is incompatible with the -**f** option.

-l *preload*
> Send *preload* number of packets as fast as possible before falling into normal mode of behavior.

-n   Numeric output only. No attempt will be made to look up symbolic names for host addresses.

-p *digits*
> Specify up to 16 pad bytes to fill out packet sent. This is useful for diagnosing data-dependent problems in a network. *digits* are in hex. For example, -**p ff** will cause the sent packet to be filled with all 1s.

-q   Quiet output—nothing is displayed except the summary lines at startup time and when finished.

-r   Bypass the normal routing tables and send directly to a host on an attached network.

-s *packetsize*
> Specify number of data bytes to be sent. Default is 56, which translates into 64 ICMP data bytes when combined with the 8 bytes of ICMP header data.

-t *n*
> Set the IP Time to Live to *n* seconds.

-v   Verbose; list ICMP packets received other than **ECHO_ RESPONSE**.

-w *n*
> Exit **ping** after *n* seconds.

-A   Adapt to return interval of packets. Like **-f ping**, sends packets at approximately the rate at which they are received. This option may be used by an unprivileged user.

-I *name*

Set source address to interface *name*. *name* may also be specified as an IP address.

-L   If destination is a multicast address, suppress loopback.

-Q *tos*

Set Quality of Service on ICMP datagrams.

-S *size*

Set send buffer (SNDBUF) size. The default is the size of one packet.

-T *option*

Set IP timestamp options. Accepted *option* values are:

tsonly

Timestamps only.

tsandaddr

Timestamps and addresses.

tsprespec *hosts*

Timestamps with prespecified hops of one or more hosts.

-M *hint*

Specify Path MTU Discovery strategy. Accepted values are **do**, **want**, or **dont**.

-R   Set the IP record route option, which will store the route of the packet inside the IP header. The contents of the record route will be printed if the **-v** option is given, and will be set on return packets if the target host preserves the record route option across echoes or the **-l** option is given.

-U   Use older **ping** behavior and print full user-to-user latency instead of network round trip time.

-V   Print version, then exit.

---

portmap   `rpc.portmap` [`options`]

NFS/NIS command. RPC program number to IP port mapper. **portmap** is a server that converts RPC program numbers to IP port numbers. It must be running in order to make RPC calls. When an RPC server is started, it tells **portmap** what port number it is listening to and what RPC program numbers it is prepared to serve. When a client wishes to make an RPC call to a given program number, it first contacts **portmap** on the server machine to determine the port number where RPC packets should be sent. **portmap** must be the first RPC server started.

Options

-d   Run **portmap** in debugging mode. Does not allow **portmap** to run as a daemon.

-v   Run **portmap** in verbose mode.

---

poweroff

poweroff [*options*]

System administration command. Close out filesystems, shut down the system, and power off. Because this command immediately stops all processes, it should be run only in single-user mode. If the system is not in runlevel 0 or 6, **poweroff** calls **shutdown -h**, then performs a poweroff.

Options

-d   Suppress writing to */var/log/wtmp*.

-f   Call **reboot** or **halt** and not **shutdown**, even when **shutdown** would normally be called. This option is used to force a hard halt or reboot.

-h   Place hard drives in standby mode before halt or poweroff.

-i   Shut down network interfaces before reboot.

-n   Suppress normal call to **sync**.

-w   Suppress normal execution; simply write to */var/log/wtmp*.

---

pppd

pppd [*tty*] [*speed*] [*options*]

System administration command. PPP stands for the Point-to-Point Protocol; it allows datagram transmission over a serial connection. **pppd** attempts to configure *tty* for PPP (searching in */dev*) or, by default, the controlling terminal. You can also specify a baud rate of *speed*. **pppd** accepts many options. Only the most common options are listed here.

Options

asyncmap *map*
> Specify which control characters cannot pass over the line. *map* should be a 32-bit hex number, where each bit represents a character to escape. For example, bit 00000001 represents the character 0x00; bit 80000000 represents the character 0x1f or _. You may specify multiple characters.

auth
> Require self-authentication by peers before allowing packets to move.

call *file*
> Read options from *file* in */etc/ppp/peers/*. Unlike the **file** option, **call** *file* may contain privileged options, even when **pppd** is not run by root.

connect *command*
> Connect as specified by *command*, which may be a binary or shell command.

crtscts
> Use hardware flow control.

debug
> Log contents of control packets to **syslogd**.

defaultroute
> Add a new default route in which the peer is the gateway. When the connection shuts down, remove the route.

nodetach
> Operate in the foreground. By default, **pppd** forks and operates in the background.

disconnect *command*
> Close the connection as specified by *command*, which may be a binary or shell command.

domain *d*
> Specify a domain name of *d*.

escape *character-list*
> Escape all characters in *character-list*, which should be a comma-separated list of hex numbers. You cannot escape 0x20-0x3f or 0x5e.

file *file*
> Consult *file* for options.

init *script*
> Run specified command or shell script to initialize the serial line.

lock
> Allow only **pppd** to access the device.

mru *bytes*
> Refuse packets of more than *bytes* bytes.

mtu *bytes*
> Do not send packets of more than *bytes* bytes.

name *name*
> Specify a machine name for the local system.

netmask *mask*
> Specify netmask (for example, 255.255.255.0).

passive, -p
> Do not exit if peer does not respond to attempts to initiate a connection. Instead, wait for a valid packet from the peer.

silent
> Send no packets until after receiving one.

[*local_IP_address*]:[*remote_IP_address*]
> Specify the local and/or remote interface IP addresses, as hostnames or numeric addresses.

Files

/var/run/pppn.pid
> **pppd**'s process ID. The *n* in *pppn.pid* is the number of the PPP interface unit corresponding to this **pppd** process.

/etc/ppp/ip-up
> Binary or script to be executed when the PPP link becomes active.

/etc/ppp/ip-down
Binary or script to be executed when the PPP link goes down.

/etc/ppp/pap-secrets
Contains usernames, passwords, and IP addresses for use in PAP authentication.

/etc/ppp/options
System defaults. Options in this file are set *before* the command-line options.

~/.ppprc
The user's default options. These are read before command-line options but after the system defaults.

/etc/ppp/options.ttyname
Name of the default serial port.

---

pr

pr [*options*] [*files*]
Convert a text file or files to a paginated, columned version, with headers. If - is provided as the filename, read from standard input.

Options
+*beg_pag*[:*end-pag*], --**pages**=[*beg_pag*[:*end-pag*]
Begin printing on page *beg_pag* and end on *end-pag* if specified.

-*num_cols*, --**columns**=*num_cols*
Print in *num_cols* number of columns, balancing the number of lines in the columns on each page.

-**a**, --**across**
Print columns horizontally, not vertically.

-**c**, --**show-control-chars**
Convert control characters to hat notation (such as ^C), and other unprintable characters to octal backslash format.

-**d**, --**double-space**
Double space.

-**D** *format*, --**date-format**=*format*
Format the header date using *format*. See the **date** command for the possible formats.

-**e**[*tab-char*[*width*]], --**expand-tabs**=[*tab-char*[*width*]]
Convert tabs (or *tab-chars*) to spaces. If *width* is specified, convert tabs to *width* characters (default is 8).

-**f**, -**F**, --**form-feed**
Separate pages with form feeds, not newlines.

-**h** *header*, --**header**=*header*
Use *header* for the header instead of the filename.

-**i**[*out-tab-char*[*out-tab-width*]], --**output-tabs**[=*out-tab-char*[*out-tab-width*]]
Replace spaces with tabs on output. Can specify alternative tab character (default is tab) and width (default is 8).

-J, --join-lines
Merge full lines; ignore **-W** if set.

-l *lines*, **--length=***lines*
Set page length to *lines* (default is 66). If *lines* is less than 10, omit headers and footers.

-m, --merge
Print all files, one per column.

-n[*delimiter*[*digits*]], **--number-lines**[=*delimiter*[*digits*]]
Number columns, or, with the **-m** option, number lines. Append *delimiter* to each number (default is a tab) and limit the size of numbers to *digits* (default is 5).

-N *num*, **--first-line-number=***num*
Start counting with *num* at the first line of the first page printed. Also see +*beg_page*.

-o *width*, **--indent=***width*
Set left margin to *width*. Does not affect the page width set with **-w** or **-W**.

-r, --no-file-warnings
Continue silently when unable to open an input file.

-s[*delimiter*], **--separator**[=*delimiter*]
Separate columns with *delimiter* (default is a tab) instead of spaces.

-S[*string*], **--sep-string**[=*string*]
Separate columns with *string*. Default is a tab with **-J** and a space otherwise.

-t, --omit-header
Suppress headers, footers, and fills at end of pages.

-T, --omit-pagination
Like **-t** but also suppress form feeds.

-v, --show-non-printing
Convert unprintable characters to octal backslash format.

-w *page_width*, **--width=***page_width*
Set the page width to *page_width* characters for multi-column output. Default is 72.

-W *page_width*, **--page-width=***page_width*
Set the page width to always be *page_width* characters. Default is 72.

--help
Print a help message and then exit.

--version
Print version information and then exit.

praliases   praliases [*options*]

System administration command. **praliases** prints the current **send-mail** mail aliases. (Usually defined in the */etc/aliases* or */etc/aliases.db* file.)

Options

-f *file*
> Read the aliases from the specified file instead of **sendmail**'s default alias files.

-C *file*
> Read **sendmail** configuration from the specified file instead of from */etc/mail/sendmail.cf*.

---

printenv   printenv [*option*] [*variables*]
printenv *option*

Print values of all environment variables or, optionally, only the specified *variables*.

Options

--help
> Print usage information and exit.

--version
> Print version information and exit.

---

printf   printf *formats* [*strings*]
printf *option*

Print *strings* using the specified *formats*. *formats* can be ordinary text characters, C-language escape characters, C format specifications ending with one of the letters **diouxXfeEgGcs** or, more commonly, a set of conversion arguments listed here.

Options

--help
> Print usage information and exit.

--version
> Print version information and exit.

Arguments

%%
> Print a single %.

%b
> Print *string* with \ escapes interpreted.

%s
> Print the next *string*.

%*n*$s
> Print the *nth* *string*.

%[-]m[.n]s

Print the next *string*, using a field that is *m* characters wide. Optionally, limit the field to print only the first *n* characters of *string*. Strings are right-adjusted unless the left-adjustment flag, -, is specified.

Examples

```
printf '%s %s\n' "My files are in" $HOME
printf '%-25.15s %s\n' "My files are in" $HOME
```

---

ps

ps [*options*]

Report on active processes. **ps** has three types of options. GNU long options start with two dashes, which are required. BSD options may be grouped and do not start with a dash, while Unix98 options may be grouped and require an initial dash. The meaning of the short options can vary depending on whether or not there is a dash. In options, *list* arguments should either be separated by commas or put in double quotes. In comparing the amount of output produced, note that **e** prints more than **a** and **l** prints more than **f** for each entry.

Options

nums, **p** *nums,* **-p** *nums,* **--pid**=*nums*
Include only specified processes, which are given in a space-delimited list.

-nums, --sid=*nums*
Include only specified session IDs, which are given in a space-delimited list.

[-]a
As **a**, list all processes on a terminal. As **-a**, list all processes on a terminal except session leaders.

[-]c
As **-c**, show different scheduler information with **-l**. As **c**, show the true command name.

-C *cmds*
Select by command name.

--cols=*cols,* **--columns**=*cols,* **--width**=*cols*
Set the output width (the number of columns to display).

-d   Select all processes except session leaders.

-e, -A
Select all processes.

e   Include environment information after the command.

[-]f, --forest
As **-f**, display full listing. As **f** or **--forest**, display "forest" family tree format, with ASCII art showing the relationships.

-g *list,* **-G** *list,* **--group**=*groups,* **--Group**=*groups*
> For **-g**, select by session leader if *list* contains numbers, or by group if it contains group names. For **-G**, select by the group IDs in *list*. **--group** selects by effective group and **--Group** selects by real group, where *groups* can be either group names or group IDs.

h, --no-headers
> Suppress header. If you select a BSD personality by setting the environment variable **PS_PERSONALITY** to **bsd**, then **h** prints a header on each page.

-H Display "forest" family tree format, without ASCII art.

--headers
> Repeat headers.

--help
> Display help information and exit.

--info
> Print debugging information.

[-]j
> Jobs format. **j** prints more information than **-j**.

[-]l
> Produce a long listing. **-l** prints more information than **l**.

L Print list of field specifiers that can be used for output formatting or for sorting.

--lines=*num,* **--rows**=*num*
> Set the screen height to *num* lines. If **--headers** is also set, the headers repeat every *num* lines.

[-]m
> Show threads.

n Print user IDs and WCHAN numerically.

-n*file,* **N***file*
> Specify the *System.map* file for **ps** to use as a namelist file. The map file must correspond to the Linux kernel; e.g., */boot/ System.map-2.4.19*.

-N, --deselect
> Negate the selection.

[-]o *fields,* **--format**=*fields*
> As **-o**, **o**, or **--format**, specify user-defined format with a list of fields to display.

[-]O *fields*
> As **-O**, is like **-o**, but some common fields are predefined. As **O**, can be either the same as **-O** in specifying fields to display, or can specify single-letter fields for sorting. For sorting, each field specified as a key can optionally have a leading + (return to default sort direction on key) or - (reverse the default direction).

r   Show only processes that are currently running.

s   Display signal format.

-s *sessions*
   Show processes belonging to the specified sessions.

-S, --cumulative
   Include some dead child process data in parent total.

[-]t*tttys,* **--tty=***ttys*
   Display processes running on the specified terminals.

T   Display all processes on this terminal.

[-]u *[users],* **--user=***users*
   As **u** with no argument, display user-oriented output . As **-u** or
   --users, display by effective user ID (and also support names),
   showing results for *users*. With no argument, **-u** displays
   results for the current user.

[-]U *users,* **--User=***users*
   As **U**, display processes for the specified users. As **-U** or **--User**,
   display processes for *users* by real user ID (and also support
   names).

v   Display virtual memory format.

[-]V, --version
   Display version information and then exit.

[-]w
   Wide format. Don't truncate long lines.

x   Display processes without an associated terminal.

X   Use old Linux i386 register format.

-y   Do not show flags; show **rss** instead of **addr**.

Sort keys

c, cmd
   Name of executable.

C, cmdline
   Whole command line.

f, flags
   Flags.

g, pgrp
   Group ID of process.

G, tpgid
   Group ID of associated tty.

j, cutime
   Cumulative user time.

J, cstime
   Cumulative system time.

k, utime
   User time.

K, stime
    System time.

m, min_flt
    Number of minor page faults.

M, maj_flt
    Number of major page faults.

n, cmin_flt
    Total minor page faults.

N, cmaj_flt
    Total major page faults.

o, session
    Session ID.

p, pid
    Process ID.

P, ppid
    Parent's process ID.

r, rss
    Resident set size.

R, resident
    Resident pages.

s, size
    Kilobytes of memory used.

S, share
    Number of shared pages.

t, tty
    Terminal.

T, start_time
    Process's start time.

U, uid
    User ID.

u, user
    User's name.

v, vsize
    Bytes of virtual memory used.

y, priority
    Kernel's scheduling priority.

Fields

%CPU
    Percent of CPU time used recently.

%MEM
    Percent of memory used.

ADDR
    Address of the process.

C, CMD, COMMAND
   The command the process is running.

ELAPSED
   Elapsed time since the start of the process.

F   Process flags:

   001
      Print alignment warning messages.

   002
      Being created.

   004
      Being shut down.

   010
      ptrace(0) has been called.

   020
      Tracing system calls.

   040
      Forked but didn't exec.

   100
      Used superuser privileges.

   200
      Dumped core.

   400
      Killed by a signal.

GROUP
   Effective group ID.

NI
   The **nice** value of the process. A higher number indicates less CPU time.

PAGEIN
   Number of major page faults.

PID
   Process ID.

PPID
   Parent process ID.

PRI
   Process's scheduling priority. A higher number indicates lower priority.

RSS
   Resident set size (the amount of physical memory), in kilobytes.

SHARE
   Shared memory.

SIZE
   Size of virtual image.

STAT
> Status:
>
> **R**   Runnable.
>
> **T**   Stopped.
>
> **D**   Asleep and not interruptible.
>
> **S**   Asleep.
>
> **Z**   Zombie.
>
> **W**   No resident pages (second field).
>
> **N**   Positive **nice** value (third field).

STIME
> Process start time.

SWAP
> Amount of swap used, in kilobytes.

TIME
> Cumulative CPU time.

TRS
> Size of resident text.

TT, TTY
> Associated terminal.

UID
> User ID.

VSZ
> Virtual memory size, in kilobytes.

WCHAN
> Kernel function in which process resides.

---

pwck

pwck [*option*] [*files*]

System administration command. Remove corrupt or duplicate entries in the */etc/passwd* and */etc/shadow* files. **pwck** will prompt for a "yes" or "no" before deleting entries. If the user replies "no," the program will exit. Alternate passwd and shadow *files* can be checked. If correctable errors are found, the user will be encouraged to run the **usermod** command.

Option

-r   Run in noninteractive read-only mode, answering all questions **no**.

Exit status

0   Success.

1   Syntax error.

2   One or more bad password entries found.

3   Could not open password files.

4   Could not lock password files.

5   Could not write password files.

pwconv

pwconv
pwunconv

System administration command. Convert unshadowed entries in */etc/passwd* into shadowed entries in */etc/shadow*. Replace the encrypted password in */etc/password* with an x. Shadowing passwords keeps them safe from password-cracking programs. **pwconv** creates additional expiration information for the */etc/shadow* file from entries in your */etc/login.defs* file. If you add new entries to the */etc/passwd* file, you can run **pwconv** again to transfer the new information to */etc/shadow*. Already shadowed entries are ignored. **pwunconv** restores the encrypted passwords to your */etc/passwd* file and removes the */etc/shadow* file. Some expiration information is lost in the conversion. See also **grpconv** and **grpunconv**.

pwd

pwd

Print the full pathname of the current working directory. See also the **dirs** shell command, built in to both **bash** and **tcsh**.

python

python

A powerful object-oriented scripting language often compared to Perl or Java. **python** drives many of the configuration scripts used in Red Hat and other Linux distributions. For more information, see *Learning Python* and *Programming Python* (both from O'Reilly).

quota

quota [*options*] [*user*|*group*]

Display disk usage and total space allowed for a designated user or group. With no argument, the quota for the current user is displayed. This command reports quotas for all filesystems listed in */etc/mtab*. Most users can display only their own quota information, but the superuser can display information for any user.

Options

-F *format*
> Show quota for the specified format. If not specified, auto-detects the format.

-g
> Given with a *user* argument, display the quotas for the groups of which the user is a member instead of the user's quotas. With no argument, shows group quotas for the current user.

-q
> Display information only for filesystems in which the user is over quota.

-s
> Try to choose units for displaying limits, space used, and inodes used.

-u
> The default behavior. When used with **-g**, display both user and group quota information.

-v
> Display quotas for filesystems even if no storage is currently allocated.

Formats

rpc
> Quota over NFS.

vfsold
> Version 1 quota.

vfsv0
> Version 2 quota.

xfs
> Quota on XFS filesystem.

---

raidstart

raidstart [*options*] [*devices*]
raidstop [*options*] [*devices*]

System administration command. Start or stop RAID *devices* as defined in the RAID configuration file, */etc/raidtab*. If option **-a** (or **--all**) is used, no *devices* need to be given; the command will be applied to all the devices defined in the configuration file.

Options

-a, --all
> Apply command to all devices defined in the RAID configuration file.

-c *file*, **--configfile** *file*
> Use *file* instead of */etc/raidtab*.

-h, --help
> Print usage message and exit.

-V, --version
> Print version and exit.

---

ramsize

ramsize [*option*] [*image* [*size* [*offset*]]]

System administration command. If no options are specified, print usage information for the RAM disk. The pair of bytes at offset 504 in the kernel image normally specify the RAM size; with a kernel *image* argument, print the information found at that offset. To change that information, specify a new *size* (in kilobytes). You may also specify a different *offset*. **rdev -r** is the same as **ramsize**.

Option

-o *offset*
> Same as specifying an *offset* as an argument.

---

ranlib

ranlib *filename*
ranlib *option*

Generate an index for archive file *filename*. Same as running **ar -s**.

Option

-v, -V, --version
> Print version information and exit.

rarpd   **rarpd** [*options*] [*interface*]

System administration command. Respond to Reverse Address
Resolution Protocol (RARP) requests. Some machines (primarily
diskless SUN machines) will use RARP requests at boot time to
discover their IP address and retrieve boot images. The request
contains the booting machine's ethernet address, and **rarpd** tells it
which IP to use. To answer requests, **rarpd** checks the *ethers* database (either the */etc/ethers* file or read from NIS+) and performs
DNS lookups as needed. **rarpd** will respond to RARP requests only
from machines for which it has a bootable image, usually stored in
the TFTP boot directory */tftpboot*. The daemon will bind to the
given *interface* if specified. This daemon replaces the kernel-based
RARP support found in kernels previous to 2.2.

Options

-a   Do not bind to the specified *interface*.

-b *directory*
      Look for boot images in the specified *directory* instead of the
      default */tftpboot*.

-d   Do not detach and run in daemon mode. Used for debugging.

-e   Answer requests without checking the TFTP boot directory.

-v   Verbose mode.

-A   Respond to ARP requestes as well as RARP requests.

---

raw   **raw** [*options*] [*rawnode* [*blockdevice*]]

System administration command. Bind a raw character device to a
block device, or query current raw device bindings. The *rawnode*
should be a device in */dev/raw*. The *blockdevice* may be specified by
filename or by its major and minor device numbers.

Options

-a   Print information on all raw device bindings. Used with option
      -q.

-h   Print usage information, then exit.

-q   Print information on binding of the specified *rawnode*, or all
      raw nodes if accompanied with the **-a** option.

---

rcp   **rcp** [*options*] *file1 file2*
                 rcp [*options*] *file ... directory*

Copy files between two machines. Each *file* or *directory* is either a
remote filename of the form *rname@rhost:path*, or a local filename.

Options

-k   Attempt to get tickets for remote host; query **krb_realmof-
      host** to determine realm.

-p   Preserve modification times and modes of the source files.

-r If any of the source files are directories, descend into each directory and recursively copy all files and directories within it. The destination must be a directory.

-x Turns on DES encryption for all data passed by **rcp**.

---

rcs

rcs [*options*] *files*

The Revision Control System (RCS) keeps track of multiple versions of files, letting you store and retrieve revisions and track the history of the files. The **rcs** command creates new RCS files and modifies attributes of existing files. See Chapter 14 for more information on RCS and its commands. See Chapter 15 for the newer and more powerful CVS system.

---

rdate

rdate [*options*] [*host...*]

TCP/IP command. Retrieve the date and time from a host or hosts on the network and optionally set the local system time.

Options

-p Print the retrieved dates.

-s Set the local system time from the host; must be specified by root.

---

rdev

rdev [*options*] [*image* [*value* [*offset*]]]

System administration command. If invoked with no arguments, show the current root filesystem in */etc/mtab* syntax. Otherwise, change the values in the kernel image that specify the RAM disk size (by default located at decimal byte offset 504 in the kernel), VGA mode (default 506), and root device (default 508). You must specify the kernel *image* to be changed, and may specify a new *value* and a different *offset*. Using **rdev** to change these values directly in an image file is discouraged. These values can all be set by a boot loader such as **lilo** or **grub**.

Options

-o *offset*
Same as specifying an *offset* as an argument. The offset is given in decimal.

-r Behave like **ramsize**.

-v Behave like **vidmode**.

-R Behave like **rootflags**.

---

rdist

rdist [*options*] [*names*]

System administration command. Remote file distribution client program. **rdist** maintains identical copies of files over multiple hosts. It reads commands from a file named *distfile* to direct the updating of files and/or directories. An alternative *distfile* can be specified with the -f option or the -c option.

Options

-a *num*

> Do not update filesystems with fewer than *num* bytes free.

-c *name [login@]host[:dest]*

> Interpret the arguments as a small *distfile*, where *login* is the user to log in as, *host* is the destination host, *name* is the local file to transfer, and *dest* is the remote name where the file should be installed.

-d *var=value*

> Define *var* to have *value*. This option defines or overrides variable definitions in the *distfile*. Set the variable *var* to *value*.

-f *file*

> Read input from *file* (by default, *distfile*). If *file* is -, read from standard input.

-l *options*

> Specify logging options on the local machine.

-m *machine*

> Update only *machine*. May be specified multiple times for multiple machines.

-n   Suppress normal execution. Instead, print the commands that would have been executed.

-o*options*

> Specify one or more *options*, which must be comma-separated.
>
> **chknfs**
>
> > Suppress operations on files that reside on NFS filesystems.
>
> **chkreadonly**
>
> > Check filesystem to be sure it is not read-only before attempting to perform updates.
>
> **chksym**
>
> > Do not update files that exist on the local host but are symbolic links on the remote host.
>
> **compare**
>
> > Compare files; use this comparison rather than age as the criteria for determining which files should be updated.
>
> **follow**
>
> > Interpret symbolic links, copying the file to which the link points instead of creating a link on the remote machine.
>
> **ignlnks**
>
> > Ignore links that appear to be unresolvable.
>
> **nochkgroup**
>
> > Do not update a file's group ownership unless the entire file needs updating.
>
> **nochkmode**
>
> > Do not update file mode unless the entire file needs updating.

nochkowner

Do not update file ownership unless the entire file needs updating.

nodescend

Suppress recursive descent into directories.

noexec

Suppress **rdist** of executables that are in *a.out* format.

numchkgroup

Check group ownership by group ID instead of by name.

numchkowner

Check file ownership by user ID instead of by name.

quiet

Quiet mode; do not print commands as they execute.

remove

Remove files that exist on the remote host but not the local host.

savetargets

Save updated files in *name.old*.

sparse

Check for sparse files, for example **ndbm** files.

verify

Print a list of all files on the remote machine that are out of date, but do not update them.

whole

Preserve directory structure by creating subdirectories on the remote machine. For example, if you **rdist** the file */foo/bar* into the directory */baz*, it would produce the file */baz/foo/bar* instead of the default */baz/bar*.

younger

Do not update files that are younger than the master files.

-p *path*

Specify the path to search for **rdistd** on the remote machine.

-t *seconds*

Specify the timeout period (default 900 seconds) after which **rdist** will sever the connection if the remote server has not yet responded.

-A *num*

Specify the minimum number of inodes that **rdist** requires.

-D   Debugging mode.

-F   Execute all commands sequentially, without forking.

-L *options*

Specify logging options on the remote machine.

-M *num*

Do not allow more than *num* child **rdist** processes to run simultaneously. Default is 4.

-P *path*

Specify path to the transport command to use on the local machine. This is normally **rsh**, but may also be **ssh**. The *path* argument may also be specified as a colon-separated list of acceptable transports to use in order of preference.

-V   Display version, then exit.

---

rdistd

rdistd *options*

System administration command. Start the **rdist** server. Note that you *must* specify the -S option unless you are simply querying for version information with -V.

Options

-D   Debugging mode.

-S   Start the server.

-V   Display the version number and exit.

---

readelf

readelf *option*[...] *elffiles*

Display information about about one or more ELF (Executable and Linking Format) object files. At least one option is required to specify the information to be displayed for each file. **readelf** does not currently work on archive files or 64-bit ELF files.

Options

-a, --all

Display all. Equivalent to **-h -l -S -s -r -d -n -V**.

-d, --dynamic

Display the dynamic section.

-D, --use-dynamic

When displaying symbols, use the symbol table in the dynamic section, not the symbols section.

-e, --headers

Display all headers. Equivalent to **-h -l -s**.

-h, --file-header

Display the ELF header at the beginning of the file.

--help

Display help information and exit.

--histogram

Display a histogram of bucket bit lengths when displaying the symbol tables.

-l, --program-headers, --segments

Display the segment headers, if any.

-n, --notes

Display the NOTE segment, if any.

-r, --relocs

Display the relocation segment, if any.

-s, --symbols, --syms

Display entries in symbol table sections, if any.

-S, --section-headers, --sections

Display the section headers, if any.

-u, --unwind

Display the unwind section, if any (currently applies only to IA64 ELF files).

-v, --version

Display version information and exit.

-V, --version-info

Display the version sections, if any.

-w[*option*], **--debug-dump**[=*option*]

Display the debug sections. If specified with an option, display only that section. The options shown here in parentheses are for **-w**; the words preceding them are for **--debug-dump**. The options are **line** (**l**), **info** (**i**), **abbrev** (**a**), **pub-names** (**p**), **ranges** (**r**), **macro** (**m**), **frames** (**f**), **frames-interp** (**F**), **str** (**s**), and **loc** (**o**).

-W, --wide

Don't break output lines at 80 columns. The default is to break them.

-x *num*, **--hex-dump**=*num*

Display a hexadecimal dump of the section *number*.

---

readlink

readlink *file*
readlink *option*

Print the contents of the symbolic link *file*, that is, the name of the file to which the link points.

Options

--help

Print usage information and exit.

--version

Print version information and exit.

---

reboot

reboot [*options*]

System administration command. Close out filesystems, shut down the system, then reboot. Because this command immediately stops all processes, it should be run only in single-user mode. If the system is not in runlevel 0 or 6, **reboot** calls **shutdown -r**.

Options

-d Suppress writing to */var/log/wtmp*.

-f Call **reboot** even when **shutdown** would normally be called.

-i Shut down network interfaces before reboot.

-n Suppress normal call to **sync**.

-w Suppress normal execution; simply write to */var/log/wtmp*.

---

rename

`rename` *from to files*

Rename *files* by replacing the first occurrence of *from* in each filename with *to*.

Example

Rename files that start with *test* so they start with *mytest*:

    % rename test mytest test*

---

renice

`renice` [*priority*] [*options*] [*target*]

Control the scheduling priority of various processes as they run. May be applied to a process, process group, or user (*target*). A privileged user may alter the priority of other users' processes. *priority* must, for ordinary users, lie between 0 and the environment variable **PRIO_MAX** (normally 20), with a higher number indicating increased niceness. A privileged user may set a negative priority, as low as **PRIO_MIN** (normally –20), to speed up processes.

Options

+num
> Specify number by which to increase current priority of process, rather than an absolute priority number.

-num
> Specify number by which to decrease current priority of process, rather than an absolute priority number.

-g   Interpret *target* parameters as process group IDs.

-p   Interpret *target* parameters as process IDs (default).

-u   Interpret *target* parameters as usernames.

---

reset

`reset` [*options*] [*terminal*]

Clear screen (reset terminal). If *terminal* is specified on the command line, the value is used as the terminal type. **reset** is a symbolic link to the **tset** command. Invoking the command as **reset** is useful for clearing your terminal when a program dies and leaves the terminal in an abnormal state. You may have to run the command with a linefeed character (usually Ctrl-J) before and after it:

    Ctrl-JresetCtrl-J

See the **tset** command for the available options.

---

resize2fs

`resize2fs` [*options*] *device* [*size*]

System administration command. Enlarge or shrink an ext2 filesystem on *device* so it has *size* blocks. The filesystem *size* cannot be larger than the underlying partition. This command changes only the filesystem size, not the underlying partition. To change the partition, use **fdisk**.

Options

-d *flags*

Print debugging information on resize activity. The value of the *flags* parameter determines what activity is reported. Compute its value by summing the numbers of the items you wish to debug:

1   Disk I/O.

2   Block relocations.

8   Inode relocations.

16   Inode table movement.

-f   Force resize, overriding safety checks.

-p   Print progress information for each resize task.

---

rev

rev [*file*]

Reverse the order of characters on each line of the specified file and print the results on standard output. If no file is specified, **rev** reads from standard input.

---

rexecd

rexecd *command-line*

TCP/IP command. Server for the **rexec** routine, providing remote execution facilities with authentication based on usernames and passwords. **rexecd** is started by **inetd** and must have an entry in **inetd**'s configuration file, */etc/inetd.conf*. When **rexecd** receives a service request, the following protocol is initiated:

1. The server reads characters from the socket up to a null byte. The resulting string is interpreted as an ASCII number, base 10.

2. If the number received in Step 1 is nonzero, it is interpreted as the port number of a secondary stream to be used for stderr. A second connection is then created to the specified port on the client's machine.

3. A null-terminated username of at most 16 characters is retrieved on the initial socket.

4. A null-terminated, unencrypted password of at most 16 characters is retrieved on the initial socket.

5. A null-terminated command to be passed to a shell is retrieved on the initial socket. The length of the command is limited by the upper bound on the size of the system's argument list.

6. **rexecd** then validates the user, as is done at login time. If the authentication was successful, **rexecd** changes to the user's home directory and establishes the user and group protections of the user.

7. A null byte is returned on the connection associated with stderr, and the command line is passed to the normal login shell of the user. The shell inherits the network connections established by **rexecd**.

Diagnostics

Username too long
   Name is longer than 16 characters.

Password too long
   Password is longer than 16 characters.

Command too long
   Command passed is too long.

Login incorrect
   No password file entry for the username exists.

Password incorrect
   Wrong password was supplied.

No remote directory
   chdir to home directory failed.

Try again
   fork by server failed.

<shellname>:...
   fork by server failed. User's login shell could not be started.

---

richtext

richtext [*options*] [*file*]

Display MIME ("richtext") files on an ASCII terminal on standard output, by means such as highlighting bold or italic text and displaying underlined text correctly. Intended primarily for use with **metamail**. If no file is specified, input is taken from standard input.

Options

-c   Don't do any formatting; simply correct the raw richtext and write the results to standard output.

-f   Use **termcap**-derived escape codes for bold and italic text, even if **richtext** was called in a pipe.

-m   In multibyte Japanese and Korean sequences, treat < as a real <, not as the start of a richtext command.

-n   Do not correct the raw richtext input.

-o   Use overstrikes for underlines.

-p   Use a pager to view the output. This option has no effect if standard input or standard output is redirected.

-s *charset*
   Use the specified character set as the default. Valid values for *charset* are **us-ascii** (default), **iso-2022-jp**, and **iso-2022-kr**.

-t   Use * and _ instead of **termcap**-derived escape codes to highlight text.

---

rlogin

rlogin [*options*] *rhost*

Remote login. **rlogin** connects the terminal on the current local host system to the remote host system *rhost*. The remote terminal

---

type is the same as your local terminal type. The terminal or window size is also copied to the remote system if the server supports it.

Options

-8   Allow an 8-bit input data path at all times.

-ec   Specify escape character *c* (default is ~).

-d   Debugging mode.

-k   Attempt to get tickets from remote host, requesting them in the realm as determined by **krb_realm-ofhost**.

-l *username*
   Specify a different *username* for the remote login. Default is the same as your local username.

-E   Do not interpret any character as an escape character.

-L   Allow **rlogin** session to be run without any output post-processing (i.e., run in **litout** mode).

---

rlogind

in.rlogind [*options*]

TCP/IP command. Server for the **rlogin** program, providing a remote login facility, with authentication based on privileged port numbers from trusted hosts. **rlogind** is invoked by **inetd** when a remote login connection is requested, and executes the following protocol:

- The server checks the client's source port. If the port is not in the range 512–1023, the server aborts the connection.

- The server checks the client's source address and requests the corresponding hostname. If the hostname cannot be determined, the dot-notation representation of the host address is used.

The login process propagates the client terminal's baud rate and terminal type as found in the **TERM** environment variable.

Options

-a   Verify hostname.

-h   Permit superuser *.rhosts* files to be used. Ignored if pluggable authentication module (PAM) support is enabled. Control through */etc/pam.conf* instead.

-l   Do not authenticate hosts via a nonroot *.rhosts* file. Ignored if pluggable authentication module (PAM) support is enabled. Control through */etc/pam.conf* instead.

-n   Suppress keep-alive messages.

-L   Do not authenticate hosts via *.rhosts* or *hosts.equiv* files. Ignored if pluggable authentication module (PAM) support is enabled. Control through */etc/pam.conf* instead.

rm	**rm** [*options*] *files*

Delete one or more *files*. To remove a file, you must have write permission in the directory that contains the file, but you need not have permission on the file itself. If you do not have write permission on the file, you will be prompted (**y** or **n**) to override.

Options

-d, --directory
> Remove directories, even if they are not empty. Available only to a privileged user.

-f, --force
> Remove write-protected files without prompting.

--help
> Print a help message and then exit.

-i, --interactive
> Prompt for **y** (remove the file) or **n** (do not remove the file).

-r, -R, --recursive
> If *file* is a directory, remove the entire directory and all its contents, including subdirectories. Be forewarned: use of this option can be dangerous.

-v, --verbose
> Verbose mode (print the name of each file before removing it).

--version
> Print version information and then exit.

--
> Mark the end of options. Use this when you need to supply a filename beginning with -.

rmail	**rmail** [*options*] *users*

TCP/IP command. Handle remote mail received via **uucp**. **rmail** transforms trace information from mail in UUCP format to the equivalent RFC 822 format, then forwards messages to **sendmail**.

Options

-D *domain*
> Use *domain* instead of **UUCP** as the UUCP host name in **From** fields.

-T Print debugging information.

rmdir	**rmdir** [*options*] *directories*

Delete the named *directories* (not the contents). *directories* are deleted from the parent directory and must be empty (if not, **rm -r** can be used instead). See also **mkdir**.

Options

--help

Print a help message and then exit.

--ignore-fail-on-non-empty

Ignore failure to remove directories that are not empty.

-p, --parents

Remove *directories* and any intervening parent directories that become empty as a result. Useful for removing subdirectory trees.

--verbose

Verbose mode; print message for each directory as it is processed.

--version

Print version information and then exit.

---

rmmod

rmmod [*options*] *modules*

System administration command. Unload a module or list of modules from the kernel. This command is successful only if the specified modules are not in use and no other modules are dependent on them.

Options

-a, --all

Autoclean modules; tag unused modules for future cleanings, and remove any currently tagged modules. Tagged modules remain tagged unless used between cleanings.

-e, --persist

Save persistent data for specified modules, or for all modules supporting persistence if none are specified. Do not unload modules.

-h, --help

Print help message then exit.

-r, --stacks

Recursively remove stacked modules (all modules that use the specified module).

-s, --syslog

Write messages to **syslogd** instead of to the terminal.

-v, --verbose

Verbose mode.

-V, --version

Print **modutils** version number and help message, then exit.

---

rootflags

rootflags [*option*] *image* [*flags* [*offset*]]

System administration command. Set *flags* for a kernel *image*. If no arguments are specified, print *flags* for the kernel image. *flags* is a

2-byte integer located at offset 498 in a kernel *image*. Currently the only effect of *flags* is to mount the root filesystem in read-only mode if *flags* is nonzero. You may change *flags* by specifying the kernel *image* to change, the new *flags*, and the byte offset at which to place the new information (the default is 498). Note that **rdev -R** is a synonym for **rootflags**. If LILO is used, **rootflags** is not needed. *flags* can be set from the LILO prompt during a boot.

Option

-o *offset*
> Same as specifying an *offset* as an argument.

---

route

route [*options*] [*command*]

TCP/IP command. Add or remove entries in the routing tables maintained by **routed**. **route** accepts two commands: **add**, to add a route, and **del**, to delete a route. The two commands have the following syntax:

> **add** [**-net** | **-host**] *address* [*modifiers*]
> **del** [**-net** | **-host**] *address* [*modifiers*]

address is treated as a plain route unless **-net** is specified or *address* is found in */etc/networks*. **-host** can be used to specify that *address* is a plain route whether or not it is found in */etc/networks*. Using route *modifiers*, you can specify the gateway through which to route packets headed for that address, its netmask, TCP mss, or the device with which to associate the route; you can also mask certain routes. Only a privileged user may modify the routing tables.

If no command is specified, **route** prints the routing tables.

Options

-n, **--numeric**
> Show numerical addresses; do not look up hostnames. (Useful if DNS is not functioning properly.)

-e, **--extend**
> Use **netstat -r** format to print routing table. Use twice to print extended information. Same as **netstat -ree**.

-h, **--help**
> Print help message, then exit.

-v, **--verbose**
> Verbose mode.

-A *family*, **--family**
> Specify an address family to use with an **add** or **del** command. *family* may be **inet**, **inet6**, **ax25**, **netrom**, **ipx**, **ddp**, or **x25**.

-C, **--cache**
> Perform command on the routing cache instead of the forwarding information base (FIB) routing table.

-F, --fib

Perform command on the forwarding information base (FIB) routing table. This is the default behavior.

-V, --version

Print version and configuration options, then exit.

Route modifiers

netmask *mask*

Use netmask **mask**.

gw *gateway*

Route packets through *gateway*.

metric *n*

Set routing metric to *n*.

mss *bytes*

Set maximum segment size for connections over this route.

reject

Cause route lookup for target to fail. Used to mask out networks from a default route.

[dev] *interface*

Associate route with specified device. When the *interface* is given as the last argument on a command line, the word **dev** is optional.

---

routed

routed [*options*] [*logfile*]

TCP/IP command. Network routing daemon. **routed** is invoked by a privileged user at boot time to manage the Internet routing tables. The routing daemon uses a variant of the Xerox NS Routing Information Protocol in maintaining up-to-date kernel routing-table entries. When **routed** is started, it uses the SIOCGIFCONF **ioctl** call to find those directly connected interfaces configured into the system and marked up. **routed** transmits a REQUEST packet on each interface, then enters a loop, listening for REQUEST and RESPONSE packets from other hosts. When a REQUEST packet is received, **routed** formulates a reply based on the information maintained in its internal tables. The generated RESPONSE packet contains a list of known routes. Any RESPONSE packets received are used to update the routing tables as appropriate.

When an update is applied, **routed** records the change in its internal tables, updates the kernel routing table, and generates a RESPONSE packet reflecting these changes to all directly connected hosts and networks.

Options

-d   Debugging mode. Log additional information to the *logfile*.

-g   Offer a route to the default destination.

-q   Opposite of **-s** option.

-s Force **routed** to supply routing information, whether it is acting as an internetwork router or not.

-t Stop **routed** from going into background and releasing itself from the controlling terminal, so that interrupts from the keyboard will kill the process.

---

rpcgen

rpcgen [*options*] *file*

Parse *file*, which should be written in the RPC language, and produce a program written in C that implements the RPC code. Place header code generated from *file.x* in *file.h*, XDR routines in *file_xdr.c*, server code in *file_svc.c*, and client code in *file_clnt.c*. Lines preceded by % are not parsed. By default, **rpcgen** produces Sun OS 4.1–compatible code.

-a Produce all files (client and server).

-5 Produce SVR4-compatible code.

-c Create XDR routines. Cannot be used with other options.

-C Produce ANSI C code (the default).

-K Produce K&R C code.

-D*name*[*=value*]
Define the symbol *name*, and set it equal to *value* or 1.

-h Produce a header file. With **-T**, make the file support RPC dispatch tables. Cannot be used with other options.

-I Produce an **inetd**-compatible server.

-K *secs*
Specify amount of time that the server should wait after replying to a request and before exiting. Default is 120. A *secs* of –1 prevents the program from ever exiting.

-l Produce client code. Cannot be used with other options.

-m Produce server code only, suppressing creation of a "main" routine. Cannot be used with other options.

-N New style. Allow multiple arguments for procedures. Not necessarily backward compatible.

-o [*file*]
Print output to *file* or standard output.

-Sc Print sample client code to standard output.

-Ss Create skeleton server code only.

-t Create RPC dispatch table. Cannot be used with other options.

-T Include support for RPC dispatch tables.

---

rpcinfo

rpcinfo [*options*] [*host*] [*program*] [*version*]

NFS/NIS command. Report RPC information. *program* can be either a name or a number. If a *version* is specified, **rpcinfo** attempts to call that version of the specified *program*. Otherwise, it attempts to find all the registered version numbers for the specified *program* by calling Version 0, and then attempts to call each registered version.

Options

-b *program version*
> Make an RPC broadcast to the specified *program* and *version* using UDP, and report all hosts that respond.

-d *program version*
> Delete the specified *version* of *program*'s registration. Can be executed only by the user who added the registration or a privileged user.

-n *portnum*
> Use *portnum* as the port number for the **-t** and **-u** options, instead of the port number given by the portmapper.

-p [*host*]
> Probe the portmapper on *host* and print a list of all registered RPC programs. If *host* is not specified, it defaults to the value returned by **hostname**.

-t *host program* [*version*]
> Make an RPC call to *program* on the specified *host* using TCP, and report whether a response was received.

-u *host program* [*version*]
> Make an RPC call to *program* on the specified *host* using UDP, and report whether a response was received.

Examples

To show all the RPC services registered on the local machine, use:

    $ rpcinfo -p

To show all the RPC services registered on the machine named **klaxon**, use:

    $ rpcinfo -p klaxon

To show all machines on the local network that are running the Network Information Service (NIS), use:

    $ rpcinfo -b ypserv *version* | uniq

where *version* is the current NIS version obtained from the results of the **-p** switch earlier in this list.

---

rpm

rpm [*options*]

The Red Hat Package Manager. A freely available packaging system for software distribution and installation. RPM packages are built, installed, and queried with the **rpm** and **rpmbuild** commands. For detailed information on RPM, see Chapter 5.

rsh   **rsh** [*options*] *host* [*command*]

Execute *command* on remote host, or, if no command is specified, begin an interactive shell on the remote host using **rlogin**.

Options
-d   Enable socket debugging.

-l *username*
Attempt to log in as *username*. By default, the name of the user executing **rsh** is used.

-n   Redirect the input to **rsh** from the special device */dev/null*. (This should be done when backgrounding **rsh** from a shell prompt, to direct the input away from the terminal.)

---

rshd   **rshd** [*options*]

TCP/IP command. Remote shell server for programs such as **rcmd** and **rcp**, which need to execute a noninteractive shell on remote machines. **rshd** is started by **inetd** and must have an entry in **inetd**'s configuration file, */etc/inetd.conf*.

All options are exactly the same as those in **rlogind**, except for -L, which is unique to **rshd**.

Option
-L   Log all successful connections and failed attempts via **syslogd**.

---

runlevel   **runlevel** [*utmp*]

System administration command. Display the previous and current system runlevels as reported in the *utmp* file. The default *utmp* file is */var/run/utmp*. See **init** for a summary of runlevels.

---

run-parts   **run-parts** [*options*] [*directory*]

System administration command. Run, in lexical order, all scripts found in *directory*. Exclude scripts whose filenames include nonalphanumeric characters (besides underscores and hyphens).

Options
--   Interpret all subsequent arguments as filenames, not options.

--test
Print information listing which scripts would be run, but suppress actual execution of them.

--umask=*umask*
Specify *umask*. The default is 022.

rup

rup [*options*] [*hosts*]

TCP/IP command. Query **statd** for system status on RPC *hosts*: current time, uptime, and load averages (the average number of jobs in the run queue).

Options

-d   Report local time on each host.

-h   Sort information by hostname.

-l   Sort information by load average.

-s   Print times in seconds. Useful for scripts.

-t   Sort information by uptime.

ruptime

ruptime [*options*]

TCP/IP command. Provide information on how long each machine on the local network has been up and which users are logged into each. If a machine has not reported in for 11 minutes, assume it is down. The listing is sorted by hostname. **ruptime** depends on **rwhod**.

Options

-a   Include users who have been idle for more than one hour.

-l   Sort machines by load average.

-r   Reverse the normal sort order.

-t   Sort machines by uptime.

-u   Sort machines by the number of users logged in.

rusers

rusers [*options*] [*host*]

TCP/IP command. List the users logged into *host*, or to all local machines, in **who** format (hostname, usernames). **rusers** depends on **rwhod**.

Options

-a   Include machines with no users logged in.

-l   Include more information: tty, date, time, idle time, remote host.

rusersd

rpc.rusersd

System administration command. Report information on users logged into the system. Answers queries from **rusers**.

rwall

rwall *host* [*file*]

TCP/IP command. Use RPC to print a message to all users logged into *host*. If *file* is specified, read the message from it; otherwise, read from standard input.

rwho

rwho [*option*]

Report who is logged on for all machines on the local network (similar to **who**). **rwho** depends on **rwhod**.

Option

-a   List users even if they've been idle for more than one hour.

---

rwhod

rwhod [*options*]

TCP/IP command. System-status server that maintains the database used by the **rwho** and **ruptime** programs. Its operation is predicated on the ability to broadcast messages on a network. As a producer of information, **rwhod** periodically queries the state of the system and constructs status messages, which are broadcast on a network. As a consumer of information, it listens for other **rwhod** servers' status messages, validates them, then records them in a collection of files located in the directory */var/spool/rwho*. Messages received by the **rwhod** server are discarded unless they originated at an **rwhod** server's port. Status messages are generated approximately once every three minutes.

Options

-a   Use both broadcast and point-to-point interfaces. This is the default.

-b   Use only broadcast interfaces.

-p   Use only point-to-point interfaces.

-u *user*
      Run daemon as specified *user*.

---

scp

scp [*options*] *file1*[...] *file2*

Securely copy files between hosts on a network, using **ssh**. Part of the OpenSSH suite of network tools. **scp** requests a password or passphrase if required. The transfer can be between two remote hosts. If more than one file is specified for *file1*, *file2* should be a directory; otherwise, only the last file in the list is copied. *file1* and *file2* can be specified in any of the following ways:

```
file
host:file
user@host:file
```

Options

-4   Use IPv4 addresses.

-6   Use IPv6 addresses.

-B   Run in batch mode. Don't ask for passwords or passphrases.

-c *cipher*
      Specify the *cipher* to be used for encrypting the data.

-C   Enable **ssh** compression.

-i *file*

Specify the file that contains the identity (private key) for RSA authentication.

-o *option*

Specify an option to pass to **ssh**.

-p   Preserve modification time, access time, and mode.

-P *port*

Connect to *port* on the remote host.

-q   Don't display the progress meter.

-r   Copy directories recursively.

-S *program*

Specify the program to use for the encrypted connection. The program must understand **ssh** options.

-v   Verbose mode.

---

screen

screen [*options*] [*command* [*args*]]

Provide ANSI/VT100 terminal emulation, making it possible to run multiple full-screen pseudo-terminals from one real terminal, and letting you manipulate and save your screen input and output, copy and paste between windows, etc.

Options

-a   Include all capabilities in each window's termcap.

-A   Adapt all windows to the size of the current terminal. Default is to try to use the previous window size.

-c *file*

Use *file* as the configuration file instead of the default *$HOME/.screenrc*.

-d   Detach session running elsewhere. With **-r**, reattach to this terminal. With **-R**, reattach to this terminal or create it if it doesn't already exist. With **-RR**, use the first session when reattaching if more than one session is available.

-D   Detach session running elsewhere, logging out before detaching. With **-r**, reattach to this terminal. With **-R**, reattach to this terminal or create it if it doesn't already exist. With **-RR**, do whatever is necessary to create a new session.

-e *xy*

Change command characters. Specify *x* as the command character (default **Ctrl-a**) and *y* as the character that generates a literal command character (default **a**). Specify in caret notation (e.g., ^A for **Ctrl-a**).

-f, -fn, -fa

Turn flow control on, off, or to automatic switching mode.

-h *num*

Specify the size of the history scrollback buffer.

-i Cause the interrupt key (usually **Ctrl-c**) to interrupt the display immediately when flow control is on. Use of this option is discouraged.

-l, -ln
Turn login mode on or off for */etc/utmp* updating.

-ls, -list
Print list of *pid.tty.host* strings identifying **screen** sessions.

-L Tell **screen** that automargin terminal has a writable last position.

-m Ignore the **$STY** environment variable and create a new session. With **-d**, start session in detached mode; useful for scripts. With **-D**, start session in detached mode but don't fork a new process; the command exits if the session terminates.

-O Use optimal output mode for terminal rather than true VT100 emulation.

-p *window*
Preselect the specified window if it exists.

-q Suppress error message printing on startup. Exit with nonzero return code if unsuccessful.

-r [*pid.tty.host*]
-r *sessionowner/*[*pid.tty.host*]
Resume detached session. No other options except **-d** or **-D** can be specified. With *sessionowner*, resume another user's detached session; requires setuid root.

-R Attempt to resume the first session found, or start a new session with the specified options. Set by default if **screen** is run as a login shell.

-s *shell*
Set the default shell, overriding the **$SHELL** environment variable.

-S *name*
Specify a name for the session being started.

-t *name*
Set the window's title.

-T *term*
Set **$TERM** to *term* instead of "screen".

-U Run in UTF-8 mode.

-v Print version information and exit.

-wipe [*match*]
Like **-ls**, but remove destroyed sessions instead of marking them dead. If a match is specified, it should be in the same form as the argument to the **-r** option.

-x Attach to a session that is not detached. Requires multi-display mode.

-X Run specified command in specified session. Requires multi-display mode, and session must not be password-protected.

Key bindings

screen commands consist of a command character (**Ctrl-a** by default) followed by another character. For many of the commands, you can also specify the character as Ctrl-*character*; e.g., **Ctrl-a Ctrl-d** as well as **Ctrl-a d**. The default key bindings are listed here. You can change the bindings for yourself in the *$HOME/.screenrc* configuration file, or for all users in */etc/screenrc*. The term in parentheses following the description is the equivalent configuration file command for changing the key binding.

Ctrl-a '
> Prompt for window name or number to switch to. (**select**)

Ctrl-a "
> List all windows for selection. (**windowlist -b**)

Ctrl-a *num*
> Switch to window *num*, where *num* is a digit in the range 0–9 or - (the blank window). (**select** *num*)

Ctrl-a Tab
> Switch input focus to next region. (**focus**)

Ctrl-a Ctrl-a
> Toggle to previously displayed window. (**other**)

Ctrl-a a
> Send the command character (**Ctrl-a**) to the window. (**meta**)

Ctrl-a A
> Prompt user to enter a name for the current window. (**title**)

Ctrl-a b
> Send a break to the window. (**break**)

Ctrl-a B
> Reopen the terminal line and send a break. (**pow-break**)

Ctrl-a c
> Create a new window with a shell and switch to it. (**screen**)

Ctrl-a C
> Clear the screen. (**clear**)

Ctrl-a d
> Detach screen from this terminal. (**detach**)

Ctrl-a D D
> Detach and log out. (**pow-detach**)

Ctrl-a f
> Toggle flow control between on, off, and auto. (**flow**)

Ctrl-a F
> Resize window to current region size. (**fit**)

Ctrl-a Ctrl-g
> Toggle visual bell mode. (**vbell**)

Ctrl-a h
> Write contents of the current window to the file *hardcopy*.n. (**hardcopy**)

Ctrl-a H

Begin/end logging of the current window to the file *screenlog*.n. (**log**)

Ctrl-a i

Show information about this window. (**info**)

Ctrl-a k

Kill current window. (**kill**)

Ctrl-a l

Refresh current window. (**redisplay**)

Ctrl-a L

Toggle window's login slot. Requires that **screen** be configured to update the **utmp** database. (**login**)

Ctrl-a m

Redisplay last message. (**lastmsg**)

Ctrl-a M

Toggle monitoring of the current window. (**monitor**)

Ctrl-a Space
Ctrl-a n

Switch to next window. (**next**)

Ctrl-a N

Show number and title of current window. (**number**)

Ctrl-a Backspace
Ctrl-a h
Ctrl-a p

Switch to previous window. (**prev**)

Ctrl-a q

Send a start signal (associated with **Ctrl-q** by terminals) to current window. (**xon**)

Ctrl-a Q

Delete all regions except the current one. (**only**)

Ctrl-a r

Toggle current window's line-wrap setting. (**wrap**)

Ctrl-a s

Send a stop signal (associated with **Ctrl-s** by terminals) to current window. (**xoff**)

Ctrl-a S

Split current region into two new regions. (**split**)

Ctrl-a t

Show system information, including time and date. (**time**)

Ctrl-a v

Display version information. (**version**)

Ctrl-a Ctrl-v

Enter digraph for entering characters that can't normally be entered. (**digraph**)

Ctrl-a w
List all windows. (**windows**)

Ctrl-a W
Toggle 80/132 columns. (**width**)

Ctrl-a x
Lock terminal. (**lockscreen**)

Ctrl-a X
Kill the current region. (**remove**)

Ctrl-a z
Suspend **screen**. (**suspend**)

Ctrl-a Z
Reset virtual terminal to its "power-on" values. (**reset**)

Ctrl-a .
Write out a *.termcap* file. (**dumptermcap**)

Ctrl-a ?
Show all key bindings. (**help**)

Ctrl-a Ctrl-
Kill all windows and terminate **screen**. (**quit**)

Ctrl-a :
Enter command-line mode. (**colon**)

Ctrl-a [
Ctrl-a Esc
Enter copy/scrollback mode. (**copy**)

Ctrl-a]
Write contents of the paste buffer to the standard input queue of the current window. (**paste**)

Ctrl-a {
Ctrl-a }
Copy and paste a previous line. (**history**)

Ctrl-a >
Write paste buffer to a file. (**writebuf**)

Ctrl-a <
Read screen-exchange file into paste buffer. (**readbuf**)

Ctrl-a =
Remove file used by **Ctrl-a <** and **Ctrl-a >**. (**removebuf**)

Ctrl-a ,
Shows where screen comes from, where it went to, and why you can use it. (**license**)

Ctrl-a _
Start/stop monitoring the current window for inactivity. (**silence**)

Ctrl-a *
List all currently attached displays. (**displays**)

script

script [*option*] [*file*]

Fork the current shell and make a typescript of a terminal session. The typescript is written to *file*. If no *file* is given, the typescript is saved in the file *typescript*. The script ends when the forked shell exits, usually with Ctrl-D or **exit**.

Options

-a   Append to *file* or *typescript* instead of overwriting the previous contents.

-f   Flush output after each write. Useful if another person is monitoring the output file.

-q   Operate in quiet mode.

-t   Write timing data to standard error. Each entry has two fields: the first is the elapsed time since the last output, and the second is the number of characters in the current output.

---

sdiff

sdiff -o *outfile* [*options*] *from to*

Find differences between the two files *from* and *to* and merge interactively, writing the results to *outfile*.

Options

--   Treat remaining options as filenames, even if they begin with -.

-a, --text
Treat all files as text and compare line-by-line.

-b, --ignore-space-change
Ignore differences in whitespace.

-B, --ignore-blank-lines
Ignore added or missing blank lines.

-d, --minimal
Use a different algorithm to find fewer changes. This option causes **sdiff** to run more slowly.

-H, --speed-large-files
Heuristically speed comparison of large files with many small scattered changes.

-i, --ignore-case
Ignore case changes.

-I *regexp*, **--ignore-matching-lines=***regexp*
Ignore any changes that insert or delete lines matching the regular expression *regexp*.

--ignore-all-space
Ignore whitespace when comparing lines.

-l, --left-column
Print only the left column of common lines.

-o *file*, **--output=***file*
Write merged output to the specified file.

-s, --suppress-common-lines
Suppress common lines.

-t, --expand-tabs
Convert tabs to spaces in the output to preserve alignment.

-v, --version
Print version information and exit.

-w *cols*, **--width=***cols*
Set the output to *cols* columns wide.

-W Ignore horizontal whitespace when comparing lines.

Interactive commands

ed Edit, then use both versions, with a header for each.

eb Edit, then use both versions.

el Edit, then use the left version.

er Edit, then use the right version.

e Edit a new version to replace the others.

l Use the left version.

r Use the right version.

s Silently include common lines.

v Verbosely include common lines.

q Quit.

---

sed

sed [*options*] [*command*] [*files*]

Stream editor. Edit one or more *files* without user interaction. See Chapter 12 for more information.

---

sendmail

sendmail [*flags*] [*address...*]

System administration command. **sendmail** is a mail transfer agent (MTA) or, more simply, a mail router. It accepts mail from a user's mail program, interprets the mail address, rewrites the address into the proper form for the delivery program, and routes the mail to the correct delivery program.

Command-line flags

-Ac
Use local submission configuration file */etc/mail/submit.cf*, even when no mail is sent from the command line.

-Am
Use configuration file */etc/mail/sendmail.cf*, even when mail is sent from the command line.

-B*type*
Set message body type. Accepted values are **7BIT** and **8BITMIME**.

-b_x_

> Set operation mode to _x_. Operation modes are:

> **a**   Run in ARPAnet mode.

> **d**   Run as a daemon.

> **D**   Run as a daemon, but remain in the foreground.

> **h**   Print persistent host status information.

> **H**   Purge expired entries from persistent host status information.

> **i**   Initialize the alias database.

> **m**   Deliver mail (the default).

> **p**   Print the mail queue.

> **s**   Speak SMTP on input side.

> **t**   Run in test mode.

> **v**   Verify addresses; do not collect or deliver.

-C _file_

> Use configuration file _file_.

-d _level_

> Set debugging level.

-F _name_

> Set full name of user to _name_.

-f _name_

> Sender's name is _name_.

-G   Relay message submission. Used by **rmail**.

-i   Do not interpret dots on a line by themselves as a message terminator.

-h _cnt_

> Set hop count (number of times message has been processed by **sendmail**) to _cnt_.

-L _identifier_

> Use the specified log _identifier_ for messages sent to **syslogd**.

-N _conditions_

> Specify conditions for delivery status notification (DSN) as a comma-separated list. Accepted values are **never**, **delay**, **failure**, and **success**.

-n   Do not alias or forward.

-O _option=value_

> Set an option specified by its long name. Options are described in the next section.

-o_Xvalue_

> Set an option specified by its short name _X_. Options are described in the next section.

-p_protocol_

> Receive messages via the _protocol_ protocol.

-q[*time*]

Process queued messages immediately, or at intervals indicated by *time* (for example, **-q30m** for every half hour).

-qp[*time*]

Same as **-q**, but create a persistent process to handle the queue instead of initiating a new process at each time interval.

-qf

Process saved messages in the queue using the foreground process.

-qG *group*

Process saved messages in the named queue *group*.

-q[!]*I substring*

Process jobs for named queues containing *substring*. Use ! to process mail for all queues not containing *substring*.

-q[!]*R substring*

Process jobs with recipients containing *substring*. Use ! to process mail for recipients not containing *substring*.

-q[!]*S substring*

Process jobs from senders containing *substring*. Use ! to process mail from senders not containing *substring*.

-R *portion*

When bouncing messages, return only the specified *portion* of the bounced message. *portion* may be **hdrs** for headers, or **full** for the full message.

-r *name*

Obsolete form of **-f**.

-t Read header for **To:**, **Cc:**, and **Bcc:** lines, and send to everyone on those lists.

-v Verbose mode.

-V *envid*

Use *envid* as the original envelope ID.

-X *file*

Log all traffic to *file*. Not to be used for normal logging.

Configuration options

Command-line configuration options are the same options normally set with an **O** in the **sendmail** configuration file. On the command line they are set using **-O** and the option's long name. Many of these options have short name variations that are used with the **-o** option. Here we document items most likely to be useful on the command line, providing both their short and long name forms. Many of the commands call for *timeout* values. These should be given as a number followed by a letter indicating the interval: **s** for seconds, **m** for minutes, **h** for hours, or **d** for days. For example, **30s** is 30 seconds, **10m** is 10 minutes, **3d** is 3 days. The default is minutes when no letter is given.

Aliasfile=*file,* **A***file*
> Use alternate alias file.

AliasWait=*min,* **a***min*
> If the **D** option is set, wait *min* minutes for the aliases file to be rebuilt before returning an alias database out-of-date warning.

BlankSub=*char,* **B***char*
> Set unquoted space replacement character.

CheckAliases, n
> When running **newaliases**, validate the right side of aliases.

CheckpointInterval=*num,* **C***num*
> Checkpoint the queue when mailing to multiple recipients. **sendmail** will rewrite the list of recipients after each group of *num* recipients has been processed.

ClassFactor=*factor,* **z***factor*
> Multiplier for priority increments. This determines how much weight to give to a message's precedence header. **sendmail**'s default is 1800.

ConnectionCacheSize=*num,* **k***num*
> Specify the maximum number of open connections to cache.

ConnectionCacheTimeout=*timeout,* **K***timeout*
> Time out connections after *timeout.*

ConnectionRateThrottle=*num*
> Restrict SMTP connections per second to *num.*

DefaultUser=*uid*[:*gid*]*,* **u***uid*[:*gid*]
> Use user ID and group ID for mailers instead of **1:1**. If no group ID is specified, the user's default group is used.

DefaultCharSet=*label*
> Use the specified label for 8-bit data.

DeliveryMode=*x,* **d***x*
> Set the delivery mode to *x*. Delivery modes are **d** for deferred delivery, **i** for interactive (synchronous) delivery, **b** for background (asynchronous) delivery, and **q** for queue only (i.e., deliver the next time the queue is run).

DialDelay=*seconds*
> Specify the number of seconds to wait before redialing after a connection fails.

DontPruneRoutes, R
> Don't prune route addresses.

EightBitMode=*mode,* **8***mode*
> Specify how to handle 8-bit input. Accepted values for *mode* are **mimefy** (convert to 7-bit), **pass** (send as is), or **strict** (bounce the message).

ErrorHeader=*text,* **E***text*
> Set error message header. *text* is either text to add to an error message, or the name of a file. A filename must include its full path and begin with a /.

ErrorMode=*x,* **e***x*

Set error processing to mode *x*. Valid modes are **m** to mail back the error message, **w** to write back the error message, **p** to print the errors on the terminal (default), **q** to throw away error messages, and **e** to do special processing for the BerkNet.

FallbackMXhost=*host,* **V***host*

Set fallback MX host. *host* should be the fully qualified domain name of the fallback host.

ForkEachJob, Y

Deliver each job that is run from the queue in a separate process. This helps limit the size of running processes on systems with very low amounts of memory.

ForwardPath=*path,* **J***path*

Set an alternative *.forward* search path.

HelpFile=*file,* **H***file*

Specify SMTP help file to use instead of */etc/mail/helpfile*.

HoldExpensive, c

On mailers that are considered "expensive" to connect to, don't initiate immediate connection.

IgnoreDots, i

Do not take dots on a line by themselves as a message terminator.

LogLevel=*n,* **L***n*

Specify log level. Default is 9.

MatchGECOS, G

Compare local mail names to the GECOS section in the password file.

MaxDaemonChildren=*num*

Restrict incoming SMTP daemon to no more than **num** child processes.

MaxHopCount=*num,* **h***num*

Allow a maximum of *num* hops per message.

MeToo, m

Send to **me** (the sender) also if I am in an alias expansion.

MinFreeBlocks=*minblocks,* **b***minblocks*

Require at least *minblocks* on the filesystem to be free.

MinQueueAge=*timeout*

Wait the specified time before processing a new job in the queue.

NoRecipientAction=*action*

Specify what headers, if any, to add to a message without recipient headers. Accepted values are **none, add-to, add-apparently-to, add-bcc,** and **add-to-undisclosed**.

OldStyleHeaders, o

If set, this message may have old-style headers. If not set, this message is guaranteed to have new-style headers (i.e., commas instead of spaces between addresses).

PostmasterCopy=*user,* **P***user*
Send copies of all failed mail to *user* (usually postmaster).

PrivacyOptions=*optionlist,* **p***optionlist*
Adjust the privacy of the SMTP daemon. The *optionlist* argument should be a comma-separated list of the following values:

public
Make SMTP fully public (the default).

needmailhelo
Require site to send HELO or ELHO before sending mail.

needexpnhelo
Require site to send HELO or ELHO before answering an address expansion request.

needvrfyhelo
Like preceding argument, but for verification requests.

noetrn
Deny requests to reverse the connection using extended TURN.

noexpn
Deny all expansion requests.

noverb
Deny requests for verbose mode.

novrfy
Deny all verification requests.

authwarnings
Insert special headers in mail messages advising recipients that the message may not be authentic.

goaway
Set all of the previous arguments (except **public**).

nobodyreturn
Don't return message body with a delivery status notification.

noreceipts
Turn off delivery status notification on success.

restrictexpand
Deny untrusted users access to aliases, forwards, or include files. Restrict **sendmail -bv** and disallow **-v**.

restrictmailq
Allow only users of the same group as the owner of the queue directory to examine the mail queue.

restrictqrun
Limit queue processing to root and the owner of the queue directory.

QueueDirectory=*dir,* **Q***dir*
Select the directory in which to queue messages.

QueueFactor=*factor,* q*factor*
Multiplier (factor) for high-load queuing. Default is 600000.

QueueLA=*load,* x*load*
Queue messages when load level is higher than *load*.

QueueTimeout=*timeout,* T*timeout*
Set the timeout on undelivered messages in the queue to the specified time (overridden by **Timeout.queuereturn**).

RecipientFactor=*factor,* y*factor*
Penalize large recipient lists by *factor*.

RefuseLA=*load,* X*load*
Refuse SMTP connections when load is higher than *load*.

ResolverOptions=*arg,* I *arg*
Use DNS lookups and tune them. Queue messages on connection refused. The *arg* arguments are identical to resolver flags without the RES_ prefix. Each flag can be preceded by a plus or minus sign to enable or disable the corresponding name server option. There must be whitespace between the I and the first flag.

RetryFactor=*inc,* Z*inc*
Increment priority of items remaining in queue by *inc* after each job is processed. **sendmail** uses 90,000 by default.

SaveFromLine, f
Save Unix-style **From** lines at the front of messages.

SendMimeErrors, j
Use MIME format for error messages.

SevenBitInput, 7
Format all incoming messages in seven bits.

StatusFile=*file,* S*file*
Save statistics in the named file.

SuperSafe, s
Always instantiate the queue file, even when it is not strictly necessary.

TempFileMode=*mode,* F*mode*
Set default file permissions for temporary files. If this option is missing, default permissions are 0600.

Timeout.queuereturn=*timeout*
Return undelivered mail that has been in the queue longer than the specified *timeout*. The default is **5d** (five days).

TimeZoneSpec=*timezone,* t*timezone*
Set name of the time zone.

UseErrorsTo, l
Do not ignore **Errors-To** header.

UserDatabaseSpec=*database,* U*database*
Consult the user *database* for forwarding information.

Verbose, v
Run in verbose mode.

sendmail support files

/usr/lib/sendmail
> Traditional location of **sendmail** binary.

/usr/bin/newaliases
> Link to */usr/lib/sendmail*; rebuilds the alias database from information in */etc/aliases*.

/usr/bin/mailq
> Prints a listing of the mail queue.

/etc/mail/sendmail.cf
> Configuration file, in text form.

/etc/mail/submit.cf
> Configuration file used for local message submissions.

/etc/mail/helpfile
> SMTP help file.

/etc/mail/statistics
> Statistics file.

/etc/aliases
> Alias file, in text form.

/etc/aliases.db
> Alias file in **dbm** format. Created by **newaliases**

/var/spool/mqueue
> Directory in which the mail queue and temporary files reside.

---

seq

> **seq** [*options*] [*first* [*increment*]] *last*

Print the numbers from *first* through *last* by *increment*. The default is to print one number per line to standard output. Both *first* and *increment* can be omitted and default to 1, but if *first* is omitted then *increment* must also be omitted. In other words, if only two numbers are specified, they are taken to be the first and last numbers. The numbers are treated as floating point.

Options

-f *format*, --format=*format*
> Write the output using the specified **printf** floating-point format, which can be one of **%e**, **%f**, or **%g** (the default).

--help
> Print help message and exit.

-s *string*, --separator=*string*
> Use *string* to separate numbers in the output. Default is newline.

-w, --equal-width
> Equalize the width of the numbers by padding with leading zeros. (Use -f for other types of padding.)

--version
> Print version information and exit.

---

setfdprm

setfdprm [*options*] *device* [*name*]

Load disk parameters used when autoconfiguring floppy devices.

Options

-c *device*
> Clear parameters of *device*.

-n *device*
> Disable format-detection messages for *device*.

-p *device* [*name* | *parameters*]
> Permanently reset parameters for *device*. You can use *name* to specify a configuration, or you can specify individual parameters. The parameters that can be specified are **dev**, **size**, **sect**, **heads**, **tracks**, **stretch**, **gap**, **rate**, **spec1**, or **fmt_gap**. Consult */etc/fdprm* for the original values.

-y *device*
> Enable format-detection messages for *device*.

setkeycodes

setkeycodes *scancode keycode*

System administration command. Assign a *keycode* event to the specified keyboard *scancode*. The kernel matches these to its own keycodes. Scancodes in the range of 1–88 are hardwired in the kernel, but the remaining scancodes can be assigned to keycodes in the range of 1–127. Use **getkeycodes** to see current assignments. Use **showkey** to discover what scancode a key is sending.

setleds

setleds [*options*]

Display or change the led flag settings (NumLock, CapsLock, and ScrollLock) for the current virtual terminal. With no options, display the current settings for all three flags. Can be used in a startup script to set the initial state of the leds.

Options

+num, -num
> Set or clear NumLock.

+caps, -caps
> Set or clear CapsLock

+scroll, -scroll
> Set or clear ScrollLock.

-D   Change both the current and the default settings. Useful for always having NumLock set, for example.

-F   Only change the flags (and their settings may be reflected by the keyboard leds). The default behavior.

-L   Change the leds but not the flags, so the leds no longer reflect the virtual terminal (VT) flags. Run **setleds -L** with no other options to restore the default behavior.

-v   Report the settings before and after the change.

setmetamode	**setmetamode** [*options*]
	Display or set Meta key handling for the current virtual terminal. With no option, print the current Meta key mode. Otherwise, set the mode and display the setting before and after the change.

Options

esc, prefix, escprefix
　Set the Meta key to send an escape sequence.

meta, bit, metabit
　Set the Meta key to set the high-order bit of the character.

setsid	**setsid** *command* [*arguments*]
	System administration command. Execute the named command and optional command *arguments* in a new session.

setterm	**setterm** [*options*]
	Set terminal attributes by writing to standard output a character string to invoke the specified attributes.

Options

For Boolean options, the default value is on. Where 8-color is specified, the possible colors are black, red, green, yellow, blue, magenta, cyan, and white. Where 16-color is specified, the possible colors include the 8-color colors, plus grey, bright red, bright green, bright yellow, bright blue, bright magenta, bright cyan, and bright white.

-appcursorkeys [on|off]
　Set cursor key application mode on or off. Virtual consoles only. Can cause problems with **vi**.

-append [*num*]
　Write a snapshot of virtual console *num* to the file specified with the **-file** option, appending the snapshot to any existing contents. With no argument, write a snapshot of the current virtual terminal.

-background *8-color*|**default**
　Set background color. Virtual consoles only.

-bfreq [*freq*]
　Set the bell frequency in Hz (default 0).

-blank [*min*]
　Set the delay before the screen blanks to the specified number of minutes. Virtual consoles only.

-blength [*millisec*]
　Set the bell duration in milliseconds (default 0).

-blink [on|off]
　Turn blinking mode on or off. If the terminal is not a virtual console, **-blink off** also turns off bold, half-bright, and reverse modes.

-bold [on|off]

Turn bold on or off. If the terminal is not a virtual console, **-bold off** also turns off blink, half-bright, and reverse modes.

-clear [all]

Clear the screen.

-clear rest

Clear from the current cursor position to the end of the screen.

-cleartabs [*tab1...tabn*]

With no arguments, clear all tab stops. Otherwise, clear the specified tab stops. Virtual consoles only.

-cursor [on|off]

Turn the cursor on or off.

-default

Set rendering options to defaults.

-dump [*num*]

Write a snapshot of virtual console *num* to the file specified with the **-file** option, overwriting any existing contents. With no argument, dump the current virtual console. Overrides **-append**.

-file *file*

Write output from the **-dump** or **-append** option to the specified file. If no filename is specified, write to the file *screen.dump* in the current directory.

-foreground *8-color*|**default**

Set foreground color. Virtual consoles only.

-half-bright [on|off]

Turn half-bright (dim) mode on or off. If the terminal is not a virtual console, **-half-bright off** also turns off bold, blink, and reverse modes.

-hbcolor *16-color*

Set color for half-bright characters. Virtual consoles only.

-initialize

Display the terminal initialization string to reset the rendering options and other attributes to their defaults.

-inversescreen [on|off]

Invert the screen colors, swapping foreground and background, and underline and half-bright. Virtual consoles only.

-linewrap [on|off]

Turn line-wrapping on or off. Virtual consoles only.

-msg [on|off]

Enable or disable the sending of kernel **printk**( ) messages to the console. Virtual consoles only.

-msglevel [*num*]

Set the console logging level for kernel **printk**( ) messages. The value of *num* can be in the range 0–8. Messages more important than the specified number are printed, with 8 printing all kernel messages, and 0 equivalent to **-msg on**. Virtual consoles only.

-powerdown [*min*]
Set the VESA powerdown interval to the specified number of minutes, from 0–60. If no value is specified for *min*, defaults to 0, disabling powerdown.

-powersave [*mode*]
Put the monitor in the specified VESA powersave mode. Specifying no mode is equivalent to **off**. The possible values of *mode* are:

on, vsync
vsynch suspend mode.

hsync
hsync suspend mode.

powerdown
Powerdown mode.

off
Turn off VESA powersaving features.

-regtabs [*num*]
Clear all existing tab stops and set a regular tab stop pattern at every *num* number (default 8). *num* is a number in the range 1–160. Virtual consoles only.

-repeat [on|off]
Turn keyboard repeat on or off. Virtual consoles only.

-reset
Display the terminal reset string to reset the terminal to its power-on state.

-reverse [on|off]
Turns reverse-video mode on or off. If the terminal is not a virtual console, **-reverse off** also turns off bold, half-bright, and blink modes.

-store
Store the current rendering options as the defaults. Virtual consoles only.

-tabs [*tab1...tabn*]
Set tab stops at the specified cursor positions, which can range from 1 to 160. Virtual consoles only.

-term *term*
Replace the value of the **TERM** environment variable with *term*.

-ulcolor *16-color*
Set color for underlining. Virtual consoles only.

-underline [on|off]
Turn underlining on or off.

sftp

sftp [*options*] *host*

An interactive file transfer program, similar to **ftp** except that it uses **ssh** to perform file transfers securely. **sftp** connects to *host* and logs in, prompting for a password if required. The host can be specified in the following ways:

> *host*
> [*user@*]*host*[:*file* [*file*] ...]
> [*user@*]*host*[:*dir*[/]]

If *user* is specified, that username is used for the login. If any files are specified, the **sftp** client automatically retrieves them after the user has been authenticated and then exits. If a directory *dir* is specified, the client starts in that directory on the remote host. **sftp** is part of the OpenSSH suite of network tools.

Options

-1   Use SSH1. The default is to use SSH2.

-b *file*
> Run in batch mode, taking commands from the specified file. Requires the use of a noninteractive authentication mechanism.

-B *bytes*
> Specify the size of the buffer **sftp** uses for file transfers. Default is 32768 bytes.

-C   Enable compression (uses **ssh -C**).

-F *file*
> Use *file* as the **ssh** configuration file instead of the default system configuration file. The systemwide file is usually */etc/ssh/ssh_config* and per-user files are *$HOME/.ssh/config*.

-o*option*
> Pass an option to **ssh**. The passed option is in the format used by **ssh_config**(5) (e.g., **-oPORT=***nn*, where *nn* is the port number). **-o** can appear more than once to pass multiple options to **ssh**. This option is useful for passing options that don't have an equivalent **sftp** command-line option.

-P *server_path*
> Connect directly to the local **sftp** server specified in *server_path*. Useful for debugging.

-R *num*
> Specify the number of requests that may be outstanding at any time (default 16).

-s *subsys*|*server_path*
> Specify the SSH2 subsystem or path to the **sftp** server on the remote system. Specifying the path is useful for using **sftp** via SSH1 or if the remote **sshd** does not have an **sftp** subsystem configured.

-S *program*

Specify the name of a program that understands **ssh** options and that you want to use for the encrypted connection.

-v   Raise the logging level.

---

sh

sh [*options*] [*file* [*arguments*]]

The standard Unix shell, a command interpreter into which all other commands are entered. On Linux, this is just another name for the **bash** shell. For more information, see Chapter 7.

---

shar

shar [*options*] *files*
shar -S [*options*]

Create shell archives ("shar" files) that are in text format and can be mailed. These files may be unpacked later by executing them with */bin/sh*. Other commands may be required on the recipient's system, such as **compress**, **gzip**, and **uudecode**. The resulting archive is sent to standard output unless the **-o** option is given.

Options

-a, --net-headers

Allows automatic generation of headers. The **-n** option is required if the **-a** option is used.

-b *bits*, **--bits-per-code=***bits*

Use **-b** *bits* as a parameter to **compress** (when doing compression). Default value is 12. The **-b** option automatically turns on **-Z**.

-c, --cut-mark

Start the shar file with a line that says "Cut here."

-d *delimiter*, **--here-delimiter=***delimiter*

Use *delimiter* for the files in the shar instead of **SHAR_EOF**.

-f, --basename

Causes only simple filenames to be used when restoring, which is useful when building a shar from several directories or another directory. (If a directory name is passed to **shar**, the substructure of that directory will be restored whether or not **-f** is used.)

-g *level*, **--level-for-gzip=***level*

Use *-level* as a parameter to **gzip** (when doing compression). Default is 9. The **-g** option turns on the **-z** option by default.

--help

Print a help summary on standard output, then exit.

-l *nn*, **--whole-size-limit=***nn*

Limit the output file size to *nn* kilobytes but don't split input files. Requires use of **-o**.

-m, --no-timestamp

Don't generate **touch** commands to restore the file modification dates when unpacking files from the archive.

-n *name*, **--archive-name**=*name*

Name of archive to be included in the header of the shar files.
Required if the **-a** option is used.

--no-i18n

Do not produce internationalized shell archives; use default
English messages. By default, **shar** produces archives that will
try to output messages in the unpacker's preferred language
(as determined by **LANG/LC_MESSAGES**).

-o *prefix*, **--output-prefix**=*prefix*

Save the archive to files *prefix*.01 through *prefix.nn* (instead of
sending it to standard output). This option must be used
when either **-l** or **-L** is used.

-p, --intermix-type

Allow positional parameter options. The options **-B**, **-T**, **-z**,
and **-Z** may be embedded, and files to the right of the option
will be processed in the specified mode.

--print-text-domain-dir

Print the directory **shar** looks in to find message files for
different languages, then immediately exit.

-q, --quiet, --silent

Turn off verbose mode.

-s *who@where*, **--submitter**=*who@where*

Supply submitter name and address, instead of allowing **shar**
to determine it automatically.

--version

Print the version number of the program on standard output,
then exit.

-w, --no-character-count

Do not check each file with **wc -c** after unpacking. The default
is to check.

-x, --no-check-existing

Overwrite existing files without checking. Default is to check
and not overwrite existing files. If **-c** is passed as a parameter
to the script when unpacking (**sh** *archive* **-c**), existing files will
be overwritten unconditionally. See also **-X**.

-z, --gzip

gzip and **uuencode** all files prior to packing. Must be
unpacked with **uudecode** and **gunzip** (or **zcat**).

-B, --uuencode

Treat all files as binary; use **uuencode** prior to packing. This
increases the size of the archive, and it must be unpacked with
uudecode.

-D, --no-md5-digest
Do not **md5sum digest** to verify the unpacked files. The default is to check.

-F, --force-prefix
Force the prefix character to be prepended to every line even if not required. May slightly increase the size of the archive, especially if **-B** or **-Z** is used.

-L *nn*, **--split-size-limit=***nn*
Limit output file size to *nn* kilobytes and split files if necessary. The archive parts created with this option must be unpacked in the correct order. Requires use of **-o**.

-M, --mixed-uuencode
Pack files in mixed mode (the default). Distinguishes files as either text or binary; binaries are uuencoded prior to packing.

-P, --no-piping
Use temporary files instead of pipes in the shar file.

-Q, --quiet-unshar
Disable verbose mode.

-S, --stdin-file-list
Read list of files to be packed from standard input rather than from the command line. Input must be in a form similar to that generated by the **find** command, with one filename per line.

-T, --text-files
Treat all files as text.

-V, --vanilla-operation
Produce shars that rely only upon the existence of **sed** and **echo** in the unsharing environment.

-X, --query-user
Prompt user to ask if files should be overwritten when unpacking.

-Z, --compress
Compress and uuencode all files prior to packing.

---

showkey   showkey [*options*]

Print keycodes, scancodes, or ASCII codes of keys pressed on the keyboard. The default is to show keycodes. In keycode and scancode mode, the program terminates 10 seconds after the last key is pressed. In ASCII mode, press Ctrl-D to exit. This command may not function properly under the X Window System, which also reads from the console device.

Options

-a, --ascii
Print the ASCII character, decimal, octal, and hexadecimal values of keys pressed.

-h, --help
Print version number and help message, then exit.

-k, --keycodes
Print keycodes associated with key-press events. This is the default mode.

-s, --scancodes
Print the keyboard scancodes associated with key-press events.

---

showmount

showmount [*options*] [*host*]

NFS/NIS command. Show information about an NFS server. This information is maintained by the **mountd** server on *host*. The default value for *host* is the value returned by **hostname**. With no options, show the clients that have mounted directories from the host. **showmount** is usually found in */usr/sbin*, which is not in the default search path.

Options

-a, --all
Print all remote mounts in the format *hostname:directory*, where *hostname* is the name of the client and *directory* is the root of the filesystem that has been mounted.

-d, --directories
List directories that have been remotely mounted by clients.

-e, --exports
Print the list of exported filesystems.

-h, --help
Provide a short help summary.

--no-headers
Do not print headers.

-v, --version
Report the current version of the program.

---

shred

shred [*options*] *files*

Overwrite a file to make the contents unrecoverable, and delete the file afterwards if requested.

Options

-   Shred standard output.

-f, --force
Force permissions to allow writing to *files*.

--help
Print help message and exit.

-n*num*, **--iterations=***num*
Overwrite files *num* times (default is 25).

-s*num***, --size=***num*

Shred *num* bytes. *num* can be expressed with suffixes (e.g., **K**, **M**, or **G**).

-u, --remove

Remove file after overwriting. **shred** does not remove the file unless this option is specified.

-v, --verbose

Verbose mode.

--version

Print version information and exit.

-x, --exact

Shred the exact file size; do not round up to the next full block.

-z, --zero

On the final pass, overwrite with zeros to hide the shredding.

---

shutdown

shutdown [*options*] *when* [*message*]

System administration command. Terminate all processing. *when* may be a specific time (in *hh:mm* format), a number of minutes to wait (in *+m* format), or **now**. A broadcast *message* notifies all users to log off the system. Processes are signaled with **SIGTERM** to allow them to exit gracefully. */etc/init* is called to perform the actual shutdown, which consists of placing the system in runlevel 1. Only privileged users can execute the **shutdown** command, although **init** may call **shutdown** with root privileges when the CTRL-ALT-DEL key combination is pressed from the console keyboard. Broadcast messages, default or defined, are displayed at regular intervals during the grace period; the closer the shutdown time, the more frequent the message.

Options

-a When called from **init**, shut down only if one of the users listed in the file */etc/shutdown.allow* is currently logged in.

-c Cancel a shutdown that is in progress.

-F Force a filesystem check (**fsck**) on reboot.

-f Reboot fast, by suppressing the normal call to **fsck** when rebooting.

-h Halt the system when shutdown is complete.

-k Print the warning message, but suppress actual shutdown.

-r Reboot the system when shutdown is complete.

-t *num*

Ensure a *num*-second delay between killing processes and changing the runlevel.

size

size [*options*] [*objfile...*]

Print the number of bytes of each section of *objfile* and its total size. If *objfile* is not specified, *a.out* is used.

Options

-d Display the size in decimal and hexadecimal.

--format=*format*
Imitate the **size** command from either System V (**--format sysv**) or BSD (**--format berkeley**).

--help
Print help message, then exit.

-o Display the size in octal and hexadecimal.

--radix=*num*
Specify how to display the size: in hexadecimal and decimal (if *num* is 10 or 16) or hexadecimal and octal (if *num* is 8).

-t, --totals
Show object totals. Works only with Berkeley format listings.

--target=*bfdname*
Specify object format by binary file descriptor name. Use **-h** for a list of supported object formats.

-x Display the size in hexadecimal and decimal.

-A Imitate System V's **size** command.

-B Imitate BSD's **size** command.

-V, --version
Print version, then exit.

---

skill

skill [*signal*] [*options*] *processes*
snice [*priority*] [*options*] *processes*

Send a signal to *processes* or reset the priority. The default signal for **skill** is **TERM**, and the default priority for **snice** is +4 but can be in the range +20 (slowest) to –20 (fastest). The selection options **-c**, **-p**, **-t**, and **-u** are not required, but can be specified to insure that *processes* are interpreted correctly.

Options

-c The next argument is a command.

-i Use interactive mode.

-l, -L
List available signals.

-n Display the process ID, but take no other action.

-p The next argument is a process ID.

-t The next argument is a tty or pty.

-u The next argument is a username.

-v Verbose mode.

slattach	**slattach** [*options*] [*tty*]

TCP/IP command. Attach serial lines as network interfaces, thereby preparing them for use as point-to-point connections. Only a privileged user may attach or detach a network interface.

Options

-c *command*
> Run *command* when the connection is severed.

-d   Debugging mode.

-e   Exit immediately after initializing the line.

-h   Exit when the connection is severed.

-l   Create UUCP-style lockfile in */var/spool/uucp*.

-L   Enable three-wire operation.

-m   Suppress initialization of the line to 8-bit raw mode.

-n   Similar to **mesg -n**.

-p *protocol*
> Specify *protocol*, which may be **slip**, **adaptive**, **ppp**, or **kiss**.

-q   Quiet mode; suppress messages.

-s *speed*
> Specify line speed.

---

sleep	**sleep** *amount*[*units*] **sleep** *option*

Wait a specified *amount* of time before executing another command. *units* may be **s** (seconds), **m** (minutes), **h** (hours), or **d** (days). The default for *units* is seconds.

Options

--help
> Print usage information and exit.

--version
> Print version information and exit.

---

snice	**snice** [*priority*] [*options*] *processes*

Reset the priority for *processes*. The default priority is +4. See **skill** for the possible options.

---

sort	**sort** [*options*] [*files*]

Sort the lines of the named *files*. Compare specified fields for each pair of lines; if no fields are specified, compare them by byte, in machine collating sequence. If no files are specified or if the file is -, the input is taken from standard input. See also **uniq**, **comm**, and **join**.

Options

-b, --ignore-leading-blanks
> Ignore leading spaces and tabs.

-c, --check
> Check whether *files* are already sorted and, if so, produce no output.

-d, --dictionary-order
> Sort in dictionary order.

-f, --ignore-case
> Fold; ignore uppercase/lowercase differences.

-g, --general-numeric-sort
> Sort in general numeric order.

--help
> Print a help message and then exit.

-i, --ignore-nonprinting
> Ignore nonprinting characters (those outside ASCII range 040–176).

-n   Sort in arithmetic order.

-k *n*[,*m*], **--key=***n*[,*m*]
> Skip *n*–1 fields and stop at *m*–1 fields (i.e., start sorting at the *n*th field, where the fields are numbered beginning with 1).

-o*file*
> Put output in *file*.

-m, --merge
> Merge already sorted input files.

-r, --reverse
> Reverse the order of the sort.

-s, --stable
> Stabilize sort by disabling last-resort comparison.

-t*c*, **--field-separator=***c*
> Separate fields with *c* (default is a tab).

-u, --unique
> Identical lines in input file appear only one time in output.

-z, --zero-terminated
> End lines with zero byte, not with newline.

--version
> Print version information and then exit.

-M, --month-sort
> Attempt to treat the first three characters as a month designation (JAN, FEB, etc.). In comparisons, treat JAN < FEB and any invalid name for a month as less than a valid month.

-S*size*, **--buffer-size=***size*
> Set the size of the main memory buffer to *size*, which may include a suffix; e.g., K (1024, the default) or M.

-T *tempdir*, **--temporary-directory=***dir*
> Directory pathname to be used for temporary files.

Examples

List files by decreasing number of lines:

```
wc -l * | sort -r
```

Alphabetize a list of words, remove duplicates, and print the frequency of each word:

```
sort -fd wordlist | uniq -c
```

Sort the password file numerically by the third field (user ID):

```
sort -nk3,4 -t: /etc/passwd
```

---

split

split [*options*] [*infile* [*prefix*]]

Split *infile* into equal-sized segments. *infile* remains unchanged, and the results are written to *prefix***aa**, *prefix***ab**, and so on. The default prefix is **x**, giving the output files **xaa**, **xab**, etc. If *infile* is - or missing, standard input is read. See also **csplit**.

Options

-*n*   Split *infile* into *n* new files.

-a *n*, --suffix-length=*n*
    Use suffixes of length *n* (default is 2).

-b *n*[b|k|m], --bytes=*n*[b|k|m]
    Split *infile* into *n*-byte segments. Alternate blocksizes may be specified:

   b   512 bytes.

   k   1 kilobyte.

   m   1 megabyte.

-C *bytes*[b|k|m], --line-bytes=*bytes*[b|k|m]
    Put a maximum of *bytes* into file; insist on adding complete lines.

-l *n*, --lines=*n*
    Split *infile* into *n*-line segments (default is 1000).

--help
    Print a help message and then exit.

--verbose
    Print a message for each output file.

--version
    Print version information and then exit.

-    Take input from the standard input.

Examples

Break *bigfile* into 1000-line segments:

```
split bigfile
```

Join four files, then split them into 10-line files named *new.aa*, *new. ab*, and so on. Note that without the -, **new.** would be treated as a nonexistent input file:

```
cat list[1-4] | split -10 - new.
```

---

ssh

ssh [*options*] **hostname** [*command*]

Securely log a user into a remote system and run commands on that system. The version of **ssh** described here is the OpenSSH client. **ssh** can use either Version 1 (SSH1) or Version 2 (SSH2) of the SSH protocol. SSH2 is preferable, as it provides better encryption methods and greater connection integrity. The hostname can be specified either as *hostname* or as *user@hostname*. If a command is specified, the user is authenticated, the command is executed, and the connection is closed. Otherwise, a terminal session is opened on the remote system. See later under "Escape characters" for functions that can be supported through an escape character. The default escape character is a tilde (~). The exit status returned from **ssh** is the exit status from the remote system or 255 if there was an error.

Options

-1   Try only SSH1.

-2   Try only SSH2.

-4   Use only IPv4 addresses.

-6   Use only IPv6 addresses.

-a   Disable forwarding of the authentication agent connection.

-A   Allow forwarding of the authentication agent connection. Can also be specified on a per-host basis in a configuration file.

-b *bind_address*
Specify the interface to transmit from when there are multiple available interfaces or aliased addresses.

-c **blowfish**|**3des**|**des**|*ciphers*
Select the cipher for encrypting the session. The default is **3des**. For SSH2, a comma-separated list of *ciphers* can also be specified, with the ciphers listed in order of preference. **des** is supported only for legacy SSH1 compatibility and otherwise should not be used.

-C   Enable compression. Useful mainly for slow connections. The default compression level can be set on a per-host basis in the configuration file with the **CompressionLevel** option.

-D *port*
Enable dynamic application-level port forwarding using *port* on the local side. Can be specified in the configuration file. Only root can forward privileged ports.

-e *char*|*^char*|**none**
Set the escape character (default ~). The escape character must be the first character on a line. If **none** is specified, disable the use of an escape character.

-f   Run interactively for user authentication, then go into background mode for command execution. Implies -**n**.

-F *configfile*
> Specify a per-user configuration file (default is *$HOME/.ssh/ config*).

-g Allow remote hosts to connect to local forwarded ports.

-i *idfile*
> Use *idfile* to read identity (private key) for RSA or DSA authentication. Default is *$HOME/.ssh/id_rsa* or *$HOME/.ssh/ id_dsa* for SSH2, or *$HOME/.ssh/identity* for SSH1. You can specify more than one **-i** option on the command line or in the configuration file.

-I *device*
> Specify a smartcard *device* from which to get the user's private RSA key.

-k Disable Kerberos ticket and AFS token forwarding. Can be set on a per-host basis in the configuration file.

-l *user*
> Log in as *user* on the remote system. Can be specified on a per-host basis in the configuration file.

-L *port:host:hostport*
> Forward *port* on the local host to the specified remote host and port. Can be specified in the configuration file. Only root can forward privileged ports. For IPv6, an alternative syntax is *port/host/hostport*.

-m *macspec*
> For SSH2, the contents of *macspec* specify message authentication code (MAC) algorithms to use. *macspec* is a comma-separated list of algorithms in order of preference.

-n Get standard input as a redirection from */dev/null*. Used to prevent reading from standard input, which is required when running **ssh** in the background. Useful for running X programs on a remote host.

-N Do not execute a remote command. Useful with SSH2 for port forwarding.

-o *option*
> Specify options in configuration-file format. Useful for specifying options that have no command-line equivalent.

-p *port*
> Specify the port on the remote host to which **ssh** is to connect. Can be specified on a per-host basis in the configuration file.

-P Use a nonprivileged port for outgoing connections. Useful if a firewall prevents connections from privileged ports.

-q Run quietly, suppressing warnings and error messages.

-R *port:host:hostport*
> Forward *port* on the remote host to the local *host:hostport*. Can be specified in the configuration file. You can forward privileged ports only if you are logged in as root on the remote host. For IPv6, an alternative syntax is *port/host/hostport*.

-s For SSH2, request invocation of a subsystem on the remote host to be used for another application such as **sftp**. The desired subsystem is specified as the remote command.

-t Force pseudo-tty allocation. Multiple -t options can be specified to force tty allocation even when **ssh** has no local tty.

-T Disable pseudo-tty allocation.

-v Verbose mode. Useful for debugging. Specify multiple -v options to increase verbosity.

-x Disable X11 forwarding.

-X Enable X11 forwarding. Can be specified on a per-host basis in the configuration file.

Escape characters

~. Disconnect.

~~ Send a single ~.

~# List forwarded connections.

~& Run **ssh** in the background at logout, while waiting for a forwarded connection or X11 sessions to terminate.

~? Display the available escape characters.

~C Open a command line. Useful for adding port forwardings when using the -L and -R options.

~R Request rekeying of the connection. Useful only for SSH2 and if the peer supports it.

~^Z
Suspend the connection.

Environment variables

DISPLAY
Set by SSH to *hostname:n* for forwarding X11 connections. *hostname* is the host where the shell is running and *n* is an integer greater than zero.

HOME
The path to the user's home directory.

LOGNAME
The same as **USER**; set only for compatibility with systems that use **LOGNAME**.

MAIL
The path to the user's mailbox.

PATH
The default **PATH** as specified when **SSH** was compiled.

SSH_ASKPASS
Can be set to the name of a program to run to open an X11 window and read the user's passphrase if **ssh** does not have an associated terminal.

SSH_AUTH_SOCK
> The path of a Unix-domain socket for communicating with the agent.

SSH_CLIENT
> Three space-separated values that contain the client IP address, the client port number, and the server port number.

SSH_ORIGINAL_COMMAND
> The original command line, including arguments, if a forced command is executed.

SSH_TTY
> The path to the tty device associated with the current shell or command. Not set if there is no associated tty.

TZ
> The time zone, passed from the SSH daemon, if it was set when the daemon was started.

USER
> The name of the user logging in.

Files

ssh uses the following files in the user's home directory:

$HOME/.rhosts
> Lists host/user pairs allowed to log in. Used with **rhosts** authentication.

$HOME/.shosts
> Like *.rhosts*, but allows *rhosts* authentication without permitting login with **rlogin** or **rsh**.

$HOME/.ssh/authorized_keys
> Lists RSA/DSA public keys that can be used to log in as this user.

$HOME/.ssh/config
> The user's configuration file.

$HOME/.ssh/environment
> Additional environment variable definitions.

$HOME/.ssh/identity, $HOME/.ssh/id_dsa, $HOME/.ssh/id_rsa
> The authentication identity of the user for SSH1 RSA, SSH2 DSA, and SSH2 RSA, respectively.

$HOME/.ssh/identity.pub, $HOME/.ssh/id_dsa.pub, $HOME/.ssh/id_rsa.pub
> The public key for user authentication for SSH1 RSA, SSH2 DSA, and SSH2 RSA, respectively.

$HOME/.ssh/known_hosts
> Contains host keys for all hosts the user has logged into that are not already in the systemwide file at */etc/ssh/ssh_known_hosts*.

$HOME/.ssh/rc
> Contains commands executed by **ssh** after the user has logged in but before the shell or command is started.

---

ssh-add

ssh-add [*options*] [*files*]
ssh-add -e|-s *reader*

Add RSA or DSA identities to the authentication agent (see **ssh-agent**), which must be running and must be an ancestor of the current process. With no arguments specified, add the files *$HOME/.ssh/id_rsa*, *$HOME/.ssh/id_dsa*, and *$HOME/.ssh/identity*. If any *files* are specified, add those instead, prompting for a passphrase if required.

Options

-d   Remove an identity from the agent instead of adding one.

-D   Delete all identities from the agent.

-e *reader*
    Remove key in specified smartcard reader.

-l   List fingerprints of all identities known to the agent.

-L   List public key parameters of all identities known to the agent.

-s   Add key in smartcard *reader*.

-t *life*
    Set maximum lifetime when adding identities to an agent. The value of *life* can be in seconds or another time format specified in **sshd**.

-x   Lock the agent with a password.

-X   Unlock the agent.

---

ssh-agent

ssh-agent [*options*] [*command* [*arguments*]]

Hold private keys used for public key authentication. **ssh-agent** is usually executed at the beginning of an X or login session; then all other windows or programs given as *command* are run as clients of **ssh-agent**. When a command is specified, the command and any arguments are executed. The agent dies when the command completes. Use **ssh-add** to add keys to the agent. Operations that require a private key are performed by the agent, which returns the results to the requestor.

Options

-a *bind_addr*
    Bind the agent to the socket **bind_addr** (default is */tmp/ssh-nnnnnnnn/agent*, where *nnnnnnnn* is a generated number).

-c   Write **csh** commands to standard output. This is the default if the environment variable **SHELL** looks like a **csh**-type shell.

-d   Debug mode.

-k   Kill the current agent.

-s   Write Bourne shell commands to standard output. This is the default if the environment variable **SHELL** does not look like a **csh**-type command.

ssh-keygen

ssh-keygen [*options*]

Generate, manage, and convert authentication keys for **ssh**.

Options

-b *bits*

    Specify the number of bits in the key. The minimum is 512 and the default is 1024.

-B   Show the bubblebabble digest (a digest represented as a string that looks like real words) for the private or public key file specified with **-f**.

-c   Change the comment in the private and public key files (for RSA1 keys only).

-C *comment*

    Specify the new comment.

-D *reader*

    Download the RSA public key from the smartcard in *reader*.

-e   Read an OpenSSH private or public key file and write it in SECSH Public Key File Format to standard output for exporting to a commercial SSH.

-f *file*

    Specify the filename of the key file.

-i   Read an SSH2-compatible unencrypted private or public key file and write an OpenSSH-compatible key to standard output. Used to import keys from a commercial SSH.

-l   Show fingerprint of public or private RSA1 key file specified with **-f**.

-N *passphrase*

    Specify the new passphrase.

-p   Change the passphrase for a private key file. Prompt for the file, the old passphrase, and twice for the new passphrase.

-P *passphrase*

    Specify the old passphrase.

-q   Operate in quiet mode.

-t *type*

    Specify the type of key to create. Possible values of *type* are **rsa1** for SSH1, and **rsa** or **dsa** for SSH2.

-U *reader*

    Upload an existing RSA private key to the smartcard in *reader*.

-y   Read a private OpenSSH-format file and print a public key to standard output.

---

ssh-keyscan

ssh-keyscan [*options*]

Gather public and private host keys from a number of hosts. Can be used in scripts.

Options

-4   Use IPv4 addresses only.

-6   Use IPv6 addresses only.

-f *file*

Read hostnames or *addrlist namelist* pairs from *file*. If - is specified instead of a filename, read hosts or *addrlist namelist* pairs from standard input.

-p *port*

Specify the port to connect to on the remote host.

-t *type*

Specify the type of key to get from the scanned hosts. Possible values are **rsa1** for SSH1 (default) or **rsa** or **dsa** for SSH2. Specify multiple values in a comma-separated list.

-T *timeout*

Specify the timeout for attempting a connection, in seconds.

-v   Verbose mode.

---

sshd

sshd [*options*]

TCP/IP command. Server for the **ssh** program, providing a secure remote login and remote execution facility equivalent to **rlogin** and **rsh**. Normally started at boot, **sshd** listens for incoming connections, forking a new daemon when one is detected. The forked daemon handles authentication, command execution, and encryption. Most implementations of **sshd** support both SSH protocols 1 and 2. The following options are those used by OpenSSH, OpenBSD's Secure Shell implementation.

Options

-b *bits*

Use the specified number of *bits* in the server key. Default is 768.

-d   Run **sshd** in the foreground and send verbose debug information to the system log. Process only one connection. Use the specified number of *bits* in the server key. This option may be specified from one to three times. Each additional **-d** increases the level of information sent to the system log.

-e   Send output to standard error instead of the system log.

-f *file*

Read configuration information from *file* instead of the default configuration file */etc/ssh/sshd_config*.

-g *seconds*

Set the grace time a client has to authenticate itself before the server disconnects and exits. The default is 600 seconds. A value of 0 means there is no limit.

-h *keyfile*

Read the host's cryptographic key from the specified *keyfile* instead of from the default file */etc/ssh/ssh_host_key* for SSH protocol 1, and the default files */etc/ssh/ssh_host_rsa_key* and */etc/ssh/ssh_host_dsa_key* for SSH protocol 2. The **-h** option may be given more than once to specify multiple keyfiles.

-i   Use when running **sshd** from **inetd**.

-k *seconds*
> Set how often the version 1 server key should be regenerated. Default value is 3600 seconds. If set to 0 seconds, the key will never be regenerated.

-o *setting*
> Pass a configuration file setting as an option.

-p *port*
> Listen for connections on *port*. The default is 22. More than one **-p** option may be specified. This option overrides ports specified in a configuration file.

-q   Send no messages to the system log.

-t   Test configuration files and keys, then exit.

-u *namelength*
> Specify the length of the remote hostname field in the UTMP structure as specifed in *utmp.h*. A *namelength* of 0 will cause **sshd** to write dotted decimal values instead of hostnames to the *utmp* file and prevent DNS requests unless required by the authentication mechanism.

-D   Do not detach from the foreground process.

-4   Use only IPv4 addresses.

-6   Use only IPv6 addresses.

---

stat

stat [**options**] *files*

Print out the contents of an inode as they appear to the **stat** system call in a human-readable format. The error messages "Can't stat file" and "Can't lstat file" usually mean the file doesn't exist. "Can't readlink file" generally indicates that something is wrong with a symbolic link.

Options

-c *format*
> Display the output as specified by *format*.

-f   Display information about the filesystem where the file is located, not about the file itself.

-l   For links, display information about the files found by following the links.

-s   For SE (Security Enhanced) Linux, show security information, if it's available, in addition to **stat**'s normal output.

-t   Print the output tersely, in a form suitable for parsing by other programs.

-v   Print version information and exit.

Output

stat and **stat -l** display the following:

- Device number
- Inode number
- Access rights
- Number of hard links
- Owner's user ID and name, if available
- Owner's group ID and name, if available
- Device type for inode device
- Total size, in bytes
- Number of blocks allocated
- I/O blocksize
- Last access time
- Last modification time
- Last change time
- Security context for SE Linux

If **-f** is specified, **stat** displays the following information about the filesystem:

- Filesystem type
- Filesystem blocksize
- Total blocks in the filesystem
- Number of free blocks
- Number of free blocks for nonroot users
- Total number of inodes
- Number of free inodes
- Maximum filename length

Format

The **printf(3)** flag characters #, 0, -, +, and space can be used in *format*. In addition, the field width and precision options can be used.

If **-c** *format* is specified, the following sequences can be used for *format*:

%a Access rights in octal

%A Access rights in human-readable form

%b Number of blocks allocated

%c SE Linux security context

%d Device number in decimal

%D Device number in hex

%f Raw mode in hex

%F File type

%g Owner's group ID

%G Owner's group name

%h Number of hard links

%i Inode number

%n Filename

%N Quoted filename. If file is a symbolic link, include path to original.

%o I/O blocksize

%s Total size, in bytes

%S SE Linux SID (security identifier)

%t Major device type in hex

%T Minor device type in hex

%u Owner's user ID

%U Owner's username

%x Last access time

%X Last access time as seconds since the Epoch

%y Last modification time (modification of the file contents)

%Y Last modification time as seconds since the Epoch

%z Time of last change (modification of the inode)

%Z Time of last change as seconds since the Epoch

If both **-c** *format* and **-f** are specified, the following sequences can be used for *format*:

%a Free blocks available to nonroot user

%b Total data blocks in filesystem

%c Total file nodes in filesystem

%d Free file nodes in filesystem

%f Free blocks in filesystem

%i Filesystem ID, **__val[0]** in hex

%I Filesystem ID, **__val[1]** in hex

%l Maximum filename length

%n Filename

%s Optimal transfer blocksize

%t Type in hex

%T Type in human-readable form

Examples

Sample output from the command **stat /**:

```
stat /
  File: "/"
  Size: 4096        Blocks: 8         IO Block: 4096
Directory
Device: 303h/771d     Inode: 2          Links: 19
```

```
Access: (0755/drwxr-xr-x)  Uid: (    0/   root)  Gid: (
0/   root)
Access: Thu Jan  2 04:02:40 2003
Modify: Wed Jan  1 23:03:20 2003
Change: Wed Jan  1 23:03:20 2003
```

Sample output with **-f**, displaying information about the filesystem:

```
stat -f /
  File: "/"
    ID: 0        0       Namelen: 255      Type: ext2/ext3
Blocks: Total: 2612475   Free: 1869472     Available:
1736735    Size: 4096
Inodes: Total: 1329696   Free: 1150253
```

---

statd

rpc.statd [*options*]

System administration command. The NFS status server, **statd**, reports server status to clients like the **rup** command.

Options

-d   Debugging mode; log verbose information to standard error.

-F   Run **statd** in the foreground.

-n *hostname,* **--name** *hostname*
Specify a name to use for the local hostname. By default this is read using the **gethostname** function.

-o *port,* **--outgoing-port** *port*
Specify the *port* that **statd** should use for its outgoing requests to other servers. When not specified, a port is assigned by **portmap**.

-p *port,* **--port** *port*
Specify the incoming *port* that **statd** should listen on. When not specified, a port is assigned by **portmap**.

-V   Print version information, then exit.

-?   Print help message, then exit.

---

strace

strace [*options*] command [*arguments*]

Trace the system calls and signals for *command* and *arguments*. **strace** shows you how data is passed between the program and the system kernel. With no options, **strace** prints a line to stderr for each system call. It shows the call name, arguments given, return value, and any error messages generated. A signal is printed with both its signal symbol and a descriptive string.

Options

-a *n*
Align the return values in column *n*.

-c   Count all calls and signals and create a summary report when the program has ended.

-d   Debug mode. Print debugging information for **strace** on stderr.

-e [*keyword*=][[!]*values*

> Pass an expression to **strace** to limit the types of calls or signals that are traced or to change how they are displayed. If no *keyword* is given, **trace** is assumed. The *values* can be given as a comma-separated list. Preceding the list with an exclamation mark (!) negates the list. The special *values* **all** and **none** are valid, as are the *values* listed with the following *keywords*.

> **abbrev**=*names*
>> Abbreviate output from large structures for system calls listed in *names*.

> **read**=*descriptors*
>> Print all data read from the given file *descriptors*.

> **signal**=*symbols*
>> Trace the listed signal *symbols* (for example, **signal**=SIGIO,SIGHUP).

> **trace**=*sets*
>> *sets* may be a list of system call names or one of the following:

file	Calls that take a filename as an argument
ipc	Interprocess communication
network	Network-related
process	Process management
signal	Signal-related

> **raw**=*names*
>> Print arguments for the given system calls in hexadecimal.

> **verbose**=*names*
>> Unabbreviate structures for the given system calls. Default is **none**.

> **write**=*descriptors*
>> Print all data written to the given file *descriptors*.

-f   Trace forked processes.

-ff   Write system calls for forked processes to separate files named *filename.pid* when using the **-o** option.

-h   Print help and exit.

-i   Print instruction pointer with each system call.

-o *filename*

> Write output to *filename* instead of stderr. If *filename* starts with the pipe symbol |, treat the rest of the name as a command to which output should be piped.

-O *n*

> Override **strace**'s built-in timing estimates, and just subtract *n* microseconds from the timing of each system call to adjust for the time it takes to measure the call.

-p *pid*

Attach to the given process ID and begin tracking. **strace** can track more than one process if more than one option **-p** is given. Type Ctrl-c to end the trace.

-q   Quiet mode. Suppress attach and detach messages from **strace**.

-r   Relative timestamp. Print time in microseconds between system calls.

-s *n*

Print only the first *n* characters of a string. Default value is 32.

-S *value*

Sort output of **-c** option by the given *value*. *value* may be **calls**, **name**, **time**, or **nothing**. Default is **time**.

-T   Print time spent in each system call.

-t   Print time of day on each line of output.

-tt   Print time of day with microseconds on each line of output.

-ttt

Print timestamp on each line as number of seconds since the Epoch.

-u *username*

Run command as *username*. Needed when tracing **setuid** and **setgid** programs.

-V   Print version and exit.

-v   Verbose. Do not abbreviate structure information.

-x   Print all non-ASCII strings in hexadecimal.

-xx Print all strings in hexadecimal.

---

strfile

strfile [*options*] *input_file* [*output_file*]
unstr [**-c** *delimiter*] *input_file*[*.ext*] [*output_file*]

strfile creates a random-access file for storing strings. The input file should be a file containing groups of lines separated by a line containing a single percent sign (or other specified delimiter character). **strfile** creates an output file that contains a header structure and a table of file offsets for each group of lines, allowing random access of the strings. The output file, if not specified on the command line, is named *sourcefile.dat*. **unstr** undoes the work of **strfile**, printing out the strings contained in the input file in the order they are listed in the header file data. If no output file is specified, **unstr** prints to standard output; otherwise, it prints to the file specified. **unstr** can also globally change the delimiter character in a strings file.

Options

Of the following options, only **-c** can be used with **unstr**. All other options apply only to **strfile**.

-c *delimiter*
> Change the delimiting character from the percent sign to *delimiter*. Valid for both **strfile** and **unstr**.

-i   Ignore case when ordering the strings.

-o   Order the strings alphabetically.

-r   Randomize access to the strings.

-s   Run silently; don't give a summary message when finished.

-x   Set the **STR_ROTATED** bit in the header **str_flags** field.

---

strings

strings [*options*] *files*

Search each *file* specified and print any printable character strings found that are at least four characters long and followed by an unprintable character.

Options

-, -a, --all
> Scan entire object files; default is to scan only the initialized and loaded sections for object files.

-e *encoding,* **--encoding**=*encoding*
> Specify the character encoding of the strings to be found. Possible values are:

b   16-bit big-endian

B   32-bit big-endian

l   16-bit little-endian

L   32-bit little-endian

s   Single-byte character, such as ASCII, ISO-8859, etc. (the default)

-f, --print-file-name
> Print the name of the file before each string.

-*min-len,* **-n** *min-len,* **--bytes**=*min-len*
> Print only strings that are at least *min-len* characters.

-o   The same as **-t o**.

-t *base,* **--radix**=*base*
> Print the offset within the file before each string, in the format specified by *base*:

d   Decimal

o   Octal

x   Hexadecimal

--target=*format*
> Specify an alternative object code format to the system default. Valid targets include **elf32-i386**, **a.out-i386-linux**, **efi-app-ia32**, **elf32-little**, **elf32-big**, **srec**, **symbolsrec**, **tekhex**, **binary**, **ihex**, and **trad-core**.

--help

> Print help message and then exit. The help message includes a list of valid targets.

-v, --version

> Print version information and then exit.

---

strip

strip [*options*] *files*

Remove symbols from object *files*, thereby reducing file sizes and freeing disk space.

Options

-F*bfdname*, **--target=***bfdname*

> Specify object format for both input and output by binary file descriptor name *bfdname*. Use option **-h** to see a list of supported formats.

-I *bfdname*, **--input-target=***bfdname*

> Expect object format *bfdname* for input.

--help

> Print help message, then exit.

-K *symbol*, **--keep-symbol=***symbol*

> Delete all symbols except the specified *symbol*. This option may be used more than once.

-N *symbol*, **--strip-symbol=***symbol*

> Remove *symbol* from the source file.

-O *bfdname*, **--output-target=***bfdname*

> Use object format *bfdname* for output.

-o *file*

> Write stripped object to *file* instead of replacing the original. Only one object file at a time may be stripped when using this option.

-p, --preserve-dates

> Preserve access and modification times.

-R *section*, **--remove-section=***section*

> Delete *section*.

-S, -g, -d, --strip-debug

> Strip debugging symbols.

-s, --strip-all

> Strip all symbols.

--strip-unneeded

> Remove symbols not needed for relocation processing.

-V, --version

> Print version and exit.

-v, --verbose

> Verbose mode.

-X, --discard-locals
Strip local symbols that were generated by the compiler.

-x, --discard-all
Strip nonglobal symbols.

---

stty

stty [*options*] [*modes*]

Set terminal I/O options for the current standard input device. Without options, **stty** reports the terminal settings that differ from those set by running **stty sane**, where ^ indicates the Ctrl key and ^` indicates a null value. Most modes can be negated using an optional - (shown in brackets). The corresponding description is also shown in brackets. Some arguments use non-POSIX extensions; these are marked with *.

Options

-a, --all
Report all option settings.

-F, --device
Open the specified device and use it instead of standard input.

-g, --save
Report settings in **stty**-readable form (i.e., hex).

--help
Print help message and exit.

--version
Print version information and exit.

Control modes

n Set terminal baud rate to *n* (e.g., 2400).

[-]clocal
[Enable] disable modem control.

[-]cread
[Disable] enable the receiver.

[-]crtscts*
[Disable] enable RTS/CTS handshaking.

cs*bits*
Set character size to *bits*, which must be 5, 6, 7, or 8.

[-]cstopb
[1] 2 stop bits per character.

[-]hup
[Do not] hang up connection on last close.

[-]hupcl
Same as previous.

ispeed *n*
Set terminal input baud rate to *n*.

ospeed *n*
Set terminal output baud rate to *n*.

[-]parenb
> [Disable] enable parity generation and detection.

[-]parodd
> Use [even] odd parity.

Flow control modes

The following flow control modes are available by combining the
ortsfl, **ctsflow**, and **rtsflow** flags:

Flag settings	Flow control mode
ortsfl rtsflow ctsflow	Enable unidirectional flow control.
ortsfl rtsflow -ctsflow	Assert RTS when ready to send.
ortsfl -rtsflow ctsflow	No effect.
ortsfl -rtsflow -ctsflow	Enable bidirectional flow control.
-ortsfl rtsflow ctsflow	Enable bidirectional flow control.
-ortsfl rtsflow -ctsflow	No effect.
-ortsfl -rtsflow ctsflow	Stop transmission when CTS drops.
-ortsfl -rtsflow -ctsflow	Disable hardware flow control.

Input modes

[-]brkint
> [Do not] signal INTR on break.

[-]icrnl
> [Do not] map CR to NL on input.

[-]ignbrk
> [Do not] ignore break on input.

[-]igncr
> [Do not] ignore CR on input.

[-]ignpar
> [Do not] ignore parity errors.

[-]inlcr
> [Do not] map NL to CR on input.

[-]inpck
> [Disable] enable input parity checking.

[-]istrip
> [Do not] strip input characters to 7 bits.

[-]iuclc*
> [Do not] map uppercase to lowercase on input.

[-]ixany*
> Allow [XON] any character to restart output.

[-]ixoff, [-]tandem
> [Enable] disable sending of START/STOP characters.

[-]ixon
> [Disable] enable XON/XOFF flow control.

[-]parmrk
> [Do not] mark parity errors.

[-]imaxbel*
> When input buffer is too full to accept a new character, [flush the input buffer] beep without flushing the input buffer.

Output modes

bs*n*
> Select style of delay for backspaces (0 or 1).

cr*n*
> Select style of delay for carriage returns (0–3).

ff*n*
> Select style of delay for formfeeds (0 or 1).

nl*n*
> Select style of delay for linefeeds (0 or 1).

tab*n*
> Select style of delay for horizontal tabs (0–3).

vt*n*
> Select style of delay for vertical tabs (0 or 1).

[-]ocrnl*
> [Do not] map CR to NL on output.

[-]ofdel*
> Set fill character to [NULL] DEL.

[-]ofill*
> Delay output with [timing] fill characters.

[-]olcuc*
> [Do not] map lowercase to uppercase on output.

[-]onlcr*
> [Do not] map NL to CR-NL on output.

[-]onlret*
> On the terminal, NL performs [does not perform] the CR function.

[-]onocr*
> Do not [do] output CRs at column 0.

[-]opost
> [Do not] postprocess output.

Local modes

[-]echo
> [Do not] echo every character typed.

[-]echoe, [-]crterase
> [Do not] echo ERASE character as BS-space-BS string.

[-]echok
> [Do not] echo NL after KILL character.

[-]echonl
> [Do not] echo NL.

[-]icanon
> [Disable] enable canonical input (ERASE, KILL, WERASE, and RPRINT processing).

[-]iexten
> [Disable] enable extended functions for input data.

[-]isig
> [Disable] enable checking of characters against INTR, SUSPEND, and QUIT.

[-]noflsh
> [Enable] disable flush after INTR or QUIT.

[-]tostop*
> [Do not] send SIGTTOU when background processes write to the terminal.

[-]xcase*
> [Do not] change case on local output.

[-]echoprt, [-]prterase*
> When erasing characters, echo them backward, enclosed in \ and /.

[-]echoctl. [-]ctlecho*
> Do not echo control characters literally. Use hat notation (e.g., ^Z).

[-]echoke [-]crtkill*
> Erase characters as specified by the **echoprt** and **echoe** settings (default is **echoctl** and **echok** settings).

Control assignments

ctrl-char c
> Set control character to *c*. *ctrl-char* is **dsusp** (flush input and then send stop), **eof**, **eol**, **eol2** (alternate end-of-line), **erase**, **intr**, **lnext** (treat next character literally), **kill**, **rprnt** (redraw line), **quit**, **start**, **stop**, **susp**, **swtch**, or **werase** (erase previous word). *c* can be a literal control character, a character in hat notation (e.g., ^Z), in hex (must begin with 0x), in octal (must begin with 0), or in decimal. Disable the control character with values of ^- or **undef**.

min *n*
> Set the minimum number of characters that will satisfy a read until the time value has expired when **-icanon** is set.

time *n*
> Set the number of tenths of a second before reads time out if the **min** number of characters have not been read when **-icanon** is set.

line *i***
> Set line discipline to *i* (1–126).

Combination modes

[-]cooked
> Same as [raw]-raw.

[-]evenp, [-]parity
> Same as [-]parenb and cs[8]7.

[-]parity
> Same as [-]parenb and cs[8]7.

ek Reset ERASE and KILL characters to Ctrl-h and Ctrl-u, their defaults.

[-]lcase
> [Unset] set **xcase, iuclc,** and **olcuc.**

[-]LCASE
> Same as [-]lcase.

[-]nl
> [Unset] set **icrnl** and **onlcr. -nl** also unsets **inlcr, igncr, ocrnl,** and **onlret, icrnl, onlcr.**

[-]oddp
> Same as [-]parenb, [-]parodd, and cs7[8].

[-]raw
> [Disable] enable raw input and output (no ERASE, KILL, INTR, QUIT, EOT, SWITCH, or output postprocessing).

sane
> Reset all modes to reasonable values.

[-]tabs*
> [Expand to spaces] preserve output tabs.

[-]cbreak
> Same as [icanon]-icanon.

[-]pass8
> Same as -parenb -istrip cs8.

[-]litout
> Same as -parenb -istrip cs8.

[-]decctlq*
> Same as -ixany.

crt
> Same as **echoe echoctl echoke.**

dec
> Same as **echoe echoctl echoke -ixany.** Additionally, set INTERRUPT to ^C, ERASE to DEL, and KILL to ^U.

Special settings

ispeed *speed*
> Specify input speed.

ospeed *speed*
> Specify output speed.

rows *rows***
> Specify number of rows.

---

cols *columns,* **columns** *columns**
    Specify number of columns.

size*
    Display current row and column settings.

speed
    Display terminal speed.

su

su [*option*] [*user*] [*shell_args*]

Create a shell with the effective user ID *user.* If no *user* is specified, create a shell for a privileged user (i.e., become a superuser). Enter EOF to terminate. You can run the shell with particular options by passing them as *shell_args* (e.g., if the shell runs **bash**, you can specify -c *command* to execute *command* via **bash**, or **-r** to create a restricted shell).

Options

-, -l, --login
    Go through the entire login sequence (i.e., change to *user*'s environment).

-c *command,* **--command**=*command*
    Execute *command* in the new shell and then exit immediately. If *command* is more than one word, it should be enclosed in quotes. For example:

        su -c 'find / -name *.c -print' nobody

-f, --fast
    Start the shell with the **-f** option, which suppresses the reading of the *.cshrc* or *.tcshrc* file. Applies to **csh** and **tcsh**.

-m, -p, --preserve-environment
    Do not reset environment variables.

-s *shell,* **--shell**=*shell*
    Execute *shell*, not the shell specified in */etc/passwd*, unless *shell* is restricted.

--help
    Print a help message and then exit.

--version
    Print version information and then exit.

sudo

sudo [*options*] [*command*]

If you are allowed, execute *command* as the superuser. Authorized users of **sudo** and the commands they are permitted to execute are listed in the **sudo** configuration file, */etc/sudoers*. If an unauthorized user attempts to run a command, **sudo** will inform an administrator via email. By default, it will send the message to the root account. Users attempting to run commands are prompted for their password. Once authenticated, **sudo** sets a timestamp for the user. For five minutes from the timestamp, the user may execute further commands without being prompted for their password. This grace period may be overriden by settings in the */etc/sudoers* file.

Options

-b   Execute *command* in the background.

-h   Print help message, then exit.

-k   Revoke user's **sudo** permissions. Similar to **-K**, but changes user's timestamp to the Epoch instead of revoking it.

-l   List all allowed and forbidden commands for the user on the current host, then exit.

-p *promptstring*
     Use the specified *promptstring* to prompt for a password. The string may contain escape codes **%u** and **%h**, which will be replaced with the current user's login name and local hostname.

-s   Run the shell specified in the **SHELL** environment variable, or the default shell specified in */etc/passwd*. If a command is given, it should be a shell script and not a binary file.

-u *user*
     Run command as the specified *user* instead of the root user. This may also be specified as a user ID number using *#uid*.

-v   Update timestamp for user. Prompt for password if necessary.

-H   Set the **HOME** environment variable to the home directory of the target user.

-K   Remove user's timestamp.

-L   List parameters that may be set as defaults for a user in the */etc/sudoers* file.

-P   Preserve initial user's group membership.

-S   Read password from standard input instead of from the console.

-V   Print version number, then exit. When run by the root user, print **sudo**'s defaults and the local network address as well.

--   Stop reading command-line arguments.

---

sum

sum [*options*] *files*

Calculate and print a checksum and the number of (1KB) blocks for *file*. If no files are specified, or *file* is -, read from standard input. Useful for verifying data transmission.

Options

-r   The default setting. Use the BSD checksum algorithm.

-s, --sysv
     Use alternate checksum algorithm as used on System V. The blocksize is 512 bytes.

Print a help message and then exit.

--version
Print the version number and then exit.

swapoff

swapoff [*options*] [*devicelist*]

System administration command. Stop making devices and files specified in *devicelist* available for swapping and paging.

Option

-a Consult */etc/fstab* for devices marked **sw**. Use those in place of the *device* argument.

-h Print help message and then exit.

-V Display version number and then exit.

swapon

swapon [*options*] *devices*

System administration command. Make the listed *devices* available for swapping and paging.

Options

-a Consult */etc/fstab* for devices marked **sw**. Use those in place of the *devices* argument.

-e Used with -**a**. Don't complain about missing devices.

-h Print help message, then exit.

-p *priority*
Specify a *priority* for the swap area. Higher priority areas will be used up before lower priority areas are used.

-s Print swap usage summaries, then exit.

-V Print version information, then exit.

sync

sync

System administration command. Write filesystem buffers to disk. **sync** executes the **sync( )** system call. If the system is to be stopped, **sync** must be called to ensure filesystem integrity. Note that **shutdown** automatically calls **sync** before shutting down the system. **sync** may take several seconds to complete, so the system should be told to **sleep** briefly if you are about to manually call **halt** or **reboot**. Note that **shutdown** is the preferred way to halt or reboot your system, as it takes care of **sync**-ing and other housekeeping for you.

sysctl

sysctl [*options*] [*key*]

System administration command. Examine or modify kernel parameters at runtime using the */proc/sys* filesystem. While many of these kernel keys can be altered by other utilities, **sysctl** provides a single interface to kernel settings.

Options

-a, -A
> Display all available values.

-e Ignore requests for unknown keys.

-n Do not print the keyname when printing values.

-p Reset keys from information specified in */etc/sysctl.conf*.

-w *key=value*
> Write a new value to the specified key.

---

syslogd

syslogd [*options*]

System administration command. **syslogd** provides both **syslogd** and **klogd** functionality. By default, it is meant to behave exactly like the BSD version of **syslogd**. While the difference should be completely transparent to the user, **syslogd** supports an extended syntax. It is invoked as **syslogd**.

syslogd logs system messages into a set of files described by the configuration file */etc/syslog.conf*. Each message is one line. A message can contain a priority code, marked by a number in angle brackets at the beginning of the line. Priorities are defined in *<sys/syslog.h>*. **syslogd** reads from an Internet domain socket specified in */etc/services*. To bring **syslogd** down, send it a terminate signal. See also **klogd**.

Options

-a *socket*
> Add *socket* to the list of sockets **syslogd** listens to.

-d Turn on debugging.

-f *configfile*
> Specify alternate configuration file.

-h Forward messages from remote hosts to forwarding hosts.

-l *hostlist*
> Specify hostnames that should be logged with just the hostname, not the fully qualified domain name. Multiple hosts should be separated by a colon (:).

-m *markinterval*
> Select number of minutes between mark messages.

-n Avoid auto-backgrounding. This is needed when starting **syslogd** from **init**.

-p *socket*
> Send log to *socket* instead of */dev/log*.

-r Receive messages from the network using an Internet domain socket with the **syslog** service.

-s *domainlist*
> Strip off domain names specified in *domainlist* before logging. Multiple domain names should be separated by a colon (:).

-v   Print version number, then exit.

-x   Disable domain name lookups for remote messages.

---

syslogd

`syslogd`

TCP/IP command. See **sysklogd**.

---

tac

tac [`options`] [`file`]

Named for the common command **cat**, **tac** prints files in reverse to standard output. Without a filename or with -, it reads from standard input. By default, **tac** reverses the order of the lines, printing the last line first.

Options

-b, --before
> Print separator (by default a newline) before the string it delimits.

-r, --regex
> Expect separator to be a regular expression.

-s *string*, **--separator=**_string_
> Specify alternate separator (default is newline).

--help
> Print a help message and then exit.

--version
> Print version information and then exit.

---

tail

tail [`options`] [`files`]

Print the last 10 lines of each named *file* (or standard input if - is specified) on standard output. If more than one file is specified, the output includes a header at the beginning of each file:

> `==>`*filename*`<==`

Options

-n[k]
> Begin printing at *n*th item from end-of-file. *k* specifies the item to count: **l** (lines, the default), **b** (blocks), or **c** (characters).

-k   Same as *-n*, but use the default count of 10.

+n[k]
> Like *-n*, but start at *n*th item from beginning of file.

+k   Like *-k*, but count from beginning of file.

-c num{**bkm**}, **--bytes** *num*{**bkm**}
> Print last *num* bytes. An alternate blocksize may be specified:
>
> **b**   512 bytes
>
> **k**   1 kilobyte
>
> **m**   1 megabyte

-f, --follow[=name|descriptor]
> Don't quit at the end of file; "follow" file as it grows and end when the user presses Ctrl-c. Following by file descriptor is the default, so **-f**, **--follow**, and **--follow=descriptor** are equivalent. Use **--follow=name** to track the actual name of a file even if the file is renamed, as with a rotated log file.

-F Identical to **--follow=name --retry**.

--help
> Print a help message and exit.

-n *num*, **--lines=***num*
> Print the last *num* lines.

--max-unchanged-stats=*num*
> Used with **--follow=name** to reopen a file whose size hasn't changed after *num* iterations (default 5), to see if it has been unlinked or renamed (as with rotated log files).

--pid=*pid*
> Used with **-f** to end when process ID *pid* dies.

-q, --quiet, --silent
> Suppress filename headers.

--retry
> With **-f**, keep trying to open a file even if it isn't accessible when **tail** starts or if it becomes inaccessible later.

-s *sec*, **--sleep-interval=***sec*
> With **-f**, sleep approximately *sec* seconds between iterations. Default is 1 second.

-v, --verbose
> With multiple files, always output the filename headers.

--version
> Print version information and then exit.

Examples

Show the last 20 lines containing instances of **.Ah**:

> `grep '\.Ah' file | tail -20`

Show the last 10 characters of variable **name**:

> `echo "$name" | tail -c`

Print the last two blocks of **bigfile**:

> `tail -2b bigfile`

---

talk

talk *person* [*ttyname*]

> Talk to another user. *person* is either the login name of someone on your own machine or *user@host* on another host. To talk to a user who is logged in more than once, use *ttyname* to indicate the appropriate terminal name. Once communication has been established, the two parties may type simultaneously, with their output appearing in separate windows. To redraw the screen, type Ctrl-L. To exit, type your interrupt character; **talk** then moves the cursor to the bottom of the screen and restores the terminal.

---

talkd

talkd [*options*]

TCP/IP command. Remote user communication server. **talkd** notifies a user that somebody else wants to initiate a conversation. A **talk** client initiates a rendezvous by sending a **CTL_MSG** of type **LOOK_UP** to the server. This causes the server to search its invitation tables for an existing invitation for the client. If the lookup fails, the caller sends an **ANNOUNCE** message, causing the server to broadcast an announcement on the callee's login ports requesting contact. When the callee responds, the local server responds with the rendezvous address, and a stream connection is established through which the conversation takes place.

Options

-d   Write debugging information to the **syslogd** log file.

-p   Log malformed packets to */var/log/talkd.packets*.

---

tar

tar [*options*] [*tarfile*] [*other-files*]

Copy *files* to or restore *files* from an archive medium. If any *files* are directories, **tar** acts on the entire subtree. Options need not be preceded by - (though they may be). The exception to this rule is when you are using a long-style option (such as --**modification-time**). In that case, the exact syntax is:

>   **tar** --*long-option -function-options files*

For example:

>   **tar** --modification-time -xvf tarfile.tar

Function options

You must use exactly one of these, and it must come before any other options:

-c, --**create**
    Create a new archive.

-d, --**diff**, --**compare**
    Compare the files stored in *tarfile* with *other-files*. Report any differences: missing files, different sizes, different file attributes (such as permissions or modification time).

--**delete**
    Delete from the archive. This option cannot be used with magnetic tape.

-r, --**append**
    Append *other-files* to the end of an existing archive.

-t, --**list**
    Print the names of *other-files* if they are stored on the archive (if *other-files* are not specified, print names of all files).

-u, --**update**
    Add files if not in the archive or if modified.

-x, --extract, --get
Extract *other-files* from an archive (if *other-files* are not specified, extract all files).

-A, --catenate, --concatenate
Concatenate a second tar file to the end of the first.

Options

[drive][density]
Set drive (0–7) and storage density (**l**, **m**, or **h**, corresponding to low, medium, or high). Not available in all versions of **tar**.

--anchored
Exclude patterns must match the start of the filename (the default).

--atime-preserve
Preserve original access time on extracted files.

-b *n*, --blocking-factor=*n*
Set blocksize to $n \times 512$ bytes.

--backup[=*type*]
Back up files rather than deleting them. If no backup type is specified, a simple backup is made with ~ as the suffix. (See also **--suffix**.) The possible values of *type* are:

t, numbered
Make numbered backups.

nil, existing
Make numbered backups if there are already numbered backups, otherwise make simple backups.

never, simple
Always make simple backups.

--checkpoint
List directory names encountered.

--exclude=*pattern*
Remove files matching *pattern* from any list of files.

-f *file*, --file=*file*
Store files in or extract files from archive *file*. Note that *file* may take the form *hostname:filename*.

--force-local
Interpret filenames in the form *hostname:filename* as local files.

-g *file*, --listed-incremental=*file*
Create new-style incremental backup.

--group=*group*
Use *group* as the group for files added to the archive.

-h, --dereference
Dereference symbolic links and archive the files they point to rather than the symbolic link.

--help
    Print help message and exit.

-i, --ignore-zeros
    Ignore zero-sized blocks (i.e., EOFs).

--ignore-case
    Ignore case when excluding files.

--ignore-failed-read
    Ignore unreadable files to be archived. Default behavior is to exit when encountering these.

-j, --bzip2, -i
    Compress files with **bzip2** before archiving them, or uncompress them with **bunzip2** before extracting them.

-l, --one-file-system
    Do not archive files from other filesystems.

-k, --keep-old-files
    When extracting files, do not overwrite files with similar names. Instead, print an error message.

-m, --touch
    Do not restore file modification times; update them to the time of extraction.

--mode=*permissions*
    Use *permissions* when adding files to an archive. The permissions are specified the same way as for the **chmod** command.

--newer-mtime=*date*
    Add only files whose contents have changed since *date* to the archive.

--no-anchor
    Exclude patterns may match anything following a slash.

--no-ignore-case
    Do not ignore case when excluding files.

--no-same-permissions
    Do not extract permissions information when extracting files from the archive. This is the default for users, and therefore affects only the superuser.

--no-recursion
    Do not move recursively through directories.

--no-same-owner
    When extracting, create files with yourself as owner.

--no-wildcards
    Don't use wildcards when excluding files; treat patterns as strings.

--no-wildcards-match-slash
    Wildcards do not match **slash** when excluding files.

--null
    Allow filenames to be null-terminated with **-T**. Override **-C**.

--numeric-owner

Use the numeric owner and group IDs rather than the names.

-o, --old-archive, --portability

Create old-style archive in Unix V7 rather than ANSI format.

--overwrite

Overwrite existing files and directory metadata when extracting from archive.

--overwrite-dir

Overwrite existing directory metadata when extracting from archive.

--owner=*owner*

Set *owner* as the owner of extracted files instead of the original owner. *owner* is first assumed to be a username, then, if there is no match, a numeric user ID.

-p, --same-permissions, --preserve-permissions

Keep permissions of extracted files the same as the originals.

--posix

Create a POSIX-compliant archive.

--preserve

Equivalent to invoking both the **-p** and **-s** options.

--record-size=*size*

Treat each record as having *size* bytes, where *size* is a multiple of 512.

--recursion

Move recursively through directories.

--recursive-unlink

Remove existing directory hierarchies before extracting directories with the same name.

--remove-files

Remove originals after inclusion in archive.

--rsh-command=*command*

Do not connect to remote host with **rsh**; instead, use *command*.

-s, --same-order, --preserve-order

When extracting, sort filenames to correspond to the order in the archive.

--same-owner

When extracting, create files with the same ownership as the originals.

--show-omitted-dirs

List directories being omitted when operating on an archive.

--suffix=*suffix*

Use *suffix* instead of the default ~ when creating a backup file.

--totals

Print byte totals.

--use-compress-program=*program*
Compress archived files with *program*, or uncompress extracted files with *program*.

-v, --verbose
Verbose. Print filenames as they are added or extracted.

--version
Print version information and exit.

--volno-file=*file*
Use/update the volume number in *file*.

-w, --interactive, --confirmation
Wait for user confirmation (**y**) before taking any actions.

--wildcards
Use wildcards when excluding files.

--wildcards-match-slash
Wildcards match / when excluding files.

-z, --gzip, --gunzip, --ungzip
Compress files with **gzip** before archiving them, or uncompress them with **gunzip** before extracting them.

-B, --read-full-records
Reblock while reading; used for reading from 4.2BSD pipes.

-C *directory,* **--directory**=*directory*
cd to *directory* before beginning **tar** operation.

-F *script,* **--info-script**=*script,* **--new-volume-script**=*script*
Implies **-M** (multiple archive files). Run *script* at the end of each file.

-G, --incremental
Create old-style incremental backup.

-K *file,* **--starting-file**=*file*
Begin **tar** operation at *file* in archive.

-L *length,* **--tape-length**=*length*
Write a maximum of *length* × 1024 bytes to each tape.

-M, --multivolume
Expect archive to be multivolume. With **-c**, create such an archive.

-N *date,* **--newer**=*date,* **--after-date**=*date*
Ignore files older than *date.*

-O, --to-stdout
Print extracted files to standard output.

-P, --absolute-names
Do not remove initial slashes (/) from input filenames.

-R, --block-number
Display archive's block number in messages.

-S, --sparse
Treat sparse files more efficiently when adding to archive.

-T *file,* **--files-from=***file*
> Consult *file* for files to extract or create.

-U, **--unlink-first**
> Remove each existing file from the filesystem before extracting from the archive.

-V *name,* **--label=***name*
> Name this volume *name.*

-W, **--verify**
> Check archive for corruption after creation.

-X *file,* **--exclude-from** *file*
> Consult *file* for list of files to exclude.

-Z, **--compress, --uncompress**
> Compress files with **compress** before archiving them, or uncompress them with **uncompress** before extracting them.

Examples

Create an archive of */bin* and */usr/bin* (**c**), show the command working (**v**), and store on the tape in */dev/rmt0*:

```
tar cvf /dev/rmt0 /bin /usr/bin
```

List the tape's contents in a format like **ls -l**:

```
tar tvf /dev/rmt0
```

Extract the */bin* directory:

```
tar xvf /dev/rmt0 /bin
```

Create an archive of the current directory and store it in a file *backup.tar*:

```
tar cvf - `find . -print` > backup.tar
```

(The - tells **tar** to store the archive on standard output, which is then redirected.)

---

tcpd   **tcpd**

TCP/IP command. Monitor incoming TCP/IP requests (such as those for **telnet, ftp, finger, exec, rlogin**). Provide checking and logging services; then pass the request to the appropriate daemon.

---

tcsh   **tcsh** [*options*] [*file* [*arguments*]]

An extended version of the C shell, a command interpreter into which all other commands are entered. For more information, see Chapter 8.

---

tee   **tee** [*options*] *files*

Accept output from another command and send it both to standard output and to *files* (like a T or fork in the road).

Options

-a, --append
> Append to *files*; do not overwrite.

-i, --ignore-interrupts
> Ignore interrupt signals.

--help
> Print a help message and then exit.

--version
> Print version information and then exit.

Example

`ls -l | tee savefile`   *View listing and save for later*

---

telinit

`telinit [option] [runlevel]`

System administration command. Signal **init** to change the system's runlevel. **telinit** is actually just a link to **init**, the ancestor of all processes.

Option

-t *seconds*
> Send SIGKILL *seconds* after SIGTERM. Default is 20.

Runlevels

The default runlevels vary from distribution to distribution, but these are standard:

0   Halt the system.

1, s, S
> Single user.

6   Reboot the system.

a, b, c
> Process only entries in */etc/inittab* that are marked with runlevel **a**, **b**, or **c**.

q, Q
> Reread */etc/inittab*.

Check the */etc/inittab* file for runlevels on your system.

---

telnet

`telnet [options] [host [port]]`

Access remote systems. **telnet** is the user interface that communicates with another host using the Telnet protocol. If **telnet** is invoked without *host*, it enters command mode, indicated by its prompt, **telnet>**, and accepts and executes the commands listed after the following options. If invoked with arguments, **telnet** performs an **open** command (shown in the following list) with those arguments. *host* indicates the host's official name, alias, or Internet address. *port* indicates a port number (default is the Telnet port).

The Telnet protocol is often criticized because it uses no encryption and makes it easy for snoopers to pick up user passwords. Most sites now use **ssh** instead.

Options

-a   Automatic login to the remote system.

-b *hostalias*
> Use **bind** to bind the local socket to an aliased address or the address of an interface other than the one that would be chosen by **connect**.

-c   Disable reading of the user's *.telnetrc* file.

-d   Turn on socket-level debugging.

-e [*escape_char*]
> Set initial **telnet** escape character to *escape_char*. If *escape_char* is omitted, no escape character is predefined.

-f   With Kerberos V5 authentication, allow forwarding of the local credentials to the remote system.

-k *realm*
> With Kerberos authentication, obtain tickets for the remote host in *realm*, instead of in the remote host's realm.

-l *user*
> When connecting to remote system and if remote system understands **ENVIRON**, send *user* to the remote system as the value for variable **USER**. Implies the -a option.

-n *tracefile*
> Open *tracefile* for recording the trace information.

-r   Emulate **rlogin**. The default escape character for this mode is a tilde (~); an escape character followed by a dot causes **telnet** to disconnect from the remote host; a ^Z instead of a dot suspends **telnet**; and a ^] (the default **telnet** escape character) generates a normal **telnet** prompt. These codes are accepted only at the beginning of a line.

-x   Turn on datastream encryption if possible.

-8   Request 8-bit operation.

-E   Disable the escape character functionality.

-F   With Kerberos V5 authentication, allow local credentials to be forwarded to the remote system, including any that were already forwarded to the local environment.

-K   Do not allow automatic login to the remote system.

-L   Specify an 8-bit data path on output.

-X *atype*
> Disable the *atype* type of authentication.

Commands

Ctrl-Z

Suspend **telnet**.

! [*command*]

Execute a single command in a subshell on the local system. If *command* is omitted, an interactive subshell will be invoked.

? [*command*]

Get help. With no arguments, print a help summary. If a command is specified, print the help information for just that command.

close

Close a Telnet session and return to command mode.

display *argument* ...

Display all or some of the **set** and **toggle** values.

environ [*arguments* [...]]

Manipulate variables that may be sent through the **TELNET ENVIRON** option. Valid arguments for **environ** are:

?   Get help for the **environ** command.

define *variable value*

Define *variable* to have a value of *value*.

undefine *variable*

Remove *variable* from the list of environment variables.

export *variable*

Mark *variable* to have its value exported to the remote side.

unexport *variable*

Mark *variable* to not be exported unless explicitly requested by the remote side.

list

Display current variable values.

send *variable*

Send the environment variable *variable*.

logout

If the remote host supports the **logout** command, close the **telnet** session.

mode [*type*]

Depending on state of Telnet session, *type* is one of several options:

?   Print out help information for the **mode** command.

character

Disable **TELNET LINEMODE** option, or, if remote side does not understand the option, enter "character-at-a-time" mode.

[-]edit

Attempt to [disable] enable the **EDIT** mode of the **TELNET LINEMODE** option.

[-]isig
>Attempt to [disable] enable the **TRAPSIG** mode of the **LINEMODE** option.

line
>Enable **LINEMODE** option, or, if remote side does not understand the option, enter "old line-by-line" mode.

[-]softtabs
>Attempt to [disable] enable the **SOFT_TAB** mode of the **LINEMODE** option.

[-]litecho
>[Disable] enable **LIT_ECHO** mode.

open[-l *user*] *host* [*port*]
>Open a connection to the named *host*. If no *port* number is specified, attempt to contact a Telnet server at the default port.

quit
>Close any open Telnet session and then exit **telnet**.

send *arguments*
>Send one or more special character sequences to the remote host. Following are the arguments that may be specified:

?   Print out help information for **send** command.

abort
>Send Telnet ABORT sequence.

ao
>Send Telnet AO sequence, which should cause the remote system to flush all output from the remote system to the user's terminal.

ayt
>Send Telnet AYT (Are You There) sequence.

brk
>Send Telnet BRK (Break) sequence.

do *cmd*
dont *cmd*
will *cmd*
wont *cmd*
>Send Telnet DO *cmd* sequence, where *cmd* is a number between 0 and 255 or a symbolic name for a specific **telnet** command. If *cmd* is **?** or **help**, this command prints out help (including a list of symbolic names).

ec
>Send Telnet EC (Erase Character) sequence, which causes the remote system to erase the last character entered.

el
>Send Telnet EL (Erase Line) sequence, which causes the remote system to erase the last line entered.

eof
>Send Telnet EOF (End Of File) sequence.

eor

Send Telnet EOR (End Of Record) sequence.

escape

Send current Telnet escape character (initially ^]).

ga

Send Telnet GA (Go Ahead) sequence.

getstatus

If the remote side supports the Telnet **STATUS** command, **getstatus** sends the subnegotiation request that the server send its current option status.

ip

Send Telnet IP (Interrupt Process) sequence, which causes the remote system to abort the currently running process.

nop

Send Telnet NOP (No Operation) sequence.

susp

Send Telnet SUSP (Suspend Process) sequence.

synch

Send Telnet SYNCH sequence, which causes the remote system to discard all previously typed (but not read) input.

set *argument value*

unset *argument value*

Set any one of a number of **telnet** variables to a specific value or to **TRUE**. The special value **off** disables the function associated with the variable. **unset** disables any of the specified functions. The values of variables may be interrogated with the aid of the **display** command. The variables that may be specified are:

? Display legal **set** and **unset** commands.

ayt

If **telnet** is in **LOCALCHARS** mode, this character is taken to be the alternate AYT character.

echo

This is the value (initially ^E) that, when in "line-by-line" mode, toggles between doing local echoing of entered characters and suppressing echoing of entered characters.

eof

If **telnet** is operating in **LINEMODE** or in the old "line-by-line" mode, entering this character as the first character on a line will cause the character to be sent to the remote system.

erase

If **telnet** is in **LOCALCHARS** mode and operating in the "character-at-a-time" mode, entering this character will send a Telnet EC sequence to the remote system.

escape

This is the Telnet escape character (initially ^]), which causes entry into the Telnet command mode when connected to a remote system.

flushoutput

If **telnet** is in **LOCALCHARS** mode and the **flushoutput** character is entered, a Telnet AO sequence is sent to the remote host.

forw1

If Telnet is in **LOCALCHARS** mode, this character is taken to be an alternate end-of-line character.

forw2

If Telnet is in **LOCALCHARS** mode, this character is taken to be an alternate end-of-line character.

interrupt

If Telnet AO is in **LOCALCHARS** mode and the **interrupt** character is entered, a Telnet IP sequence is sent to the remote host.

kill

If Telnet IP is in **LOCALCHARS** mode and operating in the "character-at-a-time" mode, entering this character causes a Telnet EL sequence to be sent to the remote system.

lnext

If Telnet EL is in **LINEMODE** or the old "line-by-line" mode, this character is taken to be the terminal's **lnext** character.

quit

If Telnet EL is in **LOCALCHARS** mode and the **quit** character is entered, a Telnet BRK sequence is sent to the remote host.

reprint

If Telnet BRK is in **LINEMODE** or the old "line-by-line" mode, this character is taken to be the terminal's **reprint** character.

rlogin

Enable **rlogin** mode. Same as using the **-r** command-line option.

start

If the Telnet **TOGGLE-FLOW-CONTROL** option has been enabled, this character is taken to be the terminal's **start** character.

stop

If the Telnet **TOGGLE-FLOW-CONTROL** option has been enabled, this character is taken to be the terminal's **stop** character.

susp

If Telnet is in **LOCALCHARS** mode or if the **LINEMODE** is enabled, the **suspend** character causes a Telnet SUSP sequence to be sent to the remote host.

tracefile

This is the file to which output generated by **netdata** is written.

worderase

If Telnet BRK is in **LINEMODE** or the old "line-by-line" mode, this character is taken to be the terminal's **worderase** character. Defaults for these are the terminal's defaults.

slc [*state*]

Set state of special characters when Telnet **LINEMODE** option has been enabled.

?   List help on the **slc** command.

check

Verify current settings for current special characters. If discrepancies are discovered, convert local settings to match remote ones.

export

Switch to local defaults for special characters.

import

Switch to remote defaults for special characters.

status

Show current status of **telnet**. This includes the peer you are connected to as well as the current mode.

toggle *arguments* [...]

Toggle various flags that control how Telnet responds to events. The flags may be set explicitly to **true** or **false** using the **set** and **unset** commands listed previously. The valid arguments are:

?   Display legal **toggle** commands.

autoflush

If **autoflush** and **LOCALCHARS** are both true, then when the **ao** or **quit** characters are recognized, Telnet refuses to display any data on the user's terminal until the remote system acknowledges that it has processed those Telnet sequences.

autosynch

If **autosynch** and **LOCALCHARS** are both true, then when the **intr** or **quit** character is entered, the resulting Telnet sequence sent is followed by the Telnet SYNCH sequence. Initial value for this **toggle** is false.

binary

Enable or disable the Telnet **BINARY** option on both the input and the output.

inbinary
> Enable or disable the Telnet **BINARY** option on the input.

outbinary
> Enable or disable the Telnet **BINARY** option on the output.

crlf
> If this **toggle** value is true, carriage returns are sent as **CR-LF**. If false, carriage returns are sent as **CR-NUL**. Initial value is false.

crmod
> Toggle carriage return mode. Initial value is false.

debug
> Toggle socket-level debugging mode. Initial value is false.

localchars
> If the value is true, **flush**, **interrupt**, **quit**, **erase**, and **kill** characters are recognized locally, then transformed into appropriate Telnet control sequences. Initial value is true.

netdata
> Toggle display of all network data. Initial value is false.

options
> Toggle display of some internal **telnet** protocol processing that pertains to Telnet options. Initial value is false.

prettydump
> When **netdata** and **prettydump** are enabled, the output from the **netdata** command is reorganized into a more user-friendly format, spaces are put between each character in the output, and an asterisk precedes any Telnet escape sequence.

skiprc
> Toggle whether to process ~/.telnetrc file. Initial value is false, meaning the file is processed.

termdata
> Toggle printing of hexadecimal terminal data. Initial value is false.

z   Suspend **telnet**; works only for **tcsh**.

---

telnetd   **telnetd** [*options*]

TCP/IP command. Telnet protocol server. **telnetd** is invoked by the Internet server for requests to connect to the Telnet port (port 23 by default). **telnetd** allocates a pseudo-terminal device for a client, thereby creating a login process that has the slave side of the pseudo-terminal serving as stdin, stdout, and stderr. **telnetd** manipulates the master side of the pseudo-terminal by implementing the Telnet protocol and by passing characters between the remote client and the login process.

The Telnet protocol is often criticized because it uses no encryption and makes it easy for snoopers to pick up user passwords. Most sites now use **ssh** instead.

Options

-a *type*

When compiled with authentication support, this option sets the authentication type. Accepted values are:

debug

Debug authentication code.

user

Allow only authenticated remote users with permission to access their accounts without giving a password.

valid

Allow only authenticated remote users. Use **login** for any additional verification needed to access an account.

none

No authentication required, but accept it if offered. Use **login** for any further verification needed to access an account.

off

Disable authentication.

-debug [*port*]

Start **telnetd** manually instead of through **inetd**. *port* may be specified as an alternate TCP port number on which to run **telnetd**.

-D *modifier(s)*

Debugging mode. This allows **telnet** to print out debugging information to the connection, enabling the user to see what **telnet** is doing. Several modifiers are available for the debugging mode:

netdata

Display data stream received by **telnetd**.

options

Print information about the negotiation of the Telnet options.

ptydata

Display data written to the pseudo-terminal device.

report

Print **options** information, as well as some additional information about what processing is going on.

-edebug

When compiled with support for encryption, enable encryption debugging code.

-h Don't print host-specific information until after login is complete.

-L *command*
> Use *command* for login instead of */bin/login*.

-n Disable checking for lost connections with TCP keep-alives.

-X *type*
> Disable authentication *type*.

---

test

test `expression`
`[expression]`

Evaluate an *expression* and, if its value is true, return a zero exit status; otherwise, return a nonzero exit status. In shell scripts, you can use the alternate form [*expression*]. This command is generally used with conditional constructs in shell programs. Also exists as a built-in in most shells.

File testers

The syntax for all of these options is **test** *option file*. If the specified file does not exist, they return false. Otherwise, they test the file as specified in the option description.

-b Is the file block special?

-c Is the file character special?

-d Is the file a directory?

-e Does the file exist?

-f Is the file a regular file?

-g Does the file have the set-group-ID bit set?

-k Does the file have the sticky bit set?

-L Is the file a symbolic link?

-p Is the file a named pipe?

-r Is the file readable by the current user?

-s Is the file nonempty?

-S Is the file a socket?

-t [*file-descriptor*]
> Is the file associated with *file-descriptor* (or 1, standard output, by default) connected to a terminal?

-u Does the file have the set-user-ID bit set?

-w Is the file writable by the current user?

-x Is the file executable?

-O Is the file owned by the process's effective user ID?

-G Is the file owned by the process's effective group ID?

File comparisons

The syntax for file comparisons is **test** *file1 option file2*. A string by itself, without options, returns true if it's at least one character long.

-nt Is *file1* newer than *file2*? Check modification date, not creation date.

-ot Is *file1* older than *file2*? Check modification date, not creation date.

-ef Do the files have identical device and inode numbers?

String tests

The syntax for string tests is **test** *option string* or **test** *string1* [!]= *string2*.

-z Is the string 0 characters long?

-n Is the string at least 1 character long?

string1 = string2
   Are the two strings equal?

string1 != string2
   Are the strings unequal?

Expression tests

Note that an expression can consist of any of the previous tests.

! *expression*
   Is the expression false?

expression **-a** *expression*
   Are the expressions both true?

expression **-o** *expression*
   Is either expression true?

Integer tests

The syntax for integer tests is **test** *integer1 option integer2*. You may substitute **-l** *string* for an integer; this evaluates to *string*'s length.

-eq Are the two integers equal?

-ne Are the two integers unequal?

-lt Is *integer1* less than *integer2*?

-le Is *integer1* less than or equal to *integer2*?

-gt Is *integer1* greater than *integer2*?

-ge Is *integer1* greater than or equal to *integer2*?

---

tftp

tftp [*options*] [*host* [*port*]]

User interface to TFTP (IPv4 Trivial File Transfer Protocol), which allows users to transfer files to and from a remote machine. The remote *host* may be specified, and optionally the *port*, in which case **tftp** uses *host* as the default host for future transfers. The version of **tftp** described here is **tftp-hpa**.

Options

-v Verbose mode.

-V Print version and configuration information and exit.

Commands

Once **tftp** is running, it issues the prompt:

```
tftp>
```

and recognizes the following commands:

? [*command...*]
help [*command...*]

> Print help information. If no command is specified, list the commands and a brief usage message. With a command, list the usage message for that command.

ascii

> Shorthand for **mode ascii**.

binary

> Shorthand for **mode binary**.

connect *hostname* [*port*]

> Set the *hostname*, and optionally the *port*, for transfers.

get *filename*
get *remotename localname*
get *filename1 filename2 filename3...filenameN*

> Get a file or set of files from the specified remote sources. The filename can be specified as *host:filename* to set both host and filename at the same time. In that case, the last host specified becomes the default for future file transfers.

mode *transfer-mode*

> Set the mode for transfers. *transfer-mode* may be **ascii**, **netascii**, **binary**, **octet**, or **image**. The default is **ascii**.

put *filename*
put *localfile remotefile*
put *filename1 filename2...filenameN remote-directory*

> Transfer a file or set of files to the specified remote file or directory. The destination can be specified as *host:filename* to set both host and filename at the same time. In that case, the last host specified becomes the default for future file transfers. If *remote-directory* is specified, the remote host is assumed to be a Unix-style system that uses / as the directory path separator.

quit

> Exit **tftp**.

rexmt *retransmission-timeout*

> Set the per-packet retransmission timeout, in seconds.

status

> Print status information: whether **tftp** is connected to a remote host (i.e., whether a host has been specified for the next connection), the current mode, whether verbose and tracing modes are on, and the values for **retransmission timeout** and **total transmission timeout**.

timeout *total-transmission-timeout*

> Set the total transmission timeout, in seconds.

trace

Toggle packet tracing.

verbose

Toggle verbose mode.

---

tftpd

in.tftpd [*options*] [*directories*]

TCP/IP command. IPv4 Trivial File Transfer Protocol server. **in. tftpd** is normally started by **inetd** and operates at the port indicated in the **tftp** Internet service description in */etc/services*. Only publicly readable files may be accessed. By default, only files that already exist and are publicly writable can be written. In addition, if any *directories* are specified, access is restricted to files in those directories. The version of **tftp** described here is **tftp-hpa**.

Options

-a [*address*][*:port*]

Specify the address and port to listen to when run in standalone mode with **-l**. By default, use the address and port in */etc/services*.

-c　Allow new files to be written. The default permissions allow anyone to read and write the files. Use **-p** or **-U** to set other permissions.

-l　Run **tftpd** in standalone mode, not from **inetd**. This mode ignores **-t**.

-m *remap-file*

Remap filenames based on rules specified in *remap-file*. Each line in the file contains an operation, an **egrep**-style regular expression (regex), and optionally a replacement pattern. If the regex matches any part of a filename, the operation is performed. The operation is specified as any of the letters shown in the next section, alone or in combination. Comment lines begin with #.

-p　Use only normal system access controls for the user specified with **-u** (the **tftpd** username).

-r *option*

Never accept the specified RFC 2347 option (see the later section "Standards"). The possible options are **blksize**, **blksize2** (not based on a standard; like **blksize** but the blocksize must be a power of 2), **tsize** (transfer size), and **timeout**.

-s　On startup, change root directory to the directory specified as *directory* on the command line. With **-s**, only one directory should be specified. Recommended for security and compatibility with certain boot ROMs.

-t *timeout*

When run from **inetd**, specify how long, in seconds, to wait for another connection before timing out and terminating the server. Default timeout is 900 (15 minutes). If server is terminated, **inetd** spawns a new server on receiving a new request.

-u *username*

Specify the name of the **tftpd** user. The default user is **nobody**.

-U *umask*

Set the umask for newly created files. Without **-p**, the default is 0. With **-p**, it is inherited from the calling process.

-v   Increase verbosity. Specify multiple times for greater verbosity.

-V   Print version and configuration information and exit.

Filename remapping rules

a   If this rule matches, refuse the request and send an "access denied" error to the client.

e   If this rule matches, execute it and then end rule processing.

g   Repeat the rule until it no longer matches. Used with **r**.

G   Apply this rule to GET (RRQ) requests only.

i   Use case-insensitive regex matching. The default is for case-sensitive matching.

P   Apply this rule to PUT (WRQ) requests only.

r   Replace the matching substring with the replacement pattern.

s   If this rule matches, execute it and then restart rule processing with the first rule.

The replacement pattern can include the following escape sequences:

\0   The entire string matching the regex.

\1...\9

The strings matched by each of the first nine substrings in the regex.

\i   The IP address of the requesting host, in dotted-quad notation.

\x   The IP address of the requesting host, in hexadecimal notation.

****   Literal backslash.

\whitespace

Literal whitespace.

\#   Literal hash mark.

Standards

- RFC 1123, Requirements for Internet Hosts—Application and Support
- RFC 1350, The TFTP Protocol (Revision 2)
- RFC 2347, TFTP Option Extension
- RFC 2348, TFTP Blocksize Option
- RFC 2349, TFTP Timeout Interval and Transfer Size Options

time [*options*] *command* [*arguments*]

Run the specified command, passing it any *arguments*, and time the execution. Note that there is also a shell **time** command, so you might need to specify the full path, usually */usr/bin/time*, to run this version of **time**. **time** displays its results on standard error. The output includes elapsed time, user CPU time, system CPU time, and other information such as memory used and number of I/Os. The output can be formatted using **printf** format strings specified with the -**f** option or the **TIME** environment variable.

Options

-- The end of the options. Anything after the -- is the command or one of its arguments.

-**a**, --**append**
Used with -**o** to append the output to *file* instead of over-writing it.

-**f** *format*, --**format**=*format*
Specify the output format. Overrides any format specified in the **TIME** environment variable.

--**help**
Print help message and exit.

-**o** *file*, --**output**=*file*
Send the output from **time** to the specified file instead of to standard error. If *file* exists, it is overwritten.

-**p**, --**portability**
Use portable output format (POSIX).

-**v**, --**verbose**
Give verbose output, providing all available information.

-**V**, --**version**
Print version information and exit.

Resources

The following resources can be specified in format strings:

c   Number of involuntary context switches because of time slice expiring.

C   Name and arguments of command being timed.

D   Average size of unshared data area, in kilobytes.

e   Elapsed real time, in seconds.

E   Elapsed real time as *hours:minutes:seconds*.

F   Number of major (I/O-requiring) page faults.

I   Number of filesystem inputs.

k   Number of signals delivered to the process.

K   Average total (data+stack+text) memory use, in kilobytes.

M   Maximum resident set size, in kilobytes.

O   Number of filesystem outputs.

p   Average unshared stack size, in kilobytes.

P   Percent of CPU used.

r   Number of socket messages received.

R   Number of minor (recoverable) page faults.

s   Number of socket messages received.

S   Total CPU seconds used by the system on behalf of the process.

t   Average resident set size, in kilobytes.

U   Total CPU seconds used directly by the process.

w   Number of voluntary context switches.

W   Number of times the process was swapped out of main memory.

x   Exit status of the command.

X   Average shared text size, in kilobytes.

Z   System page size, in bytes.

Example

Time the execution of the command **ls -l** and display the user time, system time, and exit status of the command:

```
/usr/bin/time -f "\t%U user,\t%S system,\t%x status" ls -Fs
```

---

tload

tload [*options*] [*tty*]

Display system load average in graph format. If *tty* is specified, print it to that terminal.

Options

-d *delay*

    Specify the delay, in seconds, between updates.

-s *scale*

    Specify scale (number of characters between each graph tick). A smaller number results in a larger scale.

-V   Print version information and exit.

---

top

top [*options*]

Provide information (frequently refreshed) about the most CPU-intensive processes currently running. You do not need to include a - before options. See **ps** for explanations of the field descriptors.

Options

-b   Run in batch mode; don't accept command-line input. Useful for sending output to another command or to a file.

-c   Show command line in display instead of just command name.

-C   For SMP systems, display total CPU information in addition to information for the individual CPUs.

-d *delay*

Specify delay between refreshes.

-h Print a help message and exit.

-i Suppress display of idle and zombie processes.

-n *num*

Update display *num* times, then exit.

-p *pid*

Monitor only processes with the specified process ID.

-q Refresh without any delay. If user is privileged, run with highest priority.

-s Secure mode. Disable some (dangerous) interactive commands.

-S Cumulative mode. Print total CPU time of each process, including dead child processes.

-v Print version information and exit.

Interactive commands

space

Update display immediately.

c Toggle display of command name or full command line.

f, F

Add fields to or remove fields from the display.

h, ?

Display help about commands and the status of secure and cumulative modes.

H Prompt for a process ID and show all threads for that process.

k Prompt for process ID to kill and signal to send (default is 15) to kill it.

i Toggle suppression of idle and zombie processes.

l Toggle display of load average and uptime information.

m Toggle display of memory information.

n, #

Prompt for number of processes to show. If 0 is entered, show as many as will fit on the screen (default).

o, O

Change order of displayed fields.

q Exit.

r Apply **renice** to a process. Prompt for PID and **renice** value. Suppressed in secure mode.

s Change delay between refreshes. Prompt for new delay time, which should be in seconds. Suppressed in secure mode.

t Toggle display of **processes** and **CPU states** lines.

A Sort by age, with newest first.

^L Redraw screen.

M   Sort tasks by resident memory usage.

N   Sort numerically by process ID.

P   Sort tasks by CPU usage (default).

S   Toggle cumulative mode. (See the **-S** option.)

T   Sort tasks by time/cumulative time.

W   Write current setup to *~/.toprc*. This is the recommended way to write a **top** configuration file.

Field descriptions

The first five entries in the following list describe the lines that appear at the top of the **top** display. The rest are the fields that can be displayed for each task (sizes are in kilobytes). Use the interactive **f** command to add or remove fields.

uptime
> Display the time the system has been up, and three load averages consisting of the average number of processes ready to run in the last 1, 5, and 15 minutes.

processes
> The total number of processes running when the last update was taken, shown as the number of running, sleeping, stopped, or undead tasks.

CPU states
> The percentage of CPU time spent in user mode, in system mode, on tasks with a negative nice value, and idle.

Mem
> Memory statistics, including total available memory, free memory, memory used, shared memory, and memory used for buffers.

Swap
> Swap-space statistics, including total, available, and used.

PID
> Process ID.

PPID
> Parent process ID.

UID
> User ID of task's owner.

USER
> Username of task's owner.

PRI
> Priority.

NI
> Nice value.

PAGEIN
> Page fault count.

SIZE
> Total size of the task's code, data, and stack space.

TSIZE
Code size.

DSIZE
Data plus stack size.

TRS
Resident text size.

SWAP
Size of swapped-out portion of task.

D   Size of pages marked dirty.

LC
Last-used processor, for multiprocessor systems.

RSS
Total amount of physical memory used.

SHARE
Amount of shared memory used.

STAT
State of the task. Values are **S** (sleeping), D (uninterruptible sleep), R (running), Z (zombies), or T (stopped or traced), possibly followed by < (negative nice value), N (positive nice value), or W (swapped out).

WCHAN
Address or name of the kernel function in which the task is currently sleeping.

TIME
Total CPU time used by task and any children.

%CPU
Share of CPU time since last update, as percentage of total CPU time.

%MEM
Share of physical memory.

TTY
Controlling tty.

COMMAND
Command line (truncated if too long) if task is in memory, or command name in parentheses if swapped out.

FLAGS
Task flags.

---

touch

touch [*options*] *files*

For one or more *files*, update the access time and modification time (and dates) to the current time and date. **touch** is useful in forcing other commands to handle files a certain way; for example, the operation of **make**, and sometimes **find**, relies on a file's access and modification time. If a file doesn't exist, **touch** creates it with a file-size of 0.

Options

-a, --time=atime, --time=access, --time=use
Update only the access time.

-c, --no-create
Do not create any file that doesn't already exist.

-d *time,* **--date** *time*
Change the time value to the specified *time* instead of the
current time. *time* can use several formats and may contain
month names, time zones, a.m. and p.m. strings, etc.

-m, --time=mtime, --time=modify
Update only the modification time.

-r *file,* **--reference** *file*
Change times to be the same as those of the specified *file,*
instead of the current time.

-t *time*
Use the time specified in *time* instead of the current time. This
argument must be of the format [[*cc*]*yy*]*mmddhhmm*[.*ss*], indicating optional century and year, month, date, hours, minutes,
and optional seconds.

--help
Print help message and then exit.

--version
Print the version number and then exit.

---

tr

tr [*options*] [*string1* [*string2*]]

Translate characters. Copy standard input to standard output,
substituting characters from *string1* to *string2* or deleting characters in *string1*.

Options

-c, --complement
Complement characters in *string1* with respect to ASCII
001–377.

-d, --delete
Delete characters in *string1* from output.

-s, --squeeze-repeats
Squeeze out repeated output characters in *string2*.

-t, --truncate-set1
Truncate *string1* to the length of *string2* before translating.

--help
Print help message and then exit.

--version
Print the version number and then exit.

Special characters

Include brackets ([ ]) where shown.

\a ^G (bell)

\b ^H (backspace)

\f ^L (form feed)

\n ^J (newline)

\r ^M (carriage return)

\t ^I (tab)

\v ^K (vertical tab)

\nnn

> Character with octal value *nnn*

**** Literal backslash

char1–char2

> All characters in the range *char1* through *char2*. If *char1* does not sort before *char2*, produce an error.

[*char**]

> In *string2*, expand *char* to the length of *string1*.

[*char*number*]

> Expand *char* to number occurrences. **[x*4]** expands to **xxxx**, for instance.

[:*class*:]

> Expand to all characters in *class*, where *class* can be:

> **alnum**
>> Letters and digits

> **alpha**
>> Letters

> **blank**
>> Whitespace

> **cntrl**
>> Control characters

> **digit**
>> Digits

> **graph**
>> Printable characters except space

> **lower**
>> Lowercase letters

> **print**
>> Printable characters

> **punct**
>> Punctuation

> **space**
>> Whitespace (horizontal or vertical)

upper
> Uppercase letters

xdigit
> Hexadecimal digits

[=*char*=]
> The class of characters to which *char* belongs.

Examples

Change uppercase to lowercase in a file:

```
cat file | tr 'A-Z' 'a-z'
```

Turn spaces into newlines (ASCII code 012):

```
tr ' ' '
' < file
```

Strip blank lines from **file** and save in **new.file** (or use **011** to change successive tabs into one tab):

```
cat file | tr -s "" "
" > new.file
```

Delete colons from **file** and save result in **new.file**:

```
tr -d : < file > new.file
```

---

traceroute

traceroute [*options*] *host* [*packetsize*]

TCP/IP command. Trace route taken by packets to reach network host. **traceroute** attempts tracing by launching UDP probe packets with a small TTL (time-to-live), then listening for an ICMP "time exceeded" reply from a gateway. *host* is the destination hostname or the IP number of the host to reach. *packetsize* is the packet size in bytes of the probe datagram. Default is 40 bytes.

Options

-d   Turn on socket-level debugging.

-g *addr*
> Enable the IP LSRR (Loose Source Record Route) option in addition to the TTL tests, to ask how someone at IP address *addr* can reach a particular target.

-i *interface*
> Specify the network interface for getting the source IP address for outgoing probe packets. Useful with a multi-homed host. Also see the **-s** option.

-I   Use ICMP ECHO requests instead of UDP datagrams.

-m *max_ttl*
> Set maximum time-to-live used in outgoing probe packets to *max-ttl* hops. Default is 30.

-n   Show numerical addresses; do not look up hostnames. (Useful if DNS is not functioning properly.)

-p *port*
> Set base UDP port number used for probe packets to *port*. Default is (decimal) 33434.

-q *n*
> Set number of probe packets for each time-to-live setting to the value *n*. Default is 3.

-r Bypass normal routing tables and send directly to a host on an attached network.

-s *src_addr*
> Use *src_addr* as the IP address that will serve as the source address in outgoing probe packets.

-t *tos*
> Set the type-of-service in probe packets to *tos* (default 0). The value must be a decimal integer in the range 0 to 255.

-v Verbose; received ICMP packets (other than TIME_EXCEEDED and PORT_UNREACHABLE) will be listed.

-w *wait*
> Set time to wait for a response to an outgoing probe packet to *wait* seconds (default is 5).

-x Toggle IP checksums, usually to turn them off. IP checksums are always calculated if **-I** is specified.

-z *msecs*
> Set the delay between probes, in milliseconds. The default is 0.

---

troff

troff

See **groff**.

---

true

true

A null command that returns a successful (0) exit status. See also **false**.

---

tset

tset [*options*] [*terminal*]
reset [*options*] [*terminal*]

Initialize a terminal. The terminal to be initialized is whichever is found first from the value of *terminal*, the value of the **TERM** environment variable, or the default terminal type. See also the **reset** command.

Options

-echar
> Set the erase character to *char*.

-ichar
> Set the interrupt character to *char*.

-I Do not send terminal or tab initialization strings to the terminal.

-k*char*
> Set line kill character to *char*.

-m *arg*
> Specify a mapping from a port type to a terminal, where *arg* looks like this:
>
> > [*port type*][*operator*][*baud rate*][:]*terminal type*
>
> *operator* can be any combination of < (less than), > (greater than), @ (equal), and ! (not). The terminal type is a string (e.g., **vt100** or **xterm**).

-q Print the terminal type on standard output but do not initialize the terminal.

-Q Don't display values for the erase, interrupt, and line kill characters.

-r Print the terminal type to standard error.

-s Print the shell commands that initialize the **TERM** environment variable on standard output.

-V Print the version of **ncurses** used for this program and exit.

---

tty

tty [*options*]

Print the filename of the terminal connected to standard input.

Options
--help
> Print help message and exit.

-s, --silent, --quiet
> Print nothing to standard output, but return an exit status.

--version
> Display version information and exit.

---

tune2fs

tune2fs [*options*] *device*

System administration command. Tune the parameters of a Linux Second Extended Filesystem by adjusting various parameters. You must specify the *device* on which the filesystem resides; it must not be mounted read/write when you change its parameters.

Options
-c *max-mount-counts*
> Specify the maximum number of mount counts between two checks on the filesystem.

-C *mount-count*
> Specify the mount count. For use with **-c** to force a check the next time the system boots.

-e *behavior*
> Specify the kernel's behavior when encountering errors. *behavior* must be one of:

---

continue
> Continue as usual.

remount-ro
> Remount the offending filesystem in read-only mode.

panic
> Cause a kernel panic.

-f Force completion even if there are errors.

-g *group*
> Allow *group* (a group ID or name) to use reserved blocks.

-i *interval*[**d**|**w**|**m**]
> Specify the maximum interval between filesystem checks. Units may be in days (**d**), weeks (**w**), or months (**m**). If *interval* is 0, checking will not be time-dependent.

-j Add an ext3 journal to the filesystem. If specified without -J, use the default journal parameters.

-J *jrnl-options*
> Specify ext3 journal parameters as a comma-separated list of *option=value* pairs. The specified options override the default values. Only one size or device option can be specified for a filesystem. Possible options are:

> **device**=*ext-jrnl*
>> Attach to the journal block device on *ext-jrnl*, which must exist and must have the same blocksize as the filesystem to be journaled. *ext-jrnl* can be specified by its device name, by the volume label (**LABEL**=*label*), or by the Universal Unique Identifier (UUID) stored in the journal's ext2 superblock (**UUID**=*uuid*; see **uuidgen**). Create the external journal with:
>>
>>   mke2fs -O *jrnl-dev* ext-jrnl

> **size**=*jrnl-size*
>> The size of the journal in megabytes. The size must be at least equivalent to 1024 blocks and not more than 102,400 blocks.

-l Display a list of the superblock's contents.

-L *label*
> Specify the volume label of filesystem. The label must be no more than 16 characters.

-m *percentage*
> Specify the percentage of blocks that will be reserved for use by privileged users.

-M *dir*
> Specify the filesystem's last-mounted directory.

-O *option*
> Set or clear the specified filesystem options in the filesystem's superblock. Specify multiple options as a comma-separated list. Prefixing an option with a caret (**^**) clears the option. No

prefix or a plus sign (+) causes the option to be set. Run **e2fsck** after changing **filetype** or **sparse_super**. The following options can be cleared or set:

filetype
    Save file type information in directory entries.

has_journal
    Create an ext3 journal. Same as the **-j** option.

sparse_super
    Save space on large filesystems by limiting the number of backup superblocks. Same as **-s**.

-r *num*
    Specify the number of blocks that will be reserved for use by privileged users.

-s [0|1]
    Turn the sparse superblock feature on or off. Run **e2fsck** after changing this feature.

-T *time*
    Set the time **e2fsck** was last run. The time specification is international date format, with the time optional; i.e., YYYYMMDD[[HHMM]SS]. If *time* is specified as **time-last-checked**, the current time is used.

-u *user*
    Allow *user* (a user ID or name) to use reserved blocks.

-U *uuid*
    Set the UUID of the filesystem to a UUID generated by **uuidgen** or to one of the following:

clear
    Clear the existing UUID.

random
    Randomly generate a new UUID.

time
    Generate a new time-based UUID.

---

tunelp

tunelp *device* [*options*]

System administration command. Control a line printer's device parameters. Without options, print information about device(s).

Options

-a [on|off]
    Specify whether or not to abort if the printer encounters an error. By default, do not abort.

-c *n*
    Retry device *n* times if it refuses a character. (Default is 250.) After exhausting *n*, sleep before retrying.

-i *irq*
    Use *irq* for specified parallel port. Ignore **-t** and **-c**. If 0, restore noninterrupt driven (polling) action.

-o [on|off]
Specify whether to abort if device is not online or is out of paper.

-q [on|off]
Specify whether to print current IRQ setting.

-r Reset port.

-s Display printer's current status.

-t *time*
Specify a delay of *time* in jiffies to sleep before resending a refused character to the device. A jiffy is defined as either one tick of the system clock or one AC cycle time; it should be approximately 1/100 of a second.

-w *time*
Specify a delay of *time* in jiffies to sleep before resending a strobe signal.

-C [on|off]
Specify whether to be extremely careful in checking for printer error. Obsolete; the default beginning with Linux 2.1.131.

-T [on|off]
Tell the **lp** driver whether it can trust the IRQ. Useful only if using with interrupts, to handle IRQ printing efficiently. Requires at least Linux 2.1.131.

---

ul

ul [*options*] [*names*]

Translate underscores to underlining. The process will vary by terminal type. Some terminals are unable to handle underlining.

Options

-i When on a separate line, translate - to underline instead of translating underscores.

-t *terminal-type*
Specify terminal type. By default, **TERM** is consulted.

---

umount

umount [*options*] [*directory*|*special-device*]

System administration command. Unmount a filesystem. **umount** announces to the system that the removable file structure previously mounted on the specified directory is to be removed. **umount** also accepts the *special-device* to indicate the filesystem to be unmounted; however, this usage is obsolete and will fail if the device is mounted on more than one directory. Any pending I/O for the filesystem is completed, and the file structure is flagged as clean. A busy filesystem cannot be unmounted.

Options

-a Unmount all filesystems that are listed in */etc/mtab*.

-d If the unmounted device was a loop device, free the loop device too. See also the **losetup** command.

-f   Force the unmount. This option requires kernel 2.1.116 or later.

-h   Print help message and exit.

-l   Lazy unmount. Detach the filesystem from the hierarchy immediately, but don't clean up references until it is no longer busy. Requires kernel 2.4.11 or later.

-n   Unmount, but do not record changes in */etc/mtab*.

-O *options*
Unmount only filesystems with the specified options in */etc/ fstab*. Specify multiple options as a comma-separated list. Add **no** as a prefix to an option to indicate filesystems that should not be unmounted.

-r   If unmounting fails, try to remount read-only.

-t *type*
Unmount only filesystems of type *type*. Multiple types can be specified as a comma-separated list, and any type can be prefixed with **no** to specify that filesystems of that type should not be unmounted.

-v   Verbose mode.

-V   Print version information and exit.

---

uname

uname [*options*]

Print information about the machine and operating system. Without options, print the name of the operating system (Linux).

Options

-a, --all
Combine all the system information from the other options.

-i, --hardware-platform
Print the system's hardware platform.

-m, --machine
Print the name of the hardware the system is running on.

-n, --nodename
Print the machine's hostname.

-o, --operating-system
Print the operating system name.

-p, --processor
Print the type of processor (not available on all versions).

-r, --kernel-release
Print the release number of the kernel.

-s, --kernel-name
Print the name of the kernel (Linux). This is the default action.

-v, --kernel-version
Print build information about the kernel.

--help
> Display a help message and then exit.

--version
> Print version information and then exit.

---

uncompress **uncompress** [*options*] *files*

Uncompress files that were **compress**ed (i.e., whose names end in .Z). **uncompress** takes all the same options as **compress** except **-r** and **-b**.

---

unexpand **unexpand** [*options*] [*files*]

Convert strings of initial whitespace, consisting of at least two spaces and/or tabs, to tabs. Read from standard input if given no file or a file named -.

Options
-a, --all
> Convert all, not just initial, strings of spaces and tabs.

-*nums*, -t *nums*, --tabs *nums*
> *nums* is a comma-separated list of integers that specify the placement of tab stops. If a single integer is provided, the tab stops are set to every *integer* spaces. By default, tab stops are eight spaces apart. With **-t** and **--tabs**, the list may be separated by whitespace instead of commas. This option implies **-a**.

--help
> Print help message and then exit.

--version
> Print the version number and then exit.

---

unicode_start **unicode_start** [*font* [*umap*]]

Put keyboard and console in Unicode mode, setting the font to *font* and the Unicode map to *umap* if the font doesn't have its own map. If no font is specified, use the default.

---

unicode_stop **unicode_stop**

Take keyboard and console out of Unicode mode.

---

uniq **uniq** [*options*] [*file1* [*file2*]]

Remove duplicate adjacent lines from sorted *file1*, sending one copy of each line to *file2* (or to standard output). Often used as a filter. Specify only one of **-d** or **-u**. See also **comm** and **sort**.

Options
-*n*, -f *n*, --skip-fields=*n*
> Ignore first *n* fields of a line. Fields are separated by spaces or by tabs.

+*n*, -s *n*, --skip-chars=*n*
> Ignore first *n* characters of a field.

-c, --count
> Print each line once, prefixing number of instances.

-d, --repeated
> Print duplicate lines once but no unique lines.

-D, --all-repeated[=*method*]
> Print all duplicate lines. -D takes no delimiter method. The delimiter method *method* takes one of the values **none** (default), **prepend,** or **separate.** Blank lines are used as the delimiter.

-i, --ignore-case
> Ignore case differences when checking for duplicates.

-u, --unique
> Print only unique lines (no copy of duplicate entries is kept).

-w *n*, --check-chars=*n*
> Compare only first *n* characters per line (beginning after skipped fields and characters).

--help
> Print a help message and then exit.

--version
> Print version information and then exit.

Examples

Send one copy of each line from **list** to output file **list.new**:

```
uniq list list.new
```

Show which names appear more than once:

```
sort names | uniq -d
```

---

unshar

unshar [*options*] [*files*]

Unpack a shell archive (shar file). **unshar** scans mail messages looking for the start of a shell archive. It then passes the archive through a copy of the shell to unpack it. **unshar** accepts multiple files. If no files are given, standard input is used.

Options

-c, --overwrite
> Overwrite existing files.

-d *directory*, --directory=*directory*
> Change to *directory* before unpacking any files.

-e, --exit-0
> Sequentially unpack multiple archives stored in same file. This uses the clue that many **shar** files are terminated by an exit 0 at the beginning of a line. (Equivalent to -E "exit 0".)

-E *string*, --**split-at**=*string*
> Like **-e**, but allows you to specify the string that separates archives.

-**f**, --**force**
> Same as **-c**.

--**help**
> Print help message and then exit.

--**version**
> Print the version number and then exit.

---

update

update [*options*]

System administration command. **update** is a daemon that controls how often the kernel's disk buffers are flushed to disk. **update** is also known as **bdflush**. The daemon forks a couple of processes to call system functions **flush( )** and **sync( )**. When called by an unprivileged user, no daemon is created. Instead, **update** calls **sync( )** and then exits. By default, update will wake up every 5 seconds and **flush( )** some dirty buffers. If that doesn't work, it will try waking up every 30 seconds to **sync( )** the buffers to disk. Not all of the listed options are available in every version of **update**.

Options

-d   Display the kernel parameters. This does not start the **update** daemon.

-**f** *seconds*
> Call **flush( )** at this interval. Default is 5.

-**h**   Help. Print a command summary.

-**s** *seconds*
> Call **sync( )** at this interval. Default is 30.

-**0** *percent*
> Flush buffers when the specified *percent* of the buffer cache is dirty.

-**1** *blocks*
> The maximum number of dirty blocks to write out per wake cycle.

-**2** *buffers*
> The number of clean buffers to try to obtain each time the free buffers are refilled.

-**3** *blocks*
> Flush buffers if dirty blocks exceed *blocks* when trying to refill the buffers.

-**4** *percent*
> Percent of buffer cache to scan when looking for free clusters.

-**5** *seconds*
> Time for a data buffer to age before being flushed.

-**6** *seconds*
> Time for a nondata buffer to age before being flushed.

-7 constant
> The time constant to use for load average.

-8 ratio
> How low the load average can be before trimming back the number of buffers.

---

uptime

uptime [*option*]

Print the current time, how long the system has been running, the number of users currently logged in (which may include the same user multiple times), and system load averages. This output is also produced by the first line of the **w** command.

Option

-V   Print version information and exit.

---

useradd

useradd [*options*] [*user*]

System administration command. Create new user accounts or update default account information. Unless invoked with the -D option, *user* must be given. **useradd** will create new entries in system files. Home directories and initial files may also be created as needed.

Options

-c comment
> Comment field.

-d dir
> Home directory. The default is to use *user* as the directory name under the *home* directory specified with the **-D** option.

-e date
> Account expiration *date. date* is in the format MM/DD/YYYY. Two-digit year fields are also accepted. The value is stored as the number of days since January 1, 1970. This option requires the use of shadow passwords.

-f days
> Permanently disable account this many *days* after the password has expired. A value of -1 disables this feature. This option requires the use of shadow passwords.

-g group
> Initial *group* name or ID number. If a different default group has not been specified using the **-D** option, the default group is 1.

-G groups
> Supplementary *groups* given by name or number in a comma-separated list with no whitespace.

-k [dir]
> Copy default files to the user's home directory. Meaningful only when used with the **-m** option. Default files are copied from */etc/skel/* unless an alternate *dir* is specified.

-m   Make user's home directory if it does not exist. The default is not to make the home directory.

-M   Do not create a home directory for the user, even if the system default in */etc/login.defs* is to create one.

-n   Red Hat–specific option. Turn off the Red Hat default that creates a group with the same name as the username and puts the user in that group.

-o   Override. Accept a nonunique *uid* with the **-u** option. (Probably a bad idea.)

-p *passwd*
   The encrypted password, as returned by **crypt**(3).

-r   Red Hat–specific option. Create a system account with a non-expiring password and a UID lower than the minimum defined in */etc/login.defs*. Do not create a home directory for the account unless **-m** is also specified.

-s *shell*
   Login *shell*.

-u *uid*
   Numerical user ID. The value must be unique unless the **-o** option is used. The default value is the smallest ID value greater than 99 and greater than every other *uid*.

-D *[options]*
   Set or display defaults. If *options* are specified, set them. If no options are specified, display current defaults. The options are:

   -b *dir*
      Home directory prefix to be used in creating home directories. If the **-d** option is not used when creating an account, the *user* name will be appended to *dir*.

   -e *date*
      Expire *date*. Requires the use of shadow passwords.

   -f *days*
      Number of *days* after a password expires to disable an account. Requires the use of shadow passwords.

   -g *group*
      Initial *group* name or ID number.

   -s *shell*
      Default login *shell*.

---

userdel

userdel *[option]* *user*

System administration command. Delete all entries for *user* in system account files.

Option

-r   Remove the home directory of *user* and any files contained in it.

usermod   usermod [*options*] *user*

System administration command. Modify *user* account information.

Options

-c *comment*
　　Comment field.

-d *dir*
　　Home directory.

-e *date*
　　Account expiration *date*. *date* is in the format MM/DD/YYYY; two-digit year fields are also accepted. The value is stored as the number of days since January 1, 1970. This option requires the use of shadow passwords.

-f *days*
　　Permanently disable account this many *days* after the password has expired. A value of -1 disables this feature. This option requires the use of shadow passwords.

-g *group*
　　Initial *group* name or number.

-G *groups*
　　Supplementary *groups* given by name or number in a comma-separated list with no whitespace. *user* will be removed from any groups to which it currently belongs that are not included in *groups*.

-l *name*
　　Login *name*. This cannot be changed while the user is logged in.

-L　Lock user's password by putting a ! in front of it. This option cannot be used with **-p** or **-U**.

-o　Override. Accept a nonunique *uid* with the **-u** option.

-p *pw*
　　Encrypted password, as returned from **crypt**(3).

-s *shell*
　　Login *shell*.

-u *uid*
　　Numerical user ID. The value must be unique unless the **-o** option is used. Any files owned by *user* in the user's home directory will have their user ID changed automatically. Files outside of the home directory will not be changed. *user* should not be executing any processes while this is changed.

-U　Unlock the user's password by removing the ! that **-L** put in front of it. This option cannot be used with **-p** or **-L**.

users

users [*file*]
users *option*

Print a space-separated list of each login session on the host. Note that this may include the same user multiple times. Consult *file* or, by default, */var/log/utmp* or */var/log/wtmp*.

Options

--help
> Print usage information and exit.

--version
> Print version information and exit.

usleep

usleep [*microseconds*]
usleep [*options*]

Sleep some number of microseconds (default is 1).

Options

-?, --help
> Print help information and then exit.

--usage
> Print usage message and then exit.

-v, --version
> Print version information.

uudecode

uudecode [-o *outfile*] [*file*]

Read a uuencoded file and re-create the original file with the permissions and name set in the file (see **uuencode**). The -o option specifies an alternate output file.

uuencode

uuencode [-m] [*file*] *name*

Encode a binary *file*. The encoding uses only printable ASCII characters and includes the permissions and *name* of the file. When *file* is reconverted via **uudecode**, the output is saved as *name*. If the *file* argument is omitted, **uuencode** can take standard input, so a single argument is taken as the name to be given to the file when it is decoded. With the -m option, base64 encoding is used.

Examples

It's common to encode a file and save it with an identifying extension, such as *.uue*. This example encodes the binary file *flower12.jpg*, names it *rose.jpg*, and saves it to a *.uue* file:

```
% uuencode flower12.jpg rose.jpg > rose.uue
```

Encode *flower12.jpg* and mail it:

```
% uuencode flower12.jpg flower12.jpg | mail el@oreilly.com
```

uuidgen

uuidgen [*option*]

Create a new Universal Unique Identifier (UUID) and print it to standard output. The generated UUID consists of five hyphen-separated groups of hex digits (e.g., 3cdfc61d-87d3-41b5-ba50-32870b33dc67). The default is to generate a random-based UUID, but this requires that a high-quality random-number generator be available on the system.

Options

-r   Generate a random-based UUID.

-t   Generate a time-based UUID.

---

vacation

vacation
vacation [*options*] [*user*]

Automatically return a mail message to the sender announcing that you are on vacation.

Use **vacation** with no options to initialize the vacation mechanism. The process performs several steps.

1. Creates a *.forward* file in your home directory. The *.forward* file contains:

   \user, "|/usr/bin/vacation *user*"

   user is your login name. The action of this file is to actually deliver the mail to *user* (i.e., you) and to run the incoming mail through **vacation**.

2. Creates the *.vacation.pag* and *.vacation.dir* files. These files keep track of who has sent you messages so that they receive only one "I'm on vacation" message from you per week.

3. Starts an editor to edit the contents of *.vacation.msg*. The contents of this file are mailed back to whomever sends you mail. Within its body, **$subject** is replaced with the contents of the incoming message's **Subject** line.

Remove or rename the *.forward* file to disable vacation processing.

Options

The **-a** and **-r** options are used within a *.forward* file; see the example.

-a *alias*
   Mail addressed to *alias* is actually mail for the *user* and should produce an automatic reply.

-i   Reinitialize the *.vacation.pag* and *.vacation.dir* files. Use this right before leaving for your next vacation.

-r *interval*
   By default, no more than one message per week is sent to any sender; this option changes that interval. *interval* is a number with a trailing **s**, **m**, **h**, **d**, or **w** indicating seconds, minutes, hours, days, or weeks, respectively. If *interval* is **infinite**, only one reply is sent to each sender.

Example

Send no more than one reply every three weeks to any given sender:

```
$ cd
$ vacation -I
$ cat .forward
\jp, "|/usr/bin/vacation -r3w jp"
$ cat .vacation.msg
From: jp@wizard-corp.com (J. Programmer, via the vacation
program)
Subject: I'm out of the office ...

Hi. I'm off on a well-deserved vacation after finishing
up whizprog 1.0. I will read and reply to your mail
regarding "$SUBJECT" when I return.

Have a nice day.
```

---

vdir

vdir [*options*] [*files*]

Verbosely list directory contents. Equivalent to **ls -lb**. By default, list the current directory. Directory entries are sorted alphabetically unless overridden by an option. **vdir** takes the same options as **ls**.

---

vi

vi [*options*] [*files*]

A screen-oriented text editor based on **ex**. For more information on **vi**, see Chapter 11.

---

vidmode

vidmode [*option*] *image* [*mode* [*offset*]]

System administration command. Set the video mode for a kernel *image*. If no arguments are specified, print current *mode* value. *mode* is a 1-byte value located at offset 506 in a kernel image. You may change the *mode* by specifying the kernel *image* to change, the new *mode*, and the byte offset at which to place the new information (the default is 506). Note that **rdev -v** is a synonym for **vidmode**. If **LILO** is used, **vidmode** is not needed. The video mode can be set from the LILO prompt during a boot.

Modes

-3   Prompt

-2   Extended VGA

-1   Normal VGA

0   Same as entering **0** at the prompt

1   Same as entering **1** at the prompt

2   Same as entering **2** at the prompt

3   Same as entering **3** at the prompt

n   Same as entering **n** at the prompt

-o *offset*
> Same as specifying an *offset* as an argument.

---

vim

vim

An enhanced version of the **vi** screen editor. Both **vi** and **vim** are covered in Chapter 11.

---

vmstat

vmstat [*options*] [*interval* [*count*]]

Print report on virtual memory statistics, including information on processes, memory, swap space, I/O, system and CPU usage. **vmstat** will first report average values since the last system reboot. If given a sampling period *interval* in seconds, it will print additional statistics for each interval. If specified, **vmstat** will exit when it has completed *count* reports. Otherwise, it will continue until it receives a Ctrl-C, printing a new header line each time it fills the screen.

Options

-**n** Don't print new header lines when the screen is full.

-**V** Print version number, then exit.

Fields

procs

> **r** Processes waiting for run time.
>
> **b** Uninterruptable sleeping processes.
>
> **w** Swapped but runnable processes.

memory

> **swpd**
> > Virtual memory used, in kilobytes.
>
> **free**
> > Idle memory, in kilobytes.
>
> **buff**
> > Memory used as buffers, in kilobytes.

swap

> **si** Memory swapped in from disk each second, in kilobytes.
>
> **so** Memory swapped out to disk each second, in kilobytes.

io

> **bi** Blocks sent to block devices each second.
>
> **bo** Blocks received from block devices each second.

system

> **in** Interrupts per second, including clock interrupts.
>
> **cs** Context switches per second.

cpu

us Percentage of CPU time consumed by user processes.

sy Percentage of CPU time consumed by system processes.

id Percentage of CPU time spent idle.

volname

volname [*devfile*]

Return the volume name for a device such as a CD-ROM that was formatted with an ISO-9660 filesystem. The default device file *devfile* is */dev/cdrom*.

w

w [*options*] [*user*]

Print summaries of system usage, currently logged-in users, and what those users are doing. **w** is essentially a combination of **uptime**, **who**, and **ps -a**. Display output for one user by specifying *user*.

Options

-f Toggle printing the from (remote hostname) field.

-h Suppress headings and **uptime** information.

-s Use the short format.

-u Ignore the username while figuring out the current process and CPU times.

-V Display version information.

File

/var/run/utmp

List of users currently logged in.

wall

wall [*file*]
wall [*message*]

Write to all users. Depending on your Linux distribution, **wall** uses one of the two syntaxes shown. In both versions, the default is for **wall** to read a message from standard input and send the message to all users currently logged in, preceded by "Broadcast Message from...". With the first syntax, which comes with Debian for example, if *file* is specified, **wall** reads input from that file rather than from standard input, and only the superuser can write to a terminal if the user has disallowed messages. With the second syntax, distributed by Red Hat for example, the text of the message can be included on the command line, and the message is limited to 20 lines.

watch

watch [*options*] *command* [*cmd_options*]

Run the specified command repeatedly (by default, every 2 seconds) and display the output so you can watch it change over time. The command and any options are passed to **sh -c**, so you may need to use quotes to get correct results.

Options

-d, --differences[=cumulative]
Highlight changes between iterations. If **cumulative** is specified, the highlighting remains on the screen throughout, giving a cumulative picture of the changes.

-h, --help
Display help message and exit.

-n *secs*, **--interval=***secs*
Run the command every *secs* seconds.

-v, --version
Print version information and exit.

---

wc

wc [*options*] [*files*]

Print byte, word, and line counts for each file. Print a total line for multiple *files*. If no *files* are given, read standard input. See other examples under **ls** and **sort**.

Options

-c, --bytes
Print byte count only.

-l, --lines
Print line count only.

-L, --max-line-length
Print length of longest line.

-m, --chars
Print character count only.

-w, --words
Print word count only.

--help
Print help message and then exit.

--version
Print the version number and then exit.

Examples

Count the number of users logged in:

    who | wc -l

Count the words in three essay files:

    wc -w essay.[123]

Count lines in the file named by variable **$file** (don't display filename):

    wc -l < $file

whatis

whatis *keywords*

Search the short manual page descriptions in the **whatis** database for each *keyword* and print a one-line description to standard output for each match. Like **apropos**, except that it searches only for complete words. Equivalent to **man -f**.

---

whereis

whereis [*options*] *files*

Locate the binary, source, and manual page files for specified commands/files. The supplied filenames are first stripped of leading pathname components and any (single) trailing extension of the form *.ext* (for example, *.c*). Prefixes of *s.* resulting from use of source code control are also dealt with. **whereis** then attempts to locate the desired program in a list of standard Linux directories (*/bin*, */etc*, */usr/bin*, */usr/local/bin/*, etc.).

Options

-b   Search only for binaries.

-f   Terminate the last directory list and signal the start of filenames. Required when the **-B**, **-M**, or **-S** option is used.

-m   Search only for manual sections.

-s   Search only for sources.

-u   Search for unusual entries, that is, files that do not have one entry of each requested type. Thus, the command **whereis -m -u *** asks for those files in the current directory that have no documentation.

-B *directories*
    Change or otherwise limit the directories to search for binaries.

-M *directory*
    Change or otherwise limit the directories to search for manual sections.

-S *directory*
    Change or otherwise limit the directories to search for sources.

Example

Find all files in */usr/bin* that are not documented in */usr/share/man/man1* but that have source in */usr/src*:

```
% cd /usr/bin
% whereis -u -M /usr/share/man/man1 -S /usr/src -f *
```

---

which

which [*options*] [--] [*commands*]

List the full pathnames of the files that would be executed if the named *commands* had been run. **which** searches the user's **$PATH** environment variable. **tcsh** has a built-in **which** command that has no options. To use the options with **tcsh**, specify the full pathname (e.g., */usr/bin/which*).

Options

-a, --all
> Print all matches, not just the first.

-i, --read-alias
> Read aliases from standard input and write matches to standard output. Useful for using an alias for **which**.

--read-functions
> Read shell functions from standard input and report matches to standard output. Useful for also using a shell function for **which** itself.

--skip-alias
> Ignore --**read-alias** if present. Useful for finding normal binaries while using --**read-alias** in an alias for **which**.

--skip-dot
> Skip directories that start with a dot.

--skip-functions
> Ignore --**read-functions** if present. Useful when searching for normal binaries while using --**read-functions** in an alias or function for **which**.

--skip-tilde
> Skip directories that start with a tilde (~) and executables in **$HOME**.

--show-dot
> If a matching command is found in a directory that starts with a dot, print *./cmdname* instead of the full pathname.

--show-tilde
> Print a tilde (~) to indicate the user's home directory. Ignored if the user is root.

--tty-only
> Stop processing options on the right if not on a terminal.

-v, -V, --version
> Print version information and then exit.

--help
> Print help information and then exit.

Example

```
$ which cc ls
/usr/bin/cc
ls:        aliased to ls -sFC
```

---

who

who [*options*] [*file*]
who am i

Show who is logged into the system. With no options, list the names of users currently logged in, their terminal, the time they have been logged in, and the name of the host from which they have logged in. An optional system *file* (default is */etc/utmp*) can be supplied to give additional information.

Options

am i

> Print the username of the invoking user.

--help

> Print a help message and then exit.

-i, -u, --idle

> Include idle times. An idle time of . indicates activity within the last minute; one of **old** indicates no activity in more than a day.

-l, --lookup

> Attempt to include canonical hostnames via DNS.

-m Same as **who am i**.

-q, --count

> "Quick." Display only the usernames and total number of users.

--version

> Print version information and then exit.

-w, -T, --mesg, --message, --writable

> Include user's message status in the output:

> + **mesg y** (**write** messages allowed)

> - **mesg n** (**write** messages refused)

> ? Cannot find terminal device

-H, --heading

> Print headings.

Example

This sample output was produced at 8 a.m. on April 17:

```
$ who -uH
NAME    LINE   TIME          IDLE   PID   COMMENTS
Earvin  ttyp3  Apr 16 08:14  16:25  2240
Larry   ttyp0  Apr 17 07:33    .    15182
```

Since Earvin has been idle since yesterday afternoon (16 hours), it appears that he isn't at work yet. He simply left himself logged in. Larry's terminal is currently in use.

---

whoami °

whoami

Print current user ID. Equivalent to **id -un**.

---

whois

whois [*options*] *query*[*@server*[:*port*]]
fwhois [*options*] *query*[*@server*[:*port*]]

Search a **whois** database for a domain name, IP address, or NIC name. The information returned varies, but usually contains administrative and technical contacts so that you can find a person to handle problems at that domain. By default, the command returns information on *.com*, *.net*, and *.edu* domains, but other hosts can be queried for other domains using *host* or the **-h** option.

Options

--   Indicates the end of options. A subsequent string that begins with a hyphen on the command line is taken as a query string.

-h *server*
> Query the **whois** server on the specified host. Same as *host* on the command line. By default, queries the server in the environment variable **NICNAMESERVER** or **WHOISSERVER** if either is set, otherwise queries *whois.crsnic.net*.

-n   Disable recursion.

-p *port*
> Connect to the specified port. Same as *port* on the command line. Default is 43.

-r   Force recursion when the server responds with the name of another server. The default when the default name server is used.

-t *timeout*
> Set a timeout period of *timeout* seconds.

-v   Verbose. Display the query before sending it to the server.

---

write

    write *user* [*tty*]
    message

Initiate or respond to an interactive conversation with *user*. A **write** session is terminated with EOF. If the user is logged into more than one terminal, specify a *tty* number. See also **talk**; use **mesg** to keep other users from writing to your terminal.

---

xargs

    xargs [*options*] [*command*]

Execute *command* (with any initial arguments), but read remaining arguments from standard input instead of specifying them directly. **xargs** passes these arguments in several bundles to *command*, allowing *command* to process more arguments than it could normally handle at once. The arguments are typically a long list of filenames (generated by **ls** or **find**, for example) that get passed to **xargs** via a pipe.

Options
-0, --null
> Expect filenames to be terminated by NULL instead of whitespace. Do not treat quotes or backslashes specially.

-e[*string*], **--eof**[=*string*]
> Set EOF to _ or, if specified, to *string*.

--help
> Print a summary of the options to **xargs** and then exit.

-i[*string*], **--replace**[=*string*]
> Edit all occurrences of { }, or *string*, to the names read in on standard input. Unquoted blanks are not considered argument terminators. Implies **-x** and **-l 1**.

-l[*lines*], **--max-lines**[=*lines*]

> Allow no more than *lines* nonblank input lines on the command line (default is 1). Implies **-x**.

-n *args*, **--max-args**=*args*

> Allow no more than *args* arguments on the command line. May be overridden by **-s**.

-p, **--interactive**

> Prompt for confirmation before running each command line. Implies **-t**.

-P *max*, **--max-procs**=*max*

> Allow no more than *max* processes to run at once. The default is 1. A maximum of 0 allows as many as possible to run at once.

-r, **--no-run-if-empty**

> Do not run command if standard input contains only blanks.

-s *max*, **--max-chars**=*max*

> Allow no more than *max* characters per command line.

-t, **--verbose**

> Verbose mode. Print command line on standard error before executing.

-x, **--exit**

> If the maximum size (as specified by **-s**) is exceeded, exit.

--version

> Print the version number of **xargs** and then exit.

Examples

grep for *pattern* in all files on the system:

```
find / -print | xargs grep pattern > out &
```

Run **diff** on file pairs (e.g., **f1.a** and **f1.b**, **f2.a** and **f2.b**, etc.):

```
echo $* | xargs -n2 diff
```

The previous line would be invoked as a shell script, specifying filenames as arguments. Display *file*, one word per line (same as **deroff -w**):

```
cat file | xargs -n1
```

Move files in **olddir** to **newdir**, showing each command:

```
ls olddir | xargs -i -t mv olddir/{ } newdir/{ }
```

---

xinetd

xinetd [*options*]

TCP/IP command. The extended Internet services daemon. (On some systems this replaces **inetd**.) Similar to **inetd**, **xinetd** saves system resources by listening to multiple sockets on the behalf of other server programs, invoking necessary programs as requests are made for their services. Beyond this, **xinetd** provides better logging facilities, including remote user ID, access times, and server-specific information. It also provides access control facilities. Not limited to system administration use, it can launch services that are not listed in */etc/services*. Unprivileged users can use this tool to start their own servers.

Options

-cc *num*
> Perform an internal state consistency check every *num* seconds.

-d Turn on debugging support.

-f *file*
> Read configuration from the specified *file* instead of */etc/xinetd.conf*.

-filelog *file*
> Write log messages to the specified *file*. Cannot be combined with **-syslog** or **-debug**.

-limit *num*
> Start no more than *num* concurrent processes.

-logprocs *num*
> Limit processes used to look up remote user IDs to *num*.

-p *file*
> Write **xinetd**'s process ID to *file*.

-stayalive
> Keep running even when no services have been specified.

-syslog *facility*
> Log messages to the specified **syslogd** facility. Accepted values are **daemon**, **auth**, **user**, and **local**n, where n can range from 0 to 7. Cannot be combined with **-syslog** or **-debug**. The default behavior is to write messages to **syslogd** using the **daemon** facility.

Configuration files

By default **xinetd** reads its configuration information from file */etc/xinetd.conf*. Lines in this file beginning with # are treated as comments. The entries for each service differ completely from */etc/inetd* entries. **xinetd** configuration entries for services follow the pattern:

```
service servicename
{
    attribute1 = valueset1
    attribute2 = valueset2
}
```

Some attributes allow assignment operators other than =. Other operators are +=, to add to a value set, and -=, to remove a value from a value set. There are many attributes available to control services; the following are the most common:

deny_time
> Set the time in minutes to deny access to an address that sets off a **SENSOR**. Other accepted values are **NEVER** and **FOREVER**. See the **flags** attribute.

disable

>Accept a Boolean **yes** or **no**. When disabled, **xinetd** will ignore the entry.

flags

>Accept a set of the following values defining **xinetd**'s behavior:

>**IDONLY**

>>Accept only connections when the remote user's ID can be verified by an identification server. Cannot be used with USERID logging.

>**INTERCEPT**

>>Intercept packets to ensure they are coming from allowed locations. Cannot be used with internal or multithreaded services.

>**IPv4**

>>Service is an IPv4 service.

>**IPv6**

>>Service is an IPv6 service.

>**KEEPALIVE**

>>Set flag on socket, enabling periodic checks to determine if the line is still receiving data.

>**NAMEINARGS**

>>Expect the first argument for the **server_args** attribute to be the command to run. This flag is necessary to wrap services with **tcpd**.

>**NODELAY**

>>Set socket's **NODELAY** flag.

>**NOLIBWRAP**

>>Don't use **xinetd**'s internal TCP wrapping facilities.

>**NORETRY**

>>If service fails to fork, don't try to fork again.

>**SENSOR**

>>Instead of launching a service, add IP addresses that attempt to access this service to a list of denied addresses for a time specified by the **deny_time** attribute.

group

>Specify a group ID for the server process. This may be used only when **xinetd** runs as root.

nice

>Set service priority. This attribute accepts the same values as the **renice** command.

id

>Specify a unique identifier for the service. Useful when creating multiple entries with the *servicename*. For example, two versions of the echo service, one supporting UDP and the other TCP, might be given the identifiers **echo-stream** and **echo-dgram**.

log_on_failure

Specify values to log when a server cannot be started. Accepted values are **HOST**, **USERID**, or just **ATTEMPT**.

log_on_success

Specify values to log when a server is started. Accepted values are **PID**, **HOST**, **USERID**, **EXIT**, and **DURATION**.

no_access

Specify hosts that should not be allowed access to a service. May be given as an IP address, a netmask, a hostname, a network name from */etc/networks*, or a group of IP addresses like so: **192.168.1.{10,11,12,15,32}**.

only_from

Restrict access to the service to the specified hosts. This attribute accepts the same values as **no_access**.

port

Specify the service port to listen to. This attribute is required for non-RPC services not listed in */etc/services*. If the service is listed, the value of **port** cannot differ from what is listed.

protocol

Specify protocol to use, usually **tcp** or **udp**. The protocol must be listed in */etc/protocols*. This attribute is required for RPC services as well as services not found in */etc/services*.

rpc_version

The RPC version used by the service. This can be a single number or a range of numbers from *x-y*. This attribute is required for RPC services.

rpc_number

Specify RPC ID number. This is required only for services not listed in */etc/rpc*; otherwise it's ignored.

server

The program to execute for the service. When using **tcpd** to wrap a service, also set the **NAMEINARGS** flag and use the server's program name as the first argument for **server_args**. This attribute is required for all non-internal services.

server_args

Arguments to pass to the server program.

socket_type

Specify the socket type to create. Accepted values are **stream**, **dgram**, **raw**, and **seqpacket**.

type

Describe the type of service. Accepted values are **RPC**, **INTERNAL**, and **UNLISTED**.

user

Specify a user ID for the server process. This may be used only when **xinetd** runs as root.

wait

Determine whether services should be treated as single-threaded (**yes**) and **xinetd** should wait until the server exits to resume listening for new connections, or multithreaded (**no**) and **xinetd** should not wait to resume listening. This attribute is required for all serices.

Files

/etc/xinetd.conf
Default configuration file.

/etc/xinetd.d
Common directory containing configuration files included from */etc/xinetd.conf*.

---

yacc

yacc [*options*] *file*

Given a *file* containing context-free grammar, convert *file* into tables for subsequent parsing and send output to *y.tab.c*. This command name stands for **y**et **a**nother **c**ompiler-**c**ompiler. See also **flex**, **bison**, and *lex & yacc* (O'Reilly).

Options

-b *prefix*
Prepend *prefix*, instead of *y*, to the output file.

-d Generate *y.tab.h*, producing **#define** statements that relate **yacc**'s token codes to the token names declared by the user.

-l Exclude **#line** constructs from code produced in *y.tab.c*. (Use after debugging is complete.)

-o *outfile*
Write generated code to *outfile* instead of the default *y.tab.c*.

-p *prefix*
Change the symbol **yacc** uses for symbols it generates from the default **yy** to *prefix*.

-r Produce separate files for code and tables named *y.code.c* and *y.tab.c*, respectively.

-t Compile runtime debugging code.

-v Generate *y.output*, a file containing diagnostics and notes about the parsing tables.

---

yes

yes [*strings*]
yes [*option*]

Print the command-line arguments, separated by spaces and followed by a newline, until killed. If no arguments are given, print **y** followed by a newline until killed. Useful in scripts and in the background; its output can be piped to a program that issues prompts.

Options

--help
Print a help message and then exit.

--version
Print version information and then exit.

ypbind

ypbind [*options*]

NFS/NIS command. NIS binder process. **ypbind** is a daemon process typically activated at system startup time. Its function is to remember information that lets client processes on a single node communicate with some **ypserv** process. The information **ypbind** remembers is called a *binding*—the association of a domain name with the Internet address of the NIS server and the port on that host at which the **ypserv** process is listening for service requests. This information is cached in the file */var/yp/bindings/domainname. version.*

Options

-c   Check configuration file for syntax errors, then exit.

-broadcast
>   Ignore configuration information in */etc/yp.conf* and directly request configuration information from a remote system using **ypset**.

-broken-server
>   Allow connections to servers using normally illegal port numbers. Sometimes needed for compatibility with other versions of **ypserv**.

-f *file*
>   Read configuration information, from *file* instead of */etc/yp. conf*.

-no-ping
>   Don't ping remote servers to make sure they are alive.

--version
>   Print version information then exit.

-ypset
>   Allow remote machine to change the local server's bindings. This option is very dangerous and should be used only for debugging the network from a remote machine.

-ypsetme
>   **ypset** requests may be issued from this machine only. Security is based on IP address checking, which can be defeated on networks on which untrusted individuals may inject packets. This option is not recommended.

-debug
>   Run in the foreground process instead of detaching and running as a daemon.

ypcat

ypcat [*options*] *map*

NFS/NIS command. Print values in an NIS database specified by *map* name or nickname.

Options

-d *domain*
> Specify *domain* other than default domain.

-h *host*
> Specify a **ypbind** *host* other than the default.

--help, -?
> Print help message, then exit.

-k Display keys for maps in which values are null or key is not part of value.

-t Do not translate *mname* to map name.

--version, -?
> Print version number, then exit.

-x Display map nickname table listing the nicknames (*mnames*) known and map name associated with each nickname. Do not require an *mname* argument.

---

ypchfn

ypchfn [*option*] [*user*]

NFS/NIS command. Change your information stored in */etc/passwd* and displayed when you are fingered; distribute the change over NIS. Without options, **ypchfn** enters interactive mode and prompts for changes. To make a field blank, enter the keyword **none**. The superuser can change the information for any *user*. See also **yppasswd** and **ypchsh**.

Options

-f Behave like **ypchfn** (default).

-l Behave like **ypchsh**.

-p Behave like **yppasswd**.

---

ypinit

ypinit [*options*]

NFS/NIS command. Build and install an NIS database on an NIS server. **ypinit** can be used to set up a master server, slave server, or slave copier. Only a privileged user can run **ypinit**.

Options

-m Indicate that the local host is to be the NIS master server.

-s *master_name*
> Set up a slave server database. *master_name* should be the hostname of an NIS server, either the master server for all the maps, or a server on which the database is up to date and stable.

---

ypmatch

ypmatch [*options*] *key...mname*

NFS/NIS command. Print value of one or more *keys* from an NIS map specified by *mname*. *mname* may be either a map name or a map nickname.

Options

-d *domain*

    Specify *domain* other than default domain.

-k Before printing value of a key, print key itself, followed by a colon (:).

-t Do not translate nickname to map name.

-x Display map nickname table listing the nicknames (*mnames*) known, and map name associated with each nickname. Do not require an *mname* argument.

---

yppasswd

yppasswd [*options*] [*name*]

NFS/NIS command. Change login password in Network Information Service. Create or change your password, and distribute the new password over NIS. The superuser can change the password for any *user*. See also **ypchfn** and **ypchsh**.

Options

-f Update the password information field (the **GECOS** field). Using this option is the same as **ypchfn**.

-l Update the login shell. Using this option is the same as **ypchsh**.

-p Update the password. This is the default behavior for **yppasswd**.

--help, -?

    Print help message, then exit.

--version, -?

    Print version number, then exit.

---

yppasswdd

rpc.yppasswdd [*options*]

NFS/NIS command. Server for modifying the NIS password file. **yppasswdd** handles password-change requests from **yppasswd**. It changes a password entry only if the password represented by **yppasswd** matches the encrypted password of that entry and if the user ID and group ID match those in the server's */etc/passwd* file. Then it updates */etc/passwd* and the password maps on the local server. If the server was compiled with the **CHECKROOT=1** option, the password is also checked against the root password.

Options

-D *dir*

    Specify a directory that contains the *passwd* and *shadow* files for **rpc.yppasswdd** to use instead of */etc/passwd* and */etc/shadow*. Useful to prevent all users in the NIS database from automatically gaining access to the NIS server.

-e chsh|chfn]

    Permit users to change the shell or user information in the **GECOS** field of their *passwd* entry. By default, **rpc.yppasswdd** does not permit users to change these fields.

-E *program*

Specify a program to edit the *passwd* and *shadow* files instead of **rpc.yppasswdd**. The program should return 0 for successful completion, 1 for successful completion but the **pwupdate** program should not be run to update the NIS server's maps, and anything else if the change failed.

-p *pwfile*

Specify an alternative *passwd* file to */etc/passwd*, to prevent all users in the NIS database from automatically gaining access to the NIS server.

--port *num*

Specify a port that **rpc.yppasswdd** will try to register itself, allowing a router to filter packets to the NIS ports.

-s *shadowfile*

Use *shadowfile* instead of */etc/passwd* for shadow password support.

--version

Print version information and whether the package was compiled with **CHECKROOT**.

-x *program*

Modify files using the specified *program* instead of using internal default functions. **rpc.yppasswdd** passes information to *program* in the following format:

    username o:oldpassword p:password s:shell g:gcos

Any of the fields **p**, **s**, or **g** may be missing.

---

yppoll

yppoll [*options*] *map*

NFS/NIS command. Determine version of NIS map at NIS server. **yppoll** asks a **ypserv** process for the order number and the host-name of the master NIS server for the *map*.

Options

-h *host*

Ask the **ypserv** process at *host* about the map parameters. If *host* is not specified, the hostname of the NIS server for the local host (the one returned by **ypwhich**) is used.

-d *domain*

Use *domain* instead of the default domain.

---

yppush

yppush [*options*] *mapnames*

NFS/NIS command. Force propagation of changed NIS map. **yppush** copies a new version of an NIS map, *mapname*, from the master NIS server to the slave NIS servers. It first constructs a list of NIS server hosts by reading the NIS map **ypservers** with the **-d** option's *domain* argument. Keys within this map are the ASCII names of the machines on which the NIS servers run. A map transfer request is sent to the NIS server at each host, along with

the information needed by the transfer agent to call back the
yppush. When the attempt has been completed and the transfer
agent has sent **yppush** a status message, the results may be printed
to standard error. Normally invoked by */var/yp/Makefile* after
commenting out the **NOPUSH=true** line.

Options

-d *domain*
> Specify a *domain*.

-h *host*
> Specify one or a group of systems to which a map should be
> transferred instead of using the list of servers in the **ypservers**
> map. Multiple **-h** options can be specified to create a list of
> hosts.

-p *count*
> Send maps to *count* NIS slaves simultaneously (in parallel). By
> default, **yppush** sends maps to one server at a time (serially).

-t *secs*
> Specify a timeout value in seconds. The timeout determines
> how long **yppush** will wait for a response from a slave server
> before sending a map transfer request to the next server. The
> default timeout is 90 seconds, but for big maps a longer
> timeout may be needed.

-v Verbose; print message when each server is called and for each
> response. Specify twice to make **yppush** even more verbose.

---

ypserv

ypserv [*options*]

NFS/NIS command. NIS server process. **ypserv** is a daemon
process typically activated at system startup time. It runs only on
NIS server machines with a complete NIS database. Its primary
function is to look up information in its local database of NIS
maps. The operations performed by **ypserv** are defined for the
implementor by the NIS protocol specification, and for the
programmer by the header file *<rpcvc/yp_prot.h>*. Communication
to and from **ypserv** is by means of RPC calls. On startup or when
receiving the signal SIGHUP, **ypserv** parses the file */etc/ypserv.conf*.
ypserv supports **securenets**, which can be used to restrict access to
a given set of hosts.

Options

-b, **--dns**
> Query the DNS service for host information if not found in the
> hosts maps.

-d [*path*], **--debug** [*path*]
> Run in debugging mode without going into background
> mode, and print extra status messages to standard error for
> each request. If *path* is specified, use it instead of */var/yp*.

-p *port,* **--port** *port*
> Bind to the specified port. For use with a router to filter packets so that access from outside hosts can be restricted.

-v, --version
> Print version information and exit.

Files and directories

/etc/yp.conf
> Configuration file.

/var/yp/[domainname]/
> Location of NIS databases.

/var/yp/Makefile
> *Makefile* that is responsible for creating NIS databases.

/var/yp/securenets
> **securenets** information containing netmask/network pairs separated by whitespace.

---

ypset

ypset [*options*] *server*

NFS/NIS command. Point **ypbind** at a particular server. **ypset** tells **ypbind** to get NIS services for the specified domain from the **ypserv** process running on *server*. *server* indicates the NIS server to bind to and can be specified as a name or an IP address.

Options

-d *domain*
> Use *domain* instead of the default domain.

-h *host*
> Set **ypbind**'s binding on *host* instead of the local host. *host* can be specified as a name or an IP address.

---

yptest

yptest [*options*]

NFS/NIS command. Check configuration of NIS services by calling various NIS functions. Without arguments, **yptest** queries the NIS server for the local machine.

Options

-d *domainname*
> Use *domainname* instead of the current host's default domain. This option may cause some tests to fail.

-h *host*
> Test **ypserv** on the specified *host* instead of the current host. This option may cause some tests to fail.

-m *map*
> Use the specified *map* instead of the default map.

-u *user*
> Run tests as *user* instead of as nobody.

ypwhich

ypwhich [*options*] [*host*]

NFS/NIS command. Return hostname of NIS server or map master. Without arguments, **ypwhich** cites the NIS server for the local machine. If *host* is specified, that machine is queried to find out which NIS master it is using.

Options

-d *domain*
> Use *domain* instead of the default domain.

-m [*map*]
> Find master NIS server for a map. No host can be specified with **-m**. *map* may be a map name or a nickname for a map. If no map is specified, display a list of available maps.

-t *mapname*
> Inhibit nickname translation.

-V*n*
> Version of **ypbind** (default is V2).

-x Display map nickname table. Do not allow any other options.

ypxfr

ypxfr [*options*] *mapname*

NFS/NIS command. Transfer an NIS map from the server to the local host by making use of normal NIS services. **ypxfr** creates a temporary map in the directory */var/yp/domain* (where *domain* is the default domain for the local host), fills it by enumerating the map's entries, and fetches the map parameters and loads them. If run interactively, **ypxfr** writes its output to the terminal. However, if it is invoked without a controlling terminal, its output is sent to **syslogd**.

Options

-C *tid prog ipadd port*
> This option is for use only by **ypserv**. When **ypserv** invokes **ypxfr**, it specifies that **ypxfr** should call back a **yppush** process at the host with IP address *ipadd*, registered as program number *prog*, listening on port *port*, and waiting for a response to transaction *tid*.

-c Do not send a "Clear current map" request to the local **ypserv** process.

-d *domain*
> Specify a domain other than the default domain.

-f Force the transfer to occur even if the version on the master server is older than the local version.

-h *host*
> Get the map from *host* instead of querying NIS for the map's master server. *host* may be specified by name or IP address.

-p *dir*

Use *dir* as the path to the NIS map directory instead of */var/yp*.

-s *domain*

Specify a source *domain* from which to transfer a map that should be the same across domains (such as the *services. byname* map).

zcat

zcat [*options*] [*files*]

Read one or more *files* that have been compressed with **gzip** or **compress** and write them to standard output. Read standard input if no *files* are specified or if - is specified as one of the files; end input with EOF. **zcat** is identical to **gunzip -c** and takes the options -fhLV, as described for **gzip**/**gunzip**.

zcmp

zcmp [*options*] *files*

Read compressed files and pass them uncompressed to the **cmp** command, along with any command-line options. If a second file is not specified for comparison, look for a file called *file.gz*.

zdiff

zdiff [*options*] *files*

Read compressed files and pass them, uncompressed, to the **diff** command, along with any command-line options. If a second file is not specified for comparison, look for a file called *file***.gz**.

zdump

zdump [*options*] [*zones*]

System administration command. Dump a list of all known time zones or, if an argument is provided, a specific zone or list of zones. Include each zone's current time with its name.

Options

-c *year*

Specify a cutoff year to limit verbose output. Meaningful only with -**v**.

-v Verbose mode. Include additional information about each zone.

zforce

zforce [*names*]

Rename all **gzip**ped files to *filename.gz*, unless file already has a *.gz* extension.

zgrep

zgrep [*options*] [*files*]

Uncompress files and pass to **grep**, along with any command-line arguments. If no files are provided, read from (and attempt to uncompress) standard input. May be invoked as **zegrep** or **zfgrep** and will in those cases invoke **egrep** or **fgrep**.

zic

zic [*options*] [*files*]

System administration command. Create time conversion information files from the file or files specified. If the specified file is -, read information from standard input.

Options

-d *directory*

Place the newly created files in *directory*. Default is */usr/local/ etc/zoneinfo*.

-l *timezone*

Specify a *timezone* to use for local time. **zic** links the zone information for *timezone* with the zone **localtime**.

-p *timezone*

Set the default rules for handling POSIX-format environment variables to the zone name specified by *timezone*.

-s   Store time values only if they are the same when signed as when unsigned.

-v   Verbose mode. Include extra error checking and warnings.

-y *command*

Check year types with *command*. Default is **yearistype**.

-L *file*

Consult *file* for information about leap seconds.

The source files for **zic** should be formatted as a sequence of rule lines, zone lines, and link lines. An optional file containing leap-second rules can be specified on the command line. Rule lines describe how time should be calculated. They describe changes in time, daylight savings time, and any other changes that might affect a particular time zone. Zone lines specify which rules apply to a given zone. Link lines link similar zones together. Leap lines describe the exact time when leap seconds should be added or subtracted. Each of these lines is made up of fields. Fields are separated from one another by any number of whitespace characters. Comment lines are preceded by #. The fields used in each line are listed in the next section.

Rule line fields

The format of a rule line is:

    Rule NAME FROM TO TYPE IN ON AT SAVE LETTERS

NAME

Name this set of rules.

FROM

Specify the first year to which this rule applies. Gregorian calendar dates are assumed. Instead of specifying an actual year, you may specify *minimum* or *maximum* for the minimum or maximum year representable as an integer.

TO
> Specify the last year to which this rule applies. Syntax is the same as for the *FROM* field.

TYPE
> Specify the type of year to which this rule should be applied. The wildcard - instructs that all years be included. Any given year's type will be checked with the command given with the -y option or the default **yearistype** *year type*. An exit status of 0 is taken to mean the year is of the given type; an exit status of 1 means that it is not of the given type (see -y option).

IN
> Specify month in which this rule should be applied.

ON
> Specify day on which this rule should be applied. Whitespace is not allowed. For example:
>
> **1** The 1st.
>
> **firstSun**
> > The first Sunday.
>
> **Sun>=3**
> > The first Sunday to occur before or on the 3rd.

AT
> Specify the time after which the rule is in effect. For example, you may use 13, 13:00, or 13:00:00 for 1:00 p.m. You may include one of several suffixes (without whitespace between):
>
> **s** Local standard time.
>
> **u, g, z**
> > Universal time.
>
> **w** Wall clock time (default).

SAVE
> Add this amount of time to the local standard time. Formatted like *AT*, without suffixes.

LETTERS
> Specify letter or letters to be used in time zone abbreviations (for example, S for EST). For no abbreviation, enter -.

Zone line fields

The format of a zone line is:

```
Zone NAME GMTOFF RULES/SAVE FORMAT [UNTIL]
```

NAME
> Time zone name.

GMTOFF
> The amount of hours by which this time zone differs from GMT. Formatted like *AT*. Negative times are subtracted from GMT; by default, times are added to it.

RULES/SAVE
> Either the name of the rule to apply to this zone or the amount of time to add to local standard time. To make the zone the same as local standard time, specify -.

FORMAT
> The format of time zone abbreviations. Specify the variable part with **%s**.

UNTIL
> Change the rule for the zone at this date. The next line must specify the new zone information and therefore must omit the string "Zone" and the *NAME* field.

Link line fields

The format of a link line is:

```
Link LINK-FROM LINK-TO
```

LINK-FROM
> The name of the zone that is being linked.

LINK-TO
> An alternate name for the zone that was specified as *LINK-FROM*.

Leap line fields

The format of a leap line is:

```
Leap YEAR MONTH DAY HH:MM:SS CORR R|S
```

YEAR MONTH DAY HH:MM:SS
> Specify when the leap second happened.

CORR
> Uses + or - to show whether the second was added or skipped.

R|S
> Rolling or Stationary. Describe whether the leap second should be applied to local wall clock time or GMT, respectively.

---

zless

zless *files*

Uncompress files and allow paging through them. Equivalent to running **zmore** with the environment variable **PAGER** set to **less**. See **zmore** for the available commands.

---

zmore

zmore [*files*]

Similar to **more**. Uncompress files and print them one screenful at a time. Works on files compressed with **compress**, **gzip**, or **pack**, and with uncompressed files.

Commands

space
> Print next screenful.

*i***space**
> Print next *i* lines.

---

d, ^D
Print next *i*, or 11, lines.

*i***z** Print next *i* lines or a screenful.

*i***s** Skip *i* lines. Print next screenful.

*i***f** Skip *i* screens. Print next screenful.

q, Q, :q, :Q
Go to next file or, if current file is the last, exit **zmore**.

e, q
Exit **zmore** when the prompt "--More--(Next file: *file*)" is displayed.

s Skip next file and continue when the prompt "--More--(Next file: *file*)" is displayed.

= Print line number.

*i***/***expr*
Search forward for *i*th occurrence (in all files) of *expr*, which should be a regular expression. Display occurrence, including the two previous lines of context.

*i***n** Search forward for the *i*th occurrence of the last regular expression searched for.

!*command*
Execute *command* in shell. If *command* is not specified, execute last shell command. To invoke a shell without passing it a command, enter \!.

. Repeat the previous command.

---

znew

znew [*options*] [*files*]

Uncompress **.Z** files and recompress them in **.gz** format.

Options

-9 Optimal (and slowest) compression method.

-f Recompress even if *filename***.gz** already exists.

-t Test new **.gz** files before removing **.Z** files.

-v Verbose mode.

-K If the original **.Z** file is smaller than the **.gz** file, keep it.

-P Pipe data to conversion program. This saves disk space.

4

Boot Methods

This chapter describes some techniques for booting your Linux system. Depending on your hardware and whether you want to run any other operating systems, you can configure the system to boot Linux automatically or to provide a choice between several operating systems. Choosing between operating systems is generally referred to as *dual booting*, but you can actually boot more than two.

Once your Linux system is installed, rebooting the system is generally pretty straightforward. But with the wide variety of hardware and software in use, there are many possibilities for configuring your boot process. The most common choices are:

- Boot Linux from a floppy or bootable CD, leaving any other operating system to boot from the hard drive.
- Use the Linux Loader, LILO.[*] This is the traditional method of booting and lets you boot both Linux and other operating systems.
- Use the Grand Unified Bootloader (GRUB), the GNU graphical boot loader and command shell. Like LILO, GRUB lets you boot both Linux and other operating systems. For now, GRUB runs only on i386-based systems.
- Run Loadlin, which is an MS-DOS program that boots Linux from within DOS.

Other boot managers that can load Linux are available, but we don't discuss them here. We also won't talk further about booting from a floppy or CD, except to say that whatever method you choose for booting, be sure to have a working boot disk available for emergency use. In particular, don't experiment with the files and options in this chapter unless you have a boot disk, because any error could leave you unable to boot from the hard disk. Note, though, that one of the advantages

---

[*] LILO is a boot program for i386-architecture machines. On the Alpha, the equivalent boot program is called MILO (Mini Loader), and on the SPARC, it is SILO.

of using GRUB is that if there is a problem booting from the menu, it drops you down to the command-line interface so you can enter commands directly and try to recover. Also, see "Creating a GRUB boot floppy" for information on making a GRUB boot floppy.[*]

The Boot Process

On an x86-based PC, the first sector of every hard disk is known as the *boot sector* and contains the partition table for that disk and possibly also code for booting an operating system. The boot sector of the first hard disk is known as the *master boot record* (MBR) because when you boot the system, the BIOS transfers control to a program that lives on that sector along with the partition table. That code is the *boot loader*, the code that initiates an operating system. When you add Linux to the system, you need to modify the boot loader, replace it, or boot from a floppy or CD to start Linux.

In Linux, each disk and each partition on the disk is treated as a device. So, for example, the entire first hard disk is known as */dev/hda* and the entire second hard disk is */dev/hdb*. The first partition of the first hard drive is */dev/hda1*, and the second partition is */dev/hda2*. The first partition of the second hard drive is */dev/hdb1*, and so on. If your drives are SCSI instead of IDE, the naming works the same way except that the devices are */dev/sda*, */dev/sda1*, and so on. Thus, if you want to specify that the Linux partition is the second partition of the first hard drive (as in the examples in this chapter), you refer to it as */dev/hda2*. Note, though, that GRUB has its own disk naming convention, described in "GRUB: The Grand Unified Bootloader."

Once you've made the decision to install LILO or GRUB, you still need to decide how it should be configured. If you want your system to dual-boot Linux and Windows 95/98/ME, you can install LILO or GRUB on the MBR and set it up to let you select the system to boot. Dual-booting Linux and Windows NT/2000/XP is not quite as straightforward because they use the Windows NT loader, which is installed on the MBR and expects to be the one in charge. The standard solution described in this chapter is to add Linux as an option in the NT loader and install LILO or GRUB in the Linux partition as a secondary boot loader. The result is that the NT loader transfers control to the secondary loader, which then boots Linux. See "Dual-Booting Linux and Windows NT/2000/XP" later in this chapter for more information. You can also install one of the Linux boot loaders in the MBR and use it to boot Windows—see the "Linux+WindowsNT" and the "Multiboot with GRUB" mini-HOWTOs if you're interested in doing that.

When you install the boot loader (either LILO or GRUB) on the MBR, it replaces the MS-DOS boot loader or any other boot loader that may be there, such as the Windows NT loader. If you have problems with your installation or you simply want to restore the original boot loader, you can do one of the following.

---

[*] Unfortunately, there is no standard set of instructions we can provide for making a bootable CD. Your best bet is to use a bootable installation CD for your distribution. Also, instructions and utilities are available online for making bootable CDs.

- If you're running LILO, you can boot Linux from a floppy or CD and restore the boot sector, which LILO automatically backs up:

  ```
  % /sbin/lilo -u
  ```

- If you have the capability, boot to DOS and run the **fdisk** command with a special option that rebuilds the MBR:

  ```
  C:> fdisk /mbr
  ```

- For Windows 2000 and Windows XP, which do not have an **fdisk** command, boot your computer from the Windows CD (or the Windows boot floppies if you can't boot from your CD drive). When you see "Welcome to Setup," press R (for repair) and, in Windows 2000, you then press C. Select your Windows installation from the numbered list that is displayed (there may be only one entry) and enter the administrator password at the prompt. Enter the command **fixmbr** at the command-line prompt and confirm it with **y**. After the MBR has been restored, type **exit** to reboot.

The common element in all three methods is that they replace the boot loader on the MBR with the original Microsoft boot loader. The boot loader on the MBR is the one that will be used to boot the system. This means that if you want to switch from LILO to GRUB, say, or from GRUB to LILO, you don't need to uninstall the old loader; simply install the new one.

The rest of this chapter describes the various techniques for booting Linux and the options that you can specify to configure both the boot loader and the Linux kernel. Whether you use LILO, GRUB, or Loadlin, you can pass options to the loader and specify options for the kernel.

LILO: The Linux Loader

In addition to booting Linux, LILO can boot other operating systems, such as MS-DOS, Windows 95/98/ME, or any of the BSD systems. During installation, the major Linux distributions provide the opportunity to install LILO; it can also be installed later if necessary. LILO can be installed on the MBR of your hard drive or as a secondary boot loader on the Linux partition. LILO consists of several pieces, including the boot loader itself, a configuration file (*/etc/lilo.conf*), a map file (*/boot/map*) containing the location of the kernel, and the **lilo** command (*/sbin/lilo*), which reads the configuration file and uses the information to create or update the map file and to install the files LILO needs.

One thing to remember about LILO is that it has two aspects: the boot loader and the **lilo** command. The **lilo** command configures and installs the boot loader and updates it as necessary. The boot loader is the code that executes at system boot time and boots Linux or another operating system.

The LILO Configuration File

The **lilo** command reads the LILO configuration file, */etc/lilo.conf*, to get the information it needs to install LILO. Among other things, it builds a map file containing the locations of all disk sectors needed for booting.

Note that any time you change /etc/lilo.conf or rebuild or move a kernel image, you need to rerun **lilo** to rebuild the map file and update LILO.

The configuration file starts with a section of global options, described in the next section. Global options are those that apply to every system boot, regardless of what operating system you are booting. Here is an example of a global section (a hash sign, #, begins a comment):

```
boot=/dev/hda          # The boot device is /dev/hda
map=/boot/map          # Save the map file as /boot/map
install=/boot/boot.b   # The file to install as the new boot sector
prompt                 # Always display the boot prompt
timeout=30             # Set a 3-second (30 tenths of a second) timeout
```

Following the global section, there is one section of options for each Linux kernel and for each non-Linux operating system that you want LILO to be able to boot. Each of these sections is referred to as an *image* section because each boots a different kernel image (shorthand for a binary file containing a kernel) or another operating system. Each Linux image section begins with an **image=** line.

```
image=/boot/vmlinuz    # Linux image file
  label=linux          # Label that appears at the boot prompt
  root=/dev/hda2       # Location of the root filesystem
  vga=ask              # Always prompt the user for VGA mode
  read-only            # Mount read-only to run fsck for a filesystem check
```

The equivalent section for a non-Linux operating system begins with **other=** instead of **image=**. For example:

```
other=/dev/hda1        # Location of the partition
  label=win98
  table=/dev/hda       # Location of the partition table
```

Put LILO configuration options that apply to all images into the global section of /etc/lilo.conf, and options that apply to a particular image into the section for that image. If an option is specified in both the global section and an image section, the setting in the image section overrides the global setting for that image.

Here is an example of a complete /etc/lilo.conf file for a system that has the Linux partition on /dev/hda2:

```
## Global section
boot=/dev/hda2
map=/boot/map
delay=30
timeout=50
prompt
vga=ask

## Image section: For regular Linux
image=/boot/vmlinuz
  label=linux
  root=/dev/hda2
  install=/boot/boot.b
  map=/boot/map
  read-only
```

```
## Image section: For testing a new Linux kernel
image=/testvmlinuz
  label=testlinux
  root=/dev/hda2
  install=/boot/boot.b
  map=/boot/map
  read-only
  optional                    # Omit image if not available when map is built

## Image section: For booting DOS
other=/dev/hda1
  label=dos
  loader=/boot/chain.b
  table=/dev/hda           # The current partition table

## Image section: For booting Windows 98
other=/dev/hda1
  label=win98
  loader=/boot/chain.b
  table=/dev/hda
```

Global options

In addition to the options listed here, the kernel options **append**, **read-only**, **read-write**, **root**, and **vga** (described later in "Kernel options") also can be set as global options.

backup=*backup-file*

> Copy the original boot sector to *backup-file* instead of to */boot/boot.nnnn*, where *nnnn* is a number that depends on the disk device type.

boot=*boot-device*

> Set the name of the device that contains the boot sector. **boot** defaults to the device currently mounted as root, such as */dev/hda2*. Specifying a device such as */dev/hda* (without a number) indicates that LILO should be installed in the master boot record; the alternative is to set it up on a particular partition such as */dev/hda2*.

change-rules

> Begin a section that redefines partition types at boot time for hiding and unhiding partitions. See the LILO User's Guide, which comes with the LILO distribution, for detailed information on using this option and creating a new rule set.

compact

> Merge read requests for adjacent disk sectors to speed up booting. Use of **compact** is particularly recommended when booting from a floppy disk. Use of **compact** may conflict with **linear**.

default=*name*

> Use the image *name* as the default boot image. If **default** is omitted, the first image specified in the configuration file is used.

delay=_tsecs_

Specify, in tenths of a second, how long the boot loader should wait before booting the default image. If **serial** is set, **delay** is set to a minimum of 20. The default is not to wait. See "Boot-Time Kernel Options" at the end of this chapter for ways to get the boot prompt if no delay is set.

disk=_device-name_

Define parameters for the disk specified by _device-name_ if LILO can't figure them out. Normally, LILO can determine the disk parameters itself and this option isn't needed. When **disk** is specified, it is followed by one or more parameter lines, such as:

```
disk=/dev/sda
    bios=0x80        # First disk is usually 0x80, second is usually 0x81
    sectors=...
    heads=...
```

Note that this option is not the same as the disk geometry parameters you can specify with the **hd** boot command-line option. With **disk**, the information is given to LILO; with **hd**, it is passed to the kernel. Note also that if either **heads** or **sectors** is specified, they must both be specified. The parameters that can be specified with **disk** are listed briefly here; they are described in detail in the LILO User's Guide.

bios=_bios-device-code_

The number the BIOS uses to refer to the device. See the previous example.

cylinders=_cylinders_

The number of cylinders on the disk.

heads=_heads_

The number of heads on the disk.

inaccessible

Tell LILO that the BIOS can't read the disk; used to prevent the system from becoming unbootable if LILO thinks the BIOS can read it. If this parameter is specified, it must be the only parameter.

partition=_partition-device_

Start a new section for a partition. The section contains one variable, **start=**_partition-offset_, which specifies the zero-based number of the first sector of the partition:

```
partition=/dev/sda1
    start=2048
```

sectors=_sectors_

The number of sectors per track.

disktab=_disktab-file_

This option has been superseded by the **disk=** option.

fix-table

If set, allow **lilo** to adjust 3D addresses (addresses specified as sector/head/cylinder) in partition tables. This is sometimes necessary if a partition isn't track-aligned and another operating system such as MS-DOS is on the same disk. See the _lilo.conf_ manpage for details.

force-backup=*backup-file*
> Like **backup**, but overwrite an old backup copy if one exists.

ignore-table
> Tell **lilo** to ignore corrupt partition tables.

install=*boot-sector*
> Install the specified file as the new boot sector. If **install** is omitted, the boot sector defaults to */boot/boot.b*.

lba32
> Generate 32-bit Logical Block Addresses instead of sector/head/cylinder addresses, allowing booting from any partition on hard disks greater than 8.4 GB (i.e., remove the 1024-cylinder limit). Requires BIOS support for the EDD packet call interface[*] and at least LILO Version 21-4.

linear
> Generate linear sector addresses, which do not depend on disk geometry, instead of 3D (sector/head/cylinder) addresses. If LILO can't determine your disk's geometry itself, you can try using **linear**; if that doesn't work, then you need to specify the geometry with **disk=**. Note, however, that **linear** sometimes doesn't work with floppy disks, and it may conflict with **compact**.

lock
> Tell LILO to record the boot command line and use it as the default for future boots until it is overridden by a new boot command line. **lock** is useful if there are kernel options that you need to enter on the boot command line every time you boot the system.

map=*map-file*
> Specify the location of the map file. Defaults to */boot/map*.

message=*message-file*
> Specify a file containing a message to be displayed before the boot prompt. The message can include a formfeed character (**Ctrl-L**) to clear the screen. The map file must be rebuilt by rerunning the **lilo** command if the message file is changed or moved. The maximum length of the file is 65,535 bytes.

nowarn
> Disable warning messages.

optional
> Specify that any image that is not available when the map is created should be omitted and not offered as an option at the boot prompt. Like the per-image option **optional** but applies to all images.

password=*password*
> Specify a password that the user is prompted to enter when trying to load an image. The password is not encrypted in the configuration file, so if passwords are used, permissions should be set so that only the superuser is able to read the file. This option is like the per-image version, except that all images are password-protected and they all have the same password.

---

[*] If your BIOS is dated after 1998, it should include EDD packet call interface support.

prompt

Automatically display the boot prompt without waiting for the user to press the Shift, Alt, or Scroll Lock key. Note that setting **prompt** without also setting **timeout** prevents unattended reboots.

restricted

Can be used with **password** to indicate that a password needs to be entered only if the user specifies parameters on the command line. Like the per-image **restricted** option but applies to all images.

serial=*parameters*

Allow the boot loader to accept input from a serial line as well as from the keyboard. Sending a break on the serial line corresponds to pressing a Shift key on the console to get the boot loader's attention. All boot images should be password-protected if serial access is insecure (e.g., if the line is connected to a modem). Setting **serial** automatically raises the value of **delay** to 20 (i.e., 2 seconds) if it is less than that. The parameter string *parameters* has the following syntax:

    port[,bps[parity[bits]]]

For example, to initialize COM1 with the default parameters:

    serial=0,2400n8

The parameters are:

port

The port number of the serial port. The default is 0, which corresponds to COM1 (*/dev/ttys0*). The value can be one of 0 through 3, for the four possible COM ports.

bps

The baud rate of the serial port. Possible values of *bps* are 110, 300, 1200, 2400, 4800, 9600, 19200, and 38400. The default is 2400 bps.

parity

The parity used on the serial line. Parity is specified as *n* or *N* for no parity, *e* or *E* for even parity, and *o* or *O* for odd parity. However, the boot loader ignores input parity and strips the 8th bit.

bits

Specify whether a character contains 7 or 8 bits. Default is 8 with no parity and 7 otherwise.

timeout=*tsecs*

Set a timeout (specified in tenths of a second) for keyboard input. If no key has been pressed after the specified time, the default image is booted automatically. **timeout** is also used to determine when to stop waiting for password input. The default timeout is infinite.

verbose=*level*

Turn on verbose output, where higher values of *level* produce more output. If **-v** is also specified on the **lilo** command line, the level is incremented by 1 for each occurrence of **-v**. The maximum verbosity level is 5.

Image options

The following options are specified in the image section for a particular boot image. The image can be a Linux kernel or a non-Linux operating system.

alias=*name*

Provide an alternate name for the image that can be used instead of the name specified with the **label** option.

image=*pathname*

Specify the file or device containing the boot image of a bootable Linux kernel. Each per-image section that specifies a bootable Linux kernel starts with an **image** option. See also the **range** option.

label=*name*

Specify the name that is used for the image at the boot prompt. Defaults to the filename of the image file (without the path).

loader=*chainloader*

For a non-Linux operating system, specify the chain loader to which LILO should pass control for booting that operating system. The default is */boot/chain.b*. If the system will be booted from a drive that is neither the first hard disk or a floppy, the chainloader must be specified.

lock

Like **lock** as described in the previous global options section; it can also be specified in an image section.

optional

Specify that the image should be omitted if it is not available when the map is created by the **lilo** command. Useful for specifying test kernels that are not always present.

other=*pathname*

Specify the path to a file that boots a non-Linux system. Each per-image section that specifies a bootable non-Linux system starts with an **other** option.

password=*password*

Specify that the image is password-protected and provide the password that the user is prompted for when booting. The password is not encrypted in the configuration file, so if passwords are used, only the superuser should be able to read the file.

range=*sectors*

Used with the **image** option, when the image is specified as a device (e.g., **image**=*/dev/fd0*), to indicate the range of sectors to be mapped into the map file. *sectors* can be given as the range *start-end* or as *start+number*, where *start* and *end* are zero-based sector numbers and *number* is the increment beyond *start* to include. If only *start* is specified, only that one sector is mapped. For example:

```
image=/dev/fd0
range=1+512   # take 512 sectors, starting with sector 1
```

restricted

Specify that a password is required for booting the image only if boot parameters are specified on the command line.

table=*device*

Specify, for a non-Linux operating system, the device that contains the partition table. If **table** is omitted, the boot loader does not pass partition information to the operating system being booted. Note that */sbin/lilo* must be rerun if the partition table is modified. This option cannot be used with **unsafe**.

unsafe

Can be used in the per-image section for a non-Linux operating system to indicate that the boot sector should not be accessed when the map is created. If **unsafe** is specified, then some checking isn't done, but the option can be useful for running the **lilo** command without having to insert a floppy disk when the boot sector is on a fixed-format floppy disk device. This option cannot be used with **table**.

Kernel options

The following kernel options can be specified in */etc/lilo.conf* as well as on the boot command line:

append=*string*

Append the options specified in *string* to the parameter line passed to the kernel. This typically is used to specify certain hardware parameters. For example, while BIOSes on newer systems can recognize more than 64 MB of memory, BIOSes on older systems are limited to 64 MB. If you are running Linux on such a system, you can use **append**:

```
append="mem=128M"
```

initrd=*filename*

Specify the file to load into */dev/initrd* when booting with a RAM disk. See also the options **load_ramdisk** (in "Boot-Time Kernel Options"), and **prompt_ramdisk**, **ramdisk_size**, and **ramdisk_start** in this section.

literal=*string*

Like **append**, but replace all other kernel boot options.

noinitrd

Preserve the contents of */dev/initrd* so they can be read once after the kernel is booted.

prompt_ramdisk=*n*

Specify whether the kernel should prompt you to insert the floppy disk that contains the RAM disk image, for use during Linux installation. Values of *n* are:

0   Don't prompt. Usually used for an installation in which the kernel and the RAM disk image both fit on one floppy.

1   Prompt. This is the default.

ramdisk=*size*

Obsolete; use only with kernels older than Version 1.3.48. For newer kernels, see the option **load_ramdisk** in "Boot-Time Kernel Options," as well as **prompt_ramdisk, ramdisk_size,** and **ramdisk_start** in this section.

ramdisk_size=*n*

Specify the amount of memory, in kilobytes, to be allocated for the RAM disk. The default is 4096, which allocates 4 megabytes.

ramdisk_start=*offset*

Used for a Linux installation in which both the kernel and the RAM disk image are on the same floppy. *offset* indicates the offset on the floppy where the RAM disk image begins; it is specified in kilobytes.

read-only

Specify that the root filesystem should be mounted read-only for filesystem checking (**fsck**), after which it is typically remounted read/write.

read-write

Specify that the root filesystem should be mounted read/write.

root=*root-device*

Specify the device that should be mounted as root. If the special name **current** is used as the value, the root device is set to the device on which the root filesystem currently is mounted. Defaults to the root-device setting contained in the kernel image.

vga=*mode*

Specify the VGA text mode that should be selected when booting. The mode defaults to the VGA mode setting in the kernel image. The values are case-insensitive. They are:

ask

Prompt the user for the text mode. Pressing Enter in response to the prompt displays a list of the available modes.

extended (*or* **ext**)

Select 80x50 text mode.

normal

Select normal 80x25 text mode.

number

Use the text mode that corresponds to *number*. A list of available modes for your video card can be obtained by booting with **vga=ask** and pressing Enter.

The lilo Command

You need to run the **lilo** command to install the LILO boot loader and to update it whenever the kernel changes or to reflect changes to */etc/lilo.conf*.

The path to the **lilo** command is usually */sbin/lilo*. The syntax of the command is:

```
lilo [options]
```

Some of the options correspond to *etc/lilo.conf* keywords:

Configuration keyword	Command option
boot=*bootdev*	-b *bootdev*
compact	-c
delay=*tsecs*	-d *tsecs*
default=*label*	-D *label*
disktab=*file*	-f *file*
install=*bootsector*	-i *bootsector*
lba32	-L
linear	-l
map=*mapfile*	-m *mapfile*
fix-table	-P fix
ignore-table	-P ignore
backup=*file*	-s *file*
force-backup=*file*	-S *file*
verbose=*level*	-v

These options should be put in the configuration file whenever possible; putting them on the **lilo** command line instead of in *etc/lilo.conf* is now deprecated. The next section describes those options that can be given only on the **lilo** command line; the others were described earlier.

lilo Command Options

The following list describes **lilo** command options that are available only on the command line. Multiple options are given separately; for example:

```
% lilo -q -v
```

-C *config-file*

Specify an alternative to the default configuration file (*etc/lilo.conf*). **lilo** uses the configuration file to determine what files to map when it installs LILO.

-I *label*

Print the path to the kernel specified by *label* to standard output, or an error message if no matching label is found. For example:

```
% lilo -I linux
/boot/vmlinuz-2.0.34-0.6
```

-q List the currently mapped files. **lilo** maintains a file (*/boot/map* by default) containing the name and location of the kernel(s) to boot. Running **lilo** with this option prints the names of the files in the map file to standard output, as in this example (the asterisk indicates that **linux** is the default):

```
% lilo -q
linux     *
test
```

-r *root-directory*

> Specify that before doing anything else, **lilo** should **chroot** to the indicated directory. Used for repairing a setup from a boot floppy—you can boot from a floppy but have **lilo** use the boot files from the hard drive. For example, if you issue the following commands, **lilo** will get the files it needs from the hard drive:
>
> ```
> % mount /dev/hda2 /mnt
> % lilo -r /mnt
> ```

-R *command-line*

> Set the default command for the boot loader the next time it executes. The command executes once and then is removed by the boot loader. This option typically is used in reboot scripts, just before calling **shutdown -r**.

-t   Indicate that this is a test—do not really write a new boot sector or map file. Can be used with **-v** to find out what **lilo** would do during a normal run.

-u *device-name*

> Uninstall **lilo** by restoring the saved boot sector from */boot/boot.nnnn*, after validating it against a timestamp. *device-name* is the name of the device on which LILO is installed, such as */dev/hda2*.

-U *device-name*

> Like **-u**, but do not check the timestamp.

-V   Print the **lilo** version number.

GRUB: The Grand Unified Bootloader

Like LILO, the GRUB boot loader can load other operating systems in addition to Linux. GRUB was written by Erich Boleyn to boot operating systems on PC-based hardware, and is now developed and maintained by the GNU project. GRUB was intended to boot operating systems that conform to the Multiboot Specification, which was designed to create one booting method that would work on any conforming PC-based operating system. In addition to multiboot-conforming systems, GRUB can boot directly to Linux, FreeBSD, OpenBSD, and NetBSD. It can also boot other operating systems such as Microsoft Windows indirectly, through the use of a *chainloader*. The chainloader loads an intermediate file, and that file loads the operating system's boot loader.

GRUB provides a graphical menu interface. It also provides a command interface that is accessible both while the system is booting (the native command environment) and from the command line once Linux is running.

While LILO works perfectly well, especially if you usually boot the default image, GRUB has some advantages. The graphical menu interface shows you exactly what your choices are for booting so you don't have to remember them. It also lets you easily edit an entry on the fly, or drop down into the command interface. In addition, if you are using the menu interface and something goes wrong, GRUB automatically puts you into the command interface so you can attempt to recover and boot manually. Another advantage of GRUB is that if you install a new kernel or update the configuration file, that's all you have to do; with LILO, you also have to remember to rerun the **lilo** command to reinstall the boot loader. On the other hand, if you are used to LILO, don't need to see the prompts often, and have a stable system, LILO is quick and convenient.

A GRUB installation consists of at least two and sometimes three executables, known as *stages*. The stages are:

Stage 1

Stage 1 is the piece of GRUB that resides in the MBR or the boot sector of another partition or drive. Since the main portion of GRUB is too large to fit into the 512 bytes of a boot sector, Stage 1 is used to transfer control to the next stage, either Stage 1.5 or Stage 2.

Stage 1.5

Stage 1.5 is loaded by Stage 1 only if the hardware requires it. Stage 1.5 is file-system-specific; that is, there is a different version for each filesystem that GRUB can load. The name of the filesystem is part of the filename (*e2fs_stage1_5*, *fat_stage1_5*, etc.). Stage 1.5 loads Stage 2.

Stage 2

Stage 2 runs the main body of the GRUB code. It displays the menu, lets you select the operating system to be run, and starts the system you've chosen.

If it was compiled with netboot support, GRUB can also be used to boot over a network. We don't describe that process here; see the file *netboot/README. netboot* in the GRUB source directory for detailed information.

One of the first things to understand about GRUB is that it uses its own naming conventions. Drives are numbered starting from 0; thus, the first hard drive is hd0, the second hard drive is hd1, the first floppy drive is fd0, and so on. Partitions are also numbered from 0, and the entire name is put in parentheses. So the first partition of the first drive, */dev/hda1*, is known as (hd0,0) to GRUB. The third partition of the second drive is (hd1,2). GRUB makes no distinction between IDE drives and SCSI drives, so the first drive is hd0 whether it is IDE or SCSI.

Files are specified either by the filename or by *blocklist*, which is used to specify files such as chainloaders that aren't part of a filesystem. A filename looks like a standard Unix path specification with the GRUB device name prepended; for example:

```
(hd0,0)/grub/grub.conf
```

If the device name is omitted, the GRUB root device is assumed. The GRUB root device is the disk or partition where the kernel image is stored, set with the **root** command. See "GRUB Commands" for the command descriptions.

When you use blocklist notation, you tell GRUB which blocks on the disk contain the file you want. Each section of a file is specified as the offset on the partition where the block begins plus the number of blocks in the section. The offset starts at 0 for the first block on the partition. The syntax for blocklist notation is:

```
[device][offset]+length[,offset]+length...
```

In this case, too, the device name is optional for a file on the root device. With blocklist notation, you can also omit the offset if it is 0. A typical use of blocklist notation is when using a chainloader to boot Windows. If GRUB is installed in the MBR, you can chainload Windows by setting the root device to the partition that has the Windows boot loader, making it the active partition, and then using the **chainloader** command to read the Windows boot sector:

```
rootnoverify (hd0,0)
makeactive
chainloader +1
```

In this example, the blocklist notation (+1) does not include either the device name or the offset because we set the root device to the Windows partition, and the Windows loader begins at offset 0 of that partition.

GRUB also includes a *device map*. The device map is an ASCII file, usually */boot/grub/device.map*. Since the operating system isn't loaded yet when you use GRUB to boot Linux (or any other operating system), GRUB knows only the BIOS drive names. The purpose of the device map is to map the BIOS drives to Linux devices. For example:

```
(fd0)    /dev/fd0
(hd0)    /dev/hda
```

Installing GRUB

Installing GRUB involves two stages. First, you install the GRUB files on your system, either by compiling and installing the source tarball or from a package. That puts the GRUB files in the correct locations on your system. The second step is to install the GRUB software as your boot manager. This is the step we describe in this section.

If you installed GRUB as part of your Linux installation, the distribution's installation program took care of both stages of installing GRUB, and you'll most likely see the GRUB menu when you boot Linux. If you didn't install GRUB as part of your Linux installation, you have two choices. The easiest way to install GRUB is with the **grub-install** shell script that comes with GRUB. If **grub-install** doesn't work, or if you want to do the installation manually, you can run the **grub** command and issue the installation commands yourself.

The following sections describe how to create a GRUB boot floppy and how to install GRUB.

Creating a GRUB boot floppy

You can create a GRUB boot floppy for everyday use or to have for an emergency. The following instructions make a floppy that boots to the GRUB command line:

1. From the directory where GRUB was installed (e.g., */usr/share/grub/i386-pc*), use the **dd** command to write the file *stage1* to the floppy:

   ```
   % dd if=stage1 of=/dev/fd0 bs=512 count=1
   ```

   This command writes one block, with a blocksize of 512, from the input file *stage1* to the floppy device */dev/fd0*.

2. Now write the file *stage2* to the floppy, skipping over the first block (**seek=1**) so you don't overwrite *stage1*:

   ```
   % dd if=stage2 of=/dev/fd0 bs=512 seek=1
   ```

Put together, the process looks like this:

```
% dd if=stage1 of=/dev/fd0 bs=512 count=1
1+0 records in
1+0 records out
% dd if=stage2 of=/dev/fd0 bs=512 seek=1
254+1 records in
254+1 records out
```

The boot floppy is now ready to boot to the GRUB command line.

You can also make a boot floppy that boots to the GRUB menu:

1. Create a GRUB configuration file (*/boot/grub/grub.conf*) if you don't already have one. The configuration file is described later in "The GRUB Configuration File."

2. Create a filesystem on your floppy disk. For example:

   ```
   $ mke2fs /dev/fd0
   ```

3. Mount the floppy drive and create the directory */boot/grub*:

   ```
   % mount /mnt
   % mkdir /mnt/boot
   % mkdir /mnt/boot/grub
   ```

4. Copy the *stage1*, *stage2*, and *grub.conf* GRUB images from */boot/grub* on your Linux partition to */mnt/boot/grub*.

5. Run the **grub** command. This example assumes the command is in */sbin/grub*, but it might be in */usr/sbin/grub* on your system:

   ```
   $ /sbin/grub --batch <<EOT
   root (fd0)
   setup (fd0)
   quit
   EOT
   ```

You should now be able to boot to the GRUB menu from the floppy disk you just created.

Using grub-install

GRUB comes with a shell script, **grub-install**, which uses the GRUB shell to automate the installation. The command syntax is:

```
grub-install options install-device
```

where *install-device* is the name of the device on which you want to install GRUB, specified as either the GRUB device name (e.g., (hd0)) or the system device (e.g., */dev/hda*). For example, you might issue following the command (as root):

```
# grub-install /dev/hda
```

This command installs GRUB into the MBR of the first hard drive. The **grub-install** options are:

--force-lba
> Force GRUB to use LBA mode, to allow booting from partitions beyond cylinder 1024.

--grub-shell=_file_

    Specify that _file_ is to be used as the GRUB shell. You might want to use this option to append options to **grub**. For example:

```
% grub-install --grub-shell="grub --read-only" /dev/fd0
```

-h, --help

    Print a help message on standard output and exit.

--recheck

    Force probing of a device map. You should run **grub-install** with this option if you add or remove a disk from your system. The device map is found at _/boot/grub/device.map_.

--root-directory=_dir_

    Install GRUB images in the directory _dir_ instead of the GRUB root directory.

-v, --version

    Print the GRUB version number to standard output and exit.

Installing from the GRUB command line

To install GRUB from the native command environment, make a GRUB boot floppy as described previously. You will use that floppy to boot to the GRUB command line to do the installation. If you know which partition holds the GRUB files, you're all set. Otherwise, you can find the partition with the **find** command:

```
grub> find /boot/grub/stage1
(hd0,0)
```

Here, the files are on (hd0,0). Use that information to set the GRUB root device:

```
grub> root (hd0,0)
```

Run the **setup** command to install GRUB. To install GRUB on the MBR, run **setup** as follows:

```
grub> setup (hd0)
```

If you are going to chainload Linux and want to install GRUB on the boot sector of the Linux partition, run **setup** like this:

```
grub> setup (hd0,0)
```

The GRUB Configuration File

GRUB uses a configuration file that sets up the menu interface. The configuration file is called _grub.conf_ and is found with the other GRUB files in the _/boot/grub_ directory. _grub.conf_ is also known as _menu.lst_, and at least on some distributions (e.g., Red Hat 8), _menu.lst_ is a symbolic link to _grub.conf_.

The configuration file begins with a section containing global commands that apply to all boot entries, followed by an entry for each Linux image or other operating system that you want to be able to boot. Here is an example of a global section (a hash sign, #, begins a comment):

```
default=0                            # default to the first entry
timeout=20                           # set the timeout to 20 seconds
splashimage=(hd0,0)/grub/splash.xpm.gz  # the splash image displayed with
                                     # the menu
```

Certain GRUB commands are available only in the global section of the configuration file, for use with the GRUB menu. These commands are described in the following list. All other commands can be used either in the configuration file or on the command line and are described later in "GRUB Commands."

default *num*

Set the default menu entry to *num*. The default entry is started if the user does not make a selection before the timeout time. Menu entries are numbered from 0. If no default is specified, the first entry (0) is used as the default.

fallback *num*

Specify the entry to be used if for any reason the default entry has errors. If this command is specified and the default doesn't work, GRUB boots the fallback entry automatically instead of waiting for user input.

hiddenmenu

Specify that the menu is not to be displayed. The user can press Esc before the end of the timeout period to have the menu displayed; otherwise the default entry is booted at the end of the timeout.

timeout *time*

Specify the timeout period, in seconds. The timeout is the amount of time GRUB waits for user input before booting the default entry.

title *name*

Start a new boot entry with specified *name*.

Following the global section, the configuration file includes an entry for each boot image. An entry begins with a **title** command that specifies the text that will appear on the menu for that entry when the system boots. A typical boot entry might look like this one from a Red Hat 8.0 system:

```
title Red Hat Linux (2.4.18-14)
root (hd0,1)
kernel /vmlinuz-2.4.18-14 ro root=LABEL=/ hdc=ide-scsi
initrd /initrd-2.4.18-14.img
```

This entry provides the information GRUB needs to boot to Linux. When the menu is displayed, it will include an entry that says:

```
Red Hat Linux (2.4.18-14)
```

The GRUB root is on the second partition of the first hard drive (hd0,1). The **kernel** command specifies which Linux kernel to run and passes some parameters to the kernel, and the **initrd** command sets up an initial RAM disk.

The configuration file also provides some security features, such as the ability to set passwords and to lock certain entries so only the root user can boot them. The configuration file can be set up so that a password is required to run interactively (i.e., for editing menu entries or using the command interface) or simply to protect certain menu entries while leaving other entries available to all users. See the explanation of the **password** and **lock** commands in "GRUB Commands."

In addition to providing a password feature, GRUB provides the command **md5crypt** to encrypt passwords in MD5 format, and a corresponding Linux command, **grub-md5-crypt**. **grub-md5-crypt** is a shell script that acts as a frontend to the **grub** shell, calling **md5crypt**. Passwords encrypted either directly with **md5crypt** or with **grub-md5-crypt** can be used with the **password** command to set up a GRUB password. **grub-md5-crypt** has three possible options:

--**help**
> Print help message and exit.

--**grub-shell**=*file*
> Specify that *file* is to be used as the GRUB shell.

--**version**
> Print version information and exit.

Using the Menu Interface

The most common way to use GRUB is with the menu interface. The Stage 2 loader reads the configuration file *grub.conf* and displays the menu. If a timeout is set in the configuration file, GRUB displays a countdown at the bottom of the window showing how much time is left before it boots to the default entry. Move the cursor to an entry and press Enter to boot; or, press **e** to edit the command line for that entry, **a** to modify the kernel arguments, or **c** to go to the command-line interface to issue commands manually.

If you go to the command line, you can return to the menu at any time by pressing Esc.

Selecting **a** and **e** are similar, except that **a** displays only the **kernel** command line and lets you append options to it, while **e** displays the entire boot entry for you to edit. In either case, the available editing commands are similar to those available on the shell command line. When you are through editing, press Esc to return to the main menu. Your changes take effect for this session only; the configuration file is not permanently changed.

One common use for editing a **kernel** command is to boot to single-user mode. To do that, select **a** from the menu and append the word "single" to the end of the **kernel** command. Then press Esc to return to the menu and select the entry.

The GRUB Shell

In addition to using the command line from within the GRUB menu interface (or booting directly to the command line), you can run a GRUB shell directly from the Linux command line with the **grub** command. For the most part, using the **grub** shell is the same as running in the native command-line environment. The major difference is that the shell uses operating system calls to emulate the BIOS calls that the native environment uses. That can lead to some differences in behavior.

The syntax of the **grub** command is:

```
grub [options]
```

For example:

```
% grub --no-floppy
```

The **grub** command-line options are:

--batch

Turn on batch mode for noninteractive use. Equivalent to **grub --no-config-file --no-curses --no-pager**.

--boot-drive=_drive_

Use _drive_ as the Stage 2 boot drive, specified as a decimal, hexadecimal, or octal integer. The default is hexadecimal 0x0.

--config-file=_file_

Use _file_ as the GRUB configuration file. The default is _/boot/grub/grub.conf_.

--device-map=_file_

Use _file_ for the device map. The value of _file_ is usually _/boot/grub/device.map_.

--help

Display a help message to standard output and exit.

--hold

Wait for a debugger to attach before starting **grub**.

--install-partition=_partition_

Use _partition_ as the Stage 2 installation partition, specified as a decimal, hexadecimal, or octal number. The default is hexadecimal 0x20000.

--no-config-file

Run without reading the configuration file.

--no-curses

Don't use the **curses** interface for managing the cursor on the screen.

--no-floppy

Don't probe for a floppy drive. This option is ignored if **--device-map** is also specified.

--no-pager

Don't use the internal pager.

--preset-menu

Use a preset menu, for example if your system has no console and you need to get a serial terminal set up to see messages. To use this option, compile GRUB with the **--enable-preset-menu=**_file_ option and create a menu file. See the GRUB documentation for more information.

--probe-second-floppy

Probe the second floppy drive (which is not probed by default). This option is ignored if **--device-map** is also specified.

--read-only

Do not write to any disk drives.

--verbose

Print verbose messages.

--version

Print version information and exit.

When you run **grub**, you will see something like this:

```
GRUB  version 0.92  (640K lower / 3072K upper memory)

[ Minimal BASH-like line editing is supported.  For the first word, TAB
  lists possible command completions.  Anywhere else TAB lists the possible
  completions of a device/filename. ]

grub>
```

You can now enter commands at the "grub>" prompt. Press Tab to get a brief help message, listing all the commands:

```
grub>
Possible commands are: blocklist boot cat chainloader cmp color configfile
debug device displayapm displaymem dump embed find fstest geometry halt help
hide impsprobe initrd install ioprobe kernel lock makeactive map md5crypt
module modulenounzip pager partnew parttype password pause quit read reboot
root rootnoverify savedefault serial setkey setup terminal testload testvbe
unhide uppermem vbeprobe
```

Using Tab is a quick way to remind yourself of the commands, but it can be confusing to see them all run together and wrapping across lines. You can also run the **help** command, which lists the most frequently used commands and their syntax:

```
grub> help
blocklist FILE                          boot
cat FILE                                chainloader [--force] FILE
color NORMAL [HIGHLIGHT]                 configfile FILE
device DRIVE DEVICE                     displayapm
displaymem                              find FILENAME
geometry DRIVE [CYLINDER HEAD SECTOR [  halt [--no-apm]
help [--all] [PATTERN ...]              hide PARTITION
initrd FILE [ARG ...]                   kernel [--no-mem-option] [--type=TYPE]
makeactive                              map TO_DRIVE FROM_DRIVE
md5crypt                                module FILE [ARG ...]
modulenounzip FILE [ARG ...]            pager [FLAG]
partnew PART TYPE START LEN             parttype PART TYPE
quit                                    reboot
root [DEVICE [HDBIAS]]                   rootnoverify [DEVICE [HDBIAS]]
serial [--unit=UNIT] [--port=PORT] [--  setkey [TO_KEY FROM_KEY]
setup [--prefix=DIR] [--stage2=STAGE2_  terminal [--dumb] [--timeout=SECS] [--
testvbe MODE                            unhide PARTITION
uppermem KBYTES                         vbeprobe [MODE]
```

You can add the **--all** option to see all the commands.

To get help for a specific command, add the command name (e.g., **help read**). **help** treats the text you enter as a pattern; therefore, if you enter **help find**, you'll get help for the **find** command, but if you enter **help module**, you'll get help for both **module** and **modulenounzip**.

GRUB Commands

The following sections describe two sets of commands. Both can be used at the GRUB command line. In addition, the first set can be used in the global section of the menu, and the second can be used in individual menu entries. A few commands can be used only on the GRUB shell command line; this is noted in the command entry. The commands **default, fallback, hiddenmenu, timeout,** and **title** are available only in the configuration file, for use with the menu interface. They are described in "The GRUB Configuration File."

When running commands, if you find that you aren't sure how to complete a pathname, you can use the Tab key to find the possible completions. For example:

```
grub> blocklist (hd0,1)/grub/[Tab]
Possible files are: grub.conf splash.xpm.gz menu.lst device.map stage1
stage2 e2fs_stage1_5 fat_stage1_5 ffs_stage1_5 jfs_stage1_5 minix_stage1_5
reiserfs_stage1_5 vstafs_stage1_5 xfs_stage1_5
grub> blocklist (hd0,1)/grub/stage2
(hd0,1)33306+24,33332+231
```

Command-Line and Global Menu Commands

The commands available at the command line and in the global section of the configuration file are as follows.

Boot Methods

bootp

bootp [--with-configfile]

Initialize a network device via the Bootstrap Protocol (BOOTP). This command is available only if GRUB was compiled with netboot support. If **--with-configfile** is specified, GRUB automatically loads a configuration file specified by your BOOTP server.

color

color *normal* [*highlight*]

Specify colors for the menu. *normal* represents the color used for normal menu text, while *highlight* represents the color used to highlight the line the cursor is on. Both *normal* and *highlight* are specified as two symbolic color names, for foreground and background color, separated by a slash. For example:

```
color light-gray/blue cyan/black
```

You can prefix the foreground color with **blink-** (e.g., **blink-cyan/red**) to get a blinking foreground. The colors black, blue, green, cyan, red, magenta, brown, and light-gray can be specified for foreground or background. Additional colors that can be used only for the foreground are dark-gray, light-blue, light-green, light-cyan, light-red, light-magenta, yellow, and white.

device

device *drive file*

Specify a file to be used as a BIOS drive. This command is useful for creating a disk image and/or for fixing the drives when GRUB fails to determine them correctly. The **device** command is available only from within the **grub** shell, not from the native command line. For example:

```
grub> device (fd0) /floppy-image
grub> device (hd0) /dev/sd0
```

dhcp

dhcp [--with-configfile]

Initialize a network device via the DHCP protocol. Currently, this command is just an alias for **bootp** and is available only if GRUB was compiled with netboot support. If specified with **--with-config-file**, GRUB will fetch and load a configuration file specified by your DHCP server.

hide

hide *partition*

Hide the specified partition. This is useful when you are booting DOS or Windows and there are multiple primary partitions on one disk. Hide all but the one you want to boot. Also see **unhide**.

ifconfig

ifconfig [**--server**=*server*] [**--gateway**=*gateway*] [**--mask**=*mask*] [**--address**=*address*]

Configure a network device manually. If no options are specified, displays the current network configuration. With the server address, gateway, netmask, and IP address specified, **ifconfig** configures the device. The addresses must be in dotted decimal format (e.g., 192. 168.0.4) and the options can be specified in any order.

pager

pager [*flag*]

Enable or disable the internal pager by setting *flag* to **on** (enable) or **off** (disable).

partnew

partnew *part type from to*

Make a new primary partition, *part*, specified in GRUB syntax. *type* is the partition type, specified as a number in the range 0–0xff. *from* and *to* are the starting and ending sectors, specified as absolute numbers. Some of the common partition types are:

None	0
FAT 16, lt 32M	4
FAT 16, gt 32M	6
FAT 32	0xb
FAT 32, with LBA	0xc
WIN 95, extended	0xf
EXT2FS	0x83
Linux extended	0x85
Linux RAID	0xfd
FreeBSD	0xa5
OpenBSD	0xa6
NetBSD	0xfd

parttype

parttype *part type*

Change the type of partition *part* to *type*. The type must be a number in the range 0–0xff. See **partnew** for a list of partition types.

password

password [**--md5**] *passwd* [*file*]

Set a password for the menu interface. If used in the global section of the configuration file, outside the menu entries, GRUB prompts for a password before processing an **a**, **e**, or **c** entered by the user. Once the password *passwd* has been entered, if no *file* was specified, GRUB allows the user to proceed. Otherwise, GRUB loads the file as a new configuration file and restarts Stage 2. If **password** appears in an individual menu entry, GRUB prompts for the password before continuing. Specify **--md5** to tell GRUB that the password was encrypted with the **md5crypt** command.

rarp

rarp

Initialize a network device via the Reverse Address Resolution Protocol (RARP). This command is available only if GRUB was compiled with netboot support. The use of RARP is deprecated.

serial

serial [*options*]

Initialize a serial device. The serial port is not used for communication unless **terminal** is also specified. This command is available only if GRUB was compiled with serial support.

Options

--device=*device*
> Specify the tty device to be used in the host operating system. This option can be used only in the **grub** shell.

--parity=*parity*
> Specify the parity. The possible values are **no**, **odd**, and **even**; the default is **no**.

--port=*port*
> Specify the I/O port. The value of *port* overrides any value specified for **--unit**.

--speed=*speed*
> Specify the transmission speed (default is 9600).

--stop=*num*
> Specify the number of stop bits. The value of *num* is either 1 or 2 (default is 1).

--unit=*num*
> Specify the serial port to use. The value of *num* is a number in the range 0–3; the default is 0, corresponding to COM1.

--word=*num*
> Specify the number of data bits. The value of *num* is a number in the range 5–8 (default is 8).

setkey

setkey [`to-key from-key`]

Configure the keyboard map for GRUB by mapping the key *from-key* to the key *to-key*. With no mappings specified, reset the keyboard map. **setkey** is useful for setting up international keyboards. Possible key values are letters, digits, one of the strings "alt", "backspace", "capslock", "control", "delete", "enter", "escape", "F*n*" (where *n* is one of the function key numbers), "shift", "tab", or one of the strings in the Key Value columns of the following table:

Key Value	Character	Key Value	Character
ampersand	&	asterisk	*
at	@	backquote	'
backslash	\	bar	|
braceleft	{	braceright	}
bracketleft	[	bracketright	]
caret	^	colon	:
comma	,	dollar	$
doublequote	"	equal	=
exclam	!	greater	>
less	<	minus	-
numbersign	#	parenleft	(
parenright	)	percent	%
period	.	plus	+
question	?	quote	'
semicolon	;	slash	/
space		tilde	~
underscore	_		

splashimage

splashimage *file*

Use the image in *file* as the background (splash) image. The file should be a gzipped *.xpm* (X pixmap) file, created with a 14-color palette at 640×480 resolution and specified with standard GRUB device syntax:

```
splashimage=(hd0,0)/grub/splash.xpm.gz
```

Programs that you can use to create *.xpm* files include the GIMP, **xv**, and **xpaint**.

terminal

terminal [`options`] [`console`] [`serial`]

Specify a terminal for user interaction. This command is available only if GRUB was compiled with serial support. If both **console** and **serial** are specified, GRUB uses the first terminal where a key is pressed, or the first after the timeout has expired. If neither is specified, GRUB displays the current setting.

Options

--dumb

> The terminal is a dumb terminal; if this option is not specified, the terminal is assumed to be VT100-compatible.

--lines=*num*

> The terminal has *num* lines. The default is 24.

--silent

> Suppress the prompt to hit any key (useful if your system does not have a terminal).

--timeout=*secs*

> Specify the timeout in seconds.

---

tftpserver

tftpserver *ipaddress*

Specify a TFTP server, overriding the address returned by a BOOTP, DHCP, or RARP server. The IP address must be specified in dotted decimal format. This command is available only if GRUB was compiled with netboot support. This command is deprecated; use **ifconfig** instead.

---

unhide

unhide *partition*

Unhide the specified partition. This is useful when booting DOS or Windows and there are multiple primary partitions on one disk. You can **unhide** the partition you want to boot and **hide** the others.

Command-Line and Menu Entry Commands

The commands available at the command line and in the individual menu entries of the configuration file are as follows.

---

blocklist

blocklist *file*

Print the specified file in blocklist notation, where *file* is an absolute pathname or a blocklist. For example:

```
grub> blocklist (hd0,1)/grub/grub.conf
(hd0,1)33746+2
```

---

boot

boot

Boot the operating system or chainloader that has been loaded. You need to run this command only if you are in the interactive command-line mode.

---

cat

cat *file*

Display the contents of the specified file.

---

chainloader

chainloader [--force] *file*

Load *file* as a chainloader. You can use blocklist notation to specifiy the first sector of the current partition with +1. If **--force** is specified, the file is loaded forcibly.

cmp

cmp *file1 file2*

Compare the two files *file1* and *file2*. Report differences by printing nothing if the files are identical, the sizes if they are different, or the bytes at an offset if they differ at that offset.

configfile

configfile *file*

Load *file* as the configuration file.

debug

debug

Toggle debug mode, which prints extra messages to show disk activity. The default debug mode is off.

displayapm

displayapm

Display Advanced Power Management (APM) BIOS information.

displaymem

displaymem

Display the system address space map of the machine, including all regions of physical RAM installed. For example:

```
grub> displaymem
EISA Memory BIOS Interface is present
Address Map BIOS Interface is present
Lower memory: 640K, Upper memory (to first chipset hole):
3072K
[Address Range Descriptor entries immediately follow
(values are 64-bit)]
    Usable RAM:  Base Address:  0x0 X 4GB + 0x0,
      Length:    0x0 X 4GB + 0xa0000 bytes
    Reserved:  Base Address:  0x0 X 4GB + 0xa0000,
      Length:    0x0 X 4GB + 0x60000 bytes
    Usable RAM:  Base Address:  0x0 X 4GB + 0x100000,
      Length:    0x0 X 4GB + 0x300000 bytes
```

dump

dump *from to*

Dump the contents of one file into another. The file you're dumping *from* is a GRUB file, and the file you're dumping *to* is an operating system file.

embed

embed *stage1.5 device*

Embed the specified Stage 1.5 file in the sectors following the MBR if *device* is a drive, or in the boot loader area if it is an FFS (Berkeley

Fast File System) partition (or, in the future, a ReiserFS partition). If successful, print the number of sectors the Stage 1.5 file occupies. You don't usually need to run this command directly.

find

find *file*

Search all partitions for the specified file and print the list of devices where it was found. The filename specified should be an absolute filename such as */boot/grub/stage1* or a blocklist.

fstest

fstest

Toggle the filesystem test mode, which prints data for device reads and the values being sent to the low-level routines. The **install** and **testload** commands turn off filesystem test mode. The test output is in the following format:

    <partition-offset-sector, byte-offset, byte-length>

for high-level reads in a partition, and:

    [disk-offset-sector]

for low-level sector requests from the disk.

geometry

geometry *drive* [*cylinder head sector* [*total_sector*]]

Print geometry information for *drive*. From the GRUB shell, you can specify the number of cylinders, heads, sectors, and total sectors to set the drive's geometry. If *total_sector* is omitted, it is calculated from the other values.

halt

halt [--no-apm]

Shut down the computer. The computer is halted with an APM BIOS call unless the option **--noapm** is specified.

help

help [--all] [*patterns*]

Provide help for built-in commands. With no options, show the command and any options or parameters for the most common commands. With **--all**, show the same information for all possible commands. If you specify a pattern (i.e., a partial command name) or a full command name, a more complete description of the command or commands matching the pattern is displayed.

impsprobe

impsprobe

Probe the Intel Multiprocessor Specification 1.1 or 1.4 configuration table and boot the CPUs that are found into a tight loop. This command can be used only in Stage 2.

initrd

initrd *file* [*args*]

Load an initial ramdisk *file* and pass any arguments.

install

install [*options*] *stage1_file* [**d**] *dest_dev* *stage2_file* [*addr*] [**p**]
[*config_file*] [*real_config_file*]

Perform a full GRUB install. See also the **setup** command, which
acts as a frontend to **install** and is easier to use. The Stage 2 or
Stage 1.5 file (both referred to as *stage2_file* here because they are
loaded the same way) must be in its final install location (e.g., in
the */boot/grub* directory). **install** loads and validates *stage1_file*,
installs a blocklist in the Stage 1 file for loading *stage2_file* as Stage
2 or Stage 1.5, and writes the completed Stage 1 file to the first
block of the device *dest_dev*.

Options
--force-lba

If the BIOS has LBA support but might return the incorrect
LBA bitmap (which sometimes happens), **--force-lba** forces
install to ignore the incorrect bitmap.

--stage2=os_stage2_file

This option is required to specify the operating system name
of the Stage 2 file if the filesystem where it is located cannot be
unmounted.

Parameters
addr

Specify the address at which Stage 1 is to load Stage 2 or Stage
1.5. The possible values are 0x8000 for Stage 2 and 0x2000 for
Stage 1.5. If omitted, GRUB determines the address
automatically.

config_file

Specify the location of the configuration file for Stage 2.

d   Tell Stage 1 to look for the actual disk on which *stage2_file*
was installed if it's not on the boot drive.

dest_dev

Specify the destination device. The final Stage 1 file is written
to this device.

p   If present, the partition where *stage2_file* is located is written
into the first block of Stage 2.

real_config_file

If *stage2_file* is really a Stage 1.5 file, *real_config_file* specifies
the real configuration file name and is written into the Stage 2
configuration file.

stage1_file

Specify the Stage 1 file to be written.

stage2_file

Specify the file that Stage 1 is to load for Stage 2.

ioprobe

`ioprobe` *drive*

Probe the I/O ports used for *drive* and write the results to standard output.

kernel

`kernel [--non-mem-option]` *file* `[...]`

Load the kernel image from *file*. Any text following *file* is passed on as the kernel command line. After running this command, you must reload any modules. The option **--type** specifies the kernel type and is required only for loading a NetBSD ELF kernel; GRUB automatically determines other types. The possible values of type are **linux**, **biglinux**, **freebsd**, **multiboot**, **netbsd**, and **openbsd**. For Linux, **--no-mem-option** tells GRUB not to pass the **mem=** option to the kernel.

lock

`lock`

Lock the entry until a valid password is entered. This is used in a menu entry immediately after **title** to prevent nonroot users from executing the entry. This command is most useful in conjunction with the **password** command.

makeactive

`makeactive`

Set the active partition on the root disk to GRUB's root device. Use only on primary PC hard disk partitions.

map

`map` *to from*

Map the *from* drive to the *to* drive. You need to do this when chain-loading an operating system such as Windows, if it is not on the first drive. For example, if Windows is on (hd1):

```
grub> map (hd0) (hd1)
grub> map (hd1) (hd0)
```

This swaps the mappings of the first and second hard drives, tricking Windows into thinking it's on the first drive so it can boot.

md5crypt

`md5crypt`

Prompt for a password and encrypt it in MD5 format for use with the **password** command.

module

`module` *file* `[...]`

Load the boot module *file* for a multiboot format boot image. Anything after the filename is passed as the module command line.

modulenounzip

`modulenounzip` *files*

Like **module**, except that automatic decompression is disabled.

pause

pause *messages*

Print the specified message and wait for a key to be pressed before continuing.

quit

quit

Used only from within the **grub** shell to exit from the shell. In the native command environment, use **reboot** instead, to reboot the computer.

read

read *addr*

Read a 32-bit value from memory at the specified address and display it in hex.

reboot

reboot

Reboot the system.

root

root *device* [*hdbias*]

Set the root device to the specified *device* and attempt to mount it to get the partition size (and some additional information for booting BSD kernels). If you are booting a BSD kernel, you can specify *hdbias* to tell the kernel how many BIOS drive numbers are before the current one.

rootnoverify

rootnoverify *device* [*hdbias*]

Similar to **root**, but don't attempt to mount the partition. Used when you are booting a non-GRUB-readable partition such as Windows.

savedefault

savedefault

Save the current menu entry as the default. GRUB will default to that entry the next time you boot the system.

setup

setup [*options*] *install_device* [*image_device*]

Set up installation of GRUB and run the **install** command to actually install GRUB onto the device *install_device*. Find the GRUB images on *image_device* if it is specified, otherwise use the current root device as set by the **root** command. If *install_device* is a hard disk, embed a Stage 1.5 file in the disk if possible.

Options

--force-lba

Force **install** to use LBA mode. Specify this option if your BIOS supports LBA mode but you find that GRUB isn't working in LBA mode without it.

--prefix=*dir*

> Specify the directory where the GRUB images are located. If not specified, GRUB searches for them in */boot/grub* and */grub*.

--stage2=*os_stage2_file*

> Passed to **install** to tell GRUB the operating system name of the Stage 2 file.

---

testload

testload *file*

Read the contents of a *file* in different ways and compare the results to test the filesystem code. If no errors are reported and the final output reports an equal value for the reported variables **i** and **filepos**, then the filesystem is consistent and you can try loading a kernel.

---

testvbe

testvbe *mode*

For a VBE (VESA BIOS Extension) BIOS, test the specified VESA BIOS extension mode. You should see an animation loop, which you can cancel by pressing any key.

---

uppermem

uppermem *kbytes*

Tell GRUB to assume that only the specified number of kilobytes of upper memory are installed. You should need to use this command only for old systems where not all the memory may be recognized.

---

vbeprobe

vbeprobe [*mode*]

For a VBE BIOS, probe VESA BIOS extension information. If *mode* is specified, the output shows only information for that mode; otherwise, all available VBE modes are listed.

Loadlin: Booting from MS-DOS

Loadlin is a Linux boot loader that you run from within a bootable MS-DOS partition. The system must be in real DOS mode, not in an MS-DOS window running under Windows. No installation is required; you simply copy the executable file *loadlin.exe* from the Loadlin distribution to your MS-DOS partition.* You also need a compressed Linux kernel (e.g., *vmlinuz*), which you can load from a floppy, from the DOS partition, or from a RAM disk. For example:

```
C:> loadlin c:\vmlinuz root=/dev/hda2
```

---

* If Loadlin didn't come with your Linux distribution, you can download it from any of the major Linux sites, such as the Ibiblio site at *http://www.ibiblio.org/pub/Linux*.

This example loads the Linux kernel image *vmlinuz*, passing it the boot parameter **root=/dev/hda2**, telling the kernel that the Linux root partition is */dev/hda2*. (If you are using a RAM disk, see "Boot-Time Kernel Options" later in this chapter.)

If you want to use Loadlin with Windows 95/98/ME, see the Loadlin User Guide and the Loadlin+Win95/98/ME mini-HOWTO.

Loadlin can be run directly from the DOS prompt, as in the example, or it can be invoked from CONFIG.SYS or AUTOEXEC.BAT. Like LILO, Loadlin takes both options that direct its operation and options (also referred to as *parameters*) that it passes to the kernel.

There are two ways to specify options: in a DOS file or on the Loadlin command line.

Using a Parameter File

You can store Loadlin options in a file and invoke the bootloader as follows:

```
LOADLIN @params
```

where *params* is a DOS file that contains the options you want Loadlin to run with. The Loadlin distribution comes with a sample parameter file, *test.par*, that you can use as a basis for creating your own. Each line in a parameter file contains one parameter. If you want to specify the name of the Linux kernel to use (the **image=** parameter), it must be the first entry in the file. Comments start with a hash sign (#). The entries in the parameter file can be overridden or appended on the command line. For example, to override the value of **vga** set in the parameter file:

```
C:> LOADLIN @myparam vga=normal
```

Putting Parameters on the Command Line

Another way to run Loadlin is to include options on the command line. The syntax is:

```
LOADLIN [zimage_file] [options] [boot_params]
```

zimage_file is the name of a Linux kernel to run, followed by a list of Loadlin options and/or boot options. Specifying **LOADLIN** with no parameters gives a help message listing the Loadlin options and some of the possible kernel boot options. The message is long enough that you probably want to pipe the output through a pager like **more**:

```
C:> LOADLIN | more
```

The Loadlin options are:

-clone
  Bypass certain checks. Read the LOADLIN User Guide that comes with the Loadlin distribution before using.

-d *file*
  Debug mode. Like **-t**, but sends output to *file* as well as to standard output.

-dskreset

Cause disks to be reset after loading but before booting Linux.

-noheap

For use by serious Linux hackers only; disable use of the setup heap.

-t   Test mode. Go through the loading process but don't actually start Linux. Also sets **-v**.

-txmode

Set the screen to text mode (80x25) on startup.

-v   Verbose. Print parameter and configuration information to standard output.

-wait=*nn*

After loading, wait *nn* (DOS) ticks before booting Linux.

In addition to these Loadlin options, the help message prints a number of kernel boot options that you can specify. The boot options that it prints are only a few of the many available boot options; see the BootPrompt HOWTO for a more complete list.

Dual-Booting Linux and Windows NT/2000/XP

As mentioned earlier, when you run Windows NT, its boot loader expects to be the one in charge; therefore, the standard way to dual-boot Windows NT and Linux is to add Linux as an option on the NT boot menu. This section describes how to do that. The information provided here also applies to Windows 2000 and Windows XP, which use the NT loader.

To set up dual booting with the NT loader, you need to provide the loader with a copy of the Linux boot sector. We'll describe how to do that on a computer running Windows NT with an NTFS filesystem (note that Windows NT should be installed on your system already). See the NT OS Loader+Linux mini-HOWTO for more information and other alternatives.

You should have a Linux boot floppy or CD available so that if necessary you can boot Linux before the NT boot loader has been modified. You also should have a DOS-formatted floppy to transfer the boot sector to the Windows NT partition. If you are running LILO and it is already installed, you may need to modify */etc/lilo. conf* as described later. Otherwise, install LILO or GRUB to the boot sector of the Linux partition; once the Linux boot manager is installed and you have a configuration file, you can set up the system for dual booting.

The following instructions assume your Linux partition is on */dev/hda2*. If Linux is on another partition in your system, be sure to replace */dev/hda2* in the following examples with the correct partition. The instructions also assume that you have a floppy drive to make a diskette for transferring the boot sector to your NTFS filesystem. If you don't have a floppy drive, you will have to use some other means of doing the transfer. If you have an NT FAT partition, you can mount that on Linux and transfer the file there. Other possibilities include putting it on a CD, transferring it over a network to another system while you reboot to NT, or even emailing it to yourself and reading it from the NT side.

1. If you are running LILO, specify the Linux root partition as your boot device in */etc/lilo.conf*. If you are editing */etc/lilo.conf* manually, your entry will look like this:

    ```
    boot=/dev/hda2
    ```

    and will be the same as the **root=** entry.

    If you are running GRUB, make sure your configuration file, */boot/grub/grub.conf*, includes a menu entry for booting Linux. For example:

    ```
    title Red Hat Linux (2.4.18-14)
    root (hd0,1)
    kernel /vmlinuz-2.4.18-14 ro root=LABEL=/ hdc=ide-scsi
    initrd /initrd-2.4.18-14.img
    ```

    You can then skip to Step 3.

2. Run the **lilo** command to install LILO on the Linux root partition.

3. At this point, if you need to reboot Linux, you'll have to use the boot floppy or CD because the NT loader hasn't been set up yet to boot Linux.

4. From Linux, run the **dd** command to make a copy of the Linux boot sector:

    ```
    % dd if=/dev/hda2 of=/bootsect.lnx bs=512 count=1
    ```

    This command copies one block, with a blocksize of 512 bytes, from the input file */dev/hda2* to the output file */bootsect.lnx*. Note that if you are running GRUB, the boot sector is actually the *stage1* file. (The output filename can be whatever makes sense to you; it doesn't have to be *bootsect.lnx*.)

5. Copy *bootsect.lnx* to a DOS-formatted floppy disk if that is how you are going to transfer it to NT:

    ```
    % mount -t msdos /dev/fd0 /mnt
    % cp /bootsect.lnx /mnt
    % umount /mnt
    ```

6. Reboot the system to Windows NT and copy the boot sector from the floppy disk to the hard disk. You can drag and drop the file to the hard drive, or use the command line to copy the file as in the following example:

    ```
    C:> copy a:\bootsect.lnx c:\bootsect.lnx
    ```

    It doesn't matter where on the hard drive you put the file because you'll tell the NT loader where to find it in Step 8.

7. Modify the attributes of the file *boot.ini*** to remove the system and read-only attributes so you can edit it:

    ```
    C:> attrib -s -r c:\boot.ini
    ```

8. Edit *boot.ini* with a text editor to add the line:

    ```
    C:\bootsect.lnx="Linux"
    ```

    This line adds Linux to the boot menu and tells the Windows NT boot loader where to find the Linux boot sector. You can insert the line anywhere in the **[operating systems]** section of the file. Its position in the file determines where it will show up on the boot menu when you reboot your computer.

---

* *boot.ini* is the Windows NT counterpart to */etc/lilo.conf*. It defines what operating systems the NT loader can boot.

Adding it at the end, for example, results in a *boot.ini* file that looks something like this (the **multi(0)** entries are wrapped to fit in the margins of this page):

```
[boot loader]
timeout=30
default=multi(0)disk(0)rdisk(0)partition(1)\WINNT
[operating systems]
multi(0)disk(0)rdisk(0)partition(1)\WINNT="Windows NT Server Version 4.
00"
multi(0)disk(0)rdisk(0)partition(1)\WINNT="Windows NT Server Version 4.
00 [VGA mode]" /basevideo /sos
C:\bootsect.lnx="Linux"
```

If you want Linux to be the default operating system, modify the **default=** line:

```
default=C:\bootsect.lnx
```

9. Rerun **attrib** to restore the system and read-only attributes:

```
C:> attrib +s +r c:\boot.ini
```

Now you can shut down Windows NT and reboot. NT will prompt you with a menu that looks something like this:

```
OS Loader V4.00

Please select the operating system to start:

Windows NT Workstation Version 4.00
Windows NT Workstation Version 4.00 [VGA mode]
Linux
```

Select Linux, and the NT loader will read the Linux boot sector and transfer control to LILO or GRUB on the Linux partition.

If you are using LILO and you later modify */etc/lilo.conf* or rebuild the kernel, you need to rerun the **lilo** command, create a new *bootsect.lnx* file, and replace the version of *bootsect.lnx* on the Windows NT partition with the new version. In other words, you need to rerun Steps 2–6.

 If you have any problems or you simply want to remove LILO or GRUB later, you can reverse the installation procedure: boot to Windows NT, change the system and read-only attributes on *boot.ini*, re-edit *boot.ini* to remove the Linux entry, save the file, restore the system and read-only attributes, and remove the Linux boot sector from the NT partition.

Boot-Time Kernel Options

The earlier sections of this chapter described some of the options you can specify when you boot Linux. There are many more options that can be specified. This section touches on the ways to pass options to the kernel and then describes some of the kinds of parameters you might want to use. The parameters in this section affect the kernel and therefore apply regardless of which boot loader you use.

As always with Unix systems, there are a number of choices for the boot process itself. If you are using Loadlin, you can pass parameters to the kernel on the command line or in a file.

If LILO is your boot loader, you can add to or override the parameters specified in /etc/lilo.conf during the boot process as follows:

- If **prompt** is set in /etc/lilo.conf, LILO always presents the boot prompt and waits for input. At the prompt, you can choose the operating system to be booted. If you choose Linux, you also can specify parameters.

- If **prompt** isn't set, press Control, Shift, or Alt when the word "LILO" appears. The boot prompt will then appear. You also can press the Scroll Lock key before LILO is printed and not have to wait poised over the keyboard for the right moment.

- At the boot prompt, specify the system you want to boot or press Tab to get a list of the available choices. You then can enter the name of the image to boot. For example:

    ```
    LILO boot: <press Tab>
    linux    test    dos
    boot: linux
    ```

    You also can add boot command options:

    ```
    boot: linux single
    ```

- If you don't provide any input, LILO waits the amount of time specified in the **delay** parameter and then boots the default operating system with the default parameters as set in /etc/lilo.conf.

If you are using GRUB, you can pass parameters to the kernel on the **kernel** command line, either in the configuration file or from the command-line interface. If you are booting from the GRUB menu, you can edit or add parameters by entering **e** or **a** when the menu appears.

Some of the boot parameters have been mentioned earlier. Many of the others are hardware-specific and are too numerous to mention here. For a complete list of parameters and a discussion of the booting process, see the BootPrompt HOWTO. Some of the parameters not shown earlier that you might find useful are listed next; many more are covered in the HOWTO. Most of the following parameters are used to provide information or instructions to the kernel, rather than to LILO or GRUB.

debug
Print all kernel messages to the console.

hd=cylinders,heads,sectors
Specify the hard drive geometry to the kernel. Useful if Linux has trouble recognizing the geometry of your drive, especially if it's an IDE drive with more than 1024 cylinders.

load_ramdisk=n
Tell the kernel whether to load a RAM disk image for use during Linux installation. Values of n are:

0   Don't try to load the image. This is the default.

1   Load the image from a floppy disk to the RAM disk.

mem=*size*

Specify the amount of system memory installed. Useful if your BIOS reports memory only up to 64 MB and your system has more memory installed. Specify as a number with **M** or **k** (case-insensitive) appended:

```
mem=128M
```

Because **mem** would have to be included on the command line for every boot, it often is specified on a command line saved with **lock** or with **append** to be added to the parameters passed to the kernel.

noinitrd

When set, disable the two-stage boot and preserve the contents of */dev/initrd* so the data is available after the kernel has booted. */dev/initrd* can be read only once, and then its contents are returned to the system.

number

Start Linux at the runlevel specified by *number*. A runlevel is an operating state that the system can be booted to, such as a multiuser system or a system configuration running the X Window System. A runlevel is generally one of the numbers from 1 to 6; the default usually is 3. The runlevels and their corresponding states are defined in the file */etc/inittab*. See the manpage for */etc/inittab* for more information.

ro

Mount the root filesystem read-only. Used for doing system maintenance, such as checking the filesystem integrity, when you don't want anything written to the filesystem.

rw

Mount the root filesystem read/write. If neither **ro** nor **rw** is specified, the default value (usually **rw**) stored in the kernel image is used.

single

Start Linux in single-user mode. This option is used for system administration and recovery. It gives you a root prompt as soon as the system boots, with minimal initialization. No other logins are allowed.

initrd: Using a RAM Disk

Modern Linux distributions use a modular kernel, which allows modules to be added without requiring that the kernel be rebuilt. If your root filesystem is on a device whose driver is a module (as is frequently true of SCSI disks), you can use the **initrd** facility, which provides a two-stage boot process, to first set up a temporary root filesystem in a RAM disk containing the modules you need to add (e.g., the SCSI driver) and then load the modules and mount the real root filesystem. The RAM disk containing the temporary filesystem is the special device file */dev/initrd*.

Similarly, you need to use a RAM disk if your root partition uses the ext3 filesystem and ext3 was not compiled into the kernel image. In that case, the ext3 module must be loaded with **initrd**.

Before you can use **initrd**, both RAM disk support (**CONFIG_BLK_DEV_RAM=y**) and initial RAM disk support (**CONFIG_BLK_DEV_INITRD=y**) must be compiled into the Linux kernel. Then you need to prepare the normal root file-system and create the RAM disk image. Your Linux distribution may have utilities to do some of the setup for you; for example, the Red Hat distribution comes with the **mkinitrd** command, which builds the **initrd** image. For detailed information, see the **initrd** manpage and the file *initrd.txt* (the path may vary, but is usually something like */usr/src/linux/Documentation/initrd.txt*).

Once your Linux system has been set up for **initrd**, you can do one of the following, depending on which boot loader you are using:

- If you are using LILO, add the **initrd** option to the appropriate image section:

  ```
  image=/vmlinuz
     initrd=/boot/initrd  # The file to load as the contents of /dev/initrd
     ...
  ```

  Run the **/sbin/lilo** command, and you can reboot with **initrd**.

- If you are using GRUB, add the **initrd** option to the kernel line of the configuration file boot entry, or to the **kernel** command if you are booting from the command-line interface:

  ```
  kernel /vmlinuz-2.4.18-14 ro root=LABEL=/ hdc=ide-scsi
  initrd /initrd-2.4.18-14.img
  ```

- If you are using Loadlin, add the **initrd** option to the command line:

  ```
  loadlin c:\linux\vmlinuz initrd=c:\linux\initrd
  ```

5

Red Hat and Debian Package Managers

This chapter describes the two major Linux packaging systems: the Red Hat Package Manager (RPM) and the Debian GNU/Linux Package Manager.

When you install applications on your Linux system, most often you'll find a binary or a source package containing the application you want, instead of (or in addition to) a *.tar.gz* file. A package is a file containing the files necessary to install an application. However, while the package contains the files you need for installation, the application might require the presence of other files or packages that are not included, such as particular libraries (and even specific versions of the libraries), to actually be able to run. Such requirements are known as *dependencies*.

Package management systems offer many benefits. As a user, you may want to query the package database to find out what packages are installed on the system and their versions. As a system administrator, you need tools to install and manage the packages on your system. And if you are a developer, you need to know how to build a package for distribution.

Among other things, package managers do the following:

- Provide tools for installing, updating, removing, and managing the software on your system.
- Allow you to install new or upgraded software directly across a network.
- Tell you what software package a particular file belongs to or what files a package contains.
- Maintain a database of packages on the system and their state, so you can find out what packages or versions are installed on your system.
- Provide dependency checking, so you don't mess up your system with incompatible software.
- Provide PGP, MD5, or other signature verification tools.
- Provide tools for building packages.

Any user can list or query packages. However, installing, upgrading, or removing packages generally requires superuser privileges. This is because the packages normally are installed in systemwide directories that are writable only by root. Sometimes you can specify an alternate directory to install a package into your home directory or into a project directory where you have write permission.

Both RPM and the Debian Package Manager back up old files before installing an updated package. Not only does this let you go back if there is a problem, but also ensures that you don't lose your changes (to configuration files, for example).

The Red Hat Package Manager

The Red Hat Package Manager (RPM) is a freely available packaging system for software distribution and installation. In addition to Red Hat and Red Hat–based distributions, both SuSE and Caldera are among the Linux distributions that use RPM.

Using RPM is straightforward. A single command, **rpm**, has options to perform all package management functions except building packages.* For example, to find out if the Emacs editor is installed on your system, you could say:

```
% rpm -q emacs
emacs-21.2-18
```

The **rpmbuild** command is used to build both binary and source packages.

The rpm Command

RPM packages are built, installed, and queried with the **rpm** command. RPM package names usually end with a *.rpm* extension. **rpm** has a set of modes, each with its own options. The format of the **rpm** command is:

```
rpm [options] [packages]
```

With a few exceptions, as noted in the lists of options that follow, the first option specifies the **rpm** mode (install, query, update, etc.), and any remaining options affect that mode.

Options that refer to packages are sometimes specified as *package-name* and sometimes as *package-file*. The package name is the name of the program or application, such as **gif2png**. The package file is the name of the RPM file, such as *gif2png-2.4.6-1.i386.rpm*.

RPM provides a configuration file for specifying frequently used options. The default global configuration is usually */usr/lib/rpm/rpmrc*, the local system configuration file is */etc/rpmrc*, and users can set up their own *$HOME/.rpmrc* files. You can use the **--showrc** option to show the values RPM will use for all the options that may be set in an *rpmrc* file:

```
rpm --showrc
```

---

* In older versions of RPM, the build options were part of the **rpm** command.

The **rpm** command includes FTP and HTTP clients, so you can specify an *ftp://* or *http://* URL to install or query a package across the Internet. You can use an FTP or HTTP URL wherever *package-file* is specified in the commands presented here.

Any user can query the RPM database. Most of the other functions require super-user privileges.

General options

The following options can be used with all modes:

--dbpath *path*
    Use *path* as the path to the RPM database instead of the default */var/lib/rpm*.

-?, --help
    Print a long usage message (running **rpm** with no options gives a shorter usage message).

--pipe *command*
    Pipe the **rpm** output to *command*.

--quiet
    Display only error messages.

--rcfile *filelist*
    Get configuration from the files in the colon-separated *filelist*. If **--rcfile** is specified, there must be at least one file in the list and the file must exist. *filelist* defaults to */var/lib/rpm/rpmrc:/usr/lib/rpm/redhat/rpmrc:~/.rpmrc*.

--root *dir*
    Perform all operations within the directory tree rooted at *dir*.

-v   Verbose. Print progress messages.

--version
    Print the version number of **rpm**.

-vv Print debugging information.

Install, upgrade, and freshen options

Use the **install** command to install or upgrade an RPM package. The **install** syntax is:

```
rpm -i [install-options] package_file ...
rpm --install [install-options] package_file ...
```

To install a new version of a package and remove an existing version at the same time, use the **upgrade** command instead:

```
rpm -U [install-options] package_file ...
rpm --upgrade [install-options] package_file ...
```

If the package doesn't already exist on the system, **-U** acts like **-i** and installs it. To prevent that behavior, you can **freshen** a package instead; in that case, **rpm** upgrades the package only if an earlier version is already installed. The **freshen** syntax is:

```
rpm -F [install-options] package_file ...
rpm --freshen [install-options] package_file ...
```

package-file can be specified as an FTP or HTTP URL to download the file before installing it. See "FTP/HTTP options."

The installation and upgrade options are:

--aid
> If **rpm** suggests additional packages, add them to the list of package files.

--allfiles
> Install or upgrade all files.

--badreloc
> Used with **--relocate** to force relocation even if the package is not relocatable.

--excludedocs
> Don't install any documentation files.

--excludepath *path*
> Don't install any file whose filename begins with *path*.

--force
> Force the installation. Equivalent to using all of **--replacepkgs**, **--replacefiles**, and **--oldpackage**.

-h, --hash
> Print 50 hash marks as the package archive is unpacked. Use with **-v** or **--verbose** for a nicer display.

--ignorearch
> Install even if the binary package is intended for a different architecture.

--ignoreos
> Install binary package even if the operating systems don't match.

--ignoresize
> Don't check disk space availability before installing.

--includedocs
> Install documentation files. This is needed only if **excludedocs: 1** is specified in an *rpmrc* file.

--justdb
> Update the database only; don't change any files.

--nodeps
> Don't check whether this package depends on the presence of other packages.

--nodigest
> Don't verify package or header digests.

--noorder
> Don't reorder packages to satisfy dependencies before installing.

--nopost
> Don't execute any post-install script.

--nopostun
> Don't execute any post-uninstall script.

--nopre
> Don't execute any pre-install script.

--nopreun

    Don't execute any pre-uninstall script.

--noscripts

    Don't execute any pre-install or post-install scripts. Equivalent to specifying all of **--nopre, --nopost, --nopreun**, and **--nopostun**.

--nosignature

    Don't verify package or header signatures.

--nosuggest

    Don't suggest packages that provide a missing dependency.

--notriggerin

    Don't execute any install trigger scriptlet.

--notriggerun

    Don't execute any uninstall trigger scriptlet.

--notriggerpostun

    Don't execute any post-uninstall trigger scriptlet.

--notriggers

    Don't execute any scripts triggered by package installation.

--oldpackage

    Allow an upgrade to replace a newer package with an older one.

--percent

    Print percent-completion messages as files are unpacked. Useful for running **rpm** from other tools.

--prefix *path*

    Set the installation prefix to *path* for relocatable binary packages.

--relocate *oldpath=newpath*

    For relocatable binary files, change all file paths from *oldpath* to *newpath*. Can be specified more than once to relocate multiple paths.

--repackage

    Repackage the package files before erasing. Rename the package as specified by the macro **%_repackage_name_fmt** and save it in the directory specified by the macro **%_repackage_dir** (by default */var/tmp*).

--replacefiles

    Install the packages even if they replace files from other installed packages.

--replacepkgs

    Install the packages even if some of them are already installed.

--test

    Go through the installation to see what it would do, but don't actually install the package. This option lets you test for problems before doing the installation.

Query options

The syntax for the **query** command is:

```
rpm -q [package-options] [information-options]
rpm --query [package-options] [information-options]
```

There are two subsets of query options. *Package selection* options determine what packages to query, and *information selection* options determine what information to provide.

Package selection options

package_name
> Query the installed package *package_name*.

-a, --all
> Query all installed packages.

-f *file,* **--file** *file*
> Find out what package owns *file*.

--fileid *md5*
> Query package with the specified MD5 digest.

-g *group,* **--group** *group*
> Find out what packages have group *group*.

--hdrid *sha1*
> Query package with the specified SHA1 digest in the package header.

-p *package_file,* **--package** *package_file*
> Query the uninstalled package *package_file*, which can be a URL. If *package_file* is not a binary package, it is treated as a text file containing a package manifest, with each line of the manifest containing a path or one or more whitespace-separated glob expressions to be expanded to paths. These paths are then used instead of *package_file* as the query arguments. The manifest can contain comments that begin with a hash mark (#).

--pkgid *md5*
> Query the package with a package identifier that is the given MD5 digest of the combined header and contents.

--querybynumber *num*
> Query the *num*th database entry. Useful for debugging.

-qf, --queryformat *num*
> Specify the format for displaying the query output, using tags to represent different types of data (e.g., NAME, FILENAME, DISTRIBUTION). The format specification is a variation of the standard **printf** formatting, with the type specifier omitted and replaced by the name of the header tag inclosed in brackets ({ }). For example:
>
>   %{NAME}
>
> The tag names are case-insensitive. Use **--querytags** (see "Miscellaneous options") to view a list of available tags. The tag can be followed by :*type* to get a different output format type. The possible types are:

armor
> Wrap a public key in ASCII armor.

base64
> Encode binary data as base64.

date
> Use **strftime(3)** "%c" format.

day
> Use **strftime(3)** "%a %b %d %Y" format.

depflags
> Format dependency flags.

fflags
> Format file flags.

hex
> Use hexadecimal format.

octal
> Use octal format.

perms
> Format file permissions.

shescape
> Escape single quotes for use in a script.

triggertype
> Display trigger suffix.

--specfile *specfile*
> Query *specfile* as if it were a package. Useful for extracting information from a spec file.

--tid *tid*
> List packages with the specified transaction identifier (*tid*). The tid is a Unix timestamp. All packages installed or erased in a single transaction have the same tid.

--triggeredby *pkg*
> List packages that are triggered by the installation of package *pkg*.

--whatrequires *capability*
> List packages that require the given capability to function.

--whatprovides *capability*
> List packages that provide the given capability.

Information selection options

-c, --configfiles
> List configuration files in the package. Implies **-l**.

--changelog
> Display the log of change information for the package.

-d, --docfiles
> List documentation files in the package. Implies **-l**.

--dump
> Dump information for each file in the package. This option must be used with at least one of **-l**, **-c**, or **-d**. The output includes the following information in this order:
>
> ```
> path size mtime md5sum mode owner group isconfig isdoc rdev symlink
> ```

--filesbypkg
> List all files in each package.

-i, --info
> Display package information, including the name, version, and description. Formats the results according to **--queryformat** if specified.

-l, --list
> List all files in the package.

--last
> List packages by install time, with the latest packages listed first.

--provides
> List the capabilities this package provides.

-R, --requires
> List any packages this package depends on.

-s, --state
> List each file in the package and its state. The possible states are **normal, not installed,** or **replaced.** Implies **-l**.

--scripts
> List any package-specific shell scripts used during installation and uninstallation of the package.

--triggers, --triggerscript
> Display any trigger scripts in the package.

Uninstall options

The syntax for **erase,** the uninstall command, is:

```
rpm -e package_name ...
rpm --erase package_name ...
```

The uninstall options are:

--allmatches
> Remove all versions of the package. Only one package should be specified; otherwise, an error results.

--nodeps
> Don't check dependencies before uninstalling the package.

--nopostun
> Don't run any post-uninstall scripts.

--nopreun
> Don't run any pre-uninstall scripts.

--noscripts
> Don't execute any pre-uninstall or post-uninstall scripts. Equivalent to **--nopreun --nopostun.**

--notriggerpostun
> Don't execute any post-uninstall scripts triggered by the removal of this package.

--notriggers
> Don't execute any scripts triggered by the removal of this package. Equivalent to **--notriggerun --notriggerpostun.**

--notriggerun

Don't execute any uninstall scripts triggered by the removal of this package.

--repackage

Repackage the files before uninstalling them. Rename the package as specified by the macro **%_repackage_name_fmt** and save it in the directory specified by the macro **%_repackage_dir** (by default */var/tmp*).

--test

Don't really uninstall anything; just go through the motions. Use with **-vv** for debugging.

Verify options

The syntax for the **verify** command is:

```
rpm -V|-y|--verify [package-selection-options] [verify-options]
```

Verify mode compares information about the installed files in a package with information about the files that came in the original package, and displays any discrepancies. The information compared includes the size, MD5 sum, permissions, type, owner, and group of each file. Uninstalled files are ignored.

The package selection options include those available for query mode. In addition, the following **verify** options are available:

--nodeps

Ignore package dependencies.

--nodigest

Ignore package or header digests.

--nofiles

Ignore attributes of package files.

--nogroup

Ignore group ownership errors.

--nolinkto

Ignore symbolic link errors.

--nomd5

Ignore MD5 checksum errors.

--nomode

Ignore file mode (permissions) errors.

--nordev

Ignore major and minor device number errors.

--nomtime

Ignore modification time errors.

--noscripts

Ignore any verify script.

--nosignature

Ignore package or header signatures.

--nosize

   Ignore file size errors.

--nouser

   Ignore user ownership errors.

The output is formatted as an eight-character string, possibly followed by an attribute marker, and then the filename. The possible attribute markers are:

c	Configuration file
d	Documentation file
g	Ghost file (contents not included in package)
l	License file
r	Readme file

Each of the eight characters in the string represents the result of comparing one file attribute to the value of that attribute from the RPM database. A period (.) indicates that the file passed that test. The following characters indicate failure of the corresponding test:

5	MD5 sum
D	Device
G	Group
L	Symlink
M	Mode (includes permissions and file type)
S	File size
T	Mtime
U	User

Database rebuild options

The syntax of the command to rebuild the RPM database is:

   rpm --rebuilddb [*options*]

You also can build a new database:

   rpm --initdb [*options*]

The options available with the database rebuild mode are the **--dbpath**, **--root**, and **-v** options described earlier under "General options."

Signature check options

RPM packages may have a PGP signature built into them. PGP configuration information is read from the *rpmrc* file. There are three types of digital signature options: you can check signatures, add signatures to packages, and import signatures.

The syntax of the signature check mode is:

   rpm --checksig *package_file*...
   rpm -K *package_file*...

The signature checking options **-K** and **--checksig** check the digests and signatures contained in the specified packages to insure the integrity and origin of the packages. Note that RPM now automatically checks the signature of any package when it is read; this option is still useful, however, for checking all headers and signatures associated with a package.

The following options are available for use with signature check mode:

--nogpg
  Don't check any GPG signatures.

--nomd5
  Don't check any MD5 signatures.

--nopgp
  Don't check any PGP signatures.

The syntax for adding signatures to binary packages is:

```
rpm --addsign binary-pkgfile...
rpm --resign binary-pkgfile...
```

Both **--addsign** and **--resign** generate and insert new signatures, replacing any that already exist in the specified binary packages.[*]

The syntax for importing signatures is:

```
rpm --import public-key
```

The **--import** option is used to import an ASCII public key to the RPM database so that digital signatures for packages using that key can be verified. Imported public keys are carried in headers, and keys are kept in a ring, which can be queried and managed like any package file.

Miscellaneous options

Several additional **rpm** options are available:

--querytags
  Print the tags available for use with the **--queryformat** option in query mode.

--setperms *packages*
  Set file permissions of the specified packages to those in the database.

--setugids *packages*
  Set file owner and group of the specified packages to those in the database.

--showrc
  Show the values **rpm** will use for all options that can be set in an *rpmrc* file.

FTP/HTTP options

The following options are available for use with FTP and HTTP URLs in install, update, and query modes.

---

[*] In older versions of RPM, **--addsign** was used to add new signatures without replacing existing ones, but currently both options work the same way and replace any existing signatures.

--ftpport *port*
> Use *port* for making an FTP connection on the proxy FTP server instead of the default port. Same as specifying the macro **%_ftpport**.

--ftpproxy *host*
> Use *host* as the proxy server for FTP transfers through a firewall that uses a proxy. Same as specifying the macro **%_ftpproxy**.

--httpport *port*
> Use *port* for making an HTTP connection on the proxy HTTP server instead of the default port. Same as specifying the macro **%_httpport**.

--httpproxy *host*
> Use *host* as the proxy server for HTTP transfers. Same as specifying the macro **%_httpproxy**.

The rpmbuild Command

The **rpmbuild** command is used to build RPM packages. The syntax for **rpmbuild** is:

```
rpmbuild -[b|t]step [build-options] spec-file ...
```

Specify **-b** to build a package directly from a spec file, or **-t** to open a tarred, gzipped file and use its spec file.

Both forms take the following single-character *step* arguments, listed in the order they would be performed:

p   Perform the prep stage, unpacking source files and applying patches.

l   Do a list check, expanding macros in the files section of the spec file and verifying that each file exists.

c   Perform the build stage. Done after the prep stage; generally equivalent to doing a **make**.

i   Perform the install stage. Done after the prep and build stages; generally equivalent to doing a **make install**.

b   Build a binary package. Done after prep, build, and install.

s   Build a source package. Done after prep, build, and install.

a   Build both binary and source packages. Done after prep, build, and install.

The general **rpm** options described earlier in "General options" can be used with **rpmbuild**.

The following additional options can also be used when building an **rpm** file with **rpmbuild**:

--buildroot *dir*
> Override the **BuildRoot** tag with *dir* when building the package.

--clean
> Clean up (remove) the build files after the package has been made.

--nobuild
> Go through the motions, but don't execute any build stages. Used for testing spec files.

--rmsource

Remove the source files when the build is done. Can be used as a standalone option with **rpm** to clean up files separately from creating the packages.

--rmspec

Remove the spec file when the build is done. Like **--rmsource**, **--rmspec** can be used as a standalone option with **rpmbuild**.

--short-circuit

Can be used with **-bc** and **-bi** to skip previous stages.

--sign

Add a GPG signature to the package for verifying its identity and origin.

--target *platform*

When building the package, set the macros **%_target**, **%_target_arch**, and **%_target_os** to the value indicated by *platform*.

Two other options can be used standalone with **rpmbuild** to recompile or rebuild a package:

--rebuild *source-pkgfile...*

Like **--recompile**, but also build a new binary package. Remove the build directory, the source files, and the spec file once the build is complete.

--recompile *source-pkgfile...*

Install the named source package, and prep, compile, and install the package.

Finally, the **--showrc** option is used to show the current **rpmbuild** configuration:

```
rpmbuild --showrc
```

This option shows the values that will be used for all options that can be set in an *rpmrc* file.

RPM Examples

Query the RPM database to find Emacs-related packages:

```
% rpm -q -a | grep emacs
```

Query an uninstalled package, printing information about the package and listing the files it contains:

```
% rpm -qpil ~/downloads/bash2-doc-2.03-8.i386.rpm
```

Install a package (assumes superuser privileges):

```
% rpm -i sudo-1.5.3-6.i386.rpm
```

The Debian Package Manager

Debian GNU/Linux provides several package management tools, primarily intended to facilitate the building, installation, and management of binary packages. Debian package names generally end in *.deb*. The Debian package management tools include:

dpkg

The original Debian packaging tool. Used to install or uninstall packages or as a frontend to **dpkg-deb**. Getting and installing packages is usually done with **apt-get**, but **dpkg** is still commonly used to install a package that is already on your system. In fact, **apt-get** calls **dpkg** to do the installation once it's gotten the package.

dpkg-deb

Lower-level packaging tool. Used to create and manage the Debian package archives. Accepts and executes commands from **dpkg** or can be called directly.

dselect

An interactive frontend to **dpkg**.

The Advanced Package Tool (APT)

APT is a modern, user-friendly package management tool that consists of a number of commands. The most frequently used of these commands is **apt-get**, which is used to download and install a Debian package. **apt-get** can be run from the command line or selected as a method from **dselect**. One of the features of **apt-get** is that you can use it to get and install packages across the Internet by specifying an FTP or HTTP URL. You can also use it to upgrade all packages currently installed on your system in a single operation. Note that this results in a large download and will take a long time on a slow Internet connection.

Each of these tools is described in detail in "Debian Package Manager Command Summary."

Files

Some important files used by the Debian package management tools are:

control

Comes with each package. Documents dependencies; contains the name and version of the package, a description, maintainer, installed size, and so on.

conffiles

Comes with each package. Contains a list of the configuration files associated with the package.

preinst, postinst, prerm, postrm

Scripts that can be included in a package to be run before installation, after installation, before removal, or after removal of the package.

/var/lib/dpkg/available

Contains information about packages available on the system.

/var/lib/dpkg/status

Contains information about the status of packages available on the system.

/etc/apt/sources.list

A list for APT of package sources, used to locate packages. The sources are listed one per line, in order of preference.

/etc/apt/apt.conf

The main APT configuration file.

/etc/apt/apt_preferences
>A preferences file that controls various aspects of APT, such as letting a user select the version or release of a package to install.

/etc/dpkg/dpkg.cfg
>A configuration file containing default options for **dpkg**.

Package Priorities

Every Debian package has a priority associated with it, indicating how important the package is to the system. The priorities are:

Required
>The package is essential to the proper functioning of the system.

Important
>The package provides important functionality that enables the system to run well.

Standard
>The package is included in a standard system installation.

Optional
>The package is one that you might want to install, but you can omit it if you are short on disk space, for example.

Extra
>The package either conflicts with other packages that have a higher priority, has specialized requirements, or is one that you would want to install only if you need it.

Package and Selection States

The possible states that a package can be in are:

config-files
>Only the configuration files for the package are present on the system.

half-configured
>The package is unpacked and configuration was started but not completed.

half-installed
>Installation was started but not completed.

installed
>The package is unpacked and configured.

not-installed
>The package is not installed.

unpacked
>The package is unpacked but not configured.

The possible package selection states are:

deinstall
>The package has been selected for deinstallation (i.e., for removal of everything but configuration files).

install
> The package has been selected for installation.

purge
> The package has been selected to be purged (i.e., for removal of everything including the configuration files).

Package Flags

Two possible package flags can be set for a package:

hold
> The package should not be handled by **dpkg** unless forced with the **--force-hold** option.

reinst-required
> The package is broken and needs to be reinstalled. Such a package cannot be removed unless forced with the **--force-reinstreq** option.

Scripts

In addition to the commands described in the next section, a number of shell and Perl scripts are included with the package manager for use in managing and building packages:

apt-setup
> An interactive script for adding download sources to the *sources.list* file. (Perl script)

dpkg-architecture
> Determine and set the build and host architecture for package building. (Perl script)

dpkg-checkbuilddeps
> Check installed packages against the build dependencies and build conflicts listed in the control file. (Perl script)

dpkg-buildpackage
> Help automate package building. (Shell script)

dpkg-distaddfile
> Add an entry for a file to *debian/files*. (Perl script)

dpkg-divert
> Create and manage the list of diversions, used to override the default location for installing files. (Perl script)

dpkg-genchanges
> Generate an upload control file from the information in an unpacked built source tree and the files it has generated. (Perl script)

dpkg-gencontrol
> Read information from an unpacked source tree and display a binary package control file on standard output. (Perl script)

dpkg-name
> Rename Debian packages to their full package names. (Shell script)

dpkg-parsechangelog

Read and parse the changelog from an unpacked source tree and write the information to standard output in machine-readable form. (Perl script)

dpkg-preconfigure

Let packages ask questions prior to installation. (Perl script)

dpkg-reconfigure

Reconfigure a package that is already installed. (Perl script)

dpkg-scanpackages

Create a *Packages* file from a tree of binary packages. The *Packages* file is used by **dselect** to provide a list of packages available for installation. (Perl script)

dpkg-shlibdeps

Calculate shared library dependencies for named executables. (Perl script)

dpkg-source

Pack and unpack Debian source archives. (Perl script)

dpkg-statoverride

Manage the list of stat overrides, which let **dpkg** override file ownership and mode when a package is installed. (Perl script)

Debian Package Manager Command Summary

For the **apt-** commands, options can be specified on the command line or set in the configuration file. Boolean options set in the configuration file can be overridden on the command line in a number of different ways, such as **--no-***opt* and **-***opt***=no**, where *opt* is the single-character or full name of the option.

---

apt-cache

apt-cache [*options*] *command*

Perform low-level operations on the APT binary cache, including the ability to perform searches and produce output reports from package metadata. Useful for finding out information about packages.

Commands

add *files*

Add the specified package index files to the source cache.

depends *pkgs*

For each specified package, show a list of dependencies and packages that can fulfill the dependency.

dotty *pkgs*

Graph the relationships between the specified packages. The default is to trace out all dependent packages; turn this behavior off by setting the **APT::Cache::GivenOnly** configuration option.

dump

List every package in the cache. Used for debugging.

dumpavail

Print a list of available packages to standard output, suitable for use with **dpkg**.

gencaches

Build source and package caches from the sources in the file *sources.list* and from */var/lib/dpkg/status*. Equivalent to running **apt-get check**.

pkgnames [*prefix*]

Print a list of packages in the system. If *prefix* is specified, print only packages whose names begin with that prefix. Most useful with the **--generate** option.

policy [*pkgs*]

Print detailed information about the priority selection of each specified package. With no arguments, print the priorities of each source. Useful for debugging issues related to the *preferences* file.

search *regex*

Search package names and descriptions of all available package files for the specified regular expression and print the name and short description of each matching package. With **--full**, the output is identical to that from the **show** command. With **--names-only**, only the package name is searched.

show *pkgs*

Display the package records for each specified package. Similar to running **dpkg --print-avail**.

showpkg *pkgs*

Display information about the specified packages. For each package, the output includes the available versions, packages that depend on this package, and packages that this package depends on.

stats

Display statistics about the cache.

unmet

Display the unmet dependencies in the package cache.

Options

-a, --all-versions

Print full records for all available versions. For use with the **show** commands. The configuration option is **APT::Cache::AllVersions**.

--all-names

Cause **pkgnames** to print all names, including virtual packages and missing dependencies. The configuration option is **APT::Cache::AllNames**.

-c *file*, **--config-file=***file*

Specify a configuration file to be read after the default configuration file.

-f, --full

Print full package records when searching. The configuration option is **APT::Cache::ShowFull**.

-g, --generate

Automatically regenerate the package cache rather than using the current cache. The default is to regenerate; turn it off with **--no-generate**. The configuration option is **APT::Cache::Generate**.

-h, --help

Print usage information and exit.

-i, --important

Print only important dependencies. For use with **unmet**. The configuration option is **APT::Cache::Important**.

--names-only

Search only on package names, not long descriptions. The configuration option is **APT::Cache::NamesOnly**.

-o, --option

Set a configuration option. Syntax is **-o** *group::tool=option*.

-p *file*, **--pkg-cache=**file

Use the specified file for the package cache, the primary cache used by all operations. The configuration option is **Dir::Cache::pkgcache**.

-q, --quiet

Operate quietly, producing output for logging but no progress indicators. Use **-qq** for even quieter operation. The configuration option is **quiet**.

--recurse

Run **depends** recursively, so all mentioned packages are printed once. The configuration option is **APT::Cache::RecurseDepends**.

-s *file*, **--src-cache=**file

Specify the source cache file used by **gencaches**. The configuration option is **Dir::Cache::srcpkgcache**.

-v, --version

Print version information and exit.

---

apt-cdrom

apt-cdrom [*options*] *command*

Add a new CD-ROM to APT's list of available sources. The database of CD-ROM IDs that APT maintains is */var/lib/apt/cdroms.list*.

Commands

add

Add a CD-ROM to the source list.

ident

Print the identity of the current CD-ROM and the stored filename. Used for debugging.

Options

-a, --thorough
> Do a thorough package scan. May be needed with some old Debian CD-ROMs.

-c *file*, **--config-file**=*file*
> Specify a configuration file to be read after the default configuration file.

-d *mount-point*, **--cdrom**=*mount-point*
> Specify the CD-ROM mount point, which must be listed in */etc/fstab*. The configuration option is **Acquire::cdrom::mount**.

-f, --fast
> Do a fast copy, assuming the files are valid and don't all need checking. Specify this only if disk has been run before without error. The configuration option is **APT::CDROM::Fast**.

-h, --help
> Print help message and exit.

-m, --no-mount
> Don't mount or unmount the mount point. The configuration option is **APT::CDROM::NoMount**.

-n, --just-print, --recon, --no-act
> Check everything, but don't actually make any changes. The configuration option is **APT::CDROM::NoAct**.

-o, --option
> Set a configuration option. Syntax is **-o** *group::tool=option*.

-r, --rename
> Prompt for a new label and rename the disk to the new value. The configuration option is **APT::CDROM::Rename**.

-v, --version
> Print the version information and exit.

---

apt-config

```
apt-config [options] shell args
apt-config [options] dump
```

An internal program for querying configuration information.

Commands

dump
> Display the contents of the configuration space.

shell
> Access the configuration information from a shell script. The arguments are in pairs, specifying the name of a shell variable and a configuration value to query. The value may be postfixed with */x*, where *x* is one of the following letters:

> **b**   Return true or false.

> **d**   Return directories.

> **f**   Return filenames.

> **i**   Return an integer.

Options

-c *file,* **--config-file**=*file*
> Specify a configuration file to be read after the default configuration file.

-h, --help
> Print help message and exit.

-o, --option
> Set a configuration option. Syntax is **-o** *group::tool=option.*

-v, --version
> Print the version information and exit.

---

apt-extract-templates

apt-extracttemplates [*options*] *files*

Extract configuration scripts and templates from the specified Debian package files. For each specified file, a line of output is generated with the following information:

> *package version template-file config-script*

and the template and configuration files are written to the directory specified with **-t** or **--temp-dir** or by the configuration option **APT::ExtractTemplates::TempDir**. The filenames are in the form *template.xxxx* and *config.xxxx.*

Options

-c *file,* **--config-file**=*file*
> Specify a configuration file to be read after the default configuration file.

-h, --help
> Print help message and exit.

-o, --option
> Set a configuration option. Syntax is **-o** *group::tool=option.*

-t *dir,* **--tempdir**=*dir*
> Write the extracted template files and configuration scripts to the specified directory. The configuration option is **APT::ExtractTemplates::TempDir**.

-v, --version
> Print the version information and exit.

---

apt-ftparchive

apt-ftparchive [*options*] *command*

Generate *Package* and other index files used to access a distribution source. The files should be generated on the source's origin site.

Commands

clean *config-file*
> Clean the databases used by the specified configuration file by removing obsolete records.

contents *path*
> Search the specified directory recursively. For each *.deb* file found, read the file list, sort the files by package, and write

the results to standard output. Use with **--db** to specify a binary caching database.

generate *config-file sections*
Build indexes according to the specified configuration file.

packages *paths* [*override* [*pathprefix*]]
Generate a package file from the specified directory tree. The optional override file contains information describing how the package fits into the distribution, and the optional path prefix is a string prepended to the filename fields. Equivalent to **dpkg-scanpackages**.

sources *paths* [*override* [*pathprefix*]]
Generate a source index file from the specified directory tree. The optional override file contains information used to set priorities in the index file and to modify maintainer information. The optional path prefix is a string prepended to the directory field in the generated source index. Use **--source-override** to specify a different source override file. Equivalent to **dpkg-scansources**.

Options

-c *file*, **--config-file**=*file*
Specify a configuration file to be read after the default configuration file.

--contents
Perform contents generation. If set, and package indexes are being generated with a cache database, the file listing is extracted and stored in the database. Used with **generate**, allows the creation of any contents files. The default is on. The configuration option is **APT::FTPArchive::Contents**.

-d, **--db**
Use a binary caching database. This option has no effect on **generate**. The configuration option is **APT::FTPArchive::DB**.

--delink
Enable delinking of files when used with the **External-Links** setting. The default is on; turn off with **--no-delink**. The configuration option is **APT::FTPArchive::DeLinkAct**.

-h, **--help**
Print help message and exit.

--md5
Generate MD5 sums for the index files. The default is on. The configuration option is **APT::FTPArchive::MD5**.

-o, **--option**
Set a configuration option. Syntax is **-o** *group::tool=option*.

-q, **--quiet**
Run quietly, producing logging information but no progress indicators. Use **-qq** for quieter operation. The configuration option is **quiet**.

--read-only

> Make the caching databases read-only. The configuration option is **APT::FTPArchive::ReadOnlyDB**.

-s *file*, **--source-override=***file*

> Specify a source override file. For use with the **sources** command. The configuration option is **APT::FTPArchive:: SourceOverride**.

-v, --version

> Print the version information and exit.

---

apt-get

apt-get [*options*] *command* [*package...*]

A command-line tool for handling packages. Will eventually be a backend to APT.

Commands

autoclean

> Like **clean**, but remove only package files that can no longer be downloaded.

build-dep

> Install or remove packages to satisfy the build dependencies for a source package.

clean

> Clear the local repository of retrieved package files.

check

> Update the package cache and check for broken packages.

dist-upgrade

> Like **upgrade**, but also handle dependencies intelligently. See the **-f** option for more information.

dselect-upgrade

> Used with **dselect**. Track the changes made by **dselect** to the **Status** field of available packages and take actions necessary to realize that status.

install *packages*

> Install one or more packages. Specify the package name, not the full filename. Other required packages are also retrieved and installed. With a hyphen appended to the package name, the package is removed if it is already installed.

remove *packages*

> Remove one or more packages. Specify the package name, not the full filename. With a plus sign appended to the name, the package is installed.

source *packages*

> Find source packages and download them into the current directory. If specified with **--compile**, the source packages are compiled into binary packages. With **--download-only**, the source packages are not unpacked.

update

Resynchronize the package overview files from their sources. Must be done before an **upgrade** or **dist-upgrade**.

upgrade

Install the latest versions of all packages currently installed. Run **update** first.

Options

-b, --compile, --build

Compile source packages after download. The configuration option is **APT::Get::Compile**.

-c *file*, **--config-file=***file*

Specify a configuration file to read after the default.

-d, --download-only

Retrieve package files, but don't unpack or install them. The configuration option is **APT::Get::Download-only**.

--diff-only

Download only the *diff* file from a source archive. The configuration option is **APT::Get::Diff-Only**.

-f, --fix-broken

Try to fix a system with broken dependencies. Can be used alone or with a command. Run with the **install** command if you have problems installing packages. You can run the sequence:

```
apt-get -f install
apt-get dist-upgrade
```

several times to clean up interlocking dependency problems. The configuration option is **APT::Get::Fix-Broken**.

--force-yes

Force yes. Causes APT to continue without prompting if it is doing something that could damage your system. Use with great caution and only if absolutely necessary. The configuration option is **APT::Get::force-yes**.

-h, --help

Display a help message and exit.

--ignore-hold

Ignore a hold placed on a package. Use with **dist-upgrade** to override many undesired holds. The configuration option is **APT::Get::Ignore-Hold**.

--list-cleanup

Erase obsolete files from */var/lib/apt/lists*. The default is on; use **--no-list-cleanup** to turn it off, which you would normally do only if you frequently modify your list of sources. The configuration option is **APT::Get::List-Cleanup**.

-m, --ignore-missing, --fix-missing

Ignore missing or corrupted packages or packages that cannot be retrieved. Can cause problems when used with -f. The configuration option is **APT::Get::Fix-Missing**.

--no-download

Disable package downloading; use with **--ignore-missing** to force APT to use only the packages that have already been downloaded. The configuration option is **APT::Get:: Download**.

--no-remove

Do not remove any packages; instead, abort without prompting. The configuration option is **APT::Get::Remove**.

--no-upgrade

Do not upgrade packages. Use with **install** to prevent upgrade of packages that are already installed. The configuration option is **APT::Get::Upgrade**.

-o, --option

Set a configuration option. Syntax is **-o** *group::tool=option*.

--only-source

Do not map the names specified with the **source** command through the binary table. The configuration option is **APT::Get::Only-Source**.

--print-uris

Print URIs of files instead of fetching them. Print path, destination filename, size, and expected MD5 hash. The configuration option is **APT::Get::Print-URIs**.

--purge

Tell **dpkg** to do a purge instead of a remove for items that would be removed. Purging removes packages completely, including any configuration files. The configuration option is **APT::Get::Purge**.

-q, --quiet

Quiet mode. Omit progress indicators and produce only logging output. Use **-qq** to make even quieter. The configuration option is quiet.

--reinstall

Reinstall packages that are already installed, upgrading them to the latest version. The configuration option is **APT::Get::ReInstall**.

-s, --simulate, --just-print, --dry-run, --recon, --no-act

Go through the motions, but don't actually make any changes to the system. The configuration option is **APT::Get:: Simulate**.

-t *rel, --target-release=rel, --default-release=rel*

Retrieve packages only from the specified release. The value of *rel* can be a release number or a value such as "unstable". The configuration option is **APT::Default-Release**.

--tar-only

Download only the TAR file from a source archive. The configuration option is **APT::Get::Tar-Only**.

--trivial-only
> Perform only operations that are considered trivial. The configuration option is **APT::Get::Trivial-Only**.

-u, --show-upgraded
> Print a list of all packages to be upgraded. The configuration option is **APT::Get::Show-Upgraded**.

-v, --version
> Display the version and exit.

-y, --yes, --assume-yes
> Automatically reply "yes" to prompts and run noninteractively. Abort if there is an error. The configuration option is **APT::Get::Assume-Yes**.

---

apt-sortpkgs

apt-sortpkgs [*options*] *indexfiles*

Sort the records in a source or package index file by package name and write the results to standard output. **apt-sortpkgs** also sorts the internal fields of each record.

Options
-c *file*, **--config-file=***file*
> Specify a configuration file to read after the default.

-h, --help
> Display a help message and exit.

-o, --option
> Set a configuration option. Syntax is **-o** *group::tool=option*.

-s, --source
> Order by source index field. The configuration option is **APT::SortPkgs::Source**.

-v, --version
> Display the version and exit.

---

dpkg

dpkg [*options*] *action*

A tool for installing, managing, and building packages. Serves as a frontend to **dpkg-deb**.

dpkg actions
These actions are carried out by **dpkg** itself:

-A *pkgfile*, **--record-avail** *pkgfile*
> Update the record of available files kept in */var/lib/dpkg/available* with information from *pkgfile*. This information is used by **dpkg** and **dselect** to determine what packages are available. With **-R** or **--recursive**, *pkgfile* must be a directory.

-C, --audit
> Search for partially installed packages and suggest how to get them working.

--clear-avail

Remove existing information about what packages are available.

--command-fd *n*

Accept commands passed on the file descriptor given by *n*. Note that any additional options set through this file descriptor or on the command line are not reset, but remain for other commands issued during the same session.

--compare-versions *ver1 op ver2*

Perform a binary comparison of two version numbers. The operators **lt le eq ne ge gt** treat a missing version as earlier. The operators **lt-nl le-nl ge-nl gt-nl** treat a missing version as later (where **nl** is "not later"). A third set of operators (< << <= = >= >> >) is provided for compatibility with control-file syntax. **dpkg** returns zero for success (i.e., the condition is satisfied) and nonzero otherwise.

--configure [*packages*|-a|--pending]

Reconfigure one or more unpacked *packages*. If **-a** or **--pending** is given instead of *packages*, configure all packages that are unpacked but not configured.

-Dh, **--debug=help**

Print debugging help message and exit.

--force-help

Print help message about the **--force-***list* options and exit. See the **--force-***list* option description for the possible values of *list*.

--forget-old-unavail

Forget about uninstalled, unavailable packages.

--get-selections [*pattern*]

Get list of package selections and write to standard output. With *pattern* specified, write selections that match the pattern.

--help

Print help message and exit.

-i *pkgfile*, **--install** *pkgfile*

Install the package specified as *pkgfile*. With **-R** or **--recursive**, *pkgfile* must be a directory.

-l, **--list** [*pkg-name-pattern*]

List all packages whose names match the specified pattern. With no pattern, list all packages in */var/lib/dpkg/available*. The pattern can include standard shell wildcard characters and may have to be quoted to prevent the shell from doing filename expansion.

-L *packages*, **--listfiles** *packages*

List installed files that came from the specified package or packages.

--license, **--licence**

Print **dpkg** license information and exit.

-p, --print-avail *package*
> Print the details about *package* from */var/lib/dpkg/available*.

--print-architecture
> Print the target architecture.

--print-gnu-build-architecture
> Print the GNU version of the target architecture.

--print-installation-architecture
> Print the host architecture for installation.

-r, --remove [*packages*|-a|--**pending**]
--purge [*packages*|-a|--**pending**]
> Remove or purge one or more installed *packages*. Removal gets rid of everything except the configuration files listed in *debian/conffiles*; purging also removes the configuration files. If **-a** or **--pending** is given instead of *packages*, **dpkg** removes or purges all packages that are unpacked and marked (in */var/lib/dpkg/status*) for removing or purging.

-s *packages*, **--status** *packages*
> Report the status of one or more *packages* by displaying the entry in the status database */var/lib/dpkg/status*.

-S *filename-pattern*, **--search** *filename-pattern*
> Search installed packages for a filename. The pattern can include standard shell wildcard characters and may have to be quoted to prevent the shell from doing filename expansion.

--set-selections
> Set package selections based on input file read from standard input.

--unpack *pkgfile*
> Unpack the package, but don't configure it. With **-R** or **--recursive**, *pkgfile* must be a directory.

--update-avail *pkgs-file*
--merge-avail *pkgs-file*
> Update the record of available files kept in */var/lib/dpkg/available*. This information is used by **dpkg** and **dselect** to determine what packages are available. Update replaces the information with the contents of the *pkgs-file*, distributed as *Packages*. Merge combines the information from *Packages* with the existing information.

--version
> Print **dpkg** version information and exit.

--yet-to-unpack
> Search for uninstalled packages that have been selected for installation.

dpkg-deb actions

The following actions can be specified for **dpkg** and are passed to **dpkg-deb** for execution. Also see **dpkg-deb**.

-b *dir* [*archive*], **--build** *dir* [*archive*]
  Build a package.

-c *archive,* **--contents** *archive*
  List the contents of a package.

-e *archive* [*dir*], **--control** *archive* [*dir*]
  Extract control information from a package.

-f *archive* [*control-fields*], **--field** *archive* [*control-fields*]
  Display the control field or fields of a package.

-I *archive* [*control-files*], **--info** *archive* [*control-files*]
  Show information about a package.

--fsys-tarfile *archive*
  Display the filesystem TAR file contained in a package.

-x *archive dir,* **--extract** *archive dir*
  Extract the files from a package.

-X *archive dir,* **--vextract** *archive dir*
  Extract and display the filenames from a package.

Options

dpkg options can be specified on the command line or set in the configuration file. Each line in the configuration file contains a single option, specified without the leading dash (-).

--abort-after=*num*
  Abort processing after *num* errors. Default is 50.

-B, **--auto-deconfigure**
  When a package is removed, automatically deconfigure any other package that depended on it.

-D*octal,* **--debug=***octal*
  Turn on debugging, with the *octal* value specifying the desired level of debugging information. Use **-Dh** or **--debug=help** to display the possible values. You can OR the values to get the desired output.

-E, **--skip-same-version**
  Don't install the package if this version is already installed.

--force-*list,* **--no-force-***list,* **--refuse-***list*
  Force or refuse to force an operation. *list* is specified as a comma-separated list of options. With **--force**, a warning is printed, but processing continues. **--refuse** and **--no-force** cause processing to stop with an error. The force/refuse options are:

all
  Turn all force options on or off.

architecture
  Process even if intended for a different architecture.

auto-select
  Select or deselect packages to install or remove them. Forced by default.

bad-path
Some programs are missing from the path.

confdef
Always choose the default action for modified configuration files. If there is no default and **confnew** or **confold** is also specified, use that to decide; otherwise, ask the user.

configure-any
Configure any unconfigured package that the package depends on.

conflicts
Permit installation of conflicting packages. Can result in problems from files being overwritten.

confmiss
Always install a missing configuration file. Be careful using this option, since it means overriding the removal of the file.

confnew
Always install the new version of a modified configuration file unless **confdef** is also specified. In that case, use the default action if there is one.

confold
Keep the old version of a modified configuration file unless **confdef** is also specified. In that case, use the default action if there is one.

depends
Turn dependency problems into warnings.

depends-version
Warn of version problems when checking dependencies, but otherwise ignore.

downgrade
Install even if a newer version is already installed. Forced by default.

hold
Process packages even if they are marked to be held.

not-root
Try to install or remove even when not logged on as root.

overwrite
Overwrite a file from one package with the same file from another package. Forced by default.

overwrite-dir
Overwrite one package's directory with a file from another package.

overwrite-diverted
Overwrite a diverted file with an undiverted version.

remove-essential
Remove a package even if it is essential. Note that this can cause your system to stop working.

remove-reinstreq

Remove packages that are broken and are marked to require reinstallation.

-G Don't install a package if a newer version is already installed. Same as **--refuse-downgrade**.

--ignore-depends=*pkglist*

Dependency problems result only in a warning for the packages in *pkglist*.

--new

New binary package format. This is a **dpkg-deb** option.

--no-act

Go through the motions, but don't actually write any changes. Used for testing. Be sure to specify before the action; otherwise, changes might be written.

--nocheck

Ignore the contents of the control file when building a package. This is a **dpkg-deb** option.

-O, **--selected-only**

Process only packages that are marked as selected for installation.

--old

Old binary package format. This is a **dpkg-deb** option.

-R, **--recursive**

Recursively handle *.deb* files found in the directories and their subdirectories specified with **-A**, **--install**, **--unpack**, and **--avail**.

--root=*dir*, **--admindir**=*dir*, **--instdir**=*dir*

Change default directories. **admindir** contains administrative files with status and other information about packages; it defaults to */var/lib/dpkg*. **instdir** is the directory in which packages are installed; it defaults to */*. Changing the **root** directory to *dir* automatically changes **instdir** to *dir* and **admindir** to */dir/var/lib/dpkg*.

--status-fd *n*

Send the package status information to the specified file descriptor. Can be given more than once.

dpkg-deb

dpkg-deb *action* [*options*]

Backend command for building and managing Debian package archives. Also see **dpkg**; you'll often want to use **dpkg** to pass commands through to **dpkg-deb**, rather than call **dpkg-deb** directly.

Actions

-b *dir* [*archive*], **--build** *dir* [*archive*]

Create an *archive* from the filesystem tree starting with directory *dir*. The directory must have a *DEBIAN* subdirectory containing the control file and any other control information.

If *archive* is specified and is a filename, the package is written to that file; if no *archive* is specified, the package is written to *dir.deb*. If the archive already exists, it is replaced. If *archive* is the name of a directory, **dpkg-deb** looks in the control file for the information it needs to generate the package name. (Note that for this reason, you cannot use **--nocheck** with a directory name.)

-c *archive*, **--contents** *archive*
> List the filesystem-tree portion of *archive*.

-e *archive* [*dir*], **--control** *archive* [*dir*]
> Extract control information from *archive* into the directory *dir*, which is created if it doesn't exist.

-f *archive* [*control-fields*], **--field** *archive* [*control-fields*]
> Extract information about one or more fields in the control file for *archive*. If no fields are provided, print the entire control file.

-h, **--help**
> Print help information and exit.

-I *archive* [*control-files*], **--info** *archive* [*control-files*]
> Provide information about binary package *archive*. If no control files are provided, print a summary of the package contents; otherwise, print the control files in the order they were specified. An error message is printed to standard error for any missing components.

--fsys-tarfile *archive*
> Extract the filesystem tree from *archive*, and send it to standard output in **tar** format. Can be used with **tar** to extract individual files from an archive.

--license, **--licence**
> Print the license information and exit.

--version
> Print the version number and exit.

-x *archive dir*, **--extract** *archive dir*
-X *archive dir*, **--vextract** *archive dir*
> Extract the filesystem tree from *archive* into the specified directory, creating *dir* if it doesn't already exist. **-x** (**--extract**) works silently, while **-X** (**--vextract**) lists the files as it extracts them. Do not use this action to install packages; use **dpkg** instead.

Options

-D, **--debug**
> Turn on debugging.

--new
> Build a new-style archive format (this is the default).

--nocheck

Don't check the control file before building an archive. This lets you build a broken archive.

--old

Build an old-style archive format.

---

dpkg-query

dpkg-query [*option*] *command*

Display information about packages listed in the **dpkg** database.

Commands

--help

Print help information and exit.

-l [*patterns*], **--list** [*patterns*]

List packages whose names match any of the specified patterns. With no pattern specified, list all packages in */var/lib/dpkg/available*. The pattern may need to be in quotes to avoid expansion by the shell.

-L *packages,* **--list** *packages*

List files installed on your system from each of the specified packages. This command does not list files created by package-specific installation scripts.

--license, --licence

Print the license information and exit.

-p *package,* **--print-avail** *package*

Display details for the specified package, as found in */var/lib/dpkg/available*.

-S *patterns*

Search the installed packages for filenames matching one of the specified patterns. At least one pattern must be specified.

-W [*patterns*], **--show** [*patterns*]

Like **-l**, but the output can be customized with the **--show-format** option.

--version

Print version information and exit.

Options

--admindir=*dir*

Use *dir* as the location of the **dpkg** database. The default is */var/lib/dpkg*.

--showformat=*format*

Specify the output format for **-W/--show**. The format can include the standard escape sequences **\n** (newline), **\r** (carriage return), or **** (backslash). Specify package fields with the syntax **${***var*[*;width*]**}**. Fields are right-aligned by default, or left-aligned if *width* is negative.

dpkg-split   **dpkg-split** [*action*] [*options*]

Split a binary package into smaller pieces and reassemble the pieces, either manually or in automatic mode. The automatic mode maintains a queue of parts for reassembling. Useful for transferring to and from floppy disks.

Actions

-a -o *output part*, **--auto -o** *output part*
> Add *part* to the queue for automatic reassembly, and if all the parts are available, reassemble the package as *output*. Requires the use of the **-o** (or **--output**) option, as shown.

-d [*packages*], **--discard** [*packages*]
> Discard parts from the automatic-assembly queue. If any *packages* are specified, discard only parts from those packages. Otherwise, empty the queue.

-I *parts*, **--info** *parts*
> Print information about the part file or files specified.

-j *parts*, **--join** *parts*
> Join the parts of a package file together from the *parts* specified. The default output file is *package-version.deb*.

-l, **--listq**
> List the contents of the queue of parts waiting for reassembly, giving the package name, the parts that are on the queue, and the number of bytes.

-s *full-package* [*prefix*], **--split** *full-package* [*prefix*]
> Split the package *full-package* into parts, named *prefixNofM. deb*. The prefix defaults to the *full-package* name without the *.deb* extension.

-h, **--help**
> Print help message and exit.

--license, **--licence**
> Print license information and exit.

--version
> Print version information and exit.

Options

--depotdir *dir*
> Specify an alternate directory *dir* for the queue of parts waiting for reassembly. Default is */var/lib/dpkg*.

--msdos
> Force **--split** output filenames to be MS-DOS-compatible.

-Q, **--npquiet**
> Do not print an error message for a part that doesn't belong to a binary package when doing automatic queuing or reassembly.

-O *output*, **--output** *output*
> Use *output* as the filename for a reassembled package.

> When splitting, specify the maximum part size (*num*) in kilo-
> bytes. Default is 450 KB.

---

dselect

dselect [*options*] [*action*]

A screen-oriented user frontend to **dpkg**. The primary user interface for installing and managing packages. See **dpkg** and **dpkg-deb**
for information on building packages.

Actions

If **dselect** is run with no action specified on the command line, it
displays the following menu:

```
* 0. [A]ccess   Choose the access method to use.
  1. [U]pdate   Update list of available packages, if
                possible.
  2. [S]elect   Request which packages you want on your
                system.
  3. [I]nstall  Install and upgrade wanted packages.
  4. [C]onfig   Configure any packages that are
                unconfigured.
  5. [R]emove   Remove unwanted software.
  6. [Q]uit     Quit dselect.
```

The asterisk (on the first line) shows the currently selected option.
Any of the menu items can be specified directly on the command
line as an action (**access**, **update**, **select**, **install**, **config**, **remove**,
quit) to go directly to the desired activity. For example:

% dselect access

If you enter **quit** on the command line, **dselect** exits immediately
without doing anything. An additional command-line action is
menu, which displays the menu and is equivalent to running
dselect with no action.

Options

Options can be specified both on the command line and in the
dselect configuration file, */etc/dpkg/dselect.cfg*.

--admindir *dir*
> Change the directory that holds internal data files to *dir*.
> Default is */var/lib/dpkg*.

--color *colorspec,* **--colour** *colorspec*
> Set colors for different parts of the screen, as specified by
> *colorspec* as follows:

> screenpart:[*fgcolor*],[*bgcolor*][:*attr*[+*attr*+...]]

> This option can be specified multiple times, to override the
> default colors for different screen parts. Rather than having to
> specify the colors on the command line each time you run
> **dselect**, you might prefer to set them in the configuration file.
> The possible screen parts (going from the top of the screen to
> the bottom) are:

title
> The screen title.

listhead
> The header line above the package list.

list
> The scrolling list of packages and some help text.

listsel
> The selected item in the list.

pkgstate
> The text showing the current state of each package.

pkgstatesel
> The text showing the current state of the selected package.

infohead
> The header line showing the state of the selected package.

infodesc
> The short description of the package.

info
> The text that displays information such as the package description.

infofoot
> The last line of the screen when selecting packages.

query
> Query lines.

helpscreen
> The color of help screens.

> Either the foreground color, the background color, or both can be specified for each screen part. The colors are given as the standard **curses** colors. After the color specification, you can specify a list of attributes separated by plus signs (+). The possible attributes are **normal**, **standout**, **underline**, **reverse**, **blink**, **bright**, **dim**, and **bold**. Not all attributes work on all terminals.

--expert
> Run in expert mode; don't print help messages.

-D [*file*], **--debug** [*file*]
> Turn on debugging. Send output to *file* if specified.

--help
> Print help message and exit.

--license, licence
> Print license information and exit.

--version
> Print version information and exit.

6

The Linux Shells: An Overview

The *shell* is a program that acts as a buffer between you and the operating system. In its role as a command interpreter, it should (for the most part) act invisibly. It can also be used for simple programming.

Purpose of the Shell

There are three main uses for the shell: interactive use, customizing your Linux session, and programming.

Interactive Use

When the shell is used interactively, it waits for you to issue commands, processes them (to interpret special characters such as wildcards), and executes them. Shells also provide a set of commands, known as *built-ins*, to supplement Linux commands.

Customizing Your Linux Session

A Linux shell defines *variables*, such as the locations of your home directory and mail spool, to control the behavior of your session. Some variables are preset by the system; you can define others in startup files that your shell reads when you log in, or interactively for a single session. Startup files can also contain Linux or shell commands, for execution immediately after login.

Programming

A series of individual commands (be they shell commands or other Linux commands available on the system) combined into one executable file is called a *shell script*. Batch files in MS-DOS are a similar concept. **bash** is considered a powerful programming shell, while scripting in **tcsh** is rumored to be hazardous to your health.

Shell Flavors

Many different Linux shells are available. This book describes the two most popular shells:

- The Bourne-Again shell (**bash**), which is based on the Bourne shell (**sh**). **bash** is the default Linux shell and the most commonly used.

- **tcsh**, an extension of the C shell, **csh**, that is included instead of **csh** in Linux distributions.

Most systems have more than one shell, and it's not uncommon for people to use one shell for writing shell scripts and another for interactive use. Other popular shells include the Korn shell (**ksh**) and the Z shell (**zsh**); both of these are Bourne-shell compatible.

When you log in, the system determines which shell to run by consulting your entry in */etc/passwd*. The last field of each entry calls a program to run as the default shell. For example:

Program name	Shell
/bin/sh	bash
/bin/bash	bash
/bin/csh	tcsh
/bin/tcsh	tcsh

You can change to another shell by typing the program name at the command line. For example, to change from **bash** to **tcsh**, type:

```
$ exec tcsh
```

Common Features

The following table is a sampling of features that are common to **bash** and **tcsh**.

Symbol/Command	Meaning/Action
>	Redirect output.
>>	Append output to file.
<	Redirect input.
<<	"Here" document (redirect input).
|	Pipe output.
&	Run process in background.
;	Separate commands on same line.
*	Match any character(s) in filename.
?	Match single character in filename.

Symbol/Command	Meaning/Action
!*n*	Repeat command number *n*.
[ ]	Match any characters enclosed.
( )	Execute in subshell.
" "	Partial quote (allows variable and command expansion).
' '	Preserve literal value of enclosed characters.
\	Quote following character.
$*var*	Use value for variable.
$$	Process ID.
$0	Command name.
$*n*	*n*th argument (0<*n*≤9).
$*	All arguments.
$?	Exit status.
#	Begin comment.
Tab	Complete current word.
bg	Background execution.
break	Break from loop statements.
cd	Change directories.
continue	Resume a program loop.
echo	Display output.
eval	Evaluate arguments.
exec	Execute a new shell or other program.
fg	Foreground execution.
jobs	Show active jobs.
kill	Terminate running jobs.
newgrp	Change to a new group.
shift	Shift positional parameters.
stop	Suspend a background job.
suspend	Suspend a foreground job.
umask	Set or list permissions on files to be created.
unset	Erase variable or function definitions.
wait	Wait for a background job to finish.

Differing Features

The following table is a sampling of features that differ between the two shells:

bash	tcsh	Meaning/Action
$	%	Default prompt.
>|	>!	Force redirection.
	>>!	Force append.
var=val	**set** *var=val*	Variable assignment.
export *var=val*	**setenv** *var val*	Set environment variable.

bash	tcsh	Meaning/Action
$#	$#argv	Number of arguments.
$(*command*), ``	``	Command substitution.
. *file*, source *file*	source *file*	Execute commands in *file*.
done	end	End a loop statement.
esac	endsw	End **case** or **switch**.
for/do	foreach	Loop through variables.
if [$i -eq 5]	if ($i= =5)	Sample **if** statement.
fi	endif	End **if** statement.
ulimit `	limit	Set resource limits.
read	$<	Read from terminal.
readonly	set -r	Make a variable read-only.
Tab Tab		Show possible completions.
trap 2	onintr	Ignore interrupts.
until/do	until	Begin **until** loop.
while/do	while	Begin **while** loop.

7

bash: The Bourne-Again Shell

bash is the GNU version of the standard Bourne shell—the original Unix shell—and incorporates many popular features from other shells such as **csh**, **tcsh**, and the Korn shell (**ksh**). Both **tcsh**, which is described in the following chapter, and **ksh**, which offers many of the features in this chapter, are also available on most distributions of Linux. But **bash** is the standard Linux shell, loaded by default when most user accounts are created.

If executed as part of the user's login, **bash** starts by executing any commands found in */etc/profile*. Then it executes the commands found in *~/.bash_profile*, *~/.bash_login*, or *~/.profile* (searching for each file only if the previous file is not found). Many distributions change shell defaults in */etc/profile* for all users, even changing the behavior of common commands like **ls**.

In addition, every time it starts (as a subshell or a login shell), **bash** looks for a file named *~/.bashrc*. Many system administration utilities create a small *~/.bashrc* automatically, and many users create quite large startup files. Any commands that can be executed from the shell can be included. A small sample file may look like this (each feature can be found either in this chapter or in Chapter 3):

```
# Set bash variable to keep 50 commands in history.
HSTSIZE=50
#
# Set prompt to show current working directory and history number of
# command.
PS1='\w: Command \!$ '
#
# Set path to search for commands in my directories, then standard ones.
PATH=~/bin:~/scripts:$PATH
#
# Keep group and others from writing my newly created files.
umask 022
#
# Show color-coded file types.
```

```
alias ls='ls --color=yes'
#
# Make executable and .o files ugly yellow so I can find and delete them.
export LS_COLORS="ex=43:*.o=43"
#
# Quick and dirty test of a single-file program.
function gtst () {
    g++ -o $1 $1.C && ./$1
}
#
# Remove .o files.
alias clean='find ~ -name \*.o -exec rm {} \;'
```

bash provides the following features:

- Input/output redirection
- Wildcard characters (metacharacters) for filename abbreviation
- Shell variables for customizing your environment
- Powerful programming capabilities
- Command-line editing (using **vi**- or Emacs-style editing commands)
- Access to previous commands (command history)
- Integer arithmetic
- Arithmetic expressions
- Command name abbreviation (aliasing)
- Job control
- Integrated programming features
- Control structures
- Directory stacking (using **pushd** and **popd**)
- Brace/tilde expansion
- Key bindings

Invoking the Shell

The command interpreter for **bash** can be invoked as follows:

> **bash** [*options*] [*arguments*]

bash can execute commands from a terminal (when **-i** is specified), from a file (when the first *argument* is an executable script), or from standard input (if no arguments remain or if **-s** is specified).

Options

Options that appear here with double hyphens also work when entered with single hyphens, but using double hyphens is standard coding procedure.

-, --

Treat all subsequent strings as arguments, not options.

-D, --dump-strings

For execution in non-English locales, dump all strings that **bash** translates.

--dump-po-strings

Same as **--dump-strings**, but uses the GNU **gettext** *po* (portable object) format suitable for scripting.

-c *str*

Read commands from string *str*.

--help

Print usage information and exit.

-i   Create an interactive shell (prompt for input).

-l, --login

Behave like a login shell; try to process */etc/profile* on startup. Then process *~/.bash_profile*, *~/.bash_login*, or *~/.profile* (searching for each file only if the previous file is not found).

--noediting

Disable line editing with arrow and control keys.

--noprofile

Do not process */etc/profile*, *~/.bash_profile*, *~/.bash_login*, or *~/.profile* on startup.

--norc

Do not process *~/.bashrc* on startup.

--posix

Conform to POSIX standard.

-r, --restricted

Restrict users to a very secure, limited environment; for instance, they cannot change out of the startup directory or use the > sign to redirect output.

--rcfile *file*

Substitute *file* for *.bashrc* on startup.

-s   Read commands from standard input. Output from built-in commands goes to file descriptor 1; all other shell output goes to file descriptor 2.

-v, --verbose

Print each line as it is executed (useful for tracing scripts).

--version

Print information about which version of **bash** is installed.

-x   Turn on debugging, as described under the **-x** option to the **set** built-in command later in this chapter.

The remaining options to **bash** are listed under the **set** built-in command.

Arguments

Arguments are assigned, in order, to the positional parameters **$1**, **$2**, and so forth. If the first argument is an executable script, it is assigned to **$0**; then commands are read from it, and remaining arguments are assigned to **$1**, **$2**, and so on.

Syntax

This subsection describes the many symbols peculiar to **bash**. The topics are arranged as follows:

- Special files
- Filename metacharacters
- Command-line editing
- Quoting
- Command forms
- Redirection forms
- Coprocesses

Special Files

File	Purpose
/etc/profile	Executed automatically at login.
$HOME/.bash_profile	Executed automatically at login.
$HOME/.bashrc	Executed automatically at shell startup.
$HOME/.bash_logout	Executed automatically at logout.
$HOME/.bash_history	Record of last session's commands.
$HOME/.inputrc	Initialization file for reading input in an interactive shell.
/etc/passwd	Source of home directories for ~name abbreviations.

Filename Metacharacters

Characters	Meaning
*	Match any string of zero or more characters.
?	Match any single character.
[abc...]	Match any one of the enclosed characters; a hyphen can be used to specify a range (e.g., a–z, A–Z, 0–9).
[!abc...]	Match any character *not* among the enclosed characters.
[^abc...]	Same as [!abc...].
{str1,...}	Brace expansion: match any of the enclosed strings.
~name	HOME directory of user *name*. With no *name*, HOME directory of current user.
~+	Current working directory (PWD).
~-	Previous working directory from directory stack (OLDPWD; see also the **pushd** built-in command).
~+n	The *n*th entry in the directory stack, counting from the start of the list with the first entry being 0.
~-n	The *n*th entry in the directory stack, counting from the end of the list with the last entry being 0.

Patterns can be a sequence of patterns separated by |. If any of the subpatterns match, the entire sequence is considered matching. This extended syntax resembles that of **egrep** and **awk**.

Examples

`$ ls new*`	*List* new *and* new.1
`$ cat ch?`	*Match* ch9 *but not* ch10
`$ vi [D-R]*`	*Match files that begin with uppercase D through R*

Command-Line Editing

Command lines can be edited like lines in either Emacs or **vi**. Emacs is the default. See "Line-Edit Mode" later in this chapter for more information.

vi mode has two submodes, input mode and command mode. The default is input mode; you can go to command mode by pressing Esc. In command mode, typing **a** (append) or **i** (insert) returns you to input mode.

Some users discover that the Del or Backspace key on the terminal does not delete the character before the cursor, as it should. Sometimes this problem can be solved by issuing one of the following commands (or placing it in your *.bashrc* file):

```
stty erase ^?
stty erase ^H
```

See the **stty** command in Chapter 3 for more information. On the X Window System, an alternative solution is to use the **xmodmap** command; this is not described here, as it requires some research about your terminal.

Tables 7-1 through 7-14 show various Emacs and **vi** commands.

Table 7-1. Basic Emacs-mode commands

Command	Description
Ctrl-b	Move backward one character (without deleting).
Ctrl-f	Move forward one character.
Del	Delete one character backward.
Ctrl-d	Delete one character forward.

Table 7-2. Emacs-mode word commands

Command	Description
M-b	Move one word backward.
M-f	Move one word forward.
M-Del	Kill one word backward.
M-d	Kill one word forward.
Ctrl-y	Retrieve (**yank**) last item killed.

Table 7-3. Emacs-mode line commands

Command	Description
Ctrl-a	Move to beginning of line.
Ctrl-e	Move to end of line.
Ctrl-k	Kill forward to end of line.

bash

Table 7-4. Emacs-mode commands for moving through the history file

Command	Description
Ctrl-p	Move to previous command.
Ctrl-n	Move to next command.
Ctrl-r	Search backward.
M-<	Move to first line of history file.
M->	Move to last line of history file.

Table 7-5. Emacs-mode completion commands

Command	Description
Tab	Attempt to perform general completion of the text.
M-?	List the possible completions.
M-/	Attempt filename completion.
Ctrl-x /	List the possible filename completions.
M-~	Attempt username completion.
Ctrl-x ~	List the possible username completions.
M-$	Attempt variable completion.
Ctrl-x $	List the possible variable completions.
M-@	Attempt hostname completion.
Ctrl-x @	List the possible hostname completions.
M-!	Attempt command completion.
Ctrl-x !	List the possible command completions.
M-Tab	Attempt completion from previous commands in the history list.

Table 7-6. Miscellaneous Emacs-mode commands

Command	Description
Ctrl-j	Same as Return.
Ctrl-l	Clear the screen, placing the current line at the top of the screen.
Ctrl-m	Same as Return.
Ctrl-o	Same as Return, then display next line in command history.
Ctrl-t	Transpose character left of and under the cursor.
Ctrl-u	Kill the line from the beginning to point.
Ctrl-v	Insert keypress instead of interpreting it as a command.
Ctrl-[	Same as Esc (most keyboards).
M-c	Capitalize word under or after cursor.
M-u	Change word under or after cursor to all capital letters.
M-l	Change word under or after cursor to all lowercase letters.
M-.	Insert last word in previous command line after point.
M-_	Same as M-. .

Table 7-7. Editing commands in vi input mode

Command	Description
Del	Delete previous character.
Ctrl-W	Erase previous word (i.e., erase until a blank).
Ctrl-V	Insert next keypress instead of interpreting it as a command.
Esc	Enter command mode (see Table 7-8).

Table 7-8. Basic vi command-mode commands

Command	Description
h	Move left one character.
l	Move right one character.
b	Move left one word.
w	Move right one word.
B	Move to beginning of preceding nonblank word.
W	Move to beginning of next nonblank word.
e	Move to end of current word.
E	Move to end of current nonblank word.
0	Move to beginning of line.
^	Move to first nonblank character in line.
$	Move to end of line.

Table 7-9. Commands for entering vi input mode

Command	Description
i	Insert text before current character (insert).
a	Insert text after current character (append).
I	Insert text at beginning of line.
A	Insert text at end of line.
r	Replace current character with next keypress.
R	Overwrite existing text.

Table 7-10. Some vi-mode delete commands

Command	Description
dh	Delete one character backward.
dl	Delete the current character.
db	Delete one word backward.
dw	Delete one word forward.
dB	Delete one nonblank word backward.
dW	Delete one nonblank word forward.
d$	Delete to end-of-line.
d0	Delete to beginning of line.

bash

Table 7-11. Abbreviations for vi-mode delete commands

Command	Description
D	Delete to end of line (equivalent to **d$**).
dd	Delete entire line (equivalent to **0d$**).
C	Delete to end of line; enter input mode (equivalent to **c$**).
cc	Delete entire line; enter input mode (equivalent to **0c$**).
X	Delete character backward (equivalent to **dh**).
x	Delete the current character (equivalent to **dl**).

Table 7-12. vi-mode commands for searching the command history

Command	Description
k or -	Move backward one line.
j or +	Move forward one line.
G	Move to first line in history.
/*string*	Search backward for *string*.
?*string*	Search forward for *string*.
n	Repeat search in same direction as previous.
N	Repeat search in opposite direction of previous.

Table 7-13. vi-mode character-finding commands

Command	Description
f*x*	Move right to next occurrence of *x*.
F*x*	Move left to previous occurrence of *x*.
t*x*	Move right to next occurrence of *x*, then back one space.
T*x*	Move left to previous occurrence of *x*, then forward one space.
;	Redo last character-finding command.
,	Redo last character-finding command in opposite direction.

Table 7-14. Miscellaneous vi-mode commands

Command	Description
~	Invert (toggle) case of current character(s).
_	Insert last word of previous command after cursor; enter input mode.
Ctrl-L	Clear the screen and redraw the current line on it; good for when your screen becomes garbled.
#	Prepend # (comment character) to the line and send it to the history file; useful for saving a command to be executed later, without having to retype it.

Quoting

Quoting disables a character's special meaning and allows it to be used literally, as itself. The following characters have special meaning to **bash**:

Character	Meaning
;	Command separator
&	Background execution
( )	Command grouping (enter a subshell)
{ }	Command block
|	Pipe
> < &	Redirection symbols
* ? [ ] ~ !	Filename metacharacters
" ' \	Used in quoting other characters
`	Command substitution
$	Variable substitution (or command substitution)
newline space tab	Word separators
#	Comment

The following characters can be used for quoting:

Character	Action
" "	Everything between " and " is taken literally, except for the following characters that keep their special meaning:
	$
	Variable substitution will occur.
	`
	Command substitution will occur.
	"
	This marks the end of the double quote.
' '	Everything between ' and ' is taken literally, except for another '.
\	The character following \ is taken literally. Use within " " to escape ", $, and '. Often used to escape itself, spaces, or newlines.

Examples

```
$ echo 'Single quotes "protect" double quotes'
Single quotes "protect" double quotes

$ echo "Well, isn't that \"special\"?"
Well, isn't that "special"?

$ echo "You have `ls|wc -l` files in `pwd`"
You have  43 files in /home/bob

$ echo "The value of \$x is $x"
The value of $x is 100
```

Command Forms

Syntax	Effect
cmd &	Execute cmd in background.
cmd1 ; cmd2	Command sequence; execute multiple cmds on the same line.
(cmd1 ; cmd2)	Subshell; treat cmd1 and cmd2 as a command group.
cmd1 | cmd2	Pipe; use output from cmd1 as input to cmd2.
cmd1 `cmd2`	Command substitution; use cmd2 output as arguments to cmd1.
cmd1 $(cmd2)	Command substitution; nesting is allowed.
cmd1 && cmd2	AND; execute cmd2 only if cmd1 succeeds.
cmd1 || cmd2	OR; execute cmd2 only if cmd1 fails.
{ cmd1 ; cmd2 }	Execute commands in the current shell.

Examples

```
$ cd; ls                          Execute sequentially
$ (date; who; pwd) > logfile      All output is redirected
$ sort file | pr -3 | lp          Sort file, page output, then print
$ vi `grep -l ifdef *.c`          Edit files found by grep
$ egrep '(yes|no)' `cat list`     Specify a list of files to search
$ egrep '(yes|no)' $(cat list)    Same as previous using bash command
                                  substitution
$ egrep '(yes|no)' $(<list)       Same, but faster
$ grep XX file && lp file         Print file if it contains the pattern
$ grep XX file || echo "XX not found"  Echo an error message if pattern not found
```

Redirection Forms

File descriptor	Name	Common abbreviation	Typical default
0	Standard input	stdin	Keyboard
1	Standard output	stdout	Screen
2	Standard error	stderr	Screen

The usual input source or output destination can be changed as shown in Table 7-15.

Table 7-15. I/O redirectors

Redirector	Function
> file	Direct standard output to file.
< file	Take standard input from file.
cmd1 | cmd2	Pipe; take standard output of cmd1 as standard input to cmd2.
>> file	Direct standard output to file; append to file if it already exists.
>| file	Force standard output to file even if **noclobber** is set.
n>| file	Force output from the file descriptor n to file even if **noclobber** is set.
<> file	Use file as both standard input and standard output.

Table 7-15. I/O redirectors (continued)

Redirector	Function
<< *text*	Read standard input up to a line identical to *text* (*text* can be stored in a shell variable). Input is usually typed on the screen or in the shell program. Commands that typically use this syntax include **cat**, **echo**, **ex**, and **sed**. If *text* is enclosed in quotes, standard input will not undergo variable substitution, command substitution, etc.
n> *file*	Direct file descriptor *n* to *file*.
n< *file*	Set *file* as file descriptor *n*.
>&*n*	Duplicate standard output to file descriptor *n*.
<&*n*	Duplicate standard input from file descriptor *n*.
&>*file*	Direct standard output and standard error to *file*.
<&-	Close the standard input.
>&-	Close the standard output.
n>&-	Close the output from file descriptor *n*.
n<&-	Close the input from file descriptor *n*.

Examples

```
$ cat part1 > book
$ cat part2 part3 >> book
$ mail tim < report
$ grep Chapter part* 2> error_file

$ sed 's/^/XX /' << END_ARCHIVE
> This is often how a shell archive is "wrapped",
> bundling text for distribution. You would normally
> run sed from a shell program, not from the command line.
> END_ARCHIVE
XX This is often how a shell archive is "wrapped",
XX bundling text for distribution. You would normally
XX run sed from a shell program, not from the command line.
```

To redirect standard output to standard error:

```
$ echo "Usage error:  see administrator" 1>&2
```

The following command sends output (files found) to *filelist* and sends error messages (inaccessible files) to file *no_access*:

```
$ find / -print > filelist 2>no_access
```

Variables

Preface a variable by a dollar sign ($) to reference its value. You can also optionally enclose it in braces ({ }). You can assign a value to a variable through an equals sign (=) with no whitespace on either side of it:

```
$ TMP=temp.file
```

By default, variables are seen only within the shell itself; to pass variables to other programs invoked within the shell, see the **export** built-in command.

If enclosed by brackets ([ ]), the variable is considered an array variable. For instance:

```
$ DIR_LIST[0]=src
$ DIR_LIST[1]=headers
$ ls ${DIR_LIST[1]}
```

The contents of **headers** are listed. Many substitutions and commands in this chapter handle arrays by operating on each element separately.

Variable Substitution

In the following substitutions, braces ({ }) are optional, except when needed to separate a variable name from following characters that would otherwise be considered part of the name.

Variable	Meaning
${*var*}	Value of variable *var*.
$0	Name of the program.
${*n*}	Individual arguments on command line (positional parameters); $1 \leq n \leq 9$.
$#	Number of arguments on command line.
$*	All arguments on command line.
$@	Same as $*, but contents are split into words when the variable is enclosed in double quotes.
$$	Process number of current shell; useful as part of a filename for creating temporary files with unique names.
$?	Exit status of last command (normally 0 for success).
$!	Process number of most recently issued background command.
$-	Current execution options (see the **set** built-in command). By default, **hB** for scripts and **himBH** for inter-active shells.
$_	Initially set to name of file invoked for this shell, then set for each command to the last word of the previous command.

Tables 7-16 through 7-18 show various types of operators that can be used with **bash** variables.

Table 7-16. Substitution operators

Operator	Substitution
${*varname*:-*word*}	If *varname* exists and isn't null, return its value; otherwise, return *word*.
Purpose:	Returning a default value if the variable is undefined.
Example:	${**count**:-0} evaluates to 0 if **count** is undefined.
${*varname*:=*word*}	If *varname* exists and isn't null, return its value; otherwise set it to *word* and then return its value. Positional and special parameters cannot be assigned this way.
Purpose:	Setting a variable to a default value if it is undefined.
Example:	${**count**:=0} sets **count** to 0 if it is undefined.
${*varname*:?*message*}	If *varname* exists and isn't null, return its value; otherwise, print *varname*: followed by *message*, and abort the current command or script (noninteractive shells only). Omitting *message* produces the default message "parameter null or not set."
Purpose:	Catching errors that result from variables being undefined.
Example:	{**count**:?"undefined"} prints "count: undefined" and exits if **count** is undefined.

Table 7-16. Substitution operators (continued)

Operator	Substitution
${*varname*:+*word*}	If *varname* exists and isn't null, return *word*; otherwise, return null.
Purpose:	Testing for the existence of a variable.
Example:	${**count**:+1} returns 1 (which could mean **true**) if **count** is defined.
${#*varname*}	Return the number of characters in the value of *varname*.
Purpose:	Preparing for substitution or extraction of substrings.
Example:	If ${**USER**} currently expands to **root**, ${#**USER**} expands to 4.

Table 7-17. Pattern-matching operators

Operator	Meaning
${*variable*#*pattern*}	If the pattern matches the beginning of the variable's value, delete the shortest part that matches and return the rest.
${*variable*##*pattern*}	If the pattern matches the beginning of the variable's value, delete the longest part that matches and return the rest.
${*variable*%*pattern*}	If the pattern matches the end of the variable's value, delete the shortest part that matches and return the rest.
${*variable*%%*pattern*}	If the pattern matches the end of the variable's value, delete the longest part that matches and return the rest.
${*var*/*pat*/*sub*}	Return *var* with the first occurrence of *pat* replaced by *sub*. Can be applied to $* or $@, in which case each word is treated separately. If *pat* starts with # it can match only the start of *var*; if *pat* ends with % it can match only the end of *var*.
${*var*//*pat*/*sub*}	Return *var* with every occurrence of *pat* replaced by *sub*.
${*variable*:*n*}	Truncate the beginning of the variable and return the part starting with character number *n*, where the first character is 0.
${*variable*:*n*:*l*}	Starting with character number *n*, where the first character is 0, return a substring of length *l* from the variable.

Table 7-18. Expression evaluation

Operator	Meaning
$((*arithmetic-expression*))	Return the result of the expression. Arithmetic operators are described under "Arithmetic Expressions."
Example:	TODAY=`date +%-d`; echo $(($TODAY+7)) stores the number of the current day in $TODAY and then prints that number plus 7 (the number of the same day next week).
[[$*condition*]]	Return 1 if *condition* is true and 0 if it is false. Conditions are described under the **test** built-in command.

Built-in Shell Variables

Built-in variables are set automatically by the shell and are typically used inside shell scripts. Built-in variables can use the variable substitution patterns shown earlier. When setting variables, you do not include dollar signs, but when referencing their values later, the dollar signs are necessary.

Tables 7-19 through 7-22 show the commonly used built-in variables in **bash**.

Table 7-19. Behavior-altering variables

Variable	Meaning
auto_resume	Allows a background job to be brought to the foreground simply by entering a substring of the job's command line. Values can be **substring** (resume if the user's string matches part of the command), **exact** (string must exactly match command), or another value (string must match at beginning of command).
BASH_ENV	Startup file of commands to execute, if **bash** is invoked to run a script.
CDPATH	Colon-separated list of directories to search for the directory passed in a **cd** command.
EDITOR	Pathname of your preferred text editor.
IFS	Word separator; used by shell to parse commands into their elements. The default separators are space, tab, and newline.
IGNOREEOF	If nonzero, don't allow use of a single **Ctrl-D** (the end-of-file or EOF character) to log off; use the **exit** command to log off.
PATH	Colon-separated list of directories to search for each command.
PROMPT_COMMAND	Command that **bash** executes before issuing a prompt for a new command.
PS1	Prompt displayed before each new command; see the later section "Variables in Prompt" for ways to introduce into the prompt dynamically changing information such as the current working directory or command history number.
PS2	Prompt displayed before a new line if a command is not finished.
PS3	Prompt displayed by **select** built-in command.
PS4	Prompt displayed by **-x** debugging (see "Invoking the Shell") and the **set** built-in command).

Table 7-20. History variables

Variable	Meaning
FCEDIT	Pathname of editor to use with the **fc** command.
HISTCMD	History number of the current command.
HISTCONTROL	If **HISTCONTROL** is set to the value of **ignorespace**, lines beginning with a space are not entered into the history list. If set to **ignoredups**, lines matching the last history line are not entered. Setting it to **ignoreboth** enables both options.
HISTFILE	Name of history file on which the editing modes operate.
HISTFILESIZE	Maximum number of lines to store in the history file. The default is 500.
HISTSIZE	Maximum number of commands to remember in the command history. The default is 500.

Table 7-21. Mail variables

Variable	Meaning
MAIL	Name of file to check for incoming mail.
MAILCHECK	How often, in seconds, to check for new mail (default is 60 seconds).
MAILPATH	List of filenames, separated by colons (:), to check for incoming mail.

Table 7-22. Status variables

Variable	Meaning
BASH	Pathname of this instance of the shell you are running.
BASH_VERSION	Version number of the shell you are running.
COLUMNS	Number of columns your display has.
DIRSTACK	List of directories manipulated by **pushd** and **popd** commands.
EUID	Effective user ID of process running this shell, in the form of the number recognized by the system.
GROUPS	Groups to which user belongs, in the form of the numbers recognized by the system.
HOME	Name of your home (login) directory.
HOSTNAME	Host the shell is running on.
HOSTTYPE	Short name indicating the type of machine the shell is running on; for instance, **i486**.
LINES	The number of lines your display has.
MACHTYPE	Long string indicating the machine the shell is running on; for instance, **i486-pc-linux-gnu**.
OLDPWD	Previous directory before the last **cd** command.
OSTYPE	Short string indicating the operating system; for instance, **linux-gnu**.
PPID	Process ID of parent process that invoked this shell.
PWD	Current directory.
SECONDS	Number of seconds since the shell was invoked.
SHELL	Pathname of the shell you are running.
SHLVL	Depth to which running shells are nested.
TERM	The type of terminal that you are using.
UID	Real user ID of process running this shell, in the form of the number recognized by the system.

Arithmetic Expressions

The **let** command performs integer arithmetic. **bash** provides a way to substitute integer values (for use as command arguments or in variables); base conversion is also possible.

Expression	Meaning
((*expr*))	Use the value of the enclosed arithmetic expression.

Operators

bash uses arithmetic operators from the C programming language; the following list is in decreasing order of precedence. Use parentheses to override precedence.

Operator	Meaning
-	Unary minus
! ~	Logical negation; binary inversion (one's complement)
* / %	Multiplication; division; modulus (remainder)
+ -	Addition; subtraction
<< >>	Bitwise left shift; bitwise right shift

Operator	Meaning
<= >=	Less than or equal to; greater than or equal to
< >	Less than; greater than
== !=	Equality; inequality (both evaluated left to right)
&	Bitwise AND
^	Bitwise exclusive OR
|	Bitwise OR
&&	Logical AND
||	Logical OR
=	Assign value
+= -=	Reassign after addition/subtraction
*= /= %=	Reassign after multiplication/division/remainder
&= ^= |=	Reassign after bitwise AND/XOR/OR
<<= >>=	Reassign after bitwise shift left/right

Examples

See the **let** built-in command for more information and examples.

```
let "count=0" "i = i + 1"        Assign i and count
let "num % 2"; echo $?           Test for an even number
```

Command History

bash lets you display or modify previous commands. Commands in the history list can be modified using:

- Line-edit mode
- The **fc** command

In addition, the command substitutions described in Chapter 8 also work in **bash**.

Line-Edit Mode

Line-edit mode lets you emulate many features of the **vi** and Emacs editors. The history list is treated like a file. When the editor is invoked, you type editing keystrokes to move to the command line you want to execute. On most terminals, arrow keys work in both Emacs mode and **vi** command mode. You can also change the line before executing it. See Table 7-23 for some examples of common line-edit commands. When you're ready to issue the command, press Return.

The default line-edit mode is Emacs. To enable **vi** mode, enter:

```
$ set -o vi
```

Note that **vi** starts in input mode; to type a **vi** command, press Esc first.

The mode you use for editing **bash** commands is entirely separate from the editor that is invoked for you automatically within many commands (for instance, the editor invoked by mail readers when you ask them to create a new mail message).

To change the default editor, set the **VISUAL** or **EDITOR** variable to the filename or full pathname of your favorite editor:

```
$ export EDITOR=emacs
```

Table 7-23. Common editing keystrokes

vi	Emacs	Result
k	Ctrl-p	Get previous command.
j	Ctrl-n	Get next command.
/string	Ctrl-r string	Get previous command containing string.
h	Ctrl-b	Move back one character.
l	Ctrl-f	Move forward one character.
b	M-b	Move back one word.
w	M-f	Move forward one word.
X	Del	Delete previous character.
x	Ctrl-d	Delete one character.
dw	M-d	Delete word forward.
db	M-Ctrl-h	Delete word back.
xp	Ctrl-t	Transpose two characters.

The fc Command

Use **fc -l** to list history commands, and **fc -e** to edit them. See the **fc** built-in command for more information.

Examples

`$ history`	*Display the command history list*
`$ fc -l 20 30`	*List commands 20 through 30*
`$ fc -l -5`	*List the last five commands*
`$ fc -l cat`	*List the last command beginning with cat*
`$ fc -ln 5 > doit`	*Save command 5 to file doit*
`$ fc -e vi 5 20`	*Edit commands 5 through 20 using vi*
`$ fc -e emacs`	*Edit previous command using Emacs*
`$ !!`	*Reexecute previous command*
`$ !cat`	*Reexecute last cat command*
`$ !cat foo-file`	*Reexecute last command, adding foo-file to the end of the argument list*

Command Substitution

Syntax	Meaning
!	Begin a history substitution.
!!	Previous command.
!N	Command number N in history list.
!-N	Nth command back from current command.
!string	Most recent command that starts with string.
!?string?	Most recent command that contains string.

Syntax	Meaning
!?*string*?%	Most recent command argument that contains *string*.
!$	Last argument of previous command.
!#	The current command up to this point.
!!*string*	Previous command, then append *string*.
!*N string*	Command *N*, then append *string*.
!{*s1*}*s2*	Most recent command starting with string *s1*, then append string *s2*.
^*old*^*new*^	Quick substitution; change string *old* to *new* in previous command, and execute modified command.

Variables in Prompt

Using the following variables, you can display information about the current state of the shell or the system in your **bash** prompt. Set the **PS1** variable to a string including the desired variables. For instance, the following command sets **PS1** to a string that includes the \w variable to display the current working directory, and the \! variable to display the number of the current command. The next line is the prompt displayed by the change.

```
$ PS1='\w: Command \!$ '
~/book/linux: Command 504$
```

Variable	Meaning
\a	Alarm (bell)
\d	Date in the format "Mon May 8"
\e	Escape character (terminal escape, not backslash)
\h	Hostname
\j	Number of background jobs (active or stopped)
\l	Current terminal name
\n	Newline inserted in the prompt
\r	Carriage return inserted in the prompt
\s	Current shell
\t	Time in 24-hour format, where 3:30 p.m. appears as 15:30:00
\u	User's account name
\v	Version and release of **bash**
\w	Current working directory
\A	Time in 24-hour format, where 3:30 p.m. appears as 15:30
\D{*format*}	Time in the specified format interpreted by **strftime**; an empty format displays the locale-specific current time
\H	Like \h
\T	Time in 12-hour format, where 3:30 p.m. appears as 03:30:00
\V	Version, release, and patch level of **bash**
\W	Last element (following last slash) of current working directory
\\	Single backslash inserted in the prompt
\!	Number of current command in the command history
\#	Number of current command, where numbers start at 1 when the shell starts

Variable	Meaning
\@	Time in 12-hour format, where 3:30 p.m. appears as 03:30 p.m.
\$	Indicates whether you are **root**: displays # for **root**, $ for other users
\[	Starts a sequence of nonprinting characters, to be ended by \]
\]	Ends the sequence of nonprinting characters started by \[
\nnn	The character in the ASCII set corresponding to the octal number *nnn* inserted into the prompt

Job Control

Job control lets you place foreground jobs in the background, bring background jobs to the foreground, or suspend (temporarily stop) running jobs. Job control is enabled by default. Once disabled, it can be re-enabled by any of the following commands:

```
bash -m -i
set -m
set -o monitor
```

Many job control commands take *jobID* as an argument. This argument can be specified as follows:

%n
> Job number *n*

%s
> Job whose command line starts with string *s*

%?s
> Job whose command line contains string *s*

%%
> Current job

%+
> Current job (same as preceding)

%-
> Previous job

bash provides the following job control commands. For more information on these commands, see the upcoming section "Built-in Commands."

bg
> Put a job in the background.

fg
> Put a job in the foreground.

jobs
> List active jobs.

kill
> Terminate a job.

stop
>Suspend a background job.

stty tostop
>Stop background jobs if they try to send output to the terminal.

wait
>Wait for background jobs to finish.

Ctrl-Z
>Suspend a foreground job, and use **bg** or **fg** to restart it in the background or foreground. (Your terminal may use something other than **Ctrl-Z** as the suspend character.)

Built-in Commands

Examples to be entered as a command line are shown with the **$** prompt. Otherwise, examples should be treated as code fragments that might be included in a shell script. For convenience, some of the reserved words used by multiline commands also are included.

#

>**#**

>Ignore all text that follows on the same line. **#** is used in shell scripts as the comment character and is not really a command.

#!

>**#!**_shell_

>Used as the first line of a script to invoke the named _shell_ (with optional arguments) or other program. For example:

>```
>#!/bin/bash
>```

:

>**:**

>Null command. Returns an exit status of 0. Sometimes used as the first character in a file to denote a **bash** script. Shell variables can be placed after the **:** to expand them to their values.

>**Example**

>To check whether someone is logged in:

>```
>if who | grep -w $1 > /dev/null
>    then :     # do nothing
>    # if pattern is found
>    else echo "User $1 is not logged in"
>fi
>```

.

>**.** _file_ [_arguments_]

>Same as **source**.

alias	**alias** [**-p**] [*name* [**=** *cmd*]]

Assign a shorthand *name* as a synonym for *cmd*. If =*cmd* is omitted, print the alias for *name*; if *name* is also omitted or if **-p** is specified, print all aliases. See also **unalias**.

bg	**bg** [*jobIDs*]

Put current job or *jobIDs* in the background. See "Job Control" earlier in this chapter.

bind	**bind** [*options*] **bind** [*options*] *key:function*

Print or set the bindings that allow keys to invoke functions such as cursor movement and line editing. Typical syntax choices for *keys* are "\C-t" for Ctrl-T and "\M-t" or "\et" for Esc-T (quoting is needed to escape the sequences from the shell). Function names can be seen though the -l option.

Options

-**f** *filename*
> Consult *filename* for bindings, which should be in the same format as on the **bind** command line.

-**l**
> Print all Readline functions, which are functions that can be bound to keys.

-**m** *keymap*
> Specify a keymap for this and further bindings. Possible keymaps are **emacs**, **emacs-standard**, **emacs-meta**, **emacs-ctlx**, **vi**, **vi-move**, **vi-command**, and **vi-insert**.

-**p**
> Display all functions and the keys that invoke them, in the format by which keys can be set.

-**q** *function*
> Display the key bindings that invoke *function*.

-**r** *key*
> Remove the binding attached to *key* so that it no longer works.

-**s**
> Display all macros and the keys that invoke them, in the format by which keys can be set.

-**u** *function*
> Remove all the bindings attached to *function* so that no keys will invoke it.

-**v**
> Display all Readline variables (settings that affect history and line editing) and their current settings, in the format by which variables can be set.

-**x** *key:command*
> Bind key to a shell command.

-**P**
> Display all bound keys and the functions they invoke.

bash

-S   Display all macros and the keys that invoke them.

-V   Display all Readline variables (settings that affect history and line editing) and their current settings.

Example

Bind Ctrl-T to **copy-forward-word**, the function that copies the part of the word following the cursor so it can be repasted:

```
$ bind "\C-t":copy-forward-word
```

---

break

break [*n*]

Exit from the innermost (most deeply nested) **for, while,** or **until** loop, or from the *n*th innermost level of the loop. Also exits from a **select** list.

---

builtin

builtin *command* [*arguments*]

Execute *command*, which must be a shell built-in. Useful for invoking built-ins within scripts of the same name.

---

case

```
case string
  in
    regex)
      commands
      ;;
    ...
  esac
```

If *string* matches regular expression *regex*, perform the following *commands*. Proceed down the list of regular expressions until one is found. (To catch all remaining strings, use * as *regex* at the end.)

---

cd

cd [*options*] [*dir*]

With no arguments, change to user's home directory. Otherwise, change working directory to *dir*. If *dir* is a relative pathname but is not in the current directory, search the **CDPATH** variable.

Options

-L   Force symbolic links to be followed.

-P   Don't follow symbolic links, but use the physical directory structure.

---

command

command [*options*] *command* [*arguments*]

Execute *command*, but do not perform function lookup (i.e., refuse to run any command that is neither in **PATH** nor a built-in). Set exit status to that returned by *command* unless *command* cannot be found, in which case exit with a status of 127.

Options

-p   Search default path, ignoring the **PATH** variable's value.

-v   Print the command or filename that invokes the command.

-V   Like **-v**, but also print a description of the command.

--   Treat everything that follows as an argument, not an option.

---

compgen   **compgen** [options] [word]

Generate possible completion matches for *word* for use with **bash**'s programmable completion feature, and write the matches to standard output. If *word* is not specified, display all completions. See **complete** for the options; any except **-p** and **-r** can be used with **compgen**.

---

complete   **complete** [options] names

Specify completions for arguments to each *name*, for use with **bash**'s programmable completion feature. With no options or with **-p**, print all completion specifications such that they can be reused as input.

Options

-o *comp-option*

Specify other aspects of the completion specification's behavior besides generating a completion. Possible values of *comp-option* are:

default

Use **readline**'s default filename completion if the completion specification generates no matches.

dirnames

Use directory name completion if the completion specification generates no matches.

filenames

Tell **readline** that the completion specification generates filenames so that it can process them accordingly. For use with shell functions.

nospace

Tell **readline** not to append a space to completions at the end of the line. This is the default.

-p   Print all completion specifications.

-r   Remove completion specification for each *name*, or all specifications if no names are given.

-A *action*

Specify an action to generate a list of completions. Possible actions are:

alias

Alias names. May be specified as **-a**.

arrayvar
Array variable names.

binding
readline key binding names.

builtin
Shell built-in command names. May be specified as **-b**.

command
Command names. May be specified as **-c**.

directory
Directory names. May be specified as **-d**.

disabled
Disabled shell built-in command names.

enabled
Enabled shell built-in command names.

export
Exported shell variable names. May be specified as **-e**.

file
Filenames. May be specified as **-f**.

function
Shell function names.

group
Group names. May be specified as **-g**.

helptopic
Help topic names accepted by the **help** built-in command.

hostname
Hostnames, from the file specified by **HOSTFILE**.

job
Job names, if job control is active. May be specified as **-j**.

keyword
Shell reserved words. May be specified as **-k**.

running
Names of running jobs, if job control is active.

service
Service names. May be specified as **-s**.

setopt
Valid arguments for the **-o** option to the **set** built-in command.

shopt
Valid shell option names for the **shopt** built-in command.

signal
Signal names.

stopped
Names of stopped jobs, if job control is active.

user
> Usernames. May be specified as **-u**.

variable
> Shell variable names. May be specified as **-v**.

-C *command*
> Execute the specified command in a subshell and use the output as possible completions.

-F *function*
> Execute the specified function in the current shell and take the possible completions from the **COMPREPLY** array variable.

-G *globpat*
> Expand the specified filename expansion pattern to generate the possible completions.

-P *prefix*
> Prepend the specified prefix to each possible completion after all other options have been applied.

-S *suffix*
> Append the specified suffix to each possible completion after all other options have been applied.

-W *list*
> Split the specified word list and expand each resulting word. The possible completions are the members of the resulting list that match the word being completed.

-X *pattern*
> Use the specified pattern as a filter and apply it to the list of possible completions generated by all the other options except **-P** and **-S**, removing all matches from the list. A leading ! in the *pattern* negates it so that any completion that does *not* match the pattern is removed.

---

continue

continue [*n*]

Skip remaining commands in a **for**, **while**, or **until** loop, resuming with the next iteration of the loop (or skipping *n* loops).

---

declare

declare [*options*] [*name*[*=value*]]
typeset [*options*] [*name*[*=value*]]

Print or set variables. Options prefaced by + instead of - are inverted in meaning.

Options

-a   Treat the following names as array variables.

-f   Treat the following names as functions.

-i   Expect variable to be an integer, and evaluate its assigned value.

-p   Print names and settings of all shell variables and functions; take no other action.

-r   Do not allow variables to be reset later.

-x   Mark variables for subsequent export.

-F   Print names of all shell functions; take no other action.

---

dirs

dirs [*options*]

Print directories currently remembered for **pushd/popd** operations.

Options

+*entry*
Print *entry*th entry from start of list (list starts at 0).

-*entry*
Print *entry*th entry from end of list.

-c   Clear the directory stack.

-l   Long listing.

-p   Print the directory stack, one entry per line.

-v   Like **-p**, but prefix each entry with its position in the stack.

---

disown

disown [*options*] [*jobIDs*]

Let job run, but disassociate it from the shell. By default, does not even list the job as an active job; commands like **jobs** and **fg** will no longer recognize it. When **-h** is specified, the job is recognized but is kept from being killed when the shell dies.

Options

-a   Act on all jobs.

-h   Do not pass a SIGHUP signal received by the shell on to the job.

---

echo

echo [*options*] [*strings*]

Write each *string* to standard output, separated by spaces and terminated by a newline. If no strings are supplied, echo a newline. (See also **echo** in Chapter 3.)

Options

-e   Enable interpretation of escape characters:

\a   Audible alert

\b   Backspace

\c   Suppress the terminating newline (same as **-n**)

\e   Escape character

\f   Form feed

\n   Newline

\r	Carriage return
\t	Horizontal tab
\v	Vertical tab
****	Backslash

nnn

> The character in the ASCII set corresponding to the octal number *nnn*.

\x*nn*

> The character in the ASCII set corresponding to the hexadecimal number *nn* (1 or 2 hex digits).

-n	Do not append a newline to the output.
-E	Disable interpretation of escape characters.

---

enable

enable [*options*] [*built-in* ...]

Enable (or when **-n** is specified, disable) built-in shell commands. Without *built-in* argument or with **-p** option, print enabled built-ins. With **-a**, print the status of all built-ins. You can disable shell commands in order to define your own functions with the same names.

Options

-a	Display all built-ins, both enabled and disabled.
-d	Delete a built-in command that was previously loaded with **-f**.

-f *filename*

> On systems that support dynamic loading, load the new built-in command *built-in* from the shared object *filename*.

-n	Disable each specified *built-in*.
-p	Display enabled built-ins.
-s	Restrict display to special built-ins defined by the POSIX standard.

---

eval

eval [*command args*...]

Perform *command*, passing *args*.

---

exec

exec [*options*] [*command*]

Execute *command* in place of the current shell (instead of creating a new process). **exec** is also useful for opening, closing, or copying file descriptors.

Options

-a *name*

> Tell *command* that it was invoked as *name*.

-c	Remove all environment variables from the process when the new command runs.

-l   Treat the new process as if the user were logging in.

Examples

$ **trap 'exec 2>&-' 0**   *Close standard error when shell script*
                            exits (signal 0)
$ **exec /bin/tcsh**   *Replace current shell with extended C shell*
$ **exec < infile**   *Reassign standard input to infile*

---

exit

exit [*n*]

Exit a shell script with status *n* (e.g., **exit 1**). *n* can be zero (success) or nonzero (failure). If *n* is not given, exit status will be that of the most recent command. **exit** can be issued at the command line to close a window (log out).

Example

```
if [ $# -eq 0 ]; then
    echo "Usage: $0 [-c] [-d] file(s)"
    exit 1     # Error status
fi
```

---

export

export [*options*] [*variables*]
export [*options*] [*name*=[*value*]]...

Pass (export) the value of one or more shell *variables*, giving global meaning to the variables (which are local by default). For example, a variable defined in one shell script must be exported if its value will be used in other programs called by the script. When a shell variable has been exported, you can access its value by referencing the equivalent environment variable. If no *variables* are given, **export** lists the variables exported by the current shell. If *name* and *value* are specified, **export** assigns *value* to a variable *name* and exports it.

Options

--   Treat all subsequent strings as arguments, not options.

-f   Expect *variables* to be functions.

-n   Unexport variable.

-p   List variables exported by current shell.

---

fc

fc [*options*] [*first*] [*last*]
fc -s [*oldpattern*=*newpattern*] [*command*]

Display or edit commands in the history list. (Use only one of -l or -e.) **fc** provides capabilities similar to the C shell's **history** and ! syntax. *first* and *last* are numbers or strings specifying the range of commands to display or edit. If *last* is omitted, **fc** applies to a single command (specified by *first*). If both *first* and *last* are omitted, **fc** edits the previous command or lists the last 16. A negative number is treated as an offset from the current command. The second form of **fc** takes a history *command*, replaces *old* string with *new* string, and executes the modified command. If no strings are specified, *command* is reexecuted. If no *command* is given either, the previous command is reexecuted. *command* is a number or string like *first*. See earlier examples under "Command History."

Options

-e [*editor*]
> Invoke *editor* to edit the specified history commands. The default *editor* is set by the shell variable **FCEDIT**. If **FCEDIT** is not set, the value of **EDITOR** is used, or **vi** if neither is set.

-l [*first last*]
> List the specified command or range of commands, or list the last 16.

-n Suppress command numbering from the -l listing.

-r Reverse the order of the -l listing.

-s *oldpattern=newpattern*
> Edit command(s), replacing all occurrences of the specified old pattern with the new pattern. Then reexecute.

---

fg

fg [*jobIDs*]

Bring current job or *jobIDs* to the foreground. See "Job Control."

---

for

for *x* [**in** *list*]
  do
    commands
  done

Assign each word in *list* to *x* in turn and execute commands. If *list* is omitted, **$@** (positional parameters) is assumed.

Examples

Paginate all files in the current directory and save each result:

```
for file in *
do
    pr $file > $file.tmp
done
```

Search chapters for a list of words (like **fgrep -f**):

```
for item in `cat program_list`
do
    echo "Checking chapters for"
    echo "references to program $item..."
    grep -c "$item.[co]" chap*
done
```

function	**function** *command* **{** **...** **}** Define a function. Refer to arguments the same way as positional parameters in a shell script (**$1**, etc.) and terminate with }.
getopts	**getopts** *string name* [*args*] Process command-line arguments (or *args*, if specified) and check for legal options. **getopts** is used in shell script loops and is intended to ensure standard syntax for command-line options. *string* contains the option letters to be recognized by **getopts** when running the shell script. Valid options are processed in turn and stored in the shell variable *name*. If an option letter is followed by a colon, the option must be followed by one or more arguments.
hash	**hash** [*options*] [*commands*] Search for *commands* and remember the directory in which each command resides. Hashing causes the shell to remember the association between a name and the absolute pathname of an executable, so that future executions don't require a search of **PATH**. With no arguments or only -l, **hash** lists the current hashed commands. The display shows *hits* (the number of times the command is called by the shell) and *command* (the full pathname). **Options** -d Forget the remembered location of each specified command. -l Display the output in a format that can be reused as input. -p *filename* Assume *filename* is the full path to the command and don't do a path search. -r Forget the locations of all remembered commands. -t Print the full pathname for each command. With more than one command, print the command before each full path.
help	**help** [**-s**] [*string*] Print help text on all built-in commands or those matching *string*. With **-s**, display only brief syntax; otherwise display summary paragraph also.
history	**history** [*options*] **history** [*lines*] Print a numbered command history, denoting modified commands with *. Include commands from previous sessions. You may specify how many lines of history to print.

Options

-a [*file*]

> **bash** maintains a file called *.bash_history* in the user's home directory, a record of previous sessions' commands. Ask **bash** to append the current session's commands to *.bash_history* or to *file*.

-c   Clear history list: remove all previously entered commands from the list remembered by the shell.

-d *offset*

> Delete the history entry at the specified offset from the beginning of the history list.

-n [*file*]

> Append to the history list those lines in *.bash_history* or in *file* that have not yet been included.

-p *args*

> Perform history substitution on the specified arguments and display the result on standard output. The results are not stored in the history list. Each argument must be quoted to disable normal history expansion.

-r [*file*]

> Use *.bash_history* or *file* as the history list, instead of using the working history list.

-s *args*

> Remove the last command in the history list and then add the specified arguments to the list as a single entry (but don't execute the entry).

-w [*file*]

> Overwrite *.bash_history* or *file* with the working history list.

---

if

if `test-cmds`

Begin a conditional statement. The possible formats, shown here side by side, are:

```
if test-cmds        if test-cmds        if test-cmds
   then                then                then
      cmds1               cmds1               cmds1
   fi                  else                elif test-cmds
                          cmds2               then
                       fi                        cmds2
                                               ...
                                             else
                                                cmdsn
                                             fi
```

Usually, the initial **if** and any **elif** lines execute one **test** or [ ] command (although any series of commands is permitted). When **if** succeeds (that is, the last of its *test-cmds* returns 0), *cmds1* are performed; otherwise, each succeeding **elif** or **else** line is tried.

jobs

jobs [*options*] [*jobIDs*]

List all running or stopped jobs, or those specified by *jobIDs*. For example, you can check whether a long compilation or text format is still running. Also useful before logging out. See also "Job Control" earlier in this chapter.

Options

-l   List job IDs and process group IDs.

-n   List only jobs whose status has changed since last notification.

-p   List process group IDs only.

-r   List active, running jobs only.

-s   List stopped jobs only.

-x *command* [*arguments*]

Execute *command*. If *jobIDs* are specified, replace them with *command*.

kill

kill [*options*] *IDs*

Terminate each specified process ID or job ID. You must own the process or be a privileged user. See also "Job Control" and the **killall** command in Chapter 3.

Options

-*signal*

The signal number (from **ps -f**) or name (from **kill -l**). The default is TERM (signal number 15). With a signal number of 9, the kill is unconditional. If nothing else works to kill a process, **kill -9** almost always kills it, but does not allow the process any time to clean up.

--   Consider all subsequent strings to be arguments, not options.

-l [*arg*]

With no argument, list the signal names. (Used by itself.) The argument can be a signal name or a number representing either the signal number or the exit status of a process terminated by a signal. If it is a name, the correspoding number is returned; otherwise, the corresponding name is returned.

-n *signum*

Specify the signal number to send.

-s *signal*

Specify *signal*. May be a signal name or number.

let

let *expressions*

Perform arithmetic as specified by one or more integer *expressions*. *expressions* consist of numbers, operators, and shell variables (which don't need a preceding **$**), and must be quoted if they contain spaces or other special characters. For more information and examples, see "Arithmetic Expressions" earlier in this chapter. See also **expr** in Chapter 3.

Examples
Both of the following examples add 1 to variable **i**:

```
let i=i+1
let "i = i + 1"
```

---

local   local [*options*] [*variable*[=*value*]] [*variable2*[=*value*]] ...

Without arguments, print all local variables. Otherwise, create (and set, if specified) one or more local variables. See the **declare** built-in command for options. Must be used within a function.

---

logout   logout [*status*]

Exit the shell, returning *status* as exit status to invoking program if specified. Can be used only in a login shell. Otherwise, use **exit**.

---

popd   popd [*options*]

Manipulate the directory stack. By default, remove the top directory and **cd** to it. If successful, run **dirs** to show the new directory stack.

Options

+*n*   Remove the *n*th directory in the stack, counting from 0.

-*n*   Remove the *n*th entry from the bottom of the stack, counting from 0.

-**n**   Don't do a **cd** when removing directories from the stack.

---

printf   printf *string* [*arguments*]

Format the *arguments* according to *string*. Works like the C library **printf** function. Standard **printf** percent-sign formats are recognized in *string*, such as **%i** for integer. Escape sequences such as **\n** can be included in *string* and are automatically recognized; if you want to include them in *arguments*, specify a *string* of **%b**. You can escape characters in *arguments* to output a string suitable for input to other commands by specifying a *string* of **%q**.

Examples

```
$ printf "Previous command: %i\n" "$(($HISTCMD-1))"
Previous command: 534
$ echo $PAGER
less -E
$ printf "%q\n" "\t$PAGER"
\\tless\ -E
```

The last command would probably be used to record a setting in a file where it could be read and assigned by another shell script.

pushd

pushd [*directory*]
pushd [*options*]

By default, switch top two directories on stack. If specified, add a new directory to the top of the stack instead, and **cd** to it.

Options

+*n* Rotate the stack to place the *n*th (counting from 0) directory at the top.

-*n* Rotate the stack to place the *n*th directory from the bottom of the stack at the top.

-**n** Don't do a **cd** when adding directories to the stack.

pwd

pwd [**option**]

Display the current working directory's absolute pathname. By default, any symbolic directories used when reaching the current directory are displayed, but with **-P**, or if the **-o** option to the **set** built-in is set, the real names are displayed instead.

Options

-**L** Include any symbolic links in the pathname.

-**P** Do not include symbolic links in the pathname.

read

read [*options*] [*variable1 variable2* ...]

Read one line of standard input and assign each word (as defined by IFS) to the corresponding *variable*, with all leftover words assigned to the last variable. If only one variable is specified, the entire line will be assigned to that variable. The return status is 0 unless EOF is reached, a distinction that is useful for running loops over input files. If no variable names are provided, read the entire string into the environment variable **REPLY**.

Options

-**a** *var*
　　Read each word into an element of *var*, which is treated as an array variable.

-**d** *char*
　　Stop reading the line at *char* instead of at the newline.

-**e** Line editing and command history are enabled during input.

-**n** *num*
　　Read only *num* characters from the line.

-**p** *string*
　　Display the prompt *string* to the user before reading each line, if input is interactive.

-**r** Raw mode; ignore \ as a line continuation character.

-**s** Do not echo the characters entered by the user (useful for reading a password).

-t *seconds*

Time out and return without setting any variables if input is interactive and no input has been entered for *seconds* seconds.

-u *fd*

Read input from specified file descriptor *fd* instead of standard input.

Examples

```
$ read first last address
Sarah Caldwell 123 Main Street
$ echo "$last, $first\n$address"
Caldwell, Sarah
123 Main Street
```

The following commands, which read a password into the variable **$user_pw** and then display its value, use recently added options that are not in all versions of **bash** in current use.

```
$ read -sp "Enter password (will not appear on screen)"
user_pw
Enter password (will not appear on screen)
$ echo $user_pw
You weren't supposed to know!
```

The following script reads input from the system's password file, which uses colons to delimit fields (making it a popular subject for examples of input parsing).

```
IFS=:
cat /etc/passwd |
while
read account pw user group gecos home shell
do
echo "Account name $account has user info: $gecos"
done
```

---

readonly

readonly [*options*] [*variable1 variable2...*]

Prevent the specified shell variables from being assigned new values. Variables can be accessed (read) but not overwritten.

Options

-a Treat the following names as array variables.

-f Treat the following names as functions and set them read-only so that they cannot be changed.

-p Display all read-only variables (default).

---

return

return [*n*]

Normally used inside a function to exit the function with status *n* or with the exit status of the previously executed command. Can be used outside a function during execution of a script by the . command to cause the shell to stop execution of the script. The return status is *n* or the script's exit status.

select

```
select name [ in wordlist ; ]
do
    commands
done
```

Choose a value for *name* by displaying the words in *wordlist* to the user and prompting for a choice. Store user input in the variable **REPLY** and the chosen word in *name*. Then execute *commands* repeatedly until they execute a **break** or **return**. The default prompt can be changed by setting the **PS3** shell variable.

set

```
set [options] [arg1 arg2 ...]
```

With no arguments, **set** prints the values of all variables known to the current shell. Options can be enabled (*-option*) or disabled (*+option*). Options can also be set when the shell is invoked, via **bash**. Arguments are assigned in order to **$1**, **$2**, and so on.

Options

-    Turn off **-v** and **-x**, and turn off option processing.

--   Used as the last option; turn off option processing so that arguments beginning with - are not misinterpreted as options. (For example, you can set **$1** to -1.) If no arguments are given after --, unset the positional parameters.

-a   From now on, automatically mark variables for export after defining or changing them.

-b   Report background job status at termination instead of waiting for next shell prompt.

-e   Exit if a command yields a nonzero exit status.

-f   Do not expand filename metacharacters (e.g., * ? [ ]). Wildcard expansion is sometimes called *globbing*.

-h   Locate and remember commands as they are defined.

-k   Assignment of environment variables (*var=value*) will take effect regardless of where they appear on the command line. Normally, assignments must precede the command name.

-m   Monitor mode. Enable job control; background jobs execute in a separate process group. **-m** usually is set automatically.

-n   Read commands, but don't execute. Useful for checking errors, particularly for shell scripts.

-o [*m*]
     List shell modes, or turn on mode *m*. Many modes can be set by other options. The modes can be turned off through the **+o** option. Modes are:

allexport
        Same as **-a**.

braceexpand
        Same as **-B**.

emacs
> Enter Emacs editing mode (on by default).

errexit
> Same as **-e**.

hashall
> Same as **-h**.

histexpand
> Same as **-H**.

history
> Default. Preserve command history.

ignoreeof
> Don't allow use of a single **Ctrl-D** (the end-of-file or EOF character) to log off; use the **exit** command to log off. This has the same effect as setting the shell variable **IGNOREEOF=1**.

interactive-comments
> Allow comments to appear in interactive commands.

keyword
> Same as **-k**.

monitor
> Same as **-m**.

noclobber
> Same as **-C**.

noexec
> Same as **-n**.

noglob
> Same as **-f**.

notify
> Same as **-b**.

nounset
> Same as **-u**.

onecmd
> Same as **-t**.

physical
> Same as **-P**.

posix
> Match POSIX standard.

privileged
> Same as **-p**.

verbose
> Same as **-v**.

vi
> Enable **vi**-style command-line editing.

xtrace
> Same as **-x**.

+o [*m*]

Display the **set** commands that would recreate the current mode settings or turn off mode *m*. See the **-o** option for a list of modes.

-p   Start up as a privileged user; don't process *$HOME/.profile*.

-t   Exit after one command is executed.

-u   Indicate an error when user tries to use a variable that is undefined.

-v   Show each shell command line when read.

-x   Show commands and arguments when executed, preceded by a + or the prompt defined by the **PS4** shell variable. This provides step-by-step debugging of shell scripts. (Same as **-o xtrace**.)

-B   Default. Enable brace expansion.

-C   Don't allow output redirection (>) to overwrite an existing file.

-H   Default. Enable ! and !! commands.

-P   Print absolute pathnames in response to **pwd**. By default, **bash** includes symbolic links in its response to **pwd**.

Examples

`set -- "$num" -20 -30`	*Set $1 to $num, $2 to -20, $3 to -30*
`set -vx`	*Read each command line; show it; execute it; show it again (with arguments)*
`set +x`	*Stop command tracing*
`set -o noclobber`	*Prevent file overwriting*
`set +o noclobber`	*Allow file overwriting again*

---

shift

shift [*n*]

Shift positional arguments (e.g., **$2** becomes **$1**). If *n* is given, shift to the left *n* places.

---

shopt

shopt [*options*] [*optnames*]

Set or unset variables that control optional shell behavior. With no options or with **-p**, display the settable *optnames*.

Options

-o   Allow only options defined for the **set -o** built-in to be set or unset.

-p   Display output in a form that can be reused as input.

-q   Quiet mode. Suppress normal output.

-s   Set (enable) each specified option. With no *optname*, list all set options.

-u   Unset (disable) each specified option. With no *optname*, list all unset options.

Settable shell options

Unless otherwise noted, options are disabled by default.

cdable_vars

> If an argument to the **cd** built-in is not a directory, assume that it's a variable containing the name of the directory to change to.

cdspell

> For interactive shells, check for minor errors in the name of a directory component (transposed characters, a missing character, or an extra character). Print the corrected name and proceed.

checkhash

> Check that a command found in the hash table actually exists before trying to execute it; if it is not found, do a path search.

checkwinsize

> Check the window size after each command and update **LINES** and **COLUMNS** as necessary.

cmdhist

> Attempt to save all lines of a multiline command in one history entry to facilitate re-editing.

dotglob

> Include filenames beginning with . in the results of pathname expansion.

execfail

> For a noninteractive shell, do not exit if the file specified as an argument to **exec** cannot be executed. For an interactive shell, do not exit from the shell if **exec** fails.

expand_aliases

> Expand aliases. Enabled by default for interactive shells.

extglob

> Enable the shell's extended pattern matching features for pathname expansion.

histappend

> Append the history list to the file specified by HISTFILE when the shell exits, instead of overwriting the file.

histreedit

> Give the user a chance to re-edit a failed history substitution.

histverify

> Load a history substitution into the **readline** editing buffer so it can be further edited, instead of immediately passing it to the shell parser.

hostcomplete

> Try to provide hostname completion when a word containing @ is being completed. Set by default.

huponexit

> Send SIGHUP to all jobs when an interactive login shell exits.

interactive_comments

In an interactive shell, treat any word beginning with a #, and any subsequent characters, as a comment. Set by default.

lithist

If **cmdhist** is also enabled, save multiline commands to the history file separated by embedded newlines rather than semicolons (;) when possible.

login_shell

Set by the shell if it is started as a login shell. Cannot be changed by the user.

mailwarn

Warn if a mail file has been accessed since the last time **bash** checked it.

no_empty_cmd_completion

Don't attempt to search the PATH for possible completions when completion is attempted on an empty line.

nocaseglob

Use case-insensitive filename matching during pathname expansion.

nullglob

Allow patterns that do not match any files to expand to a null string.

progcomp

Enable the programmable completion facilities. Set by default.

promptvars

Perform variable and parameter expansion on prompt strings after performing normal expansion. Set by default.

restricted_shell

Set by the shell if started in restricted mode. This option cannot be changed by the user and is not reset when the startup files are executed.

shift_verbose

Cause the **shift** built-in to print an error message when the shift count is greater than the number of positional parameters.

sourcepath

Cause the **source** built-in (.) to search the PATH to find the directory containing a file supplied as an argument. Set by default.

xpg_echo

Cause the **echo** built-in to expand backslash-escape sequences by default.

---

source

source *file* [*arguments*]

Read and execute lines in *file*. *file* does not have to be executable but must reside in a directory searched by PATH. Any *arguments* are passed as positional parameters to the file when it is executed.

| **suspend** | **suspend** [`-f`] |
| | Same as **Ctrl-Z**. |

Option

-f   Force suspend, even if shell is a login shell.

| **test** | **test** *condition* |
| | **[** *condition* **]** |

Evaluate a *condition* and, if its value is true, return a zero exit status; otherwise, return a nonzero exit status. An alternate form of the command uses **[ ]** rather than the word **test**. *condition* is constructed using the following expressions. Conditions are true if the description holds true.

File conditions

-a *file*
> *file* exists.

-b *file*
> *file* is a block special file.

-c *file*
> *file* is a character special file.

-d *file*
> *file* is a directory.

-e *file*
> *file* exists.

-f *file*
> *file* is a regular file.

-g *file*
> *file* has the **set-group-ID** bit set.

-h *file*
> *file* is a symbolic link.

-k *file*
> *file* has its sticky bit (no longer used) set.

-p *file*
> *file* is a named pipe (FIFO).

-r *file*
> *file* is readable.

-s *file*
> *file* has a size greater than 0.

-t [*n*]
> The open file descriptor *n* is associated with a terminal device (default *n* is 1).

-u *file*
> *file* has its **set-user-ID** bit set.

-w *file*
> *file* is writable.

-x *file*
> *file* is executable.

-G *file*
> *file*'s group is the process's effective group ID.

-L *file*
> *file* is a symbolic link.

-N *file*
> *file* has been modified since its last time of access.

-O *file*
> *file*'s owner is the process's effective user ID.

-S *file*
> *file* is a socket.

f1 **-ef** *f2*
> Files *f1* and *f2* are linked (refer to the same file through a hard link).

f1 **-nt** *f2*
> File *f1* is newer than *f2*.

f1 **-ot** *f2*
> File *f1* is older than *f2*.

String conditions

-n *s1*
> String *s1* has nonzero length.

-o *s1*
> Shell option *s1* is set. Shell options are described under the **set** built-in command.

-z *s1*
> String *s1* has 0 length.

s1 = *s2*
> Strings *s1* and *s2* are identical.

s1 == *s2*
> Strings *s1* and *s2* are identical.

s1 != *s2*
> Strings *s1* and *s2* are not identical.

s1 < *s2*
> String *s1* is lower in the alphabet (or other sort in use) than *s2*. By default, the check is performed character-by-character against the ASCII character set.

s1 > *s2*
> String *s1* is higher in the alphabet (or other sort in use) than *s2*.

string
> *string* is not null.

Integer comparisons

n1 **-eq** *n2*
> *n1* equals *n2*.

n1 **-ge** *n2*
> *n1* is greater than or equal to *n2*.

n1 **-gt** *n2*
> *n1* is greater than *n2*.

n1 **-le** *n2*
> *n1* is less than or equal to *n2*.

n1 **-lt** *n2*
> *n1* is less than *n2*.

n1 **-ne** *n2*
> *n1* does not equal *n2*.

Combined forms

! *condition*
> True if *condition* is false.

condition1 **-a** *condition2*
> True if both conditions are true.

condition1 **-o** *condition2*
> True if either condition is true.

Examples

Each of the following examples shows the first line of various statements that might use a test condition:

```
while test $# -gt 0       While there are arguments . . .
while [ -n "$1" ]         While the first argument is nonempty . . .
if [ $count -lt 10 ]      If $count is less than 10 . . .
if [ -d RCS ]             If the RCS directory exists . . .
if [ "$answer" != "y" ]   If the answer is not y . . .
if [ ! -r "$1" -o ! -f "$1" ]  If the first argument is not a
                              readable file or a regular file . . .
```

---

times

times

Print accumulated process times for user and system.

---

trap

trap [*option*] [*commands*] [*signals*]

Execute *commands* if any of *signals* is received. Each *signal* can be a signal name or number. Common signals include 0, 1, 2, and 15. Multiple commands should be quoted as a group and separated by semicolons internally. If *commands* is the null string (e.g., **trap ""** *signals*), then *signals* is ignored by the shell. If *commands* is omitted entirely, reset processing of specified signals to the default action. If both *commands* and *signals* are omitted, list current trap assignments. See examples at the end of this entry and under **exec**.

Options

-l   List signal names and numbers.

-p   Used with no *commands* to print the trap commands associated with each *signal*, or all signals if none is specified.

Signals

Signals are listed along with what triggers them.

0   Exit from shell (usually when shell script finishes).

1   Hang up (usually logout).

2   Interrupt (usually through **Ctrl-C**).

3   Quit.

4   Illegal instruction.

5   Trace trap.

6   Abort.

7   Unused.

8   Floating-point exception.

9   Termination.

10   User-defined.

11   Reference to invalid memory.

12   User-defined.

13   Write to a pipe without a process to read it.

14   Alarm timeout.

15   Software termination (usually via **kill**).

16   Unused.

17   Termination of child process.

18   Continue (if stopped).

19   Stop process.

20   Process suspended (usually through **Ctrl-Z**).

21   Background process has tty input.

22   Background process has tty output.

23–28
    Unused.

29   I/O possible on a channel.

Examples

```
trap "" 2        Ignore signal 2 (interrupts)
trap 2           Obey interrupts again
```

Remove a **$tmp** file when the shell program exits or if the user logs out, presses **Ctrl-C**, or does a **kill**:

```
trap "rm -f $tmp; exit" 0 1 2 15
```

type

type [*options*] *commands*

Report absolute pathname of programs invoked for *commands* and whether or not they are hashed.

Options

--   Consider all subsequent strings to be arguments, not options.

-a, -all

    Print all occurrences of *command*, not just that which would be invoked.

-f   Suppress shell function lookup.

-p, -path

    Print the hashed value of *command*, which may differ from the first appearance of *command* in the PATH.

-t, -type

    Determine and state if *command* is an alias, keyword, function, built-in, or file.

-P   Force a PATH search for each name, even if **-t** would not return a value of "file" for the name.

Example

```
$ type mv read
mv is /bin/mv
read is a shell built-in
```

typeset

typeset

Obsolete. See **declare**.

ulimit

ulimit [*options*] [*n*]

Print the value of one or more resource limits or, if *n* is specified, set a resource limit to *n*. Resource limits can be either hard (**-H**) or soft (**-S**). By default, **ulimit** sets both limits or prints the soft limit. The options determine which resource is acted on. Values are in 1024-byte increments unless otherwise indicated.

Options

--   Consider all subsequent strings to be arguments, not options.

-a   Print all current limits.

-H   Hard resource limit.

-S   Soft resource limit.

Specific limits

These options limit specific resource sizes.

-c   Core files.

-d   Size of processes' data segments.

-f	Size of shell-created files.
-l	Size of memory that the process can lock.
-m	Resident set size.
-n	Number of file descriptors. On many systems, this cannot be set.
-p	Pipe size, measured in blocks of 512 bytes.
-s	Stack size.
-t	Amount of CPU time, counted in seconds.
-u	Number of processes per user.
-v	Virtual memory used by shell.

umask

umask [*options*] [*nnn*]

Display file creation mask or set file creation mask to octal value *nnn*. The file creation mask determines which permission bits are turned off (e.g., **umask 002** produces **rw-rw-r--**).

Options

-p Display mask within a **umask** command so that a caller can read and execute it.

-S Display **umask** symbolically rather than in octal.

unalias

unalias [**-a**] *names*

Remove *names* from the alias list. See also **alias**.

Option

-a Remove all aliases.

unset

unset [*options*] *names*

Erase definitions of functions or variables listed in *names*.

Options

-f Expect *name* to refer to a function.

-v Expect *name* to refer to a variable (default).

until

```
until
  test-commands
do
  commands
done
```

Execute *test-commands* (usually a **test** or **[ ]** command); if the exit status is nonzero (that is, the test fails), perform *commands*. Repeat.

wait **wait** [*ID*]

Pause in execution until all background jobs complete (exit status 0 will be returned), or until the specified background process ID or job ID completes (exit status of *ID* is returned). Note that the shell variable **$!** contains the process ID of the most recent background process. If job control is not in effect, *ID* can only be a process ID number. See "Job Control."

Example

　　wait $!　　*Wait for last background process to finish*

while **while**
　　test-commands
　　do
　　　commands
　　done

Execute *test-commands* (usually a **test** or **[ ]** command); if the exit status is 0, perform *commands*. Repeat.

8

tcsh: An Extended C Shell

This chapter describes **tcsh**, an enhanced version of the C shell. On many versions of Linux, **tcsh** is also used as the C shell; in that case, the **tcsh** features described in this chapter work even when you run **csh**. The C shell was so named because many of its programming constructs and symbols resemble those of the C programming language.

The default shell on Linux systems is **bash**. If you want to use **tcsh**, you first need to change your default. Each user's shell preference is kept in the password table. If you are creating an account, you can set the default shell when you add the user. If the account already exists, use the **chsh** command to change the shell (see the command descriptions in Chapter 3).

Overview of Features

Features of **tcsh** include:

- Input/output redirection
- Wildcard characters (metacharacters) for filename abbreviation
- Shell variables for customizing your environment
- Integer arithmetic
- Access to previous commands (command history)
- Command-name abbreviation (aliasing)
- A built-in command set for writing shell programs
- Job control
- Command-line editing and editor commands
- Word completion (tab completion)
- Spellchecking

- Scheduled events, such as logout or terminal locking after a set idle period and delayed commands
- Read-only variables

Invoking the Shell

The shell command interpreter can be invoked as follows:

tcsh [*options*] [*arguments*]

tcsh uses syntax resembling C and executes commands from a terminal or a file. The options **-n**, **-v**, and **-x** are useful when debugging scripts.

Options

-b   Allow the remaining command-line options to be interpreted as options to a specified command rather than as options to **tcsh**.

-c   Read and execute commands specified from the argument that follows and place any remaining arguments in the **argv** shell variable.

-d   Load directory stack from *~/.cshdirs* even if not a login shell.

-e   Exit if a command produces errors.

-f   Fast startup; start without executing *.tcshrc*.

-i   Invoke interactive shell (prompt for input) even if not on a terminal.

-l   Login shell (must be the only option specified).

-m   Load *~/.tcshrc* even if effective user is not the owner of the file.

-n   Parse commands, but do not execute.

-q   Accept **SIGQUIT** when used under a debugger. Disables job control.

-s   Read commands from the standard input.

-t   Exit after executing one line of input (which may be continued with a \ to escape the newline).

-v   Display commands before executing them; expand history substitutions, but not other substitutions (e.g., filename, variable, and command). Same as setting **verbose**.

-V   Same as **-v**, but also display *.tcshrc*.

-x   Display commands before executing them, but expand all substitutions. Same as setting **echo**.

-X   Same as **-x**, but also display *.tcshrc*.

Arguments

Arguments are assigned, in order, to the positional parameters **$1**, **$2**, and so on. If the first argument is an executable script, commands are read from it, and remaining arguments are assigned to **$1**, **$2**, and so forth.

Syntax

This section describes the many symbols used by **tcsh**. The topics are arranged as follows:

- Special files
- Filename metacharacters
- Quoting
- Command forms
- Redirection forms

Special Files

Filename	Description
~/.tcshrc or ~/.cshrc	Executed at each instance of shell startup. If no ~/.tcshrc is found, **tcsh** uses ~/.cshrc if present.
~/.login	Executed by login shell after .tcshrc at login.
~/.cshdirs	Executed by login shell after .login.
~/.logout	Executed by login shell at logout.
/etc/passwd	Source of home directories for ~name abbreviations.

Filename Metacharacters

Characters	Meaning
*	Match any string of 0 or more characters.
?	Match any single character.
[abc...]	Match any one of the enclosed characters; a hyphen can be used to specify a range (e.g., a-z, A-Z, 0-9).
{abc,xxx,...}	Expand each comma-separated string inside braces.
~	Home directory for the current user.
~name	Home directory of user name.

Examples

```
% ls new*        Match new and new.1
% cat ch?        Match ch9 but not ch10
% vi [D-R]*      Match files that begin with uppercase D through R
% ls {ch,app}?   Expand, then match ch1, ch2, app1, app2
% cd ~tom        Change to tom's home directory
```

Quoting

Quoting disables a character's special meaning and allows it to be used literally, as itself. The characters in the following table have special meaning to **tcsh**.

Characters	Description
;	Command separator
&	Background execution
()	Command grouping
|	Pipe
*?[]~	Filename metacharacters
{}	String expansion characters (usually don't require quoting)
> < & !	Redirection symbols
! ^	History substitution, quick substitution
" ' \	Used in quoting other characters
`	Command substitution
$	Variable substitution
newline space tab	Word separators

The characters that follow can be used for quoting:

" " Everything between " and " is taken literally except for the following characters, which keep their special meaning:

$ Variable substitution will occur.

` Command substitution will occur.

" The end of the double quote.

\ Escape next character.

! The history character.

newline
   The newline character.

' ' Everything between ' and ' is taken literally except for ! (history).

\ The character following a \ is taken literally. Use within " " to escape ", $, and `. Often used to escape itself, spaces, or newlines. Always needed to escape a history character (usually !).

Examples

```
% echo 'Single quotes "protect" double quotes'
Single quotes "protect" double quotes

% echo "Well, isn't that "\""special?"\"
Well, isn't that "special"?

% echo "You have `ls|wc -l` files in `pwd`"
You have 43 files in /home/bob

% echo The value of \$x is $x
The value of $x is 100
```

Command Forms

Command	Action
cmd &	Execute cmd in background.
cmd1 ; cmd2	Command sequence; execute multiple cmds on the same line.
(cmd1 ; cmd2)	Subshell; treat cmd1 and cmd2 as a command group.
cmd1 | cmd2	Pipe; use output from cmd1 as input to cmd2.
cmd1 \`cmd2\`	Command substitution; run cmd2 first and use its output as arguments to cmd1.
cmd1 || cmd2	OR; execute either cmd1 or (if cmd1 fails) cmd2.
cmd1 && cmd2	AND; execute cmd1 and then (if cmd1 succeeds) cmd2.

Examples

```
% cd; ls                          Execute sequentially
% (date; who; pwd) > logfile      All output is redirected
% sort file | pr -3 | lp          Sort file, page output, then print
% vi `grep -l ifdef *.c`          Edit files found by grep
% egrep '(yes|no)' `cat list`     Specify a list of files to search
% grep XX file && lp file         Print file if it contains the pattern
% grep XX file || echo XX not found   Echo an error message if XX not found
```

Redirection Forms

File descriptor	Name	Common abbreviation	Typical default
0	Standard input	stdin	Keyboard
1	Standard output	stdout	Screen
2	Standard error	stderr	Screen

The usual input source or output destination can be changed with redirection commands listed in the following sections.

Simple redirection

Command	Action
cmd > file	Send output of cmd to file (overwrite).
cmd >! file	Same as preceding, even if **noclobber** is set.
cmd >> file	Send output of cmd to file (append).
cmd>>! file	Same as preceding, even if **noclobber** is set.
cmd < file	Take input for cmd from file.
cmd << text	Read standard input up to a line identical to *text* (*text* can be stored in a shell variable). Input usually is typed on the screen or in the shell program. Commands that typically use this syntax include **cat, echo, ex,** and **sed.** If *text* is enclosed in quotes, standard input will not undergo variable substitution, command substitution, etc.

Multiple redirection

Command	Action
cmd >& *file*	Send both standard output and standard error to *file*.
cmd >&! *file*	Same as preceding, even if **noclobber** is set.
cmd >>& *file*	Append standard output and standard error to end of *file*.
cmd >>&! *file*	Same as preceding, even if **noclobber** is set.
cmd1 |& *cmd2*	Pipe standard error together with standard output.
(*cmd*> *f1*) >& *f2*	Send standard output to file *f1* and standard error to file *f2*.
cmd	**tee** *files*	Send output of *cmd* to standard output (usually the screen) and to *files*. (See the example in Chapter 3 under **tee**.)

Examples

```
% cat part1 > book              Copy part1 to book
% cat part2 part3 >> book        Append parts 2 and 3 to same file as part1
% mail tim < report              Take input to message from report
% cc calc.c >& error_out         Store all messages, including errors
% cc newcalc.c >&! error_out     Overwrite old file
% grep Unix ch* |& pr            Pipe all messages, including errors
% (find / -print > filelist) >& no_access    Separate error messages from list of files
% sed 's/^/XX /' << "END_ARCHIVE"            Supply text right after command
This is often how a shell archive is "wrapped",
bundling text for distribution. You would normally
run sed from a shell program, not from the command line.
"END_ARCHIVE"
```

Variables

This subsection describes the following:

- Variable substitution
- Variable modifiers
- Predefined shell variables
- Formatting for the *prompt* variable
- Sample *.tcshrc* file
- Environment variables

Variable Substitution

In the following substitutions, braces ({ }) are optional, except when needed to separate a variable name from following characters that would otherwise be considered part of the name.

Variable	Description
${var}	The value of variable *var*.
${var[i]}	Select word or words in position *i* of *var*. *i* can be a single number, a range *m-n*, a range *-n* (missing *m* implies 1), a range *m-* (missing *n* implies all remaining words), or * (select all words). *i* also can be a variable that expands to one of these values.
${#var}	The number of words in *var*.
${#argv}	The number of arguments.
$0	Name of the program.
${argv[n]}	Individual arguments on command line (positional parameters); $1 \leq n \leq 9$.
${n}	Same as ${argv[n]}.
${argv[*]}	All arguments on command line.
$*	Same as {$argv[*]}.
$argv[$#argv]	The last argument.
${?var}	Return 1 if *var* is set, 0 if not.
$$	Process number of current shell; useful as part of a filename for creating temporary files with unique names.
${?name}	Return 1 if *name* is set, 0 if not.
$?0	Return 1 if input filename is known, 0 if not.

Examples

Sort the third through last arguments and save the output in a file whose name is unique to this process:

```
sort $argv[3-] > tmp.$$
```

Process *.tcshrc* commands only if the shell is interactive (i.e., the **prompt** variable must be set):

```
if ($?prompt) then
    set commands,
    alias commands,
    etc.
endif
```

Variable Modifiers

Except for **$?var**, **$$**, and **$?0**, the variable substitutions in the preceding section may be followed by one of these modifiers (when braces are used, the modifier goes inside them):

:r Return the variable's root (the portion before the last dot).

:e Return the variable's extension.

:h Return the variable's header (the directory portion).

:t Return the variable's tail (the portion after the last slash).

:gr Return all roots.

:ge Return all extensions.

:gh Return all headers.

:gt Return all tails.

:q Quote a wordlist variable, keeping the items separate. Prevents further substitution. Useful when the variable contains filename metacharacters that should not be expanded.

:x Quote a pattern, expanding it into a wordlist.

Examples using pathname modifiers

The following table shows the effect of pathname modifiers if the **aa** variable is set as follows:

```
set aa=(/progs/num.c /book/chap.ps)
```

Variable portion	Specification	Output result
Normal variable	echo $aa	/progs/num.c /book/chap.ps
Second root	echo $aa[2]:r	/book/chap
Second header	echo $aa[2]:h	/book
Second tail	echo $aa[2]:t	chap.ps
Second extension	echo $aa[2]:e	ps
Root	echo $aa:r	/progs/num /book/chap.ps
Global root	echo $aa:gr	/progs/num /book/chap
Header	echo $aa:h	/progs /book/chap.ps
Global header	echo $aa:gh	/progs /book
Tail	echo $aa:t	num.c /book/chap.ps
Global tail	echo $aa:gt	num.c chap.ps
Extension	echo $aa:e	c /book/chap.ps
Global extension	echo $aa:ge	c ps

Examples using quoting modifiers

Unless quoted, the shell expands variables to represent files in the current directory:

```
% set a="[a-z]*" A="[A-Z]*"
% echo "$a" "$A"
[a-z]* [A-Z]*

% echo $a $A
at cc m4 Book Doc

% echo $a:x $A
[a-z]* Book Doc

% set d=($a:q $A:q)
% echo $d
at cc m4 Book Doc
```

```
% echo $d:q
[a-z]* [A-Z]*

% echo $d[1] +++ $d[2]
at cc m4 +++ Book Doc

% echo $d[1]:q
[a-z]*
```

Predefined Shell Variables

Variables can be set in one of two ways; by assigning a value:

    set var=value

or by simply turning the variable on:

    set var

In the following table, variables that accept values are shown with the equals sign followed by the type of value they accept; the value is then described. (Note, however, that variables such as **argv**, **cwd**, and **status** are never explicitly assigned.) For variables that are turned on or off, the table describes what they do when set. **tcsh** automatically sets (and, in some cases, updates) the variables **addsuffix**, **argv**, **autologout**, **command**, **cwd**, **dirstack**, **echo-style**, **edit**, **gid**, **home**, **loginsh**, **logout**, **oid**, **owd**, **path**, **prompt**, **prompt2**, **prompt3**, **shell**, **shlvl**, **status**, **tcsh**, **term**, **tty**, **uid**, **user**, and **version**.

Variable	Description
addsuffix	Append / to directories and a space to files during tab completion to indicate a precise match.
afsuser	Set value to be used instead of the local username for Kerberos authentication with the **autologout** locking feature.
ampm	Display all times in 12-hour format.
argv=(args)	List of arguments passed to current command; default is ( ).
autocorrect	Check spelling before attempting to complete commands.
autoexpand	Expand history (such as ! references) during command completion.
autolist[=ambiguous]	Print possible completions when correct one is ambiguous. If **ambiguous** is specified, print possible completions only when completion adds no new characters.
autologout=logout-minutes [locking-minutes]	Log out after logout-minutes of idle time. Lock the terminal after locking-minutes of idle time, requiring a password before continuing. Not used if the **DISPLAY** environment variable is set.
backslash_quote	Always allow backslashes to quote \, ', and ".
catalog	Use tcsh.${catalog} as the filename of the message catalog. The default is tcsh.
cdpath=dirs	List of alternate directories to search when locating arguments for **cd**, **popd**, or **pushd**.
color	Turn on color for **ls-F**, **ls**, or both. Setting to nothing is equivalent to setting for both.
colorcat	Enable color escape sequence for Native Language System (NLS) support and display NLS messages in color.

Variable	Description
command	If set, hold the command passed to the shell with the -c option.
complete=enhance	When **enhance**, ignore case in completion, treat ., -, and _ as word separators, and consider _ and - to be the same.
continue=*cmdlist*	If set to a list of commands, continue those commands instead of starting new ones.
continue_args=*cmdlist*	Like **continue**, but execute the following: echo \`pwd\` $argv > ~/.cmd_pause; %cmd
correct={cmd|complete|all}	When **cmd**, spellcheck commands. When **complete**, complete commands. When **all**, spellcheck whole command line.
cwd=*dir*	Full pathname of current directory.
dextract	When set, the **pushd** command extracts the desired directory and puts it at the top of the stack instead of rotating the stack.
dirsfile=*file*	History file consulted by **dirs -S** and **dirs -L**. Default is ~/.cshdirs.
dirstack	Directory stack, in array format. **dirstack[0]** is always equivalent to **cwd**. The other elements can be artificially changed.
dspmbyte=*code*	Enable use of multibyte code; for use with Kanji. See the **tcsh** manpage for details.
dunique	Make sure that each directory exists only once in the stack.
echo	Redisplay each command line before execution; same as **csh -x** command.
echo_style={bsd|sysv|both|none}	Don't echo a newline with -n option (**bsd**), parse escaped characters (**sysv**), do both, or do neither.
edit	Enable command-line editor. Set by default for interactive shells.
ellipsis	For use with **prompt** variable. Use ... to represent skipped directories.
fignore=*suffs*	List of filename suffixes to ignore during filename completion.
gid	User's group ID.
group	User's group name.
histchars=*ab*	A two-character string that sets the characters to use in history substitution and quick substitution (default is !^).
histdup={all|prev|erase}	Maintain a record only of unique history events (**all**), do not enter a new event when it is the same as the previous one (**prev**), or remove an old event that is the same as the new one (**erase**).
histfile=*file*	History file consulted by **history -S** and **history -L**. Default is ~/.history.
histlit	Do not expand history lines when recalling them.
history=*n format*	The first word indicates the number of commands to save in the history list. The second indicates the format with which to display that list (see the "Formatting for the Prompt Variable" section for possible formats).
home=*dir*	Home directory of user, initialized from HOME. The ~ character is shorthand for this value.
ignoreeof	Ignore an end-of-file (EOF) from terminals; prevents accidental logout.
implicitcd	If directory name is entered as a command, **cd** to that directory. Can be set to **verbose** to echo the **cd** to standard output.
inputmode={insert|overwrite}	Control editor's mode.
killdup={all|prev|erase}	Enter only unique strings in the kill ring (**all**), do not enter new string when it is the same as the current killed string (**prev**), or erase from the kill ring an old string that is the same as the current string (**erase**).
killring=*num*	Set the number of killed strings to keep in memory to *num*. The default is 30. If unset or set to a number less than 2, keep only the most recent killed string.

Variable	Description
listflags=*flags*	One or more of the **x**, **a**, or **A** options for the **ls-F** built-in command. Second word can be set to path for **ls** command.
listjobs[=long]	When a job is suspended, list all jobs (in long format, if specified).
listlinks	In **ls -F** command, include type of file to which links point.
listmax=*num*	Do not allow **list-choices** to print more than *num* choices before prompting.
listmaxrows=*num*	Do not allow **list-choices** to print more than *num* rows of choices before prompting.
loginsh	Set if shell is a login shell.
logout	Indicates status of an imminent logout (**normal**, **automatic**, or **hangup**).
mail=(*n files*)	One or more files checked for new mail every 5 minutes or (if *n* is supplied) every *n* seconds.
matchbeep={never|nomatch| ambiguous|notunique}	Specifies circumstances under which completion should beep: never, if no match exists, if multiple matches exist, or if multiple matches exist and one is exact. If unset, **ambiguous** is used.
nobeep	Disable beeping.
noclobber	Don't redirect output to an existing file; prevents accidental destruction of files.
noding	Don't print "DING!" in prompt time specifiers when the hour changes.
noglob	Turn off filename expansion; useful in shell scripts.
nokanji	Disable Kanji (if supported).
nonomatch	Treat filename metacharacters as literal characters if no match exists (e.g., **vi ch*** creates new file **ch*** instead of printing "No match").
nostat=*directory-list*	Do not stat *directory-list* during completion.
notify	Declare job completions when they occur.
owd	Old working directory.
path=(*dirs*)	List of pathnames in which to search for commands to execute. Initialized from **PATH**; the default is . **/usr/ucb /usr/bin**.
printexitvalue	Print all nonzero exit values.
prompt='*str*'	String that prompts for interactive input; default is %. See "Formatting for the Prompt Variable" later in this chapter for formatting information.
prompt2='*str*'	String that prompts for interactive input in **foreach** and **while** loops and continued lines (those with escaped newlines). See "Formatting for the Prompt Variable" for formatting information.
prompt3='*str*'	String that prompts for interactive input in automatic spelling correction. See "Formatting for the Prompt Variable" for formatting information.
promptchars=*cc*	Use the two characters specified as *cc* with the %# **prompt** sequence to indicate normal users and the superuser, respectively.
pushdsilent	Do not print directory stack when **pushd** and **popd** are invoked.
pushdtohome	Change to home directory when **pushd** is invoked without arguments.
recexact	Consider completion to be concluded on first exact match.
recognize_only_executables	When command completion is invoked, print only executable files.
rmstar	Prompt before executing the command **rm ***.
rprompt=*string*	The string to print on the right side of the screen while the prompt is displayed on the left. Specify as for **prompt**.
savedirs	Execute **dirs -S** before exiting.
savehist=*max* [**merge**]	Execute **history -S** before exiting. Save no more than *max* lines of history. If specified, merge those lines with previous history saves, and sort by time.

Variable	Description
sched=*string*	Format for **sched**'s printing of events. See "Formatting for the Prompt Variable" for formatting information.
shell=*file*	Pathname of the shell program.
shlvl	Number of nested shells.
status=*n*	Exit status of last command. Built-in commands return 0 (success) or 1 (failure).
symlinks={chase|ignore|expand}	Specify manner in which to deal with symbolic links. Expand them to real directory name in *cwd* (**chase**), treat them as real directories (**ignore**), or expand arguments that resemble pathnames (**expand**).
tcsh	Version of **tcsh**.
term	Terminal type.
time='*n %c*'	If command execution takes more than *n* CPU seconds, report user time, system time, elapsed time, and CPU percentage. Supply optional %*c* flags to show other data.
tperiod	Number of minutes between executions of **periodic** alias.
tty	Name of tty, if applicable.
uid	User ID.
user	Username.
verbose	Display a command after history substitution; same as **tcsh -v**.
version	Shell's version and additional information, including options set at compile time.
visiblebell	Flash screen instead of beeping.
watch=([*n*] *user terminal...*)	Watch for *user* logging in at *terminal*, where *terminal* can be a *tty* name or **any**. Check every *n* minutes, or 10 by default.
who=*string*	Specify information to be printed by **watch**.
wordchars=*chars*	List of all nonalphanumeric characters that may be part of a word. Default is *?_-.[ ]~=.

Formatting for the Prompt Variable

tcsh provides a list of substitutions that can be used in formatting the prompt. The list of available substitutions includes:

%%
    Literal %

%/
    The present working directory

%~
    The present working directory, in ~ notation

%#
    # for the superuser, > for others

%?
    Previous command's exit status

%$*var*
    The value of the shell or environment variable *var*

%{*string*%}

Include *string* as a literal escape sequence to change terminal attributes (but should not move the cursor location); cannot be the last sequence in the prompt

\c, ^c

Parse **c** as in the **bindkey** built-in command

%b

End boldfacing

%c[[0]*n*], %.[[0]*n*]

The last *n* (default 1) components of the present working directory; if 0 is specified, replace removed components with **/<skipped>**

%d

Day of the week (e.g., Mon, Tue)

%h, %!, !

Number of current history event

%j

The number of jobs

%l

Current tty

%m

First component of hostname

%n

Username

%p

Current time, with seconds (12-hour mode)

%s

End standout mode (reverse video)

%t, %@

Current time (12-hour format)

%u

End underlining

%w

Month (e.g., Jan, Feb)

%y

Year (e.g., 99, 00)

%B

Begin boldfacing

%C

Similar to **%c**, but use full pathnames instead of ~ notation

%D

Day of month (e.g., 09, 10)

%L

Clear from the end of the prompt to the end of the display or the line.

%M

Fully qualified hostname

%P

Current time, with seconds (24-hour format)

%R

In **prompt2**, the parser status; in **prompt3**, the corrected string; and in **history**, the history string

%S

Begin standout mode (reverse video)

%T

Current time (24-hour format)

%U

Begin underlining

%W

Month (e.g., 09, 10)

%Y

Year (e.g., 1999, 2000)

Sample .tcshrc File

```
# PREDEFINED VARIABLES

set path=(~ ~/bin /usr/ucb /bin /usr/bin . )
set mail=(/usr/mail/tom)

if ($?prompt) then              # settings for interactive use
   set echo
   set noclobber ignoreeof

   set cdpath=(/usr/lib /usr/spool/uucp)
# Now I can type cd macros
# instead of cd /usr/lib/macros

   set history=100
   set prompt='tom \!% '         # includes history number
   set time=3

# MY VARIABLES

   set man1="/usr/man/man1"      # lets me do   cd $man1, ls $man1
   set a="[a-z]*"                # lets me do   vi $a
   set A="[A-Z]*"                # or           grep string $A

# ALIASES

   alias c "clear; dirs"         # use quotes to protect ; or |
   alias h "history|more"
   alias j jobs -l
   alias ls ls -sFC              # redefine ls command
   alias del 'mv \!* ~/tmp_dir' # a safe alternative to rm
endif
```

Environment Variables

tcsh maintains a set of *environment variables*, which are distinct from shell variables and aren't really part of the shell. Shell variables are meaningful only within the current shell, but environment variables are exported automatically, making them available globally. For example, shell variables are accessible only to a particular script in which they're defined, whereas environment variables can be used by any shell scripts, mail utilities, or editors you might invoke.

Environment variables are assigned as follows:

```
setenv VAR value
```

By convention, environment variable names are all uppercase. You can create your own environment variables, or you can use the predefined environment variables that follow.

The following environment variables have corresponding **tcsh** shell variables. When either one changes, the value is copied to the other.

AFSUSER
> Alternative to local user for Kerberos authentication with **autologout** locking; same as **afsuser**.

GROUP
> User's group name; same as **group**.

HOME
> Home directory; same as **home**.

PATH
> Search path for commands; same as **path**.

SHLVL
> Number of nested shell levels; same as **shlvl**.

TERM
> Terminal type; same as **term**.

USER
> User's login name; same as **user**.

Other environment variables, which do not have corresponding shell variables, include the following:

COLUMNS
> Number of columns on terminal.

DISPLAY
> Identifies user's display for the X Window System. If set, the shell doesn't set **autologout**.

EDITOR
> Pathname to default editor. See also **VISUAL**.

HOST
> Name of machine.

HOSTTYPE
> Type of machine. Obsolete; will be removed eventually.

HPATH
Colon-separated list of directories to search for documentation.

LANG
Preferred language. Used for native language support.

LC_CTYPE
The locale, as it affects character handling. Used for native language support.

LINES
Number of lines on the screen.

LOGNAME
Another name for the **USER** variable.

LS_COLORS
Colors for use with the **ls** command. See the **tcsh** manpage for detailed information.

MACHTYPE
Type of machine.

MAIL
The file that holds mail. Used by mail programs. This is not the same as the shell variable **mail**, which only checks for new mail.

NOREBIND
Printable characters not rebound. Used for native language support.

OSTYPE
Operating system.

PWD
The current directory; the value is copied from **cwd**.

REMOTEHOST
Machine name of remote host.

SHELL
Undefined by default; once initialized to **shell**, the two are identical.

TERMCAP
The file that holds the cursor-positioning codes for your terminal type. Default is */etc/termcap*.

VENDOR
System vendor.

VISUAL
Pathname to default full-screen editor. See also **EDITOR**.

Expressions

Expressions are used in @, **if**, and **while** statements to perform arithmetic, string comparisons, file testing, and so on. **exit** and **set** also specify expressions, as can the **tcsh** built-in command **filetest**. Expressions are formed by combining variables and constants with operators that resemble those in the C programming language. Operator precedence is the same as in C and can be remembered as follows:

1. * / %
2. + -

Group all other expressions inside parentheses. Parentheses are required if the expression contains <, >, &, or |.

Operators

Operators can be one of the following types.

Assignment operators

Operator	Description
=	Assign value.
+= -=	Reassign after addition/subtraction.
*= /= %=	Reassign after multiplication/division/remainder.
&= ^= |=	Reassign after bitwise AND/XOR/OR.
++	Increment.
--	Decrement.

Arithmetic operators

Operator	Description
* / %	Multiplication; integer division; modulus (remainder).
+ -	Addition; subtraction.

Bitwise and logical operators

Operator	Description
~	Binary inversion (one's complement).
!	Logical negation.
<< >>	Bitwise left shift; bitwise right shift.
&	Bitwise AND.
^	Bitwise exclusive OR.
|	Bitwise OR.
&&	Logical AND.
||	Logical OR.
{ command }	Return 1 if command is successful, 0 otherwise. Note that this is the opposite of *command*'s normal return code. The **$status** variable may be more practical.

Comparison operators

Operator	Description
== !=	Equality; inequality.
<= >=	Less than or equal to; greater than or equal to.
< >	Less than; greater than.

File inquiry operators

Command substitution and filename expansion are performed on *file* before the test is performed. Operators can be combined (e.g., **-ef**). The following is a list of the valid file inquiry operators:

Operator	Description
-b *file*	The file is a block special file.
-c *file*	The file is a character special file.
-d *file*	The file is a directory.
-e *file*	The file exists.
-f *file*	The file is a plain file.
-g *file*	The file's **set-group-ID** bit is set.
-k *file*	The file's sticky bit is set.
-l *file*	The file is a symbolic link.
-L *file*	Apply any remaining operators to symbolic link, not the file it points to.
-o *file*	The user owns the file.
-p *file*	The file is a named pipe (FIFO).
-r *file*	The user has read permission.
-s *file*	The file has nonzero size.
-S *file*	The file is a socket special file.
-t *file*	*file* is a digit and is an open file descriptor for a terminal device.
-u *file*	The file's **set-user-ID** bit is set.
-w *file*	The user has write permission.
-x *file*	The user has execute permission.
-X *file*	The file is executable and is in the path, or is a shell built-in.
-z *file*	The file has 0 size.
!	Reverse the sense of any preceding inquiry.

Finally, **tcsh** provides the following operators, which return other kinds of information:

Operator	Description
-A[:] *file*	Last time file was accessed, as the number of seconds since the epoch. With a colon (:), the result is in timestamp format.
-C[:] *file*	Last time inode was modified. With a colon (:), the result is in timestamp format.
-D *file*	Device number.
-F *file*	Composite file identifier, in the form *device:inode*.
-G[:] *file*	Numeric group ID for the file. With a colon (:), the result is the group name if known, otherwise the numeric group ID.
-I *file*	Inode number.
-L *file*	The name of the file pointed to by symbolic link *file*.
-M[:] *file*	Last time file was modified. With a colon (:), the result is in timestamp format.
-N *file*	Number of hard links.
-P[:] *file*	Permissions in octal, without leading 0. With a colon (:), the result includes a leading 0.

Operator	Description
-P*mode*[:] *file*	Equivalent to -P *file* ANDed to *mode*. With a colon (:), the result includes a leading 0.
-U[:] *file*	Numeric user ID of the file's owner. With a colon (:), the result is the username if known, otherwise the numeric user ID.
-Z *file*	The file's size, in bytes.

Examples

The following examples show @ commands and assume n = 4:

Expression	Value of $x
@ x = ($n > 10 || $n < 5)	1
@ x = ($n >= 0 && $n < 3)	0
@ x = ($n << 2)	16
@ x = ($n >> 2)	1
@ x = $n % 2	0
@ x = $n % 3	1

The following examples show the first line of **if** or **while** statements:

Expression	Meaning
while ($#argv != 0)	While there are arguments . . .
if ($today[1] = = "Fri")	If the first word is "Fri" . . .
if (-f $argv[1])	If the first argument is a plain file. . .
if (! -d $tmpdir)	If **tmpdir** is not a directory. . .

Command History

Previously executed commands are stored in a history list. You can access this list to verify commands, repeat them, or execute modified versions of them. The **history** built-in command displays the history list; the predefined variables **histchars** and **history** also affect the history mechanism. There are a number of ways to use the history list:

- Rerun a previous command
- Edit a previous command
- Make command substitutions
- Make argument substitutions (replace specific words in a command)
- Extract or replace parts of a command or word

The easiest way to take advantage of the command history is to use the arrow keys to move around in the history, select the command you want, and then rerun it or use the editing features described in "Command-Line Editing," later in this chapter, to modify the command. The arrow keys are:

Key	Description
Up arrow	Previous command.
Down arrow	Next command.
Left arrow	Move left in command line.
Right arrow	Move right in command line.

The next sections describe some tools for editing and rerunning commands. With the C shell, which does not have the command-line editing features of **tcsh**, these tools are important for rerunning commands. With **tcsh**, they are less often used, but they still work.

Command Substitution

Command	Description
!	Begin a history substitution.
!!	Previous command.
!*N*	Command number *N* in history list.
!-*N*	*N*th command back from current command.
!*string*	Most recent command that starts with *string*.
!?*string*?	Most recent command that contains *string*.
!?*string*?%	Most recent command argument that contains *string*.
!$	Last argument of previous command.
!!*string*	Previous command, then append *string*.
!*N string*	Command *N*, then append *string*.
!{*s1*}*s2*	Most recent command starting with string *s1*, then append string *s2*.
^*old*^*new*^	Quick substitution; change string *old* to *new* in previous command, and execute modified command.

Command Substitution Examples

The following command is assumed:

```
%3 vi cprogs/01.c ch002 ch03
```

Event number	Command typed	Command executed
4	^00^0	vi cprogs/01.c ch02 ch03
5	nroff !*	nroff cprogs/01.c ch02 ch03
6	nroff !$	nroff ch03
7	!vi	vi cprogs/01.c ch02 ch03
8	!6	nroff ch03
9	!?01	vi cprogs/01.c ch02 ch03
10	!{nr}.new	nroff ch03.new
11	!!|lp	nroff ch03.new	lp
12	more !?pr?%	more cprogs/01.c

Word Substitution

Colons may precede any word specifier.

Specifier	Description
:0	Command name
:n	Argument number n
^	First argument
$	Last argument
:n-m	Arguments n through m
-m	Words 0 through m; same as :0-m
:n-	Arguments n through next-to-last
:n*	Arguments n through last; same as n-$
*	All arguments; same as ^-$ or 1-$
#	Current command line up to this point; fairly useless

Word Substitution Examples

The following command is assumed:

```
%13 cat ch01 ch02 ch03 biblio back
```

Event number	Command typed	Command executed
14	ls !13^	ls ch01
15	sort !13:*	sort ch01 ch02 ch03 biblio back
16	lp !cat:3*	more ch03 biblio back
17	!cat:0-3	cat ch01 ch02 ch03
18	vi !-5:4	vi biblio

History Modifiers

Command and word substitutions can be modified by one or more of the following modifiers:

Printing, substitution, and quoting

Modifier	Description
:p	Display command, but don't execute.
:s/old/new	Substitute string new for old, first instance only.
:gs/old/new	Substitute string new for old, all instances.
:&	Repeat previous substitution (:s or ^ command), first instance only.
:g&	Repeat previous substitution, all instances.
:q	Quote a wordlist.
:x	Quote separate words.

Truncation

Modifier	Description
:r	Extract the first available pathname root (the portion before the last period).
:gr	Extract all pathname roots.
:e	Extract the first available pathname extension (the portion after the last period).
:ge	Extract all pathname extensions.
:h	Extract the first available pathname header (the portion before the last slash).
:gh	Extract all pathname headers.
:t	Extract the first available pathname tail (the portion after the last slash).
:gt	Extract all pathname tails.
:u	Make first lowercase letter uppercase.
:l	Make first uppercase letter lowercase.
:a	Apply modifier(s) following **a** as many times as possible to a word. If used with **g**, **a** is applied to all words.

History Modifier Examples

From the preceding, command number 17 is:

```
%17 cat ch01 ch02 ch03
```

Event number	Command typed	Command executed
19	!17:s/ch/CH/	cat CH01 ch02 ch03
20	!17g&	cat CH01 CH02 CH03
21	!more:p	more cprogs/01.c *(displayed only)*
22	cd !$:h	cd cprogs
23	vi !mo:$:t	vi 01.c
24	grep stdio !$	grep stdio 01.c
25	^stdio^include stdio^:q	grep "include stdio" 01.c
26	nroff !21:t:p	nroff 01.c *(is that what I wanted?)*
27	!!	nroff 01.c *(execute it)*

Special Aliases

Certain special aliases can be set in **tcsh**. The aliases are initially undefined. Once set, the commands they specify are executed when specific events occur. The following is a list of the special aliases and when they are executed:

beepcmd
 At beep.

cwdcmd
 When the current working directory changes.

jobcmd
 Before running a command or before its state changes. Like **postcmd**, but does not print built-ins.

tcsh

helpcommand
> Invoked by the **run-help** editor command.

periodic
> Every few minutes. The exact amount of time is set by the **tperiod** shell variable.

precmd
> Before printing a new prompt.

postcmd
> Before running a command.

shell *shell*
> If a script does not specify a shell, interpret it with *shell*, which should be a full pathname.

Command-Line Manipulation

tcsh offers a certain amount of functionality in manipulating the command line, including word or command completion and the ability to edit a command line.

Completion

The shell automatically completes words and commands when you press the Tab key, and notifies you when a completion is finished by appending a space to complete filenames or commands and a **/** to complete directories.

In addition, **tcsh** recognizes ~ notation for home directories; it assumes that words at the beginning of a line and subsequent to |, **&**, ;, ||, or **&&** are commands, and modifies the search path appropriately. Completion can be done midword; only the letters to the left of the prompt are checked for completion.

Related Shell Variables

- **autolist**
- **fignore**
- **listmax**
- **listmaxrows**

Related Command-Line Editor Commands

- **complete-word-back**
- **complete-word-forward**
- **expand-glob**
- **list-glob**

Related Shell Built-ins

- **complete**
- **uncomplete**

Command-Line Editing

tcsh lets you move your cursor around in the command line, editing the line as you type. There are two main modes for editing the command line, based on the two most common text editors: Emacs and **vi**. Emacs mode is the default; you can switch between the modes with:

bindkey -e   *Select Emacs bindings*
bindkey -v   *Select vi bindings*

The main difference between the Emacs and **vi** bindings is that the Emacs bindings are modeless (i.e., they always work). With the **vi** bindings, you must switch between input and command modes; different commands are useful in each mode. Additionally:

- Emacs mode is simpler; **vi** mode allows finer control.
- Emacs mode allows you to yank cut text and set a mark; **vi** mode does not.
- The command-history searching capabilities differ.

Emacs mode

Tables 8-1 through 8-3 describe the various editing keystrokes available in Emacs mode.

Table 8-1. Cursor positioning (Emacs mode)

Command	Description
Ctrl-B	Move cursor back (left) one character.
Ctrl-F	Move cursor forward (right) one character.
M-b	Move cursor back one word.
M-f	Move cursor forward one word.
Ctrl-A	Move cursor to beginning of line.
Ctrl-E	Move cursor to end of line.

Table 8-2. Text deletion (Emacs mode)

Command	Description
Del or Ctrl-H	Delete character to left of cursor.
Ctrl-D	Delete character under cursor.
M-d	Delete word.
M-Del or M-Ctrl-H	Delete word backward.
Ctrl-K	Delete from cursor to end-of-line.
Ctrl-U	Delete entire line.

tcsh

Table 8-3. Command history (Emacs mode)

Command	Description
Ctrl-P	Previous command.
Ctrl-N	Next command.
Up arrow	Previous command.
Down arrow	Next command.
cmd-fragment **M-p**	Search history for *cmd-fragment*, which must be the beginning of a command.
cmd-fragment **M-n**	Like **M-p**, but search forward.
M-*num*	Repeat next command *num* times.
Ctrl-Y	Yank previously deleted string.

vi mode

vi mode has two submodes, input mode and command mode. The default mode is input. You can toggle modes by pressing Esc; alternatively, in command mode, typing **a** (append) or **i** (insert) will return you to input mode.

Tables 8-4 through 8-10 describe the editing keystrokes available in vi mode.

Table 8-4. Command history (vi input and command modes)

Command	Description
Ctrl-P	Previous command
Ctrl-N	Next command
Up arrow	Previous command
Down arrow	Next command
Esc	Toggle mode

Table 8-5. Editing (vi input mode)

Command	Description
Ctrl-B	Move cursor back (left) one character.
Ctrl-F	Move cursor forward (right) one character.
Ctrl-A	Move cursor to beginning of line.
Ctrl-E	Move cursor to end-of-line.
DEL or Ctrl-H	Delete character to left of cursor.
Ctrl-W	Delete word backward.
Ctrl-U	Delete from beginning of line to cursor.
Ctrl-K	Delete from cursor to end-of-line.

Table 8-6. Cursor positioning (vi command mode)

Command	Description
h or **Ctrl-H**	Move cursor back (left) one character.
l or **SPACE**	Move cursor forward (right) one character.
w	Move cursor forward one word.
b	Move cursor back one word.
e	Move cursor to next word ending.
W, B, E	Like **w**, **b**, and **e**, but treat only whitespace as word separator instead of any nonalphanumeric character.
^ or **Ctrl-A**	Move cursor to beginning of line (first nonwhitespace character).
0	Move cursor to beginning of line.
$ or **Ctrl-E**	Move cursor to end-of-line.

Table 8-7. Text insertion (vi command mode)

Command	Description
a	Append new text after cursor until **Esc**.
i	Insert new text before cursor until **Esc**.
A	Append new text after end of line until **Esc**.
I	Insert new text before beginning of line until **Esc**.

Table 8-8. Text deletion (vi command mode)

Command	Description
x	Delete character under cursor.
X or **Del**	Delete character to left of cursor.
d*m*	Delete from cursor to end of motion command *m*.
D	Same as **d$**.
Ctrl-W	Delete word backward.
Ctrl-U	Delete from beginning of line to cursor.
Ctrl-K	Delete from cursor to end of line.

Table 8-9. Text replacement (vi command mode)

Command	Description
c*m*	Change characters from cursor to end of motion command *m* until **Esc**.
C	Same as **c$**.
r*c*	Replace character under cursor with character *c*.
R	Replace multiple characters until **Esc**.
s	Substitute character under cursor with characters typed until **Esc**.

Table 8-10. Character-seeking motion (vi command mode)

Command	Description
f*c*	Move cursor to next instance of *c* in line.
F*c*	Move cursor to previous instance of *c* in line.
t*c*	Move cursor just before next instance of *c* in line.
T*c*	Move cursor just after previous instance of *c* in line.
;	Repeat previous **f** or **F** command.
,	Repeat previous **f** or **F** command in opposite direction.

Job Control

Job control lets you place foreground jobs in the background, bring background jobs to the foreground, or suspend (temporarily stop) running jobs. The shell provides the following commands for job control. For more information on these commands, see "Built-in Commands."

bg   Put a job in the background.

fg   Put a job in the foreground.

jobs
> List active jobs.

kill
> Terminate a job.

notify
> Notify when a background job finishes.

stop
> Suspend a background job.

Ctrl-Z
> Suspend the foreground job.

Many job control commands take *jobID* as an argument. This argument can be specified as follows:

%n
> Job number *n*.

%s
> Job whose command line starts with string *s*.

%?s
> Job whose command line contains string *s*.

%%
> Current job.

%   Current job (same as preceding).

%+   Current job (same as preceding).

%-   Previous job.

Built-in Commands

@	**@** [*variable*[*n*]=*expression*]

Assign the value of the arithmetic *expression* to *variable*, or to the *n*th element of *variable* if the index *n* is specified. With no *variable* or *expression* specified, print the values of all shell variables (same as **set**). Expression operators as well as examples are listed under "Expressions" earlier in this chapter. Two special forms are also valid:

@ variable++
Increment *variable* by 1.

@ variable--
Decrement *variable* by 1.

#	**#**

Ignore all text that follows on the same line. # is used in shell scripts as the comment character and is not really a command.

#!	**#!***shell*

Used as the first line of a script to invoke the named *shell* (with optional arguments) or other program. For example:

#!/bin/tcsh -f

:	**:**

Null command. Returns an exit status of 0. The colon command is often put as the first character of a Bourne or Korn shell script to act as a place-holder to keep a # (hash) from accidentally becoming the first character.

---

alias	**alias** [*name* [*command*]]

Assign *name* as the shorthand name, or alias, for *command*. If *command* is omitted, print the alias for *name*; if *name* also is omitted, print all aliases. Aliases can be defined on the command line, but more often they are stored in *.tcshrc* so that they take effect upon logging in. (See the sample *.tcshrc* file earlier in this chapter.) Alias definitions can reference command-line arguments, much like the history list. Use \!* to refer to all command-line arguments, \!^ for the first argument, \!\!:2 for the second, \!$ for the last, and so on. An alias *name* can be any valid Unix command except **alias** or **unalias**; however, you lose the original command's meaning unless you type *name*. See also **unalias** and "Special Aliases."

Examples

Set the size for windows under the X Window System:

```
alias R 'set noglob; eval `resize` unset noglob'
```

Show aliases that contain the string **ls**:

```
alias | grep ls
```

Run **nroff** on all command-line arguments:

```
alias ms 'nroff -ms \!*'
```

Copy the file that is named as the first argument:

```
alias back 'cp \!^ \!^.old'
```

Use the regular **ls**, not its alias:

```
% \ls
```

---

alloc

```
alloc
```

Print totals of used and free memory.

---

bg

```
bg [jobIDs]
```

Put the current job or the *jobIDs* in the background.

Example

To place a time-consuming process in the background, you might begin with:

```
4% nroff -ms report Ctrl-Z
```

and then issue any one of the following:

```
5% bg
5% bg %          Current job
5% bg %1         Job number 1
5% bg %nr        Match initial string nroff
5% % &
```

---

bindkey

```
bindkey [options] [key] [command]
```

Display all key bindings, or bind a key to a command.

Options

-a   List standard and alternate key bindings.

-b *key*

Expect *key* to be one of the following: a control character (in hat notation, e.g., **^B**, or C notation, e.g., **C-B**); a metacharacter (e.g., **M-B**); a function key (e.g., **F-***string*); or an extended prefix key (e.g., **X-B**).

-c *command*

Interpret *command* as a shell, not editor, command.

-d *key*

Bind key to its original binding.

-e Bind to standard Emacs bindings.

-k *key*
  Expect *key* to refer to an arrow (**left**, **right**, **up**, or **down**).

-l List and describe all editor commands.

-r *key*
  Completely unbind *key*.

-s Interpret *command* as a literal string and treat as terminal input.

-u Print usage message.

-v Bind to standard **vi** bindings.

---

break

break

Resume execution following the **end** command of the nearest enclosing **while** or **foreach**.

---

breaksw

breaksw

Break from a **switch**; continue execution after the **endsw**.

---

built-ins

built-ins

Print all built-in shell commands.

---

bye

bye

Same as **logout**.

---

case

case *pattern* :

Identify a *pattern* in a **switch**.

---

cd

cd [*options*] [*dir*]

Change working directory to *dir*. Default is user's home directory. If *dir* is a relative pathname but is not in the current directory, the **cdpath** variable is searched. See the sample *.tcshrc* file earlier in this chapter.

Options

- Change to previous directory.

-l Explicitly expand ~ notation; implies -**p**.

-n Wrap entries before end-of-line; implies -**p**.

-p Print directory stack.

-v Print entries one per line; implies -**p**.

---

chdir

chdir [*dir*]

Same as **cd**. Useful if you are redefining **cd**.

complete   complete [*string* [*word/pattern/list*[:*select*]/[*suffix*]]]

List all completions, or, if specified, all completions for *string* (which may be a pattern). Further options can be specified.

Options for word

c   Complete current word only, without referring to *pattern*.

C   Complete current word only, referring to *pattern*.

n   Complete previous word.

N   Complete word before previous word.

p   Expect *pattern* to be a range of numbers. Perform completion within that range.

Options for list

Various *lists* of strings can be searched for possible completions. Some *list* options include:

(*string*)
> Members of the list *string*

$*variable*
> Words from *variable*

`*command*`
> Output from *command*

a   Aliases

b   Bindings

c   Commands

C   External (not built-in) commands

d   Directories

D   Directories whose names begin with *string*

e   Environment variables

f   Filenames

F   Filenames that begin with *string*

g   Groups

j   Jobs

l   Limits

n   Nothing

s   Shell variables

S   Signals

t   Text files

T   Text files whose names begin with *string*

u   Users

v   Any variables

x   Like **n**, but prints *select* as an explanation with the editor
command **list-choices**

X   Completions

select

select should be a glob pattern. Completions are limited to words
that match this pattern. *suffix* is appended to all completions.

---

continue   continue

Resume execution of nearest enclosing **while** or **foreach**.

---

default   default :

Label the default case (typically last) in a **switch**.

---

dirs   dirs [*options*]

Print the directory stack, showing the current directory first. See
also **popd** and **pushd**.

Options

-c   Clear the directory stack.

-l   Expand the home directory symbol (~) to the actual directory
name.

-n   Wrap output.

-v   Print one directory per line.

-L *file*
Re-create stack from *file*, which should have been created by
dirs -S *file*.

-S *file*
Print to *file* a series of **pushd** and **popd** commands that can be
invoked to replicate the stack.

---

echo   echo [-n] *string*

Write *string* to standard output; if **-n** is specified, the output is not
terminated by a newline. Set the **echo_style** shell variable to
emulate BSD and/or System V **echo** flags and escape sequences. See
also **echo** in Chapter 3 and Chapter 7.

---

echotc   echotc [*options*] *arguments*

Display terminal capabilities or move cursor on screen, depending
on the argument.

Options

-s   Return empty string, not error, if capability doesn't exist.

-v   Display verbose messages.

Arguments

baud
> Display current baud rate.

cols
> Display current column.

cm column row
> Move cursor to specified coordinates.

home
> Move cursor to home position.

lines
> Print number of lines per screen.

meta
> Does this terminal have meta capacity (usually the Alt key)?

tabs
> Does this terminal have tab capacity?

---

else

```
else
```

Reserved word for interior of **if ... endif** statement.

---

end

```
end
```

Reserved word that ends a **foreach** or **switch** statement.

---

endif

```
endif
```

Reserved word that ends an **if** statement.

---

endsw

```
endsw
```

Reserved word that ends a **switch** statement.

---

eval

```
eval args
```

Typically, **eval** is used in shell scripts, and *args* is a line of code that may contain shell variables. **eval** forces variable expansion to happen first and then runs the resulting command. This "double scanning" is useful any time shell variables contain input/output redirection symbols, aliases, or other shell variables. (For example, redirection normally happens before variable expansion, so a variable containing redirection symbols must be expanded first using **eval**; otherwise, the redirection symbols remain uninterpreted.)

Examples

The following line can be placed in the **.login** file to set up terminal characteristics:

```
set noglob eval `tset -s xterm` unset noglob
```

The following commands show the effect of **eval**:

```
% set b='$a'
% set a=hello
```

```
% echo $b          Read the command line once
$a
% eval echo $b      Read the command line twice
hello
```

Another example of **eval** can be found under **alias**.

---

exec

exec *command*

Execute *command* in place of current shell. This terminates the current shell, rather than creating a new process under it.

---

exit

exit [(*expr*)]

Exit a shell script with the status given by *expr*. A status of zero means success; nonzero means failure. If *expr* is not specified, the exit value is that of the **status** variable. **exit** can be issued at the command line to close a window (log out).

---

fg

fg [*jobIDs*]

Bring the current job or the *jobIDs* to the foreground. *jobID* can be %*job-number*.

Example

If you suspend a **vi** editing session (by pressing **Ctrl-Z**), you might resume **vi** using any of these commands:

```
% %
% fg
% fg %
% fg %vi      Match initial string
```

---

filetest

filetest -*op files*

Apply *op* file-test operator to *files*. Print results in a list. See "File inquiry operators" earlier in this chapter for the list of file-test operators.

---

foreach

foreach *name* (*wordlist*)
    commands
end

Assign variable *name* to each value in *wordlist* and execute *commands* between **foreach** and **end**. You can use **foreach** as a multiline command issued at the shell prompt (first of the following examples), or you can use it in a shell script (second example).

Examples

Rename all files that begin with a capital letter:

```
% foreach i ([A-Z]*)
? mv $i $i.new
? end
```

Check whether each command-line argument is an option or not:

```
foreach arg ($argv)
    # does it begin with - ?
    if ("$arg" =~ -*) then
        echo "Argument is an option"
    else
        echo "Argument is a filename"
    endif
end
```

---

glob

glob *wordlist*

Do filename, variable, and history substitutions on *wordlist*. No \
escapes are recognized in its expansion, and words are delimited by
null characters. **glob** is typically used in shell scripts to hardcode a
value so that it remains the same for the rest of the script.

---

goto

goto *string*

Skip to a line whose first nonblank character is *string* followed by a
colon, and continue execution below that line. On the **goto** line,
string can be a variable or filename pattern, but the label branched
to must be a literal, expanded value and must not occur within a
foreach or **while**.

---

hashstat

hashstat

Display statistics that show the hash table's level of success at
locating commands via the **path** variable.

---

history

history [*options*]

Display the list of history events. (History syntax is discussed
earlier in "Command History.")

Options

-c   Clear history list.

-h   Print history list without event numbers.

-r   Print in reverse order; show oldest commands last.

n   Display only the last *n* history commands, instead of the
number set by the **history** shell variable.

-L *file*
    Load series of **pushd** and **popd** commands from *file* in order
    to re-create a saved stack.

-M *file*
    Merge the current directory stack and the stack saved in *file*.
    Save both, sorted by time, in *file* as a series of **pushd** and **popd**
    commands.

-S *file*

> Print to *file* a series of **pushd** and **popd** commands that can be invoked to replicate the stack.

-T   Print with timestamp.

Example

To save and execute the last five commands:

```
history -h 5 > do_it
source do_it
```

---

hup

hup [*command*]

Start *command* but make it exit when sent a hangup signal, which is sent when shell exits. By default, configure shell script to exit on hangup signal.

---

if

if

Begin a conditional statement. The simple format is:

```
if (expr) cmd
```

There are three other possible formats, shown side by side:

```
if (expr) then    if (expr) then    if (expr) then
    cmds              cmds1             cmds1
endif             else              else if (expr) then
                      cmds2             cmds2
                  endif             else
                                        cmds3
                                    endif
```

In the simplest form, execute *cmds* if *expr* is true, otherwise do nothing. (Redirection still occurs; this is a bug.) In the other forms, execute one or more commands. If *expr* is true, continue with the commands after **then**; if *expr* is false, branch to the commands after **else** or **else if** and continue checking. For more examples, see "Expressions" earlier in this chapter, or the **shift** or **while** commands.

Example

Take a default action if no command-line arguments are given:

```
if ($#argv == 0) then
    echo "No filename given. Sending to Report."
    set outfile = Report
else
    set outfile = $argv[1]
endif
```

---

jobs

jobs [-l]

List all running or stopped jobs; -l includes process IDs. For example, you can check whether a long compilation or text format is still running. Also useful before logging out.

kill
kill [*options*] *IDs*

Terminate each specified process ID or job ID. You must own the process or be a privileged user. This built-in is similar to */bin/kill* described in Chapter 3 but also allows symbolic job names. Stubborn processes can be killed using signal 9.

Options

-l   List the signal names. (Used by itself.)

-signal, **-s** *signal*

The signal number or name without the SIG prefix (e.g., HUP, not SIGHUP). The command **kill -l** prints a list of the available signal names. The list varies by system architecture; for a PC-based system, it looks like this:

```
% kill -l
HUP INT QUIT ILL TRAP ABRT BUS FPE KILL USR1 SEGV USR2
PIPE ALRM TERM STKFLT CHLD CONT STOP TSTP TTIN TTOU URG
XCPU XFSZ VTALRM PROF WINCH POLL PWR SYS RTMIN RTMIN+1
RTMIN+2 RTMIN+3 RTMAX-3 RTMAX-2 RTMAX-1 RTMAX
```

The signals and their numbers are defined in */usr/include/asm/signal.h*; look in that file to find the signals that apply to your system.

Examples

If you've issued the following command:

    44% **nroff -ms report &**

you can terminate it in any of the following ways:

45% **kill 19536**	*Process ID*
45% **kill %**	*Current job*
45% **kill %1**	*Job number 1*
45% **kill %nr**	*Initial string*
45% **kill %?report**	*Matching string*

---

limit
limit [-h] [*resource* [*limit*]]

Display limits or set a *limit* on resources used by the current process and by each process it creates. If no *limit* is given, the current limit is printed for *resource*. If *resource* also is omitted, all limits are printed. By default, the current limits are shown or set; with **-h**, hard limits are used. A hard limit imposes an absolute limit that can't be exceeded. Only a privileged user may raise it. See also **unlimit**.

Option

-h   Use hard, not current, limits.

Resources

coredumpsize

Maximum size of a core dump file.

cputime

Maximum number of seconds the CPU can spend; can be abbreviated as **cpu**.

datasize

Maximum size of data (including stack).

descriptors

Maximum number of open files.

filesize

Maximum size of any one file.

maxproc

Maximum number of processes.

memorylocked

Maximum size a process can lock into memory.

memoryuse

Maximum amount of physical memory that can be allocated to a process.

vmemoryuse

Maximum amount of virtual memory that can be allocated to a process.

stacksize

Maximum size of stack.

Limit

A number followed by an optional character (a unit specifier).

For **cputime**:	*n***h** (for *n* hours)
	*n***m** (for *n* minutes)
	mm:ss (minutes and seconds)
For others:	*n***k** (for *n* kilobytes, the default)
	*n***m** (for *n* megabytes)

---

log

log

Consult the **watch** variable for list of users being watched. Print list of those who are presently logged in.

---

login

login [*user*|-p]

Replace *user*'s login shell with */bin/login*. **-p** is used to preserve environment variables.

---

logout

logout

Terminate the login shell.

---

ls-F

ls-F [*options*] [*files*]

Faster alternative to **ls -F**. If given any options, invokes **ls**.

newgrp   newgrp [-] [*group*]

Change user's group ID to specified group ID or, if none is specified, to original group ID. If - is entered as an option, reset
environment as if user had logged in with new group. Must have
been compiled into the shell; see the **version** variable.

nice   nice [+*n*] *command*

Change the execution priority for *command* or, if none is given,
change priority for the current shell. (See also **nice** in Chapter 3.)
The priority range is -20 to 20, with a default of 4. The range seems
backward: -20 gives the highest priority (fastest execution); 20
gives the lowest. Only a privileged user may specify a negative
number.

+*n*   Add *n* to the priority value (lower job priority).

-*n*   Subtract *n* from the priority value (raise job priority). Privi-
       leged users only.

nohup   nohup [*command*]

"No hangup signals." Do not terminate *command* after terminal
line is closed (i.e., when you hang up from a phone or log out). Use
without *command* in shell scripts to keep script from being terminated. (See also **nohup** in Chapter 3.)

notify   notify [*jobID*]

Report immediately when a background job finishes (instead of
waiting for you to exit a long editing session, for example). If no
jobID is given, the current background job is assumed.

onintr   onintr *label*
                   onintr -
                   onintr

"On interrupt." Used in shell scripts to handle interrupt signals
(similar to **bash**'s **trap 2** and **trap "" 2** commands). The first form is
like a **goto** *label*. The script will branch to *label*: if it catches an
interrupt signal (e.g., **Ctrl-C**). The second form lets the script
ignore interrupts. This is useful at the beginning of a script or
before any code segment that needs to run unhindered (e.g., when
moving files). The third form restores interrupt handling previously disabled with **onintr -**.

Example

   onintr cleanup   *Go to "cleanup" on interrupt*

     •

     •   *Shell script commands*

     •

   cleanup: *Label for interrupts*

```
            onintr -        Ignore additional interrupts
            rm -f $tmpfiles Remove any files created
            exit 2          Exit with an error status
```

popd

popd [options]

Remove the current entry (or the nth entry) from the directory stack and print the stack that remains. The current entry has number 0 and appears on the left. See also **dirs** and **pushd**.

Options

+*n*   Specify *n*th entry.

-l   Expand ~ notation.

-n   Wrap long lines.

-p   Override the **pushdsilent** shell variable, which otherwise prevents the printing of the final stack.

-v   Print precisely one directory per line.

printenv

printenv [variable]

Print all (or one specified) environment variables and their values.

pushd

pushd name
pushd [options]
pushd

The first form changes the working directory to *name* and adds it to the directory stack. The second form rotates the *n*th entry to the beginning, making it the working directory. (Entry numbers begin at 0.) With no arguments, **pushd** switches the first two entries and changes to the new current directory. The +*n*, -l, -n, and -v options behave the same as in **popd**. See also **dirs** and **popd**.

Examples

```
% dirs
/home/bob /usr
% pushd /etc          Add /etc to directory stack
/etc /home/bob /usr
% pushd +2            Switch to third directory
/usr /etc /home/bob
% pushd               Switch top two directories
/etc /usr /home/bob
% popd                Discard current entry; go to next
/usr /home/bob
```

rehash

rehash

Recompute the internal hash table for the **PATH** variable. Use **rehash** whenever a new command is created during the current session. This allows the **PATH** variable to locate and execute the command. (If the new command resides in a directory not listed in **PATH**, add directory to **PATH** before rehashing.) See also **unhash**.

repeat   repeat *n command*

Execute *n* instances of *command*.

Examples

Print three copies of **memo**:

    % **repeat 3 pr memo | lp**

Read 10 lines from the terminal and store in **item_list**:

    % **repeat 10 line > item_list**

Append 50 boilerplate files to **report**:

    % **repeat 50 cat template >> report**

---

sched   sched [*options*]
                      sched *time command*

Without options, print all scheduled events. The second form
schedules an event. *time* should be specified in *hh:mm* form (e.g.,
13:00).

Options

+hh:mm
      Schedule event to take place *hh:mm* from now.

-n   Remove *n*th item from schedule.

---

set   set *variable=value*
                      set [*options*] *variable*[*n*]*=value*
                      set *variable*
                      set

Set *variable* to *value* or, if multiple values are specified, set the variable to the list of words in the value list. If an index *n* is specified,
set the *n*th word in the variable to *value*. (The variable must already
contain at least that number of words.) If only *variable* is specified,
set the variable to null. With no arguments, display the names and
values of all set variables. See also "Predefined Shell Variables"
earlier in this chapter. Only one of **-f** or **-l** can be given.

Options

-f   Set only the first occurrence of a variable to keep it unique.

-l   Set only the last occurrence of a variable to keep it unique.

-r   List only read-only variables, or set specified variable to read-
       only.

Examples

    % **set list=(yes no maybe)**   *Assign a wordlist*
    % **set list[3]=maybe**   *Assign an item in existing wordlist*
    % **set quote="Make my day"**   *Assign a variable*
    % **set x=5 y=10 history=100**   *Assign several variables*
    % **set blank**   *Assign a null value to blank*

setenv

setenv [*name* [*value*]]

Assign a *value* to an environment variable *name*. By convention, *name* is uppercase. *value* can be a single word or a quoted string. If no *value* is given, the null value is assigned. With no arguments, display the names and values of all environment variables. **setenv** is not necessary for the **PATH** variable, which is automatically exported from **path**.

settc

settc *capability value*

Set terminal *capability* to *value*.

setty

setty [*options*] [+|-*mode*]

Do not allow shell to change specified tty modes. By default, act on the execute set.

Options

+*mode*
> Without arguments, list all modes in specified set that are on. Otherwise, turn on specified mode.

-*mode*
> Without arguments, list all modes in specified set that are off. Otherwise, turn off specified mode.

-a   List all modes in specified set.

-d   Act on the edit set of modes (used when editing commands).

-q   Act on the quote set of modes (used when entering characters verbatim).

-x   Act on the execute set of modes (used when executing examples). This is the default.

shift

shift [*variable*]

If *variable* is given, shift the words in a wordlist variable; i.e., *name*[2] becomes *name*[1]. With no argument, shift the positional parameters (command-line arguments; i.e., **$2** becomes **$1**. **shift** is typically used in a **while** loop. See additional example under **while**.

Example

```
while ($#argv)          While there are arguments
    if (-f $argv[1])
        wc -l $argv[1]
    else
        echo "$argv[1] is not a regular file"
    endif
    shift               Get the next argument
end
```

source

source [-h] *script* [*args*]

Read and execute commands from a shell script. With **-h**, the commands are added to the history list but aren't executed. Arguments can be passed to the script and are put in **argv**.

Example

    source ~/.cshrc

---

stop

stop *jobIDs*

Stop the background jobs specified by *jobIDs*; this is the complement of **Ctrl-Z** or **suspend**.

---

suspend

suspend

Suspend the current foreground job; same as **Ctrl-Z**. Often used to stop an **su** command.

---

switch

switch

Process commands depending on the value of a variable. When you need to handle more than three choices, **switch** is a useful alternative to an **if-then-else** statement. If the *string* variable matches *pattern1*, the first set of *commands* is executed; if *string* matches *pattern2*, the second set of *commands* is executed; and so on. If no patterns match, execute commands under the **default** case. *string* can be specified using command substitution, variable substitution, or filename expansion. Patterns can be specified using the pattern matching symbols *, ?, and [ ]. **breaksw** is used to exit the **switch**. If **breaksw** is omitted (which is rarely done), the **switch** continues to execute another set of commands until it reaches a **breaksw** or **endsw**. Following is the general syntax of **switch**, side by side with an example that processes the first command-line argument:

```
switch (string)              switch ($argv[1])
    case pattern1:               case -[nN]:
        commands                     nroff $file | lp
        breaksw                      breaksw
    case pattern2:               case -[Pp]:
        commands                     pr $file | lp
        breaksw                      breaksw
    case pattern3:               case -[Mm]:
        commands                     more $file
        breaksw                      breaksw
          .                      case -[Ss]:
          .                          sort $file
          .                          breaksw
    default:                     default:
        commands                     echo "Error—no such option"
                                     exit 1
        breaksw                      breaksw
endsw                        endsw
```

---

telltc	`telltc`
	Print all terminal capabilities and their values.
time	`time [command]`
	Execute a *command* and show how much time it uses. With no argument, **time** can be used in a shell script to time the script.
umask	`umask [nnn]`
	Display file creation mask or set file creation mask to octal *nnn*. The file creation mask determines which permission bits are turned off. With no *nnn*, print the current mask.
unalias	`unalias pattern`
	Remove all aliases whose names match *pattern* from the alias list. See **alias** for more information.
uncomplete	`uncomplete pattern`
	Remove completions (specified by **complete**) whose names match *pattern*.
unhash	`unhash`
	Stop using the internal hash table. The shell stops using hashed values and searches the **path** directories to locate a command. See also **rehash**.
unlimit	`unlimit [-h] [resource]`
	Remove the allocation limits on *resource*. If *resource* is not specified, remove limits for all resources. See **limit** for more information. With -h, remove hard limits. This command can be run only by a privileged user.
unset	`unset variables`
	Remove one or more *variables*. Variable names may be specified as a pattern, using filename metacharacters. Does not remove read-only variables. See **set**.
unsetenv	`unsetenv variable`
	Remove an environment variable. Filename matching is not valid. See **setenv**.
wait	`wait`
	Pause in execution until all child processes complete, or until an interrupt signal is received.

watchlog	`watchlog`
	Same as **log**. Must have been compiled into the shell; see the **version** shell variable.

where	`where` *command*
	Display all aliases, built-ins, and executables named *command* found in the path.

which	`which` *command*
	Report which version of command will be executed. Same as the executable **which**, but faster, and checks **tcsh** built-ins.

| **while** | ```
while (expression)
    commands
end
``` |
| | As long as *expression* is true (evaluates to nonzero), evaluate *commands* between **while** and **end**. **break** and **continue** can be used to terminate or continue the loop. |

Example

```
set user = (alice bob carol ted)
while ($argv[1] != $user[1])      Cycle through each user, checking
                                  for a match
    shift user            If we cycled through with no match...
    if ($#user == 0) then
      echo "$argv[1] is not on the list of users"
      exit 1
    endif
end
```
```

9

Pattern Matching

A number of Linux text editing utilities let you search for (and, in some cases, change) text patterns rather than fixed strings. These utilities include the editing programs **ed**, **ex**, **vi**, and **sed**, the **gawk** scripting language, and the commands **grep** and **egrep**. Text patterns (also called *regular expressions*) contain normal characters mixed with special characters (also called *metacharacters*).

Perl's regular expression support is so rich that it does not fit into this book; you can find a description in the O'Reilly books *Mastering Regular Expressions*, *Perl in a Nutshell*, *Perl 5 Pocket Reference*, or *Programming Perl*. The Emacs editor also provides regular expressions similar to those shown in this chapter.

ed and **ex** are hardly ever used as standalone, interactive editors nowadays. But **ed** can be found as a batch processor invoked from shell scripts, and **ex** commands are often invoked within **vi** through the colon (:) command. We use **vi** in this chapter to refer to the regular expression features supported by both **vi** and the **ex** editor on which it is based. **sed** and **gawk** are widely used in shell scripts and elsewhere as filters to alter text.

Filenames Versus Patterns

Metacharacters used in pattern matching are different from those used for filename expansion. When you issue a command on the command line, special characters are seen first by the shell, then by the program; therefore, unquoted metacharacters are interpreted by the shell for filename expansion. The command:

```
$ grep [A-Z]* chap[12]
```

could, for example, be interpreted by the shell as:

```
$ grep Array.c Bug.c Comp.c chap1 chap2
```

and **grep** would then try to find the pattern "Array.c" in files *Bug.c*, *Comp.c*, *chap1*, and *chap2*. To bypass the shell and pass the special characters to **grep**, use quotes:

```
$ grep "[A-Z]*" chap[12]
```

Double quotes suffice in most cases, but single quotes are the safest bet.

Note also that * and ? have subtly different meanings in pattern matching and file-name expansion by the shell.

Metacharacters, Listed by Linux Program

Some metacharacters are valid for one program but not for another. Those available to a given program are marked by a checkmark (✓) in the following table. Notes are provided after the table, and full descriptions of metacharacters are in the following section.

Symbol	ed	vi	sed	gawk	grep	egrep	Action
.	✓	✓	✓	✓	✓	✓	Match any character (can match newline in **gawk**).
*	✓	✓	✓	✓	✓	✓	Match zero or more preceding elements.
^	✓	✓	✓	✓	✓	✓	Match beginning of line or string.
$	✓	✓	✓	✓	✓	✓	Match end of line or string.
\	✓	✓	✓	✓	✓	✓	Escape following character.
[]	✓	✓	✓	✓	✓	✓	Match one from a list or range.
\(\)	✓	✓	✓				Store pattern for later replay.
\n	✓	✓	✓				Reuse matched text stored in *n*th \(\).
{}				✓			Match a range of instances.
\{ \}	✓	✓	✓		✓		Match a range of instances.
\<		✓					Match word's beginning.
\>		✓					Match word's end.
+				✓	✓	✓	Match one or more preceding elements.
?				✓	✓	✓	Match zero or one preceding elements.
|				✓		✓	Separate choices to match.
()				✓		✓	Group expressions to match.

On some Linux systems, **grep** is a link to **egrep**, so whenever you run **grep** you actually get **egrep** behavior.

In **ed**, **vi**, and **sed**, when you perform a search-and-replace (substitute) operation, the metacharacters in this table apply to the pattern you are searching for but not to the string replacing it.

In **gawk**, {} is specified in the POSIX standard and is supported by **gawk** if you run it with the **-Wre-interval** option.

In **ed**, **vi**, and **sed**, the following additional metacharacters are valid only in a replacement pattern:

Symbol	ex	sed	ed	Action
\	✓	✓	✓	Escape following character.
\n	✓	✓	✓	Reuse matched text stored in nth \(\).
&	✓	✓		Reuse previous search pattern.
~	✓			Reuse previous replacement pattern.
\e	✓			Turn off previous \L or \U.
\E	✓			Turn off previous \L or \U.
\l	✓			Change single following character to lowercase.
\L	✓			Change following characters to lowercase until \E is encountered.
\u	✓			Change single following character to uppercase.
\U	✓			Change following characters to uppercase until \E is encountered.

Metacharacters

The following characters have special meaning in search patterns:

Character	Action
.	Match any single character except newline.
*	Match any number (or none) of the single character that immediately precedes it. The preceding character also can be a regular expression (e.g., since . (dot) means any character, .* means match any number of any character—except newlines).
^	Match the beginning of the line or string.
$	Match the end of the line or string.
[]	Match any one of the enclosed characters. A hyphen (-) indicates a range of consecutive characters. A circumflex (^) as the first character in the brackets reverses the sense: it matches any one character *not* in the list. A hyphen or close bracket (]) as the first character is treated as a member of the list. All other metacharacters are treated as members of the list.
[^]	Match anything except enclosed characters.
\{n,m\}	Match a range of occurrences of the single character that immediately precedes it. The preceding character also can be a regular expression. \{n\} matches exactly n occurrences, \{n,\} matches at least n occurrences, and \{n,m\} matches any number of occurrences between n and m.
{n,m}	Like \{n,m\}. Available in **grep** by default and in **gawk** with the -**Wre-interval** option.
\	Turn off the special meaning of the character that follows.
\(\)	Save the matched text enclosed between \(and \) in a special holding space. Up to nine patterns can be saved on a single line. They can be "replayed" in the same pattern or within substitutions by the escape sequences \1 to \9.
\n	Reuse matched text stored in nth \(\).
\<	Match the beginning of a word.
\>	Match the end of a word.
+	Match one or more instances of preceding regular expression.
?	Match zero or one instance of preceding regular expression.
|	Match the regular expression specified before or after.
( )	In **egrep** and **gawk**, group regular expressions.

Many utilities support POSIX character lists, which are useful for matching non-ASCII characters in languages other than English. These lists are recognized only within [ ] ranges. A typical use would be [[:lower:]], which in English is the same as [a-z].

The following table lists POSIX character lists:

Notation	Matches
[:alnum:]	Alphanumeric characters
[:alpha:]	Alphabetic characters, uppercase and lowercase
[:blank:]	Printable whitespace: spaces and tabs but not control characters
[:cntrl:]	Control characters, such as ^A through ^Z
[:digit:]	Decimal digits
[:graph:]	Printable characters, excluding whitespace
[:lower:]	Lowercase alphabetic characters
[:print:]	Printable characters, including whitespace but not control characters
[:punct:]	Punctuation, a subclass of printable characters
[:space:]	Whitespace, including spaces, tabs, and some control characters
[:upper:]	Uppercase alphabetic characters
[:xdigit:]	Hexadecimal digits

The following characters have special meaning in replacement patterns:

Character	Action
\	Turn off the special meaning of the character that follows.
\n	Restore the nth pattern previously saved by \(and \). n is a number from 1 to 9, matching the patterns searched sequentially from left to right.
&	Reuse the search pattern as part of the replacement pattern.
~	Reuse the previous replacement pattern in the current replacement pattern.
\e	End replacement pattern started by \L or \U.
\E	End replacement pattern started by \L or \U.
\l	Convert first character of replacement pattern to lowercase.
\L	Convert replacement pattern to lowercase.
\u	Convert first character of replacement pattern to uppercase.
\U	Convert replacement pattern to uppercase.

Examples of Searching

When used with **grep** or **egrep**, regular expressions are normally surrounded by quotes to avoid interpretation by the shell. (If the pattern contains a **$**, you must use single quotes, as in **'$200'**, or escape the **$**, as in **"\$200"**.) When used with **ed**, **vi**, **sed**, and **gawk**, regular expressions are usually surrounded by **/** (although any delimiter works). Here are some sample patterns:

Pattern	Matches
bag	The string "bag"
^bag	"bag" at beginning of line or string

Pattern	Matches
bag$	"bag" at end of line or string
^bag$	"bag" as the only text on line
[Bb]ag	"Bag" or "bag"
b[aeiou]g	Second character is a vowel
b[^aeiou]g	Second character is not a vowel
b.g	Second character is any character except newline
^...$	Any line containing exactly three characters
^\.	Any line that begins with a dot
^\.[a-z][a-z]	Same, followed by two lowercase letters (e.g., **troff** requests)
^\.[a-z]\{2\}	Same as previous (**grep** or **sed** only)
^[^.]	Any line that doesn't begin with a dot
bugs*	"bug", "bugs", "bugss", etc
"word"	The string "word" in quotes
"*word"*	The string "word", with or without quotes
[A-Z][A-Z]*	One or more uppercase letters
[A-Z]+	Same (**egrep** or **gawk** only)
[A-Z].*	An uppercase letter, followed by zero or more characters
[A-Z]*	Zero or more uppercase letters
[a-zA-Z]	Any letter
[0-9A-Za-z]+	Any alphanumeric sequence

egrep or gawk pattern	Matches
[567]	One of the numbers *5*, *6*, or *7*
five|six|seven	One of the words *five*, *six*, or *seven*
80[23]?86	*8086*, *80286*, or *80386*
compan(y|ies)	*company* or *companies*

vi pattern	Matches
\<the	Words like *theater* or *the*
the\>	Words like *breathe* or *the*
\<the\>	The word *the*

sed or grep pattern	Matches
0\{5,\}	Five or more zeros in a row
[0-9]\{3\}-[0-9]\{2\}-[0-9]\{4\}	Social security number (*nnn-nn-nnnn*)

Examples of Searching and Replacing

The following examples show the metacharacters available to **sed** and **vi**. We have shown **vi** commands with an initial colon because that is how they are invoked within **vi**. A space is marked by a □; a tab is marked by *tab*.

Command	Result
s/.*/(&)/	Reproduce the entire line, but add parentheses.
s/.*/mv & &.old/	Change a wordlist (one word per line) into **mv** commands.
/^$/d	Delete blank lines.
:g/^$/d	Same as previous, in **vi** editor.
/^[□*tab*]*$/d	Delete blank lines, plus lines containing spaces or tabs.
:g/^[□*tab*]*$/d	Same as previous, in **vi** editor.
s/□□*/□/g	Turn one or more spaces into one space.
:%s/□□*/□/g	Same as previous, in **vi** editor.
:s/[0-9]/Item &:/	Turn a number into an item label (on the current line).
:s	Repeat the substitution on the first occurrence.
:&	Same as previous.
:sg	Same, but for all occurrences on the line.
:&g	Same as previous.
:%&g	Repeat the substitution globally.
:.,$s/Fortran/\U&/g	Change word to uppercase, on current line to last line.
:%s/.*/\L&/	Lowercase entire file.
:s/\<./\u&/g	Uppercase first letter of each word on current line. (Useful for titles.)
:%s/yes/No/g	Globally change a string ("yes") to another string ("No").
:%s/Yes/~/g	Globally change a different string to "No" (previous replacement).

Finally, here are some **sed** examples for transposing words. A simple transposition of two words might look like this:

```
s/die or do/do or die/          Transpose words
```

The real trick is to use hold buffers to transpose variable patterns. For example:

```
s/\([Dd]ie\) or \([Dd]o\)/\2 or\1/          Transpose using hold buffers
```

10

The Emacs Editor

The Emacs editor is found on many Unix systems, including Linux, because it is a popular alternative to **vi**. Many versions are available. This book documents GNU Emacs, which is available from the Free Software Foundation in Cambridge, MA. For more information, see the O'Reilly book *Learning GNU Emacs*.

Emacs is much more than "just an editor"—in fact, it provides a fully integrated user environment. From within Emacs you can issue individual shell commands, or open a window where you can work in the shell, read and send mail, read news, access the Internet, write and test programs, and maintain a calendar. To fully describe Emacs would require more space than we have available. In this chapter, therefore, we focus on the editing capabilities of Emacs.

To start an Emacs editing session, type:

```
emacs
```

You can also specify one or more files for Emacs to open when it starts:

```
emacs files
```

Emacs Concepts

This section describes some Emacs terminology that may be unfamiliar if you haven't used Emacs before.

Modes

One of the features that makes Emacs popular is its editing modes. The modes set up an environment designed for the type of editing you are doing, with features like having appropriate key bindings available, and automatically indenting according to standard conventions for that type of document. There are two types of modes, major and minor. The major modes include modes for various programming languages like C or Perl, for text processing (e.g., SGML or even straight text), and many more. One particularly useful major mode is Dired (Directory Editor), which has commands that let you manage directories. Minor modes set or unset features that are independent of the major mode, such as auto-fill (which controls word wrapping), insert versus overwrite, and auto-save. For a full discussion of modes, see *Learning GNU Emacs* or the Emacs Info documentation system (**C-h i**).

Buffer and Window

When you open a file in Emacs, the file is put into a *buffer* so you can edit it. If you open another file, that file goes into another buffer. The view of the buffer contents that you have at any point in time is called a *window*. For a small file, the window might show the entire file; for a large file, it shows only a portion of a file. Emacs allows multiple windows to be open at the same time, to display the contents of different buffers or different portions of a single buffer.

Point and Mark

When you are editing in Emacs, the position of the cursor is known as *point*. You can set a *mark* at another place in the text to operate on the region between point and mark. This is a very useful feature for such operations as deleting or moving an area of text.

Kill and Yank

Emacs uses the terms *kill* and *yank* for the concepts more commonly known today as cut and paste. You cut text in Emacs by killing it, and paste it by yanking it back. If you do multiple kills in a row, you can yank them back all at once.

Typical Problems

A common problem with Emacs is that the Del or Backspace key does not delete the character before the cursor, as it should, but instead invokes a help prompt. This problem is caused by an incompatible terminal setup file. A fairly robust fix is to create a file named *.emacs* in your home directory (or edit one that's already there) and add the following lines:

```
(keyboard-translate ?\C-h ?\C-?)
(keyboard-translate ?\C-\\ ?\C-h)
```

Now the Del or Backspace kill should work, and you can invoke help by pressing **C-** (an arbitrarily chosen key sequence).

Another potential problem is that on some systems, **C-s** causes the terminal to hang. This is due to an old-fashioned handshake protocol between the terminal and the system. You can restart the terminal by pressing **C-q**, but that doesn't help you enter commands that contain the sequence **C-s**. The solution (aside from using a more modern dial-in protocol) is to create new key bindings that replace **C-s** or to enter those commands as **M-x** *command-name*. This is not specifically an Emacs problem, but it can cause problems when you run Emacs in a terminal window because **C-s** and **C-q** are commonly used Emacs key sequences.

Notes on the Tables

Emacs commands use the Ctrl key and the Meta key. Most modern terminals provide a key named Alt that functions as a Meta key. In this section, the notation **C-** indicates that you should hold down the Ctrl key and press the character that follows, while **M-** indicates the same for the Meta or Alt key. As an alternative to Meta or Alt, you can press the Esc key, release it, and press the character. You might want to do this if you have problems with controlling windows capturing the Alt key (which sometimes happens).

In the command tables that follow, the first column lists the keystroke and the last column describes it. When there is a middle column, it lists the command name. The command can be executed by typing **M-x** followed by the command name; you have to do this when the binding is listed as "(none)". If you're unsure of the full command name, you can type a space, tab, or carriage return, and Emacs will list possible completions of what you've typed so far.

Because Emacs is such a comprehensive editor, containing hundreds of commands, some commands must be omitted for the sake of preserving a "quick" reference. You can browse the full command set by typing **C-h** (for help) and then **b** to get a list of the key bindings,[*] or **M-x** followed by a space or tab to get the command names.

Absolutely Essential Commands

If you're just getting started with Emacs, here's a short list of the most important commands to know:

Binding	Action
C-h	Enter the online help system.
C-x C-s	Save the file.
C-x C-c	Exit Emacs.
C-x u	Undo last edit (can be repeated).
C-g	Get out of current command operation.
C-p	Up by one line.
C-n	Down by one line.
C-f	Forward by one character.
C-b	Back by one character.
C-v	Forward by one screen.
M-v	Backward by one screen.
C-s	Search forward for characters.
C-r	Search backward for characters.
C-d	Delete current character.
Del	Delete previous character.
Backspace	Delete previous character.

---

[*] If you want to learn to create your own key bindings, see *Learning GNU Emacs* (O'Reilly).

Summary of Commands by Group

Tables list keystrokes, command name, and description. **C-** indicates the Ctrl key; **M-** indicates the Meta key.

File Handling Commands

Binding	Command	Action
C-x C-f	find-file	Find file and read it.
C-x C-v	find-alternate-file	Read another file; replace the one read currently in the buffer.
C-x i	insert-file	Insert file at cursor position.
C-x C-s	save-buffer	Save file. (If terminal hangs, **C-q** restarts.)
C-x C-w	write-file	Write buffer contents to file.
C-x C-c	save-buffers-kill-emacs	Exit Emacs.
C-z	suspend-emacs	Suspend Emacs (use **exit** or **fg** to restart).

Cursor Movement Commands

In addition to the key bindings shown in this table, you can use the arrow keys to move around in Emacs. When you are running Emacs in a graphical display environment (e.g., in the X Window System), you can also use the mouse for operations such as moving the cursor or selecting text.

Binding	Command	Action
C-f	forward-char	Move forward one character (right).
C-b	backward-char	Move backward one character (left).
C-p	previous-line	Move to previous line (up).
C-n	next-line	Move to next line (down).
M-f	forward-word	Move one word forward.
M-b	backward-word	Move one word backward.
C-a	beginning-of-line	Move to beginning of line.
C-e	end-of-line	Move to end of line.
M-a	backward-sentence	Move backward one sentence.
M-e	forward-sentence	Move forward one sentence.
M-{	backward-paragraph	Move backward one paragraph.
M-}	forward-paragraph	Move forward one paragraph.
C-v	scroll-up	Move forward one screen.
M-v	scroll-down	Move backward one screen.
C-x [	backward-page	Move backward one page.
C-x]	forward-page	Move forward one page.
M->	end-of-buffer	Move to end-of-file.
M-<	beginning-of-buffer	Move to beginning of file.
(none)	goto-line	Go to line *n* of file.
(none)	goto-char	Go to character *n* of file.

Binding	Command	Action
C-l	recenter	Redraw screen with current line in the center.
M-*n*	digit-argument	Repeat the next command *n* times.
C-u *n*	universal-argument	Repeat the next command *n* times.

Deletion Commands

Binding	Command	Action
Del	backward-delete-char	Delete previous character.
C-d	delete-char	Delete character under cursor.
M-Del	backward-kill-word	Delete previous word.
M-d	kill-word	Delete the word the cursor is on.
C-k	kill-line	Delete from cursor to end-of-line.
M-k	kill-sentence	Delete sentence the cursor is on.
C-x Del	backward-kill-sentence	Delete previous sentence.
C-y	yank	Restore what you've deleted.
C-w	kill-region	Delete a marked region (see "Paragraphs and Regions").
(none)	backward-kill-paragraph	Delete previous paragraph.
(none)	kill-paragraph	Delete from the cursor to the end of the paragraph.

Paragraphs and Regions

Binding	Command	Action
C-@	set-mark-command	Mark the beginning (or end) of a region.
C-Space	(Same as preceding)	(Same as preceding)
C-x C-p	mark-page	Mark page.
C-x C-x	exchange-point-and-mark	Exchange location of cursor and mark.
C-x h	mark-whole-buffer	Mark buffer.
M-q	fill-paragraph	Reformat paragraph.
(none)	fill-region	Reformat individual paragraphs within a region.
M-h	mark-paragraph	Mark paragraph.
M-{	backward-paragraph	Move backward one paragraph.
M-}	forward-paragraph	Move forward one paragraph.
(none)	backward-kill-paragraph	Delete previous paragraph.
(none)	kill-paragraph	Delete from the cursor to the end of the paragraph.

Stopping and Undoing Commands

Binding	Command	Action
C-g	keyboard-quit	Abort current command.
C-x u	advertised-undo	Undo last edit (can be done repeatedly).
(none)	revert-buffer	Restore buffer to the state it was in when the file was last saved (or auto-saved).

Transposition Commands

Binding	Command	Action
C-t	transpose-chars	Transpose two letters.
M-t	transpose-words	Transpose two words.
C-x C-t	transpose-lines	Transpose two lines.
(none)	transpose-sentences	Transpose two sentences.
(none)	transpose-paragraphs	Transpose two paragraphs.

Capitalization Commands

Binding	Command	Action
M-c	capitalize-word	Capitalize first letter of word.
M-u	upcase-word	Uppercase word.
M-l	downcase-word	Lowercase word.
M-- M-c	negative-argument; capitalize-word	Capitalize previous word.
M-- M-u	negative-argument; upcase-word	Uppercase previous word.
M-- M-l	negative-argument; downcase-word	Lowercase previous word.
(none)	capitalize-region	Capitalize initial letters in region.
C-x C-u	upcase-region	Uppercase region.
C-x C-l	downcase-region	Lowercase region.

Incremental Search Commands

Binding	Command	Action
C-s	isearch-forward	Start or repeat incremental search forward.
C-r	isearch-backward	Start or repeat incremental search backward.
Return	(none)	Exit a successful search.
C-g	keyboard-quit	Cancel incremental search; return to starting point.
Del	(none)	Delete incorrect character of search string.
M-C-r	isearch-backward-regexp	Incremental search backward for regular expression.
M-C-s	isearch-forward-regexp	Incremental search forward for regular expression.

Word Abbreviation Commands

Binding	Command	Action
(none)	abbrev-mode	Enter (or exit) word abbreviation mode.
C-x a -	inverse-add-global-abbrev	Define previous word as global (mode-independent) abbreviation.
C-x a i l	inverse-add-mode-abbrev	Define previous word as mode-specific abbreviation.
(none)	unexpand-abbrev	Undo the last word abbreviation.
(none)	write-abbrev-file	Write the word abbreviation file.
(none)	edit-abbrevs	Edit the word abbreviations.

Binding	Command	Action
(none)	list-abbrevs	View the word abbreviations.
(none)	kill-all-abbrevs	Kill abbreviations for this session.

Buffer Manipulation Commands

Binding	Command	Action
C-x b	switch-to-buffer	Move to specified buffer.
C-x C-b	list-buffers	Display buffer list.
C-x k	kill-buffer	Delete specified buffer.
(none)	kill-some-buffers	Ask about deleting each buffer.
(none)	rename-buffer	Change buffer name to specified name.
C-x s	save-some-buffers	Ask whether to save each modified buffer.

Window Commands

Binding	Command	Action
C-x 2	split-window-vertically	Divide the current window in two vertically, resulting in one window on top of the other.
C-x 3	split-window-horizontally	Divide the current window in two horizontally, resulting in two side-by-side windows.
C-x >	scroll-right	Scroll the window right.
C-x <	scroll-left	Scroll the window left.
C-x o	other-window	Move to the other window.
C-x 0	delete-window	Delete current window.
C-x 1	delete-other-windows	Delete all windows but this one.
(none)	delete-windows-on	Delete all windows on a given buffer.
C-x ^	enlarge-window	Make window taller.
(none)	shrink-window	Make window shorter.
C-x }	enlarge-window- horizontally	Make window wider.
C-x {	shrink-window- horizontally	Make window narrower.
M-C-v	scroll-other-window	Scroll other window.
C-x 4 f	find-file-other-window	Find a file in the other window.
C-x 4 b	switch-to-buffer-other-window	Select a buffer in the other window.
C-x 5 f	find-file-other-frame	Find a file in a new frame.
C-x 5 b	switch-to-buffer-other-frame	Select a buffer in another frame.
(none)	compare-windows	Compare two buffers; show first difference.

Special Shell Mode Characters

The following table shows commands that can be used in Shell mode. To enter Shell mode, run the command **M-x shell**.

Binding	Command	Action
C-c C-c	interrupt-shell-subjob	Terminate the current job.
C-c C-d	shell-send-eof	End-of-file character.
C-c C-u	kill-shell-input	Erase current line.
C-c C-w	backward-kill-word	Erase the previous word.
C-c C-z	stop-shell-subjob	Suspend the current job.

Indentation Commands

Binding	Command	Action
C-x .	set-fill-prefix	Prepend each line in paragraph with characters from beginning of line up to cursor column; cancel prefix by typing this command in column 1.
(none)	indented-text-mode	Major mode: each tab defines a new indent for subsequent lines.
(none)	text-mode	Exit indented text mode; return to text mode.
M-C-\	indent-region	Indent a region to match first line in region.
M-m	back-to-indentation	Move cursor to first character on line.
M-^	delete-indentation	Join this line to the previous line.
M-C-o	split-line	Split line at cursor; indent to column of cursor.
(none)	fill-individual- paragraphs	Reformat indented paragraphs, keeping indentation.

Centering Commands

Binding	Command	Action
(none)	center-line	Center line that cursor is on.
(none)	center-paragraph	Center paragraph that cursor is on.
(none)	center-region	Center currently defined region.

Macro Commands

Binding	Command	Action
C-x (	start-kbd-macro	Start macro definition.
C-x)	end-kbd-macro	End macro definition.
C-x e	call-last-kbd-macro	Execute last macro defined.
M-n C-x e	digit-argument and call-last-kbd-macro	Execute last macro defined n times.
C-u C-x (	start-kbd-macro	Execute last macro defined, then add keystrokes.
(none)	name-last-kbd-macro	Name last macro you created (before saving it).
(none)	insert-last-keyboard- macro	Insert the macro you named into a file.
(none)	load-file	Load macro files you've saved.
(none)	*macroname*	Execute a keyboard macro you've saved.
C-x q	kbd-macro-query	Insert a query in a macro definition.
C-u C-x q	(none)	Insert a recursive edit in a macro definition.
M-C-c	exit-recursive-edit	Exit a recursive edit.

Detail Information Help Commands

Binding	Command	Action
C-h a	command-apropos	What commands involve this concept?
(none)	apropos	What commands, functions, and variables involve this concept?
C-h c	describe-key-briefly	What command does this keystroke sequence run?
C-h b	describe-bindings	What are all the key bindings for this buffer?
C-h k	describe-key	What command does this keystroke sequence run, and what does it do?
C-h l	view-lossage	What are the last 100 characters I typed?
C-h w	where-is	What is the key binding for this command?
C-h f	describe-function	What does this function do?
C-h v	describe-variable	What does this variable mean, and what is its value?
C-h m	describe-mode	Tell me about the mode the current buffer is in.
C-h s	describe-syntax	What is the syntax table for this buffer?

Help Commands

Binding	Command	Action
C-h t	help-with-tutorial	Run the Emacs tutorial.
C-h i	info	Start the Info documentation reader.
C-h n	view-emacs-news	View news about updates to Emacs.
C-h C-c	describe-copying	View the Emacs General Public License.
C-h C-d	describe-distribution	View information on ordering Emacs from the FSF.
C-h C-w	describe-no-warranty	View the (non)warranty for Emacs.

Summary of Commands by Key

Emacs commands are presented next in two alphabetical lists. Tables list keystrokes, command name, and description. **C-** indicates the Ctrl key; **M-** indicates the Meta key.

Control-Key Sequences

Binding	Command	Action
C-@	set-mark-command	Mark the beginning (or end) of a region.
C-Space	(Same as preceding)	(Same as preceding)
C-]	abort-recursive-edit	Exit recursive edit and exit query-replace.
C-a	beginning-of-line	Move to beginning of line.
C-b	backward-char	Move backward one character (left).
C-c C-c	interrupt-shell-subjob	Terminate the current job.
C-c C-d	shell-send-eof	End-of-file character.
C-c C-u	kill-shell-input	Erase current line.
C-c C-w	backward-kill-word	Erase previous word.

Binding	Command	Action
C-c C-z	stop-shell-subjob	Suspend current job.
C-d	delete-char	Delete character under cursor.
C-e	end-of-line	Move to end of line.
C-f	forward-char	Move forward one character (right).
C-g	keyboard-quit	Abort current command.
C-h	help-command	Enter the online help system.
C-h a	command-apropos	What commands involve this concept?
C-h b	describe-bindings	What are all the key bindings for this buffer?
C-h c	describe-key-briefly	What command does this keystroke sequence run?
C-h C-c	describe-copying	View the Emacs General Public License.
C-h C-d	describe-distribution	View information on ordering Emacs from the FSF.
C-h C-w	describe-no-warranty	View the (non)warranty for Emacs.
C-h f	describe-function	What does this function do?
C-h i	info	Start the Info documentation reader.
C-h k	describe-key	What command does this keystroke sequence run, and what does it do?
C-h l	view-lossage	What are the last 100 characters I typed?
C-h m	describe-mode	Tell me about the mode the current buffer is in.
C-h n	view-emacs-news	View news about updates to Emacs.
C-h s	describe-syntax	What is the syntax table for this buffer?
C-h t	help-with-tutorial	Run the Emacs tutorial.
C-h v	describe-variable	What does this variable mean, and what is its value?
C-h w	where-is	What is the key binding for this command?
C-k	kill-line	Delete from cursor to end-of-line.
C-l	recenter	Redraw screen with current line in the center.
C-n	next-line	Move to next line (down).
C-p	previous-line	Move to previous line (up).
C-q	quoted-insert	Insert next character typed. Useful for inserting a control character.
C-r	isearch-backward	Start or repeat nonincremental search backward.
C-r	(none)	Enter recursive edit (during query replace).
C-s	isearch-forward	Start or repeat nonincremental search forward.
C-t	transpose-chars	Transpose two letters.
C-u n	universal-argument	Repeat the next command n times.
C-u C-x (	start-kbd-macro	Execute last macro defined, then add keystrokes.
C-u C-x q	(none)	Insert recursive edit in a macro definition.
C-v	scroll-up	Move forward one screen.
C-w	kill-region	Delete a marked region.
C-x (	start-kbd-macro	Start macro definition.
C-x)	end-kbd-macro	End macro definition.
C-x [	backward-page	Move backward one page.
C-x]	forward-page	Move forward one page.
C-x ^	enlarge-window	Make window taller.

Binding	Command	Action
C-x {	shrink-window-horizontally	Make window narrower.
C-x }	enlarge-window-horizontally	Make window wider.
C-x <	scroll-left	Scroll the window left.
C-x >	scroll-right	Scroll the window right.
C-x .	set-fill-prefix	Prepend each line in paragraph with characters from beginning of line up to cursor column; cancel prefix by typing this command in column 1.
C-x 0	delete-window	Delete current window.
C-x 1	delete-other-windows	Delete all windows but this one.
C-x 2	split-window-vertically	Divide current window in two vertically, resulting in one window on top of the other.
C-x 3	split-window-horizontally	Divide current window in two horizontally, resulting in two side-by-side windows.
C-x 4 b	switch-to-buffer-other-window	Select a buffer in the other window.
C-x 4 f	find-file-other-window	Find a file in the other window.
C-x 5 b	switch-to-buffer-other-frame	Select a buffer in another frame.
C-x 5 f	find-file-other-frame	Find a file in another frame.
C-x a -	inverse-add-global-abbrev	Define previous word as global (mode-independent) abbreviation.
C-x a i l	inverse-add-mode-abbrev	Define previous word as mode-specific abbreviation.
C-x b	switch-to-buffer	Move to the buffer specified.
C-x C-b	list-buffers	Display the buffer list.
C-x C-c	save-buffers-kill-emacs	Exit Emacs.
C-x C-f	find-file	Find file and read it.
C-x C-l	downcase-region	Lowercase region.
C-x C-p	mark-page	Place cursor and mark around whole page.
C-x C-q	(none)	Toggle read-only status of buffer.
C-x C-s	save-buffer	Save file. (If terminal hangs, **C-q** restarts.)
C-x C-t	transpose-lines	Transpose two lines.
C-x C-u	upcase-region	Uppercase region.
C-x C-v	find-alternate-file	Read an alternate file, replacing the one currently in the buffer.
C-x C-w	write-file	Write buffer contents to file.
C-x C-x	exchange-point-and-mark	Exchange location of cursor and mark.
C-x Del	backward-kill-sentence	Delete previous sentence.
C-x e	call-last-kbd-macro	Execute last macro defined.
C-x h	mark-whole-buffer	Place cursor and mark around whole buffer.
C-x i	insert-file	Insert file at cursor position.
C-x k	kill-buffer	Delete the buffer specified.
C-x o	other-window	Move to the other window.
C-x q	kbd-macro-query	Insert a query in a macro definition.
C-x s	save-some-buffers	Ask whether to save each modified buffer.
C-x u	advertised-undo	Undo last edit (can be done repeatedly).

Binding	Command	Action
C-y	yank	Restore killed text.
C-z	suspend-emacs	Suspend Emacs (use **exit** or **fg** to restart).

Meta-Key Sequences

Binding	Command	Action
M-- M-c	negative-argument; capitalize-word	Capitalize previous word.
M-- M-l	negative-argument; downcase-word	Lowercase previous word.
M-- M-u	negative-argument; upcase-word	Uppercase previous word.
M-$	spell-word	Check spelling of word after cursor.
M-%	query-replace	Search for and replace a string.
M-!	shell-command	Prompt for a shell command and run it.
M-<	beginning-of-buffer	Move to beginning of file.
M->	end-of-buffer	Move to end-of-file.
M-{	backward-paragraph	Move backward one paragraph.
M-}	forward-paragraph	Move forward one paragraph.
M-^	delete-indentation	Join this line to the previous one.
M-n	digit-argument	Repeat the next command n times.
M-n C-x e	digit-argument; call-last-kbd-macro	Execute the last defined macro n times.
M-a	backward-sentence	Move backward one sentence.
M-b	backward-word	Move one word backward.
M-c	capitalize-word	Capitalize first letter of word.
M-C-\	indent-region	Indent a region to match first line in region.
M-C-c	exit-recursive-edit	Exit a recursive edit.
M-C-o	split-line	Split line at cursor; indent to column of cursor.
M-C-r	isearch-backward-regexp	Incremental search backward for regular expression.
M-C-s	isearch-forward-regexp	Incremental search forward for regular expression.
M-C-v	scroll-other-window	Scroll other window.
M-d	kill-word	Delete word that cursor is on.
M-Del	backward-kill-word	Delete previous word.
M-e	forward-sentence	Move forward one sentence.
M-f	forward-word	Move one word forward.
(none)	fill-region	Reformat individual paragraphs within a region.
M-h	mark-paragraph	Place cursor and mark around whole paragraph.
M-k	kill-sentence	Delete sentence that cursor is on.
M-l	downcase-word	Lowercase word.
M-m	back-to-indentation	Move cursor to first nonblank character on line.
M-q	fill-paragraph	Reformat paragraph.
M-t	transpose-words	Transpose two words.
M-u	upcase-word	Uppercase word.
M-v	scroll-down	Move backward one screen.
M-x	(none)	Execute a command by typing its name.

Summary of Commands by Name

The following Emacs commands are presented alphabetically by command name. Use **M-x** to access the command name. Tables list command name, keystroke, and description. **C-** indicates the Ctrl key; **M-** indicates the Meta key.

Command	Binding	Action
macroname	(none)	Execute a keyboard macro you've saved.
abbrev-mode	(none)	Enter (or exit) word abbreviation mode.
abort-recursive-edit	C-]	Exit recursive edit and query replace.
advertised-undo	C-x u	Undo last edit (can be done repeatedly).
apropos	(none)	What functions and variables involve this concept?
back-to-indentation	M-m	Move cursor to first nonblank character on line.
backward-char	C-b	Move backward one character (left).
backward-delete-char	Del	Delete previous character.
backward-kill-paragraph	(none)	Delete previous paragraph.
backward-kill-sentence	C-x Del	Delete previous sentence.
backward-kill-word	C-c C-w	Delete previous word.
backward-kill-word	M-Del	Delete previous word.
backward-page	C-x [	Move backward one page.
backward-paragraph	M-{	Move backward one paragraph.
backward-sentence	M-a	Move backward one sentence.
backward-word	M-b	Move backward one word.
beginning-of-buffer	M-<	Move to beginning of file.
beginning-of-line	C-a	Move to beginning of line.
call-last-kbd-macro	C-x e	Execute last macro defined.
capitalize-region	(none)	Capitalize region.
capitalize-word	M-c	Capitalize first letter of word.
center-line	(none)	Center line that cursor is on.
center-paragraph	(none)	Center paragraph that cursor is on.
center-region	(none)	Center currently defined region.
command-apropos	C-h a	What commands involve this concept?
compare-windows	(none)	Compare two buffers; show first difference.
delete-char	C-d	Delete character under cursor.
delete-indentation	M-^	Join this line to previous one.
delete-other-windows	C-x 1	Delete all windows but this one.
delete-window	C-x 0	Delete current window.
delete-windows-on	(none)	Delete all windows on a given buffer.
describe-bindings	C-h b	What are all the key bindings for in this buffer?
describe-copying	C-h C-c	View the Emacs General Public License.
describe-distribution	C-h C-d	View information on ordering Emacs from the FSF.
describe-function	C-h f	What does this function do?
describe-key	C-h k	What command does this keystroke sequence run, and what does it do?

Command	Binding	Action
describe-key-briefly	C-h c	What command does this keystroke sequence run?
describe-mode	C-h m	Tell me about the mode the current buffer is in.
describe-no-warranty	C-h C-w	View the (non)warranty for Emacs.
describe-syntax	C-h s	What is the syntax table for this buffer?
describe-variable	C-h v	What does this variable mean, and what is its value?
digit-argument	M-*n*	Repeat next command *n* times.
downcase-region	C-x C-l	Lowercase region.
downcase-word	M-l	Lowercase word.
edit-abbrevs	(none)	Edit word abbreviations.
end-kbd-macro	C-x)	End macro definition.
end-of-buffer	M->	Move to end-of-file.
end-of-line	C-e	Move to end-of-line.
enlarge-window	C-x ^	Make window taller.
enlarge-window-horizontally	C-x }	Make window wider.
exchange-point-and-mark	C-x C-x	Exchange location of cursor and mark.
exit-recursive-edit	M-C-c	Exit a recursive edit.
fill-individual-paragraphs	(none)	Reformat indented paragraphs, keeping indentation.
fill-paragraph	M-q	Reformat paragraph.
fill-region	(none)	Reformat individual paragraphs within a region.
find-alternate-file	C-x C-v	Read an alternate file, replacing the one currently in the buffer.
find-file	C-x C-f	Find file and read it.
find-file-other-frame	C-x 5 f	Find a file in another frame.
find-file-other-window	C-x 4 f	Find a file in another window.
forward-char	C-f	Move forward one character (right).
forward-page	C-x]	Move forward one page.
forward-paragraph	M-}	Move forward one paragraph.
forward-sentence	M-e	Move forward one sentence.
forward-word	M-f	Move forward one word.
goto-char	(none)	Go to character *n* of file.
goto-line	(none)	Go to line *n* of file.
help-command	C-h	Enter the online help system.
help-with-tutorial	C-h t	Run the Emacs tutorial.
indent-region	M-C-\	Indent a region to match first line in region.
indented-text-mode	(none)	Major mode: each tab defines a new indent for subsequent lines.
info	C-h i	Start the Info documentation reader.
insert-file	C-x i	Insert file at cursor position.
insert-last-keyboard-macro	(none)	Insert the macro you named into a file.
interrupt-shell-subjob	C-c C-c	Terminate the current job (shell mode).
inverse-add-global-abbrev	C-x a -	Define previous word as global (mode-independent) abbreviation.
inverse-add-mode-abbrev	C-x a i l	Define previous word as mode-specific abbreviation.
isearch-backward	C-r	Start incremental search backward.
isearch-backward-regexp	M-C-r	Same, but search for regular expression.

Command	Binding	Action
isearch-forward	C-s	Start incremental search forward.
isearch-forward-regexp	M-C-s	Same, but search for regular expression.
kbd-macro-query	C-x q	Insert a query in a macro definition.
keyboard-quit	C-g	Abort current command.
kill-all-abbrevs	(none)	Kill abbreviations for this session.
kill-buffer	C-x k	Delete the buffer specified.
kill-line	C-k	Delete from cursor to end-of-line.
kill-paragraph	(none)	Delete from cursor to end of paragraph.
kill-region	C-w	Delete a marked region.
kill-sentence	M-k	Delete sentence the cursor is on.
kill-shell-input	C-c C-u	Delete current line.
kill-some-buffers	(none)	Ask about deleting each buffer.
kill-word	M-d	Delete word the cursor is on.
list-abbrevs	(none)	View word abbreviations.
list-buffers	C-x C-b	Display buffer list.
load-file	(none)	Load macro files you've saved.
mark-page	C-x C-p	Place cursor and mark around whole page.
mark-paragraph	M-h	Place cursor and mark around whole paragraph.
mark-whole-buffer	C-x h	Place cursor and mark around whole buffer.
name-last-kbd-macro	(none)	Name last macro you created (before saving it).
negative-argument; capitalize-word	M-- M-c	Capitalize previous word.
negative-argument; downcase-word	M-- M-l	Lowercase previous word.
negative-argument; upcase-word	M-- M-u	Uppercase previous word.
next-line	C-n	Move to next line (down).
other-window	C-x o	Move to the other window.
previous-line	C-p	Move to previous line (up).
query-replace	M-%	Search for and replace a string.
query-replace-regexp	(none)	Query-replace a regular expression.
quoted-insert	C-q	Insert next character typed. Useful for inserting a control character.
recenter	C-l	Redraw screen, with current line in center.
rename-buffer	(none)	Change buffer name to specified name.
replace-regexp	(none)	Replace a regular expression unconditionally.
re-search-backward	(none)	Simple regular-expression search backward.
re-search-forward	(none)	Simple regular-expression search forward.
revert-buffer	(none)	Restore buffer to the state it was in when the file was last saved (or auto-saved).
save-buffer	C-x C-s	Save file. (If terminal hangs, C-q restarts.)
save-buffers-kill-emacs	C-x C-c	Exit Emacs.
save-some-buffers	C-x s	Ask whether to save each modified buffer.
scroll-down	M-v	Move backward one screen.

Command	Binding	Action
scroll-left	C-x <	Scroll the window left.
scroll-other-window	M-C-v	Scroll other window.
scroll-right	C-x >	Scroll the window right.
scroll-up	C-v	Move forward one screen.
set-fill-prefix	C-x .	Prepend each line in paragraph with characters from beginning of line up to cursor column; cancel prefix by typing this command in column 1.
set-mark-command	C-@ or C-Space	Mark the beginning (or end) of a region.
shell-command	M-!	Prompt for a shell command and run it.
shell-send-eof	C-c C-d	End-of-file character (shell mode).
shrink-window	(none)	Make window shorter.
shrink-window-horizontally	C-x {	Make window narrower.
spell-buffer	(none)	Check spelling of current buffer.
spell-region	(none)	Check spelling of current region.
spell-string	(none)	Check spelling of string typed in minibuffer.
spell-word	M-$	Check spelling of word after cursor.
split-line	M-C-o	Split line at cursor; indent to column of cursor.
split-window-horizontally	C-x 3	Divide current window horizontally into two.
split-window-vertically	C-x 2	Divide current window vertically into two.
start-kbd-macro	C-x (	Start macro definition.
stop-shell-subjob	C-c C-z	Suspend current job.
suspend-emacs	C-z	Suspend Emacs (use **fg** to restart).
switch-to-buffer	C-x b	Move to the buffer specified.
switch-to-buffer-other-frame	C-x 5 b	Select a buffer in another frame.
switch-to-buffer-other-window	C-x 4 b	Select a buffer in another window.
text-mode	(none)	Enter text mode.
transpose-chars	C-t	Transpose two characters.
transpose-lines	C-x C-t	Transpose two lines.
transpose-paragraphs	(none)	Transpose two paragraphs.
transpose-sentences	(none)	Transpose two sentences.
transpose-words	M-t	Transpose two words.
unexpand-abbrev	(none)	Undo the last word abbreviation.
universal-argument	C-u n	Repeat the next command n times.
upcase-region	C-x C-u	Uppercase region.
upcase-word	M-u	Uppercase word.
view-emacs-news	C-h n	View news about updates to Emacs.
view-lossage	C-h l	What are the last 100 characters I typed?
where-is	C-h w	What is the key binding for this command?
write-abbrev-file	(none)	Write the word abbreviation file.
write-file	C-x C-w	Write buffer contents to file.
yank	C-y	Restore what you've deleted.

The vi Editor

vi is the classic screen-editing program for Unix. A number of enhanced versions exist, including **nvi**, **vim**, **vile**, and **elvis**. On Linux, the **vi** command is usually a link to one of these programs. The Emacs editor, covered in Chapter 10, has several **vi** modes that allow you to use the same commands covered in this chapter.

The **vi** editor operates in two modes, command mode and insert mode. The dual mode makes **vi** an attractive editor for users who separate text entry from editing. For users who edit as they type, the modeless editing of **emacs** can be more comfortable.

vi is based on an older line editor called **ex**. A user can invoke powerful editing capabilities within **vi** by typing a colon (:), entering an **ex** command, and pressing the Return key. Furthermore, you can place **ex** commands in a startup file called *~/.exrc*, which **vi** reads at the beginning of your editing session. Because **ex** commands are still an important part of **vi**, they are also described in this chapter.

One of the most common versions of **vi** found on Linux systems is Bram Moolenaar's Vi IMproved, or **vim**. On some Linux distributions, **vim** is the default version of **vi** and runs when you invoke **vi**. **vim** changes some of the basic features of **vi**, most notoriously changing the undo key to support multiple levels of undo. While seasoned users of **vi** find **vim**'s changes disturbing, those new to **vi** find **vim**'s extensive features attractive.

Fully documenting **vim** is beyond the scope of this chapter, but we do cover some of its most commonly used options and features. Beyond what we cover here, **vim** offers enhanced support to programmers through an integrated build and debugging process, syntax highlighting, extended **ctags** support, and support for Perl and Python, as well as GUI fonts and menus, function key mapping, independent mapping for each mode, and more. Fortunately, **vim** comes with a powerful help program you can use to learn more about the things we just couldn't fit into this chapter.

For more information, see the O'Reilly book *Learning the vi Editor*.

Review of vi Operations

This section provides a review of the following:

- Command-line options
- **vi** modes
- Syntax of **vi** commands
- Status-line commands

Command Mode

Once the file is opened, you are in command mode. From command mode, you can:

- Invoke insert mode
- Issue editing commands
- Move the cursor to a different position in the file
- Invoke **ex** commands
- Invoke a Linux shell
- Save or exit the current version of the file

Insert Mode

In insert mode, you can enter new text in the file. Press the Esc or Ctrl-[keys to exit insert mode and return to command mode. The following commands invoke insert mode:

a   Append after cursor
A   Append at end-of-line
c   Begin change operation (must be followed by a movement command)
C   Change to end-of-line
i   Insert before cursor
I   Insert at beginning of line
o   Open a line below current line
O   Open a line above current line
r   Replace character under cursor
R   Begin overwriting text
s   Substitute a character
S   Substitute entire line

Syntax of vi Commands

In **vi**, commands have the following general form:

    [n] operator [m] object

The basic editing *operators* are:

c   Begin a change

d   Begin a deletion

y   Begin a yank (or copy)

If the current line is the object of the operation, the operator is the same as the object: **cc**, **dd**, **yy**. Otherwise, the editing operators act on objects specified by cursor-movement commands or pattern-matching commands. *n* and *m* are the number of times the operation is performed or the number of objects the operation is performed on. If both *n* and *m* are specified, the effect is *n* × *m*.

An object can represent any of the following text blocks:

Word
>   Includes characters up to a space or punctuation mark. A capitalized object is a variant form that recognizes only blank spaces.

Sentence
>   Extends to ., !, or ? followed by two spaces.

Paragraph
>   Extends to next blank line or **nroff/troff** paragraph macro (defined by **para=** *option*).

Section
>   Extends to next **nroff/troff** section heading (defined by **sect=** *option*).

Examples

2cw
>   Change the next two words

d}   Delete up to next paragraph

d^   Delete back to beginning of line

5yy
>   Copy the next five lines into temporary buffer (for future pasting)

y]]
>   Copy up to the next section into temporary buffer (for future pasting)

Status-Line Commands

Most commands are not echoed on the screen as you input them. However, the status line at the bottom of the screen is used to echo input for the following commands:

/   Search forward for a pattern

?   Search backward for a pattern

:   Invoke an **ex** command

!   Pipe the text indicated by a subsequent movement command through the following shell command, and replace the text with the output of the shell command

Commands that are input on the status line must be entered by pressing the Return key. In addition, error messages and output from the **Ctrl-G** command are displayed on the status line.

vi Command-Line Options

The three most common ways of starting a **vi** session are:

    vi file
    vi +n file
    vi +/ pattern file

You can open *file* for editing, optionally at line *n* or at the first line matching *pattern*. If no *file* is specified, **vi** opens with an empty buffer. The command-line options that can be used with **vi** are as follows (**vim**-only options are labeled):

+[*num*]
> Start editing at line number *num*, or the last line of the file if *num* is omitted.

+/*pattern*
> Start editing at the first line matching *pattern*. (Fails if **nowrapscan** is set in your *.exrc* startup file.)

-b   Edit the file in binary mode. {vim}

-c *command*
> Run the given **vi** command upon startup. Only one -c option is permitted. **ex** commands can be invoked by prefixing them with a colon. An older form of this option, +*command*, is still supported.

--cmd *command*
> Like -c, but execute the command before any resource files are read. {vim}

-d   Run in diff mode. Works like **vimdiff**. {vim}

-e   Run as **ex** (line editing rather than full-screen mode).

-h   Print help message, then exit.

-i *file*
> Use the specified *file* instead of the default *.viminfo* to save or restore **vim**'s state. {vim}

-l   Enter LISP mode for running LISP programs (not supported in all versions).

-m   Start the editor with the **write** option turned off so the user cannot write to files. {vim}

-n   Do not use a swap file; record changes in memory only. {vim}

--noplugin
> Do not load any plug-ins. {vim}

-o[*n*]
> Start **vim** with *n* open windows. The default is to open one window for each file. {vim}

-r [*file*]
> Recovery mode; recover and resume editing on *file* after an aborted editor session or system crash. Without *file*, list files available for recovery.

-s, -s *scriptfile*

When running in **ex** mode (**-e**), suppress prompts or informative messages sent to the console. Otherwise, read and execute commands given in the specified *scriptfile* as if they were typed in from the keyboard. {vim}

-t *tag*

Edit the file containing *tag* and position the cursor at its definition. (See **ctags** in Chapter 3 for more information.)

-u *file*

Read configuration information from the specified resource file instead of default *.vimrc* resource files. If the *file* argument is **NONE**, **vim** will read no resource files, load no plug-ins, and run in compatible mode. If the argument is **NORC**, it will read no resource files but it will load plug-ins. {vim}

-v Run in full-screen mode (default).

--version

Print version information, then exit.

-w *rows*

Set the window size so *rows* lines at a time are displayed; useful when editing over a slow dial-up line.

-x Prompt for a key that will be used to try to encrypt or decrypt a file using **crypt** (not supported in all versions).

-y Modeless **vi**; run **vim** in insert mode only, without a command mode. This is the same as invoking **vim** as **evim**. {vim}

-C Same as **-x**, but assume the file is encrypted already (not supported in all versions). For **vim** this option starts the editor in **vi**-compatible mode.

-D Debugging mode for use with scripts. {vim}

-L List files that were saved due to an aborted editor session or system crash (not supported in all versions). For **vim** this option is the same as **-r**.

-M Do not allow text in files to be modified. {vim}

-N Run **vim** in a non-**vi**-compatible mode. {vim}

-O[*n*]

Start **vim** with *n* open windows arranged vertically on the screen. {vim}

-R Edit files read-only.

-S *commandfile*

Source commands given in *commandfile* after loading any files for editing specified on the command line. Shorthand for the option **-c source**. {vim}

-T *type*

Set the terminal type. This value overrides the **$TERM** environment variable. {vim}

-V[*n*]

Verbose mode; print messages about what options are being set and what files are being read or written. You can set a level of verbosity to increase or decrease the number of messages received. The default value is 10 for high verbosity. {vim}

-W *scriptfile*

Write all typed commands from the current session to the specified *scriptfile*. The file created can be used with the **-s** command. {vim}

-Z   Start **vim** in restricted mode. Do not allow shell commands or suspension of the editor. {vim}

ex Command-Line Options

While most people know **ex** commands only by their use within **vi**, the editor also exists as a separate program and can be invoked from the shell (for instance, to edit files as part of a script). Within **ex**, you can enter the **vi** or **visual** command to start **vi**. Similarly, within **vi**, you can enter **Q** to quit the **vi** editor and enter **ex**.

If you invoke **ex** as a standalone editor, you can include the following options:

+[*num*]

Start editing at line number *num*, or the last line of the file if *num* is omitted.

+/pattern

Start editing at the first line matching *pattern*. (Fails if **nowrapscan** is set in your *.exrc* startup file.)

-c *command*

Run the given **ex** command upon startup. Only one **-c** option is permitted. An older form of this option, **+**command, is still supported.

-e   Run as a line editor rather than full-screen **vi** mode (default).

-l   Enter LISP mode for running LISP programs (not supported in all versions).

-r [*file*]

Recover and resume editing on *file* after an aborted editor session or system crash. Without *file*, list files available for recovery.

-s   Silent; do not display prompts. Useful when running a script. This behavior also can be set through the older **-** option.

-t *tag*

Edit the file containing *tag* and position the cursor at its definition (see **ctags** in Chapter 3 for more information).

-v   Run in full-screen mode (same as invoking **vi**).

-w *rows*

Set the window size so *rows* lines at a time are displayed; useful when editing by a slow dial-up line.

-x   Prompt for a key that will be used to try to encrypt or decrypt a file using **crypt** (not supported in all versions).

-C   Same as **-x**, but assume the file is encrypted already (not supported in all versions).

-L   List files that were saved due to an editor or system crash (not supported in all versions).

-R   Edit files read-only; do not allow changes to be saved.

You can exit **ex** in several ways:

:x   Exit (save changes and quit).

:q!   Quit without saving changes.

:vi   Enter the **vi** editor.

Movement Commands

Some versions of **vi** do not recognize extended keyboard keys (e.g., arrow keys, Page Up, Page Down, Home, Insert, and Delete); some do. All, however, recognize the keys in this section. Many users of **vi** prefer to use these keys, as it helps them keep their fingers on the home row of the keyboard. A number preceding a command repeats the movement. Movement commands are also objects for change, delete, and yank operations.

Character

Command	Action
h, j, k, l	Left, down, up, right ($\leftarrow$, $\downarrow$, $\uparrow$, $\rightarrow$)
Spacebar	Right
Backspace	Left
Ctrl-H	Left

Text

Command	Action
w, b	Forward, backward by word (treating punctuation marks as words).
W, B	Forward, backward by word (recognizing only whitespace, not punctuation, as separators).
e	End of word (treating a punctuation mark as the end of a word).
E	End of word (recognizing only whitespace as the end of a word).
ge	End of previous word (treating a punctuation mark as the end of a word). {vim}
gE	End of previous word (recognizing only whitespace as the end of a word). {vim}
), (	Beginning of next, current sentence.
}, {	Beginning of next, current paragraph.
]], [[	Beginning of next, current section.
][, []	End of next, current section. {vim}

Lines

Long lines in a file may show up on the screen as multiple lines. While most commands work on the lines as defined in the file, a few commands work on lines as they appear on the screen.

Command	Action
0, $	First, last position of current line.
^, _	First nonblank character of current line.
+, -	First character of next, previous line.
Return	First nonblank character of next line.
n|	Column *n* of current line.
g0, g$	First, last position of screen line. {vim}
g^	First nonblank character of screen line. {vim}
gm	Middle of screen line. {vim}
gk, gj	Move up, down one screen line. {vim}
H	Top line of screen.
M	Middle line of screen.
L	Last line of screen.
nH	*n* lines after top line of screen.
nL	*n* lines before last line of screen.

Screens

Command	Action
Ctrl-F, Ctrl-B	Scroll forward, backward one screen.
Ctrl-D, Ctrl-U	Scroll down, up one-half screen.
Ctrl-E, Ctrl-Y	Show one more line at bottom, top of window.
z Return	Reposition line with cursor to top of screen.
z.	Reposition line with cursor to middle of screen.
z-	Reposition line with cursor to bottom of screen.
Ctrl-L	Redraw screen (without scrolling).

Searches

Command	Action
/pattern	Search forward for *pattern*.
/	Repeat previous search forward.
/pattern/+n	Go to line *n* after *pattern*.
?pattern	Search backward for *pattern*.
?	Repeat previous search backward.
?pattern?-n	Go to line *n* before *pattern*.
n	Repeat previous search.
N	Repeat previous search in opposite direction.
%	Find match of current parenthesis, brace, or bracket.
*	Search forward for word under cursor. Matches only exact words. {vim}
#	Search backward for word under cursor. Matches only exact words. {vim}

Command	Action
g*	Search backward for word under cursor. Matches the characters of this word when embedded in a longer word. {vim}
g#	Search backward for word under cursor. Matches the characters of this word when embedded in a longer word. {vim}
f*x*	Move forward to *x* on current line.
F*x*	Move backward to *x* on current line.
t*x*	Move forward to just before *x* in current line.
T*x*	Move backward to just after *x* in current line.
,	Reverse search direction of last **f**, **F**, **t**, or **T**.
;	Repeat last character search (**f**, **F**, **t**, or **T**).
:noh	Suspend search highlighting until next search. {vim}.

Line numbering

Command	Action
Ctrl-G	Display current filename and line number.
gg	Move to first line in file. {vim}
*n*G	Move to line number *n*.
G	Move to last line in file.
:*n*	Move to line number *n*.

Marking position

Command	Action
m*x*	Mark current position with character *x*.
`*x*	(backquote) Move cursor to mark *x*.
'*x*	(apostrophe) Move to start of line containing *x*.
``	(backquotes) Return to previous mark (or location prior to search).
''	(apostrophes) Like preceding, but return to start of line.
'''	(apostrophe quote) Move to position when last editing the file. {vim}
`[,`]	(backquote bracket) Move to beginning/end of previous text operation. {vim}
'[,']	(apostrophe bracket) Like preceding, but return to start of line where operation occurred. {vim}
`.	(backquote period) Move to last change in file. {vim}
'.	(apostrophe period) Like preceding, but return to start of line. {vim}
:marks	List active marks. {vim}

Edit Commands

Recall that **c**, **d**, and **y** are the basic editing operators.

Inserting New Text

Command	Action
a	Append after cursor.
A	Append to end of line.
i	Insert before cursor.
I	Insert at first nonblank character of line.
gI	Insert at beginning of line. {vim}
o	Open a line below cursor.
O	Open a line above cursor.
Esc	Terminate insert mode.

The following commands work in insert mode.

Command	Action
Tab	Insert a tab.
Backspace	Delete previous character.
Ctrl-E	Insert character found just below cursor. {vim}
Ctrl-Y	Insert character found just above cursor. {vim}
Ctrl-H	Delete previous character (same as Backspace).
Delete	Delete current character.
Ctrl-W	Delete previous word. {vim}
Ctrl-A	Repeat last insertion. {vim}
Ctrl-I	Insert a tab.
Ctrl-N	Insert next completion of the pattern to the left of the cursor. {vim}
Ctrl-P	Insert previous completion of the pattern to the left of the cursor. {vim}
Ctrl-T	Shift line right to next shift width. {vim}
Ctrl-D	Shift line left to previous shift width. {vim}
Ctrl-U	Delete current line.
Ctrl-V	Insert next character verbatim.
Ctrl-[	Terminate insert mode.

Some of the control characters listed in the previous table are set by **stty**. Your terminal settings may differ.

Changing and Deleting Text

The following table is not exhaustive, but illustrates the most common operations.

Command	Action
cw	Change through end of current word.
cc	Change line.
c$	Change text from current position to end-of-line.
C	Same as c$.

Command	Action
dd	Delete current line.
d$	Delete remainder of line.
D	Same as **d$**.
*n***dd**	Delete *n* lines.
dw	Delete a word.
d}	Delete up to next paragraph.
d^	Delete back to beginning of line.
d/*pattern*	Delete up to first occurrence of pattern.
dn	Delete up to next occurrence of pattern.
df*a*	Delete up to and including *a* on current line.
dt*a*	Delete up to (not including) *a* on current line.
dL	Delete up to last line on screen.
dG	Delete to end-of-file.
gqap	Reformat current paragraph to **textwidth**. {vim}
g~w	Switch case of word. {vim}
guw	Change word to lowercase. {vim}
gUw	Change word to uppercase. {vim}
p	Insert last deleted or yanked text after cursor.
gp	Same as **p**, but leave cursor at end of inserted text. {vim}
]p	Same as **p**, but match current indention. {vim}
[p	Same as **P**, but match current indention. {vim}
P	Insert last deleted or yanked text before cursor.
gP	Same as **P**, but leave cursor at end of inserted text. {vim}
r*x*	Replace character with *x*.
R*text*	Replace *text* beginning at cursor.
s	Substitute character.
*n***s**	Substitute *n* characters.
S	Substitute entire line.
u	Undo last change.
Ctrl-R	Redo last change. {vim}
U	Restore current line.
x	Delete current character.
X	Delete back one character.
*n***X**	Delete previous *n* characters.
.	Repeat last change.
~	Reverse case.
&	Repeat last substitution.
Y	Copy (yank) current line to temporary buffer.
yy	Same as **Y**.
"*x***yy**	Copy current line to buffer *x*.
ye	Copy text to end of word into temporary buffer.
yw	Same as **ye**.

Command	Action
y$	Copy rest of line into temporary buffer.
"xdd	Delete current line into buffer x.
"Xdd	Delete current line and append to buffer x.
"xp	Put contents of buffer x.
J	Join previous line to current line.
gJ	Same as J, but without inserting a space. {vim}
:j!	Same as J.
Ctrl-A	Increment number under cursor. {vim}
Ctrl-X	Decrement number under cursor. {vim}

Saving and Exiting

Writing a file means saving the edits and updating the file's modification time.

Command	Action
ZZ	Quit vi, writing the file only if changes were made.
:x	Same as ZZ.
:wq	Write and quit file.
:w	Write file.
:w file	Save copy to file.
:n1,n2w file	Write lines n1 to n2 to new file.
:n1,n2w >> file	Append lines n1 to n2 to existing file.
:w!	Write file (overriding protection).
:w! file	Overwrite file with current buffer.
:w %.new	Write current buffer named file as file.new.
:q	Quit file.
:q!	Quit file (discarding edits).
Q	Quit vi and invoke ex.
:vi	Return to vi after Q command.
%	Current filename.
#	Alternate filename.

Accessing Multiple Files

Command	Action
:e file	Edit file; current file becomes the alternate file.
:e!	Restore last saved version of current file.
:e+ file	Begin editing at end of new file.
:e+ n file	Open new file at line n.
:e#	Open to previous position in alternate (previously edited) file.
:ta tag	Edit file containing tag at the location of the tag.

Command	Action
:n	Edit next file.
:n!	Force next file into buffer (don't save changes to current file).
:n *files*	Specify new list of *files*.
:args	Display multiple files to be edited.
:rew	Rewind list of multiple files to top.

Window Commands

The following table lists common commands for controlling windows in vim. See also the **split**, **vsplit**, and **resize** commands in Chapter 3. For brevity, control characters are marked in the following list by ^.

Command	Action
:new	Open a new window.
:new *file*	Open *file* in a new window.
:sp *file*	Split the current window.
:sv*file*	Same as **:sp**, but make new window read-only.
:sn*file*	Edit next file in new window.
:clo	Close current window.
:hid	Hide current window, unless it is the only visible window.
:on	Make current window the only visible one.
:res *n*	Resize window to *n* lines.
:wa	Write all changed buffers to file.
:qa	Close all buffers and exit.
^W s	Same as **:sp**.
^W n	Same as **:new**.
^W ^	Open new window with alternate (previously edited) file.
^W c	Same as **:clo**.
^W o	Same as **:only**.
^W j, ^W k	Move cursor to next/previous window.
^W p	Move cursor to previous window.
^W h, ^W l	Move cursor to window on left/right.
^W t, ^W b	Move cursor to window on top/bottom of screen.
^W K, ^W B	Move current window to top/bottom of screen.
^W H, ^W L	Move current window to far left/right of screen.
^W r, ^W R	Rotate windows down/up.
^W +, ^W -	Increase/decrease current window size.
^W =	Make all windows same height.

Interacting with the Shell

Command	Action
:r *file*	Read in contents of *file* after cursor.
:r !*command*	Read in output from *command* after current line.
:*n*r !*command*	Like preceding, but place after line *n* (0 for top of file).
:!*command*	Run *command*, then return.
!*object command*	Send *object*, indicated by a movement command, as input to shell command *command*; replace *object* with command output.
:*n1,n2*! *command*	Send lines *n1* through *n2* to *command*; replace with output.
n!!*command*	Send *n* lines to *command*; replace with output.
!!	Repeat last system command.
!!*command*	Replace current line with output of *command*.
:sh	Create subshell; return to file with EOF.
Ctrl-Z	Suspend editor; resume with **fg**.
:so *file*	Read and execute **ex** commands from *file*.

Macros

Command	Action
:**ab** *in out*	Use *in* as abbreviation for *out*.
:**unab** *in*	Remove abbreviation for *in*.
:**ab**	List abbreviations.
:**map** *c sequence*	Map character *c* as *sequence* of commands.
:**unmap** *c*	Disable map for character *c*.
:**map**	List characters that are mapped.
:**map!** *c sequence*	Map character *c* to input mode *sequence*.
:**unmap!** *c*	Disable input mode map (you may need to quote the character with Ctrl-V).
:**map!**	List characters that are mapped to input mode.
q*x*	Record typed characters into register specified by letter *x*. If letter is uppercase, append to register.{vim}
q	Stop recording. {vim}
@*x*	Execute the register specified by letter *x*. {vim}

In vi, the following characters are unused in command mode and can be mapped as user-defined commands:

Letters
   g K q V v
Control keys
   ^K ^O ^T ^W ^X
Symbols
   _ * \ =

The = is used by **vi** if LISP mode is set. **vim** uses all of these characters, but you can create macros for function keys and multiple character commands. See **:help :map** for details. Other versions of **vi** may use some of these characters as well, so test them before using them.

Miscellaneous Commands

Command	Action
<	Shift line left to position indicated by following movement command.
>	Shift line right to position indicated by following movement command.
<<	Shift line left one shift width (default is 8 spaces).
>>	Shift line right one shift width (default is 8 spaces).
>}	Shift right to end of paragraph.
<%	Shift left until matching parenthesis, brace, bracket, etc. (Cursor must be on the matching symbol.)
=	Indent line in C-style, or using program specified in **equalprg** option. {vim}
K	Look up word under cursor in manpages (or program defined in **keywordprg**). {vim}
^[	Abort command or end input mode.
^]	Perform a tag lookup on the text under the cursor.
^\	Enter **ex** line-editing mode.
^^	(Caret key with Ctrl key pressed) Return to previously edited file.

Alphabetical List of Keys in Command Mode

For brevity, control characters are marked by ^.

Command	Action
a	Append text after cursor.
A	Append text at end-of-line.
^A	Search for next occurrence of word under cursor. Increment number in **vim** when cursor is on a number.
b	Back up to beginning of word in current line.
B	Back up one word, treating punctuation marks as words.
^B	Scroll backward one window.
c	Change text up to target of next movement command.
C	Change to end of current line.
^C	End insert mode; interrupts a long operation.
d	Delete up to target of next movement command.
D	Delete to end of current line.
^D	Scroll down half-window; in insert mode, unindent to **shiftwidth** if **autoindent** is set (or when using **vim**).
e	Move to end of word.
E	Move to end of word, treating punctuation as part of word.
^E	Show one more line at bottom of window.

Command	Action
f	Find next character typed forward on current line.
F	Find next character typed backward on current line.
^F	Scroll forward one window.
g	Unused in **vi**. Begins many multiple-character commands in **vim**.
G	Go to specified line or end-of-file.
^G	Print information about file on status line.
h	Left arrow cursor key.
H	Move cursor to home position.
^H	Left arrow cursor key; Backspace key in insert mode.
i	Insert text before cursor.
I	Insert text before first nonblank character on line.
^I	Unused in command mode; in insert mode, same as Tab key.
j	Down arrow cursor key.
J	Join previous line to current line.
^J	Down arrow cursor key; in insert mode, move down a line.
k	Up arrow cursor key.
K	Unused in **vi**. Look up word using **keywordprg** in **vim**.
^K	Unused in **vi**. Insert multiple-keystroke character in **vim**.
l	Right arrow cursor key.
L	Move cursor to last position in window.
^L	Redraw screen.
m	Mark the current cursor position in register (a–z).
M	Move cursor to middle position in window.
^M	Move to beginning of next line.
n	Repeat the last search command.
N	Repeat the last search command in reverse direction.
^N	Down arrow cursor key.
o	Open line below current line.
O	Open line above current line.
^O	Unused in **vi**. Return to previous jump position in **vim**.
p	Put yanked or deleted text after or below cursor.
P	Put yanked or deleted text before or above cursor.
^P	Up arrow cursor key.
q	Unused in **vi**. Record keystrokes in **vim**.
Q	Quit **vi** and enter **ex** line-editing mode.
^Q	Unused in **vi**. Same as ^V in **vim** (On some terminals, resume data flow.)
r	Replace character at cursor with the next character you type.
R	Replace characters.
^R	Redraw the screen.
s	Change the character under the cursor to typed characters.
S	Change entire line.

Command	Action
^S	Unused. (On some terminals, stop data flow.)
t	Find next character typed forward on current line and position cursor before it.
T	Find next character typed backward on current line and position cursor after it.
^T	Unused in command mode for **vi**. Pop tag from tagstack in **vim**. In insert mode, move to next tab setting.
u	Undo the last change made. In **vi**, a second undo redoes an undone command. **vim** supports multiple levels of undo. To redo, use **Ctrl-R**.
U	Restore current line, discarding changes.
^U	Scroll the screen upward a half-window.
v	Unused in **vi**. Enter visual mode in **vim**.
V	Unused in **vi**. Enter linewise visual mode in **vim**.
^V	Unused in command mode for **vi**. Enter blockwise visual mode in **vim**. In insert mode, insert next character verbatim.
w	Move to beginning of next word.
W	Move to beginning of next word, treating punctuation marks as words.
^W	Unused in command mode in **vi**. Begins window commands in **vim**. In insert mode, back up to beginning of word.
x	Delete character under cursor.
X	Delete character before cursor.
^X	Unused in **vi**. Decrement number in **vim** when cursor is on a number. In insert mode in **vim**, begins several commands.
y	Yank or copy text up to target of following movement command into temporary buffer.
Y	Make copy of current line.
^Y	Show one more line at top of window.
z	Reposition line containing cursor. **z** must be followed by Return (reposition line to top of screen), . (reposition line to middle of screen), or - (reposition line to bottom of screen).
ZZ	Exit the editor, saving changes.

Syntax of ex Commands

To enter an **ex** command from **vi**, type:

```
:[address] command [options]
```

An initial : indicates an **ex** command. As you type the command, it is echoed on the status line. Enter the command by pressing Return. *address* is the line number or range of lines that are the object of *command. options* and *addresses* are described in the following sections. **ex** commands are described in the alphabetical summary.

Options

! Indicates a variant command form, overriding the normal behavior.

count

The number of times the command is to be repeated. Unlike **vi** commands, the *count* comes after the command, not before it. Numbers preceding an **ex** command are considered to be part of the *address*. For example, **3d** deletes line 3; **d3** deletes 3 lines beginning with the current line.

file

The name of a file that is affected by the command. **%** stands for current file; **#** stands for previous file.

Addresses

If no address is given, the current line is the object of the command. If the address specifies a range of lines, the format is:

x,y

where *x* and *y* are the first and last addressed lines (*x* must precede *y* in the buffer). *x* and *y* may be line numbers or symbols. Using ; instead of , sets the current line to *x* before interpreting *y*.

Address Symbols

Symbol	Meaning
1,$	All lines in the file
%	All lines; same as **1,$**
x,y	Lines *x* through *y*
x;y	Lines *x* through *y*, with current line reset to *x*
0	Top of file
.	Current line
n	Absolute line number *n*
$	Last line
x-n	*n* lines before *x*
x+n	*n* lines after *x*
-[*n*]	One or *n* lines previous
+[*n*]	One or *n* lines ahead
'*x*	Line marked with *x*
"	Previous mark
/*pattern*/	Forward to line matching *pattern*
?*pattern*?	Backward to line matching *pattern*

See Chapter 9 for more information on using patterns.

Alphabetical Summary of ex Commands

ex commands can be entered by specifying any unique abbreviation. In this listing, the full name appears in the margin, and the shortest possible abbreviation is used in the syntax line. Examples are assumed to be typed from **vi**, so they include the : prompt.

abbrev

ab [*string text*]

Define *string* when typed to be translated into *text*. If *string* and *text* are not specified, list all current abbreviations.

Examples

Note: **^M** appears when you type Ctrl-V followed by Return.

    :ab ora O'Reilly & Associates, Inc.
    :ab id Name:^MRank:^MPhone:

---

append

[*address*] **a**[!]

Append new text at specified *address*, or at present address if none is specified. Add a ! to switch the **autoindent** setting that will be used during input (e.g., if **autoindent** was enabled, ! disables it). Enter new text after entering the command. Terminate input of new text by entering a line consisting of just a period.

Example

    :a   Begin appending to current line.
    Append this line
    and this line too.
    .   Terminate input of text to append.

---

args

ar

Print filename arguments (the list of files to edit). The current argument is shown in brackets ([ ]).

---

cd

cd *dir*
chdir *dir*

Change current directory within the editor to *dir*.

---

bdelete

[*n*] **bd**[!] [*n*]

Unload buffer *n* and remove it from the buffer list. Add a ! to force removal of an unsaved buffer. The buffer may also be specified by filename. If no buffer is specified, remove the current buffer. {vim}

---

buffer

[*n*] **b**[!] [*n*]

Begin editing buffer *n* in the buffer list. Add a ! to force a switch from an unsaved buffer. The buffer may also be specified by filename. If no buffer is specified, continue editing the current buffer. {vim}

---

buffers

buffers[!]

Print the listed members of the buffer list. Some buffers (e.g., deleted buffers) will not be listed. Add ! to show unlisted buffers. **ls** is another abbreviation for this command. {vim}

center	[*address*] **ce** [*width*]
	Center line within the specified *width*. If *width* is not specified, use **textwidth**. {vim}

change	[*address*] **c**[!] *text*
	Replace the specified lines with *text*. Add a ! to switch the **auto-indent** setting during input of *text*. Terminate input by entering a line consisting of just a period.

close	**clo**[!]
	Close current window unless it is the last window. If buffer in window is not open in another window, unload it from memory. This command will not close a buffer with unsaved changes, but you may add ! to hide it instead. {vim}

copy	[*address*] **co** *destination*
	Copy the lines included in *address* to the specified *destination* address. The command **t** is the same as **copy**.

Example

    :1,10 co 50   *Copy first 10 lines to just after line 50*

delete	[*address*] **d** [*buffer*]
	Delete the lines included in *address*. If *buffer* is specified, save or append the text to the named buffer.

Examples

    :/Part I/,/Part II/-1d   *Delete to line above "Part II"*
    :/main/+d   *Delete line below "main"*
    :.,$d   *Delete from this line to last line*

edit	**e**[!] [+*n*] [*file*]
	Begin editing *file*. Add a ! to discard any changes to the current file. If no *file* is given, edit another copy of the current file. With the +*n* argument, begin editing on line *n*.

Examples

    :e file
    :e#   *Return to editing the previous file*
    :e!   *Discard edits since last save*

exusage	**exu** [*command*]
	Print a brief usage message describing *command*, or a list of available commands if *command* is omitted. (In **vim** use the **help** command instead.)

file	**f** [*filename*]

Change the filename for the current buffer to *filename*. The next time the buffer is written, it will be written to file *filename*. When the name is changed, the buffer's **notedited** flag is set, to indicate you are not editing an existing file. If the new filename is the same as a file that already exists on the disk, you will need to use :w! to overwrite the existing file. When specifying a filename, the % character can be used to indicate the current filename. If no *filename* is specified, print the current name and status of the buffer.

Example

```
:f %.new
```

fold	*address* **fo**

Fold the lines specified by *address*. A fold collapses several lines on the screen into one line, which can later be unfolded. It doesn't affect the text of the file. {vim}

foldclose	[*address*] **foldc**[!]

Close folds in specified *address*, or at present address if none is specified. Add a ! to close more than one level of folds. {vim}

foldopen	[*address*] **foldo**[!]

Open folds in specified *address*, or at present address if none is specified. Add a ! to open more than one level of folds. {vim}

global	[*address*] **g**[!]/*pattern*/[*commands*]

Execute *commands* on all lines that contain *pattern* or, if *address* is specified, on all lines within that range. If *commands* are not specified, print all such lines. If ! is used, execute *commands* on all lines that don't contain *pattern*. See **v**.

Examples

```
:g/Unix/p            Print all lines containing "Unix"
:g/Name:/s/tom/Tom/  Change "tom" to "Tom" on all lines
                     containing "Name:"
```

help	**h**

Print a brief help message. Information on particular commands can be obtained through the **exusage** and **viusage** commands. (In **vim** this command provides extensive information for all commands, and neither **exusage** nor **viusage** is used.)

hide	**hid**
	Close current window unless it is the last window, but do not remove the buffer from memory. This is a safe command to use on an unsaved buffer. {vim}

insert	*address* **i**[**!**]
	Insert new text at line before the specified *address*, or at present address if none is specified. Add a **!** to switch the **autoindent** setting during input of text. Enter new text after entering the command. Terminate input of new text by entering a line consisting of just a period.

join	[*address*] **j**[**!**] [*count*]
	Place the text in the specified *address* on one line, with whitespace adjusted to provide two blank characters after a period, no blank characters after a), and one blank character otherwise. Add a **!** to prevent whitespace adjustment.

Example

   :1,5j!   *Join first five lines, preserving whitespace*

jumps	**ju**
	Print jump list used with Ctrl-I and Ctrl-O commands. The jump list is a record of most movement commands that skip over multiple lines. It records the position of the cursor before each jump. {vim}

k	[*address*] **k** *char*
	Mark the given *address* with *char*. Return later to the line with '*char*.

list	[*address*] **l** [*count*]
	Print the specified lines so that tabs display as ^I, and the ends of lines display as $. The l command is a temporary version of **:set list**.

left	[*address*] **le** [*count*]
	Left-align lines specified by *address*, or current line if no address is specified. Indent lines by *count* spaces. {vim}

map	**map**[**!**] [*char commands*]
	Define a keyboard macro named *char* as the specified sequence of *commands*. *char* is usually a single character, or the sequence #*n*, representing a function key on the keyboard. Use a **!** to create a

macro for input mode. With no arguments, list the currently defined macros.

Examples

`:map K dwwP`	*Transpose two words*
`:map q :w^M:n^M`	*Write current file; go to next*
`:map! + ^[bi(^[ea)`	*Enclose previous word in parentheses*

---

mark

[*address*] **ma** *char*

Mark the specified line with *char*, a single lowercase letter. Return later to the line with '*char*. **vim** also uses uppercase and numeric characters for marks. Lowercase letters work the same as in **vi**. Uppercase letters are associated with filenames and can be used between multiple files. Numbered marks, however, are maintained in a special **viminfo** file and cannot be set using this command. Same as **k**.

---

marks

marks [*chars*]

Print list of marks specified by *chars*, or all current marks if no chars specified. {vim}

Example

`:marks abc`   *Print marks a, b and c.*

---

mkexrc

mk[!] *file*

Create an *.exrc* file containing a **set** command for every **ex** option, set to defaults.

---

move

[*address*] **m** *destination*

Move the lines specified by *address* to the *destination* address.

Example

`:.,/Note/m /END/`   *Move text block after line containing "END"*

---

new

[*count*]**new**

Create a new window *count* lines high with an empty buffer. {vim}

---

next

n[!] [[*+command*] *filelist*]

Edit the next file from the command-line argument list. Use **args** to list these files. If *filelist* is provided, replace the current argument list with *filelist* and begin editing on the first file; if *command* is given (containing no spaces), execute *command* after editing the first such file. Add a ! to discard any changes to the current file.

Example

`:n chap*`   *Start editing all "chapter" files*

nohlsearch	**noh**
	Temporarily stop highlighting all matches to a search when using the **hlsearch** option. Highlighting is resumed with the next search. {vim}

number	[*address*] **nu** [*count*]
	Print each line specified by *address*, preceded by its buffer line number. Use **#** as an alternate abbreviation for **number**. *count* specifies the number of lines to show, starting with *address*.

open	[*address*] **o** [**/***pattern***/**]
	Enter **vi**'s open mode at the lines specified by *address* or at the lines matching *pattern*. Enter and exit open mode with **Q**. Open mode lets you use the regular **vi** commands, but only one line at a time. May be useful on slow dial-up lines.

preserve	**pre**
	Save the current editor buffer as though the system had crashed.

previous	**prev**[**!**]
	Edit the previous file from the command-line argument list.

print	[*address*] **p** [*count*]
	[*address*] **P** [*count*]
	Print the lines specified by *address*. *count* specifies the number of lines to print, starting with *address*. Add a **!** to discard any changes to the current file.

Example

    :100;+5p   *Show line 100 and the next 5 lines*

put	[*address*] **pu** [*char*]
	Restore the lines that were previously deleted or yanked from named buffer *char*, and put them after the line specified by *address*. If *char* is not specified, restore the last deleted or yanked text.

qall	**qa**[**!**]
	Close all windows and terminate current editing session. Use **!** to discard changes made since the last save. {vim}

quit	**q**[**!**]
	Terminate current editing session. Use **!** to discard changes made since the last save. If the editing session includes additional files in the argument list that were never accessed, quit by typing **q!** or by

typing **q** twice. (In **vim**, if multiple windows are open, this command will close only the current window; use **qall** to quit multiple windows.)

---

read
    [*address*] **r** *file*

Copy in the text from *file* on the line below the specified *address*. If *file* is not specified, the current filename is used.

Example

    :0r $HOME/data   *Read file in at top of current file*

---

read
    [*address*] **r** **!***command*

Read the output of Linux *command* into the text after the line specified by *address*.

Example

    :$r !cal   *Place a calendar at end-of-file*

---

recover
    rec [*file*]

Recover *file* from system save area.

---

redo
    red

Restore last undone change. Same as **Ctrl-R**. {vim}

---

resize
    res [[**+**|**-**]*n*]

Resize current window to be *n* lines high. If + or - is specified, increase or decrease the current window height by *n* lines. {vim}

---

rewind
    rew[**!**]

Rewind argument list and begin editing the first file in the list. The ! flag rewinds, discarding any changes to the current file that haven't been saved.

---

right
    [*address*] **le** [*width*]

Right-align lines specified by *address*, or current line if no address is specified, to column *width*. Use **textwidth** option if no *width* is specified. {vim}

---

sbuffer
    [*n*] **sb** [*n*]

Split the current window and begin editing buffer *n* from the buffer list in the new window. The buffer to be edited may also be specified by filename. If no buffer is specified, open the current buffer in the new window. {vim}

sbnext

[*count*] **sbn** [*count*]

Split the current window and begin editing the *count* next buffer from the buffer list. If no count is specified, edit the next buffer in the buffer list. {vim}

snext

[*count*] **sn** [[**+***n*] *filelist*]

Split the current window and begin editing the next file from the command-line argument list. If *count* is provided, edit the *count* next file. If *filelist* is provided, replace the current argument list with *filelist* and begin editing the first file. With the +*n* argument, begin editing on line *n*. Alternately, *n* may be a pattern of the form */pattern*. {vim}

split

[*count*] **sp** [**+***n*] [*filename*]

Split the current window and load *filename* in the new window, or the same buffer in both windows if no file is specified. Make the new window *count* lines high, or if *count* is not specified, split the window into equal parts. With the +*n* argument, begin editing on line *n*. *n* may also be a pattern of the form */pattern*. {vim}

sprevious

[*count*] **spr** [**+***n*]

Split the current window and begin editing the previous file from the command-line argument list in the new window. If *count* is specified, edit the *count* previous file. With the +*n* argument, begin editing on line *n*. *n* may also be a pattern of the form */pattern*. {vim}

script

sc[**!**] [*file*]

Create a new shell in a buffer that can be saved, optionally specifying *file* where the buffer can be saved. Can be used only in **vi**.

set

se *parameter1 parameter2* ...

Set a value to an option with each *parameter*, or if no *parameter* is supplied, print all options that have been changed from their defaults. For Boolean-valued options, each *parameter* can be phrased as *option* or **no***option*; other options can be assigned with the syntax *option=value*. Specify **all** to list current settings.

Examples

```
:set nows wm=10
:set all
```

shell

sh

Create a new shell. Resume editing when the shell is terminated.

source

so *file*

Read and execute **ex** commands from *file*.

Example

    :so $HOME/.exrc

stop

st

Suspend the editing session. Same as **Ctrl-Z**. Use **fg** to resume session.

substitute

[*address*] **s** [*/pattern/replacement/*] [*options*] [*count*]

Replace each instance of *pattern* on the specified lines with *replacement*. If *pattern* and *replacement* are omitted, repeat last substitution. *count* specifies the number of lines on which to substitute, starting with *address*. When preceded by the **global** (**g**) or **v** command, this command can be specified with a blank *pattern*, in which case the pattern from the **g** or **v** command is used. For more examples, see Chapter 9.

Options

c   Prompt for confirmation before each change.

g   Substitute all instances of *pattern* on each line.

p   Print the last line on which a substitution was made.

Examples

`:1,10s/yes/no/g`	*Substitute on first 10 lines*
`:%s/[Hh]ello/Hi/gc`	*Confirm global substitutions*
`:s/Fortran/\U&/ 3`	*Uppercase first instance of "Fortran" on next three lines*
`:g/^[0-9][0-9]*/s//Line &:/`	*For every line beginning with one or more digits, add the "Line" and a colon*

suspend

su

Suspend the editing session. Same as **Ctrl-Z**. Use **fg** to resume session.

sview

[*count*] **sv** [*+n*] [*filename*]

Same as the **split** command, but set the **readonly** option for the new buffer. {vim}

t

[*address*] **t** *destination*

Copy the lines included in *address* to the specified *destination*. **t** is an alias for **copy**.

Example

    :%t$ Copy the file and add it to the end

tag

[*address*] **ta**[**!**] *tag*

Switch the editing session to the file containing *tag*.

Example

Run **ctags**, then switch to the file containing *myfunction*:

```
:!ctags *.c
:tag myfunction
```

tags

tags

Print list of tags in the tag stack. {vim}

unabbreviate

una *word*

Remove *word* from the list of abbreviations.

undo

u

Reverse the changes made by the last editing command. In **vi** the undo command will undo itself, redoing what you undid. **vim** supports multiple levels of undo. Use **redo** to redo an undone change in **vim**.

unhide

[*count*] **unh**

Split screen to show one window for each active buffer in the buffer list. If specified, limit the number of windows to *count*. {vim}

unmap

unm[**!**] *char*

Remove *char* from the list of keyboard macros. Use **!** to remove a macro for input mode.

v

[*address*] **v/***pattern***/**[*commands*]

Execute *commands* on all lines not containing *pattern*. If *commands* are not specified, print all such lines. **v** is equivalent to **g!**. See **global**.

Example

```
:v/#include/d        Delete all lines except "#include" lines
```

version

ve

Print the editor's current version number.

vi

vi [**+***n*] *file*

Begin editing *file*, optionally at line *n*. Can be used only in **vi**.

view	**vie**[[**+***n*] *filename*] Same as **edit**, but set file to **readonly**. When executed in **ex** mode, return to normal or visual mode. {vim}
visual	[*address*] **vi** [*type*] [*count*] Enter visual mode (**vi**) at the line specified by *address*. Exit with **Q**. *type* can be one of -, ^, or .. (See the **z** command.) *count* specifies an initial window size.
viusage	**viu** [*key*] Print a brief usage message describing the operation of *key*, or a list of defined keys if *key* is omitted. (In **vim** use the **help** command instead.)
vsplit	[*count*] **vs** [**+***n*] [*filename*] Same as the **split** command, but split the screen vertically. The *count* argument can be used to specify a width for the new window. {vim}
wall	**wa**[**!**] Write all changed buffers with filenames. Add **!** to force writing of any buffers marked **readonly**. {vim}
wnext	[*count*] **wn**[**!**] [[**+***n*] *filename*] Write current buffer and open next file in argument list, or the *count* next file if specified. If *filename* is specified, edit it next. With the **+***n* argument, begin editing on line *n*. *n* may also be a pattern of the form */pattern*. {vim}
wq	**wq**[**!**] Write and quit the file in one command. The **!** flag forces the editor to write over any current contents of *file*.
wqall	**wqa**[**!**] Write all changed buffers and quit the editor. Add **!** to force writing of any buffers marked **readonly**. **xall** is another alias for this command. {vim}
write	[*address*] **w**[**!**] [[**>>**] *file*] Write lines specified by *address* to *file*, or write full contents of buffer if *address* is not specified. If *file* is also omitted, save the contents of the buffer to the current filename. If **>>***file* is used, write contents to the end of an existing *file*. The **!** flag forces the editor to write over any current contents of *file*.

write

[*address*] **w** !*command*

Write lines specified by *address* to *command*.

Examples

:1,10w name_list	*Copy first 10 lines to name_list*
:50w >> name_list	*Now append line 50*

X

X

Prompt for an encryption key. This can be preferable to **:set key** as typing the key is not echoed to the console. To remove an encryption key, just reset the **key** option to an empty value. {vim}

---

xit

x

Write the file if it was changed since the last write, then quit.

---

yank

[*address*] **ya** [*char*] [*count*]

Place lines specified by *address* in named buffer *char*. If no *char* is given, place lines in general buffer. *count* specifies the number of lines to yank, starting with *address*.

Example

:101,200 ya a

---

z

[*address*] **z** [*type*] [*count*]

Print a window of text, with the line specified by *address* at the top. *count* specifies the number of lines to be displayed.

Type

+   Place specified line at top of window (the default).

-     Place specified line at bottom of window.

.   Place specified line in center of window.

^   Move up one window.

=   Place specified line in center of window, and leave as the current line.

!

[*address*] !*command*

Execute Linux *command* in a shell. If *address* is specified, apply the lines contained in *address* as standard input to *command*, and replace the lines with the output.

Examples

:!ls	*List files in the current directory*
:11,20!sort -f	*Sort lines 11-20 of current file*

=	[*address*] **=**
	Print the line number of the next line matching *address*. If no address is given, print the number of the last line.
< >	[*address*]**<**[*count*] [*address*]**>**[*count*]
	Shift lines specified by *address* either left (<) or right (>). Only blanks and tabs are removed in a left shift. *count* specifies the number of lines to shift, starting with *address*.
address	*address*
	Print the line specified in *address*.
Return	*Return*
	Print the next line in the file.
@	[*address*] **@** [*char*]
	Execute contents of register specified by *char*. If *address* is given, move cursor to the specified address first. Both **star** and ***** are aliases for this command. {vim}
@@	[*address*] **@**
	Repeat the last @ command. If *address* is given, move cursor to the specified address first. {vim}
&	**&** [*options*] [*count*]
	Repeat the previous substitution (**s**) command. *count* specifies the number of lines on which to substitute, starting with *address*.
	Examples
	:s/Overdue/Paid/ *Substitute once on current line*
	:g/Status/& *Redo substitution on all "Status" lines*
~	[*address*] **~** [*count*]
	Replace the previous regular expression with the previous replacement pattern from a **substitute** (**s**) command.

vi Configuration

This section describes the following:

- The :set command
- Options available with :set
- Sample ~/.exrc file

The :set Command

The :set command lets you specify options that change characteristics of your editing environment. Options may be put in the ~/.exrc file or set during a **vi** session.

The colon should not be typed if the command is put in ~/.exrc.

Command	Action
:set x	Enable option x.
:set nox	Disable option x.
:set x=val	Give value to option x.
:set	Show changed options.
:set all	Show all options.
:set x?	Show value of option x.

Options Used by :set

The following table describes the options to :set. The first column includes the optional abbreviation, if there is one, and uses an equals sign to show that the option takes a value. The second column gives the default, and the third column describes the behavior of the enabled option.

Option	Default	Description
autoindent (ai)	noai	In insert mode, indent each line to the same level as the line above or below.
autoprint (ap)	ap	Display changes after each editor command. (For global replacement, display last replacement.)
autowrite (aw)	noaw	Automatically write (save) file if changed, before opening another file with :n or before giving a Linux command with :!.
background (bg)		Describe the background so the editor can choose appropriate highlighting colors. Default value of **dark** or **light** depends on the environment in which the editor is invoked. {vim}
backup (bk)	nobackup	Create a backup file when overwriting an existing file. {vim}
backupdir= (bdir)	.,~/tmp/,~/	Name directories in which to store backup files if possible. The list of directories is comma-separated and in order of preference. {vim}
backupext= (bex)	~	String to append to filenames for backup files. {vim}
beautify (bf)	nobf	Ignore all control characters during input (except tab, newline, or form-feed).
cindent (cin)	nocindent	Insert indents in appropriate C format. {vim}

Option	Default	Description
compatible (cp)	cp	Make **vim** behave more like **vi**. Default is **nocp** when a ~/.*vimrc* file is found. {vim}
directory= (dir)	/tmp	Name the directory in which **ex** stores buffer files. (Directory must be writable.)
edcompatible	noed-compatible	Use **ed**-like features on substitute commands.
equalprg= (ep)		Use the specified program for the = command. When the option is blank (the default), the key invokes the internal C indention function or the value of the **indentexpr** option. {vim}
errorbells (eb)	errorbells	Sound bell when an error occurs.
exrc (ex)	noexrc	Allow the execution of ~/.*exrc* files that reside outside the user's home directory.
formatprg= (fp)		The **gq** command will invoke the named external program to format text. It will call internal formatting functions when this option is blank (the default). {vim}
gdefault (gd)	nogdefault	Set the **g** flag on for substitutions by default. {vim}
hardtabs= (ht)	8	Define boundaries for terminal hardware tabs.
hidden (hid)	nohidden	Hide buffers rather than unload them when they are abandoned. {vim}
hlsearch (hls)	hlsearch	Highlight all matches of most recent search.
history= (hi)	20	Number of **ex** commands to store in the history table. {vim}
ignorecase (ic)	noic	Disregard case during a search.
incsearch (is)	noincsearch	Highlight matches to a search pattern as it is typed. {vim}
lisp	nolisp	Insert indents in appropriate LISP format. ( ), { }, [[, and]] are modified to have meaning for LISP.
list	nolist	Print tabs as ^I; mark ends of lines with $. (Use **list** to tell if tabs or spaces are at the end of a line.)
magic	magic	Wildcard characters . (dot), * (asterisk), and [ ] (brackets) have special meaning in patterns.
mesg	mesg	Permit system messages to display on terminal while editing in **vi**.
mousehide (mh)	mousehide	When characters are typed, hide the mouse pointer. {vim}
number (nu)	nonu	Display line numbers on left of screen during editing session.
paste	nopaste	Change the defaults of various options to make pasting text into a terminal window work better. All options are returned to their original value when the **paste** option is reset. {vim}
redraw (re)	noredraw	Terminal redraws screen whenever edits are made (in other words, insert mode pushes over existing characters, and deleted lines immediately close up). Default depends on line speed and terminal type. **noredraw** is useful at slow speeds on a dumb terminal: deleted lines show up as @, and inserted text appears to overwrite existing text until you press Esc.
remap	remap	Allow nested map sequences.
report=	5	Display a message on the prompt line whenever you make an edit that affects at least a certain number of lines. For example, **6dd** reports the message "6 lines deleted."
ruler (ru)	ruler	Show line and column numbers for the current cursor position. {vim}
scroll=	<1/2 window>	Amount of screen to scroll.
sections= (sect)	SHNHH HUnhsh	Define section delimiters for [[ ]] movement. The pairs of characters in the value are the names of **nroff/troff** macros that begin sections.

Option	Default	Description
shell= (sh)	/bin/sh	Pathname of shell used for shell escape (:!) and shell command (:sh). Default value is derived from **SHELL** variable.
shiftwidth= (sw)	8	Define number of spaces used by the indent commands (^T, ^D, >>, and <<).
showmatch (sm)	nosm	In **vi**, when) or } is entered, cursor moves briefly to matching (or {. (If the match is not on the screen, rings the error message bell.) Very useful for programming.
showmode	noshowmode	In insert mode, displays a message on the prompt line indicating the type of insert you are making, such as "Open Mode" or "Append Mode."
slowopen (slow)		Hold off display during insert. Default depends on line speed and terminal type.
smartcase (scs)	nosmartcase	Override the **ignorecase** option when a search pattern contains upper-case characters. {vim}
tabstop= (ts)	8	Define number of spaces that a tab indents during editing session. (Printer still uses system tab of 8.)
taglength= (tl)	0	Define number of characters that are significant for tags. Default (0) means that all characters are significant.
tags=	tags */usr/lib/tags*	Define pathname of files containing tags (see the **ctags** command in Chapter 3). By default, the system looks for files **tags** (in the current directory) and */usr/lib/tags*.
term=		Set terminal type.
terse	noterse	Display shorter error messages.
timeout (to)	timeout	Keyboard maps timeout after 1 second.
ttytype=		Set terminal type. Default is inherited from **TERM** environment variable.
undolevels= (ul)	1000	Number of changes that can be undone. {vim}
warn	warn	Display the message "No write since last change."
window= (w)		Show a certain number of lines of the file on the screen. Default depends on line speed and terminal type.
wrapmargin= (wm)	0	Define right margin. If greater than 0, automatically insert carriage returns to break lines.
wrapscan (ws)	ws	Searches wrap around either end of file.
writeany (wa)	nowa	Allow saving to any file.
writebackup (wb)	wb	Back up files before attempting to overwrite them. Remove the backup when the file has been sucessfully written.

Sample ~/.exrc File

The following lines of code are an example of a customized *.exrc* file:

```
set nowrapscan wrapmargin=7
set sections=SeAhBhChDh nomesg
map q :w^M:n^M
map v dwElp
ab ORA O'Reilly & Associates, Inc.
```

12

The sed Editor

sed is a noninteractive (stream-oriented) editor that interprets and performs the actions in a script. **sed** is said to be stream-oriented because, as with many Unix programs, input flows through the program and is directed to standard output. For example, **sort** is stream-oriented; **vi** is not. **sed**'s input typically comes from a file but can be directed from the keyboard. Output goes to the screen by default but can be captured in a file instead.

Typical uses of **sed** include:

- Editing one or more files automatically
- Simplifying repetitive edits to multiple files
- Writing conversion programs

sed operates as follows:

- Each line of input is copied into a pattern space.
- All editing commands in a **sed** script are applied in order to each line of input.
- Editing commands are applied to all lines (globally) unless line addressing restricts the lines affected.
- If a command changes the input, subsequent commands are applied to the changed line, not to the original input line.
- The original input file is unchanged because the editing commands modify a copy of the original input line. The copy is sent to standard output (but can be redirected to a file).

For more information on **sed**, see *sed & awk* (O'Reilly).

Command-Line Syntax

The syntax for invoking **sed** has two forms:

```
sed [options] 'command' file(s)
sed [options] -f scriptfile file(s)
```

The first form allows you to specify an editing command, surrounded by single quotes, on the command line. The second form allows you to specify a *scriptfile*, which is a file containing **sed** commands. If no files are specified, **sed** reads from standard input.

The following *options* are recognized:

-e *cmd*, **--expression=***cmd*
Next argument is an editing command; not needed unless specifying two or more editing commands.

-f *scriptfile,* **--file=***scriptfile*
Next argument is a file containing editing commands.

-n, **--silent**, **--quiet**
Suppress the default output; **sed** displays only those lines specified with the **p** command or with the **p** flag of the **s** command.

-V, **--version**
Display version number.

-h, **--help**
Display brief help message with command-line options.

Syntax of sed Commands

sed commands have the general form:

```
[address[,address]][!]command [arguments]
```

sed commands consist of *addresses* and editing *commands*. *commands* consist of a single letter or symbol; they are described later, alphabetically and by group. Some commands accept or expect *arguments*. Examples of arguments include the label supplied to **b** or **t**, the filename supplied to **r** or **w**, and the substitution flags for **s**. *addresses* are described in the next section.

Pattern Addressing

A **sed** command can specify zero, one, or two addresses. An address can be a line number, an increment given as a starting line number and a step amount separated by a tilde (~), the symbol **$** (for last line), or a regular expression enclosed in slashes (*/pattern/*). Regular expressions are described in Chapter 9. Additionally, \n can be used to match any newline in the pattern space (resulting from the **N** command) but not the newline at the end of the pattern space.

If the command specifies	Then the command is applied to
No address	Each input line.
One address	Any line matching the address. Some commands (**a**, **i**, **r**, **q**, and **=**) accept only one address.
Two comma-separated addresses	First matching line and all succeeding lines up to and including a line matching the second address.
An address followed by **!**	All lines that do *not* match the address.

Examples

`s/xx/yy/g`	*Substitute on all lines (all occurrences)*
`/BSD/d`	*Delete lines containing BSD*
`/^BEGIN/,/^END/p`	*Print all lines between lines that begin with BEGIN and END, inclusive*
`/SAVE/!d`	*Delete any line that doesn't contain SAVE*
`/BEGIN/,/END/!s/xx/yy/g`	*Substitute on all lines, except between BEGIN and END*
`1~2 p`	*Print all odd numbered lines*
`2~3 d`	*Delete every third line beginning with the second.*

Braces ({ }) are used in **sed** to nest one address inside another or to apply multiple commands at the same address:

```
[/address/[,/address/]]{
command1
command2
}
```

The opening curly brace must end a line, and the closing curly brace must be on a line by itself. Be sure there are no blank spaces after the braces.

Group Summary of sed Commands

In the following tables, the **sed** commands are grouped by function and are described tersely. Full descriptions, including syntax and examples, can be found afterward in the alphabetical summary.

Basic Editing

Command	Action
`a\`	Append text after a line.
`c\`	Replace text (usually a text block).
`i\`	Insert text before a line.
`d`	Delete lines.
`s`	Make substitutions.
`y`	Translate characters (like **tr** in Chapter 3).

Line Information

Command	Action
=	Display line number of a line.
l	Display control characters in ASCII.
p	Display the line.

Input/Output Processing

Command	Action
n	Skip current line and go to line below.
r	Read another file's contents into the input.
w	Write input lines to another file.
q	Quit the **sed** script (no further output).

Yanking and Putting

Command	Action
h	Copy pattern space into hold space; wipe out what's there.
H	Copy pattern space into hold space; append to what's there.
g	Get the hold space back; wipe out the pattern space.
G	Get the hold space back; append to the pattern space.
x	Exchange contents of hold space and pattern space.

Branching Commands

Command	Action
b	Branch to *label* or to end of script.
t	Same as **b**, but branch only after substitution.
:label	Label branched to by **t** or **b**.

Multiline Input Processing

Command	Action
N	Read another line of input (creates embedded newline).
D	Delete up to the embedded newline.
P	Print up to the embedded newline.

Alphabetical Summary of sed Commands

#

#

Begin a comment in a **sed** script. Valid only as the first character of the first line. (Some versions of **sed**, including the GNU version on Linux, allow comments anywhere, but it is better not to rely on this.) If the first line of the script is **#n**, **sed** behaves as if **-n** had been specified.

:

:*label*

Label a line in the script for the transfer of control by **b** or **t**. *label* may contain up to seven characters.

=

[/*pattern*/]=

Write to standard output the line number of each line containing *pattern*.

a

[*address*]a\
text

Append *text* following each line matched by *address*. If *text* goes over more than one line, newlines must be "escaped" by preceding them with a backslash. The *text* will be terminated by the first newline that is not escaped in this way. The *text* is not available in the pattern space, and subsequent commands cannot be applied to it. The results of this command are sent to standard output when the list of editing commands is finished, regardless of what happens to the current line in the pattern space.

Example

```
$a\
This goes after the last line in the file\
(marked by $). This text is escaped at the\
end of each line, except for the last one.
```

b

[*address1*[,*address2*]]b[*label*]

Transfer control unconditionally to :*label* elsewhere in script. That is, the command following the *label* is the next command applied to the current line. If no *label* is specified, control falls through to the end of the script, so no more commands are applied to the current line.

Example

Ignore lines between those that begin with **.TS** and **.TE**; resume script after **.TE**:

```
/^\.TS/,/^\.TE/b
```

c	`[address1[,address2]]c\` *text*

Replace the lines selected by the address with *text*. When a range of lines is specified, all lines as a group are replaced by a single copy of *text*. The newline following each line of *text* must be escaped by a backslash, except the last line. The contents of the pattern space are in effect deleted, and no subsequent editing commands can be applied.

Example

Replace first 100 lines in a file:

```
1,100c\
\
<First 100 names to be supplied>
```

---

d	`[address1[,address2]]d`

Delete the addressed line (or lines) from the pattern space. Thus, the line is not passed to standard output. A new line of input is read, and editing resumes with the first command in the script.

Example

Delete all blank lines (those whose first character is a line ending):

```
/^$/d
```

D	`[address1[,address2]]D`

Delete first part (up to embedded newline) of multiline pattern space created by the **N** command, and resume editing with first command in script. If this command empties the pattern space, then a new line of input is read, as if **d** had been executed.

Example

Strip multiple blank lines, leaving only one:

```
/^$/{
N
/^\n$/D
}
```

---

g	`[address1[,address2]]g`

Paste the contents of the hold space (see **h** and **H**) back into the pattern space, wiping out the previous contents of the pattern space. The example shows a simple way to copy lines.

Example

This script collects all lines containing the word *Item:* and copies them to a place marker later in the file. The place marker is overwritten.

```
/Item:/H
/<Replace this line with the item list>/g
```

G

[*address1*[,*address2*]]G

Same as **g**, except the hold space is pasted below the address instead of overwriting it. The example shows a simple way to cut and paste lines.

Example

This script collects all lines containing the word *Item*: and moves them after a place marker later in the file. The original *Item*: lines are deleted.

```
/Item:/{
H
d
}
/Summary of items:/G
```

sed

h

[*address1*[,*address2*]]h

Copy the pattern space into the hold space, a special temporary buffer. The previous contents of the hold space are obliterated. You can use **h** to save a line before editing it.

Example

```
# Edit a line; print the change; replay the original
/Linux/{
h
s/.* Linux \(.*\) .*/\1:/
p
x
}
```

Sample input:

```
This describes the Linux ls command.
This describes the Linux cp command.
```

Sample output:

```
ls:
This describes the Linux ls command.
cp:
This describes the Linux cp command.
```

H

[*address1*[,*address2*]]H

Append the contents of the pattern space (preceded by a newline) to the contents of the hold space. Even if the hold space is empty, **H** still appends a newline. **H** is like an incremental copy. See examples under **g** and **G**.

i

[*address1*]i\
text

Insert *text* before each line matched by *address*. (See **a** for details on *text*.)

Example

```
/Item 1/i\
The five items are listed below:
```

---

l

[*address1*[,*address2*]]l

List the contents of the pattern space, showing nonprinting characters as ASCII codes. Long lines are wrapped.

---

n

[*address1*[,*address2*]]n

Read next line of input into pattern space. The current line is sent
to standard output, and the next line becomes the current line.
Control passes to the command following **n** instead of resuming at
the top of the script.

Example

In the **ms** macros, a section header occurs on the line below an **.NH**
macro. To print all lines of header text, invoke this script with **sed**
-n:

```
/^\.NH/{
n
p
}
```

N

[*address1*[,*address2*]]N

Append next input line to contents of pattern space; the two lines
are separated by an embedded newline. (This command is designed
to allow pattern matches across two lines.) Using \n to match the
embedded newline, you can match patterns across multiple lines.
See example at **D**.

Examples

Like previous example, but print **.NH** line as well as header title:

```
/^\.NH/{
N
p
}
```

Join two lines (replace newline with space):

```
/^\.NH/{
N
s/\n/ /
p
}
```

---

p

[*address1*[,*address2*]]p

Print the addressed lines. Unless the **-n** command-line option is
used, this command causes duplicate lines to be output. Also, it is
typically used before commands that change flow control (**d**, **N**, **b**)

and that might prevent the current line from being output. See examples at **h**, **n**, and **N**.

P

[*address1*[,*address2*]]**P**

Print first part (up to embedded newline) of multiline pattern created by **N** command. Same as **p** if **N** has not been applied to a line.

---

q

[*address*]**q**

Quit when *address* is encountered. The addressed line is first written to output (if default output is not suppressed), along with any text appended to it by previous **a** or **r** commands.

Examples

Delete everything after the addressed line:

```
/Garbled text follows:/q
```

Print only the first 50 lines of a file:

```
50q
```

---

r

[*address*]**r** *file*

Read contents of *file* and append after the contents of the pattern space. One space must be put between the **r** and the filename.

Example

```
/The list of items follows:/r item_file
```

---

s

[*address1*[,*address2*]]**s**/*pattern*/*replacement*/[*flags*]

Substitute *replacement* for *pattern* on each addressed line. If pattern addresses are used, the pattern // represents the last pattern address specified. The following flags can be specified:

n   Replace *n*th instance of /*pattern*/ on each addressed line. *n* is any number in the range 1 to 512; the default is 1.

g   Replace all instances of /*pattern*/ on each addressed line, not just the first instance.

I   Case insensitive match. This flag is available only on GNU versions of **sed**.

p   Print the line if a successful substitution is done. If several successful substitutions are done, multiple copies of the line will be printed.

w *file*
    Write the line to a *file* if a replacement was done.

Examples

Here are some short, commented scripts:

```
# Change third and fourth quote to ( and ):
/function/{
```

```
s/"/(/3
s/"/)/4
}

# Remove all quotes on a given line:
/Title/s/"//g

# Remove first colon or all quotes; print resulting lines:
s/://p
s/"//gp

# Change first "if" but leave "ifdef" alone:
/ifdef/!s/if/    if/
```

t

[*address1*[,*address2*]]t [*label*]

Test if any substitutions have been made on addressed lines and, if so, branch to line marked by :*label*. (See **b** and :.) If *label* is not specified, control falls through to bottom of script. The **t** command is like a case statement in the C programming language or the shell programming languages. You test each case; when it's true, you exit the construct.

Example

Suppose you want to fill empty fields of a database. You have this:

```
ID: 1    Name: greg    Rate: 45
ID: 2    Name: dale
ID: 3
```

and you want this:

```
ID: 1    Name: greg    Rate: 45    Phone: ??
ID: 2    Name: dale    Rate: ??    Phone: ??
ID: 3    Name: ????    Rate: ??    Phone: ??
```

You need to test the number of fields already there. Here's the script (fields are tab-separated):

```
/ID/{
s/ID: .* Name: .* Rate: .*/&    Phone: ??/p
t
s/ID: .* Name: .*/&    Rate: ??    Phone: ??/p
t
s/ID: .*/&    Name: ??    Rate: ??    Phone: ??/p
}
```

w

[*address1*[,*address2*]]w *file*

Append contents of pattern space to *file*. This action occurs when the command is encountered, rather than when the pattern space is output. Exactly one space must separate the **w** and the filename. This command will create the file if it does not exist; if the file does exist, its contents will be overwritten each time the script is executed. Multiple write commands that direct output to the same file append to the end of the file.

Example

```
# Store tbl and eqn blocks in a file:
/^\.TS/,/^\.TE/w troff_stuff
/^\.EQ/,/^\.EN/w troff_stuff
```

x

[*address1*[,*address2*]]x

Exchange contents of the pattern space with contents of the hold space. See **h** for an example.

y

[*address1*[,*address2*]]y/*abc*/*xyz*/

Translate characters. Change every instance of *a* to *x*, *b* to *y*, *c* to *z*, etc.

Example

```
# Change item 1, 2, 3 to Item A, B, C ...
/^item [1-9]/y/123456789/ABCDEFGHI/
```

sed

13

The gawk Scripting Language

gawk is the GNU version of **awk**, a powerful pattern-matching program for processing text files that may be composed of fixed- or variable-length records separated by some delineator (by default, a newline character). **gawk** may be used from the command line or in **gawk** scripts. You should normally be able to invoke this utility using either **awk** or **gawk** on the shell command line.

With **gawk**, you can:

- Conveniently process a text file as though it were made up of records and fields in a textual database.
- Use variables to change those records and fields.
- Execute shell commands from a script.
- Perform arithmetic and string operations.
- Use programming constructs such as loops and conditionals.
- Define your own functions.
- Process the result of shell commands.
- Produce formatted reports.

For more information on **gawk**, see *sed & awk* (O'Reilly) or *Effective gawk Programming* (O'Reilly).

Command-Line Syntax

gawk's syntax has two forms:

```
gawk [options] 'script' var=value file(s)
gawk [options] -f scriptfile var=value file(s)
```

You can specify a *script* directly on the command line, or you can store a script in a *scriptfile* and specify it with **-f**. Multiple **-f** options are allowed; **awk** concatenates the files. This feature is useful for including libraries.

gawk operates on one or more input *files*. If none are specified (or if - is specified), **gawk** reads from standard input.

Variables can be assigned a value on the command line. The *value* assigned to a variable can be a literal, a shell variable (**$**name*), or a command substitution (`` `cmd` ``), but the value is available only after a line of input is read (i.e., after the **BEGIN** statement).

For example, to print the first three (colon-separated) fields of the password file, use -**F** to set the field separator to a colon:

```
gawk -F : '{print $1; print $2; print $3}' /etc/passwd
```

Numerous examples are shown later in the section "Patterns and Procedures."

Options

All options exist in both traditional POSIX (one-letter) format and GNU-style (long) format. Some recognized *options* are:

-- Treat all subsequent text as commands or filenames, not options.

-**f** *scriptfile,* --**file**=*scriptfile*
Read **gawk** commands from *scriptfile* instead of command line.

-**v** *var=value,* --**assign**=*var=value*
Assign a *value* to variable *var*. This allows assignment before the script begins execution.

-**F** *c,* --**field-separator**=*c*
Set the field separator to character *c*. This is the same as setting the variable **FS**. *c* may be a regular expression. Each input line, or record, is divided into fields by whitespace (blanks or tabs) or by some other user-definable record separator. Fields are referred to by the variables **$1**, **$2**,..., **$n**. **$0** refers to the entire record.

-**W** *option*
All -**W** options are specific to **gawk**, as opposed to **awk**. An alternate syntax is --*option* (i.e., --**compat**). *option* may be one of:

compat, traditional
Behave exactly like traditional (non-GNU) **awk**.

copyleft, copyright
Print copyleft notice and exit.

dump-variables[=*file*]
Print the name, type, and value of all global variables to the specified *file*, or to the file *awkvars.out* in the current directory if no file is specified.

help, usage
Print syntax and list of options, then exit.

lint[=**fatal**]
Warn about commands that might not port to other versions of **awk** or that **gawk** considers problematic. When **fatal** is specified, warnings are treated as fatal errors.

lint-old
Like **lint**, but compares to an older version of **awk** used on Version 7 Unix.

non-decimal-data
When reading data, interpret numbers beginning with 0 to be octal, and those beginning with 0x to be hexadecimal. (To print nondecimal numbers, use the **printf** command, as **print** prints only string representations of nondecimal numbers.)

posix
Expect exact compatibility with POSIX; disable all **gawk** extensions as if **traditional** had been specified. Ignore \x escape sequences, **, **=, the keyword **func**, and single-tab field separators. Disallow newlines after ? or : and the **fflush** function.

profile[*=file*]
Write a pretty printed version of the script being executed to the specified *file*, or to the file *awkprof.out* in the current directory if no other file is specified. When **gawk** is invoked as **pgawk** and passed this version of the program with the -f option, it will add profile data to the file inserting execution counts to the left of each statement in the program.

re-interval
Allow use of {*n,m*} intervals in regular expressions.

source=*script*
Treat *script* as **gawk** commands. Like the '*script*' argument, but lets you mix commands from files (using -f options) with commands on the **gawk** command line.

version
Print version information and exit.

Patterns and Procedures

gawk scripts consist of patterns and procedures:

```
pattern {procedure}
```

Both are optional. If *pattern* is missing, {*procedure*} is applied to all records. If {*procedure*} is missing, the matched record is printed. By default, each line of input is a record, but you can specify a different record separator through the **RS** variable.

Patterns

A pattern can be any of the following:

```
/regular expression/
relational expression
pattern-matching expression
pattern,pattern
BEGIN
END
```

Some rules regarding patterns include:

- Expressions can be composed of quoted strings, numbers, operators, functions, defined variables, or any of the predefined variables described later under "gawk System Variables."
- Regular expressions use the extended set of metacharacters and are described in Chapter 9.
- In addition, ^ and $ can be used to refer to the beginning and end of a field, respectively, rather than the beginning and end of a record.
- Relational expressions use the relational operators listed under "Operators" later in this chapter. Comparisons can be either string or numeric. For example, **$2 > $1** selects lines for which the second field is greater than the first.
- Pattern-matching expressions use the operators ~ (match) and !~ (don't match). See "Operators" later in this chapter.
- The **BEGIN** pattern lets you specify procedures that take place before the first input record is processed. (Generally, you set global variables here.)
- The **END** pattern lets you specify procedures that take place after the last input record is read.
- If there are multiple **BEGIN** or **END** patterns, their associated actions are taken in the order in which they appear in the script.
- *pattern,pattern* specifies a range of lines. This syntax cannot include **BEGIN** or **END** as a pattern.

Except for **BEGIN** and **END**, patterns can be combined with the Boolean operators || (OR), **&&** (AND), and **!** (NOT).

In addition to other regular-expression operators, GNU **gawk** supports POSIX character lists, which are useful for matching non-ASCII characters in languages other than English. These lists are recognized only within [ ] ranges. A typical use is [[:lower:]], which in English is the same as [a-z]. See Chapter 9 for a complete list of POSIX character lists.

Procedures

Procedures consist of one or more commands, functions, or variable assignments, separated by newlines or semicolons and contained within curly braces. Commands fall into four groups:

- Variable or array assignments
- Printing commands
- Built-in functions
- Control-flow commands

Simple Pattern/Procedure Examples

1. Print first field of each line (no pattern specified):

   ```
   { print $1 }
   ```
2. Print all lines that contain "Linux":

   ```
   /Linux/
   ```

3. Print first field of lines that contain "Linux":

```
/Linux/{ print $1 }
```

4. Print records containing more than two fields:

```
NF > 2
```

5. Interpret each group of lines up to a blank line as a single input record:

```
BEGIN { FS = "\n"; RS = "" }
```

6. Print fields 2 and 3 in switched order, but only on lines whose first field matches the string "URGENT":

```
$1 ~ /URGENT/ { print $3, $2 }
```

7. Count and print the number of instances of "ERR" found:

```
/ERR/ { ++x }; END { print x }
```

8. Add numbers in second column and print total:

```
{total += $2 }; END { print "column total is", total}
```

9. Print lines that contain fewer than 20 characters:

```
length( ) < 20
```

10. Print each line that begins with "Name:" and that contains exactly seven fields:

```
NF == 7 && /^Name:/
```

11. Reverse the order of fields:

```
{ for (i = NF; i >= 1; i--) print $i }
```

gawk System Variables

Variable	Description
$n	nth field in current record; fields are separated by **FS**
$0	Entire input record
ARGC	Number of arguments on command line
ARGIND	Current file's place in command line (starting with 0)
ARGV	An array containing the command-line arguments
CONVFMT	Conversion format for numbers (default is **%.6g**)
ENVIRON	An associative array of environment variables
ERRNO	Description of last system error
FIELDWIDTHS	List of field widths (whitespace-separated)
FILENAME	Current filename
FNR	Like **NR**, but relative to the current file
FS	Field separator (default is any whitespace; null string separates into individual characters)
IGNORECASE	If true, make case-insensitive matches
LINT	If true, run as if **-W lint** had been specified on the command line; if value is **FATAL**, generate fatal errors
NF	Number of fields in current record
NR	Number of the current record
OFMT	Output format for numbers (default is **%.6g**)
OFS	Output field separator (default is a blank)

Variable	Description
ORS	Output record separator (default is a newline)
RLENGTH	Length of the string matched by **match** function
RS	Record separator (default is a newline)
RT	The input text matching the record separator (RS) for the current record
RSTART	First position in the string matched by **match** function
SUBSEP	Separator character for array subscripts (default is \034)

PROCINFO Array

gawk stores information about the current process in an array named **PROCINFO**. The array contains the following fields:

Field	Description
egid	Effective group ID
euid	Effective user ID
FS	The type of field splitting being used, either **FS** or **FIELDWIDTHS**
gid	Group ID of the calling process
group*n*	Supplementary user group IDs associated with the process (**group1**, **group2**, etc.)
pgrpid	Process group ID
pid	Process ID
ppid	Parent process ID
uid	User ID of the calling process

Operators

The following table lists the operators, in order of increasing precedence, that are available in **gawk**.

Symbol	Meaning
= += -= *= /= %= ^= **=	Assignment
?:	C style conditional (*expression ? if-true-action : if-false-action*)
||	Logical OR
&&	Logical AND
in	Array membership (see **for** command)
~ !~	Match regular expression and negation
< <= > >= != == >> || &	Relational and redirection operators
(blank)	Concatenation
+ -	Addition, subtraction
* / %	Multiplication, division, and modulus
+ - !	Unary plus and minus and logical negation
^ **	Exponentiation
++ --	Increment and decrement, either prefix or postfix
$	Field reference

Variable and Array Assignments

Variables can be assigned a value with an equals sign. For example:

```
FS = ","
```

Expressions using the operators +, -, /, and % (modulo) can be assigned to variables.

Arrays can be created with the **split** function (see the listing in the "Alphabetical Summary of Commands"), or they can simply be named in an assignment statement. Array elements can be subscripted with numbers (*array*[**1**]) or with names. For example, to count the number of occurrences of a pattern, you could use the following script:

```
/pattern/ { array["/pattern/"]++ }
END { print array["/pattern/"] }
```

In **gawk**, variables need not be declared previous to their use, nor do arrays need to be dimensioned; they are activated upon first reference. All variables are stored as strings but may be used either as strings or numbers. **gawk** will use the program script context to determine whether to treat a variable as a string or a number, but the distinction also can be forced by the user. To force a variable to be treated as a string, concatenate a null to the variable:

```
var ""
```

To force a variable to be treated as a number, add 0 to it:

```
var + 0
```

Group Listing of gawk Commands

Arithmetic functions	String functions	Control flow statements	Input/output processing	Time functions	Miscellaneous
atan2	asort	break	close	mktime	and
cos	gensub	continue	fflush	strftime	compl
exp	gsub	do/while	getline	systime	delete
int	index	exit	print		function
log	length	for	printf		lshift
rand	match	if	sprintf		or
sin	split	next			rshift
sqrt	strtonum	nextfile			system
srand	sub	return			xor
	substr	while			
	tolower				
	toupper				

Alphabetical Summary of Commands

The following alphabetical list of statements and functions includes all that are available in **gawk** in Linux.

and
: `and(x,y)`

  Return the result of a bitwise AND of x and y.

asort
: `asort(array[,outarray])`

  Sort the values of the specified *array* and assign numeric indices according to each value's new position in the array. If an output array is specified, the array to be sorted is copied to the new array and the new array is sorted, leaving the original array unchanged.

atan2
: `atan2(y,x)`

  Return the arctangent of y/x in radians.

break
: `break`

  Exit from a **while** or **for** loop.

close
: `close(filename-expr)`
  `close(command-expr)`

  Close a file read by a **getline** command or a pipe. Takes as an argument the same expression that opened the pipe or file.

compl
: `compl(value)`

  Return the bitwise complement of *value*.

continue
: `continue`

  Begin next iteration of **while** or **for** loop without reaching the bottom.

cos
: `cos(x)`

  Return the cosine of x, an angle in radians.

delete
: `delete array[element]`
  `delete array`

  Delete *element* of *array*. If no element is specified, all elements are deleted.

do

```
do
    body
while (expr)
```

Looping statement. Execute statements in *body*, then evaluate *expr*. If *expr* is true, execute *body* again.

---

exit

```
exit
```

Do not execute remaining instruction, and read no new input. **END** procedures will be executed.

---

exp

```
exp(arg)
```

Return the natural exponent of *arg* (the inverse of **log**).

---

fflush

```
fflush(filename)
```

Flush output to *filename*; default is the standard output.

---

for

```
for (i=lower ; i<=upper ; i++)
    command
```

While the value of variable *i* is in the range between *lower* and *upper*, do *command*. A series of commands must be put within braces. <= or any relational operator can be used; ++ or -- can be used to increment or decrement the variable.

---

for

```
for (item in array)
    command
```

For each *item* in an associative *array*, execute *command*. Multiple commands must be put inside braces. Refer to each element of the array as *array[item]*. Elements of **gawk** arrays are stored in an order that enables access of any element in essentially equivalent time. This order may appear to be indiscriminate; if the output is desired in sorted order, you must pipe it through the **sort** command.

---

function

```
function name(parameter-list) {
    statements
}
```

Create *name* as a user-defined function consisting of **gawk** statements that apply to the specified list of parameters. Gawk accepts **func** as a synonymn for **function**.

---

gensub

```
gensub(r,s,n,t)
```

Substitute *s* for the *n*th match of regular expression *r* in the string *t*. Leave *t* unchanged, but return new string as the result. If *n* is **g** or **G**, change all matches. If *t* is not supplied, it defaults to **$0**.

getline

```
getline [varhairsp;] [<file]
command | getline [var]
```

The first form reads input from *file* or the next file on the command line, and the second form reads the output of *command*. Both forms read one line at a time, and each time the statement is executed it gets the next line of input. The line of input is assigned to **$0** and is parsed into fields, setting **NF**, **NR**, and **FNR**. If *var* is specified, the result is assigned to *var*, and neither **$0** nor **NF** is changed. Thus, if the result is assigned to a variable, the current line does not change. **getline** is actually a function, and it returns 1 if it reads a record successfully, 0 at EOF, and −1 if for some reason it is unsuccessful.

gsub

```
gsub(r,s,t)
```

Globally substitute *s* for each match of the regular expression *r* in the string *t*. Return the number of substitutions. If *t* is not supplied, it defaults to **$0**.

if

```
if (condition)
    command1
[else
    command2]
```

If *condition* is true, execute *command1*; otherwise, execute *command2*. *condition* can be an expression using any of the relational operators <, <=, ==, !=, >=, or >, as well as the pattern-matching operator ~. A series of commands must be put within braces.

Example

The following line determines whether the first word in each line starts with A, uppercase or lowercase:

```
if ($1 ~ /[Aa]*/)
```

index

```
index(substr,str)
```

Return the position of a substring in a string. Returns 0 if *substr* is not contained in *str*.

int

```
int(arg)
```

Return the integer part of *arg*.

length

```
length(arg)
```

Return the length of *arg*. If *arg* is not supplied, **$0** is assumed.

log

```
log(arg)
```

Return the natural logarithm of *arg* (the inverse of **exp**).

gawk

lshift	`lshift(value, n)`
	Bitwise command. Return the result of shifting *value* to the left by *n* bits.
match	`match(s,r)`
	Return position in *s* where regular expression *r* first matches, or 0 if no occurrences are found. Sets the value of **RSTART** and **RLENGTH**.
mktime	`mktime(datestring)`
	Convert a date given in the form *YYYY MM DD HH MM SS [DST]* into a timestamp. The time is assumed to be in the local time zone. The daylight savings time value, *DST*, may be 1 (true), 0 (false) or −1 (autodetect).
next	`next`
	Read next input line and start new cycle through pattern/procedures statements.
nextfile	`nextfile`
	Skip to the next file on the **gawk** command line and start new cycle through pattern/procedures statements.
or	`or(x,y)`
	Return the result of a bitwise OR of *x* and *y*.
print	`print [args] [destination]`
	Print *args* on output. Literal strings must be quoted. Fields are printed in the order they are listed. If separated by commas in the argument list, they are separated in the output by the character specified by **OFS**. If separated by spaces, they are concatenated in the output. *destination* is a shell redirection or pipe expression (e.g., > *file*) that redirects the default output.
printf	`printf[format [, expressions]]`
	Formatted **print** statement. Expressions or variables can be formatted according to instructions in the *format* argument. The number of *expressions* must correspond to the number specified in the format sections.
	format follows the conventions of the C-language **printf** statement. Here are a few of the most common formats:
	%s
	A string.

%d

A decimal number.

%*n.m*f

A floating-point number. *n* is the total number of digits; *m* is the number of digits after the decimal point.

%[-]*nc*

n specifies minimum field length for format type *c*. - left-justifies value in field; otherwise, value is right-justified.

Field widths are adjustable. For example, **%3.2f** limits a floating-point number to a minimum width of three digits, with two digits after the decimal point.

format also can contain embedded escape sequences, **\n** (newline) and **\t** (tab) being the most common. Spaces and literal text can be placed in the *format* argument by quoting the entire argument. If there are multiple expressions to be printed, multiple formats should be specified.

Example

Using the script:

```
{printf ("The sum on line %s is %d.\n", NR, $1+$2)}
```

the following input line:

```
5    5
```

produces this output, followed by a newline:

```
The sum on line 1 is 10.
```

---

rand	`rand( )`

Generate a random number between 0 and 1. This function returns the same series of numbers each time the script is executed, unless the random number generator is seeded using the **srand** function.

---

return	`return [expr]`

Used at end of user-defined functions to exit function, returning the value of *expr*.

---

rshift	`rshift(value, n)`

Bitwise command. Return the result of shifting *value* to the right by *n* bits.

---

sin	`sin(x)`

Return the sine of *x*, an angle in radians.

---

split	`split(string,array[,sep])`

Split *string* into elements of array *array*[**1**],...,*array*[*n*]. The string is split at each occurrence of separator *sep*. If *sep* is not specified, **FS** is used. If *sep* is a null string, a split is performed on every character. The number of array elements created is returned.

sprintf	`sprintf [format[, expression(s)]]` Return the value of one or more *expressions* using the specified *format* (see **printf**). Data is formatted but not printed.
sqrt	`sqrt(arg)` Return square root of *arg*.
srand	`srand(expr)` Use *expr* to set a new seed for random number generator. Default is time of day.
strftime	`strftime([format[,timestamp]])` Format *timestamp* according to *format*. Return the formatted string. The *timestamp* is a time-of-day value in seconds since midnight, January 1, 1970, UTC. The *format* string is similar to that of **sprintf**. (See the example for **systime**.) If *timestamp* is omitted, it defaults to the current time. If *format* is omitted, it defaults to a value that produces output similar to that of **date**.
strtonum	`strtonum(str)` Return the numeric value of string *str*. If *str* begins with 0 or 0x it will be treated as an octal or hexadecimal number. Trailing letters on *str* are ignored.
sub	`sub(r,s,t)` Substitute *s* for first match of the regular expression *r* in the string *t*. Return 1 if successful; 0 otherwise. If *t* is not supplied, the default is $0.
substr	`substr(string,m[,n])` Return substring of *string* beginning at character position *m* and consisting of the next *n* characters. If *n* is omitted, include all characters to the end of the string.
system	`system(command)` Execute the specified shell *command* and return its status. The status of the command that is executed typically indicates success (1), completion (0), or unexpected error (–1). The output of the command is not available for processing within the **gawk** script.

systime

systime( )

Return number of seconds since midnight UTC, January 1, 1970.

Example

Log the start and end times of a data processing program:

```
BEGIN {
        now = systime( )
        mesg = strftime("Started at %m/%d/%Y %H:%M:%S", now)
        print mesg
}
process data ...
END {
        now = systime( )
        mesg = strftime("Ended at %m/%d/%Y %H:%M:%S", now)
        print mesg
}
```

tolower

tolower(*str*)

Translate all uppercase characters in *str* to lowercase and return the new string.

toupper

toupper(*str*)

Translate all lowercase characters in *str* to uppercase and return the new string.

while

while (*condition*)
  command

Execute *command* while *condition* is true (see **if** for a description of allowable conditions). A series of commands must be put within braces.

xor

xor(*x,y*)

Return the result of a bitwise XOR of *x* and *y*.

14

RCS

The Revision Control System (RCS) offers *version control* (or *revision control*), a system that maintains information about a project's evolution so that project members can retrieve prior versions, track changes, and—most importantly— coordinate the efforts of the team. In a typical interaction, a developer checks out the most current code from the repository, makes changes, tests the results, and then commits those changes back to the repository when they are deemed satisfactory.

RCS can keep track of multiple file revisions, thereby reducing the amount of storage space needed. With RCS you can automatically store and retrieve revisions, merge or compare revisions, keep a complete history (or log) of changes, and identify revisions using symbolic keywords.

RCS preceded CVS and performs a similar role. RCS is more limited because it was designed to be used within a single directory and maintains a separate repository in each directory. Although RCS is no longer actively developed, it is still useful for small projects, offering fewer administrative issues than CVS. Projects with large directory structures or with team members on many different computer systems would benefit from using CVS, described in Chapter 15.

RCS uses a *locking model* to coordinate the efforts of multiple developers by serializing file modifications. Before making changes to a file, a developer must not only obtain a copy of it, but also request and obtain a lock on it from the system. This lock serves to prevent (or really, dissuade) multiple developers from working on the same file at the same time. When the changes are committed, the developer unlocks the file, permitting other developers to gain access to it.

Overview of RCS Commands

The three most important RCS commands are:

ci Check in revisions (put a file under RCS control).

co Check out revisions.

rcs Set up or change attributes of RCS files.

Two additional commands provide information about RCS files:

ident
> Extract keyword values from an RCS file.

rlog
> Display a summary (log) about the revisions in an RCS file.

You can compare RCS files with these commands:

rcsdiff
> Report differences between revisions.

rcsmerge
> Incorporate changes from two RCS files into a third RCS file.

The following command helps with configuration management:

rcsclean
> Remove working files that have not been changed.

Basic RCS Operations

Normally, you maintain RCS files in a subdirectory of your working directory called *RCS*, so the first step in using RCS should be:

```
mkdir RCS
```

Next, you place an existing file (or files) under RCS control by running the checkin command:

```
ci file
```

This creates a file called *file,v* in directory *RCS*. *file,v* is called an RCS file, and it will store all future revisions of *file*. When you run **ci** on a file for the first time, you are prompted to describe the contents. **ci** then deposits *file* into the RCS directory as revision 1.1.

To edit a new revision, check out a copy:

```
co -l file
```

This causes RCS to extract a copy of *file* from the RCS directory. You must lock the file with **-l** to make it writable by you. This copy is called a working file. When you're done editing, you can record the changes by checking the working file back in again:

```
ci file
```

This time, you are prompted to enter a log of the changes made, and the file is deposited as revision 1.2. Note that a checkin normally removes the working file. To retrieve a read-only copy, do a checkout without a lock:

co *file*

This is useful when you need to keep a copy on hand for compiling or searching. As a shortcut to the previous **ci/co**, you could type:

ci -u *file*

This checks in the file but immediately checks out a read-only copy. To compare changes between a working file and its latest revision, you can type:

rcsdiff *file*

Another useful command is **rlog**, which shows a summary of log messages.

System administrators can use the **rcs** command to set up default behavior for RCS.

General RCS Specifications

This section discusses:

- Keyword substitution
- Revision numbering
- Specifying the date
- Specifying states
- Standard options and environment variables

Keyword Substitution

RCS lets you place keyword variables in your working files. These variables are later expanded into revision notes. You can then use the notes either as embedded comments in the input file or as text strings that appear when the output is printed. To create revision notes via keyword substitution, follow this procedure:

1. In your working file, type any of the keywords listed in the next section.
2. Check the file in.
3. Check the file out again. Upon checkout, the **co** command expands each keyword to include its value. That is, **co** replaces instances of:

   $keyword$

   with:

   $keyword:value$

4. Subsequent checkin and checkout of a file will update any existing keyword values. Unless otherwise noted later, existing values are replaced by new values.

Many RCS commands have a **-k** option that provides more flexibility during keyword substitution.

Keywords

$Author$
: Username of person who checked in revision.

$Date$
: Date and time of checkin.

$Header$
: A title that includes the RCS file's full pathname, revision number, date, author, state, and (if locked) the person who locked the file.

Id
: Same as **$Header: /work/nutshell/qref.linux4/RCS/ch14,v 1.13 2003/05/23 19:00:11 emily Exp emily $**, but excludes the full pathname of the RCS file.

$Locker$
: Username of person who locked the revision. If the file isn't locked, this value is empty.

Log
: The message that was typed during checkin to describe the file, preceded by the RCS filename, revision number, author, and date. Log messages accumulate rather than being overwritten.

$Name$
: The symbolic name used to check out the revision, if there is one.

$RCSfile$
: The RCS filename, without its pathname.

$Revision$
: The assigned revision number.

$Source$
: The RCS filename, including its pathname.

$State$
: The state assigned by the **-s** option of **ci** or **rcs**.

Example values

Let's assume that the file */projects/new/chapter3* has been checked in and out by a user named *daniel*. Here's what keyword substitution would produce for each keyword, for the second revision of the file:

```
$Author: daniel $

$Date: 2003/02/25 18:21:10 $

$Header: /projects/new/chapter3,v 1.2 2003/02/25 18:21:10 daniel \
    Exp Locker: daniel $
```

```
$Id: chapter3,v 1.2 2003/02/25 18:21:10 daniel Exp daniel $

$Locker: daniel $

$Log: chapter3,v $
#Revision 1.2  2003/02/25 18:21:10  daniel
#Added section on error-handling
#
#Revision 1.1  2003/02/25 16:49:59  daniel
#Initial revision
#

$RCSfile: chapter3,v $

$Revision: 1.2 $

$Source: /projects/new/chapter3,v $

$State: Exp $
```

Revision Numbering

Unless told otherwise, RCS commands typically operate on the latest revision. Some commands have an **-r** option that is used to specify a revision number. In addition, many options accept a revision number as an optional argument. (In the command summary, this argument is shown as [R].) Revision numbers consist of up to four fields—release, level, branch, and sequence—but most revisions consist of only the release and level.

For example, you can check out revision 1.4 as follows:

```
co -l -r1.4 ch01
```

When you check it in again, the new revision will be marked as 1.5. But suppose the edited copy needs to be checked in as the next release. You would type:

```
ci -r2 ch01
```

This creates revision 2.1. You can also create a branch from an earlier revision. The following command creates revision 1.4.1.1:

```
ci -r1.4.1 ch01
```

Numbers are not the only way to specify revisions, though. You can assign a text label as a revision name, using the **-n** option of **ci** or **rcs**. You can also specify this name in any option that accepts a revision number for an argument. For example, you could check in each of your C programs, using the same label regardless of the current revision number:

```
ci -u -nPrototype *.c
```

In addition, you can specify a **$**, which means the revision number is extracted from the keywords of a working file. For example:

```
rcsdiff -r$ ch01
```

compares *ch01* to the revision that is checked in. You can also combine names and symbols. The command:

```
rcs -nDraft:$ ch*
```

assigns a name to the revision numbers associated with several chapter files.

Specifying the Date

Revisions are timestamped by time and date of checkin. Several keyword strings include the date in their values. Dates can be supplied in options to **ci**, **co**, and **rlog**. RCS uses the following date format as its default:

```
2002/10/16 02:00:00      (year/month/day time)
```

The default time zone is Greenwich Mean Time (GMT), which is also referred to as Coordinated Universal Time (UTC). Dates can be supplied in free format. This lets you specify many different styles. Here are some of the more common ones, which show the same time as in the preceding example:

```
6:00 pm lt            (assuming today is Oct. 16, 2002)
2:00 AM, Oct. 16, 2002
Wed Oct 16 18:00:00 2002 LT
Wed Oct 16 18:00:00 PST 2002
```

The uppercase or lowercase *lt* indicates local time (here, Pacific Standard Time). The third line shows **ctime** format (plus the *LT*); the fourth line is the **date** command format.

Specifying States

In some situations, particularly programming environments, you want to know the status of a set of revisions. RCS files are marked by a text string that describes their *state*. The default state is **Exp** (experimental). Other common choices include **Stab** (stable) or **Rel** (released). These words are user-defined and have no special internal meaning. Several keyword strings include the state in their values. In addition, states can be supplied in options to **ci**, **co**, **rcs**, and **rlog**.

Standard Options and Environment Variables

RCS defines the environment variable **RCSINIT**, which is used to set up default options for RCS commands. If you set **RCSINIT** to a space-separated list of options, these options will be prepended to the command-line options you supply to any RCS command. Four options are useful to include in **RCSINIT**: -q, -V, -x, and -z. They can be thought of as standard options because most RCS commands accept them.

-q[*R*]
Quiet mode; don't show diagnostic output. *R* specifies a file revision.

-V[*n*]
Emulate version *n* of RCS; useful when trading files between systems that run different versions. *n* can be 3, 4, or 5. If *n* is omitted, the command prints the version number of this version of RCS.

-xsuffixes

Specify an alternate list of *suffixes* for RCS files. Each suffix is separated by a /. On Unix systems, RCS files normally end with the characters *,v*. The **-x** option provides a workaround for systems that don't allow a comma character in filenames.

For example, when depositing a working file into an RCS file, the command:

ci -x,v/ ch01   *(second suffix is blank)*

searches in order for the RCS filenames:

RCS/ch01,v
ch01,v
RCS/ch01

-z[*zone*]

Specify the format of the date in keyword substitution. If empty, the default is to output the UTC time with no zone indication. With an argument of *LT*, the local time zone will be used to output an ISO 8601 format, with an indication of the separation from UTC. You may also specify a numeric UTC offset. For example, **-z+4:30** would output a string such as "2002-11-24 02:30:00+4:30".

Alphabetical Summary of RCS Commands

For details on the syntax of keywords, revision numbers, dates, states, and standard options, refer to the previous discussions.

ci

ci [*options*] *files*

Check in revisions. **ci** stores the contents of the specified working *files* into their corresponding RCS files. Normally, **ci** deletes the working file after storing it. If no RCS file exists, then the working file is an initial revision. In this case, the RCS file is created and you are prompted to enter a description of the file. If the RCS file exists, **ci** increments the revision number and prompts you to enter a message that logs the changes made. If a working file is checked in without changes, the file reverts to the previous revision.

The mutually exclusive options **-u**, **-l**, and **-r** are the most common. Use **-u** to keep a read-only copy of the working file (for example, so that the file can be compiled or searched). Use **-l** to update a revision and then immediately check it out again with a lock. This allows you to save intermediate changes but continue editing (for example, during a long editing session). Use **-r** to check in a file with a different release number. **ci** accepts the standard options **-q**, **-V**, **-x**, and **-z**.

Options

-d[*date*]

Check the file in with a timestamp of *date* or, if no date is specified, with the time of last modification.

-f[R]
Force a checkin even if there are no differences.

-I[R]
Interactive mode; prompt user even when standard input is not a terminal (e.g., when **ci** is part of a command pipeline).

-i[R]
Create (initialize) an RCS file and check it in. A warning is reported if the RCS file already exists.

-j[R]
Check in a file without initializing. Will report an error if file does not already exist.

-k[R]
Assign a revision number, creation date, state, and author from keyword values that were placed in the working file, instead of computing the revision information from the local environment. **-k** is useful for software distribution: the preset keywords serve as a timestamp shared by all distribution sites.

-l[R]
Do a **co -l** after checking in. This leaves a locked copy of the next revision in the working directory.

-m*msg*
Use the *msg* string as the log message for all files checked in. When checking in multiple files, **ci** normally prompts whether to reuse the log message of the previous file. **-m** bypasses this prompting.

-M[R]
Set the working file's modification time to that of the retrieved version. Use of **-M** can confuse **make** and should be used with care.

-n*name*
Associate a text *name* with the new revision number.

-N*name*
Same as **-n**, but override a previous *name*.

-r[R]
Check the file in as revision R.

-r
By itself, reverts to the default behavior of releasing a lock and removing the working file. This option overrides any **-l** or **-u** options that have been initialized by shell aliases or scripts. This behavior for **-r** is specific to **ci**.

-s*state*
Set the *state* of the checked-in revision.

-t*file*
Write the contents of *file* into the RCS file as the description, instead of prompting for it. This works only for the initial checkin.

-t-*string*

Write the specified *string* into the RCS file as the description, instead of prompting for it. This works only for initial checkin.

-T Set the RCS file's modification time to the time of the latest revision if the RCS file's time precedes the new revision.

-u[*R***]**

Do a **co -u** after checking in. This leaves a read-only copy in the working directory.

-w*user*

Set the author field to *user* in the checked-in revision.

Examples

Check in chapter files using the same log message:

```
ci -m'First round edits' chap*
```

Check in edits to *prog.c*, leaving a read-only copy:

```
ci -u prog.c
```

Start revision level 2; refer to revision 2.1 as "Prototype":

```
ci -r2 -nPrototype prog.c
```

---

co
co [*options*] *files*

Retrieve a previously checked-in revision, and place it in the corresponding working file (or print to standard output if **-p** is specified). If you intend to edit the working file and check it in again, specify **-l** to lock the file. **co** accepts the standard options **-q**, **-V**, **-x**, and **-z**.

Options

-d*date*

Retrieve latest revision whose checkin timestamp is on or before *date*.

-f[*R***]**

Force the working file to be overwritten.

-I[*R***]**

Interactive mode; prompt user even when standard input is not a terminal.

-j*R2:R3*

This works like **rcsmerge**. *R2* and *R3* specify two revisions whose changes are merged (joined) into a third file: either the corresponding working file or a third revision (any *R* specified by other **co** options).

-k*c*

Expand keyword symbols according to flag *c*, which can be:

b Like **o**, but perform its operations in binary mode, generating the previous revision's keywords and values in binary.

k Expand symbols to keywords only (no values). Useful for ignoring trivial differences during file comparison.

kv   Expand symbols to keyword and value (the default). Insert the locker's name only during a **ci -l** or **co -l**.

kvl   Like **kv**, but always insert the locker's name.

o   Expand symbols to keyword and value present in previous revision. This is useful for binary files that don't allow substring changes.

v   Expand symbols to values only (no keywords). This prevents further keyword substitution and is not recommended. Cannot be used with -l.

-l[*R*]
Same as **-r**, but also lock the retrieved revision.

-M[*R*]
Set the working file's modification time to that of the retrieved version. Use of **-M** can confuse **make** and should be used with care.

-p[*R*]
Send retrieved revision to standard output instead of to a working file. Useful for output redirection or filtering.

-r[*R*]
Retrieve the latest revision or, if *R* is given, retrieve the latest revision that is equal to or lower than *R*.

-s*state*
Retrieve the latest revision having the given *state*.

-T   Preserve the modification time of the RCS file even if a lock is added or removed.

-u[*R*]
Same as **-r**, but also unlock the retrieved revision if you locked it previously.

-w[*user*]
Retrieve the latest revision that was checked in either by the invoking user or by the specified *user*.

Examples

Sort the latest stored version of *file*:

```
co -p file | sort
```

Check out (and lock) all uppercase filenames for editing:

```
co -l [A-Z]*
```

Note that filename expansion fails unless a working copy resides in the current directory. Therefore, this example works only if the files were previously checked in via **ci -u**. Finally, here are some different ways to extract the working files for a set of RCS files (in the current directory):

`co -r3 *,v`	*Latest revisions of release 3*
`co -r3 -wjim *,v`	*Same, but only if checked in by jim*
`co -d'May 5, 2 pm LT' *,v`	*Latest revisions that were modified on or before the date*
`co -rPrototype *,v`	*Latest revisions named Prototype*

ident   ident [*option*] [*files*]

Extract keyword/value symbols from *files*. *files* can be text files, object files, or dumps.

Options

-q   Suppress warning message when no keyword patterns are found.

-V   Print version information and exit.

Examples

If file *prog.c* is compiled, and it contains this line of code:

    char rcsID[ ] = "$Author: daniel $";

then the following output is produced:

    % ident prog.c prog.o
    prog.c:
        $Author: daniel $
    prog.o:
        $Author: daniel $

Show keywords for all RCS files (suppress warnings):

    co -p RCS/*,v | ident -q

---

rcs   rcs [*options*] *files*

An administrative command for setting up or changing the default attributes of RCS files. Among other things, **rcs** lets you set strict locking (-L), delete revisions (-o), and override locks set by **co** (-l and -u). RCS files have an access list (created via -a); anyone whose username is on the list can run **rcs**. The access list is often empty, meaning that **rcs** is available to everyone. In addition, you can always invoke **rcs** if you own the file, if you're a privileged user, or if you run **rcs** with -i. **rcs** accepts the standard options -q, -V, -x, and -z.

Options

-a*users*

Append the comma-separated list of *users* to the access list.

-A*otherfile*

Append *otherfile*'s access list to the access list of *files*.

-b[*R*]

Set the default branch to *R* or, if *R* is omitted, to the highest branch on the trunk.

-c'*str*'

Set the comment character to string *str*. This option is obsolete, because RCS normally uses the preceding **Log** line's prefix when inserting log lines during checkout.

-e[*users*]
: Erase everyone (or only the specified *users*) from the access list.

-i
: Create (initialize) an RCS file, but don't deposit a revision.

-I
: Interactive mode; prompt user even when standard input is not a terminal. (New in RCS Version 5.)

-k*c*
: Use *c* as the default style for keyword substitution. (See **co** for values of *c*.) **-kkv** restores the default substitution style.

-l[*R*]
: Lock revision *R* or the latest revision. **-l** "retroactively locks" a file and is useful if you checked out a file incorrectly by typing **co** instead of **co -l**. If another user already has a lock on the file, that lock is broken, as with **-u**.

-L
: Turn on strict locking (the default). This means that everyone, including the owner of the RCS file, must use **co -l** to edit files. Strict locking is recommended when files are to be shared. (See **-U**.)

-m*R:msg*
: Use the *msg* string to replace the log message of revision *R*.

-M
: Disable email notification when breaking a lock on a file with **rcs -u**. This should be used only when there is another means to warn users that their files have been unlocked.

-n*flags*
: Add or delete an association between a revision and a name. *flags* can be:

  name:R
  : Associate *name* with revision *R*.

  name:
  : Associate *name* with latest revision.

  name
  : Remove association of *name*.

-N*flags*
: Same as **-n**, but overwrite existing *names*.

-o*R_list*
: Delete (outdate) revisions listed in *R_list*. *R_list* can be specified as *R1*, *R1:R2*, *R1:*, or *:R2*. When a branch is given, **-o** deletes only the latest revision on it.

-s*state*[*:R*]
: Set the state of the latest revision, or revision *R*, to *state*.

-t[*file*]
: Replace the RCS file description with the contents of *file* or, if no file is given, with standard input.

-t*-string*
: Replace the RCS file description with *string*.

-T Preserve the modification time of the RCS file unless a revision is removed.

-u[*R*]
Ɂ The complement of **-l**: unlock a revision that was previously checked out via **co -l**. If someone else did the checkout, you are prompted to state the reason for breaking the lock. This message is mailed to the original locker.

-U Turn on nonstrict locking. Everyone except the file owner must use **co -l** to edit files. (See **-L**.)

Examples

Associate the label **To_customer** with the latest revision of all RCS files:

```
rcs -nTo_customer: RCS/*
```

Add three users to the access list of file **beatle_deals**:

```
rcs -ageorge,paul,ringo beatle_deals
```

Delete revisions 1.2 through 1.5:

```
rcs -o1.2-1.5 doc
```

Replace an RCS file description with the contents of a variable:

```
echo "$description" | rcs -t file
```

---

rcsclean   rcsclean [*options*] [*files*]

Compare checked-out files against the corresponding latest revision or revision *R* (as given by the options). If no differences are found, the working file is removed. (Use **rcsdiff** to find differences.) **rcsclean** is useful in makefiles. For example, you could specify a "clean-up" target to update your directories. **rcsclean** is also useful prior to running **rcsfreeze**. **rcsclean** accepts the standard options **-q**, **-V**, **-x**, and **-z**.

Options

-k*c* When comparing revisions, expand keywords using style *c*. (See **co** for values of *c*.)

-n[*R*]
Ɂ Show what would happen, but don't actually execute.

-r[*R*]
Ɂ Compare against revision *R*. *R* can be supplied as arguments to other options, so **-r** is redundant.

-T Preserve the modification time of the RCS file even if a lock is added or removed.

-u[*R*]
Ɂ Unlock the revision if it's the same as the working file.

Examples

Remove unchanged copies of program and header files:

```
rcsclean *.c *.h
```

rcsdiff

rcsdiff [*options*] [*diff_options*] *files*

Compare revisions via **diff**. Specify revisions using **-r** as follows:

Number of revisions specified	Comparison made
0	Working file against latest revision
1	Working file against specified revision
2	One revision against the other

rcsdiff accepts the standard options **-q**, **-V**, **-x**, and **-z**, as well as *diff_options*, which can include any valid **diff** option. **rcsdiff** exits with a status of 0 (no differences), 1 (some differences), or 2 (unknown problem).

Options

-k*c* When comparing revisions, expand keywords using style *c*. (See **co** for values of *c*.)

-r*R1*
   Use revision *R1* in the comparison.

-r*R2*
   Use revision *R2* in the comparison. (**-r***R1* must also be specified.)

-T Preserve the modification time on the RCS file.

---

rcsmerge

rcsmerge [*options*] *file*

Perform a three-way merge of file revisions, taking two differing versions and incorporating the changes into the working *file*. You must provide either one or two revisions to merge (typically with **-r**). Overlaps are handled the same as with **merge**, by placing warnings in the resulting file. **rcsmerge** accepts the standard options **-q**, **-V**, **-x**, and **-z**. **rcsmerge** exits with a status of 0 (no overlaps), 1 (some overlaps), or 2 (unknown problem).

Options

-k*c* When comparing revisions, expand keywords using style *c*. (See **co** for values of *c*.)

-p[*R*]
   Send merged version to standard output instead of overwriting *file*.

-r[*R*]
   Merge revision *R* or, if no *R* is given, merge the latest revision.

Examples

Say you need to add updates to an old revision (1.3) of *prog.c*, but the current file is already at revision 1.6. To incorporate the changes:

```
co -l prog.c
```
(edit latest revision by adding revision 1.3 updates, then:)
```
rcsmerge -p -r1.3 -r1.6 prog.c > prog.updated.c
```

Undo changes between revisions 3.5 and 3.2, and overwrite the working file:

```
rcsmerge -r3.5 -r3.2 chap08
```

rlog

rlog [*options*] *files*

Display identification information for RCS *files*, including the log message associated with each revision, the number of lines added or removed, date of last checkin, and so on. With no options, **rlog** displays all information. Use options to display specific items. **rlog** accepts the standard options **-V**, **-x**, and **-z**.

Options

-b   Prune the display; print information about the default branch only.

-d*dates*

Display information for revisions whose checkin timestamps fall in the range of *dates* (a list separated by semicolons). Be sure to use quotes. Each date can be specified as:

date1<*date2*

Select revisions between *date1* and *date2*, inclusive.

date1 <

Select revisions made on or after *date1*.

date1

Select revisions made on or before *date1*.

-h   Display only the beginning of the normal **rlog** listing, showing the RCS pathname, working pathname, header, default branch, etc.

-l[*users*]

Display information only about locked revisions or, if *lockers* is specified, only revisions locked by the comma-separated list of *users*.

-L   Skip files that aren't locked.

-N   Don't display symbolic names.

-r[*list*]

Display information for revisions in the comma-separated *list* of revision numbers. If no *list* is given, the latest revision is used. Items can be specified as:

R1

Select revision *R1*. If *R1* is a branch, select all revisions on it.

R1.

If *R1* is a branch, select its latest revision.

R1:*R2*

Select revisions *R1* through *R2*.

:*R1*
> Select revisions from beginning of branch through *R1*.

R1:
> Select revisions from *R1* through end of branch.

-R Display only the name of the RCS file.

-s*states*
> Display information for revisions whose state matches one from the comma-separated list of *states*.

-t Same as **-h**, but also display the file's description.

-w[*users*]
> Display information for revisions checked in by anyone in the comma-separated list of *users*. If no *users* are supplied, assume the name of the invoking user.

Examples

Display a file's revision history:

```
rlog RCS/*,v | more
```

Display names of RCS files that are locked by user *daniel*:

```
rlog -R -L -ldaniel RCS/*
```

Display the "title" portion (no revision history) of a working file:

```
rlog -t calc.c
```

15

CVS

The Concurrent Versions System (CVS) is the most popular revision control system among users of free and open source software. It is particularly appropriate for highly distributed projects, with developers working on many different computer systems and even in different parts of the world.

This chapter is based on CVS Version 1.11.2.

Basic Concepts

To accommodate large projects using a hierarchy of several directories, CVS defines the concepts *repository* and *sandbox*.

The *repository* (also called an *archive*) is the centralized storage area that stores the projects' files. It is managed by the version control system and the repository administrator, and contains information required to reconstruct historical versions of the files in a project. An administrator sets up and controls the repository using the procedures and commands described later in the "CVS Administrator Reference" section.

A *sandbox* (also called a *working directory*) contains copies of versions of files from the repository. New development occurs in sandboxes, and any number of sandboxes may be created from a single repository. The sandboxes are independent of one another and may contain files from different stages of the development of the same project. Users set up and control sandboxes using the procedures and commands found in the later "CVS User Reference."

In a typical interaction with CVS, a developer checks out the most current code from the repository, makes changes, tests the results, and then commits those changes back to the repository when they are deemed satisfactory.

Locking and Merging

Some systems, such as RCS (Revision Control System) and the older SCCS (Source Code Control System), use a *locking model* that coordinates the efforts of multiple developers by serializing file modifications. This was described at the beginning of the previous chapter. The locking model is pessimistic: it assumes that conflicts *must* be avoided. Serialization of file modifications through locks prevents conflicts. But it is cumbersome to have to lock files for editing when bug-hunting. Often, developers will circumvent the lock mechanism to keep working, which is an invitation to trouble.

To handle work by multiple developers on a single file, CVS uses a *merging model* that allows everyone to have access to the files at all times and supports concurrent development. The merging model is optimistic: it assumes that conflicts are not common and that when they do occur, it usually isn't difficult to resolve them.

CVS is capable of operating under a locking model via the **-L** and **-l** options to the **admin** command. Also, CVS has special commands (**edit** and **watch**) for those who want additional development coordination support. CVS uses locks internally to prevent corruption when multiple people are accessing the repository simultaneously, but this is different from the user-visible locks of the locking model.

Conflicts and Merging

In the event that two developers commit changes to the same version of a file, CVS automatically defers the commit of the second committer's file. The second committer then issues the **cvs update** command, which merges the first committer's changes into the local file. In many cases, the changes are in different areas of the file, and the merge is successful. However, if both developers have made changes to the same area of the file, the second to commit will have to resolve the conflict. This involves examining the problematic areas of the file and selecting among the multiple versions or making changes that resolve the conflict.

CVS detects only textual conflicts, but conflict resolution is concerned with keeping the project as a whole logically consistent. Therefore, conflict resolution sometimes involves changing files other than the one CVS complained about.

For example, if one developer adds a parameter to a function definition, it may be necessary for all the calls to that function to be modified to pass the additional parameter. This is a logical conflict, so its detection and resolution is the job of the developers (with support from tools like compilers and debuggers); CVS won't notice the problem.

In any merge situation, whether or not there was a conflict, the second developer to commit will often want to retest the resulting version of the project because it has changed since the original commit. Once it passes the test, the developer will need to recommit the file.

Tagging

CVS tracks file versions by revision number, which can be used to retrieve a particular revision from the repository. In addition, it is possible to create symbolic tags so that a group of files (or an entire project) can be referred to by a single identifier even when the revision numbers of the files are not the same (which is most often the case). This capability is often used to keep track of released versions or other important project milestones.

For example, the symbolic tag **hello-1_0** might refer to revision number 1.3 of *hello.c* and revision number 1.1 of *Makefile* (symbolic tags are created with the **tag** and **rtag** commands).

Branching

The simplest form of development is *linear* development, in which there is a succession of revisions to a file, each derived from the prior revision. Many projects can get by with a completely linear development process, but larger projects (as measured by number of files, number of developers, and/or size of the user community) often run into maintenance issues that require additional capabilities. Sometimes it is desirable to do some speculative development while the main line of development continues uninterrupted. Other times, bugs in the currently released version must be fixed while work on the next version is already underway. In both of these cases, the solution is to create a *branch* (or *fork*) from an appropriate point in the development of the project. If, at a future point, some or all of the changes on the branch are needed on the main line of development (or elsewhere), they can be *merged* together (*joined*).

Branches are forked with the **tag -b** command; they are joined with the **update -j** command.

CVS Command Format

CVS commands are of the form:

```
cvs global_options command command_options
```

For example, here is a simple sequence of commands showing both kinds of options in the context of creating a repository, importing existing files, and performing a few common operations on them:

```
$ cvs -d /usr/local/cvsrep init
$ cd ~/work/hello
$ cvs -d /usr/local/cvsrep import -m 'Import' hello vendor start
$ cd ..
$ mv hello hello.bak
$ cvs -d /usr/local/cvsrep checkout hello
$ cd hello
$ vi hello.c
$ cvs commit -m 'Fixed a typo'
$ cvs tag hello-1_0
$ cvs remove -f Makefile
```

```
$ cvs commit -m 'Removed old Makefile'
$ cvs upd -r hello-1_0
$ cvs upd -A
```

Some global options are common to both user and administrator commands, and some are specific to each. The common global options are described in the next section, and the administrator and user options are described in "CVS Administrator Reference" and "CVS User Reference," respectively.

Common Global Options

Table 15-1 lists the global options that apply to both user and administrator commands.

Table 15-1. Common global options

Option	Description
-b *bindir*	Location of external RCS programs. This option is obsolete, having been deprecated at CVS versions above 1.9.18.
-T *tempdir*	Absolute path for temporary files. Overrides the setting of $TMPDIR.
-v, --version	Display version and copyright information.

Gotchas

This section clarifies a few aspects of CVS that can sometimes cause confusion.

File orientation
While directories are supported, they are not versioned in the same way as traditional files are. This is particularly important in the early evolutionary stages of a project, when the structure may be in flux. Also, if the project is undergoing major changes, the structure is likely to change. See the later section "Hacking the Repository."

Text orientation
There is no equivalent to **diff** for binary files, although CVS's support for binary files is usually sufficient. Use **admin -kb** to tell CVS a file is binary.

Line orientation
Moving a segment of code from one place in a file to another is seen as a delete (from the old location) and an unrelated add (to the new location).

CVS is not syntax-aware
As far as CVS is concerned, small formatting changes are equivalent to sweeping logic changes in the same line ranges.

CVS Administrator Reference

This section provides details on creating and configuring repositories and performing other CVS administrative tasks. A single computer can run multiple copies of the CVS server, and each server can serve multiple repositories.

Creating a Repository

Select a directory that will contain the repository files (*/usr/local/cvsrep* is used in the following examples). Use the **init** command to initialize the repository. Either set the **$CVSROOT** environment variable to the absolute path of the repository:

```
$ export CVSROOT=/usr/local/cvsrep
$ cvs init
```

or use the **-d** option to specify the absolute path to the repository:

```
$ cvs -d /usr/local/cvsrep init
```

For information on importing code, see the "CVS User Reference," especially **import** and **add**.

Setting up the password server with inetd

If your server uses **inetd** to control services and you want users to access the repository from other computers, configure the **pserver** by doing the following as root:

* Make sure there is an entry in */etc/services* similar to the following:

    ```
    cvspserver 2401/tcp
    ```

* If you are not using **tcpwrappers**, place a line like this in */etc/inetd.conf*:

    ```
    cvspserver stream tcp nowait root /usr/bin/cvs cvs --allow-root=/usr/
    local/cvsroot pserver
    ```

* Or, if you *are* using **tcpwrappers**, use a line like this:

    ```
    cvspserver stream tcp nowait root /usr/sbin/tcpd /usr/bin/cvs
    --allow-root=/usr/local/cvsroot pserver
    ```

* Once these changes are in place, restart **inetd** (or send it the appropriate signal to cause it to reread *inetd.conf*).

Setting up the password server with xinetd

If your server uses **xinetd** to control services and you want users to access the repository from other computers, configure the **pserver** by doing the following as root:

* Make sure there is a file */etc/xinetd.d/cvspserver* similar to the following:

    ```
    service cvspserver
    {
        port        = 2401
        socket_type = stream
        protocol    = tcp
        wait        = no
        user        = root
        passenv     = PATH
        server      = /usr/local/bin/cvs
        server_args = -f --allow-root=/usr/local/cvsroot pserver
    }
    ```

* Once these changes are in place, restart **xinetd** (or send it the appropriate signal to cause it to reread its configuration.

Security Issues

The following security issues need to be considered when working with CVS:

- The contents of files will be transmitted in the open over the network with **pserver** and **rsh**. With **pserver**, passwords are transmitted in the open as well.

- When using a local repository (i.e., when CVS is not being used in client/server mode), developers need write access to the repository, which means they can hack it.

- The CVS server runs as root briefly before changing its user ID.

- The *~/.cvspass* file must be kept unreadable by all users except the owner to prevent passwords from being accessible.

- A user who has authority to make changes to the files in the *CVSROOT* module can run arbitrary programs.

- Some of the options to the **admin** command are very dangerous, so it is advisable to restrict its use. This can be accomplished by creating a user group named **cvsadmin**. If this user group exists, only users in that group can run the **admin** command (except **admin -k**kflag, which is available to everyone).

Repository Structure

The CVS repository is implemented as a normal directory with special contents. This section describes the contents of the repository directory.

The CVSROOT directory

The *CVSROOT* directory contains the administrative files for the repository; other directories in the repository contain the modules. The administrative files permit (and ignore) blank lines and comment lines in addition to the lines containing real configuration information. Comment lines start with a hash mark (#).

Some of the administrative files contain filename patterns to match file and directory names. These patterns are regular expressions like those used in GNU Emacs. Table 15-2 contains the special constructions used most often.

Table 15-2. Filename pattern special constructions

Construction	Description
^	Match the beginning of the string.
$	Match the end of the string.
.	Match any single character.
*	Modify the preceding construct to match zero or more repetitions.

CVS will perform a few important expansions in the contents of the administrative files before interpreting the results. First, the typical shell syntax for referring to a home directory is *~/*, which expands to the home directory of the user running CVS, and *~user* expands to the home directory of the specified user.

In addition, CVS provides a mechanism similar to the shell's environment variable expansion capability. Constructs such as ${*variable*} will be replaced by the value of the named variable. Variable names start with letters and consist entirely of letters, numbers, and underscores. Curly brackets may be omitted if the character immediately following the variable reference is not a valid variable name character. While this construct looks like a shell environment variable reference, the full environment is not available. Table 15-3 contains the built-in variables.

Table 15-3. Administrative file variables

Variable	Description
CVSEDITOR EDITOR VISUAL	The editor CVS uses for log file editing.
CVSROOT	The repository locator in use.
USER	The name of the user (on the server, if using a remote repository) running CVS.
=*var*	The value of a user-defined variable named *var*. Values for these variables are provided by the global -s option.

To edit these files, check out the *CVSROOT* module from the repository, edit the files, and commit them back to the repository. You must commit the changes for them to affect CVS's behavior.

Table 15-4 describes the administrative files and their functions.

Table 15-4. CVSROOT files

File	Description
checkoutlist	Extra files to be maintained in *CVSROOT*.
commitinfo	Specifications for commit governors.
config	Settings to affect the behavior of CVS.
cvsignore	Filename patterns of files to ignore.
cvswrappers	Specifications for **checkout** and **commit** filters.
editinfo	Specifications for log editors (obsolete).
history	Log information for the **history** command.
loginfo	Specify **commit** notifier program(s).
modules	Module definitions.
notify	Notification processing specifications.
passwd	A list of users and their CVS-specific passwords.
rcsinfo	Template form for log messages.
readers	A list of users having read-only access.
taginfo	Tag processing specifications.
users	Alternate user email addresses for use with *notify*.
verifymsg	Specify log message evaluator program.
writers	A list of users having read/write access.

Since the *editinfo* file is obsolete, use the **$EDITOR** environment variable (or the -e option) to specify the editor and the *verifymsg* file to specify an evaluator.

Each line of the *taginfo* file contains a filename pattern and a command line to execute when files with matching names are tagged.

The checkoutlist file

Whenever changes to files in the *CVSROOT* module are committed, CVS prints the message:

```
cvs commit: Rebuilding administrative file database
```

This informs you that the checked-out copy in the repository has been updated to reflect any changes just committed. As with any other module directory in the repository, the *CVSROOT* directory contains RCS (*,v*) files that retain the history of the files. But to use the files, CVS needs a copy of the latest revision. So, when CVS prints this message, it is checking out the latest revisions of the administrative files.

If you have added files to the *CVSROOT* module (such as scripts to be called via entries in the *loginfo* file), you will need to list them in the *checkoutlist* file. This makes CVS treat them the same way as it treats the standard set of *CVSROOT* files.

Each line in this file consists of a filename and an optional error message that is displayed in case there is trouble checking out the file.

The commitinfo file

Whenever a **commit** is being processed, CVS consults this file to determine whether or not any precommit checking of the file is required. Each line of the file contains a directory name pattern, followed by the path of a program to invoke when files are commited in directories with matching names.

Aside from the usual filename-pattern syntax, there are two special patterns:

ALL
> If this pattern is present in the file, all files are passed to the specified checking program. CVS then looks for a pattern that matches the name of each particular file and runs the additional checks found, if any.

DEFAULT
> If this pattern is present in the file, all files for which there was no pattern match are sent to the specified checking program. The automatic match of every file to the **ALL** entry, if any, does not count as a match when determining whether or not to send the file to the **DEFAULT** checking program.

CVS constructs the command line for the checking program by appending the full path to the directory within the repository and the list of files being committed (this means you can specify the first few command-line arguments to the program, if necessary). If the checking program exits with a nonzero status, the **commit** is aborted.

The programs that run via this mechanism run on the server computer when a remote repository is used. Here is an example of a *commitinfo* file:

```
ALL $CVSROOT/CVSROOT/commit-ALL.pl
DEFAULT $CVSROOT/CVSROOT/commit-DEFAULT.pl
CVSROOT$ $CVSROOT/CVSROOT/commit-CVSROOT.pl
```

This example assumes you will create the script files in the *CVSROOT* module and add them to the *checkoutlist* file.

The config file

Repository configuration is specified in the *config* administrative file.

LockDir=*dir*
> Directs CVS to put its lock files in the alternate directory given instead of in the repository itself, allowing users without write access to the repository (but with write access to *dir*) to read from the repository.
>
> Version 1.11 supports this option. Version 1.10 doesn't support alternate directories for lock files and reports an error if this option is set. Older versions of CVS (1.9 and previous) don't support this option either and will not report an error. Do not mix versions that support alternate directories for lock files with versions that don't, since lock files in both places defeat the purpose of having them.

LogHistory=*types*
> Determines the types of activities that will be logged to the *history* administrative file. The special value **all** implies all the record types listed in Tables 15-19, 15-20, and 15-21. Any subset of those record types can be specified by listing them. For example, the line **LogHistory=***MAR* will log commit-related events only.

SystemAuth=*value*
> CVS tries to authenticate users via the *CVSROOT/passwd* file first; if that fails and this option is set to **yes**, CVS tries to authenticate via the system's user database. This option is used with the password server. The default is **yes**.

TopLevelAdmin=*value*
> If this option is set to **yes**, an additional *CVS* directory is created at the top-level directory when **checkout** is run. This allows the client software to detect the repository locator in that directory (see "Repository Locators"). The default is **no**.
>
> This option is useful if you check out multiple modules to the same sandbox directory. If it is enabled, you won't have to provide a repository locator after the first checkout; CVS infers it from the information in the top-level *CVS* directory created during the first checkout.

The cvsignore file

The *cvsignore* administrative file contains a list of filename patterns to ignore, just like the *.cvsignore* files that can appear in sandboxes and user home directories. Unlike the filename patterns in other administrative files, these patterns are in **sh** syntax; they are not GNU Emacs-style regular expressions. There can be multiple patterns on a line, separated by whitespace (consequently, the patterns themselves cannot contain whitespace).

There is a slight difference between filename patterns in **sh** and CVS. Since the CVS patterns are not subject to variable interpolation, a pattern such as _$* (which is one of the patterns built into CVS) will match a file named _$foo but not one named _. But, if you present the same pattern to **sh**, the **$*** part will be interpolated resulting in an effective pattern of just _, which will then match the file _, but not _$foo. This becomes particularly important if you are writing your own utilities to work with CVS and you need to implement the same policy for ignoring files.

Table 15-5 shows the most commonly used **sh**-style pattern constructs.

Table 15-5. Filename patterns for cvsignore

Construct	Description
?	Any one character.
*	Any sequence of zero or more characters.

Again, diverging from the standards used by the rest of the administrative files, the *cvsignore* file does not support comments.

The cvswrappers file

While the *cvsignore* file allows CVS to ignore certain files, the *cvswrappers* file allows you to give CVS default options for commands that work with files. Lines in this file consist of a **sh**-style filename pattern followed by a **-k** (keyword substitution mode) option and/or an **-m** (update method) option. The legal values for **-k** are described in Table 15-17. The legal values for **-m** are **COPY** and **MERGE**.

If **-m COPY** is specified, CVS will not attempt to merge the files. Instead, it presents the user with conflicting versions of the file, and the user can choose one or the other or resolve the conflict manually.

For example, to treat all files ending in *.jpg* as binary, add this line to the file:

```
*.jpg -k b
```

The history file

If this file exists, CVS inserts records of activity against the repository. This information produces displays of the **cvs history** command. The history file is not intended for direct reading or writing by programs other than CVS.

A repository set up with **cvs init** automatically has a *history* file.

The loginfo file

The *loginfo* administrative file works much like the *commitinfo* file and can use the special patterns **ALL** and **DEFAULT**. This file allows you to do something with **commit** log messages and related information.

The programs called during *loginfo* processing receive the log message on standard input. Table 15-6 shows the three codes that can pass additional information to the called programs via command-line arguments.

Table 15-6. Special loginfo variables

Variable	Description
s	Filename
V	Pre-commit revision number
v	Post-commit revision number

If a percent sign (%) followed by the desired variable is placed after the command path, CVS inserts the corresponding information as a whitespace-separated list with one entry for each file, preceded by the repository path (as with *commitinfo*). There can be only one percent sign on the command line, so if you want information from more than one variable, place the variable names inside curly brackets: %{...}. In this case, each file-specific entry has one field for each variable, separated by commas. For example, the code **%{sVv}** expands into a list like this:

```
/usr/local/cvsrep/hello Makefile,1.1,1.2 hello.c,1.8,1.9
```

It can be helpful to send email notifications each time someone commits a file to the repository. Developers can monitor this stream of notices to determine when they should pull the latest development code into their private sandboxes. For example, consider a developer doing some preparatory work in his sandbox while he awaits stabilization and addition of another developer's new library. As soon as the new library is added and committed, email notification goes out, and the waiting developer sees that the code is ready to use. So, he runs **cvs upd -d** in the appropriate directory to pull in the new library code and then sets about integrating it with his work.

It is simple to set up this kind of notification. Just add a line like this to the *CVSROOT/loginfo* file:

```
DEFAULT mail -s %s developers@company.com
```

Often, the email address is a mailing list, which has all the interested parties (developers or otherwise) on the distribution list. If you want to send messages to multiple email addresses, you can write a script to do that and have that script called via this file. Alternatively, you can use the *log.pl* program that comes as part of the CVS source distribution (located at */usr/local/src/cvs-1.11/contrib/log.pl*, assuming CVS was unpacked into */usr/local/src*). Instructions for its use are provided as comments in the file.

The modules file

The top-level directories in a repository are called *modules*. In addition to these physical modules, CVS provides a mechanism to create logical modules through the *modules* administrative file. Here are the three kinds of logical modules:

Alias

Alias modules are defined by lines of the form:

```
module_name -a alias_module ...
```

Using an alias module name in a CVS command is equivalent to using its component modules (after the **-a** option) directly.

Regular

Regular modules are defined by lines of the form:

```
module_name [options] directory file ...
```

Checking out *module_name* results in the specified files from *directory* being checked out into a directory named *module_name*. The intervening directories (if any) are not reflected in the sandbox.

Ampersand

Ampersand modules are defined by lines of the form:

```
module_name [options] &other_module ...
```

Checking out such a module results in a directory named *module_name*, which in turn contains copies of the *other_module* modules.

Table 15-7 shows the options that can define modules.

Table 15-7. Module options

Option	Description
-d *name*	Override the default working directory name for the module.
-e *prog*	Run the program *prog* when files are exported from the module; the module name is passed in to *prog* as the sole argument.
-i *prog*	Run the program *prog* when files are committed to the module; the repository directory of the committed files is passed in to *prog* as the sole argument.
-i *prog*	Run the program *prog* when files are checked out from the module; the module name is passed in to *prog* as the sole argument.
-s *status*	Assign a status descriptor to the module.
-t *prog*	Run the program *prog* when files are tagged in the module using **rtag**; the module name and the symbolic tag are passed in to *prog*.
-u *prog*	Run the program *prog* when files are updated in the module's top-level directory; the full path to the module within the repository is passed in to *prog* as the sole argument.

Alias modules provide alternative names for other modules or shortcuts for referring to collections or subdirectories of other modules. Alias module definitions function like macro definitions in that they cause commands to run as if the expanded list of modules and directories were on the command line. Alias modules do not cause the modules of their definition to be grouped together under the alias name (use ampersand modules for that). For example, the definition:

```
h -a hello
```

makes the name **h** a synonym for the **hello** module. This definition:

```
project -a library client server
```

allows you to check out all three modules of the project as a unit. If an entry in the definition of an alias module is preceded by an exclamation point (!), then the named directory is excluded from the module.

Regular modules allow you to create modules that are subsets of other modules. For example, the definition:

```
header library library.h
```

creates the **header** module, which consists of only the *library.h* file from the **library** module.

Ampersand modules are true logical modules. There are no top-level directories for them in the repository, but you can check them out to sandboxes, and directories with their names will then appear. The modules listed in the definition are below that directory. For example:

```
project &library &client &server
```

is almost the same as the alias module example given earlier, except that the submodules are checked out inside a subdirectory named *project*.

In this file, long definitions may be split across multiple lines by terminating all but the last line with backslashes (\).

The notify file

This file is used in conjunction with the **watch** command. When notifications are appropriate, this file is consulted to determine how to do the notification.

Each line of the *notify* file contains a filename pattern and a command line. CVS's notification mechanism uses the command line specified to perform notifications for files with names that match the corresponding pattern.

There is a single special-purpose variable, **%s**, that can appear in the command specification. When the command is executed, the name of the user to notify replaces the variable name. If the *users* administrative file exists, the usernames are looked up there, and the resulting values are used for **%s** instead. This allows emails to be sent to accounts other than those on the local machine. Details are sent to the notification program via standard input.

Typical usage of this feature is the single entry:

```
ALL mail %s -s "CVS notification"
```

In fact, this entry is present in the default *notify* file created when you run **cvs init** to create a repository (although it is initially commented out).

The passwd file

If you access the repository via a **pserver** repository locator (see "Repository Locators"), then CVS can have its own private authentication information, separate from the system's user database. This information is stored in the *CVSROOT/passwd* administrative file.

This feature provides anonymous CVS access over the Internet. By creating an entry for a public user (usually **anoncvs** or **anonymous**), the **pserver** can be used by many people sharing the public account. If you don't want to create a system user with the same name as the public user, or if you have such a user but it has a different purpose, you can employ a user alias to map it to something else:

```
anonymous:TY7QWpLw8bvus:cvsnoname
```

Then, make sure you create the **cvsnoname** user on the system. You can use */bin/ false* as the login shell, and the repository's root directory as the home directory for the user.

If you leave the password field empty for the anonymous user, then CVS will accept any password (as of Version 1.11). To restrict the public user to read-only access, list it in the *CVSROOT/readers* administrative file.

Additionally, CVS's private user database is useful even if you don't want to set up anonymous CVS access. You can restrict access to a subset of the system's users, provide remote access to users who don't have general system access, or prevent a user's normal system password from being transmitted in the clear over the network (see "Security Issues").

There is no **cvs passwd** command for setting CVS-specific passwords (located in the repository file *CVSROOT/passwd*). CVS-specific user and password management is a manual task.

The rcsinfo file

CVS consults this file when doing a **commit** or **import** to determine the log message editor template. Each entry in the file consists of a filename pattern and the name of the file to use as the template for module directories with matching names.

The **ALL** and **DEFAULT** special patterns apply to this file.

The readers file

If this file exists, users listed in it have read-only access.

The taginfo file

CVS consults this file whenever the **tag** or **rtag** commands are used. Entries in this file are filename patterns and program specifications. The **ALL** special pattern applies to this file.

The *taginfo* file is called with the tag, the operation being performed, the module directory name (relative to the repository root), and the filename and revision number for each affected file. The valid operations are **add** (for **tag**), **del** (for **tag -d**), and **mov** (for **tag -F**).

If the *taginfo* program returns a nonzero status, the **tag** or **rtag** command that caused its execution is aborted.

The users file

If this file exists, it is consulted during processing of the *notify* administrative file's contents. Entries in this file consist of two colon-separated fields on a single line.

The first field is the name of a user, and the second field is a value (normally the user's email address on another machine). For example:

```
john:john@somecompany.com
jane:jane@anothercompany.com
```

The verifymsg file

CVS consults this file to determine if log messages should be validated. If the program returns a nonzero status, the commit is aborted. The *verifymsg* file is called with the full path to a file containing the log message to be verified.

The **ALL** special pattern is not supported for this file, although **DEFAULT** is. If more than one pattern matches, the first match is used.

The writers file

If this file exists, users listed in it have read/write access (unless they are also listed in the *readers* file, in which case they have read-only access).

Hacking the Repository

Since the repository is a normal directory, albeit one with special contents, it is possible to **cd** into the directory and examine its contents and/or make changes to the files and directories there. For each file that has been added there will be a file with the same name followed by *,v* in a corresponding directory in the repository. These are RCS (the format, not the program) files that contain multiple versions of the file.

 Since the activities discussed in this section involve making changes directly to the repository instead of working through CVS commands, you should exercise extreme caution and have current backups when following these instructions.

Restructuring a project

Restructuring the project by moving files and directories around (and possibly renaming them) in the repository will allow the files to retain their history. The standard way to rename a file when using CVS is to rename the file in the sandbox and do a **cvs remove** on the old name and a **cvs add** on the new name. This results in the file being disconnected from its history under the new name, so sometimes it is better to do the renaming directly in the repository. However, doing this while people have active sandboxes is dangerous, as the sandboxes will contain information about a file that is no longer in the repository.

Obsolete and temporary files

When importing an entire project, all of the project's files will be added to the repository; however, if some of these files shouldn't have been added, you'll want to remove them. Doing a **cvs remove** will accomplish this, but copies of those files will remain in the repository's *.Attic* directory forever. To avoid this, you can delete the files from the repository directly before checking out sandboxes from it.

Importing

If you have an existing code base, you'll want to import it into CVS in a way that preserves the most historical information. This section provides instructions for importing projects into CVS from code snapshots or other version control systems. Except for the code snapshot import procedure, all of these are based upon conversion to RCS files, followed by placing the RCS files in the proper location in the CVS repository.

Importing code snapshots

If you have maintained project history archives manually by taking periodic snapshots of the code, you can import the first snapshot, tag it with the date or version number, and then successively overlay the updated files from later archives. Each set can then be committed and tagged in order to bootstrap a repository that maintains the prior history.

For example, first unpack the distributions (this assumes they unpack to directories containing the version numbers):

```
$ tar xvzf foo-1.0.tar.gz
$ tar xvzf foo-1.1.tar.gz
$ tar xvzf foo-2.0.tar.gz
```

Next, make a copy of the first version, import it into the CVS repository, check it out to make a sandbox (since importing doesn't convert the source directory into a sandbox), and use **cvs tag** to give it a symbolic name reflecting the project version:

```
$ mkdir foo
$ cp -R -p foo-1.0/* foo
$ cd foo
$ cvs import -m 'Imported version 1.0' foo vendor start
$ cd ..
$ mv foo foo.bak
$ cvs checkout foo
$ cd foo
$ cvs tag foo-1_0
$ cd ..
```

Now, apply the differences between Version 1.0 and 1.1 to the sandbox, commit the changes, and create a tag:

```
$ diff -Naur foo-1.0 foo-1.1 | (cd foo; patch -Np1)
$ cd foo
$ cvs commit -m 'Imported version 1.1'
$ cvs tag foo-1_1
$ cd ..
```

Apply the differences between Version 1.1 and 2.0 to the sandbox, commit the changes, and create a tag:

```
$ diff -Naur foo-1.1 foo-2.0 | (cd foo; patch -Np1)
$ cd foo
$ cvs commit -m 'Imported version 2.0'
$ cvs tag foo-2_0
```

You can now use the **log** command to view the history of the files, browse past versions of the files, and continue development under version control.

Importing from RCS

If you are migrating from RCS to CVS, following these instructions will result in a usable CVS repository. This procedure involves direct modification of the CVS repository, so it should be undertaken with caution.

Before beginning, make sure none of the files to be imported into CVS is locked by RCS. Then, create a new CVS repository and module (or a new module within an existing repository). Next, create directories in the CVS repository to mirror the project's directory structure. Finally, copy all the version files (,v) from the project (which may be in *RCS* subdirectories) into the appropriate directories in the repository (without *RCS* subdirectories).

For example, first move aside the directory under RCS control, create an empty directory to build the new CVS structure, import the directory, and then check it out to make a sandbox:

```
$ mv foo foo-rcs
$ mkdir foo
$ cd foo
$ cvs import -m 'New empty project' foo vendor start
$ cd ..
$ mv foo foo.bak
$ cvs checkout foo
```

Next, make directories and add them to the repository to match the structure in the RCS project:

```
$ cd foo
$ mkdir dir
$ cvs add dir
$ cd ..
```

Now, copy the *,v* files from the RCS project into the repository for the CVS project:

```
$ cp -p foo-rcs/*,v $CVSROOT/foo
$ cp -p foo-rcs/dir/*,v $CVSROOT/foo/dir
```

Finally, issue the **cvs update** command in the sandbox directory to bring in the latest versions of all the files:

```
$ cd foo
$ cvs upd
```

Importing from SCCS

To import from SCCS, use the *sccs2rcs* script located in the *contrib* directory of the CVS distribution to convert the files to RCS format, and then follow the preceding RCS procedure. You must have both CVS and SCCS installed for this to work. The script's comments contain additional instructions.

Importing from PVCS

To import from PVCS, use the *pvcs_to_rcs* script located in the *contrib* directory of the CVS distribution to convert the files to RCS format, and then follow the preceding RCS procedure. You must have both CVS and PVCS installed for this to work. The script's comments contain additional instructions.

Using an Interim Shared Sandbox

Projects will sometimes develop unintended environmental dependencies over time, especially when there is no pressure for the code to be relocatable. A project developed outside version control may even be initially developed in place (at its intended installation location). While these practices are not recommended, they do occur in real-world situations. CVS can help to improve the situation by encouraging relocatability from the beginning of a project.

The default mode of operation for CVS is multiple independent sandboxes, all coordinated with a central shared repository. Code that runs in this environment is necessarily (at least partially) relocatable. So, using CVS from the beginning of a project helps ensure flexibility.

However, if a project is already well underway, an interim approach can be used. For example, you could convert the development area to a single shared sandbox by importing the code into CVS and checking it back out again:

```
$ cd /usr/local/bar
$ cvs import bar vendor start
$ cd ..
$ mv bar bar.bak
$ cvs checkout bar
```

Chances are good that this approach is too aggressive and will check in more files than absolutely necessary. You can either go back and hack the repository to remove the files that shouldn't be there, or just issue the **cvs remove** command to delete them as you discover them.

In addition, there will probably be some binary files in the sandbox that were imported as text files. Wherever you see a binary file that needs to remain in the repository, you should issue the command **cvs admin -kb** *file*, then make a fresh copy from the project backup. Finally, issue the command **cvs commit** *file* to commit the fixed file back to the repository.

Having version control in place before making flexibility enhancements is a good idea, as it makes it easier to find (and possibly reverse) changes that cause trouble.

The repository locator (see "Repository Locators") is specified via the **-d** option or the **$CVSROOT** environment variable. It is stored in the various *CVS/root* sandbox files. If you are using the password server (**pserver**), the user ID of the person checking out the sandbox will be remembered. If more than one person is working with a particular sandbox, they will have to share an account for CVS access.

One way to do this is to have a neutral user account with a password known by everyone with CVS access. One person then issues the **cvs login** command with that user ID and password. Once you are no longer using a shared sandbox, this workaround won't be necessary. However, during the time you are using a shared sandbox, it is important that the developers type their real user IDs into their log messages, since all the changes will appear to have been made by the common user.

Global Server Option

The server has one global option: **--allow-root**=*rootdir*. This option is used to tell the CVS server to accept and process requests for the specified repository.

Administrator Commands

Table 15-8 lists the commands that CVS administrators can use to manage their repositories.

Table 15-8. Administrator commands

Command	Description
admin adm rcs	Perform administrative functions.
init	Create a new repository.
kserver	Run in Kerberos server mode.
pserver	Run in password server mode.
server	Run in remote server mode.

admin

```
admin
  [ -b[rev] ]
  [ -cstring ]
  [ -kkflag ]
  [ -l[rev] ]
  [ -L ]
  [ -mrev:msg ]
  [ -nname[:[rev]] ]
  [ -Nname[:[rev]] ]
  [ -orange ]
  [ -q ]
  [ -sstate[:rev] ]
  [ -t[file] ]
  [ -t-string ]
  [ -u[rev] ]
  [ -U ]
  [ files ... ]
```

The **admin** command is used to perform administrative functions. If a **cvsadmin** user group exists, then only the users in that group will be able to run **admin** with options other than -k. Options that may be used with the **admin** command are listed here.

-b[*rev*]
  Set the default branch.

-cstring
  Obsolete. Set the comment leader.

-kkflag
  Set the default keyword substitution mode.

-l[*rev*]
  Lock the specified revision.

-L Enable strict locking.

-m*rev:msg*
  Change the revision's log message.

-n*name*[:[*rev*]]
  Give the specified branch or revision the symbolic name *name*.

-N*name*[:[*rev*]]
  The same as **-n**, except that if *name* is already in use, it is moved.

-orange
  Delete revisions permanently.

-q Don't print diagnostics.

-sstate[:*rev*]
  Change the state of a revision.

-t[*file*]
  Set the descriptive text in the RCS file.

-t-*string*
  Set the descriptive text in the RCS file to *string*.

-u[*rev*]
  Unlock the specified revision.

-U Disable strict locking.

If the revision specified for **-l** is a branch, the latest revision on that branch will be used. If no revision is given, the latest revision on the default branch is used.

If the name given for **-n** is already in use, an error is generated. You can use **-N** to move a tag (change the revision associated with the tag); however, you should normally use **cvs tag** or **cvs rtag** instead.

The **-o** option is very dangerous and results in a permanent loss of information from the repository. Use it with extreme caution and only after careful consideration. See Table 15-9 for the various ways to specify ranges. There must not be any branches or locks on the revisions to be removed. Beware of interactions between this command and symbolic names.

If no *file* is specified for the **-t** option, CVS reads from standard input until it reaches the end of the file or a period on a line by itself.

The determination of the target revision for the **-u** option is the same as for **-l**.

Table 15-9. Range formats

Format	Description
rev1::rev2	Eliminate versions between *rev1* and *rev2*, retaining only enough information to go directly from *rev1* to *rev2*. The two specified versions are retained.
::rev2	The same as *rev1::rev2*, except the first revision is the branchpoint revision.
rev1::	The same as *rev1::rev2*, except the second revision is the end of the branch, and it is deleted instead of retained.
rev	Delete the specified revision.
rev1:rev2	The same as *rev1::rev2*, except the two named revisions are deleted as well.
:rev2	The same as *::rev2*, except the named revision is deleted as well.
rev1:	The same as *rev1::*, except the named revision is deleted as well.

The following options are present in CVS for historical reasons and should not be used. (Using these options may corrupt the repository.)

-a*logins*
> Append the logins to the RCS file's access list.

-A*oldfile*
> Append the access list of oldfile to the access list of the RCS file.

-e[*logins*]
> Erase logins from the RCS file's access list, or erase all if a list is not provided.

-i   Create and initialize a new RCS file. Don't use this option. Instead, use **add** to add files to a CVS repository.

-I   Run interactively. This option doesn't work with client/server CVS and is likely to be removed in a future version.

-V*n*
> This option specified that the RCS files used by CVS should be made compatible with a specific version of RCS.

-x*suffixes*
> This option used to be described as determining the filename suffix for RCS files, but CVS has always used only *,v* as the RCS file suffix.

---

init   init

Initializes the repository. Use the global **-d** option to specify the repository's directory if **$CVSROOT** isn't set appropriately.

The newly initialized repository will contain a *CVSROOT* module and nothing else. Once the repository is initialized, use other CVS commands to add files to it or to check out the *CVSROOT* module to make changes to the administrative files.

kserver   kserver

Operate as a server with Kerberos authentication, providing access to the repositories specified before the command with the --allow-root option. This command is used in the *inetd.conf* file, not on the command line. Another global option frequently used with this command is **-T** (see Table 15-1).

pserver   pserver

Operate as a password-authenticated server, providing access to the repositories specified before the command with the --allow-root option. This command is used in the *inetd.conf* file, not on the command line. Another global option frequently used with this command is -T (see Table 15-1).

server   server

The CVS client runs this command on the remote machine when connecting to a repository specified by an **:ext:** repository locator (usually via RSH or SSH).

CVS User Reference

This section provides details on connecting to a repository, the structure of sand-boxes, and using the CVS commands.

Repository Locators

CVS currently supports six methods for the client to access the repository: local, forked, external, a password server, a GSS-API (Generic Security Services API) server, and a Kerberos 4 server (most Kerberos users will want to use GSS-API). Table 15-10 describes the various repository locator types and their respective access methods.

Table 15-10. Repository access types and methods

Method	Locator format	Description
Local	*path* :**local**:*path*	If the repository directory is local to the computer from which you will access it (or appears local, such as an NFS or Samba mounted filesystem), the repository string is just the pathname of the repository directory, such as */usr/local/cvsrep*, or it can use the :**local**: prefix.
Forked local	:**fork**:*path*	This type of locator is used primarily for debugging the CVS protocol code, as it causes CVS to start (fork) a separate process to work with the repository and communicates with it using the CVS remote protocol.
External	:**ext**:*user@host:path*	External repositories are accessed via a remote shell utility, usually **rsh** (the default) or **ssh**. The environment variable $**CVS_RSH** is used to specify the remote shell program.

Table 15-10. Repository access types and methods (continued)

Method	Locator format	Description
Password server	:pserver:*user@host:path*	Password server repositories require authentication to a user account before allowing use of the repository. Public CVS servers are commonly configured this way so they can provide anonymous CVS access. See "The passwd file" earlier in this chapter for more information on anonymous CVS.
GSS-API server	:gserver:	This locator type is used for servers accessible via Kerberos 5 or other authentication mechanisms supported by GSS-API.
Kerberos server	:kserver:	This locator type is used for servers accessible via Kerberos 4.

Configuring CVS

CVS's behavior can be influenced by two classes of settings other than the command-line arguments: *environment variables* (see Table 15-11) and *special files* (see Table 15-12).

Table 15-11. Environment variables

Variable	Description
$CVS_CLIENT_LOG	Client-side debugging file specification for client/server connections. $CVS_CLIENT_LOG is the basename for the $CVS_CLIENT_LOG.in and $CVS_CLIENT_LOG.out files, which will be written in the current working directory at the time a command is executed.
$CVS_CLIENT_PORT	The port number for :kserver: locators. $CVS_CLIENT_PORT doesn't need to be set if the kserver is listening on port 1999 (the default).
$CVS_IGNORE_REMOTE_ROOT	According to the *change log*, this variable was removed from CVS with Version 1.10.3.
$CVS_PASSFILE	Password file for :pserver: locators. This variable must be set before issuing the cvs login to have the desired effect. Defaults to $HOME/.cvspass.
$CVS_RCMD_PORT	For non-Unix clients, the port for connecting to the server's rcmd daemon.
$CVS_RSH	Remote shell for :ext: locators, if not rsh.
$CVS_SERVER	Remote server program for :ext: locators, if not cvs.
$CVS_SERVER_SLEEP	Server-side execution delay (in seconds) to allow time to attach a debugger.
$CVSEDITOR	Editor used for log messages; overrides $EDITOR.
$CVSIGNORE	A list of filename patterns to ignore, separated by whitespace. (See also *cvsignore* in Table 15-4 and *.cvsignore* in Table 15-12.)
$CVSREAD	Determines read-only (if the variable is set) or read/write (if the variable is not set) for checkout and update.
$CVSROOT	Default repository locator.
$CVSUMASK	Used to determine permissions for (local) repository files.
$CVSWRAPPERS	A list of filename patterns for the cvswrappers function. See also "Repository Structure."
$EDITOR	Specifies the editor to use for log messages; see notes for $CVSEDITOR earlier in this table.
$HOME	On Unix, used to find the *.cvsrc* file.

Table 15-11. Environment variables (continued)

Variable	Description
$HOMEDRIVE	On Windows NT, used to find the *.cvsrc* file.
$HOMEPATH	On Windows NT, used to find the *.cvsrc* file.
$PATH	Used to locate programs to run.
$TEMP $TMP $TMPDIR	Location for temporary files. **$TMPDIR** is used by the server. On Unix, */tmp* (and TMP on Windows NT) may not be overridden for some functions of CVS due to reliance on the system's **tmpnam( )** function.
$VISUAL	Specifies the editor to use for log messages; see notes for **$CVSEDITOR** earlier in this table.

Despite the similarity in names, the **$CVSROOT** environment variable and the *CVSROOT* directory in a repository are not related to each other.

The "RSH" in the name of the **$CVS_RSH** environment variable doesn't refer to the particular program (**rsh**), but rather to the program CVS is supposed to use for creating remote shell connections (which could be some program other than **rsh**, such as **ssh**).

Because there is only one way to specify the remote shell program to use (**$CVS_RSH**) and because this is a global setting, users that commonly access multiple repositories may need to pay close attention to which repository they are using. If one repository requires one setting of this variable and another requires a different setting, you will have to change this variable between accesses to repositories requiring different settings. This aspect of the repository access method is not stored in the *CVS/Root* file in the sandbox (see "CVS directories," later in this chapter). For example, if you access some repositories via **rsh** and some via **ssh**, you can create the following two utility aliases (**bash** syntax):

```
$ alias cvs="export CVS_RSH=ssh; cvs"
$ alias cvr="export CVS_RSH=rsh; cvs"
```

Table 15-12 shows the files used by the CVS command-line client for server connection and client configuration information. These files reside in the user's home directory.

Table 15-12. Client configuration files

Option	Description
~/.cvsignore	Filename patterns of files to ignore.
~/.cvspass	Passwords cached by **cvs login**.
~/.cvsrc	Default command options.
~/.cvswrappers	User-specific **checkout** and **commit** filters.

The *~/.cvspass* file is really an operational file, not a configuration file. It is used by the **cvs** client program to store the repository user account password between **cvs login** and **cvs logoff**.

Some common *.cvsrc* settings are:

update -dP
> Bring in new directories and prune empty directories on **cvs update**.

diff -c
> Give output in context **diff** format.

Creating a Sandbox

In order to use CVS, you must create a sandbox or have one created for you. This section describes sandbox creation, assuming there is already a module in the repository you want to work with. See the **import** command for information on importing a new module into the repository.

1. Determine the repository locator. Talk to the repository administrator if you need help finding the repository or getting the locator syntax right.

2. If this will be your main repository, set **$CVSROOT**; otherwise, use the **-d** option when running CVS commands that don't infer the repository from the sandbox files.

3. Pick a module to check out.

4. Pick a sandbox location, and **cd** to the parent directory.

5. If the repository requires login, do **cvs login**.

6. Run **cvs checkout** *module*.

For example:

```
$ export CVSROOT=/usr/local/cvsroot
$ cd ~/work
$ cvs checkout hello
```

Sandbox Structure

This section describes the files and directories that may be encountered in sandboxes.

.cvsignore files

Sandboxes may contain *.cvsignore* files. These files specify filename patterns for files that may exist in the sandbox but that normally won't be checked into CVS. This is commonly used to cause CVS to bypass derived files.

.cvswrappers files

Sandboxes may contain *.cvswrappers* files, which provide directory-specific file handling information like that in the repository configuration file *cvswrappers* (see "The cvswrappers file" earlier in this chapter).

CVS directories

Each directory in a sandbox contains a *CVS* directory. The files in this directory (see Table 15-13) contain metadata used by CVS to locate the repository and track which file versions have been copied into the sandbox.

Table 15-13. Files in the CVS directories

File	Description
Base *Baserev* *Baserev.tmp*	The *Base* directory stores copies of files when the **edit** command is in use. The *Baserev* file contains the revision numbers of the files in *Base*. The *Baserev.tmp* file is used in updating the *Baserev* file.
Checkin.prog *Update.prog*	The programs specified in the *modules* file for options **-i** and **-u**, respectively (if any).
Entries	Version numbers and timestamps for the files as they were copied from the repository when checked out or updated.
Entries.Backup *Entries.Log* *Entries.Static*	Temporary and intermediate files used by CVS.
Notify *Notify.tmp*	Temporary files used by CVS for dealing with notifications for commands such as **edit** and **unedit**.
Repository	The name by which the directory is known in the repository.
Root	The repository locator in effect when the sandbox was created (via **cvs checkout**).
Tag	Information about sticky tags and dates for files in the directory.
Template	Used to store the contents of the *rcsinfo* administrative file from the repository for remote repositories.

Since each sandbox directory has one *CVS/Root* file, a sandbox directory corresponds to exactly one repository. You cannot check out some files from one repository and some from another into a single sandbox directory.

Client Global Options

Table 15-14 lists the global options that control the operation of the CVS client program.

Table 15-14. Client global options

Option	Description
-a	Authenticate (**gserver** only).
-d *root*	Locate the repository. Overrides the setting of **$CVSROOT**.
-e *editor*	Specify message editor. Overrides the settings of **$CVSEDITOR** and **$EDITOR**.
-f	Don't read *~/.cvsrc*. Useful when you have *.cvsrc* settings that you want to forgo for a particular command.
-H [*command*] **--help** [*command*]	Display help. If no command is specified, displays general CVS help, including a list of other help options.
-l	Don't log command in history.
-n	Don't change any files. Useful when you want to know ahead of time which files will be affected by a particular command.

Table 15-14. Client global options (continued)

Option	Description
-q	Be quiet.
-Q	Be very quiet. Print messages for serious problems only.
-r	Make new working files read-only.
-s *variable=value*	Set the value of a user variable to a given value. User variables can be used in the contents of administrative files.
-t	Trace execution. Helpful in debugging remote repository connection problems and, in conjunction with -n, in determining the effect of an unfamiliar command.
-w	Make new working files read/write. Overrides $CVSREAD. Files are read/write unless $CVSREAD is set or -r is specified.
-x	Encrypt. (Introduced in Version 1.10.)
-z *gzip_level*	Set the compression level. Useful when using CVS in client/server mode across slow connections.

Common Client Options

Tables 15-15 and 15-16 describe the options that are common to many CVS commands. Table 15-15 lists the common options with a description of their function, while Table 15-16 lists which options can be used with the user commands. In the sections that follow, details are provided only for options that are not listed here or that do not function as described here.

Table 15-15. Common options

Option	Description
-D *date*	Use the most recent revision no later than *date* (see "Date formats" for supported date formats).
-f	For commands that involve tags (via -r) or dates (via -D), include files not tagged with the specified tag or not present on the specified date. The most recent revision will be included.
-k *kflag*	Determine how keyword substitution will be performed. The space between -k and *kflag* is optional. See Table 15-17 for the list of keyword substitution modes.
-l	Do not recurse into subdirectories.
-n	Don't run module programs.
-R	Do recurse into subdirectories (the default). As of Version 1.11, CVS can work in sandboxes with directories checked out from different repositories.
-r *rev*	Use a particular revision number or symbolic tag.

Table 15-16 shows which common options are applicable to each user command.

Table 15-16. Common client option applicability

Command	-D	-f	-k	-l	-n	-R	-r
add			✓				
annotate	✓	✓		✓		✓	✓
checkout	✓	✓	✓	✓	✓	✓	✓
commit				✓	✓	✓	✓
diff	✓			✓	✓		✓	✓

Table 15-16. *Common client option applicability (continued)*

Command	-D	-f	-k	-l	-n	-R	-r
edit				✓		✓	
editors				✓		✓	
export	✓	✓	✓	✓	✓	✓	✓
help							
history	✓						✓
import			✓				
log				✓		✓	
login							
logout							
rannotate	✓	✓		✓		✓	✓
rdiff	✓	✓		✓		✓	✓
release							
remove				✓		✓	
rlog				✓		✓	
rtag	✓	✓		✓		✓	✓
status				✓		✓	
tag				✓		✓	
unedit				✓		✓	
update	✓	✓	✓	✓		✓	✓
version							
watch				✓		✓	
watchers				✓		✓	

Date formats

CVS can understand dates in a wide variety of formats, including:

ISO standard
> The preferred format is *YYYY-MM-DD HH:MM*, which would read as **2000-05-17**, or **2000-05-17 22:00**. The technical details of the format are defined in the ISO 8601 standard.

Email standard
> **17 May 2000**. The technical details of the format are defined in the RFC 822 and RFC 1123 standards.

Relative
> **10 days ago, 4 years ago**.

Common
> *month/day/year*. This form can cause confusion because not all cultures use the first two fields in this order (**1/2/2000** would be ambiguous).

Other
> Other formats are accepted, including *YYYY/MM/DD* and those omitting the year (which is assumed to be the current year).

CVS

Keyword substitutions

Table 15-17 describes the keyword substitution modes that can be selected with the **-k** option. CVS uses keyword substitutions to insert revision information into files when they are checked out or updated.

Table 15-17. Keyword substitution modes

Mode	Description
b	Binary mode. Treat the file the same as with mode **o**, but also avoid newline conversion.
k	Keyword-only mode. Flatten all keywords to just the keyword name. Use this mode if you want to compare two revisions of a file without seeing the keyword substitution differences.
kv	Keyword-value mode. The keyword and the corresponding value are substituted. This is the default mode.
kvl	Keyword-value-locker mode. This mode is the same as **kv** mode, except it always adds the lock holder's user ID if the revision is locked. The lock is obtained via the **cvs admin -l** command.
o	Old-contents mode. Use the keyword values as they appear in the repository rather than generate new values.
v	Value-only mode. Substitute the value of each keyword for the entire keyword field, omitting even the $ delimiters. This mode destroys the field in the process, so use it cautiously.

Keyword substitution fields are strings of the form $*Keyword* ...$. The valid keywords are:

Author
> The user ID of the person who committed the revision.

Date
> The date and time (in standard UTC format) the revision was committed.

Header
> The full path of the repository RCS file, the revision number, the commit date, time, and user ID, the file's state, and the lock holder's user ID if the file is locked.

Id
> A shorter form of **Header**, omitting the leading directory name(s) from the RCS file's path, leaving only the filename.

Name
> The tag name used to retrieve the file, or empty if no explicit tag was given when the file was retrieved.

Locker
> The user ID of the user holding a lock on the file, or empty if the file is not locked.

Log
> The RCS filename. In addition to keyword expansion in the keyword field, each commit adds additional lines in the file immediately following the line containing this keyword. The first such line contains the revision number and the commit date, time, and user ID. Subsequent lines are the contents of the commit log message. The result over time is a reverse-chronological list of log entries for the file. Each of the additional lines is preceded by the same

characters that precede the keyword field on its line. This allows the log information to be formatted in a comment for most languages. For example:

```
#
# foo.pl
#
# $Log: ch15,v $
#
# Revision 1.2  2000/06/09 22:10:23  me
# Fixed the new bug introduced when the last one was fixed.
#
# Revision 1.1  2000/06/09 18:07:51  me
# Fixed the last remaining bug in the system.
#
```

Be sure that you don't place any keyword fields in your log messages if you use this keyword, since they will get expanded if you do.

RCSfile

The name of the RCS file (without any leading directories).

Revision

The revision number of the file.

Source

The full path of the RCS file.

State

The file's state, as assigned by **cvs admin -s** (if you don't set the state explicitly, it will be **Exp** by default).

User Commands

The CVS client program provides the user commands defined in Table 15-18.

Table 15-18. User commands

Command	Description
ad add new	Indicate that files/directories should be added to the repository.
ann annotate	Display contents of the head revision of a file, annotated with the revision number, user, and date of the last change for each line.
checkout co get	Create a sandbox for a module.
ci com commit	Commit changes from the sandbox back to the repository.
di dif diff	View differences between file versions.
edit	Prepare to edit files. This is used for enhanced developer coordination.
editors	Display a list of users working on the files. This is used for enhanced developer coordination.

Table 15-18. User commands (continued)

Command	Description
ex exp export	Retrieve a module, but don't make the result a sandbox.
help	Get help.
hi his history	Display the log information for files.
im imp import	Import new modules into the repository.
lgn login logon	Log into (cache the password for) a remote CVS server.
lo log	Show the activity log for the file(s).
logout	Log off from (flush the password for) a remote CVS server.
pa patch rdiff	Release **diff**. The output is the format of input to Larry Wall's **patch** command. Does not have to be run from within a sandbox.
rannotate	Display contents of the head revision of a module, annotated with the revision number, user, and date of the last change for each line.
re rel release	Perform a logged delete on a sandbox.
rlog	Show the activity log for the module(s).
remove rm delete	Remove a file or directory from the repository.
rt rtag rfreeze	Tag a particular revision.
st stat status	Show detailed status for files.
ta tag freeze	Attach a tag to files in the repository.
unedit	Abandon file modifications and make read-only again.
up upd update	Synchronize sandbox to repository.
version	Display the version of the CVS client (and server, if appropriate) being used.
watch	Manage the watch settings. This is used for enhanced developer coordination.
watchers	Display the list of users watching for changes to the files. This is used for enhanced developer coordination.

add

```
add
  [ -k kflag ]
  [ -m message ]
  file ...
```

Indicate that files/directories should be added to the repository. They are not actually added until they are committed via **cvs commit**. This command is also used to resurrect files that have been deleted with **cvs remove**.

The standard meaning of the common client option **-k** applies. The only additional option that can be used with the **add** command is **-m** *message*. This option is used to provide a description of the file (which appears in the output of the **log** command).

annotate

```
annotate
  [ [ -D date | -r rev ] -f ]
  [ -F ]
  [ -l | -R ]
  file ...
```

CVS prints a report showing each line of the specified file. Each line is prefixed by information about the most recent change to the line, including the revision number, user, and date. If no revision is specified, the head of the trunk is used.

The standard meanings of the common client options **-D**, **-f**, **-l**, **-r**, and **-R** apply. There is one additional option:

-F   Annotate binary files. CVS normally skips binary files.

checkout

```
checkout
  [ -A ]
  [ -c | -s ]
  [ -d dir [ -N ] ]
  [ [ -D date | -r rev ] -f ]
  [ -j rev1 [ -j rev2 ] ]
  [ -k kflag ]
  [ -l | -R ]
  [ -n ]
  [ -p ]
  [ -P ]
  module ...
```

Copy files from the repository to the sandbox.

The standard meanings of the common client options **-D**, **-f**, **-k**, **-l**, **-n**, **-r**, and **-R** apply. Additional options are:

-A   Reset any sticky tags or dates.

-c   Copy the *module* file to standard output.

-d *dir*
    Override the default directory name.

-j *rev*
    Join branches together.

-N Don't shorten module paths.

-p Pipe the files to standard output, with header lines between them showing the filename, RCS filename, and version.

-P Prune empty directories.

-s Show status for each module from the *modules* file.

commit

```
commit
  [ -f | [ -l | -R ] ]
  [ -F file | -m message ]
  [ -n ]
  [ -r revision ]
  [ file ... ]
```

Commit the changes (if any) made to the specified files in the sandbox to the repository. If no files are specified, commit all modified files.

The standard meanings of the common client options **-l**, **-n**, **-r**, and **-R** apply. Use of the **-r** option causes the revision to be sticky, requiring the use of **admin -A** to continue to use the sandbox. Additional options are:

-f Force commit, even if no changes were made.

-F *file*

Use the contents of the file as the message.

-m *message*

Use the message specified.

diff

```
diff
  [ -k kflag ]
  [ -l | -R ]
  [ format ]
  [ [ -r rev1 | -D date1 ] [ -r rev2 | -D date2 ] ]
  [ file ... ]
```

Compare two versions of a file and display the differences in a format determined by the options. By default, the sandbox version of the file is compared to the repository version it was originally copied from.

The standard meanings of the common client options **-D**, **-k**, **-l**, **-r**, and **-R** apply. All options for the **diff** command can also be used.

edit

```
edit
  [ -a action ]
  [ -l | -R ]
  [ file ... ]
```

The **edit** command is used in conjunction with **watch** to permit a more coordinated (serialized) development process. It makes the file writable and sends out an advisory to any users that have requested them. A temporary **watch** is established and will be removed automatically when either the **unedit** or the **commit** command is issued.

The standard meanings of the common client options **-l** and **-R** apply. The only additional option that can be used with the **edit** command is **-a** *actions*. This option is used to specify the actions to watch. The legal values for actions are described in the entry for the **watch** command.

editors

```
editors
  [ -l | -R ]
  [ file ... ]
```

Display a list of users working on the files specified. This is determined by checking which users have run the **edit** command on those files. If the **edit** command has not been used, no results are displayed.

The standard meanings of the common client options **-l** and **-R** apply.

See also **watch**.

export

```
export
  [ -d dir [ -N ] ]
  [ -D date | -r rev ]
  [ -f ]
  [ -k kflag ]
  [ -l | -R ]
  [ -n ]
  [ -P ]
  module ...
```

Export files from the repository, much like the **checkout** command, except that the result is not a sandbox (i.e., *CVS* subdirectories are not created). This can be used to prepare a directory for distribution. For example:

```
$ cvs export -r foo-1_0 -d foo-1.0 foo
$ tar czf foo-1.0.tar.gz foo-1.0
```

The standard meanings of the common client options **-D**, **-f**, **-k**, **-l**, **-n**, **-r**, and **-R** apply. Additional options are:

-d *dir*

Use *dir* as the directory name instead of using the module name.

-n   Don't run any checkout programs.

-N   Don't shorten paths.

When checking out a single file located one or more directories down in a module's directory structure, the **-N** option can be used with **-d** to prevent the creation of intermediate directories.

help

```
help
```

Display helpful information about using the **cvs** program.

```
history
  [ -a | -u user ]
  [ -b string ]
  [ -c ]
  [ -D date ]
  [ -e | -x type ]
  [ -f file | -m module | -n module | -p repository ]...
  [ -l ]
  [ -o ]
  [ -r rev ]
  [ -t tag ]
  [ -T ]
  [ -w ]
  [ -x types ]
  [ -z zone ]
  [ file ... ]
```

Display historical information. To use the **history** command, you must first set up the *history* file in the repository. See "Repository Structure" for more information on this file.

When used with the **history** command, the functions of **-f**, **-l**, **-n**, and **-p** are not the same as elsewhere in CVS.

The standard meanings of the common client options **-D** and **-r** apply. History is reported for activity subsequent to the date or revision indicated. Additional options are:

-a   Show history for all users (default is current user).

-b *str*

Show history back to the first record containing *str* in the module name, filename, or repository path.

-c   Report each **commit**.

-e   Report everything.

-f *file*

Show the most recent event for *file*.

-l   Show last event only.

-m *module*

Produce a full report on *module*.

-n *module*

Report the last event for *module*.

-o   Report on modules that have been checked out.

-p *repository*

Show history for a particular repository directory.

-t *tag*

Show history since *tag* was last added to the history file.

-T   Report on all tags.

-u *name*

Show history for a particular user.

-w Show history only for the current working directory.

-x *types*

Report on specific types of activity. See Table 15-19.

-z *zone*

Display times according to the specified time zone.

The **-p** option should limit the **history** report to entries for the directory or directories (if multiple **-p** options are specified) given, but as of Version 1.10.8, it doesn't seem to affect the output. For example, to report history for the **CVSROOT** and **hello** modules, run the command:

```
cvs history -p CVSROOT -p hello
```

Using **-t** is faster than using **-r** because it only needs to search through the history file, not all of the RCS files.

The record types shown in Table 15-19 are generated by **update** commands.

Table 15-19. Update-related history record types

Type	Description
C	Merge was necessary, but conflicts requiring manual intervention occurred.
G	Successful automatic merge.
U	Working file copied from repository.
W	Working copy deleted.

The record types shown in Table 15-20 are generated by **commit** commands.

Table 15-20. Commit-related history record types

Type	Description
A	Added for the first time
M	Modified
R	Removed

Each of the record types shown in Table 15-21 is generated by a different command.

Table 15-21. Other history record types

Type	Command
E	export
F	release
O	checkout
T	rtag

import

```
import
  [ -b branch ]
  [ -d ]
  [ -I pattern ]
  [ -k kflag ]
  [ -m message ]
  [ -W spec ]
  module
  vendor_tag
  release_tag ...
```

Import an entire directory into the repository as a new module. Used to incorporate code from outside sources or other code that was initially created outside the control of the CVS repository. More than one *release_tag* may be specified, in which case multiple symbolic tags will be created for the initial revision.

The *vendor_tag* argument is used to track third-party code that may be used in your project. By using different values for this argument, you can track the third-party code separately, and upgrade that portion of your code to a new release with a subsequent **cvs import** command. Since the argument is not optional, use some conventional value such as "vendor" whenever the code being imported should not be tracked separately.

The *release_tag* argument is used to associate a symbolic tag with the initial version of every file being imported. Since this argument is not optional, use some conventional value such as "start" whenever you don't have a more meaningful value to provide.

The standard meaning of the common client option **-k** applies. Additional options are:

-b *branch*
> Import to a vendor branch.

-d Use the modification date and time of the file instead of the current date and time as the import date and time. For local repository locators only.

-I *pattern*
> Filename patterns for files to ignore.

-m *message*
> Use *message* as the log message instead of invoking the editor.

-W *spec*
> Wrapper specification.

The **-k** setting applies only to files imported during this execution of the command. The keyword substitution modes of files already in the repository are not modified.

When used with **-W**, the *spec* variable is in the same format as entries in the *cvswrappers* administrative file (see "The cvswrappers file").

Table 15-22 describes the status codes displayed by the **import** command.

Table 15-22. import status codes

Status	Description
C	Changed. The file is in the repository, and the sandbox version is different; a merge is required.
I	Ignored. The *.cvsignore* file is causing CVS to ignore the file.
L	Link. Symbolic links are ignored by CVS.
N	New. The file is new; it has been added to the repository.
U	Update. The file is in the repository, and the sandbox version is not different.

log

```
log
  [ -b ]
  [ -d dates ]
  [ -h ]
  [ -N ]
  [ -rrevisions ]
  [ -R ]
  [ -s states ]
  [ -t ]
  [ -wlogins ]
  [ file ... ]
```

Print an activity log for the files.

The standard meaning of the common client option **-l** applies. Additional options are:

-b List revisions on default branch.

-d *dates*
> Report on these dates.

-h Print header only.

-N Don't print tags.

-r[*revisions*]
> Report on the listed revisions. There is no space between **-r** and its argument. Without an argument, the latest revision of the default branch is used.

-R Print RCS filename only. The usage of **-R** here is different from elsewhere in CVS (**-R** usually causes CVS to operate recursively).

-s *states*
> Print only those revisions having one of the specified states.

-S Don't print the header if the output would otherwise be empty.

-t Print only header and descriptive text.

-w*logins*
> Report on checkins by the listed logins. There is no space between **-w** and its argument.

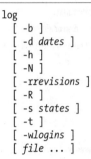

For **-d**, use the date specifications in Table 15-23. Multiple specifications separated by semicolons may be provided. For **-s**, separate
multiple states with commas.

Table 15-23. log date range specifications

Specification	Description
d1<d2 or *d2>d1*	The revisions dated between *d1* and *d2*, exclusive
d1<=d2 or *d2>=d1*	The revisions dated between *d1* and *d2*, inclusive
<d or *d>*	The revisions dated before *d*
<=d or *d>=*	The revisions dated on or before *d*
d< or *>d*	The revisions dated after *d*
d<= or *>=d*	The revisions dated on or after *d*
d	The most recent revision dated *d* or earlier

For **-r**, use the revision specifications in Table 15-24.

Table 15-24. log revision specifications

Specification	Description
rev1: rev2	The revisions between *rev1* and *rev2*, inclusive.
:rev	The revisions from the beginning of the branch to *rev*, inclusive.
rev:	The revisions from *rev* to the end of the branch, inclusive.
branch	All revisions on the branch.
branch1: branch2	All revisions on all branches between *branch1* and *branch2*, inclusive.
branch.	The latest revision on the branch.

For *rev1:rev2*, it is an error if the revisions are not on the same
branch.

login

```
login
```

Log into a remote repository. The password entered will be cached
in the *~/.cvspass* file, since a connection to the server is not maintained across invocations.

logout

```
logout
```

Log out of a remote repository. The password cached in the *~/.cvspass*
file will be deleted.

rannotate

```
rannotate
    [ [ -D date | -r rev ] -f ]
    [ -F ]
    [ -l | -R ]
    module ...
```

CVS prints a report showing each line of the specified module or
module file. Each line is prefixed by information about the most

recent change to the line, including the revision number, user, and date. If no revision is specified, the head of the trunk is used.

The **rannotate** command differs from the **annotate** command in that it refers directly to modules (and their files) in the repository rather than inferring the module based on the sandbox from which it is run. The first path component of each *module* argument must be a valid module for the repository.

The standard meanings of the common client options -**D**, -**f**, -**l**, -**r**, and -**R** apply. There is one additonal option:

-**F**   Annotate binary files. CVS normally skips binary files.

---

rdiff

```
rdiff
  [ -c | -s | -u ]
  [ { { -D date1 | -r rev1 } [ -D date2 | -r rev2 ] } | -t ]
  [ -f ]
  [ -l | -R ]
  [-V vn]
  file ...
```

Create a **patch** file that can be used to convert a directory containing one release into a different release.

The standard meanings of the common client options -**D**, -**f**, -**l**, -**r**, and -**R** apply. Additional options are:

-**c**   Use **context diff** format (the default).

-**s**   Output a summary of changed files instead of a **patch** file.

-**t**   Show the differences between the two most recent revisions.

-**u**   Use **unidiff** format.

-**V** *rcsver*

Obsolete. Used to specify version of RCS to emulate for keyword expansion. (Keyword expansion emulates RCS Version 5.)

---

release

```
release
  [ -d ]
  directory ...
```

Sandboxes can be abandoned or deleted without using **cvs release**, but using the **release** command will log an entry to the history file (if this mechanism is configured) about the sandbox being destroyed. In addition, it will check the disposition (recursively) of each sandbox file before deleting anything. This can prevent destroying work that has not yet been committed.

There is only one option that can be used with the **release** command, -**d**. The -**d** option will delete the sandbox copy if no uncommitted changes are present.

New directories (including any files in them) in the sandbox will be deleted if the -**d** option is used with **release**.

The status codes listed in Table 15-25 are used to describe the disposition of each file encountered in the repository and the sandbox.

Table 15-25. release status Codes

Status	Description
A	The sandbox file has been added (the file was created and **cvs add** was run), but the addition has not been committed.
M	The sandbox copy of the file has been modified.
P U	Update available. There is a newer version of the file in the repository, and the copy in the sandbox has not been modified.
R	The sandbox copy was removed (the file was deleted and **cvs remove** was run), but the removal was not committed.
?	The file is present in the sandbox but not in the repository.

remove

```
remove
  [ -f ]
  [ -l | -R ]
  [ file ... ]
```

Indicate that files should be removed from the repository. The files will not actually be removed until they are committed. Use **cvs add** to resurrect files that have been removed if you change your mind later.

The standard meanings of the common client options -l and -R apply. Only one other option may be used with the **remove** command, -f. When used, -f will delete the file from the sandbox first.

rlog

```
rlog
  [ -b ]
  [ -d dates ]
  [ -h ]
  [ -N ]
  [ -rrevisions ]
  [ -R ]
  [ -s state ]
  [ -t ]
  [ -wlogins ]
  [ module ... ]
```

Print an activity log for the modules.

The standard meaning of the common client option -l applies. Additional options are:

-b   List revisions on default branch.

-d *dates*
     Report on these dates.

-h   Print header only.

-N Don't print tags.

-r[*revisions*]
Report on the listed revisions. There is no space between **-r** and its argument. Without an argument, the latest revision of the default branch is used.

-R Print RCS filename only. The usage of **-R** here is different from elsewhere in CVS (**-R** usually causes CVS to operate recursively).

-s *state*
Print only those revisions having the specified state.

-t Print only header and descriptive text.

-w*logins*
Report on checkins by the listed logins. There is no space between **-w** and its argument.

For **-d**, use the date specifications in Table 15-23. Multiple specifications separated by semicolons may be provided.

For **-r**, use the revision specifications in Table 15-24.

---

rtag

```
rtag
  [ -a ]
  [ -b ]
  [ -B ]
  [ -d ]
  [ -D date | -r rev ]
  [ -f ]
  [ -F ]
  [ -l | - R ]
  [ -n ]
  tag
  file ...
```

Assign a tag to a particular revision of a set of files. If the file already uses the tag for a different revision, **cvs rtag** will complain unless the **-F** option is used. This command does not refer to the sandbox file revisions (use **cvs tag** for that), so it can be run outside of a sandbox if desired.

The standard meanings of the common client options **-D**, **-f**, **-l**, **-r**, and **-R** apply. Additional options are:

-a Search the attic for removed files containing the tag.

-b Make it a branch tag.

-B Allow movement or deletion of branch tags (used with **-d** or **-F**.)

-d Delete the tag.

-F Force. Move the tag from its current revision to the one specified.

-n Don't run any tag program from the modules file.

status   status
                        [-l | -R]
                        [-v]
                        [*file* ...]

Display the status of the files.

The standard meanings of the common client options -l and -R apply. You can use **status -v** to include tag information.

---

tag   tag
                        [-b]
                        [-c]
                        [-d]
                        [-D *date* | -r *rev*]
                        [-f]
                        [-F]
                        [-l | R]
                        tag
                        [*file* ...]

Assign a tag to the sandbox revisions of a set of files. You can use the **status -v** command to list the existing tags for a file.

The *tag* must start with a letter and consist entirely of letters, numbers, dashes, and underscores. Therefore, while you might want to tag your *hello* project with **1.0** when you release Version 1.0, you'll need to tag it with something like **hello-1_0** instead.

The standard meanings of the common client options -D, -f, -l, -r, and -R apply. Additional options are:

-b   Make a branch.

-c   Check for changes. Make sure the files are not locally modified before tagging.

-d   Delete the tag.

-F   Force. Move the tag from its current revision to the one specified.

Since the **-d** option throws away information that might be important, it is recommended that you use it only when absolutely necessary. It is usually better to create a different tag with a similar name.

---

unedit   unedit
                        [-l | -R]
                        [*file* ...]

Abandon file modifications and make the file read-only again. Watchers will be notified.

The standard meanings of the common client options -l and -R apply.

update
  [-A]
  [-C]
  [-d]
  [-D *date* | -r *rev*]
  [-f]
  [-I *pattern*]
  [-j *rev1* [-j *rev2*]]
  [-k *kflag*]
  [-l | -R]
  [-p]
  [-P]
  [-W *spec*]
  [*file* ...]

Update the sandbox, merging in any changes from the repository. For example:

cvs -n -q update -AdP

can be used to do a quick status check of the current sandbox versus the head of the trunk of development.

The standard meanings of the common client options **-D**, **-f**, **-k**, **-l**, **-r**, and **-R** apply. Additional options are:

-A Reset sticky tags.

-C Replace modified files with clean copies.

-d Create and update new directories.

-I *pattern*
    Provide filename patterns for files to ignore.

-j *revision*
    Merge in (join) changes between two revisions.

-p Check out files to standard output.

-P Prune empty directories.

-W *spec*
    Provide wrapper specification.

When using **-C**, CVS makes backups of modified files before copying the clean version. The backup files are named *.#file. revision*.

Using **-D** or **-r** results in sticky dates or tags, respectively, on the affected files (using **-p** along with these prevents stickiness). Use **-A** to reset any sticky tags or dates.

If two **-j** specifications are made, the differences between them are computed and applied to the current file. If only one is given, then the common ancestor of the sandbox revision and the specified revision is used as a basis for computing differences to be merged. For example, suppose a project has an experimental branch, and important changes to the file *foo.c* were introduced between revisions 1.2.2.1 and 1.2.2.2. Once those changes have proven stable, you want them reflected in the main line of development. From a sandbox with the head revisions checked out, run:

```
$ cvs update -j 1.2.2.1 -j 1.2.2.2 foo.c
```

CVS finds the differences between the two revisions and applies those differences to the file in your sandbox.

The *spec* used with **-W** is in the same format as entries in the *cvswrappers* administrative file (see "The cvswrappers file").

The status codes listed in Table 15-26 are used to describe the action taken on each file encountered in the repository and the sandbox.

Table 15-26. update status codes

Status	Description
A	Added. Server took no action because there was no repository file. Indicates that **cvs add**, but not **cvs commit**, has been run.
C	Conflict. Sandbox copy is modified (it has been edited since it was checked out or last committed). There was a new revision in the repository, and there were conflicts when CVS merged its changes into the sandbox version.
M	Modified. Sandbox copy is modified (it has been edited since it was checked out or last committed). If there was a new revision in the repository, its changes were successfully merged into the file (no conflicts).
P	Patched. Same as **U**, but indicates the server used a **patch**.
R	Removed. Server took no action. Indicates that **cvs remove**, but not **cvs commit**, has been run.
U	Updated. The file was brought up to date.
?	File is present in sandbox but not in repository.

version

```
version
```

Display the version of the CVS client (and server, if appropriate) being used.

watch

```
watch
  { { on | off } | { add | remove } [ -a action ] }
  [ -l | -R ]
  file ...
```

The **watch** command controls CVS's edit tracking mechanism. By default, CVS operates in its concurrent development mode, allowing any user to edit any file at any time. CVS includes this **watch** mechanism to support developers who would rather be notified of edits made by others proactively than discover them when doing an **update**. The *CVSROOT/notify* file determines how notifications are performed.

Table 15-27 shows the **watch** subcommands and their uses.

Table 15-27. watch subcommands

Subcommand	Description
add	Start watching files.
off	Turn off watching.
on	Turn on watching.
remove	Stop watching files.

The standard meanings of the common client options -l and -R apply. The only other option that can be used with the **watch** command is **-a** *action*. The **-a** option is used in conjunction with one of the actions listed in Table 15-28.

Table 15-28. watch Actions

Action	Description
all	All of the following.
commit	A user has committed changes.
edit	A user ran **cvs edit**.
none	Don't watch. Used by the **edit** command.
unedit	A user ran **cvs unedit**, **cvs release**, or deleted the file and ran **cvs update**, re-creating it.

See also **edit, editors, unedit,** and **watchers**.

---

watchers

```
watchers
  [ -l | -R ]
  [ file ... ]
```

Display a list of users watching the specified files. This is determined by checking which users have run the **watch** command on a particular file (or set of files). If the **watch** command has not been used, no results will be displayed.

The standard meanings of the common client options -l and -R apply.

See also **watch**.

16

Graphical Desktop Overview

Linux was criticized in the past for lacking an easy-to-use graphical desktop, but that has changed significantly. These days, there are several such desktops, as well as advanced alternatives aimed at experts, developers, and high-performance enthusiasts. This book covers three graphical configurations: two complete environments with their own application suites (GNOME in Chapter 17 and KDE in Chapter 18), and one traditional window manager (**fvwm2** in Chapter 19).

GNOME and KDE are the most commonly used desktops on Linux systems. KDE has been around longer, and as the default desktop for SuSE, has more of a European following. The GNOME project was started more recently, and its desktop, used as the default for Red Hat Linux, is more common in the United States. Many operating system vendors have produced unified themes for the two desktops, so that applications written with one toolkit appear consistent with those from the other.

Desktop Environments and Window Managers

The simplest graphical desktops consist of the X Window System, which displays the windows and graphics, and a *window manager*, which determines where windows are placed and how users interact with applications. A window manager, such as **fvwm2**, determines window "focus" (that is, which window is currently accepting input) and some keyboard shortcuts. Window managers often include some sort of control panel or task bar, but not always.

A desktop environment, in contrast, attempts to provide a complete experience, offering many of the tools someone would need for a typical day at the office. A desktop environment also includes more extensive cooperation between applications, ensuring that cutting and pasting text and dragging and dropping objects around the desktop work as expected, even between applications. A minimal installation would include a window manager with control panel, a file manager, and a few sample applications such as a text editor. Additional items such as games, email, calendars, office tools, and software development tools are usually available and work closely with the desktop core.

Both GNOME and KDE should look familiar to Windows and Macintosh users: they feature a desktop background with icons for files and folders, a bar with buttons and a clock at the top or bottom of the screen, and a central menu to access everything from applications to system settings. Both have more settings available than either Windows or the Macintosh OS, including support for virtual desktops, customizable key bindings, and window focus behavior. They also include or share a series of applications: office suites for word processing, spreadsheets, and presentations; groupware tools for email, calendar, and address-book management; and image processing, web, and software development tools for artists, programmers, and system administrators.

While GNOME and KDE offer entire suites of applications and configuration tools and serve as both software and software development platform, **fvwm2** focuses strictly on handling windows and the desktop background. **fvwm2** does not include other applications, and is customized with configuration files the way that all Linux and Unix applications used to be. It is, in fact, almost endlessly customizable—as long as you are willing to edit the right files. Some developers of software for GNOME or KDE will admit to using **fvwm2** or another window manager on their own systems, because they have customized it to work exactly as they wish.

Desktop Differences: Development

The differences between KDE and GNOME matter more to developers than to the average user. If you choose to develop software based on one of these platforms, your choice of toolkit and desktop environment will probably be based on two factors: language and license. The GNOME libraries (the main widget set is called Gtk+) are written in C, and the KDE libraries (notably Qt) in C++. For both desktops, bindings for other languages, such as Perl, Python, and Java, are available and popular, so the choice comes down to the architecture you prefer.

Licensing is slightly more complicated. Qt, the base toolkit for KDE software, is controlled by TrollTech, Inc., and is available under a dual licensing scheme: free for the development of open software, and proprietary for the development of proprietary software. Most GNOME libraries are available for open or proprietary development at no charge. Visit *http://developer.gnome.org* and *http:// developer.kde.org* for more details on building software with these tools.

17

GNOME

One of the two popular desktop environments used with Linux, GNOME is provided as the default desktop for Red Hat, Debian, and several other popular distributions. As a graphical environment, GNOME provides users with a highly customizable user interface and consistent functionality of common GUI features such as menus, toolbars, and buttons. In addition, it offers users a growing set of native applications to create a productive computing system. The number and quality of applications are a testament to the developer-friendly GNOME libraries; many GNOME technologies are also used in nongraphical or totally unrelated software. GNOME is distributed with most Linux distributions, and you can also get it from the GNOME web site (*http://www.gnome.org*) or from Ximian (*http://www.ximian.com*), a company that specializes in the GNOME desktop.

GNOME stands for "GNU Network Object Model Environment," and although the name is admittedly obscure, it does point to one of GNOME's core technologies: its CORBA-based objects. CORBA (Common Object Request Broker Architecture) specifies methods that allow interaction among applications through the sharing and embedding of component objects. For example, a spreadsheet created by Gnumeric (a GNOME spreadsheet program) can be placed as an object into an AbiWord document, and the Nautilus file browser can display images, web pages, and so forth by embedding an image viewer and HTML display engine. GNOME uses two libraries to do this: ORBit, (*http://orbit-resource.sourceforge.net*), which provides an Object Request Broker (ORB), and Bonobo (*http://developer.ximian.com/articles/whitepapers/bonobo*), which is designed to simplify the task of creating reusable software components and compound documents.

This edition of *Linux in a Nutshell* covers a GNOME desktop based on the GNOME 2 platform, which is included in Red Hat 8.0, Mandrake 9.0, and SuSE 8.1, among other distributions. The new platform differs from the previous version, GNOME 1.4, in a number of significant ways. Overall, the new platform has brought increased performance and stability, more coherent and powerful developer tools, and a friendlier, simpler interface.

You do not need to be familiar with earlier versions of GNOME to use GNOME 2. If you are familiar with earlier versions and want to know what's new, or if you are curious about the history of the project, see "History and Changes in GNOME 2" at the end of this chapter for additional background information.

Desktop Overview

Figure 17-1 shows the default GNOME desktop. The left side of the screen contains icons that are shortcuts to open applications, files, or URLs. The top icon is a link to the user's home folder; when double-clicked, it launches the Nautilus file manager to display the folder's contents. The other icons include shortcuts to the floppy drive and CD-ROM and links to web pages. In general, double-clicking on an icon leads to the most logical operation, so clicking folder icons displays folder contents, clicking application icons launches applications, and clicking a file opens the file in its most appropriate application (see "File Associations (MIME Types)" for information on how to choose which one). A button or icon you can press to start an application is called a *launcher*. You can drag and drop the icons around the desktop to arrange them as you like, or drag them onto the Trash icon to get them out of your way.

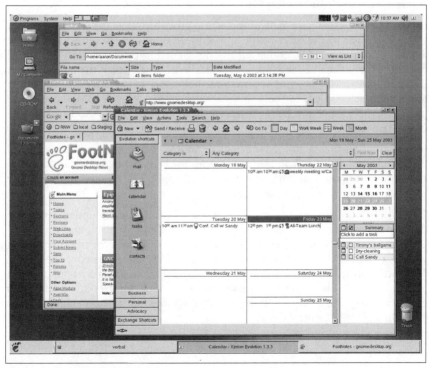

Figure 17-1. The GNOME desktop

You can also right-click on any blank space in the desktop and get a context menu that allows you to:

- Open a new file manager window.
- Create a new folder.
- Create an application launcher.
- Open a new terminal window.
- Run scripts or executable files you place in your scripts folder (*~/.gnome2/ nautilus-scripts*).
- Clean up the icons on the desktop.
- Copy, paste, or cut selected files.
- Change your desktop background.
- Display the contents of any mounted disk in the file manager.

The bars across the top and bottom of the screen are called *panels*. Some distributions and configurations use only one, and others use more than two. GNOME allows you to create a variety of panels and choose their placement, size, and behavior. The one at the top, called the menu panel, is perhaps the most common and important. It may be slightly different in some distributions of GNOME, but it generally consists of two menus on the left, and a clock and application switcher on the right. Some systems may also include other small applications, called applets; see "GNOME Panel Applets" for more information.

If you do not have a menu panel, the desktop probably offers the GNOME menu, which is similar to the Start menu in Microsoft Windows. On most systems, it appears in the lower left corner and is designated with a GNOME foot logo, earning it the nickname "the foot menu." In Red Hat 8.0, click the red hat to get the same menu with a list of applications, help, and a few other tools, plus the logout and screen-locking tools. If you want to add this GNOME menu to a panel, right-click on any blank space in the panel and select Add to Panel → GNOME Menu.

In general, the panel is a primary means of finding and opening applications and managing your desktop. You can add buttons to the panel to launch any application on your system; you can also include small applications, called applets, in the panel. For more information, see "The Panel."

GNOME allows you an enormous number of configuration options for your desktop environment. You can right-click on just about anything and get a pop-up menu (called a *context menu*) containing specific actions for that item and a way to configure its properties. General configuration settings are contained in the GNOME Control Center. You can access this tool by selecting System and then Settings in your menu panel (on some systems, look for Desktop Preferences under the Programs or Applications menu). For more information about settings, see "The GNOME Control Center."

Adding Desktop Icons

Desktop icons offer convenient double-click access to your most important files, applications, and links. The items displayed on your desktop exist as files in the *.gnome-desktop* directory of your home directory. Anything you add to that directory will appear on the desktop.

To add an icon that launches an application, select New Launcher. This opens the Desktop Entry Properties dialog box as shown in Figure 17-2. Provide the name of the launcher (this will be the text displayed underneath the icon), a comment (the tooltip that appears when the pointer is over the icon), and the command used to run the application. After you click OK, the new launcher icon appears on your desktop.

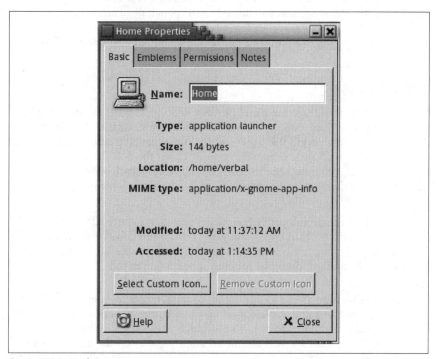

Figure 17-2. Desktop entry properties

A convenient use of desktop icons is to provide shortcuts to frequently used files or folders. Adding shortcuts is easiest from the file manager (Nautilus). Display the directory containing the item for which you want a shortcut on your desktop, right-click on the item, and select Make Link. Then click on the new link and drag it to the desktop, which has the underlying effect of moving it to your *~/.gnome-desktop* folder. You can copy an item instead of moving it by pressing the Ctrl key while selecting and dragging the item.

GNOME

The Panel

The GNOME panel can contain several different types of objects. The most obvious are the buttons for the menu and application launchers. You also can use a button to open a *drawer*, which is a subpanel containing additional launchers. There are a few special types of buttons used for logging out of the session and locking the screen. Finally, small programs called applets can be run on the panel. The Workspace Switcher, the Window List, and the clock are examples of panel applets.

As with many other things in GNOME, you can find settings for the panel by looking in the Panel menu under the GNOME menu, or by right-clicking on the panel itself. In both cases, there are options to add new launchers or applets to the panel; to adjust the style, size, and display of the panel; or to create new panels on the desktop. The menu panel does not have a properties dialog, as it is preconfigured. If you wish, you can remove it or replace it with an edge panel that is more to your liking.

Additional Panels

You can create more than one panel on your desktop. This is useful if you have different sets of applications used for specific but common tasks. For example, if you do a lot of work on graphics, you can dedicate a panel to launch your favorite graphics tools. To create a new panel, right-click on the default panel and select Add New Panel, or, from the GNOME menu, select Panel → Add New Panel. There are five different types of panels available from the submenu:

Edge panel
> The style of the default panel. It stretches across one entire edge of the screen. Arrow buttons on each end of the panel are used to collapse the panel to the side of the screen. Clicking on the remaining visible arrow button of a collapsed panel will cause the panel to appear again in full.

Corner panel
> A panel that is anchored to one corner of the screen and extends just enough to fit the buttons and applets it contains. A corner panel can be hidden by clicking the arrow button that is at the edge of the screen. The arrow button farthest from the edge will anchor an aligned panel on the opposite side of the screen.

Sliding panel
> Like a corner panel, except that instead of being anchored to a corner, it can be placed anywhere along the edge of the screen. This is similar to the Dock in Macintosh OS X.

Floating panel
> A panel that can be placed anywhere on the screen.

Menu panel
> A special type of preconfigured edge panel. It is a thin bar that stretches across the top of the screen and contains drop-down menus and a clock. Users of the Macintosh will find it quite familiar.

All of the panels except the menu panel can be moved by middle-clicking (or clicking the left and right buttons simultaneously) and dragging the panel to another part of the screen. They can also be configured individually from the Panel menu in its context (right-click) menu. Right-click and select Panel → Properties to open a properties dialog. Your options vary depending on panel type, but the complete list is:

Position
> This option does not appear for floating panels. For other types, choose a position by clicking the location on a diagram of a screen. You can also move all four configurable types of panels without this dialog by middle-clicking and dragging to a new location.

Orientation
> This option is available only for floating panels. It lets you choose whether the panel should be vertical or horizontal. Other panels are aligned with the screen edges.

Autohide
> Check this box to have the panel hide itself automatically. A small amount of the panel will be left showing; bring the mouse pointer over that bit, and the panel will reappear. This functions similarly to the Microsoft Windows task bar.

Show Hide Buttons, Arrows on Hide Buttons
> At each end of the panel is a hide button with an arrow. Click the button, and the panel shrinks into it. Click again, and the panel reappears. Uncheck these boxes to get rid of the buttons or to remove the arrow labels from them. The buttons are slightly smaller if they are unlabeled.

A second tab of the preferences window allows you to choose a background for your panel. Normally, a panel is light gray, but you can choose a color or even an image to go behind your buttons. If you choose an image, you can also scale or stretch it to fit the panel more accurately.

Adding an Application Launcher to the Panel

One of the conveniences of the panel is creating launcher icons that allow you one-click access to frequently used applications. To add an application, right-click the panel and select Add to Panel → New Launcher. You can also right-click launchers in your menus and choose Add This Launcher to Panel, or simply drag launchers to the panel.

To customize the launcher, right-click on it and select Properties. Here, you can enter a name for the application, a comment to be used as a tooltip, and the command used to open the application. (This is similar to creating a launcher, as shown in "Adding Desktop Icons.") Click on the icon button to select the image to be used for the button on the panel. If the application is to be run in a terminal window—that is, if it is a text-based program normally invoked from the shell—check the box labeled Run in Terminal.

Launcher buttons can be placed in any position and order you want on the panel. To move a launcher button, right-click it and select Move, or middle-click and drag it. The mouse pointer will change shape, indicating that you can drag the button to another position. Click to set the new position of the button.

 The middle mouse button has two features that are often overlooked. First, it can be used to paste whatever text is currently selected, without a copy command. Second, it can be used to move items such as the Workspace Switcher Applet that cannot be moved with the left mouse button. (In the Workspace Switcher Applet, left clicking and dragging moves individual windows among the workspaces, rather than moving the applet itself.)

GNOME Panel Applets

As mentioned earlier, GNOME offers small applications that run inside the panel, called panel applets. Some will already be in your panel by default. To add more, right-click on a blank space in the panel and select one of the items under Add to Panel → Applet. The two most important GNOME panel applets are the Workspace Switcher Applet and the Window List Applet.

Workspaces and the Workspace Switcher

GNOME allows you to create extra screen real estate by multiplying your desktop with workspaces. You can keep a few windows open in each workspace instead of choosing between clutter and closing windows. For example, you might keep your mail program open in one workspace with a few messages open in separate windows, then have one or two browser windows open in a second workspace, and a spreadsheet in a third.

The workspaces are drawn in miniature on your panel in the Workspace Switcher Applet, which at first looks like a series of small grey boxes. Drawn inside each workspace, you can see the individual windows you have open, and even drag them from one workspace to another with the left mouse button. You can navigate these workspaces with the keyboard shortcuts Ctrl+Alt+Left, Ctrl+Alt+Right, Ctrl+Alt+Up, and Ctrl+Alt+Down, or by clicking one of the workspaces in the Workspace Switcher Applet.

Most systems give you four workspaces by default, although some stick with one or two. To create more, open the Workspace Switcher Applet preferences tool by right-clicking on the Workspace Switcher Applet and selecting Preferences. There, you can select not only the number of workspaces, but also their names and their layout in columns and rows.

The Window List Applet

The Window List Applet applet lets you keep track of open windows. It displays a button on the panel for each window you have open. Clicking on a button in the tasklist will bring that window to the foreground, reopening it if it was minimized.

You can right-click on any of the buttons for an application to get a context menu that allows you to interact with the window for that application, and close, minimize, maximize, un-maximize, move, or resize it.

To set the way the Window List Applet behaves, right-click on an empty space in the window list or on the small "handle" on its left side, and select Preferences. This will open a dialog box that allows you to set the following options:

Window List content
> You can show the windows from all your workspaces, or just from the workspace you are currently in.

When restoring minimized windows
> This setting matters only if you choose to display windows from all your workspaces. The default setting, "Restore to current workspace," means that minimized windows you restore with the Window List Applet will appear on your current workspace. If you select "Restore to native workspace," the windows will appear in the workspace where you were last using them. In other words, you can choose to have your windows appear either where you are now or where you were last using them.

Window grouping
> One of the more useful Window List Applet features is window grouping. If you have several windows open for a particular application, the Window List Applet can save space by combining all the entries for that application. Then, instead of a button for each window, you'll have a menu for the whole application. For example, if you have one Galeon web browser window open, you will have a button that shows the Galeon icon and the title of the page for that window. If you have five open, the Window List Applet will show "Galeon (5)," and clicking the button will offer you a choice of which window to focus. You can set the applet never to group windows, to group windows only when it runs out of space, or to group windows whenever it can.

Window List size
> Choose a minimum and maximum size for your window list applet. The applet will grow between these sizes depending upon how many windows you have open.

Miscellaneous applets

In addition to the Window List and Workspace Switcher Applets, there are roughly a dozen other applets in five categories. You can find the complete list of applets by right-clicking on the panel and selecting Add to Panel → Applet.

Accessories
> A clock, a dictionary, a stock ticker, and a weather report.

Amusements
> A fish that tells your fortune, and some googly eyes that follow your mouse pointer.

Internet
> A modem traffic monitor and a mail checker.

Multimedia
> A CD player and volume control.

GNOME

Utility

The largest category: a battery charge monitor, international character and keyboard layout tools, a mini command line, a system load monitor, a system event notification area, and the Workspace Switcher and Window List Applets.

The GNOME Menu and the Menu Panel Menus

Because different distributions organize their menus differently, you're best off exploring them yourself or referring to the documentation for your particular system. For the most part, however, the menus have similar contents: applications, help files, settings or preferences tools, utilities and system administration tools, and a few special items like Log Out and Run Command. The major difference is whether these items are split into several menus, as in the menu panel, or put in a single place, as in the GNOME menu.

There are, however, a number of common tasks related to menu items that do not vary across distributions, and we'll describe those here. First, there are context menus for individual menu items. To see them, right-click on a menu item (this is easier if you do not keep the left mouse button pressed while navigating your menus). The possible actions are:

Add this launcher to panel

Add the item as a launcher in the panel. If you have more than one panel, the launcher will be added to the first panel. You can then drag the launcher to wherever you actually want it.

Put into run dialog

Display this item as a shortcut in the Run Program dialog.

Entire menu

The two items here, "Add this as menu to panel" and "Add this as drawer to panel," allow you to add the entire submenu containing the launcher to your panel as either a drawer (a portion of panel that stays open when a menu might close) or as a menu.

The menu customization tools are one of the simplest and most obvious improvements in the GNOME 2 platform. To alter your menus, just open your Nautilus file manager and type "applications:///" into the location bar. The Applications display represents your menus and submenus as folders, with item launchers in them. Drag items around and move, copy, delete, or rename them as you see fit.

To add a submenu, right-click in an empty spot in the folder and select New Folder, then rename the folder, or right-click on it to set its name and icon.

To add a launcher, right-click in an empty spot in the folder and select New Launcher, then enter the name of the application, type in any pop-up text you want to describe it, and enter or browse for the command that starts the application itself. If you're not sure where that is, look in the */usr/bin* directory, or use the **which** or **locate** commands (see Chapter 2) to find it.

The GNOME Control Center

The GNOME Control Center (Figure 17-3) is where most customization and configuration of your desktop environment takes place. There are several ways to open it: you can click the toolbox button on your panel, select items in the Preferences section of the GNOME menu, or choose Settings in the System menu. The Control Center is also one place where different distributions vary significantly. The tools covered in this section appear in most distributions, but you may find a slightly different set that is organized in a different fashion.

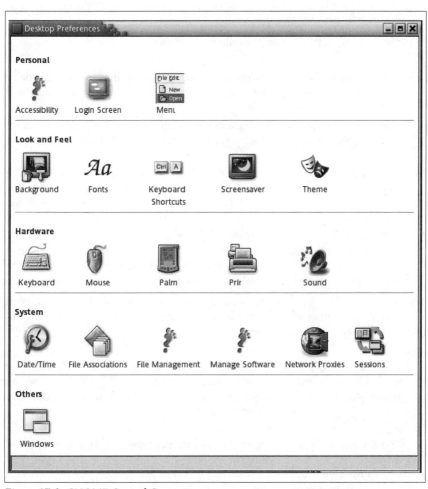

Figure 17-3. GNOME Control Center

Personal Settings

These settings control the system information pertaining most directly to you.

Accessibility

The Accessibility tool, new in GNOME 2, handles the various settings related to making a computer easier to use for people with disabilities.

There are three sections to the tool: Basic, Filters, and Mouse, plus the option to turn all the accessibility options on or off at once. To set any option, you must first click the "Enable keyboard accessibility" checkbox.

In the Basic section, you can set the following options:

Features
> You can set the features to turn off automatically if they are unused, or to emit a keyboard beep when turned on or off. This helps prevent confusion if they are turned on accidentally.
>
> The Import Feature Settings button is relevant only to those migrating from CDE to GNOME 2, and allows you to import CDE accessibility settings.

Sticky Keys
> Sticky Keys allows you to press key combinations such as Ctrl+R by pressing only one key at a time. If you choose to enable the sticky keys feature, you can also set it to beep when used, and to turn off if a normal key combination is pressed.

Repeat Keys
> Key repeat can be troublesome for people with limited mobility. To turn it off, uncheck this box. Alternately, you can use the sliders to adjust the delay before key repeating begins, and the speed at which keys are repeated.

The Filters section handles the way that the system can ignore accidental keypresses. Individuals with limited dexterity may wish to use these features to prevent extraneous key inputs.

Slow Keys
> Check the Enable Slow Keys button to have the system accept only keys that are held down, and ignore keys that are tapped quickly. You can set an amount of time before a keypress is registered, and also set beeps for keypress, key acceptance, or key rejection.

Bounce Keys
> The Bounce Keys feature ignores duplicate keypresses: if you hit a key and then accidentally hit it again, the system will ignore the second input. You can set the amount of time the system will wait before accepting another key, and have it beep when it rejects a duplicate.

Toggle Keys
> Some keypresses toggle individual features on and off. Enabling the Toggle Keys function will have the system beep once when a toggle is turned on, and twice when it is turned off.

The mouse accessibility settings allow you to control the mouse pointer with the keyboard arrows instead of with the mouse itself. Click the Enable Mouse Keys checkbox to turn this feature on.

There are three settings for the Mouse Keys feature. You can set sliders for the maximum speed, the acceleration rate, and the delay between pressing the arrow key and the time that the mouse pointer actually begins to move.

Menus

The Menus button in the Control Center takes you to the special Nautilus view called Applications, which is a file display of your menu tree. There, you can edit the menus as though they were files. You can drag and drop items to move, add, or delete them, and change their names or descriptions by right-clicking on them and selecting Properties.

Password

Open this tool to change your password. You will be asked for your current password and your new password. You will have to type the new password twice to confirm it.

The tool may reject passwords if they are not long enough or are too easy to guess.

Look and Feel Settings

These sections provide settings for the overall look of your desktop by letting you choose the background, screensaver, theme, and keyboard shortcuts.

Background

Selects images, colors, and dispay effects for the part of the display that lies behind windows and menus. To use an image, select one from the list of default backgrounds, or add another by clicking the Add Picture button and selecting a file from your disk. Then choose how you want the image fitted to your screen. For very small images or tile patterns, choose Tiled; for larger images or those exactly the size of the screen, choose Centered. Images that are a different shape from the screen may be scaled to fit, or scaled symmetrically until the entire image fits on the screen. You can also choose No Image and just use a color. If the image doesn't exactly fit the screen, you'll see the background color behind it.

In the color section, select either a solid, single color, or a horizontal or vertical gradient of two colors. If you select a gradient, the color will fade from the first color to the second one, down or across the screen. Click the color box to select the colors.

Fonts

Here, choose the fonts you want GNOME to use in different situations, and how it should draw those fonts on your screen.

The top half of the font dialog displays the fonts your system uses; click on the current font to change it.

Application Font
> The font used in dialog boxes, text areas, and menus.

Desktop Font
> The font used to display desktop icon labels.

Window Title Font
> The font used in window titles.

Terminal Font
> The font used in the terminal emulator. This should be a monospaced font such as Courier.

The bottom half of the font dialog is taken up with font rendering options. Font rendering determines the method used to draw the actual fonts on your screen. You have four options:

Monochrome
> Render the fonts only in black and white. This can lead to letters being somewhat jagged, but is faster.

Best Shapes
> Also known as "antialiasing," this is considered the highest quality and is recommended for most standard monitors.

Best Contrast
> Make sure that the letters are displayed in the sharpest possible contrast. Recommended for the visually impaired.

Subpixel Smoothing (LCDs)
> This optimization method is best for flat-panel (LCD) monitors.

Screensaver

Contains settings for the screensaver. You can choose from a list of available screensavers (including a random setting). Input the number of minutes of inactivity before the screensaver starts and whether you will be required to give your password before going back to the desktop. Power management settings are available here if your system is configured for them.

Keyboard Shortcuts

The Keyboard Shortcuts tool lets you choose the key combinations that will execute a wide range of actions, from opening the Run Command dialog or taking a screenshot to moving windows between workspaces.

To choose a new keyboard shortcut, click the action you want to change and then type a new accelerator. Setting a shortcut that conflicts with an existing GNOME shortcut will disable the old shortcut. Setting a shortcut that conflicts with one for any other application will usually override the application's shortcut.

Theme Selector

Themes provide a consistent overall style to the many widgets and components used by GNOME. A number of basic themes are included with the *gtk-engines* package, and you can download and install additional themes from *http://gtk.themes.org*.

Any themes installed on your system are listed in the Theme Selector. You can select one, and the theme will be applied to the desktop immediately.

If you have downloaded a theme and wish to install it, click the Install New Theme button. Provide the name and location of the *.tar.gz* or *.tgz* file and click OK. The new theme will be installed in the */usr/share/themes* directory and be available for you to use on your desktop.

Hardware Settings

In some systems this section is called Peripherals. It includes tools that allow you to control the way your system works with hardware and peripheral devices such as your mouse and keyboard. If you have installed PalmOS device software, you may also have Palm Pilot configuration tools. Some systems also include a printer configuration tool here.

Keyboard

Contains settings for keyboard autorepeat and sounds. You can set the repeat rate of a pressed key and the delay before it starts. You also can enable keyboard clicks and their volume. Settings can be previewed by typing in the Test Settings textbox.

Three sliders adjust the volume, pitch, and duration of the keyboard bell. Click the Test button to hear the bell's new settings.

Mouse

Lets you configure the mouse for either a right-handed user or a left-handed user. If you configure for a left-handed user, all documentation about the left button applies to the right button, and vice versa. You also can set the acceleration and threshold (sensitivity) of the mouse.

Sound

This tool sets up a sound scheme for various actions. You can enable or disable all system sounds by checking the box "Start the sound server when I log in." To add sounds to particular events, check the box "Play sounds for specific events."

The rest of the window contains a listing of events, sorted by application. Each event with an associated sound has the name of the file played when it occurs. Select an event from the listing and click Play to hear its assigned sound.

To change the sound for an event, click on the event and then enter the name of the file or click Browse to choose a file to play.

System Settings

The System Settings category contains settings that relate to the internal operation of your desktop and operating system, such as the time or the way that files are associated with applications.

Date and Time

You will need your system's root password to change the date and time, since time affects all users on the system. The appearance of the time tool itself may vary depending on the operating system you use, but it will present you with options for choosing the time, date, and time zone for your system.

In addition, most time and date tools allow you to set one or more network time servers with which to synchronize, so your clock will never be inaccurate.

File Associations (MIME Types)

This tool also varies between operating systems. On most it is called File Associations, but on some it is called MIME Types. It allows you to set the applications that open particular files or handle particular network protocols. There are a bewildering number of file types listed here, sorted by category. For example, HTML documents are in the World Wide Web section of the Documents category, and have filenames ending in *.htm* and *.html*.

To add a new type of document, click the Add button. A dialog will open asking for the category/type listing for the file type and the extensions to associate with it. Then, choose an application (if any) that handles that document. Optionally, you can supply up to two regular expressions to identify the type. For example, if you installed the RealPlayer music software and wanted to add RealAudio music files to your system, you would list the *.ram*, *.rm*, and *.ra* file extensions (but not *.rpm*, which is used for the RPM software package format), and place the MIME type in the Audio category. Then, you would enter the name of your RealAudio application.

To edit an existing file association, select its listing and click the Edit button. You will see a dialog box in which you can choose an icon to be used for the file type, add or remove file extensions, and supply commands that will open, view, and edit this type of file. To delete a type, select it from the list and click the Delete button.

You can also choose protocol handlers, the applications that work with various internet services. To change your web browser to Galeon, you would open the World Wide Web (*http://*) item in the Internet Services section and set it to run */usr/ bin/galeon*. Some distributions replicate this ability in a tool called URL Handlers, described next.

URL Handlers

Not all distributions have this tool, as it replicates some of the functionality from the File Associations tool. The URL Handlers tool allows you to adjust the settings for special URL launchers used by the GNOME help system. The defaults for protocols such as HTTP, FTP, and Mail are already set and likely handled by your default web browser (for example, Galeon). The special URLs are *ghelp*, *info*, and *man* (i.e., GNOME help files, command *info* files, and *man* files). The defaults use the help browser for these types of files.

Manage Software

Not all distributions have this tool, which opens the Ximian Red Carpet software management application. You can use Red Carpet to install, remove, or update the software on your computer. There isn't room to describe this tool completely, but you can find complete instructions in its help menu.

Network Proxies

A *proxy* is a system that stands between your computer and the Internet, handling all the connections for you. If your system uses a proxy, you can name it here to allow all GNOME applications to take advantage of it.

You may set a proxy for HTTP, Secure HTTP (HTTPS), FTP, and Socks transactions. To do so, click the "Manual proxy configuration" radio button and enter the name of the proxy and, if necessary, the port number. Leave an entry blank if you do not use a proxy for that protocol.

Some networks have automatic proxy configuration, which allows you to enter a single URL and let the computer set the proxy names and port numbers. If this is the case, click the "Automatic proxy configuration" radio button and enter the URL for your proxy configuration host.

Sessions

This tool controls session management—that is, what happens when you log in and log out. The options are divided into three categories: general session options, settings for the current session, and startup programs. If you create multiple session types, you can choose among them when you log in. Most distributions have at least a few different sessions created for you in advance; you can select among them at the login screen.

The Session Options tab contains:

Show splash screen on login
> Normally, GNOME displays a "splash screen" image to show you what's going on as it starts up. If you prefer not to have this appear, uncheck this box.

Prompt on logout
> Normally, when you select the Log Out item from your System menu or GNOME menu, you will be asked if you really want to log out, and whether you would like to shut down, restart, or just log out. If you want the system to log out without confirmation, uncheck this box.

GNOME

Automatically save changes to session
> When you log out and leave applications running, GNOME will normally remember that the application was running, and start that application again the next time you log in. If you prefer not to have that happen, uncheck this box.

Sessions:
> You can create alternate sessions and select them from the GNOME login screen before you log in. You could, for example, create a "work" session that would start your calendar and spreadsheet as soon as you logged in, and turn down the volume on your speakers. Another session might turn the volume up and start your web browser and a game. To make changes to a session beyond renaming it, log into that session and change it there.

The Current Session tab shows the programs that are running right now. Each application is assigned a number to indicate the order in which it is started (lower numbers are first). You can also assign a style to each application, which determines how it starts, restarts, or quits.

Normal
> The application starts automatically when you log in and runs until you quit.

Restart
> The application starts when you log in, and restarts itself if you stop it or if it crashes. The Metacity window manager and the panel have this style because they need to be running at all times.

Trash
> The application doesn't start when you log in.

Settings
> The application starts before other applications and is used to store configuration settings. Very few applications get this style.

The Startup Programs tab allows you to start an application every time you log in, whether or not it's running when you log out. To add a program to your list of startup applications, click the Add button and enter its name or select it by clicking Browse and selecting it in the filesystem.

Advanced Settings Control with GConf

GConf is the name of the GNOME configuration database. It acts as a central repository for settings and other shared system data, much like the Registry in Microsoft Windows. It uses XML files stored in the *~/.gconf* directory to associate keys and values that multiple applications can access. It's possible to change those values with a text editor, but the gconf-editor application provides a much easier way to adjust variables and settings. It displays keys and their values in a convenient heirarchical fashion, together with any explanation of the key and its available values.

The gconf-editor program is not generally supported and is not the recommended tool for general-purpose configuration. It does not have an Undo feature; if you break something and can't figure out how to fix it, you can revert to the system default GConf database. To do so, log out, log into a command-line or non-GNOME environment (Ctrl+Alt+F1 will get you a virtual console in most systems), and delete the *.gconf* directory in your home directory. The default settings for GNOME applications will be restored when you next start your applications. Do not delete your *.gconf* directory while running GNOME.

To begin working with GConf keys, run the "gconf-editor" command at the command line or in the "Run Program..." dialog. The editor has a filesystem tree on the left, and an area on the right that is used to display keys and values. There are five groups of keys at the top level, but only two are really relevant to most users: *apps*, where you'll set preferences for applications, and *desktop*, which stores most of the keys set by the GNOME Control Center. There are too many keys and values to list here, but the examples in the rest of the section should give you a feel for what you can do with them.

Note that most of these configuration variables are loaded only when a program starts, so changes will not take effect until you restart the relevant application.

Window managers and window behavior

The window manager is the individual piece of software that handles the particulars of placement, movement, and border style of the windows on your desktop. The default GNOME 2 window manager is called Metacity.

Except for themes, almost none of the Metacity options are settable in the standard GNOME Control Center. To set them, select "apps" and then "metacity" in the gconf-editor. Metacity has a "general" category, where most of the options are set, plus a number of key bindings for window and workspace control. The most commonly changed items are:

auto_raise
If the box is checked, windows that get mouse focus automatically come to the front of the screen. If you set the focus mode to **sloppy** and leave this box unchecked, you can type into windows that are in the background. In the default focus mode, this setting has no effect.

focus_mode
GNOME 1.2 and 1.4 users will remember this feature, which lets you choose how windows get the keyboard focus. The default behavior is **click:** you must click on a window to bring it into focus. Other possible values are **enter-exit** (window focus comes to a window when the mouse does, and leaves when the mouse does) and **sloppy** (window focus comes to a window when the mouse enters it, and stays until the mouse enters another window).

animation_style
Choose the style of animation for moving, resizing, and minimizing windows. Your options are **wireframe**, **thin**, **opaque**, and **none**.

wrap_style

    This item is a good example of the sort of feature that has been removed, hidden, or abstracted away in GNOME 2. The settings chosen here determine what happens when you use the key combination (normally Ctrl-Alt-Arrow, and set in the **global_keybindings** section of the Metacity keys) to try to move beyond the defined borders of your virtual desktops. If the value is **none**, you will not move any further. If the value is **classic**, movement leads you to the next workspace in number: going right from the rightmost workspace in a row will take you to the first workspace in the next row, and moving down from the bottom workspace in a column will take you to the top workspace in the next column. If you select **toroidal**, the workspaces behave as though they were on a globe: moving from the end of one row will take you back to the beginning of the same row.

The panel

As mentioned earlier, many panel options have been left out of the Panel Preferences tool that you get when you right-click on the panel. Some of the items you can adjust with gconf-editor are:

panel_show_delay *and* **panel_hide_delay**

    If you have a panel set to automatically hide itself when you leave it alone, these values are the time in milliseconds that you leave it alone before it hides itself, and the time it takes to appear when you move the mouse to its side of the screen.

tooltips-enabled

    Some people don't like tooltips in their panels. Setting this key to false (unchecking the box) will turn them off.

enable-animations *and* **panel_animation_speed**

    When you hide or show a panel, it slides on and off the screen smoothly. These values allow you to turn off animation entirely or have it move faster or slower.

History and Changes in GNOME 2

Most new software releases add features, and a major complaint among users is of steadily increasing complexity, or "feature creep." The GNOME 2 desktop is distinctive in that, while adding a few features, it has also removed some features.

Many configuration formats have changed between GNOME 1.4 and GNOME 2.0 as applications have moved to using the GConf system. You will need to reconfigure most, if not all, of your applications when you upgrade.

New features include:

- Font smoothing (antialiased fonts).
- Marked speed increases in the Nautilus file manager.

- Tabbed browsing (press Ctrl-T to create a new tab) in both Galeon and Mozilla web browsers.

- Internationalization support, including proper handling of right-to-left languages.

- Accessibility tools for people with visual or mobility impairments.

- Control Center more smoothly integrated with the rest of the system.

Removed features include:

- Edge flipping (dragging items from one desktop to another) is no longer available; use keyboard shortcuts or the Workspace Switcher Applet instead.

- Detachable menus have been disabled; you can turn them on with the gconf-editor tool.

- It is no longer possible to choose window placement algorithms. Some versions of GNOME ship without window focus options and leave them only as gconf keys.

- GNOME 1.x made a distinction between two types of virtual desktops. *Workspaces* assumed the creation of multiple distinct desktops, whereas *viewports* assumed that you were creating a single, large desktop and displaying only a portion of it. Few people ever fully understood the distinction, and it has been removed from Metacity and the Workspace Switcher. As a result, windows moved to the edge of the screen no longer appear in the next workspace over, and it is not possible to create a three-dimensional array of virtual desktop areas.

- Application display fonts, themes for window borders and application buttons, and the virtual filesystem's HTTP proxy have been given simplified configuration tools that appear in only one place. Several other Control Center tools have been eliminated, and the term "capplet" has been removed from the GNOME vocabulary.

- Both menu configuration tools (gmenu and the menu display options tool) have been replaced by the ability to edit menus in Nautilus (type the location "applications:///" into Nautilus).

- Many of the less important panel options are available only in the gconf-editor, including panel movement speed, the delay before hiding the panel when using the automatic hiding option, menu caching, and the option to display an image on the left side of the GNOME and Programs menus.

- There are far fewer panel applets. Notably, there is only one clock applet rather than five (nobody admits to thinking five clocks were ever necessary) and there are only two applets in the "Amusements" category: eyes that track the mouse, and the fish that tells your fortune.

- The Nautilus file manager also has fewer options. Notably, speed has been improved to the point that the Performance Tradeoffs are no longer necessary, the User Levels feature has been removed, the theme, font, and HTTP proxy settings have been moved to the Control Center, and the Help display has been moved to a dedicated help browser called **yelp**.

GNOME

Most of these feature removals stem from switching from Sawfish to the much simpler Metacity window manager. However, all of the features that ended up being removed had initially sprung from one of the major pitfalls of any software project, especially open projects where making an executive decision is harder. When developers disagree, it is often easier politically to create an option than to find an acceptable compromise or enforce a "correct" decision. However, each preference, option, and feature adds another layer of complexity, making the software harder to support, debug, and integrate with the rest of the desktop.

The clearest example in GNOME is window management software. The window manager is important and complex software: it controls window placement and ordering, controls event handling and focus, and so forth. Without a window manager, your desktop would not be functional as you know it. At the same time, window managers have to be completely unobtrusive, or they interfere with the use of applications. Most computer users do not know or care what window managers are, and have certainly never started a window manager by hand themselves.

When GNOME 1.0 was released, it allowed users to select among various window managers, including **twm** and **icewm**. The majority of users and distributions used a window manager called Enlightenment, which quickly grew from being a window manager to being a desktop environment in its own right. Running GNOME and Enlightenment at once became increasingly redundant, so for GNOME 1.2 and 1.4, users and distributors switched to Sawfish, which was small, fast, and highly configurable.

In fact, there were so many combinations of settings that it was hard to test, and it kept getting larger and more complex. By the time GNOME 2.0 was on the way, Sawfish was slow, large, and impossible to maintain. The Sawfish maintainer had abandoned it, and nobody was willing to continue the project.

The GNOME development team was determined not to repeat the process. Metacity, the GNOME 2 window manager, is small, fast, and simple. The GNOME Control Center is designed around the assumption that most users do not care to pick or know their window manager, and that developers do not care to bear the burden of code complexity caused by interacting with multiple window management systems. It's still possible to switch window managers, and those who wish to do so can do it by editing their ~/.gnome-session files.

The GNOME 2 series of releases (2.0 and 2.2 have been released as of this writing; 2.4 and 2.6 are planned) aims to choose good defaults rather than offer limitless options, and considers simplicity and usability to be as important as adding additional behavior. The desktop is kept as simple as possible so that it does not distract from the actual functionality of the applications that are based upon it and that are its real reason for existence. The applications themselves are not shying away from new features or new capabilities, but for the most part share the goals of simplicity and ease of use.

The K Desktop Environment (KDE) is an open source software project that provides a consistent, user-friendly, contemporary desktop for Unix and Linux systems. KDE is not simply a window manager like **fvwm**, but a whole desktop environment including services to assist end users, application developers, and system administrators in standardizing the look and feel of their applications and configuring their systems. The KDE interface makes full use of drag-and-drop functionality so that, for instance, you can grab an icon for a text file in the file manager and drag it to a text editor window to open it. Full network integration of KDE applications allows you to transparently access files from other computers or FTP sites and manipulate them as if they were local.

KDE also implements a standard help system based on HTML. Applications that display a Help button offer a specific file of documentation for that application in the help viewer.

One goal of KDE is to provide the user with system information and configuration through easy-to-use graphical interfaces on the desktop. The KDE Control Center is a central utility for desktop and application configuration, as well as a source of information for important system components. The Information module of the Control Center can retrieve and display status information for your processor, memory, PCI bus, network devices, and many other hardware components on your system.

A wide variety of applications has been developed to take advantage of KDE's features and provide the user with a wealth of productive applications. The base package comes with programs such as a mail client, a calendar and organizer, a CD player, image viewers, chat programs, and more.

Most Linux distributions ship with KDE and allow you to set it up as the default session environment when you install the operating system. If you are installing KDE separately, download and install the KDE packages (you can find them at *ftp://ftp.kde.org*, among other places). You can also use this link if you want to upgrade your version of KDE with the current official version.

Red Hat 8.0 has introduced a new look and feel called Bluecurve. For the most part, the applications and services offered on the KDE desktop under Bluecurve are the same as those described here, but they may appear in different places or have different names and icons. For instance, the startup menu at the bottom left corner of the screen, which displays a large K in vanilla KDE, displays a red hat in Bluecurve.

To set KDE as your desktop environment, look for the X initialization files in your home directory. Depending on your distribution and how you log in, look for *.xinitrc*, *.xsession*, or *.Xclients* in your home directory. If none of these files exist, create a new *.xinitrc* file. Edit the file to remove any window manager references that may exist and add **startkde** on a line at the end of the file. If you are logging in through the KDE or GNOME display manager, there may be a Session tab or icon that allows you to select KDE as your desktop environment. In that case, you do not need to update or add an initialization file.

Desktop Overview

Figure 18-1 shows a typical KDE desktop. The bar across the bottom of the screen is the panel. It contains buttons for the main menu (often referred to as the K menu), the window list, the desktop pager, and the taskbar, as well as other buttons used to launch applications. The taskbar is used to keep track of application windows running on the desktop.

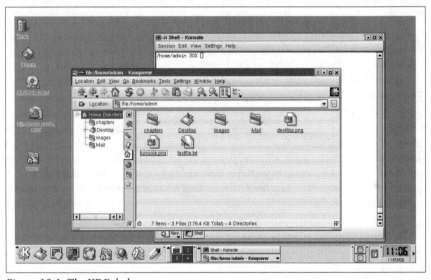

Figure 18-1. The KDE desktop

The desktop displays several open application windows and contains icons that can be used to launch applications with a single click. Several icons are placed on the desktop by default. The Trash icon is a link to a special desktop folder to which you can drag files that you want to delete. There are also icons that link to a mounted CD-ROM and an unmounted floppy drive.

Application Windows

Each KDE window has a titlebar with common buttons on the right for minimize, maximize, and close. On the left side of the titlebar, there is a small icon (or a dash if an icon isn't specified by the application) and a button that looks like a pushpin. The icon opens the window menu that contains a number of different functions you can apply to the window, such as sending it to another desktop. The pushpin button is used to stick or unstick the window to the screen. If you click on the pushpin, the window becomes sticky and appears on all of the virtual desktops. The button appears pushed in when a window is sticky. Click the button again to unstick a window.

The window menu contains standard window commands: Maximize, Iconify, Move, Resize, Sticky, Always on Top, and Close. There is also a command that lets you send the window to another virtual desktop.

Double-click on a window's titlebar to "shade" the window. Shading a window causes it to roll up and disappear into the titlebar, making space on the desktop.

The Konqueror File Manager and Web Browser

One of the most important KDE applications is Konqueror. Konqueror is both a graphical file manager and an Internet browser. Any time you click a folder icon, such as the Home folder button on the panel, a Konqueror window opens, displaying the contents of the directory. Konqueror also provides the underlying engine for the Help Center and the Control Center. Figure 18-2 shows a Konqueror file manager window displaying a home directory. Files and directories are shown as icons by default, but you can use the View menu to view contents with more detail.

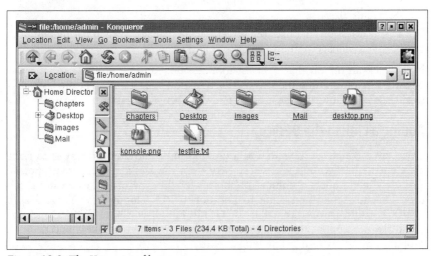

Figure 18-2. The Konqueror file manager

Like other web browsers, Konqueror has a toolbar that contains back and forward buttons for stepping through your selection history, a home button, reload, and stop. The Location bar uses URL addressing for both network addresses and local filesystems. These features are therefore available to the file manager aspect of Konqueror as well as to the web browser aspect. Depending on the URL you enter, Konqueror opens either in browser or file manager mode. You can also split the screen into multiple windows and have, for example, one window open to your home directory and another window open to a web site. If you want, you can even open a terminal window from Konqueror, making it an almost complete working environment.

The Konsole Terminal Emulator

If you are used to working in a terminal window, you can still do that in KDE. Konsole, KDE's terminal emulation program, can be started from the K menu or from a button on the panel. Once a Konsole window is running, you can open new terminal sessions in a single Konsole window, saving space on your desktop. To start a new session, go to the Session menu and pick the session type you want to open, or select a session type by clicking the New button at the bottom of an open Konsole window. The choices are:

New Shell
> Opens a new Konsole terminal shell.

New Linux Console
> Opens a session that emulates a text-only Linux terminal.

New Midnight Commander
> Opens a session with the Midnight Commander file manager.

New Root Console
> Opens a root console session.

New Root Midnight Commander
> Opens a root Midnight Commander session.

New Screen Session
> Opens a session that uses the **screen** screen manager, which permits multiple virtual terminals to share a single physical terminal.

If you pick an option that opens a root session, Konsole prompts for the root password before starting the session. Each session adds a button at the bottom of the Konsole window; use the buttons to switch between sessions.

Adding a Link to the Desktop

There are a couple of ways to add a desktop link. The simplest way is to right-click on the background and select New from the Desktop menu that appears. The New menu offers a number of choices for the type of link to create: Directory, Link to Application, Link to Location (URL), Floppy Device, Hard Disc, CD/DVD-ROM Device, Text File, or HTML File. If you have KOffice installed, you'll also see options to add Office documents. When you make a selection, the properties window for that link type appears.

The properties window varies slightly depending on the type of link, but for most links you need to specify a name for the link file, the label for the icon, and the executable command or file location. You can also set the permissions for the link file and select a new icon.

The following example shows how to create an application desktop link that opens the Kate text editor. First, right-click on the desktop and select New → Application. The properties window opens, showing four tabs: General, Permissions, Execute, and Application.

The General tab shows "Link to Application" in the text box. That text represents both the name of the link file being created and the text that appears under the icon on the desktop. Enter a filename that reflects the purpose of the link; in Figure 18-3, it is *Kate*.

The tab also displays an image of the icon that will appear on the desktop and additional information about the file. The default icon for an application is a picture of a gear. You can change the icon by clicking the button showing the current icon. This opens a window that displays a set of default KDE icons found on your system. Pick the one you like and click OK.

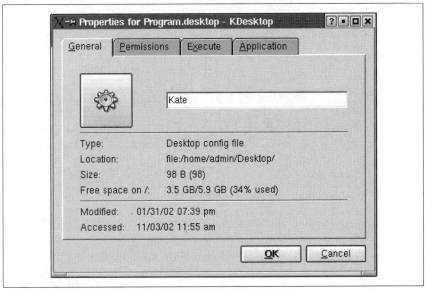

Figure 18-3. General tab of desktop link properties

Because you created the link file, the permissions allow you to use it. If you want to adjust the permissions, go to the Permissions tab. The next step is to supply the command used to open the application. On the Execute tab, type in the command, or click the Browse button to locate the file (Figure 18-4).

The final step is to supply a tooltip comment. Fill in the Comment box on the Application tab with a description of the application (Figure 18-5). Click the OK button to finish the configuration. If you want to change a property of your link later, right-click on the icon and choose Properties.

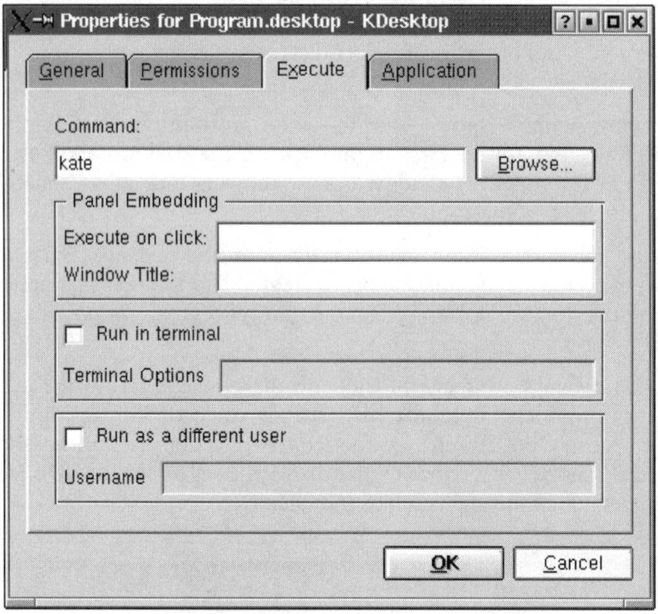

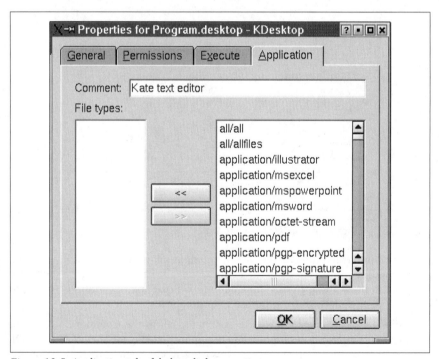

Figure 18-4. Execute tab of desktop link properties

Figure 18-5. Application tab of desktop link properties

When you create a link to a URL, a window appears with the text "New Link To Location (URL)" and an empty text box (Figure 18-6). Enter the URL in the text box and click the OK button.

Figure 18-6. Desktop window for URL link

Entering a new directory link is similar to entering a URL link, except the prompt above the text box reads "New Directory." Enter the path to the directory, and click the OK button.

For a new device link, select the appropriate device and set the link name and permissions if needed. On the Device tab, select the device from the drop-down list. That sets the device location, such as */dev/fd3*, and displays the mount point as well.

You can also add a link to the desktop by dragging an item from a file manager window. You can do this with any file or directory. After you drag the item to the desktop, a small pop-up window asks whether you want to copy, move, or link the item. Copy simply makes a copy of the item in the Desktop directory; move removes the item from its original location and places it in the Desktop directory. If you choose link, the desktop icon contains a symbolic link that points to the item's current location.

The Desktop Folder

Everything that appears on the desktop exists in the *~/Desktop* folder. If you open this folder in the file manager, you may see directories for Templates and Autostart, as well as files for the CD-ROM and floppy drive and any other links you have set. When KDE starts, it scans the contents of the Desktop directory and creates icons for each item.

Desktop links that launch applications, URLs, or files are configured in the background by *.desktop* files. These are simple text files that contain all the information that you set for a link in the link properties dialog boxes. Although all configuration of desktop links is handled thoroughly by the configuration pop-up windows, the contents of *.desktop* files may be of interest. The following example shows the *.desktop* file for a link to the Kate text editor:

```
# KDE Config File
[Desktop Entry]
Comment[en-US]=The Kate text editor
Encoding=UTF-8
Exec=kate
Icon=
```

KDE

```
MimeType=
Name[en-US]=Kate
Path=
ServiceTypes=
SwallowExec=
SwallowTitle=
Terminal=false
TerminalOptions=
Type=Application
X-KDE-SubstituteUID=false
X-KDE-Username=
...
```

As you can see, the syntax is simple and straightforward. The items filled in on the properties windows are listed on each line of the file. The **Type** line identifies the kind of link file. In this example, Kate is an application; **Type=URL** would indicate an Internet address link file. The **Name** line lists the name of the application, **Comment** lists the comment you added to describe the application, **Exec** lists the command, **Icon** identifies the icon image file for an icon other than the default, and so on. Unspecified options have empty values. The **Name** and **Comment** lines include the language in square brackets.

The Panel

The panel is the control bar across the bottom of the screen, used to find and launch applications and navigate among windows and desktops. It contains the K menu (identified by the KDE K logo), which organizes the installed KDE applications into submenus; the Desktop Access button, which minimizes all open windows to display a clean desktop; and the desktop pager and the taskbar. Additional buttons that open applications, directories, and URLs can be added to the panel.

The Desktop Pager

Like most window managers, **kwin** (KDE's window manager) can divide your workspace into multiple desktops. Different application windows can be open on each desktop, reducing the amount of clutter on your screen. You can switch among desktops by using the desktop buttons on the panel. The panel displays a grid of buttons called the *pager*. The pager has one button for each virtual desktop, and shows images of the open windows or their names (1, 2, 3, etc., by default). Clicking on a button switches your screen to the corresponding desktop.

Clicking the wider vertical bar to the left of the pager opens a Desktop Pager window. If your version of KDE does not have that bar, right-click on the pager itself and select Launch Pager. The Desktop Pager has larger buttons for each desktop and an actual icon for each application running on that desktop, making it easier to tell what applications are running.

You can configure the number of virtual desktops and their names in the Control Center by selecting Look & Feel → Desktop and clicking the Number of Desktops tab.

The Taskbar

The taskbar runs in the panel and helps you keep track of running applications. It contains buttons to identify each open application window. If the button for an application is clicked, that becomes the current active window. When you iconify a window, you can raise it again by clicking its button on the taskbar. If a window has been iconified, its taskbar button contains a parenthesized text label. If multiple instances of one type of window are running, they are represented by a single button in the taskbar, with a small up-arrow on the right. Click the button to display a list of the instances and select the one you want.

Clicking the wider vertical bar to the left of the taskbar displays a menu divided into sections for each desktop and items for each window they contain. (This window list is also accessible by middle-clicking on the desktop background.) For example, if desktop 2 contains an open Konqueror window, you can click on its entry in the window list, and the window manager switches you to desktop 2 and activates the Konqueror window.

You can add an external taskbar to the desktop, either in place of or in addition to the one running in the panel. The external taskbar runs along one edge of the desktop, usually the top or bottom. You can configure the location and other settings of the external taskbar in the Control Center by selecting Panel → Extensions.

Adding an Application Link to the Panel

The simplest way to add an application button to the panel is by dragging an icon from the desktop to the panel. This copies the link from the desktop. Any application listed in the K menu can be easily added to the panel. From the K menu, choose Panel → Add Application, then select from the submenus or items that are listed. The choices you have are the same items that appear on the K menu.

To remove a button from the panel, right-click on an empty place on the panel to bring up the panel menu, and select Remove. That displays another menu that lets you remove applets such as the pager or taskbar, buttons that start applications, or special buttons such as the K menu or the Desktop Access button. You can also right-click on an icon and select Remove.

Running an Application on the Panel

A swallowed application, or applet, is a program that runs on the panel instead of in a desktop window. A swallowed application can be a small utility that monitors network activity or provides mail notification, for example. The lock/login applet, the **klipper** clipboard applet, and the clock are examples of swallowed applications, as are the pager and the taskbar when they're running in the panel. Add other applets by selecting Add → Applet from the panel menu and selecting the applet you want.

KDE

The KDE Control Center

The KDE Control Center contains a number of configuration tools, called *modules*, that allow you to configure and view information about your system. You can configure the desktop, window behavior and decoration, input devices, and any other important part of your system here.

The Control Center is split into two windows: the left window shows a hierarchical list of installed modules, and the right window displays the modules when they are selected. (You can also run individual Control Center modules by selecting the one you want from the Preferences option on the K menu.) Start the Control Center from the panel button with an icon of a circuit board in front of a terminal, or from the K menu. Many of the modules can also be accessed directly from their applications, by right-clicking on the application icon and selecting Preferences, or by right-clicking on the titlebar of the running application window and selecting Configure.

Context-sensitive help is available for Control Center modules by clicking on the question mark on the titlebar and then on the setting for which you want help. You can get a brief general help message for the currently open module by clicking the Help tab in the left window; each help message also contains a link to the module's manual. Or you can get help by opening the Help Center, selecting Applications → Preferences, and then choosing a module.

The middle tab in the left Control Center window lets you search. You can enter a term in the text box at the top to narrow the list of keywords, or scroll through the keywords. When you find the one you want, click on it to highlight it. The Results box at the bottom will display a list of modules for which the term applies; select a module from the list and that module will appear in the right-hand window. For example, selecting the keyword **audio** displays the results Sound, Sound Server, System Bell, and System Notifications. If you select Sound Server from that list, you can view or change the Sound Server settings.

The following sections describe the modules. The number and type of available Control Center modules vary depending on your Linux distribution and which version of KDE you are running. You may find that some of the modules described here are not on your system, that you have others that we don't describe, or that some of the specifics are different. In general, however, these descriptions should give you a good idea of how to go about configuring your KDE desktop.

File Browsing

The File Browsing modules are used to set file associations and to configure Konqueror's file management features.

File Associations

This module associates a filename extension with an application so that clicking on a file with that extension automatically opens the application with the file loaded. The utility divides files into various types based on the MIME standard used for email and the Web. Thus, under the text types you can find the **html** type. The file extensions *.htm*, *.HTM*, *.html*, and *.HTML* are associated with the **html** file type.

The window initially has only a text box where you can enter a filename pattern to search for the matching application and a list of known applications. You can also add and remove types from the list.

When you select an application from the Known Types list, the right side of the window displays options for that file type. The General tab shows the patterns associated with the application; you can add others or select one of the patterns to remove it from the list. Clicking on the icon image opens the Select Icon window for choosing a different icon to use with that file type. Application Preference Order lists the applications associated with that type. You can add applications to the list with the Add button; select an entry to activate the other buttons. You can then move the entry up or down on the list, edit it, or remove it from the list.

On the Embedding tab, the set of radio buttons determines whether a file is viewed in Konqueror or in an application window.

File Manager

This module contains configuration settings for the Konqueror file manager. The Behavior tab sets some global options, such as whether opening a directory also opens a new Konqueror window or if you want a dialog box to show the progress of a network file download. On the Appearance tab, you can set your choice of font, font size, and text color. Other options on this tab include whether to wrap or truncate icon text, underline filenames on the desktop, or display the file size in bytes (otherwise kilobytes or megabytes are shown for large files) in tree, detailed list, and text view modes. The Trash tab determines whether you'll be asked for confirmation when moving a file to the trash, deleting it, or shredding it. For every file type checked on the Previews tab, the Konqueror file manager displays a mini-preview of the file contents instead of an icon.

Information

The Information modules allow you to view status information about various system components. There are no configuration settings here, but if you need to see information about your processor or what PCI devices you have installed, use these modules. Information is provided for the following system components:

- Block devices
- Devices
- DMA-Channels
- Interrupts
- IO-Ports
- Memory
- Network interfaces
- Partitions

- PCI
- PCMCIA
- Processor
- Protocols
- Samba status
- SCSI
- Sound
- USB devices
- X-Server

Look & Feel

The Look & Feel modules determine the appearance of the KDE desktop and configure it to work in a way that is comfortable for you.

Background

This module sets the desktop background. It allows you to specify a background for each virtual desktop or just one background for all of them. Select the desktop you want to configure from the list, or check the Common Background box.

On the Background tab at the bottom of the window, select whether you want a flat (Solid color) background, a pattern, or one of several gradients from the Mode drop-down box. If you select a pattern, click the Setup box, and the Select Background Pattern window will open. Select a pattern from the choices or add your own, and click OK. For a pattern or gradient, choose colors for Color 1 and Color 2 by clicking on the color bars. For a flat background, choose a color from the Color 1 color bar.

On the Wallpaper tab, you can choose No Wallpaper, Single Wallpaper, or Multiple Wallpaper. If you are using wallpaper, the Mode setting determines how the image file is laid out. You can choose a tiled layout, or various centered or scaled options. If you want to use an image file as wallpaper on the background, select it from the drop-down list, or click the Browse button to look for the image on the filesystem. To use multiple wallpapers, click the Setup Multiple button. Set the time interval that each wallpaper remains on the screen. The Mode button lets you cycle through wallpaper patterns in order or randomly. Choose the wallpapers to use from the list, or click the Add or Remove button to add or remove files from the list. When viewing available wallpapers, right-click the display and choose Thumbnail Previews to see what they'll look like.

The Advanced tab sets a blending pattern for a multicolored background. The choices range from no blending to horizontal or vertical blending to various patterns and intensities.

Colors

The Colors module allows you to select the colors for the various window widgets, the components used to build windows. You can select the colors based on a scheme installed on your system. Select one of the available schemes from the list, and click Apply to change the color scheme. You can also set colors for individual components. The top portion of the tab shows sample window components. Click on the component you want to configure, such as the active titlebar or window background, to select it, or select a component from the widget color list. Click the color bar under the list to open the color selector dialog box and choose your color. Other choices are to set the contrast of the component with the Contrast slider and to apply the colors to non-KDE applications.

Desktop

The Desktop module sets preferences for the visual display of your environment. You can determine the appearance of your desktop and the number of virtual desktops, the actions taken by mouse buttons, and other options.

On the Desktop tab, select the options you want. Enable Desktop Menu places a copy of the desktop menu as a menubar at the top of the screen. Enable Icons on Desktop lets you place icons on the desktop for easy access. If you also set Show Hidden Files on Desktop, all files in the Desktop directory are displayed, including hidden files. Programs in Desktop Window lets you set a running application such as **xearth** as your desktop background. From the list of file types under "Show Previews for," select any for which you want a preview displayed on the desktop instead of an icon. Under "Clicks on the desktop," select the action to be taken on a left, right, or middle mouse-button click.

From the Appearance tab, select your preferred font, font size, and text color. You can also select a background color if you want to view the background box of the label. By default, the background is transparent, allowing the desktop background to be visible. Finally, you can choose to have filenames underlined.

The Number of Desktops tab sets the number of virtual desktops you can divide your workspace into. The default is 4, and you can use up to 16. The slider selects the number of desktops. The desktops are listed, numbered 1 through 16. For each enabled desktop, the listing has a usable text box next to it. You can type in a label for each desktop that will be shown in the pager display on the panel. The default labels are Desktop 1 through Desktop 16.

The Paths tab lets you set the path to the desktop, trash, and Autostart directories and to the default path for documents. In most cases, you won't need to change the defaults.

Fonts

The Fonts module sets the default fonts used on your display. You can set the font for the following listed selections: General, Fixed Width, Toolbar, Window Title, and Taskbar. Click the Choose button for the font you want to change, and the Select Font window appears. From this, you can select the font you want, choose if you want it to be bold or italic, and select the point size. A sample of the selected font is displayed at the bottom of the window. You can also check the box labeled "Use Anti-Aliasing for fonts" to make the fonts appear smoother on the screen.

Icons

This module controls the display and behavior of icons on the desktop. The module has two tabs, Theme and Advanced.

On the Theme tab, select an icon theme. The sample icons at the top are displayed in the current theme. After selecting a theme, select Install New Theme to install it. At the bottom of the window, you can add a new theme to the list by entering the path in the text box or clicking the button at the right to open a File dialog window. You can also remove any theme except the default.

Icons are used for many purposes: in the file manager, on the panel, and so on. The Advanced tab configures icons individually for different uses. First, select the use that you want to configure from the list. For that use, select a size from the Size list, or "Double-sized pixels" to get very large, but somewhat blurry, icons. You can also choose to have the icons animated. The icon images at the bottom show how the icon will appear normally (default), when it is active (i.e., when the cursor is over it), and when it is disabled.

For each use, you can set special effects. Clicking the Set Effect button displays the Set Default Icon Effect window. From that window, select an effect and move the slider to determine the amount of that effect. For instance, choosing the To Gray effect for Active causes an icon to turn gray when you put the cursor on it. (To Gray is probably more appropriate for Disabled.) If you choose Colorize, the Color option becomes active so you can pick a color.

Launch Feedback

The Launch Feedback module has two options to provide visual feedback while an application is starting, so you know something is happening. If you check the box Enable Busy Cursor, a mini-icon appears and tracks the cursor. Under the Enable Busy Cursor option, checking Enable Blinking causes the icon to blink. Enable Taskbar Notification causes the taskbar entry to show a revolving timer while the application starts. Both options let you set a timeout, which has a maximum of 99 seconds. When the timeout period is over, the visual feedback stops, even if the application is not yet fully started.

Panel

The panel configuration module controls the panel's appearance, the panel's behavior, and the K menu layout, and it configures any extensions that are enabled.

On the Position tab, you can choose to place the panel at the top, bottom, left side, or right side of the screen by clicking the appropriate radio button. You can set the panel alignment to Left, Center, or Right. Five settings are available to set the size of the panel to either Tiny, Small, Medium, Large, or Custom. In the Length section, you can move the slider to set the amount of the width or height of the desktop that the panel occupies. If you set it to less than 100% and click the "Expand to fit required size" button, the panel will expand to take up as much room as it needs to fit all the icons.

The Hiding tab, shown in Figure 18-7, is divided into sections that provide options for hiding the panel when you want more visible desktop space to use as a work area. The Hide Buttons section contains checkboxes that enable the display of a hide button at one or both sides of the panel. Clicking on a hide button causes the panel to roll up into that side and disappear, leaving only a button you can click to have the panel reappear. Move the slider in the Hide Button Size section to set the size of the hide button. Checking the box in the Manual Hide Animation section enables the panel to use a sliding visual effect when you show or hide it with its side arrow buttons. The slider sets the speed of this animation. You can have the panel autohide (i.e., disappear when not being used) by checking the "Enable automatic hide" button and moving the slider to set the amount of time after the pointer has left the panel that the panel will hide. The panel reappears when you move the mouse over it. Checking the "Show panel when switching desktop" box causes the panel to reappear when you move to a different desktop. It appears on the new desktop and then hides again. You can set "Enable automatic hide animation" and move the slider to set the animation speed.

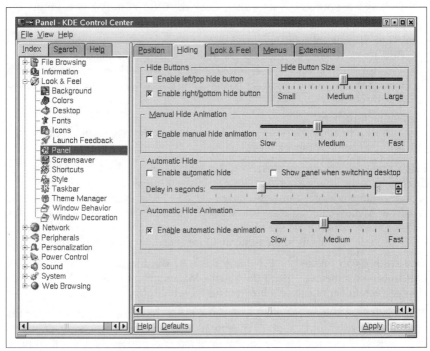

Figure 18-7. Panel hiding configuration

The Look & Feel tab contains settings for the appearance of the panel and its icons. Each icon is on a tile that by default is transparent, so all you see is the icon. If you set "Enable background tiles," the tiles are shown, and the settings in the middle of the window are enabled so you can enable or disable different tile types and set the background colors individually. The tile types are K-Menu, Quickbrowser, Application Launcher, Legacy Application Launcher, Window List, and Desktop Access.

KDE

Also on the Look & Feel tab, the "Enable icon zooming" setting causes icons to zoom large when you pass the mouse over them, so they appear to pop out at you. The "Show tooltips" option displays tooltips when you move the mouse over icons on the panel. To see an image on the panel background, set "Enable background image" and either enter the path to the image or browse to find one.

The Menus tab contains settings for the K menu and other menu layouts. Settings for the K menu include:

Show side image
　Show a small image next to each menu entry.

Show "Bookmarks" submenu
　Include a Bookmarks menu that shows your Konqueror bookmarks and lets you edit them.

Show "Recent Documents" submenu
　Display a list of recently used files. Click the Clear History box to empty the list.

Show "Quick Browser" submenu
　Add a browser menu for easy access to files without running the file manager. The top-level entries are Home Directory, Root Directory, and System Configuration to start from the user's home directory, the root directory, and */etc*, respectively.

Detailed menu entries
　Include a brief description of each menu item. If the box is not checked, only the application name is shown.

Below these settings are two columns, Available Menus and Selected Menus. The first column contains menus that are not in the K menu but can be added. The second column contains those you have selected to add. Highlight an entry in the Available Menus column and click the right-pointing arrow to move it to the Selected Menus column; do the reverse to unselect an entry. Click the Apply button to add the selected menus to the K menu. Once added, they stay in the Selected list.

To have browser menus show hidden files (i.e., dot files), select "Show hidden files in browser menus." Move the slider "Maximum browser menu entries" to change the number of entries a browser menu will display.

The Quick Start section is at the top of the K menu. Its entries consist of either the most recently used or the most frequently used applications, depending on which radio button is selected. Set the maximum number of entries shown in the Quick Start section if you want to change the default, which is 5.

The Extensions tab is active if you have added any extensions, such as a child panel or an external taskbar (by right-clicking on the panel and selecting Add → Extension). For each extension, you can locate it to the left, right, top, or bottom of the desktop, set automatic hide options, enable hide buttons, and specify the hide button size.

Screensaver

This module sets up your screensaver. A list of available screensavers is shown with a preview window. If you want to use a screensaver, check the Enable Screensaver box and select the screensaver you want to use. The Setup button opens a dialog box that contains specific configuration settings for each screensaver. For a full-screen test of the screensaver, click the Test button.

The Settings section allows you to set the amount of time the system is inactive before the screensaver starts. Type in the number of minutes in the Wait For box to set this time. If you check the Require Password box, the user must supply a password before returning to the desktop. You can also check the box "Show Password as Stars" to display the password text as asterisks instead of leaving the field blank. The Priority control lets you adjust the priority that the screensaver process has when it is run. If you have lots of important server activity, for example, set the priority to low so the performance of other programs does not suffer.

Shortcuts

Shortcuts are key combinations that do something to your desktop or application. By default, for example, Alt-F4 closes the current window. That's a global shortcut; there are also shortcuts used in specific applications.

You can choose the scheme used for shortcuts by selecting the KDE defaults or the current scheme if you have customized the shortcuts. The bottom section of the tab allows you to edit the selected keyboard shortcut. You can choose no key for the action, the default key, or a custom key. If you select custom, the Define Shortcut dialog appears. Here you can set or modify the primary or alternate shortcut. Click the X in the box pointing to the current shortcut, then click Multi-Key if you want to use any modifiers (Shift, Ctrl, or Alt). Finally, press the key or key combination on the keyboard that you want to use. Click Apply to save the change to the current scheme, or click New Scheme and then Save to save them as a new scheme.

The Modifier Keys tab shows the modifier keys for the current keyboard. It is not used for configuration, but is there simply to provide information.

Style

The Style module contains settings for the display of windows and icons. Choose a style from the Widget Style list on the Style tab. The bottom half of the window previews the selected style. If you check Enable GUI Effects on the Effects tab, you can set effects such as fade or animation for ComboBox, ToolTip, and Menu effects. You can also make menus translucent and specify the type and degree of translucency or opacity. (Note that translucency uses more system resources, so you might not want to use these effects on a slower system.) The Miscellaneous tab offers several toolbar and visual appearance options.

Taskbar

The Taskbar module configures the taskbar, both in the panel and on the desktop. It is not used to set where on the desktop the taskbar appears (do that

KDE

from Panel → Extensions). To add or remove the taskbar from the panel, right-click on the panel and select Add or Remove and then Taskbar. To place the taskbar directly on the desktop or to remove it from the desktop, use the Extensions tab in the Panel module.

The Taskbar module settings include the following:

Show windows from all desktops
> The taskbar shows all windows, regardless of which desktop they are on. You can then select a task and move directly to that desktop with that window active.

Show window list button
> Add a menu button at the left edge of the taskbar that displays, when clicked, a list of all desktops and their windows. This is particularly useful if "Show windows from all desktops" is unchecked, since it lets you select a window on another desktop.

Group similar tasks
> Combine multiple instances of any application into a single taskbar entry. The entry shows a small up-arrow. When you click on the arrow, a list of the instances appears and you can select the one you want.

Sort tasks by virtual desktop
> Order the taskbar by desktop.

Show application icons
> Show the application's icon along with the text on each taskbar entry.

The Actions section sets an action for each of the left, middle, and right mouse buttons. The possible actions for each are Show Task List, Show Operations Menu, Cycle Through Windows, Activate Task, Raise Task, Lower Task, and Minimize Task.

Theme Manager

Themes provide an overall visual style to your desktop, so you get an integrated look instead of having to configure items individually. A theme can determine the color scheme of windows, the font styles, icons, background, and even sound events for your desktop. Several themes are installed by default with KDE, and many more are available at *http://kde.themes.org* for download.

The Installer tab, shown in Figure 18-8, lists the themes you have installed on your system. These include global themes, which are stored in *$KDEDIR/share/ apps/kthememgr/Themes*, and local themes, which you have installed or customized and stored in *~/.kde/share/apps/kthememgr/Themes*. You can edit and save local themes. Global themes cannot be altered by individual users.

If you select a theme from the list, a sample desktop image using the theme is displayed on the tab with a short text description. To apply a new theme, select from the list and click the Apply button. The selected theme is copied to your theme manager work directory (*~/.kde/share/apps/kthememgr/Work*).

You can also manage installed themes on the Installer tab. To install a new theme that you have downloaded, click the Add button. Specify the filename and location of the theme's *.tgz* file in the pop-up dialog box and click OK. The Save As

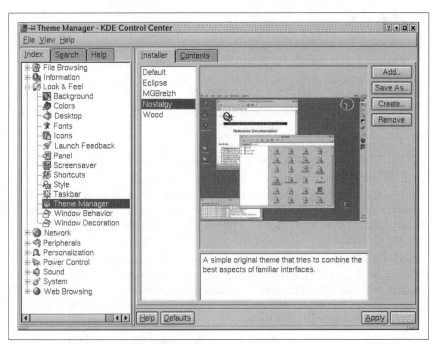

Figure 18-8. Theme Manager Installer tab

button saves the currently configured theme as a separate local package without altering the original theme. The Create button works similarly, allowing you to copy your current working theme as a new local theme package. The Remove button deletes a local theme or inactivates a global theme.

The Contents tab shows the components that are configured by a theme. A theme may not have settings available for all the listed components. If a theme configures a specific component, it is listed as available. Otherwise, the component is listed as empty. Use the checkboxes to select which theme components you want to use. If you choose not to activate a specific component, information on that component from a previous theme will be used if its information is still in the theme manager work directory. If you don't want this to happen, activate the component even if it is listed as empty, and default settings will be used.

Window Behavior

The modules in the Window Behavior module allow you to set the look and functionality of window titlebars, mouse button actions, and focus and placement policy.

On the Focus tab, the Focus Policy section sets the policy for giving a window keyboard focus and an active titlebar. The drop-down list contains four focus styles:

Click to Focus
> This default focus policy requires a mouse click in a window to give it focus and raise it (bring it to the foreground).

Focus Follows Mouse

This setting causes a window to receive focus when the mouse pointer enters it. It does not come to the foreground unless the Auto Raise button is checked. The window maintains focus until the pointer enters another window.

Focus Under Mouse

This setting is similar to the Focus Follows Mouse setting, except that the window loses focus when the mouse pointer moves out of it. If the pointer is not in a window, no window has focus.

Focus Strictly Under Mouse

This setting is similar to Focus Under Mouse, but is stricter in interpreting when the mouse leaves the window.

For all the focus policies except Click to Focus, the Auto Raise and Click Raise boxes are available. One of these must be checked to be able to raise windows to the foreground. Auto Raise raises a window after a short delay, which you can set with the Delay slider.

The Keyboard section determines behavior when you use the keyboard to switch windows or desktops. In KDE mode, a box appears showing the window you are about to switch to. In CDE mode, no box appears. Check "Traverse windows on all desktops" if you want to move through all windows on all desktops. (CDE is an older desktop distributed with some commercial Unix systems.)

The Actions tab (Figure 18-9) configures the actions of mouse buttons on the various window components. Drop-down lists contain several options, such as raise or lower, for the left, middle, and right buttons. For each of the components, you can choose what happens when a mouse button is clicked. For instance, by default, right-clicking in a titlebar brings up an Operations menu.

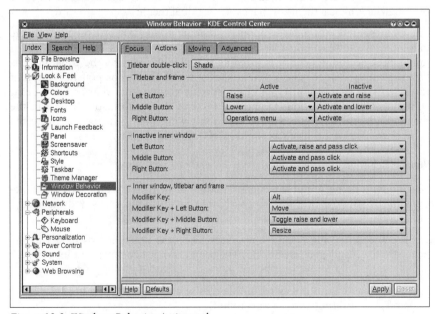

Figure 18-9. Windows Behavior Actions tab

The Moving tab sets window and snap zone options. The Windows section of the tab has the following settings:

Display Content in Moving Windows
Enable the display of window contents when the window is moved.

Display Content in Resizing Window
Enable the display of window contents when the window is resized.

Animate Minimize and Restore
Enable animation and activate the slider, which controls the animation speed.

Allow Moving and Resizing of Maximized Windows
Allow the use of the border on a maximized window to move or resize the window.

Placement
Choose Smart, Cascade, or Random window placement from the drop-down list to determine the initial placement of new windows on the desktop. Smart placement attempts to keep windows as uncluttered as possible. Cascade attempts to place windows in a cascaded pattern, so at least an edge of each window is visible. Random placement puts each new window randomly on the desktop.

The Snap Zones section sets the width of the zone within which a window will snap to the desktop border at the edge of the screen ("Border snap zone") or to another window ("Window snap zone"). Both zones are set with sliders and default to 10 pixels.

The Advanced tab sets options for configuring window shading, the use of Xinerama, and active desktop borders. In the Shading section, check Animate to animate window shading and unshading, and check Enable Hover to cause a shaded window to unshade if the mouse pointer remains over the titlebar for the number of milliseconds determined by moving the Delay slider.

Xinerama is a feature of XFree86 that allows multiple monitors to be treated as one big monitor. KDE supports Xinerama; the Xinerama section is available only if Xinerama support was compiled into KDE.* The following checkboxes configure the use of Xinerama:

Enable Xinerama Support
Enable the use of Xinerama with KDE.

Enable Window Resistance Support
Provide some resistance when a window moves to the edge of one monitor screen so that it doesn't accidentally move onto the next.

Enable Window Placement Support
Provide support for positioning windows on any portion of the logical desktop, regardless of which monitor it falls on. If window placement support is enabled, a new window appears on the screen where the mouse pointer is.

Enable Window Maximize Support
Permit windows to be maximized across multiple monitors.

---

* The screens also need to be configured in */etc/X11/XF86Config*.

Active desktop borders enable you to switch between desktops by moving the mouse pointer to an adjacent screen edge. In the Active Desktop Borders section, the choices are:

Disabled
Turn off active desktop borders.

Only When Moving Windows
Enable active borders only when moving windows across the edge, not when moving the mouse across.

Always Enabled
Active borders are enabled both for moving windows and for moving the mouse across the edge to another desktop.

The Desktop switch-delay slider sets a delay time for the switch to the adjacent desktop. Set this time to a comfortable setting that doesn't cause an unwanted desktop switch every time you move the pointer to the screen edge. The slider is active unless active borders have been disabled.

Window Decoration

The Window Decoration module sets preferences for the appearance of KDE windows. There are three tabs: General, Buttons, and Configure.

The Buttons tab configures the layout of buttons that appear on the titlebars of windows. It is available only if you check "Use custom titlebar button positions" on the General tab. There are five buttons: minimize (dot), maximize (square), sticky (pushpin), close (X), and menu (dash or application-specified icon). Each button has three placement options, specified by radio buttons: left, right, or off. You can place no more than three buttons on one side of the titlebar.

The options available on the Configure tab vary according to the window decoration style selected on the General tab. Depending on the style, they affect the appearance of the titlebar and buttons, and the width of the window frame. The tab itself shows the name of the current style. For some styles, no configuration options are available.

Network

The Network modules configure a number of networking features on your system. These modules don't configure the network itself, but set your personal preferences and configuration options. The primary networking modules in the Control Center include Email, Preferences, SOCKS, and Window Shares. These modules are described here. Depending on your Linux distribution and what applications you have installed, you may also see modules such as Kisdndock, which configures ISDN docking options; LAN Browsing to configure LISa, the LAN Information Server, which provides a TCP/IP-based "network neighborhood" for your network; and News Ticker, which is a news ticker applet that runs on the panel and provides running access to current news from sites you specify.

Email

The Email module provides a place for you to specify some basic pieces of information that KDE may use for email-related purposes. In the User Information section, you can specify your Full Name, Organization, Email Address, and Reply-To Address. In the Preferred Email Client section, enter the name of the email client you want KDE to use on your behalf. The default client is KDE's KMail, but you can enter another client or click the Browse button to find available clients. Check the Run in Terminal box if you use a text-based email client such as Pine.

Preferences

The Preferences module sets timeout values for "Socket read," "Proxy connect," "Server connect," and "Server response." If your connection is slow and you find that you are getting frequent timeouts, you might want to increase the values. This module also has an FTP Options section where you can check "Enable passive mode (PASV)" if you want to permit passive FTP transfers because you are behind a firewall, and you can check "Mark partially uploaded files" so that they appear in a directory listing with a *.part* extension until the transfer is complete.

SOCKS

The SOCKS module enables SOCKS support in KDE applications. SOCKS is a protocol that executes proxy requests on behalf of a client. If you have SOCKS installed and working, you can check the box "Enable SOCKS support." At that point, additional options become available. Click "Auto detect" to have KDE try to determine which SOCKS implementation you are using, or click NEC SOCKS or Dante if you are using one of those. Finally, if KDE can't detect your SOCKS implementation, you can enter one or more paths in the "Additional library search paths" section for KDE to search. Click the Test button to test your SOCKS support.

Windows Shares

The Windows Shares module configures your Samba client if you are running Samba on your network to communicate with Windows systems. This module configures the client, not the Samba server, so that Konqueror can access shared Windows filesystems from other computers.

Enter your default username, default password, and workgroup in the three text boxes at the top of the window. Check the box "Show hidden shares" if you want to see shares whose names end with a dollar sign ($).

Note that entering your password and having KDE store it on the system is a security risk. If you don't enter your name or password and they are required to access the shared Windows system, you will be prompted for them. That's less convenient, but safer.

Password

The Password module is available in some distributions, including Red Hat 8 with Bluecurve, allowing you to change your login password. This module prompts you for your current password and new password, and then asks you to re-enter the new password.

Peripherals

The modules here control the configuration of the keyboard and mouse. These settings affect only your use of KDE; they don't modify the global X server settings. Some distributions may include other modules in this section, such as a Digital Camera module that lets you add and configure one or more digital cameras.

Keyboard

This module configures your primary keyboard layout and any additional layouts (if you work in more than one language, for example). Use it also to configure other keyboard options.

The Layout tab determines your keyboard layouts if you check "Enable keyboard layouts." In the Configuration section, three drop-down lists are available to set your keyboard model, primary country and language layout, and a primary variant. The options on the variant drop-down list vary depending on which primary layout you select, but generally include different keymaps for the same language.

In the "Additional layouts" section, select any other layouts you may want to use. You can also select a variant for each. The additional layouts include variations such as the Dvorak keyboard layout, in addition to language layouts. The list of layouts shows a flag image for each layout. When you enable layouts, a button is added to the system tray in the panel that allows you to switch between your selected layouts. The button contains the flag for the current layout. Click the flag to cycle through the layouts.

The Options tab sets the Switching Policy to one of Global, Window Class, or Window. The policy determines whether a layout switch happens globally, by window class, or on a window-by-window basis. The Xkb Options section sets Xkb (X keyboard) options; you can check the box Reset Old Options to reset your options to the defaults as defined in your */etc/X11/XF86Config* file. The rest of this section consists of five drop-down lists used to set the behavior of certain keys.* Each can be left blank or set to one of the listed options. The drop-down lists are:

CapsLock Key Behavior
> Sets whether the Caps Lock key uses internal capitalization or acts as a shift lock key, in each case with or without canceling caps.

---

* Depending on your Linux distribution, you may not see all the lists described here.

Third-Level Choosers
Sets the key or keys that can be used as an ISO 9995 third-level chooser. ISO 9995 is a multipart ISO standard that specifies keyboard layouts for text and office systems. The choices are Any of the Win-keys, Left Win-key, Right Control, Right Win-key, or Menu key.

Control Key Position
Determines the position of the Control key. The choices are Control Key at Bottom Left, Control Key at Left of "A", Make CapsLock an Additional Control, or Swap Control and CapsLock.

Use keyboard LED to show alternative group
Sets one of Scroll_Lock LED, Caps_Lock LED, or Num_Lock LED to show an alternative group as defined by ISO 9995.

Group Shift/Lock behavior
Determines what key is used to switch groups. Some of the options change the group until it is changed again, while others change the group only while the key is pressed. The choices are: Left Win-key changes group, Both Win-keys switch group while pressed, R-Alt switches group while pressed, Both Shift keys together change group, Right Win-key changes group, Left Win-key switches group while pressed, Caps Lock key changes group, Right Alt key changes group, or Alt+Shift changes group.

The Advanced tab configures the keyboard repeat (i.e., holding a key down repeats the character until you release the key). Check the "Keyboard repeat" box to enable keyboard repeat, and use the slider to set the keyclick volume. If you don't want to hear keyclicks, set the slider to 0. Note that your keyboard may not support changing the keyclick volume. The section "NumLock on KDE startup" determines the state of the NumLock key when KDE starts. Click Turn on, Turn off, or Leave unchanged.

Mouse

This module configures the movement and button layout of your mouse.

On the General tab, the Button Mapping section sets the mouse to be right-handed or left-handed. In the Icons section, select either "Single-click to open files and folders" or "Double-click to open files and folders." If you select single-click, you also have the option to check "Change pointer shape over icons" and "Automatically select icons." If you select "Automatically select icons," move the slider to determine how long the pointer can remain over the icon before it is selected. If you select double-click to open, then a single click selects an icon. Check "Visual feedback on activation" or "Large cursor" to select either of those options.

On the Advanced tab, the Pointer Acceleration slider determines how fast the pointer moves on your screen when you move your mouse. Lower values move the pointer more slowly for small mouse movements, giving you finer control. Higher values let you cross the screen more quickly. The Pointer Threshold slider sets the distance (in pixels) that the mouse must move before pointer movement occurs. The Double Click Interval slider sets the maximum time that can pass between two clicks and still be considered a double-click. The Drag Start Time slider sets the amount of time that has to pass after you click a button and start to

KDE

move the mouse before it is considered a drag operation. The Drag Start Distance slider sets the distance (in pixels) that the mouse must move with a button clicked before it is considered a drag operation. The Mouse Wheel Scrolls By slider determines how many lines are scrolled for one mouse wheel movement.

Personalization

The Personalization modules cover configuration options that don't fit neatly into any of the other categories.

Accessibility

The Accessibility module sets configuration options to make the system more accessible. The Bell tab sets the audible bell to one of "Use System bell" or "Use customized bell." If you choose a customized bell, use the text box to enter the path to the sound you want, or select Browse. You can set a visible "bell" by checking "Use visible bell" and then either "Invert screen" or "Flash screen." Select a color by clicking the color button and use the slider to set the duration of the inversion or flashing.

The Keyboard tab has three settings to make the keyboard easier to use:

Use sticky keys
> Pressing one of the Ctrl, Alt, or Shift keys and then releasing it to press another key is treated as a multi-key combination for the next keypress. For example, to enter Ctrl-Tab with sticky keys enabled, press Ctrl, release it, and then press Tab. You can also check "Lock sticky keys." In that case, pressing Ctrl, Alt, or Shift once behaves the same as "Use sticky keys"; pressing the key twice leaves it in the modified mode until you press it again to release it.

Use slow keys
> Each key must be held down for the amount of time specified by the Delay slider to be recognized as a key press. This protects you from accidental keystrokes.

Use bounce keys
> The amount of time specified by the Delay slider must pass between two key presses for the second one to be recognized. This protects you from accidentally hitting multiple keys if you type fast.

The Mouse tab sets values for using the arrow keys on the numeric keypad to move the mouse pointer instead of having to use a mouse, trackball, or other device. The possible settings are Acceleration Delay, Repeat Interval, Acceleration Time, Maximum Speed, and Acceleration Profile. If you don't have a numeric keypad (e.g., on a laptop computer), the numeric keypad keys are usually available on the keyboard, accessed with a function (fn) key.

Country & Language

The Country & Language module sets the preferred locale settings for your programs. The Locale tab has a drop-down list for selecting your country. When you select a country, the language or languages generally used in that country appear in the Languages box. You can add a language to the list from the Add

Language drop-down list, or select a language and click Remove Language to remove one from the list. The bottom portion of the tab shows the default appearance of numbers, money, dates, and time for that country and language. Use the remaining tabs to change these defaults. As you change the settings, the examples at the bottom of the window (which are shown on all the tabs) also change, so you can see how they will look with the new settings.

The Numbers tab lets you set the character used for the decimal symbol, thousands separator, positive sign, and negative sign.

The Money tab lets you set the character to be used for the currency symbol, decimal symbol, thousands separator, and fract (fractional) digits, i.e., the number of digits after the decimal point. In the sections positive and negative, check the "Prefix currency symbol" box to have the currency symbol appear before the positive or negative sign, and then select where the sign should be placed from the drop-down list. The possible positions are:

Parentheses around
　　Display the value in parentheses. For example, you might select this option to display negative numbers in parentheses rather than showing a minus sign.

Before quantity money
　　Display the sign after the currency symbol and before the value.

After quantity money
　　Display the sign after the value and before the currency symbol.

Before money
　　Display the sign before both the value and the currency symbol.

After money
　　Display the sign after both the value and the currency symbol.

The Time & Dates tab has the following settings: Time format, Date format, Short date format, and Start week on Monday. Select the time and date formats from drop-down lists or enter a format into the appropriate text box. Check the "Start week on Monday" box if you want Monday rather than Sunday to start a new week. The time and date formats are specified with the following codes; the table shows the time codes first, then the date codes.

Code	Replaced by
HH	The two-digit hour on a 24-hour clock.
hH	The hour on a 24-hour clock, using one or two digits as appropriate.
PH	The two-digit hour on a 12-hour clock.
pH	The hour on a 12-hour clock, using one or two digits as appropriate.
MM	The minute, using two digits.
SS	The second, using two digits.
AMPM	Replaced with either "am" or "pm" as appropriate; primarily for use with a 12-hour clock setting.
YYYY	The four-digit year.
YY	The two-digit year.
MM	The two-digit month.
mM	The month, using one or two digits as appropriate.

KDE

Code	Replaced by
MONTH	The full name of the month.
SHORTMONTH	The abbreviated name of the month.
DD	The two-digit day of the month.
dD	The day of the month, using one or two digits as appropriate.
WEEKDAY	The full day of the week.
SHORTWEEKDAY	The abbreviated day of the week.

Crypto

The Crypto module controls the configuration of the OpenSSL implementation of the Secure Sockets Layer (SSL) and Transport Layer Security (TLS) network protocols. Use this module to configure SSL for use with KDE applications, and to manage your personal certificates and known certificate authorities. The module has six tabs: SSL, OpenSSL, Your Certificates, Authentication, Peer SSL Certificates, and SSL Signers.

If you do not have OpenSSL installed, each of the tabs displays the message "SSL ciphers cannot be configured because this module was not linked with OpenSSL." If you do have OpenSSL installed, you probably still should not make any configuration changes unless you are familiar with SSL and know what you are doing. For more information on using and configuring OpenSSL, see the O'Reilly book *Network Security with Open SSL.*

At the bottom of the SSL tab are some checkboxes. If OpenSSL is installed, you'll see five checkboxes; if it is not installed, only the last three are shown and available. The checkboxes are:

Use EGD
> Use the entropy-gathering daemon (EGD) to initialize the pseudo-random number generator. Entropy is basically a measure of randomness; SSL requires random numbers for such functions as creating public and private keys, and EGD is a Perl script that gathers entropy.

Use entropy file
> Use the file whose path you specify in the text box or by browsing as the source of entropy for the pseudo-random number generator.

Warn on leaving SSL mode
> See a warning when you leave an SSL-enabled site.

Warn on sending unencrypted data
> See a warning when you are about to send unencrypted data over the network with a web browser.

At the top of the SSL tab are three checkboxes that enable TLS support (if it's available), SSL v2 support, and SSL v3 support. These options are followed by two columns containing a list of SSL v2 and SSL v3 ciphers. You can check or uncheck the ciphers individually to select the ones you want to use, or use the buttons below the lists to select them in groups: Most Compatible, US Ciphers Only, Export Ciphers Only, or Enable All.

The OpenSSL tab lets you specify the path to your SSL libraries or use the Browse button to locate them. Then click on the Test button to test your settings.

The Your Certificates tab shows a list of certificates that KDE knows about and lets you manage them with a set of buttons on the right-hand side. The buttons are Import, Export, Remove, Unlock, Verify, and Change Password.

The Authentication tab lets you specify a default certificate from the drop-down button and a default action or policy. The possible policies are Send, Prompt, and Don't Send. You can also add or remove hosts and host certificates, and set one of the same three actions for each.

The Peer SSL Certificates tab lets you Export, Remove, or Verify peer organizations, and set a policy of Accept, Reject, or Prompt for each.

The SSL Signers tab lets you Import, Remove, or Restore organizations to a list of signing organizations, and determine whether to accept for site signing, accept for email signing, or accept for code signing.

Konsole

The Konsole module configures the Konsole terminal emulator. It has four tabs: General, Schema, Session, and Write Daemon.

The General tab has settings to determine general Konsole behavior:

Use Konsole as default terminal application
Set Konsole as your default terminal.

Show Terminal Size when Resizing
Display the number of characters and lines as you resize the terminal. The display changes as you change the size, showing the current dimensions.

Show Frame
Put a frame around the terminal window. If the frame is turned on, a narrow edge appears inside the Konsole window around the portion that represents the terminal itself. This option does not affect the border around the entire Konsole window.

Warn for Open Sessions on Quit
Konsole warns you if you still have open sessions when you quit out of Konsole.

Blinking Cursor
The cursor blinks inside the Konsole window, making the cursor easier to find.

Require Ctrl key for drag and drop
Require the use of the Ctrl key for dragging and dropping text. Konsole allows you to drag text and drop it into other applications.

Line Spacing
Use the up or down arrows to set the line spacing. The default value is Normal, which is single-spacing.

Double Click
The text box shows a default set of characters (besides letters and digits) that are treated as part of a word when you double-click to select a word. You can add or remove characters from this set.

KDE

The Schema tab sets up the appearance of the Konsole window. The Schema box in the center of the tab shows the available schemas with the current one highlighted. The current schema also is shown in the Title box at the top. Check the box under the list of schemas to set the highlighted one as the default or click the Remove Schema button to remove it from the list. You can also set up a color scheme and add a background image to your Konsole sessions.

The Session tab lets you set properties for the different types of Konsole sessions. Pick the session type from the list in the Session section of the tab, and then enter or change the name, the command to execute, and the default directory in the General section. You can select an icon by clicking on the image of the current icon, pick a font size from the Font drop-down menu, enter or change the setting of the **TERM** environment variable, set the keyboard type (e.g., Linux console, VT100, or XTerm), and set the color schema for that session type.

The Write Daemon tab has a single checkbox, whose effect is to start the write daemon when KDE starts up. You should generally leave this box checked.

Passwords

The Passwords module has three settings that determine how passwords are treated when you run privileged operations. Note that there are security implications to these settings. If you are not in a secure location, be careful of setting options that may make things easier for you but may also open security holes. The settings are:

Echo characters as
> Determines if and how your password is echoed on the screen as you enter it. Each character can be shown as one star, three stars, or not at all.

Remember passwords
> KDE will remember passwords so they don't have to be entered each time.

Timeout
> If "Remember passwords" is checked, this option becomes available to set the period of time for the passwords to be remembered. For example, you might set a timeout period of an hour if you are temporarily doing work that requires superuser privileges.

Session Manager

The Session Manager module controls the configuration of your KDE sessions. Check the "Confirm logout" box if you want KDE to ask for confirmation before logging you out. The confirmation box lets you change your mind and cancel the logout, or proceed to log out, with or without saving your current session information. If you check the "Save session for future logins" box, the logout confirmation box will also have that option checked by default; you can uncheck it when you log out to have your next session revert to the previously saved session.

The section "Default action after logout" has three options that control what action takes place by default when you log out. Check one of: Login as Different User, Turn Off Computer, and Restart Computer. The default action applies only if you logged in through the **kdm** display manager. You can always choose a different option if you let the system prompt you for confirmation.

Spell Checking

The Spell Checking module configures the KDE spell checker, KSpell. You can check either or both of "Create root/affix combinations not in dictionary" and "Consider run-together words as spelling errors." Select a dictionary from the drop-down list of dictionaries available on your system; also select the language encoding to use from another drop-down list, and whether to use international ISpell or ASpell as the underlying spell-checking client program. International ISpell is an interactive spell-checking program that understands many European languages. ASpell is similar to ISpell, but it is smarter about suggesting alternative spellings.

Power Control

The Power Control modules configure the energy-saving and battery settings for your system. The Energy module applies to all systems that have a monitor with energy-saving capabilities; the remaining modules apply to laptop or other battery-powered systems using the Linux Advanced Power Management (APM) or Advanced Configuration and Power Interface (ACPI) features.

The Laptop Power Control module is available only if your system supports APM and you set the setuid bit for the APM binary file. (Do this as root with the command **chmod u+s /usr/bin/apm**. But be aware that there are security issues with turning on the setuid bit.) In addition, both the Low Battery Critical and Low Battery Warning modules add Suspend and Standby to the possible options if this file is setuid. Suspend mode is designed for times when you want to stop working (especially on a laptop), but want to be able to restart where you left off. Open applications are preserved in memory, the CPU remains active at a low level, and the hard drive is shut down. Standby mode shuts the computer down almost completely, but continues to draw a small amount of power so that it wakes up quickly when you restart it. Nothing is saved in memory.

Battery Monitor

Check the Show Battery Monitor box in the Battery Monitor module to turn on the visual display of the battery's status. Then you can set the frequency with which the status should be checked. You can also change the icons that appear when there is no battery, the battery is not charging, or the battery is plugged in and charging by clicking on the icon that you want to change and selecting a new one.

Energy

If your hardware supports power management, you can enable it by checking the Enable Display Energy Saving box in the Energy module. Then use the sliders to set the amount of idle time before the system goes to standby mode, then to suspend mode, and finally turns off.

Laptop Power Control

This module configures how and when the automatic power-down feature takes effect. You can set the behavior separately for Not Powered, when the computer is running off the battery, and Powered, when it is plugged into a power supply. For

KDE

each case you can set it to suspend, go into standby mode, or turn off. Then set the amount of idle time before the power management takes effect. It's common to set a shorter delay for battery power to save the battery.

Low Battery Critical

The Low Battery Critical module sets a trigger time for notifying you that your battery is almost out of power. The time tells you how many minutes are left before the battery runs out of power. The remaining options determine what happens when that threshold is reached. The first two choices are Run Command and Play Sound. Each has a text box where you can enter the path to the command or the sound. The remaining options are System Beep, Notify, Suspend, and Standby. Suspend and standby are available only if */usr/bin/apm* has the setuid bit on.

Low Battery Warning

The Low Battery Warning module is like the Low Battery Critical module, except that it notifies you sooner when the battery is running low. The trigger time is set to a higher number, so if both warnings are set, you will first get a warning that the power is getting low, and then the power-critical warning when it is about to run out. The other options are the same.

Sound

The modules contained in this section configure the keyboard bell and other system sounds. The basic modules described here are Midi, Sound Server, System Bell, and System Notifications. You may also have other Sound modules, such as Audio CD IO-Slave, which configures the program that lets you make *.wav*, *.mp3*, or Ogg Vorbis files from audio CDs or DVDs, or Mixer, which configures a sound mixer.

Midi

The Midi module sets the Midi device to use. Select the device you want from the list, and if you want to use a Midi map, check Use Midi Mapper and enter the path to the map file or click the Browse button to search for it.

Sound Server

The Sound Server module configures the aRts sound server, which is a simulation of an analog real-time synthesizer used by KDE for multimedia support. On the General tab, check "Start aRts soundserver on KDE startup" to enable the aRts server. This makes the rest of the checkboxes available:

Enable network transparency
> Allow the server to respond to sound requests that come in over the network. Uncheck if you want the server to respond only to local requests.

Exchange security
> Check this box if you also checked the "Enable network transparency" box. It allows security information to be exchanged across the network.

Run soundserver with realtime priority
> If your system supports real-time scheduling, check this box to have the sound server run at a high priority. Note that you may need root privileges for this option to take effect.

Autosuspend if idle
> The sound server will suspend itself if it has been idle for the number of seconds that you specify in the combination box. Having the server suspend itself frees the sound card for other applications.

Display messages using
> Specify the application that will display aRts messages and enter the application to change it from the default **artsmessage**.

Whether or not you enable the sound server, you can set the level of messages to be displayed from the Message Display drop-down list. The choices are Errors, Warnings, Informational, and Debug. Messages at the selected level or higher are displayed.

The Sound I/O tab configures the sound itself if the sound server is enabled. Choose the Sound I/O method from the drop-down list. The choices are Auto-detect, Threaded Open Sound System, No Audio Input/Output, and Open Sound System. The default Autodetect is usually fine. Similarly, you can set the Sound quality to Autodetect, 16 bits (high), or 8 bits (low). Between the two drop-down lists are four checkboxes: "Enable full duplex operation," "Use custom sound device," "Use custom sampling rate," and "Other custom options." Select full-duplex operation if you need to record and play sound at the same time. Use the custom options if you have particular requirements that make the defaults unsuitable. See the context-sensitive help to determine if you should check one of these boxes. The slider at the bottom of the tab labeled "Audio buffer size (response time)" determines how responsive the sound is. Moving the slider to the left speeds up response time, while moving it to the right slows it down. Faster response time has a cost, though, as it uses more of the CPU.

System Bell

This module configures the system bell. Checking "Use System Bell instead of System Notification" enables the other options, which you can set with sliders or directly in the combination boxes. Volume sets the volume of the bell, measured as a percentage of the maximum possible volume; Pitch sets the tone of the slider in Hz; and Duration determines how long the beep lasts, in milliseconds. To listen to your settings, click the Test button.

System Notifications

This module allows you to enable and configure sound events for different applications. Most of the window is taken up with a tree listing of applications and events. For each event, you can select among four choices for how you want to be notified:

Log to file
> Log the event to a file, specified in the Filename text box below.

Play sound

Play the sound contained in the file specified in the Filename text box below. You can also check the box "Use external player" to use a particular media player and enter the path to the player in the text box.

Show messagebox

Display the notification in a message box displayed in the program's window.

Standard error output

Write the message to the standard error output.

You can select more than one option. For example, you might want to hear a sound and also have the event logged to a file.

The volume slider lets you determine the sound volume, and the long button at the bottom of the window switches between "Enable all sounds" and "Disable all sounds" to turn sound on or off for all applications at once.

System

The system modules set configuration options that have a systemwide effect. For that reason, most of them require you to enter the root password before you can make changes. Other modules, like the Font Installer module, let you make changes in your home directory without the root password, but require it for global changes. To enter the root password, click the Administrator Mode button in the lower-right corner of the window and enter the password in the window that appears. A red border appears around the module window to indicate that you are in administrator mode. Administrator mode does not carry over across modules. You must enter the root password for each module you want to use in administrator mode.

In addition to the modules described here, other modules that you might find depending on your distribution and KDE version include Boot Manager (LILO), Linux Kernel Configurator, Alarm Daemon, and XML RPC Daemon.

Date & Time

The Date & Time module lets you set the system date and time. The window has a calendar in the upper left corner of the window, and a clock in the upper right. Set the date by selecting a month from the drop-down list and setting the year in the combination box. Then select the correct date from the calendar. Set the time by entering the correct hour, minutes, and seconds in the boxes under the clock. The current time zone is displayed under the clock; you can choose a new time zone by selecting a location from the drop-down list and click Apply to see the new time zone displayed.

Font Installer

The Font Installer module installs new fonts onto the system. If you want to install a font globally, click the Administrator Mode button and enter the root password; otherwise the font will be installed in your home directory. The two columns on the Fonts tab show the directory from which the font will be installed on the left and the directory to which it will be installed on the right. To install the font from a different location, click the Change Folder button and select a new location. If you highlight a font in one of the columns, a preview appears in the box at the bottom of the window. To install a font, select it from the first column and click the Install button.

The Anti-Alias tab lets you set up options for antialiasing with the XRender Extension. If your system is not capable of using this extension, the checkboxes under the Configuration File text box are grayed out. If they are available, you can check "Exclude range" and enter the end points of the range to exclude certain point sizes from antialiasing, and check "Use sub-pixel hinting."

If you are in administrator mode, you can click the Advanced button to set up rules for matching font families and establish any desired include directives specifying additional font files. The Include Directives tab has two sections. Any files listed in the top section, Include, must be available. Files in the bottom section, Include If, are included if they are found, but aren't required.

The Settings tab has customization settings for five aspects of font installation:

Appearance
> The Appearance settings customize the look and operation of the Font Installer module. The settings are:
>
> *Mode*
>> Select Advanced or Basic mode. In advanced mode, the full font directory and file hierarchy are shown in the columns on the Fonts tab, and you can install Speedo and bitmap fonts in addition to TrueType and Type 1. In basic mode, only the font files are shown in the columns on the Fonts tab, and you can install only TrueType and Type 1 fonts.
>
> *Font Lists*
>> Select whether to display the fonts on the Fonts tab in left and right columns or top and bottom columns.
>
> *Custom preview string*
>> Check this box and enter the string if you want to see characters other than the alphabet for the font preview on the Fonts tab.

Folder & Files
> When you select the Font Installer module, it searches for the correct folders (directories) and files. Use these settings to make any changes or add any missing entries for the fonts folder, the font configuration file, and the encodings folder. You can also check the Ghostscript, Fontmap file box and set the path to the file to enable configuration of Ghostscript. Check the CUPS folder box and set the path if you are using CUPS (the Common Unix Print System) and want to enable its configuration.

Install/Uninstall
> To configure font install and uninstall operations, check "Fix TrueType Postscript names table" to automatically fix the names table when you install TrueType fonts; this corrects any problems that sometimes occur with TrueType fonts. You can also specify a file to which fonts should be moved when they are uninstalled.

StarOffice

Check the box to configure fonts for StarOffice, and specify a folder and a printer file. These options need to be set only for versions of StarOffice before Version 6. OpenOffice and later versions of StarOffice don't need this section.

X System

This section sets some X Window System font configuration options:

Configure X to only use ... encoding

Check this box and select an encoding from the drop-down list to specify an encoding for X to use.

Generate AFMs, with ... encoding

Check this box and select an encoding from the drop-down list to generate the Adobe Font Metric (AFM) files used by programs such as StarOffice to display font sizes correctly.

Command to Refresh X's Font List

This section lets you select the command to use after adding or removing fonts to refresh the internal font list. The choices are:

- **xset fp rehash**: This command resets the font path, which causes the font server to reread its database.

- **/etc/rc.d/init.d/xfs restart**: This command restarts the X font server. You must be in administrator mode to use this command.

- Custom: Check this box to use a command of your own choosing, and enter the command in the text box.

Login Manager

The KDE login manager, **kdm** (KDE display manager), is the program that controls the graphical login screen. This module lets you configure the graphical style of the login screen and set some default display options, such as prelisted users and available session environments.

The Appearance tab lets you edit the greeting string displayed on the login screen. Certain special characters, such as **%s** and **%n** in the default greeting string, can be used; they are replaced as follows:

Sequence	Replaced by
%d	The current display
%h	The host name
%m	The machine (hardware) type
%n	The node name
%r	The operating system version
%s	The operating system
%%	A single %

You can choose a logo if you want one, or select Show Clock to display a clock instead of a logo. To select a logo other than the default KDE logo, click the logo image and select another image file. A drop-down list offers you a choice of GUI styles for the login screen. Use the Echo Mode drop-down list to choose whether to replace each character of the password with a single star, three stars, or no echo. The Language option lets you select the default character encoding for **kdm**.

The Fonts tab lets you choose the font style and size for the Greeting, Fail, and Standard screen messages. Select which type you want to configure from the drop-down list and click the Change Font button. The pop-up window shows a list of available fonts and lets you set the point size. Click the OK button to close the pop-up window. The font you have chosen is displayed in the Example area of the tab.

The Background tab lets you select the background for the login screen. See the earlier description of the Background module in the Look & Feel section for a detailed description of the options on this tab.

The Sessions tab configures session settings. There are two drop-down lists at the top that set who is allowed to shut down the system from the console and remotely. The choices for both are Everybody, Only root, and Nobody. The default for the console is Everybody; the default for remote shutdown is Only root.

The Commands section allows you to set the commands used for shutdown and restart. In the Lilo section, check "Show boot options" to enable the LILO boot options to be displayed in the Shutdown menu. The Session Types section configures the list of session types available to the user from the login screen. The Default list contains the various environments that are installed on your system, such as KDE and GNOME. You can add a new type or remove a type from the listing.

The Users tab lets you show a list of users on the login screen. The users are listed by username with a logo displayed for each user. To log in, you can simply click your logo to automatically enter your name into the login box, but you still must supply your password. The tab contains listings labeled "Remaining users," "Selected users," and "No-show users." You can select names from the lists and use the arrow buttons to move them from one box to another. Two options are available for who to display on the login screen. You can place names in the "Selected users" list and click the "Show only selected users" button, or you can click the "All but no-show" button to display users in both the "Remaining users" and "Selected users" lists. No-show users are user IDs that are used to control access-restricted system resources (e.g., **root**, **news**, and **nobody**). They are never displayed on the login screen. You can add the names of other users to the no-show list. Check the "Sort users" box to display the images in alphabetical order.

You can select a different default image by clicking on the image button and choosing another image file. You can also select a unique image for each user by highlighting the user in one of the lists and selecting an image file for that user.

Users whose image is not shown on the login screen can still log in; the only difference is that they have to enter their login name as well as their password.

The Convenience tab offers options that make logging in easier and more automatic. The drawback to the convenience options is that they are potential security risks, because they make it easy for someone without a valid login ID to access the

KDE

system. Therefore, conveneince options should be used only on a system that is in a secure environment. The sections on the Convenience tab are:

Automatic login

If you check the box "Enable auto-login" in this section, you log in normally to KDE, but if you then use Ctrl-Alt-Backspace to kill the X server, **kdm** will log you in automatically when it comes up again. If you check the box "Truly automatic login" and select a username from the drop-down box, **kdm** will automatically log you in to that account when it comes up.

Preselect User

kdm can be configured to start up with a username already entered in the Name field. Select None if you do not want this option, Previous to have the previously logged-in user preselected, or Specify to choose a user from the drop-down list. Check the Focus password box to leave the cursor in the password field after preselecting the user. The alternative is to leave it in the user box so you can select a different username.

Password-less login

Check the "Enable password-less logins" box if you want users to be able to log in without entering a password. Then move users from the "Password required" list to the "Skip password" list, to identify users who can log in without entering their password.

Miscellaneous

Check the box "Automatically log in again after X server crash" to have **kdm** log you in automatically when X restarts after a crash.

Printing Manager

The Printing Manager module configures the KDE print manager, KDEPrint. KDEPrint is a frontend to your system's printing subsystem that provides an interface layer between KDE applications and the printing subsystem. Therefore, the details for using the Printing Manager module may vary depending on the printing subsystem in use.

Any application can use KDEPrint by printing to *$KDEDIR/bin/kprinter* instead of */usr/bin/lpr*. KDEPrint supports all the usual Linux printing subsystems, with an emphasis on CUPS.

The configuration window has a row of icons on the top. If you select Administrator Mode for this module, all the icons are available except for features you don't have installed. Otherwise, you can select only certain icons. From left to right, the icons are:

- Add printer/class
- Add special (pseudo) printer
- Start/Stop printer
- Enable/Disable job spooling
- Set as local default
- Set as user default
- Remove

- Configure
- Test printer
- Printer tools
- Restart server
- Configure server
- Configure manager
- Refresh view
- Show/Hide printer details
- View
- Orientation
- Toggle printer filtering

Below the icons is a large window that lists all available printers or pseudo-printers. A pseudo-printer lets you send print output somewhere other than to a printer, such as a file or a fax. At the bottom of the window is a drop-down list of print systems that shows the print system in use. Below that is a window with four tabs. The tabs provide detailed information for the printer currently highlighted in the printer list. The Information tab shows information such as the type, state, and location of the printer. The Jobs tab lists current jobs and their status. The Properties tab displays current property settings and lets you change them. The Instances tab shows individual printers and lets you configure them.

Web Browsing

The Web Browsing modules let you configure the Konqueror web browser.

Cache

The Cache module controls the use of a local cache to save copies of web pages you have visited. Using a cache lets Konqueror display pages without going back to the remote web site, which saves time and Internet access at the cost of using disk space and not always seeing the current version of a page. If you use the cache, you can always press Konqueror's Reload button to get the latest version.

The Use Cache button is checked by default. Uncheck it if you do not want any pages stored in a cache on your system. The Policy section controls how up to date the cache is kept and whether to read first from the cache or the Web. Check one of these options:

Keep cache in sync
Before displaying a page from the cache, verify that it is still valid and, if not, reread it from the remote site.

Use cache if possible
Display a page from the cache if it is there, otherwise read it from the remote site.

Offline browsing mode
Display a page from the cache if it is there, otherwise do not display it. Do not attempt to reread the page from the remote site.

In the "Disk cache size" box, enter the cache size you want. Click the Clear Cache button at any time to empty the cache.

Cookies

The Cookies module sets Konqueror's cookie policy and lets you manage individual cookies. This module has two tabs: Policy and Management.

On the Policy tab, check the Enable Cookies box to enable web sites to store cookies on your system. Then check one of the options in the Default Policy section:

Ask for confirmation before accepting cookies
> Konqueror asks you to confirm your acceptance of every cookie. Each time a web site wants to store a cookie, a window pops up asking if you want to accept the cookie. At that time, you can choose to apply your response to just that cookie, all cookies from the domain, or all cookies.

Accept all cookies by default
> Konqueror accepts and stores all cookies. If you select this policy, you will never be asked for confirmation. You can go to the Management tab later to remove cookies you don't want.

Reject all cookies by default
> Konqueror refuses to accept any cookies. Selecting this policy can result in your not being able to use certain web sites that require you to accept their cookies. You can change this policy later for all cookies or for a particular domain.

The Domain Specific Policy section lets you override the default policy for cookies from certain domains. This section lists domains for which you have specifically chosen to accept or reject cookies. Click the New button to add a domain. Click on a domain in the list to change the policy for that domain or to delete it from the list. The Delete All button deletes the entire list. The possible policies are Accept, Reject, and Ask.

The Management tab lets you manage cookies stored by Konqueror. The top portion lists the cookies hierarchically by domain and host. Select a domain and click Delete to delete all cookies from that domain, or select an individual cookie from the Host column and click Delete to delete just that cookie. If an individual cookie is selected, the Cookie Details portion of the tab shows the content, expiration date, and other information for that cookie. The Delete All button deletes all cookies stored by Konqueror, and the Reload List button reloads the list of stored cookies if more have been saved since you selected this module.

Enhanced Browsing

The Enhanced Browsing module controls the use of Internet keywords and web shortcuts by Konqueror—two features designed to make web browsing easier. Click the Enable Internet Keywords box to enable the use of Internet keywords. This lets you enter words such as company names without having to enter a full URL. For example, the use of Internet keywords would let you enter *oreilly* instead of the full URL *http://www.oreilly.com*. If you enable Internet keywords, you can also use the Fallback Search Engine drop-down list to pick the search engine to use if what you entered isn't found as an Internet keyword.

Check the Enable Web Shortcuts box to enable the use of web shortcuts. These are shortcuts that are not known Internet keywords, but have much the same purpose. A predefined list of shortcuts is provided. For example, *gg* is a shortcut for Google. This means that you can enter *gg:KDE* anywhere a URL is expected, and KDE searches Google for references to KDE. You can add your own shortcuts by clicking Add, or select an entry in the list and click Change to change its associated shortcuts or Delete to remove it from the list. The character sequence \{@} in a shortcut causes the shortcut to prompt the user for a string (such as a term in a query) and to plug the user's string into the shortcut at that point.

Konqueror Browser

This module configures settings used for Konqueror's web browsing functionality. It has five tabs: HTML, Appearance, Java, JavaScript, and Plugins.

On the HTML tab, checking the box "Enable completion of forms" causes Konqueror to store your responses as you fill in forms and automatically fill in the same information in other forms. Move the "Maximum completions" slider to set the maximum number of responses Konqueror will remember. Check the box "Change cursor over links" to have Konqueror display a different cursor when the pointer is over a link. The link cursor is a hand with a finger pointing to the link. If you check the box "Right click goes back in history," right-clicking on a web page acts like the Back button and takes you back a page. Check the box "Automatically load images" to have Konqueror load embedded images as it loads a web page. Check the box "Allow automatic delayed reloading/redirecting" to allow Konqueror to honor reload or redirect requests from the remote host. Choose an option from the Underline Links drop-down box to determine if and when links should be underlined. Select Enable to always underline links, Disable to never underline them, or Only on Hover to underline links only when the mouse pointer is directly over the link. Finally, you can enable or disable animations, or set them to be shown only once.

The Appearance tab sets fonts, font sizes, and the default encoding. Use the top slider to set the minimum font size and the lower slider to set the medium font size. Then specify your preferred fonts. The text boxes let you set standard, fixed, serif, sans serif, cursive, and fantasy fonts. Use the Default Encoding drop-down box to set the default language encoding. Just above this box, you can set a font size adjustment for the encoding.

The Java tab controls whether you will permit web pages to run Java applets. This tab lets you turn Java on globally, or set a policy on a host- or domain-specific basis. You can also turn Java on globally and then selectively turn it off for certain hosts or domains. To set policy by domain, click the Add button to specify a domain. A dialog box appears for you to enter the host or domain name and specify a policy of Reject or Accept. If you change your mind, you can click the Change or Delete button to change the policy or delete the entry. If you enable Java globally, you can also set the following Java Runtime Settings.

KDE

Show Java Console
Open a Java console window for the use of Java applets.

Use Security Manager
Run a security manager that prevents Java applets from accessing your file-system or perfoming other insecure actions. Normally, you should leave this box checked to protect your system.

Shutdown Applet Server when inactive
Shut down the Java Applet Server when no Java applet is running. This frees up resources when no applet is running, but causes a new applet to take slightly longer to start. If you choose this option, you can also move the Applet Server Timeout slider to set the number of seconds with no applet activity before the server shuts down.

Path to java executable, or "java"
Enter the path to the Java executable in the text box, or *java* to have Konqueror find Java in your path.

Additional Java Arguments
Enter any arguments for the Java virtual machine in this text box.

KDE does not implement any Java functionality itself; it relies on an external Java virtual machine. Therefore, you must already have Java installed on your system in order for these settings to have any effect.

The JavaScript tab controls whether you will permit web pages to run JavaScript code. Check the box to enable JavaScript globally, or set a policy on a host- or domain-specific basis, as you did for Java. As with Java, you can turn JavaScript on globally and off selectively for certain hosts or domains. Finally, set the policy you want for JavaScript web pop-ups. The possible policies are:

Allow
Allow all JavaScript pop-ups.

Ask
Ask for permission before displaying a JavaScript pop-up.

Deny
Don't allow any JavaScript pop-ups.

Smart
Allow only JavaScript pop-ups that have been activated by the user with a mouse click or keyboard operation.

On the Plugins tab, check Enable Plugins Globally to allow the use of plug-ins.

Netscape Plugins

The Konqueror browser can use Netscape plug-ins to display various types of web content. The Netscape Plugins module lets you tell Konqueror where to find the plug-ins on the system.

The Scan tab contains a list of directories for Konqueror to scan when looking for Netscape plug-ins. Initially, it contains a list of directories where plug-ins are typically found. You can add or delete entries from the list with the New and Remove buttons, or move around in the list with the Up and Down buttons. Or you can simply click on the entry you want with the first mouse button. Click the Scan for New Plugins button to have Konqueror rescan the directories in the list. You can also check the box labeled "Scan for new plugins at KDE startup" to run the scan each time KDE starts.

The Plugins tab contains a list of plug-ins that Konqueror found when it scanned the directories listed on the Scan tab. Check the box labeled "Use artsdsp to pipe plugin sound through aRts" if you want to use the analog real-time synthesizer to play sound.

Proxy

If your system is behind a firewall, you may need to use a proxy server for HTTP and FTP services. The Proxy module lets you enable the use of a proxy and configure it. Check the Use Proxy box to enable the use of a proxy server. The remaining options are:

Automatically detected script file
Konqueror will automatically find the setup configuration script file.

Specified script file
Specify the location of the script file, and enter the path to the file in the Location text box.

Preset environment variables
Check this box if your system has preset environment variables such as **$HTTP_PROXY** for graphical and nongraphical applications to share proxy configuration information, and click the Setup button to provide the environment variable names.

Manually specified settings
Provide the proxy server locations manually, and click the Setup button to provide the information.

Prompt as needed
Konqueror will prompt as needed for login information.

Use automatic login
Check this box if you have login information set up for your proxy server in the file *$KDEHOME/share/config/kionetrc*.

Stylesheets

The Stylesheets module contains settings for the use of CSS (Cascading Style Sheets) in Konqueror. On the General tab, choose the stylesheet. Check "Use default stylesheet" to use the Konqueror default; check "Use user-defined stylesheet" to specify a different stylesheet, and enter the path to the stylesheet in the text box. Or check "Use accessibility stylesheet defined in 'Customize' tab" and go to the Customize tab to define the stylesheet.

On the Customize tab, select a font family and check the box if you want to use that family for all text, overriding custom font settings. Select a base font size and check the box if you want to use that font size for all elements, overriding custom font size settings. Select a color scheme: Black on White, White on Black, or Custom. If you select Custom, also select a background and foreground color by clicking on the Background and Foreground color buttons. You can use the same color for all text, overriding any custom color settings. Check the box "Suppress images" if you don't want any images automatically displayed, "Suppress background images" to prevent display of background images. Click the Preview button to see the effect of your choices.

User Agent

The User Agent module allows you to specify the user-agent string reported by the browser for sites that may not recognize Konqueror, or anything that's not a major commercial web browser. Check the box "Send browser identification" to send information about your browser; it is recommended that you leave this checked for the use of host sites that customize the page they send depending on the browser. The user-agent string contains the name and version number of the client program making the request. The default for Konqueror at the time of this writing is "Mozilla/5.0(compatible;Konqueror/3)". Check the boxes below the default identification to customize the information sent; the example is updated to reflect your choices. The options are:

Add operating system name
Adds the name of your operating system to the identification; e.g., Linux.

Add operating system version
If you checked the box to add the operating system name, you can also check this box to add the version.

Add platform name
Adds the name of your platform; e.g., X11.

Add machine (processor) type
Adds information about your processor; e.g., i586.

Add your language setting
Adds your language; e.g., en_US.

You can set the identification string individually for certain hosts or domains by clicking the New button. Enter the host or domain name in the dialog box that opens, and select the identity from the drop-down box. A description appears in the Alias box. Click the OK button to add the entry to the list. The Update list box updates the list of identities that are shown in the drop-down list. You can also change and delete individual entries in the list, or delete all of them at once with the Delete All button.

19

An Alternative Window Manager: fvwm2

Among the most appealing characteristics of a Linux system are its flexibility, its independence from industry-dominating standards, and the degree of control a user has over his own working environment. Most flavors of Linux come with a default desktop environment replete with handy tools and menus and a consistent look and feel. The most widely used of these desktop environments are GNOME and KDE, the customization of which are detailed in Chapter 17 and Chapter 18, respectively. Both of these environments put a PC-like wrapper around what is basically a no-frills Unix-based system suitable for personal computers. For some people this is a good thing. But if you want a basic, functional desktop, and you're comfortable editing configuration files to customize your environment, you might instead try the **fvwm2** window manager.

fvwm2 is the latest generation of a window manager called **fvwm**. **fvwm** predates both GNOME and KDE as a program that can provide multiple virtual screens to expand your desktop real estate. The letters *vwm* stand for virtual window manager, but the original meaning of the *f* has been forgotten and has led to much speculation. In fact, among the latest group of the program's developers are a number of cat lovers who claim the *f* stands for *feline*.

The first important concept you should understand in order to work with **fvwm2** is that your desktop can be larger than the area of your screen. In fact, **fvwm2** allows you to have acres of desktop real estate in the form of virtual screens, or pages. In a typical default environment, you might have a single desktop composed of four virtual screens/pages arranged in a two-by-two grid.

You can run applications on any of the screen pages you want and navigate the entire desktop in a variety of ways. If the default environment doesn't suit you, you can specify a grid of any size you like. How about three screens across and two down? No problem.

And if that still isn't enough space for you, you can also have multiple desktops, each composed of multiple pages. You might use separate desktops for different applications or different projects. **fvwm2** provides the tools to navigate whatever space you design.

fvwm2 is also customizable in a vast number of other ways; the most significant are summarized in this chapter. What it all boils down to is maximum workspace and maximum flexibility.

Running fvwm2

Your Linux distribution may include a reasonably current version of **fvwm2**; if not, you can download it from *http://www.fvwm.org*. If you're running GNOME or KDE, the easiest way to switch over to **fvwm2** is to edit your X client's startup file to invoke the window manager and then restart X. If you start X from the Linux command line with the **startx** command, the startup file is *.xinitrc*; if you start X from one of the graphical display managers (XDM, GDM, or KDE) and you are running Red Hat Linux, the file is probably *.Xclients*; otherwise, it is *.xsession*.

Here is an excerpt from a simple startup file that has been edited to run **fvwm2**:

```
xterm -geometry +50+0 &
xterm -geometry -0+0&
exec fvwm2
```

fvwm2 provides GNOME support as a compile-time option. As this is being written, the current stable version of **fvwm2** is 2.4.15. The next major release, currently in development as the 2.5 series, will also support KDE compliance. In addition, **fvwm2** now supports Xinerama as a compile-time option. Xinerama is a feature of recent versions of XFree86 that permits multiple monitors to be treated logically as a single monitor (of course, each of these monitors needs its own video card).

Configuration Files

The key to how **fvwm2** works is the configuration file it reads at startup or restart. The systemwide configuration file is called *system.fvwm2rc* and usually lives in the directory */etc/X11/fvwm2*. The typical *system.fvwm2rc* file that gets distributed should create a simple but perfectly workable environment. We'll take a look at one in the next section. There's no guarantee that the file on your system will create the same layout, but you'll get the idea.

If you want to customize **fvwm2** to suit your needs, you need to make a copy of *system.fvwm2rc* called *.fvwm2rc* and put it in your home directory. This personal configuration file takes precedence over the systemwide file. You can edit your *.fvwm2rc* file to adapt the window manager to your needs.

There are a few simple rules for editing your *.fvwm2rc* file. First, any line that begins with a pound sign (#) is a comment (i.e., is not interpreted as part of the window manager definition). Second, a plus sign (+) at the beginning of a line means to repeat the first terms from the previous line. The section "Making the WinList Part of Your Default Environment," later in this chapter, illustrates the use of this syntax. The final thing to keep in mind is that life will be simpler if you weave your own definitions into the file, respecting its current contents and their order. So, for instance, if you decide to define some function keys, put your new lines in the section of the file that already deals with keys.

In terms of **fvwm2** customization, there's some good news and some bad news. The good news is that you can make an extraordinary number of changes to the way **fvwm2** looks and operates. That's also the bad news. The window manager has dozens of configuration options, many very handy and easy to use, others complex and even arcane. The sum total can make the configuration file syntax daunting to anyone who isn't accustomed to serious tinkering. In fact, you could get dizzy considering the possibilities.

The **fvwm2** manpage gives all the configuration options and illustrates their use; you may also want to consult the manpages for the **fvwm2** modules, introduced in the next section. The web site *http://www.fvwm.org* is the definitive source for **fvwm2** documentation, news, source code, and updates.

This chapter will help you cut to the chase in performing some of the more basic and useful customizations, as well as some tricky but handy upgrades.

A Modular Approach

fvwm2 has been designed to allow the interested user to devise new components, known as *modules*. A typical module is the Pager (FvwmPager), which provides a map of the desktop space and a way to navigate it, as we'll see a little later in the chapter. The Pager is a default module in just about any desktop environment.

FvwmWinList is another useful module. Though not as ubiquitous as the Pager, it is just as useful. The module displays the WinList, which is a small window that provides a list of all the windows running on all pages of all desktops. The WinList is another navigation tool, allowing you to switch the pointer focus to any application you have running and switch the screen view so that you can use that application. We'll talk more about this later.

A module is actually a separate program from **fvwm2** but works in concert with it, passing commands to be executed to the window manager. Most configurations of **fvwm2** have a Root menu with an FvwmModules submenu from which you can start certain of these programs. (Naturally, the list of modules on the menu is configurable.) You might also edit your *.fvwm2rc* file to run modules in other ways (when you type certain keys, when other events happen, etc.).

Since a module is a separate program, users can write their own modules without adversely affecting **fvwm2**. Note, however, that you must configure **fvwm2** to start the module's process; you cannot start a module from the command line. Note also that while some modules, like the Pager, are intended to be used for the entire session, others simply perform a function and exit (e.g., RefreshWindow). Since modules are programs in their own right, many of them have their own manpages too.

Implementing Window Manager Customizations

If you edit your *.fvwm2rc* file, simply restart **fvwm2** to have the changes implemented. In most environments, there will be a menu item that restarts the window manager. The vanilla setup we started with offers the item Exit Fvwm on the Root menu. If you select that item, you'll get a submenu titled Really Quit Fvwm? that contains several entries, including Restart Fvwm. When you select Restart Fvwm, your configuration changes should be implemented. A slower but just as effective way is to quit the X session and start it again (presuming your session startup file includes **fvwm2**).

A Quick Tour of the fvwm2 Environment

In any desktop environment with multiple virtual screens/pages, you can work on only a single screenful at a time. But **fvwm2** makes it easy to run applications on different pages, move applications between pages, and switch the view between pages. If you refer to a particular window all the time, you can even arrange for it to appear on every page of every desktop. (We'll come back to this concept of "sticky" windows.) And you're not limited to viewing a page proper or keeping a window entirely on a single page.

Figure 19-1 shows an example of a typical **fvwm2** environment. Notice the long horizontal box in the bottom right corner of the figure. This box is the FvwmButtons module (also called the *button bar*). FvwmButtons is generally used to house a number of tools and applications to which the user needs frequent access. Often these are other **fvwm2** modules.

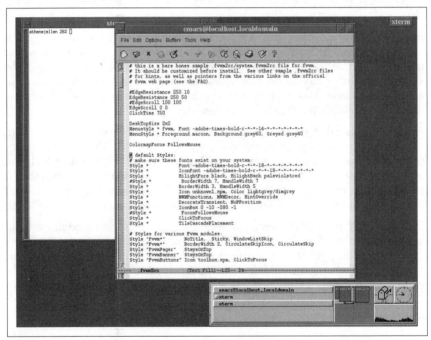

Figure 19-1. A typical fvwm2 environment

In this sample configuration, FvwmButtons contains two other modules: the Icon Manager (FvwmIconMan) on the left, and the Pager (FvwmPager) in the middle.

At the far right you can also see three small application windows: **xbiff** (a mailbox that indicates when you have new email messages), **xclock**, and **xload** (a graphic representation of your system's workload).

The Icon Manager and the Pager are tools that let you monitor what's happening in your environment and manipulate the windows running there. The Icon Manager shows an entry for every conventional window currently on your display. If that window is iconified, the Icon Manager entry is preceded by a square that has a three-dimensional appearance. You can iconify and deiconify any window on the current page by clicking the first pointer button on the corresponding entry in the Icon Manager. (The Icon Manager always shows the windows on the current page; for a similar tool that reflects what's running on every page on every desktop, check out the WinList, described later in this chapter.)

Think of the Pager as a tiny mirror of your entire desktop(s). In a typical default environment with a single desktop composed of two-by-two screen pages, the Pager shows a small grid of four partitions separated by dotted lines. These partitions correspond to the desktop's four virtual screen pages. (If you configure for multiple desktops, a solid line is used to show the border between desktops. The section "Using Multiple Desktops" later in this chapter tells you how to set this up.)

Each application you run appears in miniature in the Pager window. Applications with small windows are fairly hard to spot in miniature, but a blip representing them is there if you look closely. The miniature version of a larger client, like **xterm**, should have a readable label.

Whatever operations you perform on windows on the desktop (move, iconify, resize, and so on) are mirrored in the Pager. But the Pager is more than a monitor of activity—it's also a tool. Thus, you can move the miniature versions by clicking the second pointer button and dragging, and the actual windows will be moved. The Pager can also help you move windows between pages and desktops and select the area to be displayed on your monitor (which does not have to correspond to a page proper). You can select an area by right-clicking on the pager.

In addition to the desktop tools, **fvwm2** is commonly configured to provide a set of cascading menus beginning from the Root menu. Click the first pointer button on the root window to reveal the Root menu. The Root menu is usually a good way to start a new terminal emulator window. If you start with the default environment for your system, the Root menu is likely to have submenus like Fvwm Modules, Fvwm Window Ops (which offers items like moving, resizing, and closing windows), Fvwm Simple Config Ops (for changing focus policies, how paging works, etc.), and Exit Fvwm (for restarting or exiting the window manager, starting another one, etc.).

This chapter assumes you know how to perform basic window manager operations. We're not going to teach you how to use the Pager or all the menu items. But we will show you how to change the number of desktops the Pager shows, add menu items, configure keyboard shortcuts, and make other useful customizations.

Specifying Click-to-Type Focus

Most versions of **fvwm2** are configured to use the pointer focus model (Focus-FollowsMouse or MouseFocus in the configuration file). This means you need to move the pointer into a window in order to type in it, post an application menu, and so forth. However, **fvwm2** provides other options.

Two other focus policies are available: click-to-type focus (ClickToFocus), which requires you to click the pointer on the window in order to type in it, and the very handy SloppyFocus, which is like pointer focus with a twist—the focus does not leave the last window that had it until you move it into another window that takes over the focus. This can come in handy, particularly with terminal emulator windows like **xterm** and **rxvt**. You can actually move the pointer out of the way—accidentally or on purpose—and still continue to type in the window.

The best part of **fvwm2**'s way of handling focus policy is that you can mix and match what windows use what type of focus. All the settings for focus policy are used as arguments to the Style variable. (Style takes several arguments that determine the appearance and behavior of a particular client or window manager component. See Style on the **fvwm2** manpage for more information about this versatile option.)

In the following excerpt from a configuration file, the first line makes pointer focus the default for all applications (the asterisk is a wildcard). The subsequent lines specify the exceptions to this rule. The button bar works better with click-to-type focus, as do **xman** (the manpage viewer) and **xmag** (a magnification tool). The two terminal emulators benefit from sloppy focus.

```
Style "*"            FocusFollowsMouse
Style "FvwmButtons"  Icon toolbox.xpm, ClickToFocus
Style "xman"         Icon xman.xpm, RandomPlacement, ClickToFocus
Style "xmag"         Icon mag_glass.xpm, RandomPlacement, ClickToFocus
Style "XTerm"        Icon xterm.xpm, SloppyFocus, IconBox -70 1 -1 -140
Style "rxvt"         Icon term.xpm, SloppyFocus, IconBox -70 1 -1 -140
```

In our sample configuration, the Simple Config Ops submenu of the Root menu offers three items that let you change the focus policy on the fly for the current window manager session: Sloppy Focus, Click to Focus, and Focus Follows Mouse. Note, however, that these items supersede what's in your configuration file for all applications. If you want to recover the more specialized definitions in your configuration file, you'll have to restart the window manager.

Raising the Focus Window Automatically

If you're using pointer focus (FocusFollowsMouse), you might want to consider also using the FvwmAuto module to automatically raise the focus window to the top. If we add the following line to our *.fvwm2rc* file, the focus window is automatically raised after the pointer has been in it for 200 milliseconds (one-fifth of a second):

```
Module FvwmAuto 200
```

The delay is important and makes FvwmAuto much more practical. When pointer focus is in effect, an autoraise feature can make the display seem chaotic: when

---

you move the pointer across the screen, the focus hits several windows and they are raised in a distracting shuffle. With an autoraise delay, you can avoid the shuffling by moving the pointer quickly to the window you want to focus on.

If you use ClickToFocus mode by default, the autoraise feature is built in and you don't have to make this modification.

Of course, those who adapt to using the FvwmWinList module to transfer focus will have their windows raised automatically, without having to edit their .fvwm2rc file or even move the pointer off the WinList.

One of your menus may also be configured to offer an item that turns on autoraise on the fly and another item that turns it off again. In some default setups, the Fvwm Modules menu features AutoRaise and Stop AutoRaise for these purposes.

Changing the Size of the Desktop

Many default configuration files have a default desktop of two screen pages across by two screen pages down, which in the configuration file is defined using the line:

```
DeskTopSize 2x2
```

It's easy to change the size of your desktop by editing the dimensions of the grid. Thus, the following line creates a desktop of three pages across by two pages down:

```
DeskTopSize 3x2
```

You don't have to have multiple pages in both directions. You can have a desktop of one page above another above another:

```
DeskTopSize 1x3
```

You don't even have to have multiple pages at all:

```
DeskTopSize 1x1
```

But then why use **fvwm2**?

Of course, the number of pages you select will depend on your space needs and style of working and whether you will use more than one desktop (described in the next section). If you configure for multiple desktops, each one will have the same DeskTopSize. So if you want a desktop for work and one for play, you may not need each one to have many pages. Two desktops of three-by-three, for instance, would give you a total of 18 pages to get lost on. However, some people, such as graphical artists, may welcome a larger workspace.

Using Multiple Desktops

In order to work with multiple desktops, you simply have to configure the Pager to display the number of desktops you want. Each desktop will have the same number of pages, the number you specified using DeskTopSize.

To specify more than one desktop, you'll need to edit a line that looks something like this one:

```
*FvwmButtons(2x2 Frame 2 Swallow(UseOld) "FvwmPager" "Module FvwmPager 0 0")
```

This line incorporates the Pager into the FvwmButtons module (the button bar). The two numbers at the end of the definition line (0 0) give the range of desktops visible. The first desktop is number 0, and in this case the last desktop is also number 0 (i.e., there is only one).

If you want two desktops, change the final number to a 1:

```
*FvwmButtons(1x2 Frame 2 Swallow(UseOld) "FvwmPager" "Module FvwmPager 0 1")
```

The following line creates a Pager with four desktops, numbered 0 through 3:

```
*FvwmButtons(1x2 Frame 2 Swallow(UseOld) "FvwmPager" "Module FvwmPager 0 3")
```

Few people require this much space. But even if you add only a single desktop, you may have to change the overall dimensions of the Pager, and thus of the button bar that contains it, in order to have a reasonably sized view of your various desktops. You may also have to reallocate the space you have so that the Pager gets a large enough area.

There are a few relevant sizes you can tinker with to make room for a Pager that shows multiple desktops:

- The dimensions of the button bar (FvwmButtons module)
- The number of columns the button bar is divided into
- How many of those columns the Pager takes up

A typical FvwmButtons module might be 520 pixels wide and 100 pixels high, starting in the lower right corner of the screen:

```
*FvwmButtonsGeometry 520x100-1-1
```

And it might be configured as two rows and five columns (the sizes of which are entirely dependent on FvwmButton's geometry):

```
*FvwmButtons(Frame 2 Padding 2 2 Container(Rows 2 Columns 5 Frame 1 Padding
10 0))
```

In this particular setup, the Pager takes up a one-column by two-row section of the FvwmButtons module:

```
*FvwmButtons(1x2 Frame 2 Swallow(UseOld) "FvwmPager" "Module FvwmPager 0 1")
```

The Icon Manager takes up three columns:

```
*FvwmButtons(3x2 Frame 2 Swallow "FvwmIconMan" "Module FvwmIconMan")
```

And the remaining column is occupied by the desktop applications (e.g., **xbiff**, **xclock**, **xload**) that run within a container in the FvwmButtons module:

```
*FvwmButtons(1x2 Frame 0 Container(Rows 2 Columns 2 Frame 0))
*FvwmButtons(Frame 2 Swallow(UseOld,NoHints,Respawn) "xbiff" 'Exec exec
xbiff -bg bisque3')
*FvwmButtons(Frame 3 Swallow(UseOld,NoHints,Respawn) "xclock" 'Exec exec
xclock -bg
bisque3 -fg black -hd black -hl black -padding 0 update 1')
*FvwmButtons(2x1 Frame 2 Swallow(UseOld,NoHints,Respawn) "xload" 'Exec exec
xload -bg bisque3 -fg black -update 5 -nolabel')
```

Notice that the container is subdivided into two rows and two columns. The top row contains **xbiff** and **xclock**, and the bottom row contains **xload**, using both columns.

Back to the issue of multiple desktops. If you want two desktops, set that up by changing the number of the final desktop to a 1 at the end of this line, as we did earlier:

```
*FvwmButtons(1x2 Frame 2 Swallow(UseOld) "FvwmPager" "Module FvwmPager 0 1")
```

Then, to make the Pager big enough to display both desktops adequately, add some pixels to the width of the button bar. Here's an extra hundred added to the 520 we started with:

```
*FvwmButtonsGeometry 620x100-1-1
```

And let's also reallocate the available five columns so that the Icon Manager takes up only two (rather than the three it started with), and give the extra column to the Pager. The section with the applications remains a single column wide:

```
*FvwmButtons(2x2 Frame 2 Swallow "FvwmIconMan" "Module FvwmIconMan")
*FvwmButtons(2x2 Frame 2 Swallow(UseOld) "FvwmPager" "Module FvwmPager 0 1")
*FvwmButtons(1x2 Frame 0 Container(Rows 2 Columns 2 Frame 0))
```

Figure 19-2 shows our new double desktop reflected in the updated button box. This is just one sample customization. With your individual needs and display specifics, you can imagine how complicated this can get. But it's easy to test your changes by simply restarting the window manager.

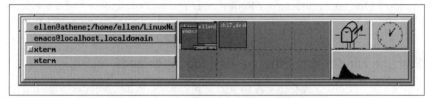

Figure 19-2. The modified FvwmButtons module shows two desktops in the Pager

Making the Same Window Appear on Every Page

A window that appears on every virtual screen page is called a sticky window because it "sticks" to the screen. Some windows are designated as sticky in the *system.fvwm2rc* file, among them **xbiff**, programs ending in *lock* (e.g., clock programs such as **xclock** and **oclock**), and all the **fvwm2** modules (because you need the button bar, Pager, etc., on every page).

If you want a window to be sticky, you need to specify that in your *.fvwm2rc* file. The specification requires you to use the Style variable, followed by the client's name, and the parameter Sticky. The Style variable is used to set many different characteristics. Here are some lines you might see in a configuration file to establish that a window is sticky, among other things:

```
Style "xbiff"     NoTitle, Sticky, WindowListSkip, ClickToFocus
Style "*lock"     NoTitle, NoHandles, Sticky, WindowListSkip, ClickToFocus
Style "Fvwm*"     NoTitle, Sticky, WindowListSkip
```

Notice that the Style variable can recognize a wildcard character (*) to widen the scope of the definition. The value **Fvwm*** encompasses all **fvwm2** modules.

Now try adding the following line, which specifies that an application called **xpostit** will stick:

```
Style "xpostit"      Sticky
```

Practically speaking, you probably also want to specify that **xpostit** uses click-to-type focus and doesn't appear on the WinList, so this definition is better:

```
Style "xpostit"      Sticky, WindowListSkip, ClickToFocus
```

In most cases, you'll want only small windows that you run a single instance of (and that you use frequently) to be sticky. Having a terminal emulator like **xterm** appear on every page would take up too much space. However, if you do want a client like **xterm** to follow you around, be sure to give that instance of the program a distinctive name using the **-name** option.

For example, in your X session startup file you can run an **xterm** you name **mailwindow**:

```
xterm -name mailwindow &
```

Then, to make that window appear on every page, add the following line to your .fvwm2rc file:

```
Style "mailwindow"  Sticky
```

If you want to make a particular window sticky temporarily, look for an Fvwm Window Ops menu under your Root menu. You will commonly find a toggle to (Un)Stick a Window. Or, you can set up such a menu item yourself; see "Customizing Menus" later in this chapter.

Starting Windows on Different Desktops and Pages

There's an obvious, low-tech way to start applications on different desktops and on different pages within a desktop: switch the view to the desktop and page you want (using the Pager, keyboard shortcuts, or whatever method you like), open a terminal emulator window (e.g., using the Root menu), then run whatever program you want. Voilà—the application window opens on the current desktop and page.

But there are two automated ways to accomplish the same thing. In the first method, you specify in your .fvwm2rc file that certain programs appear on certain desktops and/or pages automatically when you run them. You do this using **fvwm2**'s Style variable, which takes two relevant options: StartsOnPage and StartsOnDesk.*

StartsOnPage takes up to three numeric arguments. If there is only one argument, it corresponds to the number of the desktop on which to open the application. If there are three arguments, the second and third additionally identify the page using an X,Y coordinate scheme. We'll come back to this in a moment. Two arguments alone are interpreted as the X and Y coordinates of the page.

---

* There is also a StartsOnScreen option that specifies which screen to start a window on if you have Xinerama enabled.

And what about the closely associated StartsOnDesk variable? StartsOnDesk takes only one argument: the desk number. But since you can set this with Starts-OnPage, along with the more specific page address, in practice there is no need to use StartsOnDesk at all. Although it's still supported, StartsOnDesk is an older option that has been replaced by StartsOnPage.

Now back to desktop and page addressing. Let's consider the addressing scheme of a single two-by-two desktop. Just as the first desk is addressed as number 0, the first page on a desk is 0,0. The next page to the right is 1,0. The third page clockwise (the lower-right quadrant) is 1,1. And the fourth page clockwise (the lower-left quadrant) is 0,1.

Supposing there are at least two desktops of four pages each, the following definition says that when you run an **xterm** called "bigxterm" it is opened on the second desktop (number 1) in the lower-left quadrant (0,1):

```
Style "bigxterm"    StartsOnPage 1 0 1
```

Once you make this update to your *.fvwm2rc* file and restart the window manager, running the command:

```
xterm -name bigxterm &
```

opens the window where you want it.

You can accomplish the same thing using X resource syntax on the command line. This strategy may even be a little more practical than putting the definitions in your *.fvwm2rc* file because you won't have to define many different instances of the various programs (bigxterm, littlexterm, mailwindow, or whatever). The **-xrm** option (recognized by many X clients) lets you specify an X resource variable on the command line:

```
xterm -xrm '*Page: 1 0 1' &
```

You can even put a series of such lines in your X session startup file in order to open applications wherever you want them on your desktop(s) when you log in.

While it looks as if these two methods of opening windows on different desktops/pages (the Style variable with StartsOnPage and the **-xrm** command-line option) produce identical results, there is actually a subtle difference in behavior. When you use Style with StartsOnPage and you specify only the desktop number, the window is opened on the first page (0,0) of that desk. If you give the same information on the command line (using **-xrm**), the destination page of the new window is related to the page you're on when you run the command. The new window appears on the analogous page of the desktop you specify.

You have one more alternative if you're interested in opening a window on a different page within the current desktop. Run a window with the **-geometry** option and supply large enough coordinates to place it on a particular page in the desktop. If you use a desktop three pages square, the following line places a window in the middle page of the nine-page grid:

```
xterm -geometry +1200+1200 &
```

Keep in mind, however, that display-specific characteristics play a big part in gauging these distances, and they are not easy to guess.

If It's Too Hard (or Easy) to Move the Pointer Between Pages

If you're navigating the desktop by moving the pointer and you find it either too easy or too difficult to go from one page to the next, there's a configuration file variable you can customize. The aptly named EdgeResistance variable lets you adjust how easy it is to move the pointer beyond the perimeter of the current page.

The variable takes two parameters. The first, which is more relevant to the problem at hand, is the number of milliseconds the pointer must remain at the screen edge before you move onto the next page. The second parameter, which has to do with the way a window is moved between pages, is the number of pixels over the edge of the screen a window's border must move before it moves partially off the screen. Typical default settings are:

```
EdgeResistance 250 10
```

Some people find that the EdgeResistance they're working with is too low, with the inconvenient result that they inadvertently knock the pointer off the current screen page. If this is your problem, you can increase the first parameter:

```
EdgeResistance 500 10
```

A first parameter between 500 and 1000 greatly enhances the resistance. The maximum resistance is 10000, which actually makes it impossible to page over.

If you have the opposite problem and have to bounce the mouse against what feels like a hard rubber wall in order to page over, try reducing the first number:

```
EdgeResistance 100 10
```

In a typical default configuration, **fvwm2** is set up with menu options that let you change your paging options on the fly. A number of these options are located in the Root menu, in the Fvwm Simple Config Ops menu. Thus, you can toggle the ability to page on and off with Full Paging On and All Paging Off.

All Paging Off limits you to keeping the pointer on the current page. You might prefer this if you're going to be working on that page for a while and you don't want to worry about knocking the pointer onto another page. You can toggle paging back on with the Full Paging On menu item. There are other items to constrain paging in different ways (e.g., Horizontal Paging Only, Vertical Paging Only). The Partial Paging item lets you move the pointer so that the view straddles two adjacent pages; the area you see will be highlighted in the Pager window.

The item Full Paging & Edge Wrap actually expands the range of paging possibilities. Normally when you reach the edge of a desktop, you can't move the pointer beyond it. With this item selected, you can drag the pointer beyond the edge of the desktop and it wraps around to the page on the other side (either horizontally or vertically). Thus, if you have the pointer in the upper-right page of a two-by-two desktop, and you drag the pointer off the right edge, it wraps around to the upper-left page of that desktop.

Underlying all these menu items is the EdgeScroll variable. Here are the Edge-Scroll parameters that map to the various menu items:

```
Full Paging ON          EdgeScroll 100 100
All Paging OFF          EdgeScroll 0 0
```

```
Horizontal Paging Only      EdgeScroll 100 0
Vertical Paging Only        EdgeScroll 0 100
Partial Paging              EdgeScroll 50 50
Full Paging & Edge Wrap     EdgeScroll 100000 100000
```

EdgeScroll's two parameters specify the percentage of a page to scroll when you reach the border of the page. The first parameter is for horizontal moves, the second for vertical. If the horizontal and vertical percentages are multiplied by 1000, scrolling will wrap around at the edge of the desktop. **EdgeScroll 100000 100000** will wrap for both horizontal and vertical moves.

Rather than rely on menu items like these, you can make any of these options the default behavior by putting the EdgeScroll variable on its own line in your *.fvwm2rc* file. See the **fvwm2** manpage and check out the *system.fvwm2rc* file for guidance.

Note that none of these variations lets you scroll from one desktop to another. The next section shows how to configure some keyboard shortcuts to do just that.

Adding Keyboard Shortcuts

The *system.fvwmrc* file that we started with offers little in the way of keyboard shortcuts, or accelerators, for window management functions. But if you're one of those users who prefer to keep their hands on the keyboard and off the mouse as much as possible, you can easily define keys in your *.fvwm2rc* file to perform a variety of functions.

Navigating the Desktop

The Pager is a great tool for getting around one or more desktops, but many people hate using the mouse. You can configure certain keys and key combinations to let you move around in various ways.

Add the following lines to your *.fvwm2rc* file to set up key combinations to scroll one page in any direction on the desktop using Ctrl plus an arrow key. The view scrolls in the direction of the arrow.

Each definition uses the Key variable followed by:

1. The name of the key
2. The context (location) in which it must be typed
3. Any modifying keys that must also be held down
4. The action initiated by the key or key combination

Thus, in the following example, the first definition line says that pressing the left arrow key (Left) in any (A) context, while also holding down the Ctrl (C) key scrolls the screen one page to the left on the current desktop:

```
# Press arrow + Control in any context
# to scroll by one page in the direction of the arrow
Key Left        A       C       Scroll -100 0
Key Right       A       C       Scroll +100 +0
Key Up          A       C       Scroll +0  -100
Key Down        A       C       Scroll +0  +100
```

Table 19-1 summarizes the functionality.

Table 19-1. Key combinations to change the page

Key combination	Moves view
Control, right arrow key	One page to the right
Control, left arrow key	One page to the left
Control, up arrow key	One page up
Control, down arrow key	One page down

The Scroll variable takes the same parameters as EdgeScroll, which was explained in the previous section. See the **fvwm2** manpage for more information. Note that the key combinations we've defined let you get around a single desktop but won't let you advance to another desktop. We'll deal with that contingency later.

Here's another possible key binding. This one advances the view to every page in the desktop in order, and finally wraps back to the first page. You use the Tab key while holding down Control, again in any context. The definition line looks like:

```
# Press Tab + Control in any context to scroll
# by one page with wrap scrolling
Key Tab        A      C      Scroll 100000 0
```

Table 19-2 summarizes another page-changing combination.

Table 19-2. Another key combination to change the page

Key combination	Moves view
Control, Tab	To the next page in the desktop

Since application windows can straddle pages, there may be times when you want the screen to display a screenful other than a page proper. (You might also want to look at windows on two different pages at once.) The following shortcuts scroll the view one-tenth of a page at a time. Instead of Control, these shortcuts use the so-called Meta key. This is a symbolic name—the actual key that serves the Meta function varies from keyboard to keyboard. In many cases, the key labeled Alt serves as the Meta key. Here are the configuration file definition lines:

```
## Press arrow + meta key in any context
## to scroll by 1/10 of a page in the direction of arrow
Key Left       A      M      Scroll -10 +0
Key Right      A      M      Scroll +10 +0
Key Up         A      M      Scroll +0   -10
Key Down       A      M      Scroll +0   +10
```

These lines establish the functionality outlined in Table 19-3.

Table 19-3. Key combinations to scroll the page by 1/10

Key combination	Moves view
Meta, left arrow key	One-tenth of a page to the left
Meta, right arrow key	One-tenth of a page to the right

Table 19-3. Key combinations to scroll the page by 1/10 (continued)

Key combination	Moves view
Meta, up arrow key	One-tenth of a page up
Meta, down arrow key	One-tenth of a page down

If you have more than one desktop, you can also create shortcuts to move between desktops. The following two shortcuts let you go back and forth between desktops in a two-desktop environment:

```
## Press Control + Return in any context
## to scroll forward by 1 desktop
Key Return          A      C        Desk 1 1 1
## Press Shift + Control + Return in any context
## to scroll back by 1 desktop
Key Return          A      SC       Desk -1 0 0
```

Table 19-4 summarizes these shortcuts.

Table 19-4. Key combinations to scroll to the next desktop

Key combination	Moves view
Control, Return	One desktop ahead
Shift, Control, Return	One desktop back

The second and third parameters to the Desk variable constrain the paging so that you can't page beyond the first or second desktops. (Theoretically, you can page outside the view of the Pager!) If you have more than two desktops, you will need to edit these definitions. See the **fvwm2** manpage for more about the Desk variable.

Moving the Pointer

The previous section outlines some keyboard shortcuts you can define to scroll the page view. But you can also define shortcuts to move the position of the pointer on the screen. If you prefer using the keyboard to the mouse, these shortcuts can come in handy. They employ the CursorMove variable, also described on the **fvwm2** manpage.

The keyboard accelerators in the first group move the cursor symbol one-tenth of a screen at a time. The first definition line says that pressing the left arrow key in any (A) context, while also holding down the Shift (S) and Meta (M) keys, moves the cursor one-tenth of a page in the direction of the arrow:

```
## Press Shift + Meta + arrow in any context
## to move the pointer by 1/10 of a page in direction of arrow
Key Left           A      SM       CursorMove -10   +0
Key Right          A      SM       CursorMove +10   +0
Key Up             A      SM       CursorMove +0    -10
Key Down           A      SM       CursorMove +0    +10
```

Table 19-5 summarizes the commands.

Table 19-5. Key combinations to move the pointer by 1/10 of the page

Key combination	Moves pointer
Meta, Shift, left arrow key	One-tenth of a page to the left
Meta, Shift, right arrow key	One-tenth of a page to the right
Meta, Shift, up arrow key	One-tenth of a page up
Meta, Shift, down arrow key	One-tenth of a page down

If you want as much control moving the pointer with keystrokes as you do moving it by hand, you can specify shortcuts to move it a mere one percent of a page at a time:

```
## Press Shift + Control + arrow in any context
## to move the pointer by 1% of a page in direction of arrow
Key Left          A          SC          CursorMove -1 0
Key Right         A          SC          CursorMove +1 +0
Key Up            A          SC          CursorMove +0 -1
Key Down          A          SC          CursorMove +0 +1
```

Table 19-6 summarizes the commands.

Table 19-6. Key combinations to move the pointer by 1 percent of the page

Key combination	Moves pointer
Shift, Control, left arrow key	One percent of a page to the left
Shift, Control, right arrow key	One percent of a page to the right
Shift, Control, up arrow key	One percent of a page up
Shift, Control, down arrow key	One percent of a page down

Menu and Window Manipulation

So far we've limited our keyboard shortcuts to scrolling the view and moving the pointer. But you can create keyboard bindings for any window manager function.

Here are some sample bindings to perform simple window operations and to display a few menus:

```
# Keyboard accelerators
Key F1          A          M          Iconify
Key F2          A          M          Move
Key F3          A          M          Resize
Key F4          A          M          Popup "RootMenu"
Key F5          A          M          Popup "Misc-Ops"
Key F6          A          M          Popup "Utilities"
Key F7          A          M          Popup "Module-Popup"
Key F10         A          M          Restart fvwm2
Key F12         A          SM         Close
```

These are just sample bindings; you may want to set up your own keyboard short-cuts to do entirely different things. But these bindings illustrate some of the possibilities, as well as potential problems.

In our sample definition lines, the first binding specifies that if you press the F1 function key while holding down the Meta (M) key, with the pointer in any (A) context, the focus window is iconified (or deiconified). Meta-F2 lets you initiate moving the focus window, while Meta-F3 starts a resize operation.

Note that if you've adopted the keyboard bindings to move the pointer (as described in the previous section), you can perform the move and resize opera-tions entirely with keystrokes. For example, use Meta-F2 to begin a move, drag the window outline by moving the pointer symbol using the appropriate keyboard shortcuts, then press the Return key to complete the operation.

In addition, we've set up function keys to pop up four different menus, the contents of which are predefined in the *.fvwm2rc* file. Once a menu is popped up, you can use the up and down arrow keys to highlight items on the menu, right and left keys to move down and up through submenus (cascading menus), the Return key to select an item, and Esc to pop down the menu without making a selection.

Because we're doing a lot of tinkering with **fvwm2** customization, we have set up Meta-F10 to restart the window manager. This is much faster than bringing up menus.

We've also created a key combination to close the focus window: Shift-Meta-F12. Certainly it's handy to be able to get rid of a window with a keyboard shortcut, but you don't want it to be too easy or you may do it by mistake. Having an extra modifying key (Shift) and using the very last function key (F12) require you to act deliberately in closing a window using this method.

Customizing Menus

Among the window manager features and functions defined in the configuration file are the contents of menus. The *system.fvwm2rc* file generally defines a number of menus intended to be useful to a large percentage of people. But the menus you have and what they offer are basically up to you.

Typically the Root menu is defined as follows:

```
AddToMenu RootMenu    "Root Menu"              Title
+                     "XTerm"                  Exec exec xterm
+                     "Rxvt"                   Exec exec rxvt
+                     " "                      Nop
+                     "Remote Logins"          Popup Remote-Logins
+                     " "                      Nop
+                     "Utilities"              Popup Utilities
+                     " "                      Nop
+                     "Fvwm Modules"           Popup Module-Popup
+                     "Fvwm Window Ops"        Popup Window-Ops
+                     "Fvwm Simple Config Ops" Popup Misc-Ops
+                     " "                      Nop
```

```
+                   "Refresh Screen"       Refresh
+                   "Recapture Screen"     Recapture
+                   ""                     Nop
+                   "Exit Fvwm"            Popup Quit-Verify
```

You use the AddToMenu variable to create a menu. The first parameter that AddToMenu takes is the name of the menu, in this case RootMenu. The menu name is used to reference the menu elsewhere in the configuration file (e.g., to specify a key binding to pop up the menu). Note that the AddToMenu variable and the menu name are automatically repeated on each line of the menu definition, as indicated by the plus sign.

Each line of the definition creates a line on the menu as seen by the user; types of lines include the menu title, a menu item proper, a blank line, and a separator. The third component of each line specifies the text that appears on that line. The fourth component specifies the window manager function to be performed.

The first line of our example specifies the menu title. Lines with empty text fields ("") together with the Nop ("No operation") function create divider lines on the menu.

The Popup function is worth looking at more closely. Popup specifies that a menu is displayed; the menu name is given as an argument to Popup. When Popup is invoked from another menu, it creates a submenu (or cascading menu). This sample Root menu definition has six submenus, named Remote-Logins, Utilities, Module-Popup, Window-Ops, Misc-Ops, and Quit-Verify. These menus would also be defined using the AddToMenu command elsewhere in the configuration file.

You can start from the default menus in the *system.fvwm2rc* file and use the **fvwm2** manpage to modify the existing menus or create your own. It is simple to replace definition lines in the template menus, and not much more difficult to write a new entry or even a menu from scratch.

You can also change how the menus are displayed. Perhaps you don't want a bunch of cascading menus off the Root menu. In the previous section we set up some function keys to display certain menus. That's one option. You might instead specify pointer buttons to display various menus. In a typical default, the first pointer button displays the Root menu and the second displays the Window Ops menu. But since most Window Ops functions (e.g., Move, Resize, Iconify) are available using the pointer directly on parts of a window, you may instead choose to have the second pointer button display another menu (e.g., Utilities).

The WinList: Switching the Focus

FvwmWinList is an **fvwm2** module that lets you keep track of all the application windows on your many screen pages. Generally the WinList is configured to let you switch the focus to whatever window you want, but you can set it up to perform other operations.

In a typical environment, you can start the WinList from the Fvwm Modules menu on the Root menu. If you prefer to configure **fvwm2** to start the WinList automatically, see "Making the WinList Part of Your Default Environment." (You might also configure a keyboard shortcut to start the WinList module; see "Adding Keyboard Shortcuts" for details.)

Some of WinList's appearance and behavior can be customized. We'll see some example module definition lines later. If you are using that example configuration, WinList performs the following operations:

First mouse button click
> Switch the focus to the window in question. If the window is iconified, de-iconify. Switch the screen view so that the page with the window is displayed.

Second mouse button click
> Iconify/deiconify window; the page displayed does not change.

Third mouse button click
> Display a pop-up box containing information about the window in question (e.g., dimensions in pixels, whether it is sticky, permanent, or transient, etc.). Pop down the box by clicking any mouse button on it.

One of the interesting features of the WinList is that none of these commands moves the pointer to the focus window. Instead, the pointer stays on the entry in the WinList that corresponds to the focus window.

In theory, you could simply keep the pointer on the WinList and do all your navigation from there—except when you want to work with the FvwmButtons module or another of the windows that don't normally appear in the WinList.

Distinguishing Multiple Instances of Windows in WinList

The primary limitation of the WinList is that it can be difficult to tell which window in the list is which. Each entry in the WinList gives the text that appears in the corresponding window's titlebar. (If the titlebar is suppressed, it gives the text that would normally appear.) If you tend to run the same program many times simultaneously—e.g., multiple **xterm**s—they all look alike in the WinList. (The one difference is that iconified windows have entries surrounded by parentheses.)

If you get attached to using the WinList, you should probably specify different titles for multiple instances of the same window. The standard X options **-title** or **-name** will do the trick. Note, however, that while **-title** changes only the text in the titlebar, **-name** literally changes the name of the application. Thus it affects how resources and configuration file parameters are assigned.

Making the WinList Part of Your Default Environment

If you want to make the WinList part of your default environment, edit your configuration file to have the FvwmWinList module run at both initialization and restart of the window manager. In the following example, we've added the third and sixth lines for these purposes:

```
AddToFunc InitFunction    "I" Module FvwmButtons
+                "I" exec xsetroot -mod 2 2 -fg \#554055 -bg \#705070
+                "I" Module FvwmWinList
```

```
AddToFunc RestartFunction "I" Module FvwmButtons
+              "I" exec xsetroot -mod 2 2 -fg \#554055 -bg \#705070
+              "I" Module FvwmWinList
```

These lines specify that the FvwmWinList module is run whenever you start or restart the window manager. The WinList window appears in the bottom left corner of the screen.

As an alternative, you might make the WinList appear as a pop-up menu. The following definition binds the module to the third pointer button when it is held down on the root window (this may not be as handy as having the module present all the time):

```
Mouse 3        R      A       Module FvwmWinList Transient
```

But running a module is different from specifying how it looks and behaves. Like a number of other modules (FvwmButtonBox, FvwmPager, etc.), the various characteristics of the FvwmWinList module are defined elsewhere in the configuration file. Here are some typical definition lines:

```
######################FvwmWinList######################
*FvwmWinListBack #908090
*FvwmWinListFore Black
*FvwmWinListFont -adobe-helvetica-bold-r-*-*-10-*-*-*-*-*-*-*
*FvwmWinListAction Click1 Iconify -1,Focus
*FvwmWinListAction Click2 Iconify
*FvwmWinListAction Click3 Module "FvwmIdent" FvwmIdent
*FvwmWinListUseSkipList
*FvwmWinListGeometry +0-1
```

The first three lines specify the background color, foreground color, and text font used for the application. The next three define the actions that first, second, and third mouse button clicks invoke when they occur within the WinList. UseSkip-List tells the WinList not to list any windows that are assigned the Style classification WindowListSkip elsewhere in the configuration file. (Generally all module windows are classified thus and do not appear in the WinList.) The final line specifies the location at which the window should appear (bottom left corner).

The WinList is also a sticky window; it appears on every page on every desktop. But the configuration file can be confusing. This characteristic is specified elsewhere in the file, using the Style option:

```
Style "Fvwm*"        NoTitle, Sticky, WindowListSkip
```

This line specifies that all modules (including the WinList) have no titlebars, are sticky, and do not appear on the WinList. In the case of the FvwmWinList module, having it appear as an entry on itself would be more than a little confusing.

Index

Symbols

& (ampersand), 572
  ex, 719
  logical AND, 133
< > (angle brackets) ex, 719
* (asterisk), 572, 578
  multiplication operator, 132
@ (at)
  ex, 719
  tcsh, 649
' (backquote), 583
\ (backslash), 573
! (bang), 573
  ex, 718
  shell invocation, ftp, 152
!~ (bang tilde), gawk, 737
{ } (braces), sed command, 725
[ ] (brackets), 573, 578
^ (caret), gawk, 737
: (colon)
  ex editor, 689
  pattern search, expr, 133
  sed, 727
  :set command (ex), 720
  tcsh null command, 649
$ (dollar), 573
  execute macro command, ftp, 152
  gawk, 737
  prompt, xiii
  sed, 724

. (dot), 594
?? (double question marks), 32
" " (double quotes), 573
= (equals)
  ex, 719
  sed, 727
\(\) (escaped parentheses), 142
/ (forward slash)
  division operator, 132
  sed command, 724
#! (hash bang), 594
  tcsh shell, 649
(hash mark), 512, 573
  in shell scripts, 594
  sed, 727
  tcsh shell, 649
- (hyphen) and metamail command, 283
- (minus operator), 132
% (modulo operator), 132
: (null command), 594
( ) (parentheses), 573
% (percent), 573
  bash job ID argument, 593
  prompt, xiii
| (pipe), 572, 578
  as logical OR symbol, 133
+ (plus) operator, 132
  fvwm2, 878
? (question mark), 572, 578
  ftp help command), 157

About the Authors

Ellen Siever is a writer and editor specializing in Linux and other open source topics. In addition to *Linux in a Nutshell*, she coauthored *Perl in a Nutshell*. She is a longtime Linux and Unix user, and was a programmer for many years before deciding that writing about computers was more fun.

Stephen Figgins is a programmer, animal tracker, musician, and lifelong learner. He honed many of his computer skills while working as O'Reilly's book answer guy. Now living in Lawrence, Kansas, he works as a writer, editor, and consultant.

Aaron Weber is a technical writer for Ximian, Inc. and wrote the manual for Ximian Evolution, Red Carpet, and Red Carpet Enterprise, and was a contributor to *Running Linux*, Fourth Edition. He's also published in Interex Enterprise Solutions (*http://interex.com*) and Boston's Weekly Dig (*http://www.weeklydig.com*), and is the host of secretlyironic.com.

Colophon

Our look is the result of reader comments, our own experimentation, and feedback from distribution channels. Distinctive covers complement our distinctive approach to technical topics, breathing personality and life into potentially dry subjects.

The animal featured on the cover of *Linux in a Nutshell* is an Arabian horse. Known for its grace and intelligence, the Arabian is one of the oldest breeds of horse, with evidence of its existence dating back 5000 years. The Arabian was instrumental as an ancestor to other popular breeds, most notably the Thoroughbred in the 17th and 18th centuries. Possibly one of the more characteristic horse breeds, the typical Arabian has large expressive eyes and nostrils, small ears, and a short, sturdy back. Its stamina suits it particularly well for endurance riding, where the breed dominates the sport. Its wonderful temperament makes the Arabian an all-around favorite riding horse in North America, although it also can be found in more specialized competitions such as dressage, jumping, and reining.

Emily Quill was the production editor and copyeditor for *Linux in a Nutshell*, Fourth Edition. Derek Di Matteo, Claire Cloutier, Genevieve d'Entremont, Mary Brady, and Colleen Gorman provided quality control. Derek Di Matteo and Jamie Peppard provided production assistance. John Bickelhaupt wrote the index.

Edie Freedman designed the cover of this book, using a 19th-century engraving from the Dover Pictorial Archive. Emma Colby produced the cover layout with QuarkXPress 4.1 using Adobe's ITC Garamond font.

David Futato designed the interior layout. This book was converted by Joe Wizda to FrameMaker 5.5.6 with a format conversion tool created by Erik Ray, Jason McIntosh, Neil Walls, and Mike Sierra that uses Perl and XML technologies. The text font is Linotype Birka; the heading font is Adobe Myriad Condensed; and the code font is LucasFont's TheSans Mono Condensed. The illustrations that appear in the book were produced by Robert Romano and Jessamyn Read using Macromedia FreeHand 9 and Adobe Photoshop 6. The tip and warning icons were drawn by Christopher Bing.